DRAFTING CONTRACTS

ASPEN COURSEBOOK SERIES

DRAFTING CONTRACTS
How and Why Lawyers Do What They Do
Third Edition

Tina L. Stark
*Professor in the Practice of Law (retired) and
The first Executive Director of the Center for Transactional Law
and Practice
Emory University School of Law*

Monica L. Llorente
*Senior Lecturer
Northwestern Pritzker School of Law*

To contact Customer Service, e-mail customer.service@aspenpublishing.com, call 1-800-950-5259, or mail correspondence to:

Aspen Publishing
Attn: Order Department
1 Wall Street
Burlington, MA 01803

Cover Credit: incomible/Shutterstock.com

Printed in the United States of America.

1 2 3 4 5 6 7 8 9 0

ISBN 978-1-5438-0390-7

Library of Congress Cataloging-in-Publication Data

Library of Congress Cataloging- in- Publication Data application is in process.

SUSTAINABLE FORESTRY INITIATIVE

Certified Chain of Custody
At Least 10% Certified Forest Content
www.sfiprogram.org
SFI-O1028

ABOUT ASPEN PUBLISHING

Aspen Publishing is a leading provider of educational content and digital learning solutions to law schools in the U.S. and around the world. Aspen provides best-in-class solutions for legal education through authoritative textbooks, written by renowned authors, and breakthrough products such as Connected eBooks, Connected Quizzing, and PracticePerfect.

The Aspen Casebook Series (famously known among law faculty and students as the "red and black" casebooks) encompasses hundreds of highly regarded textbooks in more than eighty disciplines, from large enrollment courses, such as Torts and Contracts, to emerging electives, such as Sustainability and the Law of Policing. Study aids such as the *Examples & Explanations* and the *Emanuel Law Outlines* series, both highly popular collections, help law students master complex subject matter.

Major products, programs, and initiatives include:

- **Connected eBooks** are enhanced digital textbooks and study aids that come with a suite of online content and learning tools designed to maximize student success. Designed in collaboration with hundreds of faculty and students, the Connected eBook is a significant leap forward in the legal education learning tools available to students.
- **Connected Quizzing** is an easy-to-use formative assessment tool that tests law students' understanding and provides timely feedback to improve learning outcomes. Delivered through CasebookConnect.com, the learning platform already used by students to access their Aspen casebooks, Connected Quizzing is simple to implement and integrates seamlessly with law school course curricula.
- **PracticePerfect** is a visually engaging, interactive study aid to explain commonly encountered legal doctrines through easy-to-understand animated videos, illustrative examples, and numerous practice questions. Developed by a team of experts, PracticePerfect is the ideal study companion for today's law students.
- The **Aspen Learning Library** enables law schools to provide their students with access to the most popular study aids on the market across all of their courses. Available through an annual subscription, the online library consists of study aids in e-book, audio, and video formats with full text search, note-taking, and highlighting capabilities.
- Aspen's **Digital Bookshelf** is an institutional-level online education bookshelf, consolidating everything students and professors need to ensure success. This program ensures that every student has access to affordable course materials from day one.
- **Leading Edge** is a community centered on thinking differently about legal education and putting those thoughts into actionable strategies. At the core of the program is the Leading Edge Conference, an annual gathering of legal education thought leaders looking to pool ideas and identify promising directions of exploration.

For Bobby and Mort Weisenfeld, my mother- and father-in-law, who have always treated me as if I were their daughter

For their son Dave, my best friend and beloved husband

and

For their grandson Andy, my wondrous treasure

Tina L. Stark

A mis amigos y a mi familia,

especially to my children,

Jack and Lucía,

who share their love, curiosity, challenges, and happiness with me, every day.

I hope they are as proud of me as I am of them.

For anyone signing a contract anytime soon:

Read and question everything before you sign,

If it's already in the contract — it's supposed to happen,

If it's not in the contract — it's not going to happen,

And I hope this book helps with the rest . . .

Monica L. Llorente

About the Authors

TINA L. STARK

It was 2006 when Aspen published the First Edition of *Drafting Contracts: How and Why Lawyers Do What They Do*. At that time, there was no market for a contract drafting textbook. Only a smattering of law schools even offered a course. Aspen and Tina decided to push forward anyhow. Their mantra was, "If we build it, they will come."

And come they did. Professors quickly recognized the book's groundbreaking pedagogy and the seminal role it would play in teaching contract drafting. With so few professors having transactional expertise, Tina mentored anyone who sought her help. Eventually, many in the Academy conflated Tina and the textbook. Professors stopped referring to the textbook by its title. Instead, it was *Tina's Book*.

Tina joined Emory University School of Law in 2007 as its first Professor in the Practice of Law, and was the founding Executive Director of that school's Center for Transactional Law and Practice. There, she pioneered a multi-year integrated transactional skills curriculum. During her stewardship, she transformed the nascent transactional curriculum into one that is nationally acclaimed.

In joining Emory, Tina wanted to persuade law schools to embrace the teaching of transactional skills as a core element of preparing law students for practice. She pursued that goal with fervor and quickly recruited others to join with her. Fifteen-plus years later, similar law school curricula are ubiquitous.

But Tina knew from the beginning of her efforts that the imprimatur of the American Association of Law Schools would be essential to the emerging discipline's ultimate legitimacy and growth. So, in April 2010, she proposed to the AALS that it create a new section, the Section on Transactional Law and Skills. It took the work of many people and a petition signed by over 200 professors and deans, but the new section was created. And Tina was its first chair.

Tina has received multiple accolades. In 2012, she was awarded the prestigious *Burton Award for Outstanding Contributions to Legal Writing Education*. In the same year, she was chosen as one of 26 professors from a nationwide search to be included in the study, *What the Best Law Teachers Do*. When Tina retired from teaching, Emory honored her by creating the *Tina L. Stark Award for Excellence in the Teaching of Transactional Law and Skills*.

In 2019, the Legal Writing Institute conferred on Tina the *Golden Pen Award*, which honors those who "make significant contributions to the cause of better and more effective legal writing." In announcing her award, the LWI also included this excerpt from one of the nominations:

> [Tina is] a world-renowned educator—a pioneer in the field of teaching transactional law and skills. She is revered in teaching circles of legal writing and transactional drafting professors and well-respected by professors who teach transactional doctrine.

In addition to her textbook, Tina has published numerous law review articles and is the editor-in-chief and co-author of *Negotiating and Drafting Contract Boilerplate*.

Before becoming a full-time academic, Tina was a commercial banker at Irving Trust Company and a corporate law partner at Chadbourne & Parke LLP. At the firm, Tina had a broad-based transactional practice, including acquisitions and dispositions, recapitalizations, financing transactions, and general corporate counseling.

Tina retired from Chadbourne in 1993. For the next 14 years, through her consulting business and as an adjunct professor at Fordham Law School, she taught courses in transactional skills worldwide. She is now known internationally for her expertise in legal education and the teaching of transactional law and skills.

Tina graduated from Brown University with honors. After attending New York University School of Law, she clerked for Judge Jacob D. Fuchsberg of the New York State Court of Appeals.

MONICA L. LLORENTE

Monica L. Llorente has been drafting and reviewing contracts for over 20 years. Throughout her career, she has made significant contributions in both the private and public sectors by creating and developing new organizations, policies, and agreements.

Llorente started her legal career as an attorney in the Corporate & Securities Department of Baker & McKenzie, where she focused on both domestic and international mergers, acquisitions, and strategic alliances of publicly and closely held corporations, limited liability companies, and partnerships. Then, she went on to direct and develop the Children's Law Pro Bono Project at Northwestern's Bluhm Legal Clinic, where she created and implemented a fundraising plan; established intake, case placement, and evaluation procedures; and expanded the number of cases handled per year from approximately 30 to more than 120.

Through the years, Llorente has co-founded a number of organizations, including Dignity in Schools, a national organization of advocates, policymakers, and other stakeholders that reviews and revises juvenile justice and school expulsion policies; and the Transforming School Discipline Collaborative, an organization based in Illinois that supports school districts in implementing equitable and non-exclusionary disciplinary practices. Llorente's experience and passion for contract negotiations and drafting have been essential to developing these organizational structures and to creating agreements between various stakeholders.

More recently, Llorente has focused on helping different types of students and organizations with their contract drafting, form agreements, and training efforts. She has also expanded to support various types of artists in the issues they face in contract negotiations and agreements. Furthermore, Llorente has played an integral role in many crucial legislative and judicial efforts. For example, she was appointed by U.S. Senators Dick Durbin and Tammy Duckworth to the Judicial Screening Committee, the U.S. Attorney Screening Committee, and the U.S. Marshal Screening Committee.

Currently, as a Senior Lecturer at the Northwestern Pritzker School of Law, Llorente teaches Business Associations, Contract Drafting, Creating Change as a Lawyer, and Public Interest Law courses.

Llorente has been fortunate to have worked with individuals and entities of all types and sizes, and in various types of transactions. For this reason, she has had many opportunities to think about drafting contracts from different perspectives. In doing so, she always tries to focus on what each specific party needs and wants from that particular agreement. Through the years, her broad scope of experience has pushed her to think outside the box when problem solving and addressing risk allocation in contracts. Llorente has worked with many hundreds of drafters and students from across the world on a variety of issues. They have shared their wisdom and experiences with her, further strengthening her abilities as a professor. She hopes that this practice and teaching experience will bring new insights and real-life examples to Tina Stark's original, seminal text.

Summary of Contents

Online materials and updates for using artificial intelligence and technology in contract drafting is available on the Casebook Connect Resources page and the Aspen Website.

Contents

Online materials and updates for using artificial intelligence and technology in contract drafting is available on the Casebook Connect Resources page and the Aspen Website.

Preface to the Third Edition

From a single student signing an apartment lease to the merger of enormous corporations, almost every business relationship in the world is governed by a contract. While not every layperson needs to know how to draft a contract, every law student, lawyer, businessperson, and layperson should understand the six essential contract concepts that are the building blocks for any type of business agreement. *Drafting Contracts: How and Why Lawyers Do What They Do*, Third Edition, offers an accessible yet thorough approach to understanding these building-block concepts.

While some may hold that the skill of contract drafting can only be learned in practice, there are steps one can take before going into practice to get a running start. With the explanations, real-life scenarios, and exercises in this text, students can learn to think and draft like an attorney, and others who already have some experience in drafting can further hone their skills.

This edition would not have been possible without the strong foundation, incredible insights, and hard work of Tina L. Stark. In the Third Edition, you will find her innovative approach for understanding and drafting any type of business contract with the building-block concepts, along with detailed descriptions and examples of each part of an agreement. As in previous editions, you will continue to find a strong emphasis on teaching contract drafting in the real-world context of business transactions and developing drafting skills through practice-based examples and sample documents. Furthermore, many of the same topics continue to be relevant to current and future drafters, such as how to write clearly and avoid ambiguity, how to best organize a contract and individual provisions, and how to add value to a deal. I am honored to be following in Tina L. Stark's footsteps and to have the opportunity and responsibility to carry her work forward.

In keeping with Tina L. Stark's approach of bridging law school and practice, I have sought input from students, academics, and practitioners. As a result, the Third Edition has been updated to reflect recent developments in practice, including the initial effects of COVID-19 on drafting (such as its impact on force majeure provisions). Online materials and updates on using artificial intelligence and technology in contract drafting can be found on the Casebook Connect Resources page and on the Aspen website.

Coverage of a number of topics has been expanded, including issues relating to qualifiers, endgame mechanisms (such as limitations on liability and specific indemnity tools and provisions), and professional responsibility.

The Third Edition has been reorganized into **Parts A** through **E**.

- **Part A** introduces the six contract concepts for drafting and illustrates how to translate the business terms of a deal into these concepts.
- **Part B** explains how to draft each contract concept and how to best include them as provisions in agreements.
- **Part C** provides a thorough overview of the structure and parts of a contract, from preamble to signature lines, schedules, and exhibits.
- **Part D** focuses on Drafting Clearly and Unambiguously, mirroring Part 3 from previous editions.
- **Part E** consolidates those chapters that address skills, techniques, processes, and professional responsibility considerations when putting a contract together.

A summary chapter for study and review concludes each part, A through E, with a capsule overview of all topics covered in that section of the book.

I am excited that the Third Edition will be available on the Casebook Connect platform, where you will find more content and links. Some of the exercises, agreements, and specific explanations formerly located in Part 7 or 8 or in the Exhibit section of previous editions can now be found on the Casebook Connect Resources page and at www.aspenpublishing.com.

Students and colleagues, I look forward to receiving feedback about your experiences learning and teaching with the Third Edition. I welcome your input for my future work on the Fourth Edition.

Monica L. Llorente
December 2023

PREFACE TO THE SECOND EDITION

The following discussion occurred in 2005 between the publisher's editors and me—before I signed the contract for the First Edition:

Person 1: It's a great idea.
Person 2: But there's no market.
Persons 1 and 2 and me: If we build it, they will come.

And you came—in numbers I never thought possible. Enough of you came, you could *almost* say that Contract Drafting has become a mainstream course. Indeed, enough of you came, that the publisher said, "Write a Second Edition." So, here it is.

HIGHLIGHTS OF THE SECOND EDITION

1. The Second Edition retains the same organizational structure and pedagogy as the First Edition, but with two additions. First, students will spend more time learning how to work with precedents. For example, the textbook includes a well-drafted House Purchase Agreement that students can use as a precedent for the Car Purchase Agreement. Second, students will learn contract analysis—how to read a contract. The Teachers' Manual includes the pedagogy and many of the textbook's exercises do double-duty, so teaching this new skill will fit easily into most syllabi.

2. Most chapters have expanded discussions of their respective content, along with new exercises.

3. The Second Edition virtually completely overhauls Chapter 15—Endgame. It now discusses in detail common contractual remedies and provides a multitude of exemplars. The exemplars come from a host of contracts, so students can see the provisions at work. Among the contracts from which the provisions have been taken are a grocery supply agreement, a construction agreement, a theater lease, and a movie distribution agreement.

4. Chapter 16—General Provisions now includes examples of well-drafted provisions, so that students have basic precedents going forward.

5. Scattered throughout the book and in Chapter 32 are multiple well-drafted exemplars for students. These exemplars are more than bare bones contracts. The Chapter 32 exemplars are populated with annotations that explain associated business and legal issues and ask questions designed to

help students problem solve the agreement's drafting. These annotations give students context for what they are reading and help avert a *mindless markup*. I call the pedagogy for using the annotations *guided reading*.

6. The textbook has revised the *Aircraft* Purchase Agreement exercise. By omitting some provisions and redrafting others, the APA more directly addresses the significant issues. The memos giving instructions are also more targeted. In addition, Chapter 32 includes exemplars of action sections and endgame sections in acquisition agreements so that students gain practice working with precedents. This move reduces the textbook's narrative discussions on acquisitions — a topic not all professor want to teach.

7. The poorly drafted, much-maligned *Asset Purchase Agreement* appears no longer in the textbook's appendices. But it's on the website for anyone who grew attached to it.

8. The website will include significant new material:

   (a) Multiple exercises not included in the textbook

   (b) Standard comments that you can use when grading some of the more significant exercises. They are in a Word document, listed in order by section number. All you need to do is copy and paste the comment into a Word Comment bubble — and then tailor as necessary. These standard comments work because students regularly make the same mistakes because provisions target a specific pedagogic issues. So, when a student errs in her drafting, the error probably resembles the same error of previous students. I update these comments regularly, so please check the website right before you use the comments.

   (c) Proposed grading suggestions. The grading document allocates to each drafting, business or legal issue a number of points reflective of the issue's difficulty; for example, fewer points for the preamble and more points for the action sections. The website provides detailed information on how to use the grading documents.

Tina L. Stark
November 2013

PREFACE TO THE FIRST EDITION

Drafting Contracts brings a new approach to the teaching of contract drafting. It emphasizes the nexus between the business deal and the contract, both in the material taught and in the exercises students work on. In addition, it teaches students to think critically about the law and the transaction they are memorializing.

To draft a contract well, a drafter must know the rules of good writing — and more. Among other things, a drafter must

- understand the business deal;
- know how to use the contract concepts to reflect the parties' deal accurately; and
- be able to draft and recognize nuances in language that change the deal.

In addition, a good drafter knows how to add value to a deal by discerning and resolving business issues.

Drafting Contracts reflects a real world approach to contract drafting, bringing together years of real world contract drafting experience and law school teaching.

Although new to the market, the materials in Drafting Contracts have been used in law school classrooms for more than 13 years, including use of the manuscript at more than ten schools.

Drafting Contracts teaches students through narration and drafting exercises. The exercises are numerous, permitting a professor to choose the ones most appropriate for his or her class. As designed, the exercises in later chapters incorporate material from earlier chapters, so that students practice what they have already learned while integrating new skills. Professors need not, however, teach the materials in *Drafting Contracts* in the order set out. The book is sufficiently flexible that professors can reorder the chapters to suit any curriculum.

This book's organization reflects its pedagogy. Part 1 teaches the material that is the course's foundation. Its chapters introduce students to the building blocks of contracts: representations and warranties, covenants, rights, conditions, discretionary authority, and declarations. These chapters do more, however, than define the terms. They show how and why a drafter chooses a specific contract concept by teaching the analytic skill of *translating the business deal into contract concepts*.

In Part 2, *Drafting Contracts* sets out the framework of an agreement and works through it from the preamble to the signature lines, in each instance discussing the business, legal, and drafting issues that occur in each part of a contract. After these chapters, in Part 3, *Drafting Contracts* turns to the rules for good drafting and to techniques to enhance clarity and to avoid ambiguity. Although the chapters in this Part concentrate on more traditional drafting issues, they nonetheless remain sensitive to how the business deal affects drafting in subtle ways.

In Part 4, students learn how to look at a deal from the client's business perspective and how to add value to a transaction by identifying business issues using the five-prong framework of money, risk, control, standards, and endgame.

In Part 5, students learn the drafting process, from organizing the initial contract to amending the signed agreement. Students also learn how to analyze and comment on a contract that another lawyer has drafted.

Drafting Contracts directly addresses ethical issues unique to contract drafting, both through textual material and exercises in Part 6. The book's final part, Part 7, provides supplementary exercises.

Drafting Contracts is designed for use in an upper-level drafting course but can be integrated into a variety of other courses, including a first-year writing or contracts course, a mergers and acquisitions course, a transactional simulation course, a transactional clinic, and an upper-level writing survey course. The Teachers Manual suggests appropriate chapters and exercises for each of these uses.

The Teachers Manual is detailed. For exercises that require the redrafting of a provision, the TM includes the original provision, a mark-up showing the changes, the final version, and Notes explaining the answer. For exercises that require free drafting, the TM includes an example of a good answer along with Notes explaining the answer. In addition, the TM provides answers to commonly asked questions and tips on how to present material.

The *Drafting Contracts* website will also be a resource available to professors and students. First, professors will have access to an electronic version of the TM, so anything in it can be copied and incorporated into class notes. Second, professors will be able to download PowerPoint slides and additional exercises. Third, the website will include Word and WordPerfect versions of each provision in a large, readable font. These provisions can be projected on a screen in the same way that a PowerPoint slide can be projected. Once projected, the professor and students can work through the revision together. The website will also have additional exercises to give professors even more choices for assignments. Finally, to minimize the word processing that students do, the website will include electronic versions of the longer exercises.

Drafting Contracts teaches contract drafting in a new way. It teaches students how to think like deal lawyers and how to reflect that thinking in the contracts they draft.

Tina L. Stark
May 2007

Acknowledgments

MONICA L. LLORENTE

In line with Tina L. Stark's legacy of building a bridge between law school and practice, while working on this Third Edition, I solicited significant input from students, law professors, and practitioners. Therefore, I have many people to thank, and fear that I may have left out a few people in this section. Please forgive any oversights and know that your help was tremendously appreciated.

Every student I have had has had an impact on this edition in some way—Thank you for your thirst and passion for knowledge, your constant questioning of anything that doesn't seem quite right, and your trust and willingness to work together to improve our classes, our practice, and our profession. More specifically, I deeply appreciate the following research assistants, who I could not have accomplished this edition without: Cai Chen, Kathleen Drake, Savannah Markel, Branden Phillips, Sarah Roman-Jakob, Akiva Ungar, Monica Yue Zhang, Baruch Zimmerman. Additionally, the following teacher's assistants: Jonathan Arnold, Efrem Berk, Alexandra Edmonds, Clarissa Galaviz Lizarraga, Angela Gallagher, Cynthia Gu, Karen Hsu, Jane Lee, Gianna Miller.

To my incredible colleagues at Northwestern—Thank you for believing in me and what I do, always finding a way to make things happen, being the best sounding board one could ask for, and making our work and lives fun and enjoyable, especially in the most difficult moments. In particular, I am especially grateful for working with: Ronald Allen, Jesse Bowman, Christel Bridges, Jane Brock, Janet Brown, Lindsay Brown, Lynn Cohn, Michelle Falkoff, Andre Fiebig, the Finance & HR & Library teams, Mark Frazer, Daniel Gandert, Paul Gowder, María Amparo Grau Ruiz, Annamarie Jedziniak, Emily Kadens, Daniel Linna, Bruce Markell, Chris Martin (now at Wake Forest), Stephan Martone, Czarina Morgan, Wendy Muchman, Ellen Mulaney, David Schwartz, Sarah Reis, Judith Rosenbaum, Brian Silbernagel, Carole Silver, Alyson Smith, J. Samuel Tenenbaum (who read and commented on every single chapter and made sure I stopped to eat—invaluable), John Thornton, Cindy Wilson.

Now, to my other amazing friends and, basically, family outside of Northwestern— Muchísimas gracias por TODO—You hear me out at all hours of the day and night, you are incredibly supportive yet challenge me to be better each day. Not sure what I would do without you, especially: Jasmine Abdel-khalik, Arthur Acevedo, Laura Carrillo, Marjunette de Magistris, Andrew Fraker, Morgan Kinney, David Llorente, María Jesús López Martínez, Cheron McNeal, Maribel Núñez Mora Fernández, Regina Trillo, Kate Wargin.

And, of course, this would not have been possible without the following incredible production and management teams, who have worked long hours to bring this Third Edition to life: Aspen (Denise Clinton, Natalie Danner, Stacie Goosman, Mary Sanger, Joe Terry), The Froebe Group (Jess Barmack — a true partner who carried us to the finish line with grace, humor, unconditional support, endless energy, and photos of puppies & ponies, Susan Boulanger, Susan McClung, Suzanne Rapcavage), S4Carlisle (Rajesh N., Ravindran Santhanam).

Finally, I want to thank my friends from all over the world, especially my Culver people—I could fill pages in this book with your names and the amazing things you have done in the past year that have sustained me and allowed me to live, love, and thrive despite the challenges I have faced. Some of you even worked with me side-by-side on

Zoom, Teams, Focusmate, etc., and from different time zones. You shared your company, offered your motivation constantly, and kept me on track. You made this book happen. Thank you.

Monica L. Llorente
December 2023

TINA L. STARK

I began writing the manuscript of *Drafting Contracts: How and Why Lawyers Do What They Do* in the early aughts. I had, however, been working on the book since 1993, when I started teaching as an adjunct. It was then that I began researching what I thought I knew.

I was stunned by how much I needed to learn. I collected and filed everything: cases, law review articles, precedents, draft chapters, and miscellany. I housed my treasure trove of paper materials in ten steel drawers. (I had no computer in 1993.)

But the paper I squirreled away barely competed with the books I amassed. I bought full sets of Williston, Corbin, and *Words & Phrases*. My library was comprised of whatever I could find on legal writing, volumes on English legal history and the history of the English language, subject matter treatises on almost anything transactional (both old and modern), early dictionaries and grammar books, 19th-century compendia of precedents, and 18th-century fill-in-the-blank printed documents.

Given what seemed to be never-ending research, I was proud and relieved when, in 2007, Aspen published the First Edition of *Drafting Contracts: How and Why Lawyers Do What They Do*. They published the Second Edition in 2014, and now, in 2023, Aspen is publishing the Third Edition.

I regret the gap between the Second and Third Editions. Typically, the customary period between editions is three or four years. This gap was longer.

As some of you know, I have wrestled with chronic medical problems since 1992. The last five years have been particularly challenging, and despite my best efforts (my really, truly best efforts), I was unable to deliver a finished manuscript. Therefore, Aspen made the right call, asking me to submit the manuscript in its then-current state. They had decided that a co-author should finish the book. I understood. They had given me more time than I could have reasonably expected. New co-author Monica Llorente of Northwestern Pritzker School of Law has extensive experience teaching contract drafting and brings her expertise to the Third Edition of *Drafting Contracts: How and Why Lawyers Do What They Do*.

I wish to thank Tina Boudreaux, Senior Professor of the Practice, Tulane Law School; and Nadelle Grossman, Associate Dean for Academic Affairs and Professor of Law, Marquette University Law School. I also thank Joan E. Neal, Professor from Practice, The University of Chicago Law School; and Jane Scott, Associate Professor of Legal Writing, St. John's University School of Law.

During my years teaching in the Academy, both as an adjunct and full-time, I worked with more than 20 research assistants. With that number of students, statistically, at least a few should have failed to meet my unrealistically high expectations. But that was not the case. The students all brought their A-game to our work. Importantly, they gave me their friendship. I thank them for all of it.

As always, I thank my husband, Dave Weisenfeld, who has made, and now makes, all things possible. He is particularly skilled at helping me swat back the hard balls that life throws our way. I love him dearly. I also thank our son, Andy, for his love and unbridled pride in my success as *Professor Stark*. Somehow, my millennial son believes my working was a good thing and did not shortchange him during his childhood. In listing family members to whom I am grateful, I would be remiss not to mention Erin Weisenfeld, my daughter-in-law, who makes my son smile every day. For that, I will always be grateful. And then, there's my grandson, Kieran, eight-months-old as of this writing. What to say? Imagine every splendiferous(!) thing a grandmother could say, and consider it said.

I was a full-time professor in the Academy for only five years. But they were intellectually rewarding and great fun. Thank you for having let me be part of our joint endeavor of educating law students.

Tina L. Stark
November 8, 2023

ACKNOWLEDGMENTS TO THE SECOND EDITION

I first thank my adopters and would-be adopters. You waited patiently for this Second Edition. Unfortunately, life intervened, and earlier publication was not a realistic possibility. During this time, my publisher graciously delayed publication and supported me through a difficult time. The mantra was, "We will publish when you are ready." I will always be most grateful to Carol McGeehan (Publisher, Aspen Publishers) and Dana Wilson (my editor) for the many kindnesses they showed during my extended illness.

I also thank my adopters for taking the time to send me suggestions. As for my students, it was a joy to teach them, and the book is better because of their uncensored critiques—which were always given with a smile.

During the writing of this edition, I had superb help from my research assistants, both those from Emory and BU: Connor Alexander, Kasey Chow, Trey Flaherty, Roy Hakimian, Blake Kamaroff, Lisa Prestamo, Melissa Softness, and Sam Taylor. I particularly thank Anna Katz who worked with me at the pressured end of the writing process, juggling multiple projects with panache and good humor.

I give most special thanks to Nancy Stein who read every word, commented on substance and style, and worked tirelessly to make the book right. She also provided solace and dear friendship during difficult times. I am delighted to call her my friend.

I also thank Terry Lloyd, my longtime friend and colleague. His financial acumen added depth and accuracy to Chapter 22—Numbers and Financials Provisions. Any errors are mine.

Only a publisher who values and pursues excellence can publish a quality textbook. For me, Aspen is that publisher. Dana Wilson skillfully guided me throughout the writing process, providing wise counsel, good humor, and compassion. I look forward to working with her on the Third Edition. Julie Nahil copy edited the book, paying extraordinary attention to substance, style, and formatting. Her questions were perceptive and her proposed changes often added elegance to the text. Sharon Ray, the compositor, did a wonderful job designing and formatting the book. The exemplars in Chapter 32 required formatting work rarely seen in textbooks. Sharon inserted, by hand, each annotation, revising repeatedly until each page was correct. No computer program could accomplish what I envisaged. Sharon did.

Finally, I have three family members to thank.

First, to my mother, Cookie Stark. In 2007, she told me that I had to take the Emory job because it was what I always wanted. That permission was a gift. She was

75 years old, when daughters are supposed to be hanging around. But she gave me her blessing to leave. It was a gift that only a special mother could give.

Second, to my husband, Dave. Your love embraces me and makes possible everything I do. My words are inadequate.

Finally, to my son, Andy. Your pursuit of life inspires me and brings me a mother's joy. You are happy, and I could want nothing more. Besides, you're a stitch.

The author gratefully acknowledges permission from the following sources to use excerpts from their works:

ACKNOWLEDGMENTS TO THE FIRST EDITION

I began this book in 1993 when I first began teaching at Fordham Law School. Unfortunately, the text was only in my head. It took another ten years before I began to put the words on a page. This lengthy gestation has led to a long list of people to thank.

I begin by thanking my students. They were the first to encourage me to write this book. Through the years, their comments and insights challenged me to rethink and clarify my ideas.

While writing this book, I had the help of the following practitioners and professors: Helen Bender, Robin Boyle, Ruthie Buck, Sandra Cohen, Carl Felsenfeld, John Forry, Eric Goldman, Morton Grosz, Carol Hansell, Charles Hoppin, Vickie Kobak, Terry Lloyd, Lisa Penland, Nancy Persechino, and Sally Weaver. Their input and that of Aspen Publishers's anonymous reviewers greatly improved this book's quality.

I thank my colleague Alan Shaw for his intellectual generosity and careful review of the manuscript. In addition, I am grateful to Peter Clapp, someone whom I have never met, but who gave me line-by-line comments on almost every chapter.

Richard Green at Thelen Reid Brown Raysman & Steiner LLP was most helpful. He not only reviewed chapters, but also graciously arranged for his firm's word processing wonders to turn my typed pages into a manuscript.

While working on this book, I had the enthusiastic and dedicated support of my student research assistants: Hannah Amoah, Stephen Costa, Sarah Elkaim, and Noel Paladin-Tripp. I thank Fordham Law School for its generous support of this book.

I also thank Rick Garbarini for his good work and friendship.

Richard Neumann of Hofstra Law School played a pivotal role in this book's publication by introducing me to Richard Mixter at Aspen Publishers. I thank them and Carol McGeehan at Aspen for having had the imagination to envisage a contract drafting textbook market, even when one barely existed.

Others at Aspen also played important roles. Barbara Roth expertly shepherded me through the writing and design process, and Sarah Hains and Meri Keithley artfully designed the book's pages to showcase the contract provision examples. In addition, Kaesmene Harrison Banks skillfully guided the book through production on a tight timeframe, and Lauren Arnest meticulously copy-edited the manuscript.

Finally, I thank my husband Dave and son Andy. Their unwavering love, support, and encouragement make everything I do possible. They also make me laugh — at myself.

The author gratefully acknowledges permission from the following sources to use excerpts from their works:

American Bar Association, ABA Informal Opinion 86-1518. © 1986 by the American Bar Association. Reprinted with permission. Copies of ABA Ethics Opinions are available from Service Center, American Bar Association, 321 North Clark Street, Chicago, IL 60610, 1-800-285-2221.

American Bar Association, ABA *Model Rules of Professional Conduct*, 2006 Edition. © 2006 by the American Bar Association. Reprinted with permission. Copies of ABA *Model Rules of Professional Conduct*, 2006 Edition are available from Service Center, American Bar Association, 321 North Clark Street, Chicago, IL 60610, 1-800-285-2221.

Gulfstream Aerospace Corporation, Gulfstream G550 photo and technical data. © Gulfstream Aerospace Corporation. Reprinted by permission.

Shaw, Alan, excerpts from Fordham Law School course materials. Reprinted by permission.

Stark, Tina L., *Thinking Like a Deal Lawyer*, 54 J. Leg. Educ. 223, 223-224 (June 2004). Excerpts appear in *Drafting Contracts* Sections 2.3 and 3.1. Reprinted by permission.

Stark, Tina L. et al. eds, *Negotiating and Drafting Contract Boilerplate*, ALM Properties, Inc. 2003. All material from *Negotiating and Drafting Contract Boilerplate* is used with permission of the publisher—ALM Publishing (www .lawcatalog.com); copyright ALM Properties, Inc. 2003. All Rights Reserved.

Contract Concepts Explained

CHAPTER ONE

A Few Words About Contracts and This Book

I. INTRODUCTION

A contract is a promise or a set of promises for the breach of which the law gives a remedy, or for the performance of which the law in some way recognizes as a duty.[1]

A well-drafted contract is clear and effective, and its organization is cohesive and thoughtful. But drafting a contract requires more than good writing and organizational skills. To be a great drafter, you need to develop keen analytical skills; strong negotiation skills; an informed understanding of your client's business, industry, and interests; detailed knowledge of relevant business transactions and the laws that govern them; and a discerning eye for detail.

The following are also helpful: a great power of concentration, physical stamina, mental acuity, tenacity, the ability to multitask, and a sense of humor. Finally, a drafter must enjoy working with colleagues to create a product—namely, the contract.

II. CONTRACTS

A. WHAT DOES A CONTRACT DO?

Parties use a written contract to set out their interests, their expectations, and the rules that will govern their relationship and the transactions between them. These rules generally include the following:

- The statements of facts that each party made that induced the other to enter the transaction.
- Each party's promises as to its future performance.
- The events that must occur before each party is obligated to perform.
- Permissions or choices for the parties to act in particular ways under certain circumstances.
- How the contract will end, including the events that constitute breach and the remedies for breach.
- The general policies that govern the parties' relationship.

---

1. *Restatement (Second) of Contracts* § 1-2 (1981).

The rules in a contract constitute a set of private laws that the signing parties agree to follow. Courts will enforce these rules, subject to applicable mandatory laws or public policy, just as they would uphold public laws that apply to the general public. Therefore, judges and attorneys may speak of contracts as **private law**.

Judges and attorneys also refer to contracts as **planning documents**. Unlike documents produced in the context of ongoing litigation, which look back in time to analyze facts that already happened, contracts focus on the present and look forward to the parties' future relationship in order to document their joint plans on particular matters.

B. WHAT ARE YOUR GOALS WHEN DRAFTING A CONTRACT?

When drafting, you are trying to create a document that serves multiple purposes. You may not be able to accomplish all of them sometimes, but you should try.

When drafting a contract, you should do the following:

- Accurately memorialize the business deal.
- Draft clearly and unambiguously.
- Resolve problems with realistic solutions.
- Include sufficient specific information that the parties know their rights and obligations, but retain enough flexibility to enable the parties to cope with changing circumstances.
- Advance the client's goals and reduce the risks.
- Give both parties enough of what they need so that they leave the negotiating table feeling that they negotiated a good deal.
- Anticipate challenges and disputes and provide ways of resolving them, so that a question or dispute between the parties can be easily answered or resolved by looking at the relevant provisions in the contract.

You must take great care to properly reflect the parties' relationship and think in depth about the rules that should govern that relationship, because the parties will use the contract to solve any problems that may arise going forward. Often, parties will have the same goal but differ as to how to resolve a specific issue. A well-written contract can bridge such differences, giving all parties enough of what they need that they will agree to the contract. A well-drafted contract avoids misunderstandings and provides ways to resolve any possible future challenges.

C. WHAT IS THE CONTEXT WITHIN WHICH CONTRACTS ARE DRAFTED?

You will draft most contracts in a different atmosphere from that in which a litigator would draft a memo or brief. Litigators are out to win in an active litigation case before reaching any type of settlement phase. They want to defeat their adversaries in court, and cooperation is not generally a big part of their strategy. When you are doing deals and drafting contracts, you will find that neither party wants to give in on every issue, but each is prepared to compromise to get the deal done.

As a transactional lawyer, your language differs from that of a litigator. While litigators talk about their **adversaries** or **opposing counsel**—those whom they will battle with through a war of words—transactional lawyers and their clients talk about **the other side**, or **counterparties**. These phrases acknowledge that the interests of the parties are not necessarily aligned, but they are not as adversarial as the opposing parties in a litigation matter. The language of contract drafting reflects a different kind of relationship. The parties are competitive, but the work of drafting is performed in the context of a cooperative venture.[2] Each party may be willing to walk away from the deal, but each also has an incentive to find a way to do the deal.

Drafters do not usually write agreements for the parties from scratch every time, and, instead, they use precedent or a standard form as the basis for a new agreement. **Precedent** is a contract from an earlier transaction. A **standard form**, also known as a model or template, usually has different possible provisions you can choose from and that can be adjusted to a real transaction, even possibly annotated with brief explanations and instructions. Drafters think of precedent or a standard form as a template that they can tailor for their specific transaction.

D. WHY SHOULD YOU LEARN TO DRAFT IF YOU PLAN TO LITIGATE?

If you plan to litigate, you should learn to draft, for two reasons. First, you will regularly draft contracts as a litigator. Litigating parties settle more often than they go to trial. The settlement that they reach is a business deal and must be memorialized clearly and accurately. Failure to do so can lead to more disputes and further litigation. Second, knowing how to draft a contract will make you a better litigator. Many of the cases that you litigate will grow out of contract disputes. To represent your client properly, you should be able to analyze a contract and its provisions. If you understand how and why a drafter wrote a provision in a specific way, you will be able to craft more persuasive legal arguments.

III. ABOUT THIS BOOK

A. DOES THIS BOOK COVER ALL KINDS OF CONTRACTS?

There is no end to the variety of contracts that parties may use. Contracts can be oral or written, formal or informal, drafted by sophisticated parties or drafted on the back of a restaurant receipt over cocktails.[3] There are many ways to organize and categorize contracts. This book focuses primarily on the drafting of **business contracts** and less on standard-form consumer contracts. Consumer contracts include the terms and conditions of a Wi-Fi network that you would click on while spending time at a cafe or the general release and waiver of liability that you would sign before skydiving. The style and substance of these consumer contracts differ substantially from those of most business contracts.

There is a wide array of business contracts, and different business contracts can vary in how they are negotiated and approached. The scope of the phrase *business contracts* is intended to be broad and encompassing and to cover most negotiated contracts, whatever the topic or dollar amount. Business contracts may include an agreement for the sale of a used car, a lease, an employment agreement, an agreement for the construction of an office tower, a distribution agreement, or a settlement between litigating adversaries. Although there are unique issues to each type of business contract, this book focuses more on the concepts and parts of an agreement that are common to most business contracts with common examples and exceptions.

---

2. Settlement and divorce negotiations, which occur within the litigation context but involve drafting contracts, can be more cooperative in nature, like drafting other business contracts, or more competitive, like other parts of the litigation process. The nature of settlement and divorce negotiations will depend on the parties involved and the circumstances surrounding the matter.

3. *See Lucy v. Zehmer,* 196 Va. 493 (Sup. Ct. Va., 1954).

This book focuses on a style of drafting called **contemporary commercial drafting** for business contracts. This style of drafting draws on the principles of plain English that promote clarity through simpler language, shorter sentences, and thoughtful formatting, among other things. However, plain English drafters make their contracts even more reader-friendly by adopting an informal tone. Because plain English contracts are thought to be more easily understood, most standard-form consumer contracts are drafted in plain English. Indeed, many consumer protection statutes require that consumer contracts, such as insurance contracts, be in plain English.

Contemporary commercial drafting differs from the plain English approach when it comes to the business contract's length, thoroughness, and substance. A plain English contract's provisions are pared down to their essentials, while a business contract, written with a contemporary commercial drafting approach, is heftier, retaining all provisions that might add value or protect against risk.

Carl Felsenfeld, one of the first proponents of plain English, explained the difference between these two kinds of contracts as follows:

> The plain English movement requires a new drafting approach. Each provision [of a consumer contract] must be analyzed one at a time against the specific transaction and the type of protection required. Many of the traditional legal provisions may well be found essentially unnecessary.
>
> It is basic to this approach that one must regard drafting for a consumer transaction as quite different from drafting for a business transaction. . . . Traditionally, many of the carefully drafted provisions that cluttered up consumer documents, while important, perhaps even essential to a business transaction really added very little to the typical consumer loan. . . . The point is that consumer drafting must be regarded as a separate process from business drafting. A legal principle derived from this, while perhaps extreme, does lead the way: "In a business transaction, if a risk can be perceived draft for it. In a consumer transaction, unless a risk seems likely, forget it."[4]

B. WHAT WILL THIS BOOK TEACH YOU?

This book will teach you how to think about writing a business contract and how to write a business contract. To write a contract, you need to learn the basic principles of contract drafting, such as using defined terms for terms that you use throughout your contract; using those defined terms consistently; avoiding ambiguity; stating clearly who has the duty to do what, and when and how; tabulating to promote clarity; and being consistent in your use of language and formatting. To think about writing a contract, you have to learn how businesspeople and their lawyers think about a transaction and the contract that memorializes it.

Some of the questions that lawyers and their clients consider include the following:

- What are the client's business goals?
- How can the contract frustrate or further those goals?
- What risks are inherent in the transaction?
- What business issues does a provision raise, and how can the drafting resolve them?

---

4. Carl Felsenfeld, "Language Simplification and Consumer Legal Forms," remarks made at a program on simplified legal drafting, American Bar Association, New York City, Aug. 7, 1978, in F. Reed Dickerson, *Materials on Legal Drafting* 267 (2d ed., Little, Brown & Co. 1986). *See also* Carl Felsenfeld & Alan Siegel, *Writing Contracts in Plain English* 28-29 (West 1981).

- Does a provision give the other side too much control?
- Do the representations and warranties allocate too much risk to the client?
- How can the drafter change a covenant's standard of liability to reduce the client's risk?
- Should a particular event result in a breach or termination of the contract?
- What remedies are appropriate if a party breaches the contract?

Asking and answering these and other questions are the enjoyable part of contract drafting and what will make you stand out as a great contract drafter.

CHAPTER TWO

The Building Blocks of Contracts: The Six Contract Concepts

I. TRANSLATING THE BUSINESS DEAL INTO CONTRACT CONCEPTS

Before you start drafting a contract for a client, your client will usually have already negotiated part of the deal with the other party or parties and have come to an agreement as to some of the key business terms, such as price and timing of the transaction in question. The usual deal timeline and drafting process are explained in more detail in Chapter 32 on page 495, but the following summary will help you start to understand how a client's business issues are translated by the drafter into contract concepts.

After some type of initial negotiation, the parties will contact their lawyers. If you are one of these lawyers, you or one of the lawyers representing the other party or parties would typically put together a list summarizing the key business terms to which all parties have agreed. The next step would be for all the parties to review and confirm those key business terms. At this point in the deal, the parties may decide to enter into a more formal, written agreement, such as a letter of intent, term sheet, or memorandum of understanding. Any of these may be binding or nonbinding but would be preliminary to a more final business contract.

Before you begin to draft the more final contract, such as the purchase agreement, lease, or employment agreement, you must learn and understand the key business terms that are important to your client and those to which the parties have already agreed.[1] These key business terms of the deal are the deal lawyer's *facts*. The drafter must look at each specific issue agreed to — the terms of the deal — and translate each one into contract language. Drafters use the following six contract concepts to translate the business terms of a deal into contract language:

1. Representations.
2. Warranties.
3. Covenants.
4. Discretionary Authority.

---

1. Furthermore, as explained in more detail in Chapter 32 on page 501, you will need to understand your client's business, industry, and interests well, among other things, in order to better identify issues and problem-solve throughout the drafting process and transaction timeline. This is how successful contract drafters add value to the deal and their client's business, as discussed in more detail throughout Chapter 30.

     5. Declarations.

     6. Conditions.

Drafters use these concepts as the building blocks for creating a contract. With them, they express the parties' interests, expectations, and rules for their relationship. The best drafters assemble these contract concepts in a particular order within a contract with clear and thoughtful wording in order to best reflect the terms of the deal and the interests and expectations of their client.

Each contract concept serves a different business purpose and has different legal consequences. The analytical skill of determining which contract concept best reflects each issue or term of the business deal is known as **translating the business deal into contract concepts**, or **the translation skill**. Chapters 3 through 7 teach the translation skill by looking at each of the contract concepts in depth and demonstrating how to identify and use them in a contract. After that, in Chapters 8 through 12, you will learn how to best draft these same contract concepts.

II. CAPSULE DEFINITIONS OF THE SIX CONTRACT CONCEPTS

The following quick definitions introduce you to the six contract concepts, covered in more detail in the chapters to come. Once you understand how and why these concepts are used in specific ways, you can learn how to draft contracts that are clear and unambiguous and, thus, more effectively express the parties' interests, expectations, and rules for their relationship more effectively.

Note that only representations, warranties, covenants, and conditions to an obligation usually give rise to a cause of action in court if something goes wrong and the parties need to resort to litigation.

1. A **representation** is a statement of a past or present fact given by one party, made as of a moment in time and intended to induce reliance from the other party.

2. A **warranty** is a promise by the maker of a statement that the statement is true, which includes two promises:
   - The explicit promise that what is stated is true.
   - The promise to pay appropriate damages to the recipient of the statement if the statement is not true.

3. A **covenant** is a promise to do or not do something, also known as *a promise to perform*. A covenant creates both an obligation or duty to perform and the related right to receive the promising party's performance.

4. **Discretionary authority** gives a party a choice or permission to act and does not impose any obligation or liability.

5. A **declaration** is a fact or policy to which both parties agree, generally a definition or policy for the management of the contract. Certain general provisions, like one specifying what the governing law of the contract is, would constitute such a policy.

6. A **condition** is a state of facts that must exist before one of the following can happen:
   - A party is obligated to perform (*condition to an obligation*).
   - A party may exercise their discretionary authority (*condition to discretionary authority*).
   - A different fact or policy to which both parties agree has substantive consequences (*condition to a declaration*).

   The condition must be satisfied before the obligation, discretionary authority, or declaration is applicable.

You may already be familiar with most of these concepts, especially if you have taken a course focused on the theory behind contracts, like a first-year law school contracts course. In the chapters that follow, you will learn about the legal aspects and business purposes of each concept and how contract lawyers apply these contract concepts in practice.

Note that we will be using the purchase of a house as the factual basis for much of our discussion of contract concepts. The same concepts that apply to this example can be applied to all other types of business contracts.

CHAPTER THREE

Understanding Representations and Warranties

I. INTRODUCTION

Imagine that Sally has listed her house for sale and Bob is interested in purchasing it. However, before Bob agrees to buy the house, he wants to learn more about it. All that he knows now is the location of the home, its price, and its style—a two-story, Cape Cod–style home that is painted brown. He asks Sally the following questions during a telephone call:

- When was the house built?
- How old is the roof?
- Do all the appliances work?
- Is the house wired for Wi-Fi and cable television, and is the wiring functioning properly?
- Is there a swimming pool?
- Is there a swimming pool water heater? If so, does it use propane gas for fuel? If so, how much propane gas is in the tank?
- What color are the living room walls, and when were they last painted?
- How much property comes with the house?

Sally responds to Bob by telling him the following:

- The house was built in 1953, along with other houses in the neighborhood.
- The roof is four years old.
- All the appliances are in excellent condition.
- The house is wired for Wi-Fi and cable television, and the wiring is functioning properly.
- Yes, a swimming pool is on the property.
- Yes, a swimming pool water heater is on the property, and it uses propane gas for fuel. The tank is exactly one-half full of propane gas.
- The living room's walls are painted eggshell white and were painted one year ago. Sally mentions that she has been thinking of painting them a pale blue to coordinate with her furniture.
- The house is on a one-acre lot.

After hearing Sally's answers, Bob visits the house and immediately decides that it is perfect for him. He and Sally agree on a $200,000 purchase price. Bob then calls his lawyer and asks her to draw up the contract and include within it the information that Sally has told him. Bob tells his lawyer that he relied on Sally's answers when deciding to buy the house.

How does the lawyer include the information from Bob's questions and Sally's answers in the contract? She will use **representations and warranties**, which are two of the six contract concepts.

II. REPRESENTATIONS

A. DEFINITION OF A REPRESENTATION

> A **representation** is
> - A statement[1] of a past or present fact given by one party[2]
> - Made as of a moment in time[3]
> - Intended to induce reliance from the other party[4]

Assume that Sally and Bob sign a contract today for the sale of the house and that, in the contract, Sally tells Bob the following: The Seller represents and warrants that the roof is four years old.

Let's put aside the warranty for now and concentrate on the idea that Sally's statement about the roof is a *representation*. She made that statement *(a statement of present fact)* today, at the signing of the agreement *(a moment in time)*. Had she made the statement a year ago, the roof would have been three years old, and if she were to make the statement in a year, it would be five years old. In addition, she made the statement to convince Bob to purchase the house *(to induce reliance from the other party)*.

The representation that the roof is four years old is a statement about a present fact. In the conversation with Bob, Sally also made a statement about a past fact when she said, "The house was built in 1953, along with other houses in the neighborhood."

Although a party can make representations with respect to present and past facts, a party generally cannot do so with respect to future events or matters, sometimes referred to as *future facts*.[5] The concept of *future facts* is a contradiction. Facts are statements about matters that are known—matters that have occurred in the past or exist in the present. No one can know the future, so statements about the future cannot be facts. They are mere speculative statements or opinions.[6] (Note that

---

1. *See Restatement (Second) of Contracts* § 159 (1981) (Section 159 states that "[a] misrepresentation is an assertion that is not in accord with the facts."). Turning the definition from a negative statement to a positive one, we obtain a definition of representation: a true assertion of fact. The *Restatement* uses *assertion* and *statement* synonymously; this book will use *statement*.

2. *Id.* at cmt. c ("[F]acts include past events as well as present circumstances but do not include future events."); *see Misrepresentation by Promisor of Real Intention as Misstatement of Existing Fact*, 4 U. N.Y.U. L. Rev. 5, 5 (1926) (author not listed). ("Misrepresentations, in order to support an action in fraud, must, among other things, relate *to a fact existing or past*. Statements as to future events, merely promissory in character, are not actionable.") (citations omitted; emphasis added).

3. *Id.* at cmt. c ("An assertion must relate to something that is a fact at the time the assertion is made in order to be a misrepresentation."); *see Spreitzer v. Hawkeye State Bank*, 779 N.W.2d 726, 735 (Iowa 2009) ("[A] representation must be false at the time it was made to support a claim of fraud, and a representation that was true cannot serve as the basis for a claim of fraud. . . ." (citation omitted)).

4. *See Harold Cohn & Co., Inc. v. Harco Int'l, LLC*, 804 A.2d 218, 223-224 (Conn. App. 2002).

5. *See supra* n. 2 and the accompanying text.

6. *See Restatement (Second) of Contracts* § 159 (1981) ("An assertion is one of opinion if it expresses only a belief, without certainty, as to the existence of a fact or expresses only a judgment as to quality, value, authenticity, or similar matters.")

this book uses the phrase *future matters* to describe something in the future that could become a fact after time has elapsed.)

Practitioners in certain practice areas sometimes include future matters along with their representations in their agreements, but they should avoid doing so and should look at addressing those issues separately. In that context, the future matters may be primarily meant as warranties (or even covenants).

More typically, courts find that statements of representations cannot be drafted with respect to the future, holding that statements about future events are opinions or speculation.[7] Thus, a recipient of a representation with respect to the future usually cannot justifiably rely on that statement.[8]

The following are rare exceptions that you are not likely to run into in practice, especially when starting out, but are worth mentioning.

A recipient may rely on a *future fact* — an opinion — if the speaker purports to have special knowledge of the *fact*, stands in a fiduciary relationship to the recipient, and has secured the recipient's confidence.[9]

In addition, what may seem more like a future statement has been held to be one of existing fact if

> a quality is asserted which inheres in the article so that, at the time the representation is made, the quality may be said to exist independently of future acts or performance of the one making the representation, independently of other particular occurrences in the future, and independently of particular future uses or requirements of the buyer.[10]

Moreover, a party has a cause of action when another party promises to perform but knows that it will not.[11] This is known as **promissory fraud**. In this context, the promise as to the future fraudulently misrepresents a present fact — the misrepresenting party's state of mind.[12] While this cause of action exists, courts disfavor it because it risks converting ordinary breach of contract claims into tort actions, which bring with them the potential award of punitive damages.[13]

B. REPRESENTATIONS AND REMEDIES

In the context of contract concepts, representations, like warranties, covenants, and conditions to an obligation, can give rise to a cause of action in court and allow a party to sue if there is an issue with a provision based on a representation.[14] For example, in the event that one of Sally's representations about the house turns out to be untrue and Bob suffers damages as a result, Bob could sue Sally. The same is not

---

7. *See, e.g., Next Cent. Commun. Corp. v. Ellis*, 171 F. Supp. 2d 1374, 1379-1380 (N.D. Ga. 2001).

8. *Glen Holly Ent., Inc. v. Tektronix, Inc.*, 100 F. Supp. 2d 1086, 1093 (C.D. Cal. 1999).

9. *Outlook Windows Partn. v. York Int'l Corp.*, 112 F. Supp. 2d 877, 894 (D. Neb. 2000) (citing *Burke v. Harman*, 574 N.W.2d 156, 179 (Neb. App. 1998)).

10. *Nyquist v. Foster*, 268 P.2d 442, 445 (Wash. 1954).

11. *Levin v. Singer*, 175 A.2d 423, 432 (Md. 1961); *but see Bower v. Jones*, 978 F.2d 1004, 1011-1012 (7th Cir. 1992) (stating that Illinois does not recognize promissory fraud as a cause of action except if the promise is part of a scheme to accomplish fraud; but noting, however, that the exception has been viewed as swallowing the rule); *see generally* Ian Ayres & Gregory Klass, *Insincere Promises: The Law of Misrepresented Intent* (Yale U. Press 2005).

12. *Palmacci v. Umpierrez*, 121 F.3d 781, 786-787 (1st Cir. 1997).

13. *See Rosenblum v. Travelbyus.com, Ltd.*, 2002 WL 31487823 at *3 (N.D. Ill.).

14. Note that the only causes of action referenced here would have to be ones relating to the contract concepts. Parties to a failed agreement that want to pursue litigation usually have more causes of action available pursuant to contracts law, torts law, other branches of law, and statutes.

necessarily true for discretionary authority, declarations, and conditions coupled with discretionary authority or declarations. This distinction is why deal lawyers focus on representations, warranties, covenants, and conditions with an obligation, and why you should use them as much as possible in your drafting, when you are trying to bind the parties more and provide for further remedies.

If a provision is included in a contract as a representation, then the party receiving the representation (Bob, in our house example) may have a cause of action against the party giving the representation (Sally); if that representation is not true, the party giving the representation (Sally) knows that it is not true when she makes it, and the party receiving the representation (Bob) justifiably relies on it.[15] Representations are a common law concept. As such, they carry with them common law remedies. The differences among these remedies can directly affect which cause of action is the most favorable for a plaintiff to plead.

A party can make three types of misrepresentations: innocent,[16] negligent,[17] and fraudulent.[18] Litigation alleging any of these types of misrepresentations is a suit in tort.[19] Typically, innocent and negligent misrepresentations must be *material* to support a remedy.[20] With respect to fraudulent misrepresentations, the law varies by jurisdiction. In some jurisdictions, a misrepresentation need not be material for it to be fraudulent,[21] while in others, it must.[22]

If a misrepresentation is innocent or negligent, the usual remedies are avoidance and restitutionary recovery.[23] **Avoidance** permits the injured party to unwind the contract.[24] Both lawyers and courts often refer to this as **rescission. Restitutionary recovery** requires each party to return to the other what they received, either in kind, or, if necessary, in money.[25]

---

15. *See Restatement (Second) of Torts* § 537 (1977) ("The recipient of a fraudulent misrepresentation can recover against its maker for pecuniary loss resulting from it if, but only if . . . (a) he relies on the misrepresentation in acting or refraining from action, and (b) his reliance is justifiable."). *See generally* 37 Am. Jur. 2d *Fraud and Deceit* § 239 (2001) for a list of cases from multiple jurisdictions addressing the issue of justifiable reliance.

16. *See Bortz v. Noon*, 729 A.2d 555, 563-564 (Pa. 1999); *Restatement (Second) of Torts* § 552C (1977) (misrepresentations in sales, rental, or exchange transactions).

17. *See Liberty Mut. Ins. Co. v. Decking & Steel, Inc.*, 301 F. Supp. 2d 830, 834 (N.D. Ill. 2004); *Restatement (Second) of Torts* § 552 (1977) (information negligently supplied for the guidance of others).

18. *See Tralon Corp. v. Cedarapids, Inc.*, 966 F. Supp. 812, 826-827 (N.D. Iowa 1997) *aff'd* 205 F.3d 1347 (8th Cir. 2000).

19. This will often result in two claims. Party A sues based on misrepresentation and refuses to move forward with the contract, and Party B claims the statement was true and sues for breach of contract. Often, a contract will require the truth of representations and warranties as a condition of closing, of payment, or some other performance. The litigation might be about one party's failure to go forward based on inaccuracy of a representation, countered by the other party's assertion that the representation was true and, thus, the first party is in breach of the contract.

20. *See Restatement (Second) of Contracts* § 164 (1981).

21. *See Sarvis v. Vt. State Colleges*, 772 A.2d 494, 498 (Vt. 2001). *Compare Restatement (Second) of Contracts* § 164 (1981) (providing that a fraudulent misrepresentation need not be material to make it voidable) *with Restatement (Second) of Torts* § 538 (1977) (providing that reliance on a fraudulent representation is not justifiable unless the matter misrepresented is material).

22. *See Tralon Corp.*, 966 F. Supp. 812 at 826-827 ("the required elements of fraudulent misrepresentation under Iowa law: '(1) a material (2) false (3) representation coupled with (4) scienter and (5) intent to deceive, which the other party (6) relies upon with (7) resulting damages to the relying party.'")

23. *See Norton v. Poplos*, 443 A.2d 1, 4-5 (Del. 1981) (innocent misrepresentation); *Patch v. Arsenault*, 653 A.2d 1079, 1081-1083 (N.H. 1995) (negligent misrepresentation). Damages have been awarded in cases of innocent and negligent misrepresentation. *See Restatement (Second) of Torts* §§ 552B and 552C (1977); *see generally* Dan B. Dobbs, *Dobbs' Law of Remedies* vol. 2, § 9.2(2), 554-556 (2d ed., West 1993).

24. *See Kavarco v. T.J.E., Inc.*, 478 A.2d 257, 261 (Conn. App. 1984); *see generally* E. Allan Farnsworth, *Farnsworth on Contracts* § 4.09 (4th ed., Aspen Publishers 2004).

25. *Farnsworth on Contracts*, at § 2.24. Some cases hold that the injured party is also entitled to reliance damages. *See In re Letterman*, 799 F.2d 967, 974 (5th Cir. 1986).

A fraudulent misrepresentation is a misstatement made with **scienter**, which means the party knew the statement was false, or the party made the statement recklessly without knowledge of its truth.[26] In either case, an injured party has a choice of remedies.

First, the injured party who received the representation may void the contract and seek restitution,[27] just as with innocent and negligent misrepresentations.

Alternatively, the injured party may affirm the contract, retain the benefits from the contract, and sue for damages based on a claim of fraudulent misrepresentation,[28] which is sometimes referred to as the *tort of deceit*. Lawyers sometimes refer to affirming the contract as **standing on the contract**.

If an injured party decides to affirm or stand on the contract by suing for fraudulent misrepresentation, the measure of damages depends on which state's law governs the contract. Most states use the **benefit of the bargain** measure of damages,[29] with the minority using the **out-of-pocket** measure of damages.[30]

The benefit of the bargain measure of damages results in a higher damages award and is the measure of damages that a party generally receives on a contract breach. The benefit of the bargain is equal to the value that the property was represented to be minus the actual value. So if the property was represented to be worth $10,000 but was actually only worth $3,000, the damages would be $7,000:

Value if as represented	$10,000
Actual value	− 3,000
Damages	$7,000

Out-of-pocket damages are equal to the amount the plaintiff paid for the property minus the actual value. Thus, if the plaintiff paid $5,000 for the property that was only worth $3,000, it could recover only $2,000 in damages:

Amount paid	$5,000
Actual value	− 3,000
Damages	$2,000

The injured party's damages claim could also include punitive damages,[31] which, of course, can be significantly larger than general damages.

In this discussion, false representations have been referred to as *misrepresentations*. Although some lawyers speak of *breaches of representations*, that terminology is incorrect. A breach is a violation of a promise. Because representations are not promises, they cannot be breached. Instead, a party makes *misrepresentations*. It is correct, however, to speak of *breaches of warranties*, as warranties *are* promises.

---

26. *See Bortz v. Noon*, 729 A.2d 555, 560 (Pa. 1999).

27. *See Smith v. Brown*, 778 N.E.2d 490, 497 (Ind. App. 2002).

28. *See Stebbins v. Wells*, 766 A.2d 369, 372 (R.I. 2001); *A. Sangivanni & Sons v. F. M. Floryan & Co.*, 262 A.2d 159, 163 (Conn. 1969) ("Fraud in the inducement of a contract ordinarily renders the contract merely voidable at the option of the defrauded party, who also has the choice of affirming the contract and suing for damages. . . . [in which event] the contract remains in force").

29. *See, e.g., Lightning Litho, Inc. v. Danka Indus., Inc.*, 776 N.E.2d 1238, 1241-1242 (Ind. App. 2002).

30. *See Reno v. Bull*, 124 N.E. 144, 146 (N.Y. 1919). Some states follow neither rule exclusively, but instead have a more flexible approach that varies the damage award based on specific factors. *See, e.g., Selman v. Shirley*, 85 P.2d 384, 393-394 (Or. 1938).

31. *See generally Dobbs' Law of Remedies* vol. 2, § 9.2(5), 565-568.

III. WARRANTIES

A. DEFINITION OF A WARRANTY

A warranty differs from a representation, so the terms *representation* and *warranty* should not be used interchangeably. They are different concepts, even though they are often used together. A good drafter should understand how they are different and how they will be interpreted by the courts within the relevant jurisdiction.

The term **warranty** has been interpreted differently in many contexts. For example, even within the Uniform Commercial Code (UCC), you will find different types and interpretations of warranties. In this book, we do not seek to categorize and show you how to draft every type of warranty. We simply focus on the meaning of warranty as a contract concept when drafting business contracts, which is as follows:

> A **warranty** is a promise[32] by the maker of a statement that the statement is true.[33]

There are two promises that exist in this definition. First, there is the explicit promise that is stated. Second, the party making the statement is also promising to pay appropriate damages to the party receiving the statement if the explicit promise is not true. If a provision is included in a contract as a warranty (Sally's statement that the roof is four years old), then the party receiving the warranty (Bob) may have a cause of action against the party giving the warranty (Sally). Sally would have to pay appropriate damages to Bob if her statement about the age of the roof is not true.

If the warranty is used with a condition, the breach of the warranty by one party may permit the other party not to perform a particular act that otherwise they would have had to perform.[34] Often, a contract will require the truth of representations and warranties as a condition of closing, of payment, or some other performance.

Depending on the purpose they serve, warranties can be paired with representations or can stand alone in a business contract. For this reason, you need to think about how to best include a business issue that relates to a warranty. Chapter 8 on page 56 goes into more depth on how to approach drafting these two types of warranties.

In the context of a contract that has representations and warranties paired together, the statements referenced in the definition of warranty are those that the party made in the representation.[35] Thus, a warranty requires the party who made the statement to pay damages to the other party if the statement of past or present fact in the representation was false and the recipient was damaged. The warranty acts as an indemnity.[36]

---

32. A promise is a commitment to do or not to do something made in such a way that the person receiving the commitment justifiably believes that a commitment has been made. *Restatement (Second) of Contracts* § 2. *See generally* Chapter 4 on page 25.

33. *See CBS Inc. v. Ziff-Davis Publg. Co.*, 554 N.Y.S.2d 449, 452-453 (1990). This is not the UCC definition of a warranty, but the common law one on which this book will focus.

34. *See* Chapter 6 on page 45.

35. Do not equate a statement *in* a representation with a representation itself. A representation is more than a statement of fact and has multiple elements, as you can see from its definition, presented earlier in this chapter on page 14.

36. *Metro. Coal Co. v. Howard*, 155 F.2d 780, 784 (2d Cir. 1946) (Judge Learned Hand). Judge Learned Hand provided the following useful definition: "A *warranty* is an assurance by one party to a contract of the existence of a fact upon which the other party may rely. It is intended precisely to relieve the promisee of any duty to ascertain the fact . . . ; it amounts to a promise to indemnify the promisee for any loss if the fact warranted proves untrue, for obviously the promisor cannot control what is already in the past." *Metropolitan Coal Co. v. Howard*, 155 F.2d 780, 784 (2d Cir. 1946). Thus, the word *warranty* should be used to refer to an agreement to protect the recipient against loss if the *representations* are not true.

Here are examples of representations and warranties paired together:

Examples—Representations and Warranties Together

Organization. The Developer represents and warrants to the Client that the Developer is a corporation duly organized, validly existing, and in good standing under the laws of their jurisdiction of incorporation.

Corporate Action to Authorize. The Developer represents and warrants to the Client that the Developer has taken all necessary corporate action to authorize the execution, delivery, and performance of this Agreement.

If warranties stand on their own without representations because they are *promises*, they may promise that anything is true: either a past or present fact, a statement as to the future, or a statement that by necessity cannot be proven.

Most stand-alone warranties in a contract will be as to future matters. For example, parties may warrant that certain thresholds will be reached and, if they are not, then remedies will be provided. Here are simple examples of some stand-alone warranty provisions, but note that you would want to draft more specific provisions:

Examples—Stand-Alone Warranties

Warranty. The Builder warrants the House will never burn down.[37]

Warranty. The Owner warrants that the Boat's engine will be repaired on the date of the sale to the Buyer.

Warranty. The Company warrants that the Products sold by the Company to the Consumer are free from defects in materials and workmanship for 12 months.

B. WARRANTIES AND REMEDIES

Warranties, like representations, are common law concepts. As such, they carry with them common law remedies. The purpose behind warranties is to get the parties to disclose information and provide for damages if the information is not true or accurate.

If a provision is included in a contract as a warranty, then the party receiving the warranty may have a cause of action against the party providing that warranty if the statement is not true. Alternatively, the party receiving the warranty (Bob in the house example) may not need to perform (i.e., buy the house) if the statement is not true.

If we look again at the three warranty provisions provided as examples earlier in this chapter, those three warranties share a common denominator: The promisor may not know if the statements are or will be true. Nonetheless, the promisor *warrants* or stands behind the statement as though they could cause it to be true. In the

---

37. This example is based on *Restatement (Second) of Contracts* § 2, cmt. c, Illustration 1. This provision written as a stand-alone warranty includes a promise from the Builder to pay for costs if the House burns down.

context of warranties, not knowing or not being sure of a statement is *immaterial*.[38] Generally, it does not matter to the court if the recipient of a warranty knew that the statement was false and did not rely on it:

> The critical question is not whether the buyer believed in the truth of the warranted information . . . , but "whether [the buyer] believed [it] was purchasing the [seller's] promise [as to its truth]."[39]

This question has at its core the role of reliance as an element of a cause of action for breach of warranty, which has tortured lawyers and courts for centuries. The confusion stemmed from the uncertainty as to what *reliance* meant in the context of a warranty. Was it that the warranty's recipient had relied on the statement actually being true (as with a representation), or had the recipient relied on the *promise* that the statement was true, and the implied promise of damages if the statement were false? Through the years, the concept of reliance and who needs to prove what to recover damages in such a cause of action for breach of warranty have evolved, as we shall see.

American scholars extensively debated and analyzed warranties concerning the sale of goods during much of the twentieth century.[40] Codification of the law of warranty concerning the sale of goods in the Uniform Sales Act, and subsequently in the UCC, did little to resolve the debate about whether reliance was a required element of a cause of action for breach of warranty.[41] Outside the context of the sale of goods, there is not much academic writing about warranties, despite the use of warranties in all kinds of commercial agreements (e.g., leases, licenses, and acquisition, credit, settlement, and entertainment agreements).[42]

The evolution of warranties outside the UCC context, which is our focus here, relies heavily on the 1990 case of *CBS Inc. v. Ziff-Davis Publishing Company*. In that case, New York's highest state court held that a warranty was contractual, and that reliance was not an element in a cause of action for its breach.[43] The Second Circuit, the appellate federal court that includes New York within its circuit, has

---

38. UCC § 2-313. ("Express warranties by the seller are created as follows: (a) Any affirmation of fact or promise made by the seller to the buyer which relates to the goods and becomes part of the basis of the bargain creates an express warranty that the goods shall conform to the affirmation or promise. (b) Any description of the goods which is made part of the basis of the bargain creates an express warranty that the goods shall conform to the description.")

39. *CBS Inc. v. Ziff-Davis Publg. Co.*, *supra* n. 33 on page 18, at 453 (*quoting Ainger v. Mich. Gen. Corp.*, 476 F. Supp. 1209, 1225 (S.D.N.Y. 1979), *aff'd*, 632 F.2d 1025 (2d Cir. 1980).

40. *See, e.g.,* James J. White, *Freeing the Tortious Soul of Express Warranty Law*, 72 Tul. L. Rev. 2089 (June 1998); George Gleason Bogert, *Express Warranties in Sale of Goods*, 33 Yale L. J. 14 (1923); Samuel Williston, *What Constitutes an Express Warranty in the Law of Sales?*, 21 Harv. L. Rev. 555 (1908); *see also* Thomas Williams Saunders, *Warranties and Representations: Fraudulent Representations on the Sale of Personal Chattels*, 10 W. Jurist 586 (1876) (discussing then-contemporary English cases).

41. *See generally* White, *supra* n. 12, at 2094-2098; Sidney Kwestel, *Freedom from Reliance: A Contract Approach to Express Warranty*, 20 Suffolk U. L. Rev. 959 (Winter 1992).

42. After *CBS*, scholarly and practitioner writing on reliance's role as an element in a cause of action for breach of warranty outside the UCC context increased. *See, e.g.,* Bill Payne, *Representations, Reliance & Remedies: The Legacy of Hendricks v. Callahan*, 62 Bench & Bar Minn. 30 (Sept. 2005); Robert J. Johannes & Thomas A. Simonis, *Buyer's Pre-Closing Knowledge of Seller's Breach of Warranty*, 75 Wis. Law. 18 (July 2002); Sidney Kwestel, *Express Warranty as Contractual — The Need for a Clear Approach*, 53 Mercer L. Rev. 557 (Winter 2002); Matthew J. Duchemin, *Whether Reliance on the Warranty is Required in a Common Law Action for Breach of an Express Warranty*, 82 Marq. L. Rev. 689 (Spring 1999); Frank J. Wozniak, *Purchaser's Disbelief in, or Nonreliance upon, Express Warranties Made by Seller in Contract for Sale of Business as Precluding Action for Breach of Express Warranties*, 7 A.L.R. 5th 841 (1992).

43. *CBS Inc. v. Ziff-Davis Publg. Co.*, *supra* n. 33 on page 18.

qualified the *CBS* decision by holding that a party waives their cause of action for breach of warranty and can no longer continue with the claim, if the party knows that a warranty is false and does not explicitly preserve their rights to the claim.[44] Nonetheless, the *CBS* decision leaves open whether New York's Court of Appeals at the state level would agree with the Second Circuit at the federal level.[45]

Since this important *CBS* decision, the majority of courts addressing the issue of reliance have agreed with the *CBS* court, holding that reliance is not an element of a cause of action for breach of warranty.[46] In addition, courts have roundly criticized the small number of decisions holding to the contrary.[47] Thus, the modern view is that warranty has shed its tort origins[48] and is a promise like any other in a contract.[49] Because state law governs this issue, be sure you know the law in the state whose law governs the transaction.

IV. WHY A PARTY SHOULD RECEIVE BOTH REPRESENTATIONS AND WARRANTIES

Most practitioners, regardless of which party they represent, will pair representations and warranties together, whenever possible, to create certainty for their clients, third

---

44. *See Galli v. Metz*, 973 F.2d 145, 151 (2d Cir. 1992) (holding that where a buyer closes with full knowledge that the facts disclosed by the seller are not as warranted, the buyer may not sue on the breach of warranty, unless it expressly preserves the right to do so); *Rogath v. Siebenmann*, 129 F.3d 261, 264-265 (2d Cir. 1997) (requiring the express preservation of rights when the seller is the source of knowledge of the warranties' falsity).

45. *CBS Inc. v. Ziff-Davis Publg. Co.*, *supra* n. 33 on page 18, at 454, *505-506, **1002 ("We see no reason why Ziff-Davis should be absolved from its warranty obligations under these circumstances. A holding that it should because CBS questioned the truth of the facts warranted would have the effect of depriving the express warranties of their only value to CBS — that is, as continuing promises by Ziff-Davis to indemnify CBS if the facts warranted proved to be untrue (*see Metropolitan Coal Co. v. Howard*, at 784). Ironically, if Ziff-Davis's position were adopted, it would have succeeded in pressing CBS to close despite CBS's misgivings and, at the same time, would have succeeded in *defeating* CBS's breach of warranties action because CBS harbored these *identical misgivings*.") (emphasis in the original).

46. *See Grupo Condumex, S.A. v. SPX Corp.*, 2008 WL 4372678 at *4 (No. 3:99CV7316, N.D. Ohio, Sept. 19, 2008) ("Declining to impose an obligation on a party claiming damages for breach of warranty to prove reliance on the warranty conforms to the current views of a majority of other jurisdictions." *Mowbray v. Waste Mgmt. Holdings, Inc.*, 189 F.R.D. 194, 200 (D. Mass.); *see Power Soak Sys. v. EMCO Holdings, Inc.*, 482 F. Supp. 2d 1125, 1134 (W.D. Mo. 2007) ("The modern trend is that a buyer need not rely on a seller's express warranty in order to recover for the seller's subsequent breach of the express warranty."); *Southern Broadcast Group, LLC v. GEM Broadcasting, Inc.*, 145 F. Supp. 2d 1316, 1321-1324 (M.D. Fla. 2001) (citing cases applying Illinois, Pennsylvania, Connecticut, Montana, New York, New Mexico, Indiana, and Massachusetts law); *Norcold Inc. v. Gateway Supply Co.*, 154 Ohio App. 3d 594, 601, 798 N.E.2d 618 (2003) (also recognizing that a "decisive majority of courts' have held that reliance is not an element for claim of breach of warranty").

47. Cases holding to the contrary follow. *Hendricks v. Callahan*, 972 F.2d 190 (8th Cir. 1992) (applying Minnesota law), and *Land v. Roper Corp.*, 531 F.2d 445 (10th Cir. 1976) (applying Kansas law), are criticized by *Giuffrida v. Am. Family Brands, Inc.*, 1998 WL 196402 at *4 (E.D. Pa. Apr. 23, 1998); *S. Broad. Group, LLC v. GEM Broad., Inc.*, 145 F. Supp. 2d 1316, 1321 (M.D. Fla. 2001); *Mowbray v. Waste Mgt. Holdings, Inc.*, 189 F.R.D. 194, 200 (D. Mass. 1999). *Middleby Corp. v. Hussman*, 1992 WL 220922 (N.D. Ill. 1992) (applying Delaware law), is criticized by *Vigortone AG Prods., Inc. v. AG Prods. Inc.*, 316 F.3d 641, 649 (7th Cir. 2002); *Kazerouni v. De Satnick*, 228 Cal. App. 3d 871 (2d Dist. 1991), is distinguished by *Telephia v. Cuppy*, 411 F. Supp. 2d 1178 (N.D. Cal. 2006).

48. *CBS Inc. v. Ziff-Davis Publg. Co.*, *supra* n. 33 on page 18, at 453, 503, 1001 ("This view of 'reliance' — i.e., as requiring no more than reliance on the express warranty as being a part of the bargain between the parties — reflects the prevailing perception of an action for breach of express warranty as one that is no longer grounded in tort, but essentially in contract."); *see also Ainger v. Mich. Gen. Corp.*, 476 F. Supp. 1209, 1224-1225 (S.D.N.Y. 1979), *aff'd*, 632 F.2d 1025 (2d Cir. 1980) ("Transplanting tort principles into contract law seems analytically unsound.").

49. *Glacier Gen. Assur. Co. v. Cas. Indem. Exch.*, 435 F. Supp. 855, 860 (D. Mont. 1977) ("The warranty is as much a part of the contract as any other part, and the right to damages on the breach depends on nothing more than the breach of warranty.").

parties, and any courts that may be involved in the future. However, there are specific instances where warranties stand alone. Cases of warranties standing alone usually deal with future facts that have not yet occurred (e.g., a washing machine breaking down in the future and a company warranting their performance for a specific period of time).

As the previous sections in this chapter have made clear, a party who receives both representations and warranties obtains multiple benefits. To summarize, these benefits include the following:

1. A party may void the contract and receive restitution only if that party receives representations.
2. A party may sue for punitive damages only by claiming a fraudulent misrepresentation.
3. If a party cannot prove justifiable reliance on a representation, that party can still sue for breach of warranty.
4. If a state follows the out-of-pocket rule for damages for fraudulent misrepresentations, a party can still recover the greater benefit of the bargain damages by suing for breach of warranty.
5. A breach of warranty claim may be easier to prove than a fraudulent misrepresentation claim. As noted earlier, to prove fraudulent misrepresentation, a plaintiff must demonstrate scienter—that the defendant knowingly made a false representation. Because proving a party's state of mind can be difficult, a breach of warranty claim, which has no such requirement, may be the easier claim to win.[50]
6. Tort claims are not limited by the limitations agreed to in the contract.

The following chart summarizes the remedies associated with representations and warranties.

INNOCENT AND NEGLIGENT MISREPRESENTATIONS	FRAUDULENT MISREPRESENTATIONS	WARRANTIES
■ Avoidance and restitutionary recovery	■ Avoidance and restitutionary recovery *or* ■ Damages: ■ Out-of-pocket damages *or* ■ Benefit of the bargain damages ■ Punitive damages (rare)	■ Benefit of the bargain damages

V. REPRESENTATIONS AND WARRANTIES IN ACTION

Now that you have a better understanding of representations and warranties, let's return to our house purchase hypothetical. Remember that Sally told Bob that the roof was four years old.

For Bob to have a cause of action for fraudulent misrepresentation, Sally must have known that her statement (regarding the age of the roof) was false when she made it,

---

50. *See* W. Page Keeton, Dan B. Dobbs, Robert E. Keeton & David G. Owen, *Prosser and Keeton on Torts* § 107, 741 (5th ed. West 1984).

that Bob must have relied on Sally's statement, and that Bob's reliance must have been justifiable.[51] That is, Bob must not have known that Sally's statement was false.

For example, let's say that Bob's contractor had inspected the roof before Bob closed on the purchase of the house and told Bob that the roof is much older than four years. If Bob purchased the house anyway, then he could not justifiably rely on Sally's representation that the roof is four years old. If this were the case, Bob would not have a cause of action for misrepresentation with respect to the roof's age because his contractor had told him that it was older than Sally *represented*.

However, Bob would have had the ability not to close on the transaction if the warranty were material and untrue. Also, Bob might have a separate cause of action for breach of warranty based on Sally's statement about the roof's age.[52] Because Sally also *warranted* the roof's age, Bob would be able to sue for a breach of warranty post-closing — so long as he told Sally when they were closing that he was reserving his right to make such a claim. In reality, if this issue was important for Bob, he would most likely walk away from the transaction, as opposed to closing and then suing for breach of warranty. Instead, Bob could also try to negotiate a lower purchase price and continue with the transaction.

Deal lawyers almost always negotiate paired representations and warranties. For example, in the house purchase agreement between Sally and Bob, the representations and warranties article would be introduced with the following language:

> ### Example—Language Introducing Representations and Warranties
>
> The Seller *represents and warrants* to the Buyer as follows:

In a contract, every statement in the sections that follow this lead-in language would be both a representation and a warranty. Nonetheless, as we discussed, courts may differ in how they identify representations and warranties. For this reason, it is very important to draft them as clearly as possible to make the intent of the parties evident to all parties, third parties, and any court that has to interpret the contract.

In the purchase agreement between Sally and Bob, Sally's representations and warranties would resemble the following:

> ### Example—Representations and Warranties for the Sally and Bob House Purchase Transaction
>
> **Seller's Representations and Warranties.** The Seller represents and warrants to the Buyer as follows:
>
> (a) The house was built in 1953, along with the other houses in the neighborhood.
> (b) The roof is four years old.
> (c) All the appliances are in excellent condition.
> (d) The house is wired for Wi-Fi and cable television, and the wiring is functioning properly.

---

51. *See supra* n. 15 on page 16.
52. *See S. Broad. Group, LLC v. Harco Int'l, LLC*, 145 F. Supp. 2d 1316, 1321-1324 (M.D. Fla. 2001), *aff'd*, 49 Fed. Appx. 288 (11th Cir. 2002) (table); *see also Shambaugh v. Lindsay*, 445 N.E.2d 124, 125-127 (Ind. App. 1983).

> (e) A swimming pool is on the property.
> (f) A swimming pool water heater is on the property, and it uses propane gas for fuel. The propane gas tank is on the property.
> (g) The tank is exactly one-half full of propane gas.
> (h) The living room's walls are painted eggshell white and were painted one year ago.
> (i) The house is on a one-acre lot.

Finally, as discussed earlier in this chapter, when determining whether a party made a misrepresentation and breached a warranty, a statement's truthfulness is determined by comparing the statement to reality as of the moment in time when the statement was made, not when the determination of truthfulness is made.[53]

Therefore, Sally's representation and warranty regarding the color of the living room's walls' are truthful, so long as the living room walls were painted eggshell white when she stated that they were that color at the time of the signing of the purchase agreement. If Sally painted the walls in a different color between the signing of the agreement and the closing, Bob would not have a cause of action for misrepresentation or breach of warranty.

If Bob did not like the new color, then, to obtain a remedy, he would need to rely on a cause of action other than one based on a representation and warranty that only needed to be true at the time of the signing of the purchase agreement. The walls would have needed to be eggshell white only up to the date of the signing of the purchase agreement, and, after that, Sally could have painted them a different color. To better protect himself, Bob would have needed a covenant in the purchase agreement not allowing Sally to make any changes between the signing of the agreement and the closing. Such covenants will be discussed further in Chapter 4 on page 29. Also, Bob would have needed to include a condition in the purchase agreement allowing him to walk away from the deal if the representations and warranties are not true also as of the closing, not just as of the signing of the agreement, which will be explained in more detail in Chapter 11 on page 117.

In practice, if you are including important business issues in a contract, you should make sure that the issues are included as representations, warranties, covenants, conditions to an obligation, or all four. We will talk more later about how you do not just have to pick one of the contract concepts, and, in fact, you are encouraged to draft a business issue using a variety of concepts.

---

53. *See Union Bank v. Jones*, 411 A.2d 1338, 1342 (Vt. 1980) and n. 3 on page 14 of this chapter.

CHAPTER FOUR

Understanding Covenants

I. INTRODUCTION

Now that you have learned about representations and warranties, we will move on to the third contract concept, covenants.

Imagine that Bob and Sally are moving forward with the sale of the house, as described in Chapter 3. Bob and Sally agreed to a price of $200,000. Also, to make sure that Bob gets appropriate title to the house, Bob and Sally agreed that Sally will obtain, fill out, sign, and give to Bob any specific documents that their lawyers say are needed to properly transfer the title of the house from Sally to Bob.

Both Bob and Sally have made promises to each other about things that they will do in the future relating to the purchase price and documents to transfer title. They both have specific duties and obligations to each other that they must perform in the future relating to these two issues. To incorporate these promises, duties, and obligations into the contract, the lawyers use **covenants**.

II. DEFINITION

> A **covenant** is a promise to do or not to do something.[1]

A covenant is called a **promise** in the *Restatement (Second) of Contracts*[2] and creates a **duty** to perform if a contract has been formed.[3] That duty to perform is called an **obligation**.[4] Therefore, if a business issue in question is included in the contract as a covenant, the party giving the covenant has a duty to perform and has an obligation under the contract. In this section, we will look at examples of covenants that would appear in the house purchase agreement between Bob and Sally.

Along with the duty to perform, the covenant creates a **right** to the performance for the party receiving the covenant. This right is the flip side of the duty to perform.

---

1. *Restatement (Second) of Contracts* § 2(1) (1981).
2. *Id.*
3. *Id.* at §§ 1, 2 cmt. a (1981).
4. *Id.* at § 1 cmt. b.

Note that some practitioners use the terms *covenant, obligation, duty,* and *promise* interchangeably; but each term has different meanings and consequences depending on various factors, such as jurisdiction. These terms have had different meanings throughout the history of contract law and were interpreted in various ways depending on the context in which they were used.

Let's bring this full circle back to Bob and Sally. To incorporate into the contract Bob's promise of payment of the purchase price and Sally's promise of delivery of the necessary documents to transfer title to the assets being sold to Bob, the lawyers will use covenants because these events will occur in the future. The specific covenants that Bob and Sally will make to address each other's concerns will resemble the following:[5]

Examples—Covenants from Buyer and Seller

Purchase Price. The Buyer shall pay the purchase price of $200,000 to the Seller.

Seller's Closing Deliveries. The Seller shall execute and deliver to the Buyer

(a) the House;

(b) a general warranty deed for the House, substantially in the form of **Exhibit A;**[6] and

(c) any other instrument of transfer that may be necessary or appropriate to vest in the Buyer good title to the House.

Although these covenants relate to an acquisition, all types of contracts have covenants. Parties include covenants when they agree to perform whatever legal acts are necessary to successfully complete the business transaction. For example, in other types of agreements, covenants may be included where a party promises to sell trademarked goods only within a limited geographic area, or to use only a specific brand of pipe in the construction of a building, or to build kitchen cabinets and paint them white, or to not compete against the other party for a year after an employment relationship ends, or to not disclose confidential information. All of these examples could be drafted in the form of a covenant within a contract.

One covenant common to all types of contracts is the **subject matter performance provision**, covered in more detail in Chapter 16 on page 209. In this provision, each party covenants to the other that they will perform the main subject matter of the contract. So, in our house contract hypothetical, since the main

---

5. Note that the examples in these early chapters have been kept much simpler to focus on the issues that we are covering in that particular example. Therefore, these examples include a limited use of the defined terms and do not utilize other important best practices, such as always including *when, how,* and other conditional words in a covenant. Definitions and defined terms are covered in Chapter 15 on page 183, and Chapter 9 on page 71 covers how to best draft covenants and how important it is to include more specific information.

6. Exhibit A would be the form for the general warranty deed of the house. An exhibit is usually located at the end of a contract and is a separate agreement or other document relating to the contract and that which the parties want treated as part of the contract. Exhibits may or may not have already been signed when the parties sign the contract. To facilitate keeping track of the exhibits, some drafters bold the references to them the first time that they are used. See Chapter 20 on page 313 for more information on exhibits.

subject matter of the contract is the purchase and sale of a house, the subject matter performance provision would be:

Example—Subject Matter Performance Provision with Covenants

Purchase and Sale. At the Closing, the Seller shall sell and transfer title to the House to the Buyer, and the Buyer shall pay for and buy the House from the Seller.

III. THE RELATIONSHIP BETWEEN COVENANTS, OBLIGATIONS, AND RIGHTS

When a party promises to perform through a covenant in a contract, that promise has two consequences that matter for our understanding of covenants. First, the party that made the promise *is obligated to perform* that which was promised. Second, the party to whom performance was promised has a legally enforceable *right to that performance or compensatory damages*. The obligation to perform and the right to the performance or compensatory damages are related to each other, since they are the flip side of each other. If one exists, so does the other.

Let's take a closer look at the relationship between rights and obligations within the concept of a covenant by going back to our hypothetical and looking at a related agreement.

Assume that the house Bob is buying is in Glendale, Kentucky, and that the Glendale School District has just decided to hire Bob's partner, Mark Chin, to be a fifth-grade schoolteacher. The Glendale School District and Mark Chin summarize their agreement in a short employment contract that includes the following:

Examples—Covenants from Both Parties

2.1 Employment of Chin.[7]

(a) **Glendale Covenants**. Glendale shall hire Chin to perform all the customary duties of a fifth-grade schoolteacher on the terms stated in the Glendale Teachers' Manual, for the period beginning on August 1, 20__, and ending at 5:00 PM on July 31, 20__.

(b) **Chin Covenants**. Chin shall work for Glendale and perform all the customary duties of a fifth-grade schoolteacher on the terms stated in the Glendale Teachers' Manual, for the period beginning on August 1, 20__, and ending at 5:00 PM on July 31, 20__.

First, Section 2.1(a) states Glendale's covenant or promise to hire Chin. Using the verb *shall* plus another verb signals a covenant, as explained in more detail in Chapter 9 on page 73. That promise has two common law consequences. First, Glendale becomes obligated to perform their promise by hiring Chin. Second, Chin gains the right to Glendale's performance. That neither the obligation nor the right is

---

7. The terms *Chin* and *Glendale* would be defined elsewhere in the agreement.

explicit is irrelevant. They are both common law consequences of the promise, and common law consequences do not need to be explicit.

Although Section 2.1(a) states Glendale's covenant or promise, it does not state Chin's promise. The fact that Chin has the right to be hired under Section 2.1(a) does not obligate him to work for Glendale if he is hired. Chin's promise to work for Glendale is presented in Section 2.1(b). That promise also has two consequences: Chin is obligated to perform by teaching for Glendale, and Glendale has a right to that performance from Chin.

IV. COVENANTS AND REMEDIES

Covenants are important because, like representations and warranties, they are common law concepts that carry their own common law remedies. As discussed previously, only representations, warranties, covenants, and conditions to an obligation usually give rise to a cause of action in court and allow one party to sue another if there is an issue with the provision. If you are including an important business issue in a contract, you should make sure that this issue is included as representations, warranties, covenants, conditions to obligations, or more than one of these contract concepts.

If a provision is included in a contract as a covenant, then the party receiving the covenant may have a cause of action against the party promising the covenant, if the party making the promise does not perform. If a party makes a promise to perform but does not perform, this is called a **breach of covenant**. In general, a breach of a covenant entitles the injured party to sue for damages[8] and, if the facts are appropriate, specific performance.[9] The calculation of the damages will usually be the benefit of the bargain damages, which are equal to the value that the property was represented to be in minus the actual value of the property (instead of only out-of-pocket damages that the party incurred). If the breach is so material that it is a breach of the whole contract that cannot be cured, then a party may have a right to cancel the contract, as well as other remedies.[10,11] See Chapter 3 on page 17 for more information on the benefit of the bargain damages.

If a party breaches a covenant, they may not necessarily have also made a misrepresentation and breached a warranty. First, as is often the case, the party may not have made a representation and warranty on the same topic as the covenant. Second, even if they have made a representation and warranty on the same topic, recall that a misrepresentation and breach of warranty are determined *as of the time the representation and warranty was made*. Therefore, their status is fixed and unaffected by a covenant breach, which refers specifically to promises to be performed in the future. If a representation and warranty was true at the time it was made, then no misrepresentation or breach of warranty would have occurred just because a related covenant is breached in the future. (See the discussion of covenants in acquisitions and financings later in this chapter, on page 29, for an example of where a representation and warranty was true at the time it was made and there was no misrepresentation or breach of warranty, but the party breached a covenant.)

---

8. *See generally Dobbs' Law of Remedies* vol. 3, § 12.2, 21-50.

9. *See generally id.* at § 12.8, 189-245. For more on specific performance, see Chapter 17, page 254.

10. *See* UCC § 2-106(4), 2-612, 2-703 (2004).

11. There is the argument that, if UCC §2-601 applies, the breach need not be material for the aggrieved party to cancel. Or, under the common law, the parties can deem any breach, no matter how immaterial, as a sufficient basis for cancellation.

V. COVENANTS IN ACQUISITION AGREEMENTS AND FINANCINGS

Acquisition and financing contracts can seem more complicated because the parties will usually sign the agreement on one date but not finalize the transaction in question until a later date. To learn more about the terms and concepts that come up in acquisitions and financings, especially relating to covenants, let's go back to our hypothetical.

Imagine that after Bob and Sally have agreed to a purchase price for the house, Bob tells Sally that he cannot immediately purchase the house because he first needs to get a mortgage. He would like to delay the actual purchase for two months. He wants to apply for a mortgage so that he can use borrowed funds to pay for part of the purchase price. This is a common ask in this kind of transaction because most home buyers need a mortgage to finalize a purchase, so Sally agrees to sign the house purchase agreement on January 5th, and delay the actual sale of the house until March 3rd.

Lawyers refer to the actual finalization of an acquisition or loan as a **closing**. In this case, the actual sale of the house or closing would be on March 3rd, and that is when Bob and the bank giving him the loan would provide Sally with the full purchase price and Sally would give the house to Bob. During a closing, the parties perform at the same time the promises that constituted consideration. In an acquisition, a closing is the moment when the seller transfers the seller's property to the buyer and the buyer pays the seller. In a financing, a closing would be the moment when the bank actually distributes the money of the loan to the borrower and the borrower agrees to repay the loan under the particular terms of the agreement.

Generally, parties agree to hold the closing on a specific date, the **closing date**. The difference between a closing and the closing date and how each term is used may matter, so be sure to be precise and distinguish between the two. You will often find both terms in an acquisition or financing agreement. Practitioners generally conceive of closings and closing dates as limited to acquisitions and financings, one-off transactions that do not involve an ongoing relationship. Therefore, neither an employment agreement nor a lease would have a closing or closing date because the parties perform throughout the agreement's term, not once simultaneously, and the parties have an ongoing relationship. Instead, employment agreements and leases would have a date when the agreement was signed or from which the agreement was effective.

Because of the way that acquisitions and financings are structured, there is a gap period between the signing of the agreement and the closing of the transaction. A gap period is a routine feature of acquisitions and financings, but it is not present in most other transactions. The **gap period** is the time period that begins on the date that the agreement is signed by the parties and ends on the closing date when the closing occurs and the parties finalize the transaction. This gap period may be necessary for multiple reasons. First, a buyer may need to obtain financing, as in Bob's case for the purchase of the house. Second, the parties may need to obtain consents to the transaction or to the transfer of particular assets. Finally, the buyer may want to perform **due diligence,** if they did not previously do so. Due diligence is the corporate equivalent of test-driving a car before purchasing it. To be sure that a target company or assets are worth purchasing, the buyer-to-be examines, among other things, the seller's contracts, equipment, financial statements, and anything else that may be relevant.[12]

---

12. Because companies and assets can change in the time between the beginning of due diligence and the closing, buyers often want to include a *no material adverse change clause* to ensure their interest in the company is preserved. Then, if anything occurs that negatively affects the company or the assets, the buyer has the right to walk away or other rights specified in the agreement.

Not all acquisitions have gap periods. The signing and closing may happen at the same time: a **simultaneous sign and close**. Parties often turn to this form of closing when time is short, negotiations continue to the last minute, or both.

If there is a gap period, the agreement will often include covenants that the parties need to perform during the gap period. Let's go back to our hypothetical to examine covenants during a gap period. So, as Bob and Sally negotiate the sale of the house, Bob tells Sally how he would like her to maintain the house during the gap period between the signing of the agreement and the closing and what he expects at closing. Specifically, Bob does not want the living room walls painted in any way because he really likes the color. In addition, he wants to make sure that the propane gas tank will be at least one-third full of propane gas when he gets the house. Sally agrees to both of Bob's requests. To incorporate Sally's agreement into the purchase contract, the lawyers use covenants.

The specific covenants that Sally will make to address Bob's concerns will resemble the following:

Examples—Covenants from Sally to Bob Regarding House Purchase

Article 2—Purchase and Sale

From the date of this Agreement to the Closing Date, the Seller and the Buyer shall perform as follows:

2.4 Instruments of Transfer; Payment of Purchase Price.

(a) **Seller's Deliveries**. At the Closing, the Seller shall execute and deliver to the Buyer

> (i) the House with a propane gas tank that is at least one-third full;

> (ii) a general warranty deed, substantially in the form of **Exhibit A**; and

> (iii) any other instrument of transfer that may be necessary or appropriate to vest in the Buyer good title to the House.

Article 5—Seller's Covenants

From the date of this Agreement to the Closing Date, the Seller shall perform as follows:

5.1 Paint.   The Seller shall not paint or allow any other person to paint the living room walls of the House.

First, Section 2.4(a)(i) includes the covenant from Sally that she will make sure that the propane gas tank is at least one-third full at the closing. In this case, Bob does not care at what level the propane gas tank is during the gap period, presumably so long as there are no issues with the tank. He only really cares that the tank is one-third full by the closing, when he receives the house. Also, notice that Sections 2.4 (ii) and (iii) incorporate the covenants that we discussed earlier in this chapter regarding the documents that will be necessary to transfer title at closing.

Section 5.1 above includes the covenant from Sally that she will not paint the living room walls nor allow any other person to do so. This covenant is for a promise to *not* do something during the gap period. Acquisition agreements commonly have an article like this with many sections like Section 5.1, with covenants from the seller that involve obligations between signing and closing, and such agreements have the same type of article, though shorter, with covenants from the buyer that should be performed during the gap period.

The following timeline of the home purchase between Bob and Sally shows how covenants can be included in the purchase agreement to cover different time periods in the transaction:

Example 1 — Timeline of the House Purchase Transaction Between Bob and Sally

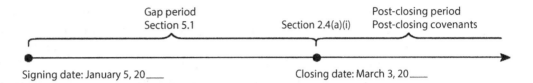

The following timelines of an acquisition agreement and a license agreement show how representations, warranties, covenants, and conditions can be used at different stages of each transaction.

Example 2 — Timeline of an Acquisition Agreement

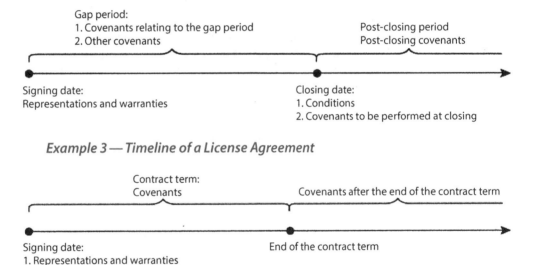

Example 3 — Timeline of a License Agreement

Example 2 shows the timeline of an acquisition agreement. As we have seen, in this type of transaction, the parties use covenants during the gap period to control the seller's actions with respect to the subject matter of the contract (e.g., the house). Buyers also provide covenants during the gap period, such as promising to obtain financing and any necessary consents to go forward with the transaction on their side. However, an acquisition agreement also has covenants that are unrelated to the gap period. Some covenants, such as confidentiality provisions, apply both before and after closing. Other covenants apply only at closing, such as the promise to pay the purchase price and the promise to transfer the assets (the subject matter performance covenants). Finally, some covenants apply only to the post-closing period, such as indemnities and noncompetition provisions. These concepts will all be explained further as you go through this book. This is simply an overview.

In acquisitions and financings, it is important to understand the relationship between representations, warranties, and covenants that have to be performed during the gap period. For example, assume that, at the signing of the contract, Sally represents and warrants that the walls of the living room are eggshell white and covenants to maintain their color until closing. Then, during the gap period, Sally decides that she wants blue walls for her last few weeks in the house, and she paints them. By doing so, Sally breaches her covenant not to paint the walls, giving Bob a cause of action for breach of the covenant. However, Bob will not have a cause of action for misrepresentation or breach of warranty because the walls were eggshell white when Sally represented and warranted as of the signing of the agreement their color as eggshell white. As will be explained further in Chapter 16 on page 223, to have a cause of action for misrepresentation or breach of warranty, Bob would need to include provisions in the purchase agreement that **bring down** the representations and warranties from the signing date to the closing date. In other words, a provision that states that the representations and warranties are true as of the signing date and as of the closing date.

The timeline of a license agreement differs from the timeline of an acquisition agreement (see Example 3 on previous page). The license agreement has no gap period, and the term begins and ends on agreed-on dates.[13] Each party covenants to the other as to their behavior during the term. The licensee promises to use their commercially reasonable efforts[14] to manufacture and market products using the trademark, to pay license fees, and to submit for approval a prototype of each product. In turn, the licensor promises not to license the trademark to anyone else, to defend the trademark, and to promptly approve or disapprove each prototype submitted for approval. Occasionally, covenants relate to the period after the term. For example, the contract will typically set out the parties' obligations post-term with respect to any unsold inventory that the licensee owns at the end of the term and any confidentiality provisions.

---

13. Sometimes the parties sign on a date before the term begins. The period between the signing and the beginning of the term differs from the gap periods in acquisition agreements. During the license agreement's gap period, generally, no covenants must be performed or conditions satisfied. Instead, the delayed beginning of the term is for administrative ease, so that the term begins either on the first day of a month or immediately after one party's relationship with a third party concludes. For example, a licensor and a licensee may negotiate and sign a license agreement in October, but the license term will not begin until January 1, the day after the licensor's current arrangement with another licensee terminates.

14. Drafters often use general qualifiers *like commercially reasonable efforts* to reduce a party's risk. However, as explained further in Chapter 9 on page 88, drafters should take the time to be more specific and thoughtful in their drafting and the standards that they are setting, especially if the issue is important.

CHAPTER FIVE

Understanding Discretionary Authority and Declarations

I. INTRODUCTION

Let's explore the fourth and fifth contract concepts: discretionary authority and declarations. Discretionary authority and declarations are two different concepts and are not used together, as representations and warranties are. However, this book covers them in one chapter because they are both straightforward and easy to explain.

II. DISCRETIONARY AUTHORITY

> A party with **discretionary authority** has a choice, or permission, to act in some way.[1]

A party who has discretionary authority is sometimes said to have an **option** or a **privilege**.[2] The party with discretionary authority *may* exercise that authority, but is *not required* to do so. However, once the party does exercise that authority, the other party is bound by the decision of the party holding the discretionary authority to exercise it.

In this chapter, we focus on *contractual* discretionary authority. That is, the parties have negotiated and agreed that a party should have a choice of action if certain criteria are met. Using the concept of discretionary authority to draft a business issue generally benefits the party with the discretionary authority because they have the option to act or not act. On the other hand, the party without discretionary authority is subject to the consequences of those actions of the party that does have discretionary authority.

Drafters often refer to discretionary authority as *having a right, being entitled to do something, or having permission to do something*, which can make it easy for anyone to confuse with other contract concepts, especially covenants. However,

---

1. *See Aroostook Valley Railroad Co. v. Bangor & Aroostook Railroad Co.*, 455 A.2d 431, 433 (Me. 1983).

2. *See, e.g., Armstrong Paint & Varnish Works v. Continental Can Co.*, 301 Ill. 102, 107-108 (1921); *Smith v. St. Paul & D. R. Co.*, 60 Minn. 330, 332 (1895).

if discretionary authority provided a party with a right, as that concept may be interpreted by a court, then a borrower taking on a loan through financing would have an obligation or duty that went along with that right. Make sure that you do not think of discretionary authority as a *right* or an *entitlement*. Discretionary authority does not provide rights, obligations, duties, or promises. To provide for those types of mechanisms and causes of action, make sure that you are using covenants, as described in Chapter 4 on page 28.

The following provisions from Bob and Sally's contract demonstrate how discretionary authority can be used:

> ### Examples—Discretionary Authority in House Purchase Agreement
>
> **Use of House.** During the period between the date of this Agreement and the Closing, the Seller may rent the House to one or more third parties.
>
> **Notice.** A party shall use one of the following methods of delivery, when sending any notice to the other party, but the party sending the notice may choose which method: registered mail, personal delivery, or overnight courier.

In the Use of House provision, Sally Seller has the absolute discretion to rent her house to anyone she chooses. In contrast, in the Notice provision, the parties have limited the exercise of discretion. There, the party giving notice may choose how to notify the other party but must use the previously agreed-on methods. The notifying party has discretion, but within some boundaries.

A grant of discretionary authority often appears as an exception to a prohibition. In that case, the discretionary authority may not be stated explicitly, but you should make every effort to draft it explicitly. Compare the examples below.

> ### Examples—Stating Discretionary Authority Explicitly
>
> #### Not Recommended—Because Not Stated Explicitly:
> **Sale of Assets.** The Borrower shall not invest in any business, except a business that one of the Borrower's subsidiaries owns.
>
> #### Recommended—Redrafted to State Explicitly:
> **Sale of Assets.** The Borrower shall not invest in any business, except the Borrower *may* invest in a business that one of the Borrower's subsidiaries owns.

When discretionary authority is embedded in an exception, either party may have that discretionary authority. The party who has it will depend on the drafting, as we will see in the three examples of an anti-assignment provision on the next page. In these examples, the house purchase agreement prohibits the buyer from assigning his rights under the agreement but grants the Seller the discretionary authority to consent to an assignment.

The examples that follow allocate to the Buyer the risk of how the Seller will exercise their discretionary authority and demonstrate the consequences of each change in wording. In Example 1, the agreement imposes no constraints on how the Seller may exercise the discretionary authority. Therefore, this first example is high risk for the Buyer. By contrast, in Example 2, the agreement limits the Buyer's risk because that provision requires the Seller to act reasonably. Example 3 differs from the first two in that the Seller is no longer the party with the discretionary authority. Instead, the Buyer is the party with the discretionary authority. Here, the contract language limits the grant of discretionary authority in the *except* clause. The Buyer may assign, but only to his wife. The Buyer's wife is also specifically named, so, if he divorces and remarries, the Buyer cannot assign his rights to his new wife. Therefore, in Example 3, the Seller has limited risk despite having granted discretionary authority to the other party.

Examples—Discretionary Authority in an Exception

1—Seller's Discretionary Authority Not Stated Explicitly with No Limits:
   Assignment. The Buyer shall not assign any of the Buyer's rights under this Agreement without the Seller's prior written consent.

2—Seller's Discretionary Authority Not Stated Explicitly with Limits:
   Assignment. The Buyer shall not assign any of the Buyer's rights under this Agreement without the Seller's prior written consent, which consent the Seller shall not unreasonably withhold.

3—Switch to Buyer's Discretionary Authority Stated Explicitly with Limits:
   Assignment. The Buyer shall not assign any of the Buyer's rights under this Agreement, except that the Buyer may assign the Buyer's rights to the Buyer's wife, Lara Raskin.

III. DECLARATIONS

A **declaration** is a fact or policy to which both parties agree, generally a definition or policy for the management of the contract.

Practitioners sometimes refer to declarations as **mutual statements of fact** and agree that they are included in agreements primarily for informational purposes — to clarify, expand, or limit the meaning of the representations, warranties, covenants, and conditions.[3]

There are two main types of declarations: definitions and policies. The definitions are usually included in the definitions article, often at the beginning of the agreement, but they may not be. Many of the policies are included in the general provisions article, which is usually toward the end of the agreement. Definitions are discussed in more detail in Chapter 15 on page 183, while general provisions are explored in Chapter 18 on page 263. Here are examples of each of these types of declarations:

Examples—Declarations

Definition:
   "Storage Space" means the 2,500 square feet of storage space shown on the drawing attached to this Lease as **Exhibit A.**

Policy in General Provisions:
   Successors and Assigns. This Agreement binds and benefits the parties and their respective successors and permitted assigns.

---

3. Practical Law Com. Transactions, *Drafting or Reviewing a Com. Cont,* https://1.next.westlaw .com/2-531-1345?isplcus=true&transitionType=Default&contextData=%28sc.Default%29 (last visited Sept. 24, 2022).

Neither party has stated the fact or policy to induce the other party to act, so neither party may rely on declarations in the same way as one would rely on representations and warranties. A party cannot sue on a declaration to obtain damages because no rights or remedies are associated with a declaration.[4] Only representations, warranties, covenants, and conditions to an obligation provide the parties with a cause of action and common law remedies.

Even though a party cannot directly access remedies through a declaration in the same way as through a representation, warranty, covenant, or condition to an obligation, declarations can have substantive legal consequences when used with one of these other contract concepts, such as when a drafter uses a definition in a covenant. Furthermore, declarations that relate to policies can also have substantive legal consequences because they often dictate how the parties will handle disputes and how to interpret different parts of the agreement. The next sections explain these issues in more detail.

A. USING DEFINITIONS

All definitions are declarations. As explained in more detail in Chapter 15 on page 183, definitions are used to compress long, complex ideas into a shorter, more digestible form to ease the reading and understanding of the contract. Definitions have no substantive legal consequences on their own. However, definitions are often used within representations, warranties, covenants, and conditions to an obligation, which give parties a right to a cause of action and remedies. For instance, the following definition of the purchase price might appear in Sally and Bob's purchase agreement:

> *Example—Definition That Is a Declaration in the House Purchase Agreement*
>
> **"Purchase Price"** means $200,000.

Although the parties have declared a legal result by including the definition in the contract, standing alone, the definition of Purchase Price has no substantive legal consequences within the contract. This provision cannot be breached. Neither party has made a representation and warranty about it or promised to do anything in the future with respect to it. Instead, the definition must be *kicked into action* by another provision or the definition serves to better inform another provision — for example, Bob's covenant to pay the Purchase Price at the closing:

> *Example—Definition within a Covenant*
>
> **Payment of Purchase Price.** The Buyer shall pay the Purchase Price to the Seller at the Closing.

Only by including this second provision does Bob have a duty to pay the purchase price and Sally have a remedy if Bob fails to pay. Definitions are often used within

---

4. *See Third-Party "Closing" Opinions: A Report of the TriBar Opinion Committee*, 53 Bus. Law. 592, 605-606, 620 (1998).

covenants for terms that are still being negotiated or may possibly change through the negotiation or transaction process. This way, if the *Purchase Price*, for example, is changed from $200,000 to $190,000, the parties only need to change the definition as opposed to searching and replacing every instance where that amount is stated within the document.

B. USING POLICIES

Parties use declarations in a business contract to establish policies that the parties will follow during their contractual relationship. A classic example is the governing law provision:

> *Example—General Provision That Is a Declaration*
>
> **Governing Law.** The laws of Michigan govern all matters arising under or relating to this Agreement.

This provision establishes a policy. When the parties litigate a dispute, the courts will use Michigan law to interpret any disputed provision. A governing law may well determine a dispute's outcome, so this type of provision does have substantive legal consequences at that time. For example, Michigan law may differ greatly from Nevada law so which law governs does matter.

As with a definition standing on its own, the governing law provision has no rights or remedies associated with it and cannot be breached. However, unlike definitions that must be *kicked into action* or inserted into another provision to have a substantive effect, the governing law provision is a policy that has consequences on its own without having to be included with a different contract concept.

The contents of declarations are often litigated by parties. Here is a common declaration from a website agreement:

> *Example—Declaration from Website Agreement*
>
> **Rights to Programming.** The Website is a work made for hire and all rights in the Website vest in the Client. Despite the preceding sentence, the Developer retains all rights to all programming or software that the Developer creates or has created outside of this Agreement and uses in the Website.

Both sentences are declarations. Were the parties to dispute who owned a piece of code, they would litigate whether that code was part of the *work made for hire*[5] or *programming or software*. That determination could have serious financial consequences for the parties. But the damages awarded would not be because of a

---

5. As defined by the Copyright Act (17 U.S.C.A. No. 101), a "work made for hire" is:
(1) a work prepared by an employee within the scope of his or her employment; or
(2) a work specially ordered or commissioned for use as a contribution co a collective work, as a part of a motion picture or other audiovisual work, as a translation, as a supplementary work, as a compilation, as an instructional text, as a test, as answer material for a test, or as an atlas, if the parties expressly agree in a written instrument signed by them that the work shall be considered a work made for hire.

statement that a party made as of a moment in time to induce the other party to act (a representation); or because of a promise that if a statement is false, one party will indemnify the other party (a warranty); or because of a breach of a party's obligation to perform (the obligation that flows from the covenant).

Similarly, although neither party could sue the other for damages based on a governing law provision, a party could sue claiming that the governing law should be that of another state (say, Wisconsin). The determination of that claim alone would not subject a party to liability. However, liability might result when a court adjudicated the substantive claim (e.g., negligence) according to Wisconsin law rather than Michigan law.

CHAPTER SIX

Understanding Conditions

I. INTRODUCTION

The final, sixth contract concept is conditions, which would be coupled with obligations, discretionary authority, or declarations. Conditions appear in all types of agreements and are often found in endgame provisions, where parties plan for what may happen if particular future scenarios arise that require the parties to substantively change or end their relationship (as explained further in Chapter 17 on page 229). In this chapter, we use conditions to obligations to demonstrate the main features of conditions.

II. CONDITIONS TO OBLIGATIONS

A. DEFINITION

Let's use Sally and Bob's real estate transaction to take a closer look at conditions to obligations.

After negotiating the purchase price of the house, Bob tells Sally that he needs to obtain a mortgage, and the application process will take about six weeks. He also tells Sally that while he is quite confident that he will obtain the mortgage, he does not want to be obligated to buy Sally's house if he cannot obtain the mortgage.

Sally agrees.

To establish the mortgage as a contractual prerequisite to Bob's obligation to buy Sally's house, the purchase contract will include a **condition to an obligation**.

> A **condition to an obligation** is a state of facts that must exist before a party is obligated to perform.[1]

---

1. The *Restatement (Second) of Contracts* § 224 (1981) defines a condition as "an event, not certain to occur, which must occur, unless its nonoccurrence is excused, before performance under a contract becomes due." However, this book uses the shorthand definition in the text. In addition, this textbook discusses two other types of conditions: *conditions to discretionary authority* and *conditions to declarations*. See Section III on page 46 *infra* (conditions to discretionary authority) and Section IV on page 47 *infra* (conditions to declarations).

As discussed previously in Chapter 4 on page 27, both obligations and rights are consequences of covenants and the flip side of each other. In other words, a provision that may be stated as a condition to an *obligation* may also be stated as a condition to a *right*. However, in practice, lawyers rarely draft a condition to a right, but are encouraged instead to draft a condition to an obligation (for various reasons, which we will discuss in Chapter 11 on page 114). One reason for this is that by setting out the party who is obligated and how they are obligated makes the instructions more clear and less ambiguous for the parties to the agreement, third parties, and, if necessary, the courts. Therefore, our primary focus in this section will be on conditions to obligations.

Uncertainty is the main characteristic of a condition. For a state of facts to be a condition, those facts cannot be certain to occur. The passage of time cannot be a condition because time will *always* pass.[2] Therefore, the following example cannot be a condition to an obligation:

> **Example—Not a Condition Due to Lack of Uncertainty**
>
> On January 7, 20___, the Contractor shall begin the work.

The passage of time overnight until January 7th arrives cannot be a condition to the contractor's obligation to begin work because January 7th is certain to come. This is not a condition, and, instead, is a covenant.

Conditions act as prerequisites to the obligation to perform.[3] Those prerequisites are a set of facts that need to exist before a party is obligated to perform. When the state of facts exists that triggers a party's obligation to perform, a condition is said to have been **satisfied** or **fulfilled**.

The consequence of a condition to an obligation is that a promisor has no contractual obligation to perform *unless* the condition to their performance is first satisfied. Likewise, if the conditions to an obligation are *not* satisfied—the prerequisite set of facts do *not* occur and do *not* exist—then an obligation is not triggered and not yet enforceable. In other words, unless the conditions to an obligation were satisfied, a party cannot be said to have breached their obligation to perform because they had no obligation to perform. First, the condition is satisfied, then the obligation is triggered, and then the promisor must perform. If the promisor does not perform, then there is a **breach of promise**.

Note that conditions are never performed, and thus never breached. Therefore, saying that conditions have been *performed* would be confusing and incorrect.

Also note that a condition to an obligation is not a condition to the making of a covenant. Instead, such a condition is a state of facts that must exist before a party must perform the *obligation* that flows from a covenant—a promise that was already made.

---

2. *Restatement (Second) of Contracts* § 224, cmt. b (1981).

3. However, the party with the obligation cannot insist on a condition being satisfied if the condition remains unsatisfied because of something that that party did. *See Amies v. Wesnofske*, 255 N.Y. 156, 162-163, 174 N.E. 436 (1931) ("If a promisor himself is the cause of the failure of performance of a condition upon which his own liability depends, he cannot take advantage of the failure. (*Williston on Contracts*, vol. 2, § 677; *Dolan v. Rodgers*, 149 N.Y. 489; *Matter of Casualty Co.* [*Bliss Co. Claim*], 250 N. Y. 410, 419.) 'It is a well-settled and salutary rule that a party cannot insist upon a condition precedent, when its non-performance has been caused by himself.' (*Young v. Hunter*, 6 N. Y. 203.)") "It is as effective an excuse of performance of a condition that the promisor has hindered performance as that he has actually prevented it." *Williston on Contracts*, vol. 2, § 677.

In the purchase agreement between Bob and Sally, the condition to the obligation and the obligation to perform should be drafted as shown in the two Correct Examples below, using *must* (preferable) or *shall* (also acceptable), and not using *is obligated*, as shown here in the Incorrect Example. As will be discussed in more detail in Chapter 11 on page 110, best practice is to use *must* to signal a condition and include elsewhere an interpretive provision stating that *must* signals a condition.

> *Examples—Condition to an Obligation in the House Purchase Agreement*
>
> *Incorrect:* **Obligation to Purchase.** If the Buyer obtains a mortgage, then the Buyer is obligated to buy the House.
>
> *Correct:* **Obligation to Purchase.** If the Buyer obtains a mortgage, then the Buyer must buy the House.
>
> *Correct:* **Obligation to Purchase.** If the Buyer obtains a mortgage, then the Buyer shall buy the House.

In the Correct Examples above, the *if* clause states the condition to the obligation. The *then* clause states the obligation to perform.

The Incorrect Example above states the condition to an obligation, as in the Correct Examples. But it also explicitly states that *the Buyer is obligated to buy*. Although that language states the common law consequence of the Buyer's promise, it is not promissory language. A court may find that this provision imposes no duty. For the parties and the courts to be able to enforce a promise, a contract should have a clearer promise.

Note that many conditions to obligations are drafted as one sentence in the *if/then* format, which presents the issues in chronological order. *If* something happens, *then* a party is obligated to do something. But the statements do not have to be ordered chronologically. In fact, the condition to an obligation and the obligation need not appear in the same sentence or even the same section of a contract. However, a contract must have both the condition to an obligation and the obligation. They are a matched pair. Whether they appear together or separately is irrelevant. Chapter 11 on page 107 explains in greater detail how to draft conditions.

B. CONDITIONS PRECEDENT VS. CONDITIONS SUBSEQUENT

Although many lawyers refer to a condition as a condition precedent or a condition subsequent, the *Restatement (Second) of Contracts* has eliminated the use of those terms and instead simply uses the term *condition*.[4] Because a lawyer could draft most provisions as either a condition precedent or a condition subsequent, distinguishing in practice between the two conditions was problematic and did not make sense.

The difference between a condition precedent and a condition subsequent was important because the type of condition determined which party had the evidentiary burden of proving the condition.[5] While a **condition precedent** was defined as a state of facts that had to exist before there was an obligation to perform (which is now known simply as a *condition*), a **condition subsequent** was defined as a state

---

4. *Restatement (Second) of Contracts* § 224, Reporter's Note (1981).
5. Timothy Murray, *Corbin on Contracts* § 39.11 (Matthew Bender).

of facts that took away a preexisting obligation.[6] The *Restatement* has recharacterized the condition subsequent as the discharge of an obligation.[7]

> **Example—Condition Subsequent**
>
> **Promise and Discharge.** The Borrower promises to pay the Bank $500,000 on or before December 31, 20____. If Guarantor pays the Bank $500,000 on or before December 31, 20____, then the Owner's obligation to pay the Bank is discharged.

In this example, the first sentence is the Borrower's absolute promise to pay the Bank $500,000. The second sentence (the condition subsequent) ends the obligation if Guarantor pays the Bank.

C. WALK-AWAY CONDITIONS VS. ONGOING CONDITIONS

You can think of conditions to obligations as having two subcategories: **walk-away conditions** and **ongoing conditions**. These classifications depend on the *type of obligation* that must be performed *if the condition is satisfied*. (Note that the *Restatement* does not separate conditions into these categories, and these terms are not always used by practitioners or the courts, but we use them in this book to help you understand how conditions operate.

- A **walk-away condition** is a condition that must be satisfied before a party is obligated to perform their subject matter performance obligation.[8]
- An **ongoing condition** is a condition that must be satisfied before a party is obligated to perform an obligation that *is not* a subject matter performance obligation.

As Chapter 16 on page 209 explains in more depth, the subject matter performance provisions are the covenants that state the parties' promise to perform the main subject matter of the contract. Therefore, for example, in an acquisition agreement, where the main subject matter of the contract is the purchase and sale of the business, the subject matter performance provisions are the parties' reciprocal promises to buy and sell that business. Similarly, in a lease where the main subject matter of the contract is the rental of specific premises, the subject matter performance provisions are the landlord's promise to lease the premises to the tenant and the tenant's reciprocal promise to rent the premises from the landlord.

A party will want a walk-away condition in the contract if there is a condition that they want satisfied before that party is obligated to perform their subject matter performance obligation. They are most frequently seen in acquisition and financing agreements. In contrast, ongoing conditions can appear in any kind of contract. Let's return to Sally and Bob's real estate transaction as an example.

Let's assume that the $200,000 purchase price for Sally's house already takes into account the water damage to the living room ceiling from a leaky roof. Bob worries that the leaks could cause additional damage during the period between the

---

6. *Restatement of Contracts* § 250 (1932).

7. *Restatement (Second) of Contracts* § 224, Reporter's Note (1981).

8. Some overzealous attorneys will make every obligation contingent on satisfaction of every condition even though they may not intend to walk away if some minor conditions are not satisfied.

signing and the closing, which is a reasonable concern. Therefore, he offers Sally the following deal: Bob will pay 110 percent of the cost of repairs for Sally to have the roof repaired no later than ten business days after the contract's signing. Sally agrees. Here's the condition and the obligation between Bob and Sally:

Example—Condition for House Purchase Agreement

Roof Repair. If the Seller repairs the roof to the Buyer's reasonable satisfaction no later than ten business days after the date of this Agreement, the Buyer shall pay the Seller at Closing

(a) the Purchase Price *plus*
(b) an amount equal to 110% of the cost of the repairs, as evidenced by receipts.

Sally's timely repair of the roof is a condition to Bob's obligation to pay 110 percent of the cost of repairs in addition to the purchase price. Bob's obligation to pay this additional amount is separate from his obligation to buy the house, which is his subject matter performance obligation. Therefore, the failure to satisfy the condition as to the roof repairs only affects Bob's obligation to pay the additional amount, not any other provision. Because the remainder of the contract provisions continue and have ongoing relevance, this condition is an *ongoing condition*.

In contrast, Bob securing a mortgage is a walk-away condition. If he does not secure a mortgage, the condition is not satisfied, and Bob is not obligated to perform his subject matter performance obligation — the purchase of the house.

Now, here is the tricky part: At this point, if Bob does not get the mortgage that he needs, he is not obligated to perform, but he may choose whether to perform. Practitioners also call this choice a **walk-away right**. Here are Bob's options:

1. Bob may choose not to perform and not buy the house. That nonperformance would not be a breach because Bob had no obligation to purchase the house if he was not able to get a mortgage.[9] The obligation to perform was never triggered by the satisfaction of the condition.
2. Bob may choose to perform by buying the house, even though he does not have the obligation to buy the house. Why would he do so? The purchase of the house may ultimately be more important to him than the satisfaction of the condition. If Bob does buy the house,[10] as a technical legal matter, he waives the failure to satisfy the condition.

The choice is not contractual.[11] The choice is the *common law consequence* of a failed walk-away condition. Accordingly, many agreements do not explicitly state that a party may choose whether to perform in these circumstances.

---

9. Note that if the condition is within the buyer's control, then the buyer has an implied obligation to attempt to satisfy the condition in good faith. Here, for example, Bob would have an obligation to *apply* for financing, at the very least.

10. The circumstances may have changed. For example, Bob may have inherited money or decided to sell some stock to have access to more cash. Alternatively, Bob may have tied the financing condition to obtaining financing at a certain rate, but he may have found that he can obtain the financing only at a higher rate. Bob may waive the condition and finance at a higher rate.

11. This choice—although a form of discretionary authority—differs from the discretionary authority discussed in Chapter 5 on page 33, which is *contractual* discretionary authority. Contractual discretionary authority exists because the parties agreed to it as a business term. It is not the common law consequence of the failure to satisfy a walk-away condition.

Nonetheless, the agreement may explicitly provide additional consequences that flow from the existence of the choice not to perform. For example, the agreement could automatically terminate. Alternatively, the agreement could give one or both parties the discretionary authority to terminate immediately, thereby permitting termination, but not requiring it. By not requiring termination, the agreement may extend the deadline by which the walk-away condition may be satisfied. Often, the agreement terminates automatically if the condition is not satisfied by the new deadline.

The following diagram depicts the relationship between

- the satisfaction of a walk-away condition and the obligation to perform, on the one hand, and
- the failure to satisfy the walk-away condition and the choice of whether to walk away or perform, on the other hand.

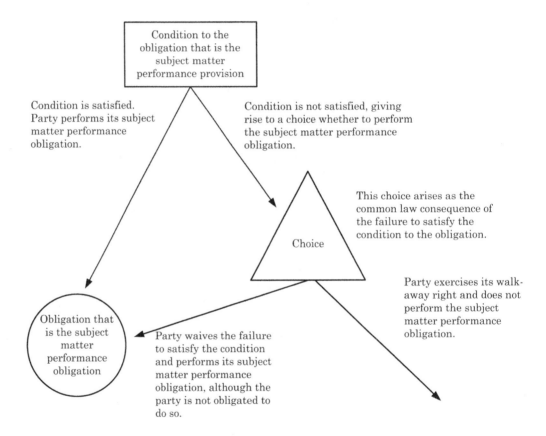

The rectangle represents the condition to the obligation to perform the subject matter performance provision. If the condition is satisfied (the left side of the diagram), the party must perform the subject matter performance obligation (the circle). If the condition is not satisfied (the right side of the diagram), the party has a choice (the triangle) that is the common law consequence of the failure to satisfy the condition. In this event, the party may choose to perform (ending up at the circle), or it may walk away, not perform, and not be in breach — despite its nonperformance. Again, the nonperformance is not a breach because the obligation to perform was never triggered.

D. RELATIONSHIP BETWEEN CONDITIONS AND COVENANTS IN ACQUISITION AGREEMENTS AND FINANCINGS

In acquisitions and financings, there is sometimes a close relationship between the closing conditions and certain covenants that a party must perform between the signing of the agreement and the closing date, the period referred to as the **gap period**. The closing conditions are the conditions that must be satisfied before a party is obligated to finalize the transaction, so they are walk-away conditions.

Let's use the house purchase as an example. Suppose that the kitchen is a wreck, and Bob wants Sally to renovate it before the closing date. If Sally agrees to do the work, the parties can use both covenants and conditions to implement and memorialize their business deal. First, Sally can promise to renovate the kitchen before the closing date. Second, the performance of that covenant can be a condition to Bob's obligation to perform (i.e., to buy the house).

> *Example—Covenant and Condition to Closing for House Purchase Agreement*
>
> **Covenant: 3.2 Kitchen Renovation.** The Seller shall renovate[12] the kitchen no later than the Closing Date.
>
> **and**
>
> **Condition to Closing: 8.2 Kitchen Renovation.** It is a condition to the Buyer's obligation to buy the House that the Seller must have performed the Seller's covenant in Section 3.2.[13]

Because the parties have used two provisions to implement their business deal, if Sally does not renovate the kitchen, both provisions must be consulted to determine the consequences.

Let's assume that Sally never renovates the kitchen and thus breaches her covenant. In that event, Bob has a cause of action for breach and may sue Sally for damages. However, Bob has an additional remedy. The covenant breach means that the related condition was not satisfied. Therefore, on or before the closing date, Bob may choose whether to perform or walk away. No matter which of these actions Bob chooses, he retains his right to sue Sally for damages because she breached her covenant to renovate the kitchen.

In this example, two contract concepts were involved (covenant and condition to an obligation), so Bob has claims under each. Each of these contract concepts exists independent of the other.[14] In these types of circumstances, the buyer (in this case, Bob) would probably walk away from the deal.

Although satisfaction of a walk-away condition may rest on the performance of a covenant, it need not. A condition may be completely unrelated to any covenant. For example, Bob might quite reasonably insist that, before closing, he must have received a licensed engineer's report stating that the house has no structural problems.

---

12. In a real contract, the parties would include more detail regarding the specific work to be performed by the seller in renovating the kitchen.

13. Bob would probably be quite unhappy with this vague standard. In a real-world situation, the parties would negotiate alternative language, providing more detailed standards.

14. In either scenario, as a matter of good practice, the buyer should formally notify the seller that it is reserving its right to sue for breach. Also, the role of misrepresentations and warranties would be considered independently, assuming that the contract included them.

> *Example—Condition for House Purchase Agreement Not Related to Covenant*
>
> **Engineer's Report.** It is a condition to the Buyer's obligation to buy the House that the Buyer must have received a licensed engineer's report stating the House has no structural damage.

Securing the clean report would then be a walk-away condition, giving Bob a walk-away right if not satisfied. In the way that it is currently drafted in the example above, it would not be based on Sally's performance of a covenant. However, to strengthen Bob's claims, Bob may want to add a covenant stating that Sally must obtain that engineer's report before the closing date so that it is clear who has the obligation of securing the engineer's report. If this ends up being too much risk for Sally, the provision can be further revised by saying that Sally has to make reasonable efforts to secure the engineer report or, even better, list specific steps that Sally needs to take to minimize her risk and state the parties' expectations more clearly. Risk allocation of this type will be discussed for each contract concept in Part B.

III. CONDITIONS TO DISCRETIONARY AUTHORITY

> A **condition to discretionary authority** is a state of facts that must exist before a party may exercise their discretionary authority, which means before they have a choice or permission to act in some way.

As with conditions to obligations, an *if / then* sentence structure often signals a condition to discretionary authority. In addition, as with conditions to an obligation and the obligation, the condition to discretionary authority and the discretionary authority are a matched pair. If a contract includes a condition to discretionary authority, it must also include the discretionary authority.

A classic example of the interplay between a condition and discretionary authority occurs in a loan agreement. Assume that to finance his purchase of the house, Bob takes out a loan and mortgages the house. In one of the later sections of the bank's loan agreement, that agreement lists the events that constitute an event of default and provides for what happens if one of those events occurs:

> *Example—Condition to Discretionary Authority*
>
> **Remedies.** If an Event of Default occurs and is continuing, then the Bank may accelerate the Loan and foreclose on the Bank's security [Bob's house] . . . .

Here, the Bank has no authority to accelerate the loan and foreclose unless an event of default has occurred and is continuing.[15] The condition must first be satisfied. Once this state of facts exists, the Bank must decide whether they wish to

---

15. The *is continuing* language is needed and favors a borrower. It precludes a bank from exercising their remedies if a borrower cures an event of default.

exercise the stated contractual remedies. The bank does not have to do so, as they have discretion. The bank could sue, waive the default, or grant Bob extra time to comply with the loan covenant.

Remember that discretionary authority is not a *right* or an *entitlement*, even though drafters often refer to discretionary authority as *having a right or permission or being entitled to do something*. For instance, in the preceding example, some practitioners might characterize the Bank's choice of whether to exercise their remedies as a right. But, if it were a right, a borrower would have a correlative obligation or duty, and they do not. However, the discretion must still be exercised in good faith.

IV. CONDITIONS TO DECLARATIONS

> A **condition to a declaration** is a state of facts that must exist before a different fact or policy as to which both parties agree has substantive consequences.

In the same way that obligations and discretionary authority can be subject to conditions, so can a declaration that is a policy, but this is not likely to happen with a definition. Here is an example of a condition to a declaration:

Example—Condition to a Declaration

Consequences of Assignment. If any party purports to assign their rights under this Agreement in breach of this Section, those assigned rights are void.[16]

Here, the entire provision establishes a policy, but the policy consists of a condition and the declaration together. That policy does not have substantive contractual consequences for the parties until the condition is satisfied. A party must purport to assign their rights before the provision, as a whole, voids the assignment. An assignment satisfies the condition in the *if* clause, which in turn triggers the effectiveness of the policy.

---

16. The law is split on whether such a clause renders the assignment null, or whether such an assignment is simply a breach of contract by the assignor. Also, under UCC § 9-406, restrictions on assignments of rights to receive payments are void themselves.

CHAPTER SEVEN

Summary of Contract Concepts Explained

The building blocks of a contract are the following six concepts: representations, warranties, covenants, discretionary authority, declarations, and conditions. The quick definitions, remedies, and questions in the table that follows will help you recall what you have learned about these concepts. Before drafting, use the questions in the fourth column to identify the business issues that you need to include in the contract and translate those issues into the appropriate contract concepts. Once you know which concepts best express the business issues, you can draft the necessary contract provisions.

When reviewing a contract, use the questions in the fourth column to identify the business issues that need to be included in the contract and determine whether the appropriate contract concepts are being used to address those issues. Then, based on this analysis, you can suggest revisions to the contract.

CONTRACT CONCEPT	DEFINITION	REMEDIES	QUESTIONS TO ASK
Representation (Chapter 3, page 14)	▪ A representation is a statement of past or present fact given by one party, ▪ made as of a moment in time, and ▪ intended to induce reliance from the other party.	▪ Representations can give rise to a cause of action in court and allow a party to sue if there is an issue with a provision based on a representation. ▪ Generally, a remedy may be available if the maker knows that their statement is false when they make it and the recipient justifiably relies on the facts represented. ▪ A party can make three types of misrepresentations: innocent, negligent, and fraudulent.	▪ Has a party said something on which the other party is relying?

CONTRACT CONCEPT	DEFINITION	REMEDIES	QUESTIONS TO ASK
		■ For an innocent misrepresentation or a negligent misrepresentation, avoidance (unwinding the contract) and restitutionary recovery (each party returns to the other party what they received in kind or in money, also known as *recission*) may be available. ■ For a fraudulent misrepresentation, an injured party has a choice of remedies, such as: (1) voiding the contract and seeking restitution (as with innocent and negligent misrepresentations), or (2) standing on the contract and suing for damages (either out-of-pocket or benefit of the bargain, depending on the jurisdiction) and possibly punitive damages.	
Warranty (Chapter 3, page 18)	■ A warranty is a promise by the maker of a statement that the statement is true. ■ In the definition of a warranty, two promises exist: (1) the explicit promise that the statement is true, and (2) the implicit promise to pay appropriate damages to the recipient of the statement if the statement is not true.	■ Warranties can give rise to a cause of action in court and allow the party receiving the warranty to sue if the statement is not true. ■ Generally, benefit of the bargain damages would be available.	■ Has a party said something on which the other party is relying?
Covenant (Chapter 4, page 25)	■ A covenant is a promise to do or not to do something. ■ A covenant establishes a duty or obligation to perform and is also known as a *promise to perform*. ■ The party receiving the covenant has a right to the performance of that promise. (This right is the flip side of the promissor's obligation to perform.)	■ Covenants can give rise to a cause of action in court and allow the party receiving the covenant to sue if the party making the promise does not perform. ■ Generally, benefit of the bargain damages would be available. ■ If appropriate, specific performance would be available.	■ Has a party promised to do something in the future?

CONTRACT CONCEPT AND CHAPTER	DEFINITION	REMEDIES	QUESTIONS TO ASK
		■ If the breach is so material that it is a breach of the whole contract that cannot be cured, then a party may have a right to cancel, as well as other remedies.	
Discretionary Authority (Chapter 5, page 33)	■ Discretionary authority gives a party a choice, or permission, to act in some way. ■ Discretionary authority is also known as an option or a privilege. ■ Discretionary authority is *not* a right or entitlement because it does not impose any obligation or liability.	■ Not applicable; there is no remedy. ■ If a party would want a remedy, then make it a representation, warranty, covenant, and / or condition to an obligation.	■ Does a party have a choice, or have they been given permission to do something? ■ Would you want a monetary (or other) remedy if the other party has discretionary authority and they do or do not act? Or, is this business issue important enough that you would want a remedy regardless?
Declaration (Chapter 5, page 35)	■ A declaration is a fact or policy to which both parties agree, generally a definition or policy for the management of the contract. ■ Also known as *mutual statements of fact.* ■ There are two main types of declarations that can be found in a contract: definitions and policies.	■ Not applicable; there is no remedy. ■ If a party would want a remedy, then make it a representation, warranty, covenant, and / or condition to an obligation.	■ Is the business issue or provision a definition, or does it establish a policy? ■ Would a party want a monetary or other remedy if it were not true or appropriate?
Condition to an Obligation (Chapter 6, page 39)	■ Condition to an obligation is a state of facts that must exist before a party is obligated to perform. ■ Once the state of facts exists sometime in the future, the condition is satisfied or fulfilled and the party must perform. ■ *Walk-away condition to an obligation*: A condition that must be satisfied before a party is obligated to perform its subject matter performance obligation (a promise to perform the main subject of the contract).	■ A condition to an obligation cannot be breached. ■ If the state of facts fails to exist, the obligation to perform then is not triggered. ■ If the obligation is triggered and not performed, then the party that had to perform has not met their obligation and there may be a breach of a promise.	■ Does the business issue or provision require that one thing must happen before a party is obligated to do something? ■ Are there events that have to occur in chronological order? ■ Are the parties uncertain as to whether those events will occur? ■ Is the business issue or provision phrased in an *if / then* sentence structure, or can it be?

CONTRACT CONCEPT AND CHAPTER	DEFINITION	REMEDIES	QUESTIONS TO ASK
	▪ *Ongoing condition to an obligation*: A condition that must be satisfied before a party is obligated to perform an obligation that *is not* a subject matter performance obligation.	If a walk-away condition is not satisfied, the party for whose benefit the condition exists may: (1) choose to waive the failure of the condition and perform the subject matter performance obligation; or (2) choose not to perform the subject matter performance obligation without being in breach and walk away from the relationship.	▪ If the condition is not met, does one of the parties want the option to walk away, or would they be satisfied still continuing with the contract? If they plan to continue with the contract, do they want to receive something else in exchange for the condition not having been met?
Condition to Discretionary Authority (Chapter 6, page 46)	▪ Condition to discretionary authority is a state of facts that must exist before a party may exercise their discretionary authority. ▪ The condition must be satisfied first, before the discretionary authority is applicable.	▪ Not applicable; there is no remedy.	▪ Must an event occur before a party has a choice or permission to do or not do something? ▪ Are there events that have to occur in chronological order? ▪ Are the parties uncertain as to whether those events will occur? ▪ Is the business issue or provision phrased in an *if / then* sentence structure, or could it be structured that way?
Condition to a Declaration (Chapter 6, page 47)	▪ Condition to a declaration is a state of facts that must exist before a different fact or policy to which both parties agree has substantive consequences. ▪ The condition to a declaration must be satisfied before the declaration is applicable.	▪ Not applicable; there is no remedy.	▪ Must an event occur before the fact or policy is triggered or has substantive consequences? ▪ Are there events that have to occur in chronological order? ▪ Are the parties uncertain as to whether those events will occur? Is the business issue or provision phrased in an *if / then* sentence structure, or can it be?

How to Draft the Contract Concepts

CHAPTER EIGHT

Drafting Representations and Warranties

I. INTRODUCTION: CHAPTERS 8 TO 12

As you learned in Chapters 1 through 7, the building blocks of contracts are the following contract concepts: representations, warranties, covenants, discretionary authority, declarations, and conditions. You want to use these building blocks as the starting point when drafting contract provisions to accurately set out the business issues that you need in your agreement. In Chapters 8 through 12, we will discuss how to best draft each of these contract concepts.

II. THE LANGUAGE INTRODUCING REPRESENTATIONS AND WARRANTIES

As mentioned in Chapter 3 on page 21, representations and warranties in a business contract are often paired together. You should not use representations by themselves, but you may want to use warranties in a contract on their own under specific circumstances.

When you draft the representations and warranties together, the language introducing representations and warranties is simple, as in the following example:

> *Example—Language Introducing Representations and Warranties*
>
> **2.1 Party A Representations and Warranties.** Party A represents and warrants to Party B as follows:

This type of lead-in sentence plainly states the parties' intent: that a party both represents and warrants the statements that follow. Each statement listed after this lead-in sentence will be considered both a representation and a warranty. Nothing else is needed. Using *represents and warrants* together, rather than either term alone, makes your contract clearer and does not allow any ambiguity as to the contract's meaning. This type of lead-in sentence plainly states the parties' intent: that a party both represents and warrants the statements that follow.

Using just *represents* or just *warrants* could create different legal consequences because each of these terms has a different substantive meaning. Using only one raises the possibility that the parties intended the consequences of only that term, which invites problems if what the parties really intended was represents *and* warrants.

Note that the phrase *represents and warrants* differs from other couplets and triplets where the two or three words used in the phrase may have the same meaning, such as *made* and *entered into*, or *sole* and *exclusive*.[1] In cases like those, where the words have the same meaning, you can safely omit all but one of the words without changing the phrase's meaning.

One of the most important jobs that you have when drafting is to plan ahead and explore different legal possibilities and alternatives.[2] A careful drafter anticipates the business and legal problems that a provision might pose and then drafts the document in such a way as to take into account any possible consequences. By using both *represents* and *warrants* together, you reduce a client's risk by explicitly saying what the parties mean, which is a key principle of good drafting.

As described in Chapter 3 on page 14, the parties in a contract provide representations and warranties as of a *particular moment in time*. The standard lead-in language introducing representations and warranties in a contract makes it so that representations and warranties are given by the parties *as of the date in the preamble*, the preamble being the first or introductory paragraph of the agreement. For example, if a bank and their borrower are amending and restating their credit agreement because of changes in the loan, the representations and warranties would be made as of the date in the amended and restated agreement's preamble.

However, the parties to a contract may want a different or additional date for representations and warranties to take effect. For example, the bank might insist that the borrower's representations and warranties be true as of two dates: first, the date of the amended and restated agreement; and second, the date of the original credit agreement.[3] This way, the amended and restated agreement does not eliminate any of the bank's rights or remedies arising from any misrepresentation or breach of warranty in the original credit agreement. The introductory language may look like the following:

> *Example—Language Introducing Representations and Warranties with Other Dates*
>
> **2.1 Borrower Representations and Warranties.** Borrower represents and warrants the following as of the date of this Amended and Restated Agreement and as of the date of the Original Agreement:

III. DRAFTING THE SUBSTANCE OF REPRESENTATIONS AND WARRANTIES

This section discusses how to craft the statements that constitute representations and warranties. By virtue of the introductory language referred to earlier, these

---

1. *See* Chapter 22 on page 334.

2. *See* Louis M. Brown, *The Law Office — A Preventive Law Laboratory*, 104 U. Pa. L. Rev. 940, 945-946 (1956).

3. There may be an exception, where the facts covered have changed. For example, this would not be appropriate if the representation covered solvency, sales revenue, or something similar that had declined or changed in some material way since the original agreement.

statements do double duty, serving as both representations and warranties. An example of such a statement that serves as both may be the following:

> ### Example—Statement Serving as Both Representation and Warranty
>
> The Seller is a corporation duly organized, validly existing, and in good standing under the laws of the state of Delaware, with all requisite corporate power and authority to own, operate, and lease the Seller's properties, and to carry on the Seller's business as now being conducted.

If the statement is not true[4] and the statement's recipient suffered any damages, the statement's recipient may have a cause of action for misrepresentation and for breach of warranty against the statement's maker, which will require that the statement's maker pay damages to the statement's recipient.

This section covers *best practices for drafting representations and warranties*, including knowing what you should include, drafting them with past or present facts, making sure to use the active voice instead of the passive voice, and using qualified representations and warranties. This chapter ends with guidance on how to draft stand-alone warranties and exercises to practice your drafting skills on representations and warranties.

A. CONTENT AND QUESTIONS TO ASK

The content of an agreement's representations and warranties can vary greatly depending on the type of transaction and the parties involved. To determine what you should include as representations and warranties, you will need to talk to your client. You will need to ask your client what information they were relying on when they entered into the transaction—information that the other party provided. That particular information provided by the other party and on which your client relied is what you need to have in order to draft the representations and warranties.

Also, you will want to consult any binding or non-binding written agreement or list of business issues that the clients have put together and agreed to already, if any. You will want to limit the representations and warranties that your client gives, so you will have to ask your client what they feel comfortable representing and warranting. You may not even want to offer any representations and warranties from your client to the other party, but instead wait to see which ones they request. You can use the summary chart in Chapter 7 on page 49 as a guide. Also, you should look at form agreements or precedent for the type of agreement that you are drafting. Furthermore, make sure that you understand what is common in the relevant industry to best protect your client, or if not, research those industry standards.

At times, representations and warranties are also used after the contract is signed to better manage the contract and relationship between the parties. For example, many ongoing commercial contracts make the truth of some or all of the representations and warranties a condition of continued performance.

---

4. You must work to verify representations and warranties before closing a deal. For example, if you are buying a used car, you may want to hire a mechanic to verify that the car is in the condition that the seller has represented and warranted. Also, if you are doing any kind of transaction with a company, you would want to verify that they are organized, validly existing, and in good standing under the laws of their jurisdiction of incorporation by checking with the relevant state authorities.

Even though the content of the representations and warranties will vary from agreement to agreement, most contracts that have an entity as a party share a set of **foundational representations and warranties**, assurances about core, fundamental facts that are a prerequisite to most deals. More specifically, these representations and warranties address whether a party exists as a legal entity, which type of legal entity and in which jurisdiction, whether they have the authority to conduct their business and to enter into the transaction, and whether their counterparty has enforceable rights and remedies against them if they breach. For a simple example of such a foundational representation and warranty, see the next section.

Parties often make *parallel or reciprocal* foundational representations and warranties. *Parallel or reciprocal* representations and warranties use the same words for each party, so the parties are assuming equivalent risks. On the other hand, parties with substantial negotiating leverage limit even these representations and warranties to the greatest extent possible. The rationale is, "Why take any risk? The other side is getting our money or the benefit of working with us. What more do they need?" Commercial banks are known for refusing to give borrowers any foundational representations and warranties.

B. PAST OR PRESENT FACTS

Generally, the facts in a representation and warranty statement must relate to a state of affairs that exists in the present or existed in the past but not in the future.[5] With respect to those facts that presently exist, draft the representation and warranty in the present tense, as follows:

Example—Representation and Warranty Statement in Present Tense

    Organization; Good Standing. The Seller *is* a corporation duly organized, validly existing, and in good standing under the laws of the state of Delaware, with all requisite corporate power and authority to own, operate, and lease the Seller's properties, and to carry on the Seller's business as now being conducted.

Be careful not to use *currently* or *presently* in a representation and warranty statement. Using these types of words relating to time in any kind of transaction could create confusion regarding which moment in time the representations and warranties are made.

For example, remember that in an acquisition, there is often the date of the purchase agreement (when it is signed), a gap period (between signing the agreement and the closing date), and the final closing date (when the purchase price and assets are exchanged). In an acquisition agreement, there are often representations and warranties that are made *as of the date of the purchase agreement*. In addition, there are provisions in the purchase agreement drafted as conditions that state that the parties will close on the transaction only if the representations and warranties are also true *as of the closing date*. Using *currently* or *presently* in the representations and warranties of a purchase agreement could affect the meaning of the conditions that provide that the representations and warranties must be true both as of the signing of the purchase agreement and on the closing date.

---

5. *Restatement (Second) of Contracts* § 159 cmt. c (1981).

If you need to include a fact that occurred in the past in a representation and warranty, draft the statement in a tense that expresses that time horizon. Statements in representations and warranties with respect to the past are generally drafted in the past tense or the present perfect tense, like the following:

Example—Representation and Warranty Statement in Past Tense

Board Authorization. The Borrower's board of directors *authorized* the Borrowings on September 26, 20__.

Example —Representation and Warranty Statement in Present Perfect Tense

Tax Returns and Payments. The Parent and each Subsidiary *have duly filed* all federal, state, and local tax returns and reports required to be filed, and each of them *has duly paid or established* adequate reserves for the proper payment of all taxes and other governmental charges on it or its properties, assets, income, franchises, licenses, or sales.

As mentioned in Chapter 3 on page 14, statements of paired representations and warranties should not be drafted with respect to facts that are expected to materialize in the future. The following representation and warranty from an acquisition agreement shows an error with respect to *future facts* that drafters commonly make:

Example—Incorrect Representation and Warranty Statement with Future Facts

3.8 Consents. The Seller has obtained all consents required in connection with the execution and delivery of this Agreement. The Seller *will have obtained* before Closing all consents required in connection with the consummation of the transactions that this Agreement contemplates.

As the statement in the second sentence is phrased in terms of the future, a recipient may not justifiably rely on that statement because it is not a clear representation and warranty, covenant, or condition to an obligation. However, that sentence was included with the best of intentions. The seller intended to reassure the buyer by stating that the seller would obtain all the consents before closing, even though they had not yet done so. In essence, the seller was *promising* the buyer that they would obtain them. Statements in paired representations and warranties with respect to the future should probably be drafted as covenants. Note that when drafting these covenants, you will also want to tie them to explicit conditions, so that there is no obligation to close or move forward in any way until the covenant has been performed (in this case, the consents being obtained). Then, your client will be better protected. Remember to think carefully and coordinate how the various contract concepts and parts of the agreement work with each other.

To correctly carry out the seller's intent from the example above, the provision should be redrafted as two provisions: one as a representation and warranty and the other as a covenant.

By breaking out the covenant from the representation and warranty, we clearly lay out the past and present facts that the seller can represent and warrant and the responsibilities that the seller has going forward to obtain the consents that are still outstanding.

Example—Correct Representation and Warranty Statement and Covenant with Future Facts

3.1 Seller Representations and Warranties. Seller represents and warrants to Buyer as follows:

(i) **Consents**. The Seller has obtained all consents required in connection with the execution and delivery of this Agreement. Except as listed in **Schedule 3.8**,[6] the Seller has obtained all consents required in connection with the consummation of the transactions that this Agreement contemplates.

4.1 Seller Covenants. From the date of this Agreement to the Closing, the Seller shall perform as follows:

(i) **Consents**. The Seller shall obtain all the consents listed in **Schedule 3.8** before the Closing.

Making sure that you are using the correct contract concepts is essential to preserving any possible causes of action for your client, as well as ensuring that the parties know what has already occurred and what they still need to do.

C. ACTIVE VERSUS PASSIVE VOICE

Treatises, commentators, and practitioners usually advise drafters to use the active voice over the passive voice for clarity and to avoid ambiguity when drafting any provision, regardless of which contract concept you are using. When one uses the active voice, the subject of the sentence acts on an object. When one uses the passive voice, the subject of the sentence is acted on by an actor. Sometimes, when one uses the passive voice, the actor is dropped from the sentence entirely, creating the possibility of ambiguity. Sentences in the active voice tend to be shorter, be easier to read, be clearer, and have a stronger impact. Here are some examples of representations and warranties in the active and passive voice:

While you should generally draft paired representations and warranties in the active voice, there can be exceptions. Sometimes the voice used makes a substantive difference, and a change in the subject of the sentence or in the order of the words

---

Examples—Voice in Representation and Warranty Statement

Recommended in Active Voice:
Taxes. The Seller paid the taxes on the Property when due.

Not Recommended in Passive Voice:
Taxes. The taxes on the Property were paid when due.
Taxes. The taxes on the Property were paid when due by the Seller.

---

6. A schedule is usually located at the end of an agreement and is used to disclose information relating to representations and warranties. See Chapter 20 on page 312 for more on schedules.

can alter the meaning. For example, when purchasing a used parachute, a buyer wants to know the *total* number of times the parachute has been used, not how many times the *seller* has used it, as follows:

When the issue is the action rather than the actor, the passive voice is appropriate. You can use settings in a word-processing application to help you spot the use of the passive voice.

Examples—Representation and Warranties Exception to Active Voice

Incorrect in Active Voice:

Prior Use. The Seller has used the parachute three times.

Correct in Passive Voice:

Prior Use. The parachute has been used five times.

IV. RISK ALLOCATION IN REPRESENTATIONS AND WARRANTIES

Each representation and warranty establishes a standard of liability. If a statement is false and does not reflect reality, then the standard has not been met and the party making the statement is subject to liability. By establishing standards of liability, representations and warranties serve an important business purpose. They are a **risk allocation** mechanism. This means that the degree of risk that each party assumes with respect to a statement varies depending on how broadly or narrowly the statement is drafted. In this section, we will explore how to draft flat and qualified representations and warranties and how to use knowledge, materiality, efforts, and other qualifiers in representations and warranties.

A. FLAT OR QUALIFIED REPRESENTATIONS AND WARRANTIES

Let's go back to the house purchase example that we looked at in Part A. When Sally told Bob that the propane gas tank was exactly one-half full, she declared this as a precise, absolute statement, without any room for flexibility or variation of any kind. This would be considered a **flat representation and warranty**. Saying that the propane gas tank is exactly one-half full is a high-risk statement for Sally because if she is even a little wrong, Bob has a cause of action for misrepresentation and breach of warranty. He might not have a claim for a great deal of money, but he could certainly bring a nuisance suit and hope for a quick settlement and price reduction. In addition, if this representation and warranty is a condition to closing, Sally has given Bob a reason not to close.

Sally could have reduced her risk by making a less precise statement. She could have made a **qualified representation and warranty**. For example, she could have said, "[T]he tank is *approximately* half full." Then if the propane gas tank had been less than one-half of its capacity, Sally might still have been able to contend that her statement was true. Her risk of having made a false statement would have been reduced. However, Bob would have assumed a greater risk with respect to Sally's statement about the amount of fuel in the tank. Originally, Bob would have had a cause of action if the tank was even a little less than half full. Now, to prove a misrepresentation and breach of warranty, Bob must argue what *approximately* means. The risk allocation has shifted more of the risk to Bob.

To see how risk allocation works in a more sophisticated context, imagine that you are the general counsel of a $100 million company that is selling all of the company's shares in a wholly owned subsidiary, which is defined in the stock purchase agreement as the Target. Your current task is to negotiate the *no litigation* representation and warranty that appears in the stock purchase agreement, where you would disclose whether the Target is involved in any litigation.[7] You know that the statement needs to be qualified to account for possible circumstances (e.g., a lawsuit could have been filed, but not served, so your client may not know yet about this lawsuit). But how would you qualify the representation and warranty?

Immediately following this paragraph are five versions of a *no litigation* representation and warranty. The first version is the original language in the form agreement that you chose to use. The subsequent versions represent the evolution of your thinking with respect to what kind of qualifications would be appropriate. Read all of the versions and see if you can explain how each version changes the risk allocation.

Examples—Flat and Qualified Representations and Warranties

1—Flat:

No Litigation. No Litigation is pending or threatened against the Target.

2—Qualified with Disclosure Schedule:

No Litigation. Except as stated in **Schedule 3.14,** no Litigation is pending or threatened against the Target.

3—Qualified with Disclosure Schedule + Knowledge:

No Litigation. Except as stated in **Schedule 3.14,** no Litigation is pending or, to the Seller's knowledge, threatened against the Target.

4—Qualified with Disclosure Schedule + Specific on Who Has Knowledge:

No Litigation. Except as stated in **Schedule 3.14,** no Litigation is pending or, to the knowledge of any of the Seller's officers, threatened against the Target.

5—Qualified with Disclosure Schedule + Specific on Who Has Knowledge + Knowledge Definition:

No Litigation. Except as stated in **Schedule 3.14,** no Litigation is pending or, to the Knowledge of any of the Seller's three executive officers, threatened against the Target. For the purpose of this representation and warranty, "Knowledge" means, cumulatively,

(a) each executive officer's actual knowledge; and
(b) the knowledge that each executive officer would have had after a diligent investigation.

Example 1 is how the representation and warranty appeared in the stock purchase form agreement or precedent that you chose to use; it is a flat representation and warranty. You immediately recognize its most obvious flaw: It is probably false. Virtually every company has some litigation going on, and the target is no exception. If the representation and warranty is not changed, the seller (your client) is at great

---

7. In an acquisition agreement, a *no litigation* representation and warranty details what litigation exists so a buyer can determine if that litigation presents a significant risk to the business that they are buying. Similar representations and warranties exist in other agreements. For example, in an intellectual property licensing agreement, the licensor generally represents and warrants that there is no litigation challenging the licensor's ownership of the intellectual property.

risk because they know that the statement is probably false. A cause of action for misrepresentation could allege fraud. Therefore, the first qualification is that the representation and warranty must allow the parties to include any exceptions to the statement that there is no pending or threatened litigation and list those exceptions in some detail so the buyer is aware of them. The typical way to do this is to list them on a **disclosure schedule** and then refer to the schedule in the representation and warranty. Example 2 does this. Note that it is common for representations and warranties, especially in an acquisition, to include these and any other schedules that are part of the agreement. For a more detailed discussion of schedules, see Chapter 20 on page 312.

On further review, you see that the representation and warranty actually makes two statements: one about pending litigation and the other about threatened litigation. At first, you do not see this as a concern since the disclosure schedule can qualify the representation and warranty not only with respect to pending litigation, but also with respect to known, threatened litigation. But what if the seller does not know of an existing, threatened litigation against the target? Perhaps some party is claiming that a product malfunctioned and intends to sue, but it is an unknown, threatened litigation to the seller. You realize that it would be unfair for the seller (your client) to assume this risk, so you ask the buyer's counsel for a knowledge qualification with respect to unknown, threatened litigation. He agrees, so you redraft the representation and warranty as set forth in Example 3. Parties often agree to such a qualification, and a buyer's first draft may even already include it.

The representation and warranty in Example 3 decreases the seller's risk of liability but increases the buyer's risk. Because the seller is no longer making a representation and warranty about unknown, threatened litigation, the buyer will have no cause of action if unknown, threatened litigation against the target exists.

Example 4 addresses the problem of what constitutes the seller's knowledge. In the hypothetical, the seller is a corporation, an entity formed when its certificate of incorporation was filed with the appropriate governmental authority. As it is not a living, breathing human being, what constitutes the seller's knowledge is not immediately apparent. Is it the knowledge of the company's managers, or the knowledge of everyone from the president to any lower-level employee?

From your perspective as seller's general counsel, it seems unfair for the seller to be liable for the knowledge of every company employee. Accordingly, you request that the representation and warranty be further qualified so that the seller is responsible only for the seller's officers' knowledge. The qualification in Example 4 uses the phrase *to the knowledge of any of the Seller's officers*. Thus, if any one or more of the seller's officers knows of any threatened litigation, the seller is responsible for a misrepresentation and breach of warranty. If *any* were replaced with *each,* however, then possibly all three of the seller's officers would have to know of the threatened litigation to cause a misrepresentation or breach of warranty. Therefore, keep in mind how important word usage is and how one simple word change can make a difference.

With the change in Example 4, the seller no longer takes a risk as to the knowledge of just any employee. However, the seller's decrease in risk means that the buyer's risk has proportionally increased. If a lower-level employee knows of a threatened litigation, the buyer will have no cause of action against the seller because their representation and warranty is true: No officer knew. Thus, should the threatened litigation turn into actual litigation and result in an award of damages, the buyer would be obligated to pay it.

At this point, however, you decide that even *knowledge of any of the Seller's officers* is too great a risk. Therefore, you go back and ask the buyer's counsel to change the qualification so that it reads *knowledge of any of the Seller's three executive officers*, which is the language in the first sentence of Example 5.

Unfortunately, the buyer's counsel says: "Enough. If knowledge is limited to three executive officers, they could walk around with blinders on doing their best to acquire no knowledge of threatened litigation. This is too much risk for the buyer to assume." The buyer's counsel instead proposes to define *knowledge* as the aggregate actual knowledge of each of the executive officers and their **imputed knowledge**; that is, the knowledge that each executive would have had if the executive had performed a diligent inquiry. This is the compromise language in the remainder of Example 5. The seller has limited their risk to the knowledge of the three executive officers, while, at the same time, the buyer has eliminated their risk of the executive officers' intentional avoidance. In practice, the parties often negotiate the definition of *knowledge*.

Notice how the standard of liability — and, therefore the risk — shifted each time the no litigation representation and warranty changed. The same process of risk allocation occurs each time that a drafter changes any other representation and warranty. If the statement changes, the standard changes, and the risk shifts. Therefore, when drafting the substance of representations and warranties, look closely at each word and ask whether it establishes the appropriate standard.

Understanding the impact of risk allocation is essential to fulfilling your role as a counselor. Clients too often misunderstand the purpose of representations and warranties and think that the time spent negotiating them is mere **wordsmithing**.[8] By explaining to a client that the wording of the representations and warranties can affect potential liability, you have explained that money is on the table, something that clients readily understand.

B. KNOWLEDGE, MATERIALITY, EFFORTS, AND OTHER QUALIFIERS

As demonstrated in the examples above, drafters often use **knowledge, materiality, efforts, good faith, and other qualifiers** to reduce a maker's risks. For example, a materiality qualifier reduces a maker's risks by limiting a representation and warranty's focus to the most important facts. Material is a vague term, requiring a test of facts and circumstances, and there is no easy definition for what is or may be material in every context. What may be material in one context may not be material in another context. Generally, something is material if it would affect a person's decision.[9] Compare the following:

Examples—Flat and Qualified Representations and Warranties

1 — Flat — High Risk to Borrower:
   Defaults. The Borrower is not in default under any agreement.

2 —Qualified with Materiality Qualifier — Less Risk to Borrower:
   Defaults. The Borrower is not in default under any material agreement.

---

8. *Wordsmithing* has a negative connotation, suggesting that a lawyer redrafts language for no substantive reason, wasting time and money.

9. *See TSC Industries, Inc. v. Northway, Inc.*, 426 U.S. 438 (1976); *Barrington Press, Inc. v. Morey*, 752 F.2d 307, 310 (7th Cir. 1985).

In Example 1, a borrower with $200 million in sales misrepresents the facts if they have failed to pay the rent for even one month on one of their 450 photocopiers. But the borrower may not have misrepresented the facts if the representation is that shown in Example 2. Exercise 8B on page 68 looks at the various ways in which materiality qualifiers can be drafted.

Practitioners often use knowledge, materiality, efforts, good faith, and other qualifiers in their agreements. In part, practitioners do so to minimize transaction costs so they don't have to spend as much time or the client's money negotiating every single issue. However, you should be very careful with how you use qualifiers, and you should not simply throw them into a provision figuring that it limits your client's risk in some way and the parties will know what *knowledge, material, best efforts, good faith,* or *reasonable care* mean.

By including terms like this in your drafting without being more specific and really talking through with your client and the other side to establish what these terms mean, you are deferring to the courts as to what their interpretation of the provision will be. Studies have shown that courts differ in their interpretation of these terms, and it is not really clear what the hierarchy of these terms is.[10] How these terms are interpreted by the courts may depend on a number of factors, including the jurisdiction and case law in that jurisdiction, what is included in the rest of the contract, etc.[11] In fact, contract experts have continuously declared that these types of terms are "nonverifiable and therefore not contractible," even though practitioners continue to rely on them so much.[12]

Instead of including a general qualifier like *material* or *best efforts*, take the time to be more specific and thoughtful in your drafting and the standards that you are setting, especially if it is an important issue. Remember that your job includes documenting properly the relationship between the parties and planning for possible issues that may arise. For example, let's say that your client is purchasing a company, so your client is the buyer. You are going to want to know from the seller that there are no problems with the company's contracts. The seller may ask you to limit the representation and warranty to material contracts. Instead of simply throwing in the word *material* in front of *contracts*, take the time to ask your client and think through what *material* means in this context: Is it contracts over $5,000 and/or contracts from particular parties? Don't assume that what the seller thinks is material is what your client or you will think is material. All three of you may have different opinions on the definition.

The same principle applies in the context of a lease. If a residential or commercial landlord represents and warrants that the apartment is in *good condition*, what does that mean? Be clearer and make sure to include any exceptions, possibly even with photos to document the condition of the premises, depending on the circumstances and who your client is in this matter. Sometimes the best way to do this is by creating a defined term, such as *Good Condition*, with a detailed definition of what that term means. You can define almost any qualifier. Other examples of defined terms that are qualifiers include *Seller's Knowledge* and *Material Contracts*.

---

10. Julian Narko & Sarath Sanga, *A Statistical Test for Legal Interpretation: Theory and Applications*, 38 Journal of Law, Econ., and Org., 539-569 (2022).

11. *Id.* at 540.

12. Robert E. Scott & George G. Triantis, *Incomplete Contracts and the Theory of Contract Design*, 56 Case W. Rsrv. L. Rev. 187, 196 (2005).

V. DRAFTING WARRANTIES THAT STAND ALONE

When a warranty is coupled with a representation, one party promises to pay appropriate damages to the other if facts currently existing or that existed in the past are not true. Separately, outside of a representation and warranty paired together, a party may want another party to warrant that a state of facts will exist in the future, and they will want to be paid appropriate damages if that state of facts does not occur.[13] Here is an example of a stand-alone warranty requested (or required) by a retailer concerning the future condition of a product that will be packaged and shipped by the manufacturer in the future. The retailer would ask the manufacturer for the following stand-alone warranty regarding these future facts:

Example— Stand-Alone Warranty Regarding Future Facts

Warranty. The Manufacturer warrants to the Retailer that the Product as packaged and shipped from the Manufacturer's plant *will be free* from defects in material and workmanship and *will function and perform* in accordance with Manufacturer's specifications for a period of one year from the date of retail purchase.[14]

Here, the retailer is not relying on the truthfulness of the underlying statements, which are future facts. Instead, the retailer is relying on the manufacturer's promise that the manufacturer will pay damages if that state of facts does not exist in the future.[15] Thus, a statement that deals with the future cannot be a paired representation and warranty, but it can be a warranty that stands alone.

Occasionally, a party might also make only a warranty instead of a paired representation and warranty as a matter of risk allocation. Typically, this occurs when a party refuses to represent a *fact* because the parties do not know for sure if a fact is true or if the information needed to verify that fact is not available. However, the parties agree that the party who would be making the paired representation and warranty should be liable if the fact as stated is not true. Deal lawyers refer to this practice as **representing over the fact**. For example, suppose that the buyer of a manufacturing business asks the seller to represent and warrant that existing claims against their products do not exceed $1.5 million. If the seller does not know, the seller might quite reasonably refuse to make a paired representation and warranty. Nonetheless, the parties might agree that, as a matter of risk allocation, the seller should be financially responsible for any pending claims that exceed $1.5 million. In this circumstance, some lawyers may permit their clients to make the requested representation and warranty without qualification, even though it is not the best practice.

Best practice suggests accomplishing the desired risk allocation through using a stand-alone warranty instead of making the paired representation and warranty. The seller should probably warrant, but not represent, the dollar amount of the claims. This would accomplish the risk allocation without the seller possibly making a misrepresentation. Parties should understand that truthfulness in a contract matters.

---

13. *See S. Cal. Enterprises, Inc. v. D.N. & E. Walter & Co.*, 178 P.2d 785, 789-791 (Cal. App. 2d Dist. 1947).

14. *See* James J. White, Robert S. Summers & Robert A. Hillman, *Uniform Commercial Code* vol. 1, § 12-9 (6th ed. West 2012) (discussing what constitutes warranty of future performance under UCC § 2-725(2)).

15. *See Wright v. Couch*, 54 S.W.2d 207, 209-210 (Tex. App. 1932).

A seller could be unpleasantly surprised if the buyer *forgets* that the representation was merely risk allocation and sues for fraudulent misrepresentation, including punitive damages. Moreover, a buyer might not even have a cause of action for misrepresentation if the seller successfully argues that the buyer could not have justifiably relied on the representation. Ironically, in that event, the buyer ends up where they could have started — with a cause of action for breach of warranty.

The use of a warranty on a stand-alone basis has increased since the *CBS, Inc. v. Ziff-Davis Publishing Co.*[16] decision, which made clear that a warranty was a separate contract concept with a separate cause of action from a paired representation and warranty. For example, lawyers drafting software contracts are often advised to draft only warranties.[17]

When the parties do not know for sure if a fact is true or if the information needed to verify that fact is not available, they can address this matter in various ways as well, separate from doing a stand-alone warranty. For example, first, the seller could make the representation and warranty *to the best of Seller's knowledge* — assuming that the seller had the knowledge of the facts. Then the seller could promise to indemnify the buyer with respect to the representation and warranty, but without regard to the knowledge qualifier in another provision of the agreement. That is, for the purposes of the indemnity, the representation and warranty would be flat, a precise, absolute statement, without any room for flexibility or variation of any kind. However, this could end up being a little bit more complicated and confusing.

Another possible way would be that the parties could address this issue only as a type of indemnity, which is described in more detail in Chapter 17 on page 249, where the seller would agree to indemnify the buyer for claims in excess of $1.5 million in another provision of the agreement. This second option would be using covenants and conditions, so if the seller does not indemnify the buyer, there would be a breach of covenant and condition to an obligation. Both of these additional methods accomplish the parties' business goals without the seller misrepresenting the facts.

---

16. *See generally CBS Inc. v. Ziff-Davis Publ'g. Co.*, 553 N.E.2d 997 (N.Y. 1990).

17. H. Ward Classen, *A Practical Guide to Software Licensing for Licensees and Licensors*, 48-50 (4th ed. ABA 2011) (generally with respect to the differences between representations and warranties), 49 (while noting the differences between representations and warranties, the author states that "given that most licensees are willing to accept only a warranty and not require the licensor to provide a representation in the belief one is as good as the other, the licensor should refrain from including any representations in its agreement.").

VI. EXERCISES

A. EXERCISE 8A: VOICE

If you were selling the horse in the examples below, which one of the following two representations and warranties would you prefer, and why? For guidance on this exercise, review Section III in this chapter on page 56, titled "Drafting the Substance of Representations and Warranties."

1. **Additional Races**. Sam Jockey has not raced the Horse since the Kentucky Derby.
2. **Additional Races**. The Horse has not raced since the Kentucky Derby.

B. EXERCISE 8B: MATERIALITY AND OTHER QUALIFIERS

In the examples that follow, the provisions are representations and warranties and a definition from a loan agreement. In a loan agreement, a bank requires representations and warranties from a borrower in the same way that a buyer requires representations and warranties from a seller. Both the buyer and the bank are making investments. The buyer is investing in the house by buying something from the seller, and the bank is investing in the borrower by making a loan to the borrower. Both the buyer and the bank need as much information as possible before they make their respective decisions to invest.

The bank will use the representations and warranties as a risk allocation mechanism to establish standards of liability, which, if breached by the borrower, will provide the bank with remedies.

Each of the examples that follow has qualifications, but each differs from the others. Exercise 8B is intended to familiarize you with these differences and how they affect the business deal. Although most of the examples are of different representations and warranties, several examples are different versions of the same representation and warranty. In reality, of course, only one version would appear in the agreement. If you would like to review more information before doing this exercise, review Section IV.A in this chapter on page 61 titled "Flat or Qualified Representations and Warranties" and Section IV.B. in this chapter on page 64 titled "Knowledge, Materiality, Efforts, and Other Qualifiers." There are five parts to this exercise.

1. *Examples a–c.*
Review Examples a through c below and answer the following questions:

- Would the bank or the borrower have asked for the change in language from Example a to Example b, and what would have been their argument for asking for the change?
- If the first draft of the contract used the representation and warranty in Example b, which party would have asked to change the language to Example c?
- If the bank were to agree to Example c, what risk would the bank be taking?

Example a — **Purchase and Sale Orders**. Listed in **Schedule 3.10** is each purchase and sale order to which the Borrower is a party.

Example b — **Purchase and Sale Orders**. Listed in **Schedule 3.10** is each material purchase and sale order to which the Borrower is a party.

Example c — **Purchase and Sale Orders**. Listed in **Schedule 3.10** is each purchase and sale order to which the Borrower is a party and that involves future payments in excess of $100,000.

2. *Examples d–e.*

The representations and warranties in Examples d and e deal with the parties being in default under an agreement, which means not doing something that is required by an agreement or being in violation of an agreement. Example d answers the question of whether entering into this agreement creates a conflict or a default under any other agreement to which the borrower is a party. Example e answers the question of whether the borrower is currently in default under any other agreement to which the borrower is a party. Both examples include materiality qualifications. Which example is more favorable to the borrower, and why?

Example d — **Noncontravention**. The Borrower's execution and delivery of this Agreement does not conflict with or create a default under any agreement to which the Borrower is a party, except for any conflict or default that would not materially adversely affect the business or financial condition of the Borrower.

Example e — **Other Material Agreements**. The Borrower is not in default under any Material Agreement, except for any default that does not materially adversely affect the Borrower.

The following would be included in the "Definitions" section of the agreement: "**Material Agreement**" means any agreement that involves future payments in excess of $50,000.

3. *Examples f–g.*

Would the borrower prefer the language in Example f or Example g? Why?

Example f — **Regulatory Compliance**. The Borrower is in compliance in all material respects with all federal, state, local, and foreign laws and regulations applicable to the Borrower.

Example g — **Regulatory Compliance**. The Borrower is in compliance with all federal, state, local, and foreign laws and regulations applicable to the Borrower, except for those instances of noncompliance that would not materially adversely affect the Borrower's financial condition, business, or results of operations.

4. *Examples h–i.*

In Example h, would the borrower prefer the *material adverse change* qualification in subsection (i) or subsection (ii)? Why? What is the effect of the words "severally or in the aggregate" in Example i?

Example h — **No Material Adverse Change**. Since the date of the Financial Statements,
  (i) no material adverse change has occurred in the financial condition, operations, or business of the Borrower and the Subsidiaries taken as a whole; and
  (ii) no property or asset of the Borrower or any Subsidiary has suffered material damage, destruction, or loss.

***Example i*—Leases**. With respect to each lease listed in **Schedule 3.11**,

(i) no default has occurred and is continuing; and

(ii) no event has occurred and is continuing which, with notice or lapse of time or both, would constitute a default on the Borrower's part, except for those defaults, if any, that

 (A) are not material in character, amount, or extent; and

 (B) do not, severally or in the aggregate, materially detract from the value, or interfere with the present use, of the property subject to the lease.

5. *Examples j–k.*

List all of the qualifications in Example j, and what are the most important words or phrases in the definition of "Material" in Example k?

***Example j*—Litigation**. Except as set forth in **Schedule 3.14**, no litigation is pending or, to the knowledge of any of the Borrower's officers, threatened that might, severally or in the aggregate, materially adversely affect the financial condition of the business, assets, or prospects of the Borrower and the Subsidiaries taken as a whole.

***Example k*—"Material"** means an event, condition, matter, change, or effect (either alone or in combination with any one or more other events, conditions, matters, changes, or effects) that impacts or that is reasonably likely to impact the Borrower's condition (financial or otherwise), in an amount in excess of $10,000.

CHAPTER NINE

Drafting Covenants

I. DRAFTING THE SUBSTANCE OF COVENANTS

This section covers best practices for drafting covenants, the promises that parties make to each other about doing or not doing something. Remember that if a party does not perform as the covenant states they must perform, the other party will have a cause of action for breach of covenant.

Best practices for drafting covenants include being specific about what you include, using the active voice instead of the passive voice, being consistent about which verb you use to signal a covenant (preferably the verb *shall*), knowing how to incorporate the performance and actions of third parties into the contract, and being intentional about risk allocation in these provisions.

This chapter ends with a more in-depth explanation of covenants in acquisition agreements and financings, and exercises that relate to covenants.

A. CONTENT AND QUESTIONS TO ASK

As with representations and warranties, the content of an agreement's covenants can vary greatly depending on the type of transaction and the parties involved. To determine what you should include as covenants, you should talk to your client to find out what your client and the other party (or parties) have promised to do and not do, so that you can draft those as covenants. Also, you should consult any binding or not binding written agreement or list of business issues that all the parties have put together and agreed to already. You can use the quick definitions and questions in the Chapter 7 contract concepts summary table as a guide. Remember to look at form agreements or precedent for the type of agreement or provision that you are drafting and make sure to understand or research what is common in the industry in which you are working to best protect your client.

Here are the questions that you should be asking yourself when drafting covenants:

- **Who** is obligated to whom?
- **What** is the obligation?
- **When** must the obligation be performed?
- **Where** will the performance take place?

- **Why** must a party perform?
- **How** is the obligation performed?
- **How much,** if performance involves money or any other type of item?

When you are drafting covenants in response to these questions, ask yourself whether there are different options and which options would be best for your client. You may not have the answers to all these questions from the first discussion with your client. You may need to return to your client with follow-up questions to get all the information that you need to draft the covenants in more detail. Usually, the more specific you are, the better it will be for the parties going forward because the expectations for each party will be clearer.

The following are examples of covenants, annotated with the questions that they address within the provision so you can see how the questions play into drafting the covenant provisions:

Examples—Covenants Answering the Relevant Questions

Samples. No later than 60 days before an Item is to be shipped to the Retail Stores [*answers* ***when*** *must the obligation be performed—consider whether it should be shorter or longer*], the Manufacturer shall submit a sample of that Item to the Licensor [*answers* ***who*** *is obligated to whom*] for Licensor's approval [*answers* ***why*** *a party must perform*]. The Licensor [*answers* ***who*** *is obligated to whom*] shall approve or reject the sample and notify [*answers* ***what*** *the obligation is*] the Manufacturer of the Licensor's decision [*answers* ***how*** *the obligation is to be performed*] no later than three business days after the date of the Licensor's receipt of the Item [*answers* ***when*** *the obligation must be performed*] for approval.

Delivery of Disputed Amount. No later than five days after the Escrow Agent's receipt of the Release Notice [*answers* ***when*** *the obligation must be performed—consider whether it should be later or sooner*], the Escrow Agent shall deliver to the party set forth in the Release Notice [*answers* ***who*** *is obligated to whom*] a certified check [*answers* ***how*** *the obligation is to be performed—consider whether a wire transfer would be better*] in an amount equal to the Disputed Amount [*answers* ***how much***, *if performance involves money or any other type of item*], payable to the order of the party set forth in the Release Notice.

Condition of Premises at End of Term. The Tenant [*answers* ***who*** *is obligated to whom*] shall leave [*answers* ***what*** *the obligation is*] the Premises [*answers* ***where*** *the performance will take place*] broom clean [*answers* ***how*** *the obligation is to be performed—consider whether this is the proper standard depending on whom you are representing*] when the Tenant vacates the Premises at the end of the Term [*answers* ***when*** *the obligation must be performed—consider what happens if the Tenant leaves earlier*].

When drafting or reviewing the substance of a covenant, make sure that your client is promising something that is entirely in their control so they will be able to meet their obligation.[1] Promising something that is not under your client's control would be a high-risk covenant because an outside event or third party controls whether your client breaches the covenant. For example, imagine that Herald Stadium Productions Inc. asks your client, Preston Presentations Inc., to sign a contract that includes the following provision:

Example—Covenant Where Your Client Has No Control Is High Risk

McCrary Concert. Preston shall present a concert on July 4, 20__, at Herald Stadium at which Sir Paul McCrary is the lead act.

This covenant presents no problem if your client has already arranged that Sir Paul will perform. If they have not, your client is in serious risk of breaching this covenant. Sir Paul could just say "No." Also, what happens if Sir Paul suddenly is not able to perform, or there is a problem with the Herald Stadium venue? Your client may not have as much control in this situation, so you may want to think twice about what you're obligating your client to do. See also Section IV in this chapter on page 91 for more information on how to deal with third parties through covenants.

B. ACTIVE VS. PASSIVE VOICE

Like representations and warranties, try to always draft covenants using the active voice. Then, it is clear who has the obligation to do what, and you can avoid any confusion or ambiguity.

Examples—Voice in Covenants

Incorrect in Passive Voice:

End of Term Repairs. The premises *shall be painted* by the Tenant in the last month of the lease term.

Correct in Active Voice:

End of Term Repairs. The Tenant shall paint the premises in the last month of the lease term.

C. VERBS IN COVENANTS

This section discusses when to use *shall* and when to use *will,* as well as some exceptions. We recommend that you use *shall* to indicate a covenant and *will* to indicate the future, as in declarations, which is still the most common practice in the context of business contracts. However, what is most important is that you be consistent about which verbs you use and how you use them throughout the contract, so the meaning of provisions are clear, and so that it will be very clear to the parties, others involved in the transaction, and the courts when you are signaling a covenant.

---

1. *See, e.g., World of Boxing LLC v. King,* 56 F. Supp. 3d 507, 512-515 (S.D.N.Y. 2014) (inability to control whether boxer would pass drug test did not excuse party from breach when he had promised that the boxer would participate in boxing bouts).

Note that an exception would be when you are drafting a covenant that begins with a negative subject, such as: "no party" or "neither party." Then, you can use *may*, such as: "No party may hire the other party's employees for a period of two years after the termination of this Agreement."

1. Use *Shall* in Covenants

When drafting covenants, use *shall* to establish clearly that a party is promising to perform. If the name of a party does not come before the word *shall*, then *shall* is incorrect. If the name of the party comes before the word *shall*, *shall* is usually correct, but there are three exceptions, which will be discussed later in this section. To begin, here is an example of a covenant using *shall* correctly:

> *Example—Correct Use of* Shall
>
> **Regular Exercise**. The Athlete *shall* exercise regularly to maintain himself in top physical condition.

Courts have interpreted *shall* to mean *will*,[2] *may*,[3] and a *condition*. Yet courts have continuously clarified that covenants will be enforced, even when the language is not perfect.[4] They have interpreted the intention of the parties to be more important than the use of *will* or *shall* and have stated that both *will* and *shall* denote mandatory covenants.[5] Even using the words *will* and *shall* interchangeably has indicated covenants.[6]

However, using *will* and *shall* interchangeably is still not recommended. The case law that exists relating to what is a covenant comes from contracts that were not clear enough (e.g., how they used *will* and *shall*). By using *shall* to signal a covenant, and *will* to signal the future, as in a declaration, you are more likely to avoid any type of dispute.

Note that the same issue of clarity and consistency comes up when signaling conditions with *must* instead of *shall*, as explained in more detail in Chapter 11 on page 110. Therefore, in business contracts, we recommend that you use *shall* for covenants and do not use *will* for covenants. Furthermore, as with conditions, to be even clearer, it is helpful to have an **interpretive section** in your contract, which is a separate provision, usually part of the definitions at the beginning of the contract or the general provisions at the end of the contract, stating that the verb *shall* signals a covenant.

---

2. *Cunningham v. Long*, 135 A. 198, 201 (Me. 1926) (stating that when looked at in the context of the other contract provisions, "shall" plainly had an element of futurity).

3. The Supreme Court of the United States noted in an opinion that "(t)hough 'shall' generally means 'must,' legal writers sometimes use, or misuse, 'shall' to mean 'should,' 'will,' or even 'may.'" *See* note 9, *Gutierrez de Martinez v. Lamagno*, 515 U.S. 417, 432 (1995). The dissent viewed "shall" as carrying "normally uncompromising directive." *Id*. at 439.

4. *In re Universal Serv. Fund Tel. Billing Prac. Litig.*, 619 F.3d 1188, 1196 (10th Cir. 2010) (A promise is a manifestation of intention to act or refrain from acting, as a result, words such as agree, will, or shall, are not required to form a contractual promise under New York law.); *see also Blue Ocean Int'l Bank LLC v. Golden Eagle Cap. Advisors, Inc.*, 408 F. Supp. 3d 57, 59 (D.P.R. 2019); *Vogt-Nem, Inc. v. M/V Tramper*, 263 F. Supp. 2d 1226, 1231 (N.D. Cal. 2002); *Terra Int'l, Inc. v. Mississippi Chem. Corp.*, 922 F. Supp. 1334, 1358 (N.D. Iowa 1996), *aff'd*, 119 F.3d 688 (8th Cir. 1997); *Frediani & Delgreco, S.P.A. v. Gina Imports, Ltd.*, 870 F. Supp. 217, 220 (N.D. Ill. 1994).

5. *Blue Ocean Int'l Bank LLC v. Golden Eagle Cap. Advisors, Inc.*, 408 F. Supp. 3d 57, 59 (D.P.R. 2019).

6. *Frediani & Delgreco, S.P.A. v. Gina Imports, Ltd.*, 870 F. Supp. 217, 220 (N.D. Ill. 1994).

The mixing of verbs happens often, for example, when you have a lot of different lawyers from different parties working on a contract. Know that it is not going to be worth your time, your client's money, or any negotiating capital that you have for you to go through the other side's precedent and change every verb in the contract. Thus, you will probably be limited in the changes that you can make to the contract and should not change the initial verb used, if its use is consistent. What is likely to happen is that one of the lawyers will add a new provision (taken from a different precedent or drafted from scratch) and not pay attention to the verbs being used to signal covenants and not make the necessary changes to make sure that new provision works properly within that contract. Therefore, especially be careful when you or others are cutting and pasting from different contracts or when you or others are adding isolated provisions into a contract. No matter what, especially if you have to use precedent that uses *will* for covenants, be consistent about which verbs you use for what provision throughout the contract, so that the meaning of provisions are clear and the parties, others involved in the transaction, and the courts know clearly when you are signaling a covenant.

Remember that the practice of consumer contracts is different from the practice of business contracts, and, therefore, the recommendations in this book do not necessarily apply to consumer contracts, as we discussed in Chapter 1 on page 5. In fact, there are consumer protection statutes that require that consumer contracts be written in plain English and some statutes even mandate the use of *will* and do not allow for the use of *shall*. There also tends to be a trend and disposition for businesses to move more towards using plain English in contracts, so the significance and use of *shall* may be shifting in the coming years.

Most commentators agree that sophisticated commercial contracts should use *shall* to signal a covenant.[7] However, some commentators advocate for banning *shall* completely from our legal language, because, as you can see from the examples that directly follow, practitioners sometimes misuse *shall* in practice.[8] They would propose the alternatives *will* and *must*.[9] But neither of those alternatives provides the perfect remedy. Assume that drafters stop using *shall* in their contracts. A drafter would then need to use *will*, *must*, or a different word to signal a covenant. But, as *will* is already used often for the future, it would need to do double duty, creating the possibility of ambiguity. If a drafter uses *will* instead of *shall*, there may still be confusion as to whether *will* denotes a covenant, discretionary authority, or a future event. Courts will need to construe *will* instead of *shall*.[10] Would a court then try to interpret the meaning of *will* by using as precedent the cases analyzing whether *shall* was intended to signal a covenant, the future, or discretionary authority? The use of *must* instead of *shall* creates the same problem because drafters use it to signal a condition.

For now, we recommend using *shall* for covenants as much as you can in business contracts, always putting the name of one of the parties to the agreement as the subject before *shall,* and phrasing provisions as much as possible in the active voice.

---

7. *See* Kenneth A. Adams, *A Manual of Style for Contract Drafting* 64-65 (5th ed. 2023); Scott J. Burnham, *Drafting and Analyzing Contracts* §§ 16.2 and 17.6.1 (3d ed. 2003); Robert C. Dick, *Legal Drafting in Plain Language* 93 (3d ed. 1995); F. Reed Dickerson, *The Fundamentals of Legal Drafting* 214 (2d ed. 1986); Lenné Espenschied, *Contract Drafting, Powerful Prose in Transactional Practice* 139 (2010).

8. *See* Bryan A. Garner, *A Dictionary of Modern Legal Usage* 940 (2d ed. 1995); Joseph Kimble, *The Many Misuses of Shall*, 3 Scribes J. Leg. Writing 6s1, 69-71 (1992); Bryan A. Garner, *Shall We Abandon Shall?*, Am. Bar. Ass'n J. (Aug. 1, 2012).

9. For example, some commentators would argue that "[t]he advantage of will is that nobody—nobody—misuses this word in any of the myriad ways in which lawyers misuse shall. Nobody writes will instead of may or should or is entitled to. In American English, will is the ordinary verb of promise." Bryan A. Garner, *Shall We Abandon Shall?*, Am. Bar. Ass'n J. (Aug. 1, 2012).

10. *See Doe I v. Wal-Mart Stores, Inc.*, 572 F.3d 677, 681-682 (9th Cir. 2009) (issue whether the phrase "will undertake" created a covenant or discretionary authority).

When looking at a provision in a contract that uses *shall*, you must first determine whether the parties intend the provision to be one of the following:

- a covenant (as in Example 1, below);
- a statement of discretionary authority or permission (as in Example 2);
- a declaration in the present tense (as in Example 3);
- a provision trying to bind a nonparty (as in Example 4); or
- a condition (as in Examples 5 and 6).

You may need to make the necessary corrections, as recommended in the examples below, to make sure that you are using the contract concept that best captures the business issue and the intent of the parties, while also using *shall* in the right way. You should draft your provision as clearly as possible so that it is obvious which contract concept you are using.

Here are some common ways in which *shall* is misused by drafters, with suggestions for correcting these misuses:

Examples—Using Covenants and Shall Correctly

1—Incorrect Use of Shall and Passive Voice:
Maintenance of the Premises. The outside of the Premises shall be maintained by the Landlord, and the inside of the Premises shall be maintained by the Tenant.

1—Correct Use of Shall and Active Voice:
Maintenance of the Premises. The Landlord shall maintain the outside of the Premises, and the Tenant shall maintain the inside of the Premises.

2—Incorrect Use of Shall and Passive Voice:
Forum. An action shall be permitted to be filed to enforce this Agreement in the Supreme Court of the State of New York.

2—Correct Discretionary Authority with May and Active Voice:
Forum. A party may file and maintain an action to enforce this Agreement in the Supreme Court of the State of New York.

3—Incorrect Use of Shall and Passive Voice:
Governing Law. This Agreement shall be governed by the laws of Nebraska, without regard to its conflict of laws principles.

3—Correct Declaration in the Present Tense and More Specific:
Governing Law. Without regard to Nebraska's conflict of laws principles, the laws of Nebraska govern all matters arising under or relating to this Agreement, including torts.

4—Incorrect Use of Shall and Passive Voice with Third Parties:
Arbitration. The arbitrators shall render a decision promptly.

4—Correct Use of Shall Binding the Parties to the Agreement:
Arbitration. The parties shall instruct the arbitrators to render a decision promptly.

4—Correct Verb with Third Parties:
Arbitration. The arbitrators are to render a decision promptly.

5—Incorrect Use of Shall and Passive Voice:
Notice. The Event Notice shall be given to the Insurance Company no later than ten days after the Insured Event.

5—Correct Condition with the **Then** *Part of* If / Then *Drafted Separately:*

Notice. The Insured must give the Event Notice to the Insurance Company no later than ten days after the Insured Event.

6—Incorrect Use of Shall *Because Notice Not a Party:*

Purchase of Shares. If a Stockholder wants to purchase any of the Shares referred to in the Offer, the Stockholder shall give notice no later than three days after it receives the Offer, and the notice shall state . . . .

6—Correct Use of Shall *with Party Before* Shall:

Purchase of Shares. If a Stockholder wants to purchase any of the Shares referred to in the Offer, the Stockholder shall deliver a notice no later than three days after receiving the Offer. The Stockholder shall include the following information in the notice:

Note, in Example 5, the drafters only included the *then* part of the *if / then* structure of a condition. If it helps you to understand it better, imagine that the correct answer in Example 5 could also be drafted as: "If there is an Insured Event, the Insured must give the Event Notice to the Insurance Company no later than ten days after the Insured Event."

The other contract concepts mentioned in these examples — discretionary authority, declarations, and conditions — will be covered in more detail in the remaining chapters of Part B.

2. Exceptions: When *Shall* Is Not Recommended

If the name of a party to the agreement comes before the word *shall, shall* is usually correct, but, as mentioned above, there are at least three exceptions.

First, do not use *shall* with a form of the verb *to be,* as in the incorrect example below. Instead, delete *shall* and change the verb *to be* to its present tense form, as in the correct examples below. Once redrafted, you will be able to see that the provision is a condition to a declaration or a condition to an obligation. Depending on how you want to allocate risk between or among the parties, the provision can be drafted in different ways:

Examples 1—Do Not Use Shall + Verb To Be

Incorrect to Use Shall + Verb To Be:

Suspension of Performance. If a *Force Majeure Event* occurs and is continuing, the Affected Party *shall be excused* from the performance to the extent prevented from performing.

Correct to Use Present Tense in Condition to a Declaration:

Suspension of Performance. If a *Force Majeure Event* occurs and is continuing, the Affected Party is excused from the performance to the extent prevented from performing.

Correct to Use Shall in Condition to an Obligation:

Suspension of Performance. If a *Force Majeure Event* occurs and is continuing, the Non-Affected Party shall excuse the Affected Party from the performance to the extent prevented from performing.

Second, do not use *shall* with a form of the verb *to have* or *to have to* (to be in possession of something or to have to do something). If you find yourself in a situation where you think using *shall* and *have* seems right, reconsider and explore other options because it is very likely that you are not using the right contract concept. Depending on the intent and construction of the sentence, different corrections are appropriate. For example, are the parties really intending to create a covenant or a condition? If they intend a covenant, then you do not need to use *have*. If they intend a condition, you may want to consider joining the *if* and *then* parts of the provision to make it clearer, as in the examples that follow. If you keep them separate, consider using *must* instead to clearly signal a condition.

Alternatives to using *shall* with the verb *to have* are illustrated in the following examples:

Examples 2A—Do Not Use Shall + Verb To Have

Incorrect Use of Shall + *Verb* To Have

Consent. The Seller shall have obtained the Landlord's consent.
Consent. The Seller shall have the Landlord's consent.

Correct Use of Shall:

Consent. If the Seller sublets the Apartment, the Seller shall obtain the Landlord's consent.

Correct Use of Must:

Consent. If the Seller sublets the Apartment, the Seller must have obtained the Landlord's consent.

Alternatively, if the parties intended the sentence with *shall have* to be a statement of discretionary authority, replace *shall have* with *may*.

Examples 2B—Incorrect Use of Shall + Verb To Have Because Discretionary Authority

Incorrect Use of Shall:

Termination. The Publisher *shall have the right* to terminate this Agreement if the Author does not complete the Work by the Deadline.

Correct with May:

Termination. The Publisher may terminate this Agreement if the Author does not complete the Work by the Deadline.

Third, the use of *shall* is incorrect if the name of a party comes before *shall* in a clause that establishes a condition or other circumstances under which an event may occur, as in the first incorrect example below in Example 3. Clue words and phrases that begin these clauses include *if, when, as, in the event of, provided,* and *that.* These clauses are properly drafted in the present tense, so that whenever the circumstances occur, the clause applies.

However, note that *shall* is appropriate to use in the second part of a condition provision that establishes the obligation if the condition is satisfied. So, no *shall* in the *if* part of the condition, but you can use *shall* in the *then* part of the provision.

Here are some examples of how to use *shall* correctly in conditions:

> ### Examples 3—Do Not Use **Shall** *in If Clause of Condition*
>
> *Incorrect Because* **Shall** *in If Clause:*
> **Late Payment**. If the Borrower shall fail to pay interest when due, the Bank may declare the Borrower to be in default.
>
> *Correct with Present Tense in If Clause:*
> **Late Payment**. If the Borrower fails to pay interest when due, the Bank may declare the Borrower to be in default.
>
> *Incorrect Use of* **Shall** *in Clause Stating the Condition:*
> **Deposit of Funds**. The Bank shall deposit the funds to any account that the Borrower shall designate in a written notice.
>
> *Correct Use of Present Tense in Clause Stating the Condition:*
> **Deposit of Funds**. The Bank shall deposit the funds to any account that the Borrower designates in a written notice.

The three exceptions that we have just discussed are the most common exceptions, but not the only ones because contracts can be complicated. See the second example on page 81 to see another exception that does not fall within any of these three. It is a good idea to always test each use of *shall* by asking yourself whether a party is promising to do or not do something. If no party is making a promise, then the use of *shall* is incorrect.

The chart that follows summarizes the tests in this section:

TEST WHETHER *SHALL* IS CORRECT

IF THE NAME OF A PARTY DOES NOT COME BEFORE *SHALL*	IF THE NAME OF A PARTY COMES BEFORE *SHALL*
Shall is always incorrect.	*Shall* is generally correct, but at least three exceptions exist. 1. If *shall* is coupled with the verb *to be*, *shall* is incorrect. 2. If *shall* is coupled with the verb *to have*, *shall* is incorrect. 3. If *shall* is in a clause that establishes a condition, *shall* is incorrect (clue words: *if, when, as, in the event of, that*, and *provided*).

3. When to Use *Will*

While we are recommending using *shall* to signal an obligation, *will* is already a popular verb in practice for signaling an obligation, even in business contracts, for several reasons. First, *will* is preferred for consumer contracts, and some statutes even mandate its use. *Will* tends to be easier to understand and is less intimidating than *shall*.

Second, commercial lawyers frequently use *will* in letter agreements where they believe an informal tone is appropriate. For example, employers often request their lawyers to draft an employment agreement with a senior executive as a letter. The friendly, informal tone becomes another part of charming their new employee. In these letters, drafters often use *will* instead of *shall*.

Finally, commercial lawyers have started to extend this practice of using *will* to other types of agreements besides employment agreements and consumer contracts, in which *will* has been in use for some time. Some sophisticated parties in these other types of agreements are choosing to shift from *shall* to *will* for various reasons, including that it makes agreements easier to read and implement for all parties involved. Therefore, the other side is more likely today to give you precedent that has *will* everywhere to signal an obligation. As mentioned earlier, you probably should not spend your time, your client's resources, or negotiating capital changing every *will* to *shall.* Focus on fixing what you can to make the contract clear, consistent, and unambiguous.

You should be aware that courts have recognized that *will* has multiple meanings. It has been interpreted to signal a covenant, a condition, or a declaration. For example, *will* has been interpreted to state either the present tense[11] or the future, depending on the contract and facts in question. Courts look at the intent of the parties and the rest of the agreement to determine the right intent in that particular provision. Therefore, simply switching from *shall* to *will* for covenants may not resolve all issues, as discussed previously in this chapter on page 75. So, what is important is that you apply uniformity and consistency in your use of *will* and any other verb.

There are some circumstances where you would want to use *will* instead of *shall* or another verb. Under these circumstances, you would not be using *will* to signal a covenant or obligation.

First, use *will* instead of *shall* or a different verb if a provision states a party's opinion, determination, or belief about the future.

Example—Correct Use of Will for Party's Opinion on Future

Amendments. As a condition to the effectiveness of each amendment, each party must obtain the authorization of

(a) its Board of Directors and
(b) its stockholders

if, in the judgment of that party's Board of Directors, the amendment *will* have a material adverse effect on the benefits intended under this Agreement to that party and its stockholders.

This rule makes sense when viewed in the context of the rule that representations cannot be in the future because they then would not be facts, but instead would be opinions. Here, in a condition, an opinion about the future is called for and so *will* is appropriately used.

Second, use *will* when the provision states that a party or a nonparty (Person A) will take action in the future, and Person A is not the contract party promising to perform a covenant, nor are they the person to whom discretionary authority has been granted. See this example:

---

11. *See Milner v. Dudrey,* 362 P.2d 439, 443 (1961) ("The use of future tense may under some circumstances constitute present action. The word 'will' when used as an auxiliary verb (as in the sentence above quoted) is sometimes used in the present tense.")

> *Example—Correct Use of* Will *for Party Not Promising to Perform*
>
> **Subcontractor for Painting**. The Contractor shall use commercially reasonable efforts to find a subcontractor who *will* paint the House for less than $5,000.

In the example above, the contractor, a party, promises to find a subcontractor (Person A) who *will do* something in the future (paint the house). *Shall* is an incorrect signal to follow the subcontractor because this is not the provision that obligates the subcontractor to paint the house for less than $5,000. Presumably, the subcontractor is not a party to this agreement, so to bind the contractor better on what the subcontractor has to do, you would have to explore options in Section IV on page 91 regarding how to deal with third parties. Furthermore, you would want to explore having the subcontractor be a party to this agreement or a subsequent agreement and possibly already laying out in this first agreement what will be included in the subsequent agreement with the subcontractor.

The example below involves both parties to the agreement, but the provision's primary purpose is to describe the owner's discretionary authority, which is choosing the paint color that the subcontractor (Person A) will use in the future. *Shall* is not the correct signal to follow contractor. That part of the provision is not a promise by the contractor to paint the House the chosen color. That requires a separate covenant.

> *Example—Correct Use of* Will *for Third Party*
>
> **Choice of Color**. The Owner may choose the color that the Contractor will paint the House.

Third, use *will* if a provision contrasts the present with the future or the past with the future.

> *Example—Correct Use of* Will *for Contrast Between Past and Future*
>
> **Right to Deposit on Termination**. When the Lease terminates, the Landlord has the right to retain the Deposit to pay for expenses that the Landlord has incurred or will incur to repair the Tenant's damage to the Premises. The Landlord shall return any retained proceeds that the Landlord does not use no later than three days after repairing the damage.

Fourth and finally, use *will* if a provision warrants future performance of a good or a future state of facts.

> *Example—Correct Use of* Will *for Warranting Future Performance or Facts*
>
> **Warranty**. The Manufacturer warrants to the Retailer and the eventual consumer that the Product as packaged and shipped from the Manufacturer's plant *will be free* from defects in material and workmanship and *will function and perform* in accordance with Manufacturer's specifications for a period of one year from the date of retail purchase.

In this provision, the manufacturer promises that if a state of facts does not exist in the future, then they are responsible as described in the warranty's other provisions. *Shall* would be incorrect in this provision because the product is not promising anything about its future performance. Of course, this provision can also be redrafted as a condition to an obligation with an obligation from the manufacturer.

4. Example of *Shall* and *Will* in a Covenant

The following example demonstrates the proper use of both *shall* and *will,* as described in the previous sections of this chapter. In the agreement from which this provision is excerpted, the General Partner is a party and the limited partners are not.

Example—Correct Use of Shall *and* Will *in the Same Provision*

Obligation to Find Investors. The General Partner *shall* use commercially reasonable efforts to find at least ten limited partners, each of whom *will* invest $1 million in the Partnership.

First, the provision obligates the general partner to find unidentified persons or entities to be investors. Therefore, the drafter appropriately used *shall* to signal the General Partner's obligation. Second, the provision describes the characteristics of these unidentified persons. They must be persons willing to be "limited partners." But the purpose of *will* is to signal future acts that are not yet the subject of obligations, which is precisely what the *will* clause does. It describes what these unidentified nonparties will do in the future — once the general partner finds them and they become limited partners in accordance with some future agreement. At that point, the drafters will memorialize the limited partners' promises to invest, using *shall* to signal the obligations in those future agreements.

5. *Has the Right, Entitled,* and *Is Permitted*

As a general rule, do not state that a party *has the right, is entitled*, or *is permitted* to do something. State the provision as a covenant using *shall* and the active voice, so that it is clear which party is obligated to do what. Recall from Chapter 4 on page 25 that a right is the flip side of an obligation. Therefore, you could draft these provisions as either a covenant and its obligation, or as a right. However, it's better to draft them as covenants for two reasons. First, a covenant is easier to carry out and understand because it explicitly states that a party has an obligation to perform. The statement of a right is not always that explicit. When a provision is cast as a right, the parties and, later, a litigator, must first establish who has the obligation to perform. While usually it is not an insurmountable task, it adds an unnecessary issue and step to the litigation. Second, a covenant facilitates the drafting of the full scope of a party's obligations.

Examples—Use of Has the Right *and* Shall

Acceptable Use of Has the Right:

Air-conditioning. The Tenant *has the right* to air-conditioning for the Premises during the summer.

Better Use of Shall and More Specific Limitations:

Air-conditioning. The Landlord *shall air-condition* the Premises until 5:00 p.m. each weekday during the summer, unless the Tenant requests that the air-conditioning remain on longer on a weekday or turned on for one or both weekend days. The Landlord shall comply with the Tenant's request and shall bill the Tenant at the regular rate plus 15%. The Tenant may make one or more requests, all of which this Section governs.

If a party insists on a statement of their rights, state the right, preferably using the word *right,* but pair it with a covenant. But be careful—if the covenant and the right are inconsistent, the contract will be ambiguous. There are exceptions to this rule, as we shall discuss next.

Example—Right Paired with Covenant

Author's Right to Book Copies. The Author has the right to receive 20 free copies of the Book, and the Publisher *shall provide* the Author with those copies no later than ten days before the Publication Date.

Parties often do state just one party's rights when stating their entitlement to a remedy.

Examples—Right if Entitlement to a Remedy

1—**Equitable Relief**. If the Executive breaches the Executive's duty of confidentiality, the Company has the right to equitable relief.

2—**Return of Deposit**. If the Tenant does not return the Premises in broom clean condition, the Landlord *has the right* to retain the amount of the Deposit equal to the cost of the appropriate cleaning.

In Example 1, the flip side of the Company's right to equitable relief is the Executive's implied obligation (from a promise) not to contest that equitable relief is appropriate.[12] Similarly, in Example 2, the flip side of the Landlord's right to the Deposit is the Tenant's implied obligation (from a promise) not to seek the Deposit's return.

Check all contract provisions to confirm that the party indeed has a right and not a choice between remedies, because drafters often misuse *has the right to, is entitled to*, and *is permitted to* in order to signal discretionary authority.

In Example 1 below, the sentence should be drafted using language of discretionary authority to make clear that the bank has a choice of remedies. As you can see in Example 2 and will be explained in more detail in Chapter 10 on page 97, *may* is the correct term to signal discretionary authority in a remedy when the remedies include a choice.

---

12. *See* Thomas R. Haggard, *Legal Drafting: Process, Technique, and Exercises* 409 (West 2003).

> *Examples—Use of* Right, Entitled, *and* Permitted *When Really Discretionary Authority*
>
> ***Incorrect:*** **Bank Remedies**. If the Borrower makes a material misrepresentation, the Bank [has the right] [is entitled][is permitted] to accelerate the Loan or to take any other action that law or this Agreement permits.
>
> ***Correct Use of May:*** **Bank Remedies**. If the Borrower makes a material misrepresentation, the Bank *may* accelerate the Loan or take any other action that law or this Agreement permits.

6. *Is Obligated, Is Responsible, Warrant, Agree,* and Other

Do not use *is obligated, is responsible, warrants,* or *agrees* instead of *shall*. First, *is obligated* does not necessarily signal the same thing as *shall*. If you are using *shall* to signal a covenant, be consistent and always use *shall*. Do not use *is obligated* interchangeably because it could cast doubt on the intent of the parties.

While practitioners should abstain from using *is obligated* as a synonym for *shall,* some practitioners believe *is obligated* can be useful at times. For example, the parties may want to contrast what a party *is not obligated to do* with what *it is obligated to do* as follows:

> *Example— Acceptable Use of* Obligated
>
> **Roof Maintenance**. X shall maintain the roof in its present condition. Without otherwise limiting the generality of the preceding covenant, X *is not obligated to* replace the roof although X *is obligated to* make spot repairs.

Here, the parties are trying to avoid litigating the meaning of *maintain the roof* by explicitly addressing one aspect of the meaning of *maintain*. However, remember that the word *obligation* is also useful as a tool when a practitioner is explaining the business deal in legal terms to their client since the common law talks extensively, as already discussed, of obligations in covenants and conditions.

Also, do not say that a party *is responsible* for doing something; use *shall* instead.

> *Examples—Do Not Use* Responsible
>
> ***Incorrect:*** **Costumes**. The Performer *is responsible* for designing and making her own costume.
>
> ***Correct Using*** **Shall:** **Costumes**. The Performer *shall* design and make her own costume.

Do not use *warrant* as a synonym for *shall* either. Drafters should limit their use of *warrant* as a verb to promises that a statement is true, as discussed in Chapter 3 on page 18. A party who warrants is not promising to take or refrain from taking an action. There is no promise of performance.

Finally, do not use any form of *agree*; use *shall* instead. *Agree* is not needed because the words of agreement state that *the parties agree.*

> **Examples— Do Not Use Agree**
>
> **Incorrect: Capital Contribution.** Each Limited Partner *agrees* to contribute $100,000 to the limited partnership before January 1, 20__.
>
> **Correct Use of Shall: Capital Contribution.** Each Limited Partner *shall* contribute $100,000 to the limited partnership before January 1, 20__.

D. NEGATIVE COVENANTS

As noted in Chapter 4 on page 25, covenants include promises both to do and not to do something. Some drafters refer to these promises as *affirmative* and *negative covenants*. This distinction is generally not important, except in the context of a loan agreement where covenants are classified for convenient reference.[13] There, affirmative covenants generally require a borrower to *maintain prudent business practices,*[14] including payment of taxes, maintenance of equipment, maintenance of existence, compliance with laws, and the keeping of proper business and financial records. Other affirmative covenants require the borrower to provide the bank with current financial information.

In contrast, negative covenants typically prohibit actions that the borrower might take if the loan agreement were not in effect and that would significantly change the borrower's structure or business operations.[15] For example, negative covenants prohibit mergers, debt, and the granting of security interests. Breaches of these covenants generally require that the borrower intended to perform the act that violated the covenant. Banks generally grant a borrower a grace period to cure a breach of an affirmative covenant, as it may be unintentional.[16] Breaches of negative covenants generally eventually result in an immediate event of default.[17] Once a company has merged, for instance, the merger can rarely be undone.

When you are drafting and want a party to promise not to do something, use *shall not* after the party's name.

> **Example—Negative Covenant with Shall Not *for One Party***
>
> **Participation in Other Sports.** The Athlete *shall not* participate in any sport other than baseball.

If you want two or more parties to promise not to do something, use a negative subject, such as *neither party* or *no party*, and the verb *may* instead of *shall not*, as in Example 1 below.[18] If *shall* were used instead of *may,* as in Example 2 below, the substantive meaning of the sentence would change. To determine how the

---

13. *See* Richard Wight, Warren Cooke & Richard Gray, *The LSTA's Complete Credit Agreement Guide* § 7.1 (2d ed., McGraw-Hill 2009) ("Covenants can be divided into three categories: financial covenants, affirmative covenants, and negative covenants. . . . There is no substantive effect to these classifications; they are purely a matter of convenience of reference.").

14. Michael A. Leichtling, Barry A. Dubin & Jeffrey J. Wong, 1 *Commercial Loan Documentation Guide* § 11.01 (2020).

15. Sandra Schnitzer Stern, *1 Structuring and Drafting Commercial Loan Agreements,* 5.01[1], 6.01[1] (2012).

16. Stern, *supra* n. 15, at 8.01[2] (2019); Leichtling et al., *supra* n. 14, at § 11.01.

17. Stern, *supra* n. 15, at 8.05[2].

18. *See INEOS Polymers Inc. v. BASF Catalysts,* 553 F.3d 491, 500 (7th Cir. 2009) (stating that "neither party may" constitutes an "absolute bar to assignment of contractual rights."); *see also Balmoral Racing Club, Inc. v. Churchill Downs, Inc.,* 953 F. Supp. 2d 885, 895 (N.D. Ill. 2013).

substantive meaning has changed, replace *shall* with *is obligated to*, as in Example 3. Examples 2 and 3 do not prohibit the parties from assigning. Instead, they state that no party is obligated to assign its rights.

---

*Examples—Negative Covenants with **May** for Two or More Parties*

1—Correct: **Anti-assignment**. Neither party *may* assign any of its rights under this Agreement.

2—Incorrect: **Anti-assignment**. Neither party *shall* assign any of its rights under this Agreement.

3—Incorrect: **Anti-assignment**. Neither party *is obligated to* assign any of its rights under this Agreement.

Sometimes you may have to draft an exception to an affirmative covenant. In these cases, the party giving a covenant has made a promise, but they do not have to perform certain specific duties or obligations that fall under that covenant. For these exceptions, you can use *is not obligated to.* In Example 1, the monetary limit is an exception to the general duty to *use commercially reasonable efforts.* In Example 2, another provision not included here obligates the Company to provide an indemnity. Example 2 states the circumstances of the exception.

Examples—Obligated as Exception to Affirmative Covenant

*1—***Landlord's Consent**. The Seller shall use commercially reasonable efforts to obtain the Landlord's consent, but in using those efforts, the Seller *is not obligated to* spend more than $10,000.

*2—***No Obligation to Indemnify**. The Company *is not obligated to* indemnify the Executive for the Executive's actions if such actions were outside the scope of the Executive's duties as stated in Section 3.

E. COVENANTS POSING AS DECLARATIONS

Sometimes drafters write a provision so that it appears to be a declaration, but it should really be a covenant. Test whether a declaration is appropriate by asking whether your client would want to have access to remedies when it comes to that provision. If the answer is *yes*, then redraft the provision as a covenant. Of course, it might also be a representation and warranty, depending on the context, so make sure that it does not have to be drafted as those instead or as well. Here is an example of a covenant posing as a declaration:

Examples—Covenants Posing as Declarations

1—Incorrect as Declaration:
Security Deposit. The security deposit will be $3,000, due concurrently with the parties' execution and delivery of this Agreement.

2—Correct Declaration with Covenant:
Security Deposit. The security deposit is $3,000, and the Tenant shall pay the security deposit to the Landlord by certified check concurrently with the parties' execution and delivery of this Agreement.

> *3 — Correct as Covenant:*
> **Security Deposit.** The Tenant shall pay the Landlord a $3,000 security deposit by certified check concurrently with the parties' execution and delivery of this Agreement.

A quick read of Example 1 gives us the impression that the provision is a declaration that defines the amount of the security deposit. However, a closer read reveals that the provision should be drafted to include both a declaration and a covenant, as in Example 2, or as a covenant that includes the information in the declaration, as in Example 3.

II. RISK ALLOCATION IN COVENANTS

In the same way that representations and warranties are a risk allocation mechanism, so are covenants. The allocation manifests itself in terms of how absolute a party's promises are. The business differences between the different ways of expressing a party's obligations are **the degrees of obligation**.[19]

For example, let's say that an owner of a local store is selling their business because they are retiring. The seller has five years left on a commercial lease with Landlord Corp. for the space where the store is located. As part of selling the business, the seller wants to include, and the buyer wants to assume, the lease with Landlord Corp.

To effect this acquisition, the seller must assign their rights under the lease to the buyer, but the seller's lease prohibits the seller from doing so. Therefore, the buyer insists that the seller must promise to obtain the landlord's consent to the assignment. Review the following examples of covenants and see if you can determine how the risk allocation shifts depending on the degree of the seller's obligation.[20] You will see that the provisions drafted in the table that follows change the seller's risk, but differently in each one.

RISK ALLOCATION EXAMPLES	SELLER'S PERSPECTIVE	BUYER'S PERSPECTIVE
1 — **Consents.** The Seller shall obtain from Landlord Corp. the consent allowing the Seller to assign the Lease to the Buyer.	I would not want this consent provision. This is the equivalent of a *flat representation*, so I would be making an absolute promise to obtain consent, which would expose me to tremendous risk.	This may be a good covenant for me, as the Buyer! If the Seller obtains Landlord Corp.'s consent, then I am immediately in a position to start running the business that the seller had had on the same premises.

---

19. Thank you to Alan Shaw from Fordham University School of Law for coining this phrase, *degrees of obligation.*

20. These covenants are based on covenants that Alan Shaw drafted. *See generally W. Willow-Bay Ct., LLC v. Robino-Bay Ct. Plaza, LLC,* No. CIV.A. 2742-VCN, 2007 WL 3317551 (Del. Ch. Nov. 2, 2007), *aff'd,* 985 A.2d 391 (Del. 2009), as corrected (Nov. 30, 2009) (discussing how a party's liability changes as the degree of obligation changes from an absolute promise to obtain consents to a promise qualified by best efforts).

RISK ALLOCATION EXAMPLES	SELLER'S PERSPECTIVE	BUYER'S PERSPECTIVE
	The promise I would be making here is dangerous because I would have no control over the outcome: Landlord Corp. has no obligation to consent, and it could just as easily refuse consent as grant it. Since I have no control over the outcome, there is risk in that I may not be able to avoid breaching the covenant. Therefore, I would not agree to this provision so drafted. I would rather reduce my risk by lowering my degree of obligation.	If the Seller does not obtain the consent, then that would give me the right to sue Seller for damages, so I should still come out whole. If the current lease's rent is below market value, my damages might be equal to the rent I would have to pay for comparable leased property minus the rent the Seller is paying under their lease. However, I would rather think of other possibilities because I do not want the alternative to be resorting to litigation. It may be helpful to be more specific in this provision and separately negotiate an additional provision where the Seller has to pay me an amount as indemnification if they do not get the consent.
2—**Consents.** The Seller shall use commercially reasonable efforts[21] to obtain from Landlord Corp. the consent allowing the Seller to assign the Lease to the Buyer.	I prefer this provision to the one above. It does not require me to obtain consent. Instead, this standard requires only that I use commercially reasonable efforts in trying to obtain consent. This change *substantially reduces* my degree of obligation and, therefore, my risk. Now, the covenant focuses on my degree of effort, rather than on my success in obtaining a specific result. So long as I use commercially reasonable efforts to obtain consent, I have performed, leaving the Buyer with no cause of action for breach, even if Landlord Corp. refuses to consent. But I wonder, how do I know for sure that I've made a commer-	This second provision shifts risk to me, so I prefer the first provision, above. However, it wouldn't be unreasonable for the Seller to expect me to assume a portion of their increased risk, but I don't see why I should. The Seller may have to offer Landlord Corp. a lot of money to consent to assigning me the lease, which may be enough for the seller to do in order to fulfill their obligation. If Landlord Corp. refuses to consent in this case, then it may not really be the seller's fault. Commercially reasonable efforts can be vague at times. I wonder if we should be more specific about what this means.

---

21. Instead of using the qualifier of commercially reasonable efforts, you would want to draft a more specific standard to establish more clearly for the parties what this means. Your client and the other party, along with your research and knowledge of the industry, would help you establish this standard. See Chapter 8 on page 64 for more information on qualifiers.

RISK ALLOCATION EXAMPLES	SELLER'S PERSPECTIVE	BUYER'S PERSPECTIVE
	cially reasonable effort? I'm not sure I know exactly what that means. It seems pretty vague. Assuming that I perform, then the Buyer will have to bear the increased costs associated with any higher rent that the new landlord requires. This shifts some of my risk to the Buyer. The decrease in my risk directly increases the Buyer's risk.	If, despite their commercially reasonable efforts, the Seller cannot obtain consent from Landlord Corp., then I will be in a difficult position where I may have to offer Landlord Corp. even more or find a different location.
3 — Consents. The Seller shall use commercially reasonable efforts to obtain from Landlord Corp. the consent allowing the Seller to assign the Lease to the Buyer. For purposes of this provision, the Seller is deemed to have used its commercially reasonable efforts if it offers Landlord Corp. at least $10,000 as an inducement to consent to the assignment.	I think this would probably be the best of these three for myself. Hopefully, the buyer will agree to it and won't insist on a provision like the first one. This third provision addresses the concerns I had with the first two provisions. For one thing, it's less vague than the second one. Instead of only referring to "commercially reasonable efforts," it states how much money I am required to spend to try to induce Landlord Corp. to grant consent, *capping that amount* at $10,000. I like that I know I will be in compliance with this covenant once I offer $10,000 (and no more than that) to Landlord Corp. in exchange for its grant of consent.	This third provision is much more clear and precise. Of these first three, this provision would probably be the best, both for myself and, if I'm being generous, for the Seller.
4 — Consents. The Seller shall request that Landlord Corp. consent to the Seller's assignment of the Lease to the Buyer.	I think this provision is the best of these four because it totally eliminates my obligation to obtain consent from Landlord Corp. Instead, all I am required to do is *request* consent from Landlord Corp. With this provision, my degree of obligation is minimal, and my risk much lower than in the preceding three provisions.	I do not like this fourth provision because it has me assuming *almost all the risk* with respect to the Seller's failure to obtain consent! There's no way that I would agree to this.

As you can see from these examples, a drafter can change a covenant significantly by using different degrees of obligation. In the example mentioned previously regarding how the seller should maintain the equipment between signing and closing: Should the equipment be maintained *in good condition, ordinary wear and tear excepted*, or *in accordance with industry standards*? As the obligation changes, so does the standard of liability. The covenant becomes harder or easier for the promisor to perform, and therefore it becomes more or less likely that the promisor might be found in breach of the standard.

Good drafting requires that you carefully examine each covenant in the context of the client's business deal to determine the appropriate standard of liability. As a general rule, if your client is making the covenant, the degree of obligation should be as weak as possible, while the reverse would be true if your client has the right to receive the performance. No matter what, your provisions should be clear and as specific as possible so that the parties are on the same page on what the standard is and what each party has to do to meet that standard.

III. MORE ON COVENANTS IN ACQUISITION AGREEMENTS AND FINANCINGS

The modern acquisition agreement often combines the pre- and post-closing covenants of both parties into one article. Because each covenant may relate to a different time period, each covenant must state the time period and party to which it applies. The following excerpt from a purchase agreement is typical. The italicized language has been added to emphasize the language related to the time period.

Example—Article with Pre- and Post-Closing Covenants for Both Parties in Acquisition Agreement

Article VIII[22] Covenants

8.1 Access to Information. *Prior to Closing*, Sellers shall permit Purchaser . . . to have reasonable access, during normal business hours and on reasonable advance notice, to the Books and Records and senior management personnel of Sellers pertaining to the Purchased Assets . . .

8.2 Conduct of the Business Pending the Closing. Except as otherwise expressly contemplated by this Agreement . . . , *during the period from and after the date hereof until the Closing Date*, Sellers:

    (a) shall use commercially reasonable efforts to conduct the Business in the Ordinary Course of Business . . .

    (c) will maintain in full force and effect policies of insurance that provide casualty, property damage and general liability coverage for the Purchased Assets comparable in all material respects in amount and scope of coverage to that now maintained by or on behalf of Sellers . . . .

8.3 Cooperation; Consents and Filings.

    (a) *From and after the date hereof until the Closing Date*, Sellers, Purchaser and Guarantor will each cooperate with each other and use (and will cause their respective representatives to use) commercially reasonable efforts . . . (i) to take, or to cause to be taken, all actions, and to do, or to cause to be done, all things reasonably necessary, proper or advisable on its part under this Agreement . . . to consummate and make effective the transactions contemplated by this Agreement as promptly as practicable . . . .

---

22. Excerpt from Article VIII of the Settlement and Purchase and Sale Agreement among ASARCO LLC, AR Silver Bell, Inc., Copper Basin Railway, Inc., ASARCO Santa Cruz, Inc., Sterlite (USA), Inc. and Sterlite Industries (India) LTD, dated as of March 6, 2009. *See* Sterlite Industries (India) Ltd., Annual and Transition Report of Foreign Private Issuers (Form 20F, Ex-4.42) (July 10, 2009).

> **8.4 Preservation of Records**. Subject to the other provisions of this Agreement, Purchaser and Guarantor shall . . . preserve and keep in their possession all records held by them on and after the date hereof relating to the Purchased Assets, *for a period of seven years or such longer period as may be required by Applicable Law* . . . .

Another drafting style for covenant articles in acquisition agreements begins the article with an unnumbered introductory paragraph. It states that a specific party promises to perform the following obligations from signing to closing. Numbered sections follow the introductory paragraph, each section addressing a different subject. When drafters use this style instead, they put the post-closing covenants in a separate article. Here is an example of the article that relates to the pre-closing covenants of the Seller using this different drafting approach:

Example—Article with Pre-Closing Covenants for One Party in Acquisition Agreement

Article 4 — Seller's Covenants

The Seller shall do the following beginning on the date of this Agreement and ending on the Closing Date:

4.1 Consents. The Seller shall use commercially reasonable efforts to obtain all consents.

4.2 Maintenance of Machinery. The Seller shall maintain the Machinery in its current condition.

IV. HOW TO DEAL WITH THIRD PARTIES

You should not draft a provision that appears to bind a third party that is not a party to the contract. If they are not a party to the agreement, that provision is not a covenant binding them because you cannot bind a party that is not a party to the agreement. Even if you use *shall* after that third party's name, that party will not necessarily be bound. For example, contracts often include arbitration provisions in which the parties state the arbitrators' obligations. A typical provision might be as Example 1 that follows. The use of *shall* is inappropriate because the arbitrators are not parties to the agreement and cannot be obligated to do anything. Example 2 provides an appropriate redraft. The wording in Example 2 creates a declaration, a policy statement. As an alternative, the agreement can obligate the parties to instruct the arbitrators how to act, as in Example 3. Some drafters prefer Example 3 because it reflects the reality of what will happen if the parties arbitrate their controversies.

Examples—Drafting for Third Parties

1 — Incorrect Because You Cannot Use Shall to Bind Nonparties:

Choice of Law. The arbitrators shall interpret all controversies arising under or relating to this Agreement, including torts, in accordance with the laws of Missouri.

> *2—Correct Use of Present Tense Declaration for Nonparties:*
> **Choice of Law**. The arbitrators are to interpret all controversies arising under or relating to this Agreement, including torts, in accordance with the laws of Missouri.
>
> *3—Correct Use of Covenant Involving Nonparties:*
> **Choice of Law**. The parties shall instruct the arbitrators to interpret all controversies arising under or relating to this Agreement, including torts, in accordance with the laws of Missouri.

Drafters also use *shall cause* or *shall not permit* when one of the parties to the contract is more responsible for a result, but a third party has to perform in order to achieve that result. For example, suppose that a contractor is obligated to construct a building on land that has an underground gas tank, but the contractor does not do this type of work. Part of the deal might be that the gas tank is to be removed by someone else before construction begins, and the owner is going to arrange for that separately. In the negotiations, the owner might object to a covenant that the owner is obligated to remove the tank. A provision like this is often drafted—incorrectly—in the passive voice without stating who is to perform, as in Example 1 below. But covenants should establish who has the obligation to perform, as Example 2 and 3 do correctly. Example 3 further lowers the risk for the owner by bringing in the qualifier of reasonable efforts, but as discussed in more detail in Chapter 8 on page 65, we would encourage you to draft more specifically what *reasonable efforts* means in this case.

> ### Examples—Third Parties and Which Verbs to Use
>
> *1—Incorrect Because of Use of Shall Be and Passive Voice with No Actor*
> **Removal of Gas Tank**. The underground gas tank shall be removed from the Land no later than five Business Days before the Start Date.
>
> *2—Correct Because of Use of Shall Cause and Active Voice with Owner Responsible*
> **Removal of Gas Tank**. The Owner shall cause the underground gas tank to be removed from the Land no later than five Business Days before the Start Date.
>
> *3—Correct Because of Use of Shall, Active Voice with Owner Responsible, and Qualifier*
> **Removal of Gas Tank**. The Owner shall use reasonable efforts to cause the underground gas tank to be removed from the Land no later than five Business Days before the Start Date.

A similar problem occurs when a parent corporation sells the shares of a subsidiary. A buyer often wants the subsidiary to take various actions during the gap period, but the parent, not the subsidiary, is party to the agreement. To achieve the desired result, have the parent *cause* the subsidiary to perform in a certain way.[23] In the example below, the covenant is the seller's. Their obligation is to cause a certain result: the target's maintenance of the equipment in accordance with industry standards.

---

23. As an alternative, some buyers require the target to become a party to the stock purchase agreement and to agree to perform certain obligations during the gap period.

Example—Correct Because of Use of Shall Cause *and Active Voice with Seller Responsible*

Equipment. The Seller shall cause the Target to maintain the Target's equipment in accordance with industry standards.

V. EXERCISES

A. EXERCISE 9A: CORRECT DRAFTING ERRORS

Mark up the following provisions by deleting language that is not needed and adding language that would be more appropriate. As you redraft these provisions, remember to follow best drafting practices, such as keeping verbs together, avoiding legalese, using the active voice, following the proper use of *shall* to indicate covenants binding the appropriate party, etc.

1. Use of Proceeds. The Borrower shall not use, and hereby specifically agrees not to use, directly or indirectly, the Borrowing's proceeds for any purpose, except that stated in this Section 3.4.

2. Fees and Expenses. The fees of the Escrow Agent and all expenses reasonably incurred by the Escrow Agent in performing its obligations hereunder shall be borne one-half by Rapid Transportation and one-half by Eagle.

3. Discharge. No employee may be discharged without two weeks' notice.

4. Disputes. The parties have decided to submit all disputes arising under or relating to this Agreement to binding arbitration before the American Arbitration Association and under the rules of that Association. The lawyers' expenses related to the arbitration shall be paid as the arbitrators may direct.

B. EXERCISE 9B: DRAFT COVENANTS

Draft the following provisions. You may need more than one sentence. Do not draft any definitions—just use a defined term that you think works in that context.

1. Sam Student wants to rent an apartment. The landlord was leery of renting it to a student, but he agreed to do so because Sam said that he would return the apartment in good condition and broom clean. How would you draft covenants that cover this information?

_____

_____

2. Same facts as in question 1, plus the following: Sam wanted it made clear that he had not agreed to repair any damage that existed when he moved into the apartment. Draft this provision as a nonobligation. It should be a follow-on sentence to the provision that you wrote for the previous question.

_____

_____

3. Private Equity LLP is borrowing money from Big Bank N.A. The bank does not want the borrower to merge or sell substantially all of its assets without the bank's consent. The bank agreed it would not unreasonably withhold its consent. How would you draft covenants that cover this information?

_____

_____

4. A seller and buyer have entered into a Confidentiality Agreement, in accordance with which each party has agreed "to hold in strict confidence and not disclose to any nonsignatory information acquired in connection with the transaction." A nonsignatory is a third party that is not a party to the Confidentiality Agreement (not the seller or the buyer). The seller is concerned that the buyer has three subsidiaries, and that word will leak out. How can you protect the seller with a buyer's covenant?

_____

_____

EXERCISE 9C: RISK ALLOCATION IN COVENANTS

The following provisions relate to how a seller has to maintain their plants, structures, and equipment between the signing of a purchase agreement and the closing date. You may find it helpful to read through all six examples first to note the differences.

For each of the following examples, determine the following:

- Would one of the parties, the seller or the buyer, prefer this provision? If so, why?
- What issues come up because of the language used?

1. **Maintenance**. Seller shall maintain Seller's plants, structures, and equipment in good operating condition and repair.

2. **Maintenance**. Seller shall maintain Seller's plants, structures, and equipment in good operating condition and repair, subject only to ordinary wear and tear.

3. **Maintenance**. Seller shall maintain Seller's plants, structures, and equipment in customary operating condition and repair.

4. **Maintenance**. Seller shall maintain Seller's plants, structures, and equipment in accordance with industry standards.

5. **Maintenance**. Seller shall steam clean, oil, and otherwise maintain each piece of Seller's equipment as described in Exhibit B.

6. **Maintenance**. Seller shall not permit Seller's plants, structures, and equipment to be in a state of operating condition and repair that would materially and adversely affect the operations of Seller.

CHAPTER TEN

Drafting Discretionary Authority Provisions and Declarations

I. DRAFTING DISCRETIONARY AUTHORITY PROVISIONS

This section covers best practices for drafting discretionary authority provisions, which are provisions where one party has a choice or permission to do something. Best practices for drafting these provisions include using *may*. A lot of the other best practices that we discussed in the representations, warranties, and covenant sections earlier in Chapters 8 and 9 also apply to discretionary authority, such as drafting as clearly as possible, being specific about what you include, drafting in the active, not passive voice, and being intentional about risk allocation in these provisions.

A. CONTENT AND QUESTIONS TO ASK

As with representations, warranties, and covenants, the content of an agreement's discretionary authority provisions can vary greatly depending on the type of transaction and the parties involved. To determine what you should include as discretionary authority provisions, you will need to find out if your client and the other party have a choice or permission to do something and what that something is.

You often find provisions with discretionary authority in the action, endgame, and general provisions articles in an agreement. These parts of the agreement are discussed in more detail in Chapters 16 (page 209), 17 (page 229), and 18 (page 263).

B. VERB: USE *MAY* FOR DISCRETIONARY AUTHORITY

Use *may* to grant a party discretionary authority,[1] rather than *has the right to, is entitled to,* or *is permitted.* Using words like *right, entitled,* or *permission* can make the parties, courts, and anyone else involved with the agreement think of covenants or other contract concepts and remedies, which creates confusion.

---

1. *See In re Oneida Ltd.*, 400 B.R. 384, 391 (Bankr. S.D.N.Y. 2009); *Burgess Mining & Constr. Corp. v. City of Bessemer*, 312 So. 2d 24, 28 (Ala. 1975); *McMaster v. McIlory Bank*, 654 S.W.2d 591, 594 (Ark. App. 1983). *See also N.W. Traveling Men's Ass'n v. Crawford*, 1906 WL 1865 (Ill. App. 1 Dist.) ("'May' does not mean 'shall,' and is not so construed in private contracts. It is only in the case of statutes by which public rights are involved that this construction is sometimes adopted *ex debito*

Moreover, the other terms (*right, entitled, permission*) are just a long way of saying *may*.[2] See the following example:

Examples—Discretionary Authority

Giving a Party a Choice:
Events of Default. If an Event of Default occurs and is continuing, the Bank *may* waive the Event of Default or exercise its remedies.

Giving a Party Permission or Authorization:
Capital Expenditures. The Borrower shall not make any capital expenditures, except that the Borrower *may* make capital expenditures in connection with the Bridge Project.

Although most provisions use *may* to signal a grant of discretionary authority, sometimes a provision only implies that grant, as in the following anti-assignment provision:

Example—Implied Discretionary Authority:

Anti-assignment. The Tenant shall not assign the Tenant's rights under this Lease, without the prior written consent of the Landlord.

Here, the landlord has the option to consent to an assignment or not consent to an assignment. Therefore, the landlord has discretionary authority.

Occasionally, using *may* alone does not properly express the parties' intent. Assume that a retailer and a manufacturer agree that the manufacturer will create a product in one of two colors and that the manufacturer will decide which color. Look at the proposed provision.

Examples—Discretionary Authority Where Using May *Is Not Enough*

1—Incorrect with May:
Color of the Product. The Manufacturer may manufacture the Product in green or blue.

2—Incorrect with May *and* Only:
Color of the Product. The Manufacturer may manufacture the Product *only* in green or blue.

---

justiticœ."); but *see Carleno Coal Sales, Inc. v. Ramsay Coal Co.*, 270 P.2d 755, 756 (Colo. 1954) (en banc) (construing the clause "[T]he party not at fault *may* give to the defaulting party 60 days written notice [of termination]." (emphasis in the original)). The drafting error in this clause is that *may* was intended to give the party not at fault discretionary authority to give a notice of termination, but the 60 days was intended to be mandatory. The ambiguity arose because the two matters were merged into one sentence.

2. *See, e.g., Kattas v. Sherman*, 32 A.D.3d 496, 498 (N.Y. 2d Dept. 2006) (quoting the following contract language: "[S]hould said Certificate of Occupancy not be able to issue as a matter of right, then and in that event, either party shall be entitled to cancel this Contract." (emphasis in opinion omitted)).

> *3—Incorrect with* **Shall:**
>
> **Color of the Product.** The Manufacturer shall manufacture the Product in green or blue.
>
> *4—Correct with* **Shall** *and* **May:**
>
> **Color of the Product.** The Manufacturer shall manufacture the Product in green or blue and may choose which color.

Example 1 does not say what it means: that the manufacturer is obligated to make the product in one of the two colors, but they may choose between these two colors. As drafted, the provision does not prohibit the manufacturer from making the product in colors other than green or blue. In similar situations, courts have refused to interpret a provision as if the word *only* had been included in the sentence.[3] However, inserting *only* does not necessarily fix the problem, as seen in Example 2.

Example 2 limits the colors, but it still does not obligate the manufacturer to make the product in green or blue. Simply adding *shall* does not work either, as can be seen in Example 3. By using *shall* in this way, the Manufacturer is obligated to make the Product, but the provision does not state who has the discretionary authority to determine the Product's color. Curing this drafting problem is simple. The provision should say what it means, as in Example 4.

When drafting a provision of discretionary authority that gives a party permission, consider whether the exercise of that permission acts as a condition to the performance of the other party. If so, the correlative obligation must be drafted. For example, consider the following provision:

> *Example—Discretionary Authority That Serves Like a Condition*
>
> **Nonselling Stockholder Purchases.** On receipt of a Sales Notice, each Nonselling Stockholder may purchase from the Selling Stockholder the number of Shares equal to [insert formula] by delivering a Purchase Notice to the Selling Stockholder.

This provision gives a nonselling Stockholder permission (discretionary authority) to purchase shares, which permission the nonselling stockholder may or may not exercise. *If* the nonselling stockholder does exercise its discretionary authority (as to some or all of the shares), *then* the selling stockholder is obligated to sell the number of shares that the nonselling stockholder wants to purchase. Therefore, one party having discretionary authority is not the same as the other party having an obligation to perform. The contract must include a specific covenant obligating the other party to perform if you want them to have to do or not do something, as in the example above.

You should also know that a provision granting discretionary authority to do something cannot prohibit a party from doing anything else. For example, here is language that resulted in litigation:

---

3. *See Pravin Banker Assocs., Ltd. v. Banco Popular Del Peru*, 109 F.3d 850, 856 (2d Cir. 1997).

Example— Incorrect Discretionary Authority That Does Not Limit

Assignment and Delegation. The Bank may assign all or any part of its rights in the Loan to any Qualified Bank Transferee.[4]

The court interpreted this as explicit permission to assign all or any part of its rights in a loan to qualified bank transferees, but not to the exclusion of other transferees (i.e., not Qualified Bank Transferees). The grant of permission to assign did not imply a prohibition on other assignments.

This provision could have been fixed in either one of two ways to limit the assignment to only qualified bank transferees:

Examples—Correct Discretionary Authority That Does Limit

1 — **Assignment and Delegation**. The Bank may assign all or any part of its rights in the Loan *but only* to a Qualified Bank Transferee.

2 — **Assignment and Delegation**. The Bank shall not assign all or any part of its rights in the Loan to any Person, except to a Qualified Bank Transferee.

Example 2 is preferable because it creates a duty for the Bank not to assign all or any part of its rights to any Person, except to a Qualified Bank Transferee. Any assignment in contravention of the provision would be a breach entitling the borrower to damages. When drafting discretionary authority, you should always consider whether you should be drafting covenants related to the same issue, as in this example, instead of or in addition to that discretionary authority.

C. DISCRETIONARY AUTHORITY VS. HAVING A RIGHT

Lawyers sometimes negotiate whether an equitable remedy can or should be drafted as a right rather than discretionary authority.[5]

Example— Equitable Remedy Provision with Discretionary Authority

Equitable Relief. If the Executive *breaches* the Executive's duty of confidentiality, the Company *may* seek equitable relief.

Here, *may* is being used in the sense of permission. In other words, this provision states: *The Company has the Executive's permission to seek equitable relief.* Many parties in the company's position would be quite unhappy with this provision because, from a business perspective, a company would expect more from this endgame provision. As stated, this provision provides no more than what would already be true without it: that the company can go into

---

4. Tina L. Stark, *Assignment and Delegation, in Negotiating and Drafting Contract Boilerplate* ch.3, 71-72 (Stark et al. eds., ALM Publg. 2003); *see Pravin Banker Assocs., Ltd. v. Banco Popular Del Peru*, 109 F.3d 850, 856 (2d Cir. 1997). The provision is from the case and could be more concisely drafted.

5. *See* Chapter 5 on page 33 and Chapter 17 on page 254.

court to seek a temporary injunction or not do so. Instead, the company would want an acknowledgment that if they go into court, the executive agrees that the court should award equitable relief if the executive breached their duty of confidentiality. In essence, the company wants a liquidated damages provision, which is about equitable relief, rather than money. Liquidated damages are discussed in more detail in Chapter 17 on page 246.

To provide the company with this remedy, you, representing the company, would change the provision from one of discretionary authority or permission to one of a right. This would give the company the right to equitable relief and the executive the obligation not to interfere with that right, as follows:

Example—Recommended Equitable Remedy Provision with **Having the Right**

> **Equitable Relief**. If the Executive breaches the Executive's duty of confidentiality, the Company *has the right* to equitable relief.

This issue also arises in endgame provisions outside the context of equitable relief, such as in the following provision:

Example—Endgame Provision with **May**

> **Deposit**. The Landlord *may* keep the Deposit if the Tenant remains in possession of the Apartment after the Term.

Technically, the provision could be read as a condition to discretionary authority: *If the Tenant stays in the Apartment, the Landlord may keep the Deposit.* Under the stated circumstances, the landlord has the tenant's permission to keep the deposit, but the discretionary authority to return it. Both parties would probably agree that the previous sentence inaccurately documents their intent and agreement. Somewhat reasonably, the landlord could argue that there is no choice involved in this remedy because no reasonable businessperson would give away money. Therefore, some drafters would argue that the proper way to describe the landlord's legal relationship with the deposit is that the landlord has a right to the deposit that cannot be taken away, and the tenant has the obligation not to seek the return of the deposit. So, instead of using discretionary authority, some drafters will choose to draft this provision as a right as follows:

Example—Endgame Provision with **Have the Right**

> **Deposit**. The Landlord *has the right to* keep the entire Deposit if the Tenant remains in possession of the Apartment after the Term.

D. DISCRETIONARY AUTHORITY POSING AS A DECLARATION

In the same way that covenants can pose as declarations, a grant of discretionary authority can pose as a declaration, as follows:

> *Examples— Discretionary Authority Posing as a Declaration*
>
> ***Incorrect:* Counterparts.** Execution of this Agreement in counterparts is permissible.
>
> ***Correct:* Counterparts.** The parties may execute this Agreement in counterparts.

This last example is preferable because it brings together various drafting best practices, including using the active voice and the appropriate contract concept and corresponding verb. Notice too that the parties are given permission and choice to execute in counterparts (which means that each party can sign a separate copy of the agreement and exchange signature pages).

E. RISK ALLOCATION IN DISCRETIONARY AUTHORITY PROVISIONS

When drafting a provision that grants discretionary authority, you will have to consider how broad or narrow the grant of discretion should be, which is a matter of the allocation of risk. If your client will be exercising the discretionary authority, then the following guidelines generally apply in order to better protect your client:

- Draft the grant as broadly as possible as to type, matter involved, time, etc. to give your client as much discretionary authority as possible. This reduces the risk to your client because then they will have more options.
- Draft any condition to the exercise of discretionary authority so it can be easily satisfied. This reduces the risk to your client by facilitating their ability to exercise the discretionary authority when they wish and to make it easier for them to achieve the desired result.

If the other party will be exercising their discretionary authority, then do the following:

- As much as possible, narrow the grant of discretionary authority as to type, matter involved, time, etc., so the other side has a more limited choice or permission to act. This reduces the risk that your client will be subject to the other party's discretionary authority.
- Draft any condition to the exercise of the discretionary authority so it applies only in the most limited circumstances. This reduces the risk for your client because it will make it harder for the other party to meet the condition, and it will limit the consequences for your client if the other party meets the condition.

Therefore, when drafting a grant of discretionary authority, you must determine whether to provide for:

- an unrestricted grant of discretionary authority, which would probably be for your client (Example 1 below), or
- a more limited grant of discretionary authority that requires a party be reasonable or sets a similar standard for the party's exercise of discretion, which would probably be for the party that is not your client (Example 2 below).

> *Examples—Unrestricted and Restricted Grants of Discretionary Authority*
>
> *1—Unrestricted:*
> **Anti-assignment**. The Tenant shall not assign the Tenant's rights under this Lease, without the prior written consent of the Landlord, and the Landlord may give or withhold that consent in the Landlord's sole discretion.
>
> *2—Restricted by Reasonableness Standard:*
> **Anti-assignment**. The Tenant shall not assign the Tenant's rights under this Lease, without the prior written consent of the Landlord, and the Landlord shall not unreasonably withhold that consent.

In some jurisdictions, courts hold that public policy considerations can override a provision in a contract that grants a party sole discretion or an unrestricted grant of discretionary authority. For example, courts have concluded that such unrestricted grants of discretionary authority must be exercised in good faith to put into effect the parties' intent.[6] The courts often rely on the implied covenant of good faith and fair dealing in these circumstances. If the court finds that one of the parties acted in bad faith, the court will not honor the provision granting that party sole discretion.[7]

II. DRAFTING DECLARATIONS

This section covers best practices for drafting declarations, which are facts or policies to which both parties agree. Generally, these are definitions or policies for the management of the contract. You often find declarations in the definitions article of an agreement (discussed in more detail in Chapter 15 on page 183), and in the general provisions article (discussed in more detail in Chapter 18 on page 263).

A lot of the other best practices that we discussed in the representations, warranties, covenant, and discretionary authority sections in Chapters 8 and 9 and earlier in this chapter also apply to declarations, such as drafting as clearly as possible, being specific about what you include, drafting in the active voice, and being intentional about risk allocation. An additional best practice for drafting declarations is to use the present tense.

A. CONTENT AND QUESTIONS TO ASK

As with representations, warranties, covenants, and discretionary authority provisions, the content of an agreement's declarations can vary greatly depending on the type of transaction and the parties involved. To determine what you should include as declarations you will need to talk to your client to find out whether your client and the other party have agreed to specific facts or policies, such as definitions or policies for the management of the contract.

To test whether a fact or policy should be included as a declaration, ask yourself: Would a party want monetary damages if the legal consequences were not as stated?

---

6. *See, e.g., White Stone Partners, LP v. Piper Jaffray Cos., Inc.*, 978 F. Supp. 878, 882 (D. Minn. 1997); *In re Syngenta AG MIR 162 Corn Litigation*, MDL No. 2591, 2017 WL 2080601 at *8 (D. Kan. May 15, 2017).

7. *See id.*

If the answer is *no*, then the provision should probably be a declaration. If the answer is *yes*, then the provision should be drafted as a representation, warranty, covenant, and/or condition to an obligation, because only those contract concepts have monetary remedies in the event of misrepresentation or breach.

B. PRESENT TENSE

Draft declarations using the present tense, since these provisions have continuing effect throughout a contract's life.[8] If drafted this way, a declaration always applies to the current situation, no matter when it occurs during the life of the contract and the transaction. Here are a few examples:

> ### Examples—Correct Declarations in Present Tense
>
> **Governing Law**. The laws of Idaho govern all matters, including torts, arising under or relating to this Agreement.
>
> **Salary**. The Executive's salary is $3,000 per week.
>
> **Merger**. This Agreement is the parties' complete and exclusive agreement on the matters contained in this Agreement.
>
> **Termination**. This Agreement terminates on the date that is the later of the date that the Lender releases the Collateral and the date the Lender returns to the Borrower its Note marked "Paid."

C. RISK ALLOCATION IN DECLARATIONS

Declarations can also be used as a risk allocation mechanism. You determine how much risk your client takes on when you draft and agree to a declaration in a contract. In drafting declarations and assessing your client's risk, focus on carefully reading the definitions and policy matters. Think about, research, and tailor the declarations to what would be most beneficial to your client. For example, do you have a choice between New York and Delaware for the governing law? Would one of these states' governing law pose less risk for your client in this transaction than the other? Do you need to add a definition for a concept that you need to use and set clear and specific standards in the contract to manage parties' expectations and further reduce risk?

Some drafters tend to overlook the declarations or use the same ones for each contract, even if the circumstances are different. Try not to do that, especially if you have the time and resources to review and revise an agreement and the client has issues that must be covered in declarations. To learn more about how to better draft declarations like definitions and general provisions and to see more examples, see Chapter 15 on page 183 and Chapter 18 on page 263.

---

8. As stated by Reed Dickerson, "[A provision should speak] as of the time it is being read, not merely as of the time it took effect." F. Reed Dickerson, *The Fundamentals of Legal Drafting* 185 (2d ed. Little, Brown & Co. 1986).

III. EXERCISES

A. EXERCISE 10A: CORRECT DRAFTING ERRORS

Mark up the following provisions to correct the drafting errors, focusing particularly on the verbs that you are using and the purposes for those verbs:

1. Alterations. The Tenant shall be permitted to alter the Premises if the Tenant shall have submitted its architectural plans to the Landlord at least 60 days before it wants to begin construction.

2. Withdrawal from LP. No limited partner shall have the right to withdraw from the LP without the previous written consent of all the other partners.

CHAPTER ELEVEN

Drafting Conditions

I. INTRODUCTION

Conditions can be followed by either an obligation, discretionary authority, or a declaration. The sections below explain how to best draft each type of condition. Note that the focus in this chapter is the condition to an obligation, which gives parties access to more common law remedies than the other conditions. Therefore, we will use conditions to an obligation to demonstrate the primary issues that come up with conditions and best practices in drafting.

II. CONDITIONS TO OBLIGATIONS

There are various techniques for drafting conditions to obligations. Especially when you are starting out, we recommend that you try to fit the fact pattern into an *if / then* formulation because it creates a provision that is easy for parties to understand and follow. It also makes it very clear that what you want is a condition.

The part of the provision in the *if* section is what we refer to as the *condition*. It will be the event that needs to occur first. The part of the provision in the *then* section is what happens if the condition is met or satisfied. This is where you clearly draft who the actor is and what they are required to do or not allowed to do.

It is very important to draft a condition very clearly to avoid it being misinterpreted as a different contract concept, especially a covenant.

A. CONTENT AND QUESTIONS TO ASK

As with all the other contract concepts, the content of an agreement's conditions to an obligation, or any other condition, can vary greatly depending on the type of transaction and the parties involved. To determine what you should include as a condition to an obligation, you will need to talk to your client to find out if a relationship exists between two events and whether one must happen before the other event or issue comes into play. If this is the case, you will have to gather specific information about the event that comes first, so that you can set out that condition and standard in the agreement in detail. Finally, you will draft the obligation that comes into play if that condition does occur. Just as you would when drafting a covenant, when you draft the obligation, you will want to be specific as to who has the obligation, when the obligation can be performed, how it should be performed, etc.

If you are assessing a contract and are not sure whether a provision is written as a condition, try to fit the fact pattern presented into the *if / then* format. *If* this happens, *then* a party is obligated to perform. If you can put the fact pattern into that format, then draft the business issue as a condition.

B. DIFFERENT TECHNIQUES TO SIGNAL A CONDITION

In this section, we discuss drafting conditions that would apply to any type of agreement. Apart from the techniques discussed here, there are further considerations to take into account when drafting the conditions articles in acquisition and financing agreements, which are described in further detail in Section IV on page 116.

Courts dislike conditions because they often result in a party giving up a right.[1] So, courts regularly construe a provision to be a covenant if there is ambiguity as to whether the contract concept is a covenant or a condition.[2] Courts may go to great lengths to obtain the result-oriented decision they think is fair. Then, if a party breaches the covenant or there is any other cause of action, that party may have to pay damages.

To signal a condition, a lawyer usually precedes the condition with one of the following words or phrases: *if / then,*[3] *must,*[4] *when,*[5] *subject to,*[6] *provided that,*[7] *if, conditioned on,* and *on.*[8] Unfortunately, using these words does not guarantee that a court will construe the provision as a condition.[9]

When you are drafting, you and your client want as much clarity, certainty, and predictability as possible. You want to predict as best as possible how a court will interpret a provision, and you want to leave as little as possible to chance. Therefore, if you include a condition, you want to make sure that you do so with language that properly signals a condition.

Use one or more of the following four drafting techniques to increase the likelihood that a court will interpret a provision as a condition rather than as a covenant:

1. *See Restatement (Second) of Contracts* § 227(2) and cmt. d (1981).

2. *See* Samuel Williston, *Williston on Contracts* vol. 13, § 38.13 (4th ed. 2000), and the cases cited therein.

3. *Oppenheimer & Co. v. Oppenheim, Appel, Dixon & Co.,* 86 N.Y.2d 685, 691, 660 N.E.2d 415 (1995) ("'if' and 'unless and until' are unmistakable language of condition").

4. *See In re Kirkbride,* 409 B.R. 354, 357-358 (E.D.N.C. 2009); *Stewart-Smith Haidinger, Inc. v. Avi-Truck, Inc.,* 682 P.2d 1108, 1115 (Alaska 1984).

5. *Amies v. Wesnofske,* 255 N.Y. 156, 161, 174 N.E. 436 (1931) ("The employment of such words as 'when,' 'after,' or 'as soon as,' clearly indicate that a promise is not to be performed except upon a condition. (*Williston on Contracts,* vol. 2, § 671.)").

6. *See Burgess Const. Co. v. M. Morrin & Son Co.,* 526 F.2d 108, 113 (10th Cir. 1975) (*subject to* usually indicates a condition). *See also F. W. Berk & Co. v. Derecktor,* 301 N.Y. 110, 113, 92 N.E.2d 914 (1950); *but see Stonehill Capital Mgmt., LLC v. Bank of the W.,* 28 N.Y.3d 439, 451, 68 N.E.3d 683 (2016) (*subject to* was formulaic in an auction bid form and so not a condition).

7. Despite the regular use of *provided that* to signal a condition, drafters should avoid it because of its potential to create ambiguity. *See* Chapter 25 on page 371.

8. *See Ross v. Harding,* 391 P.2d 526, 531 (Wash. 1964); *see Restatement (Second) of Contracts* § 226 cmt. a (1981).

9. *Cedar Point Apts., Ltd. v. Cedar Point Inv. Corp.,* 693 F.2d 748 n. 9 (8th Cir. 1982), *cert. denied,* 461 U.S. 914 (1983).

Drafting Conditions Technique 1

State that a provision is a condition.[10]

Example—Drafting Conditions Technique 1

Claims. It is a condition to the Insurer's obligations under this Agreement that the Owner give the Insurer written notice of any Loss no later than ten days after the day of the Loss.

Drafters derive an advantage from an express statement of the parties' intent, as per Technique 1. This provision explicitly declares the condition of the owner giving written notice before the insurer is obligated to do anything under the agreement. Notice also that this is an example of a stand-alone provision, which means that it states only the condition, not the promise to perform. The insurer's promise to perform is elsewhere in the contract. This separation of the condition and the related obligation is common.

A second approach used by drafters is to include less information about the condition, and to focus on what happens next and the consequences if the condition is not met. By stating the legal consequences of a condition that has not been satisfied, the provision establishes the remedy intended, a remedy associated with conditions, not covenants.

Drafting Conditions Technique 2

State the intended consequences of a condition that has not been satisfied.

Example—Drafting Conditions Technique 2

Failed Notice. The Owner's failure to give written notice of any Loss no later than ten days after the day of the Loss relieves the Insurer of the Insurer's obligation to the Owner for any Loss.

Technique 2 does not expressly state a condition, so there is still some risk to using this technique on its own. Therefore, to be safe and engage in best practices that maximize clarity and certainty, you would probably want to use Techniques 1 and 2 together. Again, the condition and the obligation may be in separate sections of the agreement. The following provision combines Techniques 1 and 2:

Example—Drafting Conditions Techniques 1 and 2

Claims. It is a condition to the Insurer's obligations under this Agreement that the Owner give the Insurer written notice of any Loss no later than ten days after the day of the Loss. The Owner's failure to give written notice of any Loss no later than ten days after the day of the Loss relieves the Insurer of the Owner's obligation to the Owner for any Loss.

---

10. *See Royal Bank of Canada v. Beneficial Fin. Leasing Corp.*, No. 87 CIV. 1056 (JMC), 1992 WL 167339, at *5 (S.D.N.Y. June 30, 1992), quoting John D. Calamari & Joseph M. Perillo, *The Law of Contracts,* § 11-7, at 442 (3d ed. 1987).

Technique 3 focuses on using the verb *must* to signal a condition and includes a separate provision stating that the verb *must* signals a condition. Although many commentators agree that using *must* signals a condition,[11] practitioners, on the whole, have yet to adopt the use of *must* as standard practice. Also problematic for the use of *must,* some courts have previously interpreted *must* to mean a covenant, as though *shall* had been used.[12] To avoid any confusion, the best practice when using *must* to signal a condition is to pair the condition with an interpretive provision. Drafters typically place the interpretive provision either in the interpretive subsection of a definitions section or as a separate section in the general provisions. As with the first two techniques, the condition and its covenant appear in different sections of the agreement.[13]

Here is a description and example of Technique 3:

Drafting Conditions Technique 3

Use must[14] *and insert an interpretive provision to indicate that* must *signals a condition.*

Example—Drafting Conditions Technique 3

Claims. The Owner *must* give the Insurer written notice of any Loss no later than ten days after the day of the Loss.

and

Use of *Must*. The use of *must* in this Agreement signals a condition.

Finally, if instead of using *must,* you want to use *shall* in a condition, we recommend that you put the matter you are trying to cover into the *if / then* format, as shown by Technique 4 below. By using this technique, you keep the statement of the condition (the *if* clause) with the obligation that is triggered when the condition is satisfied (the *then* clause) and you make it clear that there is a condition that needs to be satisfied before there is an obligation. The *if* clause first states the condition to the obligation, and the *then* clause uses *shall* to signal the promise.[15] Together, they present the information that the parties need to follow in chronological sequence: first, the condition that must be satisfied, then the party's promise to perform and, by implication, the obligation that is the consequence of the covenant.

Drafting Conditions Technique 4

Construct the condition using an if / then *formulation.*

Example—Drafting Conditions Technique 4

Bonus. *If* the Contractor completes construction before the Deadline, *then* the Owner shall pay the Contractor a $5,000 bonus no later than five business days after the construction is complete.

---

11. *See* Kenneth A. Adams, *A Manual of Style for Contract Drafting* 115-116 (5th ed. 2023); F. Reed Dickerson, *The Fundamentals of Legal Drafting* 214 (2d ed. 1986).

12. *See* Samuel Williston, *Williston on Contracts* vol. 13, § 38.13 (4th ed. 2000), and the cases cited therein.

13. Remember: The condition is not a condition to a covenant but to the obligation that flows from the covenant. Drafting practice is to state the covenant not the obligation.

14. *See In re Kirkbride*, 409 B.R. 354, 357-358 (E.D.N.C. 2009); *Stewart-Smith Haidinger, Inc. v. Avi-Truck, Inc.*, 682 P.2d 1108, 1115 (Alaska 1984).

15. *See Adirondack Transit Lines, Inc. v. United Transp. Union, Local 1582*, 305 F.3d 82, 87 (2d Cir. 2002) and the cases and treatises cited therein.

C. DRAFTING CONDITIONS USING THE *IF / THEN* FORMAT

This section provides you with general guidelines you can follow when drafting conditions in the *if / then* format, and a step-by-step process for how to draft the *if* and *then* parts of the provision.

1. Drafting the *If* Clause

Once the parties have decided that a condition is appropriate, they must decide on the state of facts that must exist before a party is obligated to perform. This state of facts is the standard that the parties set out in the *if* clause.

For example, assume that there is an agreement between the landlord of a commercial building and a tenant who owns a store in that building. Their agreement holds that the landlord will maintain the premises in the ordinary course of business but will make immediate repairs under certain circumstances. The parties and the drafter must then determine what those circumstances would be. Those particular circumstances are thought of as the *standard.*

Here is the provision *before* the parties have negotiated the standard:

Example—Blank If Clause Standard to Be Drafted

Maintenance of the Premises. The Landlord shall maintain the Premises in the ordinary course of business. Despite the preceding sentence, if [state of facts to be inserted], the Landlord shall make immediate repairs.

The tenant might propose that the landlord's obligation be activated whenever *an unsafe condition* exists. The landlord might object to this standard, noting its vagueness and the failure to consider a danger's extent or immediacy. Consistent with these concerns, the landlord might propose instead that their obligation be activated only when *a significant, imminent danger* exists. This alternative standard would reduce the landlord's risk that they would be obligated to perform. Here are the two versions of the provision:

Examples—Different Standards in If Clause

1—Unsafe Condition Standard:
Maintenance of the Premises. The Landlord shall maintain the Premises in the ordinary course of business. Despite the preceding sentence, if *an unsafe condition* exists, the Landlord shall make immediate repairs.

2—Significant, Imminent Danger Standard:
Maintenance of the Premises. The Landlord shall maintain the Premises in the ordinary course of business. Despite the preceding sentence, if *a significant, imminent danger* exists, the Landlord shall make immediate repairs.

In deciding how a condition should be tailored, a drafter should consider whether the client *will be obligated to perform once the condition is satisfied,* or whether the client *will have the right to the benefit of the other side's performance.*

Remember that parties are not obligated to satisfy conditions. Therefore, a drafter needs to focus on *how satisfaction of the condition affects their client.*

If the consequence of the condition being satisfied is that the *other* party becomes obligated to perform in favor of your client, then, arguably, the hurdle of the condition should not be set too high. If your client has the right to performance, consider choosing objective, fact-based standards, which are more difficult to contest. For example, if we are setting a standard relating to a temperature, using *frigid* is a subjective standard, while stating *below 32 degrees Fahrenheit* is an objective, fact-based standard.

If your client is to be obligated to perform, conditions that are hard to satisfy will benefit them because performance will be delayed or prevented. A classic way to achieve this goal is to draft a condition with a *subjective standard* (e.g., frigid temperature), because judgment can always be questioned and litigated. However, even if your client is obligated to perform, you probably still want to draft the condition clearly, with an objective standard, so there is no disagreement between the parties and everyone knows what to expect going forward.

These drafting techniques relate to risk allocation in determining how much risk your client takes on. See Section III in this chapter for more information on risk allocation in conditions to an obligation.

Although many conditions depend on facts occurring, a condition can also be based on the *failure* of facts to occur.[16] For example, a condition to a bank's obligation to lend could be the absence of product liability litigation against the borrower.

When drafting the substance of a condition, keep in mind two other considerations. First, a party's own actions cannot be a condition to its own obligations. If they could, a party could claim that it was not obligated to perform because the condition to performance had not been satisfied—even though the party's own inaction caused the condition not to be satisfied. That is exactly the problem with the following condition.

> ### Example—Incorrect If Standard Since Party Controls Condition and Obligation
>
> **PB&J**. If Devon buys all the ingredients for a PB&J sandwich at the grocery store, Devon must clean his room.

Here, the *if* clause fails to state a true condition because Devon—who would be the party obligated to perform if the condition were satisfied—controls whether the condition is satisfied. Stated simply, a party cannot control the satisfaction of a condition that would trigger that party's obligation to perform.[17]

Second, the passage of time cannot be a condition because it is certain that time will pass.[18] There should be some uncertainty as to whether a condition will be satisfied. For example, the following provision does not state as clearly as possible the condition to an obligation and its related obligation.

> ### Examples—Passage of Time Cannot Be a Condition
>
> ***Not As Good:*** **Payment**. If 30 days from the date of completion have elapsed, then the Owner must pay the Contractor on the 30th day.[19]

---

16. *Restatement (Second) of Contracts* § 224 cmt. b (1981).

17. *Rogier v. Am. Testing & Engr. Corp.*, 734 N.E.2d 606, 621 (Ind. App. 2000) ("[A] party may not rely on the failure of a condition precedent to excuse performance where that party's own action or inaction caused the failure. When a party retains control over when the condition will be fulfilled, it has an implied obligation to make a reasonable and good faith effort to satisfy the condition. (citation omitted.) 'The *Hamlin* doctrine prevents a party from acts of contractual sabotage or other acts in bad faith by a party that causes the failure of a condition.' (citation omitted.").

18. *Restatement (Second) of Contracts* § 224 cmt. b (1981).

19. Example based on *Restatement (Second) of Contracts* § 224 cmt. b, Illustration 2 (1981).

> ***Better:* Payment**. If the Contractor completes the Proposed Work, then the Owner must pay the Contractor within 30 days of completion.

Remember to state the condition in the *if* clause using the present tense because it does not change over time. You are then stating directly what the condition is, and the use of *if / then* is sufficient to indicate the passage of time and chronological order.

Also, do not use *shall* or *must* in the *if* clause. In particular, if you use *shall* in the *if* clause, that creates a linguistic battle between *if* and *shall,* resulting in ambiguity. With *if,* you would be signaling a condition, but by using *shall* in that same clause, you would be signaling a covenant. See the following examples or more information:

Examples—Verbs in If *Clause*

1—Incorrect Verb Tense:

Payment for Demolition. If the Warehouse has been demolished, then the Owner must pay the Contractor.

1—Correct Use of Present Tense:

Payment for Demolition. If the Warehouse is demolished, then the Owner must pay the Contractor.

2—Incorrect Use of Shall:

Termination. If the Contractor *shall complete* construction before the Deadline, then the Owner shall pay the Contractor a $5,000 bonus no later than five Business Days after the construction is complete.

2—Incorrect Use of Shall Have:

Termination. If the Contractor *shall have completed* construction before the Deadline, then the Owner shall pay the Contractor a $5,000 bonus no later than five Business Days after the construction is complete.

2—Incorrect Use of Must:

Termination. If the Contractor *must complete* construction before the Deadline, then the Owner must pay the Contractor a $5,000 bonus no later than five Business Days after the construction is complete.

2—Correct Use of Present Tense:

Termination. If the Contractor *completes* construction before the Deadline, then the Owner shall pay the Contractor a $5,000 bonus no later than five Business Days after the construction is complete.

---

2. Drafting the *Then* Clause

When you draft the *then* clause, you should make sure that you include which party has the obligation to perform, state explicitly what the obligation is, write in the active voice, and avoid negative language if possible. More important, as discussed earlier, best practice is to use *must* to signal a condition, and to include elsewhere an interpretive provision stating that *must* signals a condition. If you use *shall* to signal the obligation in the *then* clause, make sure that you state the provision clearly in that *if / then* format.

> ## Examples—Use of Shall *and Obligation in* Then *Clause*
>
> **Correct: Termination**. If the Contractor *completes* construction before the Deadline, then the Owner shall pay the Contractor a $5,000 bonus no later than five Business Days after the construction is complete.
>
> **Correct: Mortgage**. If the Buyer obtains a mortgage, then the Buyer shall purchase the House on the Closing Date.

Be up front and do not hide what really must happen by using negatives, as in this example:

> ## Example—Incorrect Because Negatives and Obligated
>
> **Mortgage**. If the Buyer does *not* obtain a mortgage, the Buyer is *not* obligated to purchase the House on the Closing Date.

When faced with a condition presented in the negative, reconceptualize it so that it states what must occur in the positive. Similarly, if the obligation is not clear, reconceptualize the *then* clause so that it states which party has an obligation to perform and what that obligation is, as shown in the two correct examples above. Furthermore, as discussed relating to covenants in Chapter 9 on page 82, do not state that a party *has a right, is entitled,* or *is permitted* to do something; instead, use the techniques for drafting conditions detailed in this section.

III. RISK ALLOCATION IN A CONDITION TO AN OBLIGATION

Parties use conditions in several ways to allocate risk. First, including a condition is itself a risk allocation. By agreeing to a condition, the parties have agreed that the *performing party* has no obligation to perform if the condition is not satisfied. Thus, the party who benefits from performance if the condition is satisfied has more risk than the other party because the condition may not be met. The party who benefits from performance does not get that benefit if the condition is not met.

Let's go back to our initial house purchase example where Bob is buying a house from Sally, but Bob needs a mortgage to do so. If Bob and Sally have agreed that if Bob gets a mortgage, then Bob has to buy the house. Sally bears the risk that the condition might not be satisfied. If Bob does not get a mortgage, then Bob does not have to buy the house, and Sally needs to find a new buyer.[20]

Second, parties allocate risk by choosing to frame a business issue as a condition rather than as a covenant. A classic example occurs in the insurance context, where a party who is insured must notify their insurer of a loss as a condition to the insurer's payment. Let's assume that Bob purchases the house and that, shortly afterward, someone breaks in and steals his large-screen television. Bob reviews his homeowner's insurance policy and discovers that the insurance company must receive notice of the loss no later than 10 days after the loss occurs. Unfortunately, the notice that Bob sends is received 12 days late. If the notice provision is a covenant, then Bob has

---

20. Note that the condition to an obligation is explained here in the positive. Often, deal lawyers will phrase it in the negative, more complex manner, such as: If Bob does not obtain a mortgage, Bob is not obligated to purchase the house.

breached the contract. In that event, the insurance company may remain obligated to pay Bob for his loss, depending on the wording of the other provisions in the contract, but they may be entitled to damages, if any. For example, Bob's damages might be the additional expense that he incurs when he purchases the replacement television at full price rather than at a sale that took place during the initial 10-day period. However, it is not likely that the contract with the insurance company is drafted with such a covenant.

Instead, it is more likely that the contract includes a condition to cover this issue, and the result differs dramatically. Then, if the provision is a condition and the notice is late, Bob fails to satisfy the condition to the insurance company's obligation to perform. This failure means that the insurance company's obligation to pay Bob is never triggered, and Bob forfeits his right to receive the insurance proceeds. Thus, the use of a condition places the risk of a late notice squarely on Bob, the homeowner. Courts dislike forfeitures and regularly construe them as covenant provisions, even though the language suggests that the provisions are conditions.[21]

Third, parties allocate risk by choosing the standard that establishes the state of facts that must exist before the obligation to perform arises. Each party's risk then depends on how difficult or easy it is to meet the standard and how much control they have over the ability to meet that standard. For example, assume that as a condition to Bob's obligation to buy the house, Sally's lawyer must deliver an opinion addressing, among other things, environmental matters. That condition could be formulated in several ways. Here are three ways, and note how even minor drafting revisions change the standard and shift risk:

> ### Examples— Different Standards in Conditions Shifting Risk
>
> #### 1—Satisfactory Opinion:
> **Opinion of Seller's Counsel**. The Seller's lawyers must have delivered to the Buyer an opinion of counsel *satisfactory* to the Buyer.
>
> #### 2—Reasonably Satisfactory Opinion:
> **Opinion of Seller's Counsel**. The Seller's lawyers must have delivered to the Buyer an opinion of counsel *reasonably satisfactory* to the Buyer.
>
> #### 3—Opinion Substantially in the Form of Exhibit:
> **Opinion of Seller's Counsel**. The Seller's lawyers must have delivered to the Buyer an opinion of counsel *substantially in the form of Exhibit B.*

Example 1 is high risk for Sally, as the standard of *satisfactory to the Buyer* seems to give Bob unrestricted discretion in deciding whether the opinion is acceptable. Example 2 is somewhat less risky to Sally, as it constrains Bob's determination. Here, the reasonable person standard has been imported into the contract. The opinion must be *reasonably satisfactory*. Example 3 substantially reduces Sally's risk, as she and her lawyer will know what is required because they will have negotiated and agreed on the opinion that the lawyer must give. As explained in further detail in Chapter 8 on page 64, we recommend setting out more specific standards, as in Example 3, instead of relying on qualifiers, as in Examples 1 and 2.

Fourth, parties allocate risk by deciding whose obligations are subject to the satisfaction of which conditions. For example, Bob may insist that before he is obligated to buy the house, he wants an appropriate test to conclude that the house's

---

21. Williston, *13 Williston on Contracts* § 38.13 (Richard A. Lord ed., 4th ed., 2000), and the cases cited therein.

water meets certain safety standards. To incorporate that requirement into the contract, the parties might use the following condition:

> ### Example—Stating Whose Conditions and Obligations
>
> **Water Safety.** It is a condition to the Buyer's obligation to buy the House that the Buyer must have received test results that conclude that the House's water is safe to use for all residential purposes.

This condition would be a condition only to Bob's obligation to close, not to Sally's. Why? Because the test is only for Bob's benefit. It is part of his due diligence, part of his risk assessment. If the water is not satisfactory and he is willing to waive the failure of the condition, Sally should not be able to ruin the deal by being able to walk away from the deal if the water is not satisfactory.

IV. CONDITIONS IN THE CONDITIONS ARTICLE OF AN ACQUISITION OR FINANCING AGREEMENT

This section outlines some of the most important characteristics of conditions articles in acquisition and financing agreements. You can find an example of an actual conditions article from an acquisition agreement online on the CasebookConnect Resources page and on the Aspen website product page for this book.

A. INTRODUCTORY PARAGRAPH IN A CONDITIONS ARTICLE

Conditions articles appear almost exclusively in acquisition and financing agreements. Generally, these articles begin with an unnumbered introductory paragraph that establishes that each condition in the article is a condition to the party's obligation to close on the transaction.

The example below is an introductory paragraph in a conditions article from an acquisition agreement:

> ### Example—Unnumbered Introductory Paragraph
>
> The Buyer is obligated to consummate the transactions that this Agreement contemplates only if each of the following conditions has been satisfied or waived on or before the Closing Date:

The couplet *satisfied* or *waived* in this example tells us that the buyer must finalize the purchase if the listed conditions are satisfied. If one of the conditions has not been satisfied, but the buyer still wants to close on the transaction, then the buyer may waive that condition and close. Technically, the contractual statement that the buyer may waive is not necessary because the buyer may waive a condition as a matter of common law.[22]

---

22. *See* Williston, *supra* n. 2, at vol. 13, § 39.17; *Restatement (Second) of Contracts* § 225(1) (1981).

After the introductory paragraph, as in the example above, you would generally find a list of conditions that must be met before the Buyer has to close.

Remember that the phrase *is obligated to* does not take the place of the main covenant from which the obligations flow. That main covenant is the subject matter performance provision in the action sections, where the parties exchange the general promises of what they will do as memorialized in that agreement.[23] For example, for a Buyer, that covenant may be similar to: "The Buyer shall purchase_____ ."

B. VERB: USE *MUST*

The proper way to signal a condition in a conditions article is to join the verb *must* or *must have* with one or more words that signal different time periods or dates relating to the acquisition or financing.

Examples—Different Time Periods

1—Time — On the Signing Date:
Seller's Representations and Warranties. The Seller's representations and warranties *must have been true on the signing date.*

2—Time — Every Day During the Period Between Signing and Closing:
Seller's Representations and Warranties. The Seller's representations and warranties must have been true on the signing date and *throughout the period* from the signing date to and including the Closing Date [standard exceptions are typically added here].

In Example 1, *must have been* signals a time period in the past. The addition of *on the signing date* adds specificity to a date during that period. In Example 2, *must have been* once again signals a time period in the past, and the remainder of the sentence establishes the beginning and ending dates of the time period.

Here are a few more examples relating to different time periods:

Examples—Different Time Periods

3—Time — Unspecified Date Between Signing and Closing:
Seller's Covenants. The Seller *must have performed* all of the Seller's covenants contained in this Agreement to be performed by the Seller *on or before the Closing Date.*

4—Time — Unspecified Date Between Signing and Closing:
Seller's Trademark and Patent Counsel's Opinion. The Seller's Trademark and Patent counsel *must have delivered the Opinion, dated the Closing Date*, reasonably satisfactory to Buyer's counsel.

In Examples 3 and 4, *must have* describes the time period between signing and closing, but without pinpointing a specific date. Example 4 has a bit of a twist. Even though the condition does not specify the opinion's delivery date, practitioners almost always deem their opinions delivered on the closing date. If there were to be a

---

23. For more on subject matter performance provisions, *see* Chapter 16 on page 209.

gap between the delivery and the closing date, the opinion could become inaccurate during that time period, putting the lawyer at risk of being sued. No gap means no risk of facts changing.

While you will want to favor the use of *must* in conditions, as mentioned earlier, you will find practitioners that use *shall* in the conditions article. Two versions of the same set of acquisition agreement conditions follow. In Example 1, the conditions are properly stated, using *must*. In Example 2, *shall* replaces *must,* which you are likely to see in practice.

Example 3 includes only a few of the conditions and highlights variations that practitioners use to address certain fact patterns.

Examples—Acquisition Agreement Articles on Conditions with Different Verbs

1—Best Practice with Use of Must:

Article 8—Conditions to the Buyer's Obligations

The Buyer is obligated to consummate the transactions that this Agreement contemplates only if each of the following conditions has been satisfied or waived on or before the Closing Date:

8.1 Seller's Representations and Warranties. The representations and warranties of the Seller set forth in this Agreement

(a) must have been true on the date this Agreement was executed and delivered; and

(b) must be true on and as of the Closing Date with the same force and effect as though made on and as of the Closing Date, except as affected by transactions that this Agreement contemplates.

8.2 Seller's Covenants. The Seller *must have performed* all of its covenants contained in this Agreement to be performed by it on or before the Closing Date.

8.3 Seller's Closing Certificate. The Buyer *must have received* a certificate of the Seller, executed on behalf of the Seller by the President or any Vice President of the Seller, dated the Closing Date, reasonably satisfactory to the Buyer's counsel, certifying the satisfaction of the conditions in Section 8.1 and Section 8.2.

8.4 Seller's Trademark and Patent Counsel's Opinion. The Seller's trademark and patent counsel must have delivered to the Buyer an opinion, dated the Closing Date, reasonably satisfactory to the Buyer's counsel.

8.5 The Manufacturing Facility. The Seller must have demolished the Manufacturing Facility and removed all debris from the Manufacturing Facility.

2—Common to See with Use of Shall:

Article 8—Conditions to the Buyer's Obligations

The Buyer is obligated to consummate the transactions that this Agreement contemplates only if each of the following conditions has been satisfied or waived on or before the Closing Date:

8.1 Seller's Representations and Warranties. The representations and warranties of the Seller set forth in this Agreement

(a) shall have been true on the date this Agreement was executed and delivered; and

(b) shall be true on and as of the Closing Date with the same force and effect as though made on and as of the Closing Date, except as affected by transactions that this Agreement contemplates.

8.2 Seller's Covenants. The Seller *shall have performed* all of its covenants contained in this Agreement to be performed by it on or before the Closing Date.

8.3 Seller's Closing Certificate. The Buyer *shall have received* a certificate of the Seller, executed on behalf of the Seller by the President or any Vice President of the Seller, dated the Closing Date, reasonably satisfactory to the Buyer's counsel, certifying the satisfaction of the conditions in Section 8.1 and Section 8.2.

8.4 Seller's Trademark and Patent Counsel's Opinion. The Seller's trademark and patent counsel *shall have delivered* to the Buyer an opinion, dated the Closing Date, reasonably satisfactory to the Buyer's counsel.

8.5 The Manufacturing Facility. The Seller *shall have demolished* the Manufacturing Facility *and removed* all debris from the Manufacturing Facility.

In Examples 1 and 2, the introductory language specifies the Closing Date as the deadline by which all of the conditions must be satisfied. But that deadline may not reflect the entire business deal because the individual conditions can have their own deadlines. Example 3, below, addresses this possibility in two ways. First, the introductory language omits any reference to a deadline to satisfy conditions. Second, each condition states its own deadline.

Examples—Acquisition Agreement Articles on Conditions with Different Verbs

3—Best Practice with Use of Must and More Accurate Deadlines:

Article 8—Conditions to the Buyer's Obligations

The Buyer is obligated to consummate the transactions that this Agreement contemplates only if each of the following conditions has been satisfied or waived:

[Sections 8.1 and 8.2 intentionally omitted.]

8.3 Seller's Closing Certificate. The Buyer must have received *on the Closing Date* a certificate of the Seller, executed on behalf of the Seller by the President or any Vice President of the Seller, dated the Closing Date, reasonably satisfactory to the Buyer's counsel, certifying to the satisfaction of the conditions in Section 8.1 and Section 8.2.

[Section 8.4 intentionally omitted.]

8.5 The Manufacturing Facility. The Seller must have demolished the Manufacturing Facility and removed all debris from the Manufacturing Facility no later than ten Business Days before the Closing Date.

8.6 Shareholder Approval. The Seller's shareholders must have authorized the sale that this Agreement contemplates *no later than December 23, 20__*.

C. MIRROR CONDITIONS

In the conditions article, some conditions may apply to only one party, while other conditions may apply to all parties. When you have conditions that apply to both parties, make sure to include those conditions in the list of conditions for both parties, not just one. Also, list those conditions in the same order on both parties' lists, and try to mirror the language of these conditions as much as possible.

A classic example of a condition that affects both parties is in this next example, from an acquisition agreement. It is a condition for obtaining specific governmental approvals in which each party wants to decide for themselves whether they will risk proceeding with the transaction if all governmental approvals have not yet been obtained. To address that risk, each party insists that they have the following condition in their own list of conditions to closing, so that the provision requiring all governmental approvals be obtained before closing is listed twice — once on the seller's list of conditions, and once on the buyer's list of conditions:

> ### Example—Seller's and Buyer's Condition to Closing Same for Both
>
> **Governmental Consents.** The Seller and the Buyer must have obtained all Governmental Consents.

If the parties obtain the governmental consents, the condition is satisfied and the Seller is obligated to perform. However, if the parties do not obtain the governmental consents and thus, the condition is not satisfied, the seller has the common law right to choose whether to perform. Should the seller choose not to perform, that nonperformance is not a breach because the seller's obligation to perform was not triggered. The buyer has a mirror condition, so the same goes for the buyer, in that the buyer has a choice of whether to perform or not. Performing in this case would mean going forward with the closing and finalizing the transaction in question. The consequences for the buyer parallel those of the seller.

In contrast, if a private equity firm is buying the assets of the seller, the private equity firm may want to have a signed employment contract with the seller's key executive to be a condition to its obligation to close. However, that condition should be a condition only to the buyer's obligation to close because the executive's signed contract benefits the buyer exclusively. The seller should not be able to walk away and end the deal if the buyer is willing to waive the failure of the condition.

D. CONSEQUENCES OF A FAILED CONDITION

When drafting conditions in a conditions article, omit from that article the consequences of failing to satisfy a specific condition. The language introducing the conditions already provides that a party is obligated to perform only if all of the conditions are satisfied or waived. Put all specific consequences relating to the failure to satisfy a condition in the endgame provisions, which are discussed further in Chapter 17 on page 229.

E. RELATIONSHIP BETWEEN COVENANTS AND CONDITIONS IN AN ACQUISITION OR FINANCING AGREEMENT[24]

In acquisition agreements, a common condition to the buyer's obligation to close is that the seller and the buyer must have performed all of their covenants to be performed on or before the closing.[25] But not every condition in an acquisition agreement is tied into a covenant. Sellers often try to limit their risk by insisting that certain matters be handled with just a condition, not a condition and a covenant.

For example, delivery of an opinion letter from the seller's lawyers is generally a condition to a buyer's obligation to close. A seller is generally willing to risk the buyer's refusal to close if the seller's lawyers refuse to deliver their opinion. If that happens, the seller's risk is probably limited to their transaction costs. But, if the seller also *promises* that their lawyers will deliver their opinion letter in the covenants article of the agreement, then the seller's risk substantially increases. In that case, the lawyers' failure to deliver their opinion puts the seller in breach of a covenant, making the seller liable for damages to the buyer.

Therefore, when you are considering risk allocation in such acquisition and financing agreements, you want to think carefully about whether you want only a closing condition on the issue, or a condition and a covenant relating to the same issue, in the different parts of the agreement. A number of factors will affect your decision including who your client is, your client's interests, and the amount of risk that they are able to assume.

V. CONDITIONS TO DISCRETIONARY AUTHORITY

A party's exercise of discretionary authority may be subject to the satisfaction of one or more conditions. Drafters often establish the relationship between a condition and the exercise of discretionary authority by using the *if/then* format discussed earlier in the *Conditions to Obligations* section.

When drafting the *if* clause, follow the guidelines that were set out earlier in this chapter on page 111 for how to draft the *if* clause in conditions to obligations. For example, always use a present tense verb.

When drafting the *then* clause, follow the guidelines that were set out earlier in Chapter 10 on page 113 for how to draft discretionary authority provisions. As in the following examples, use the verb *may:*

> ### Examples—Conditions to Discretionary Authority
>
> *1*—**Sales to Other Persons.** If the Manufacturer *builds* more than 500 units of the Product in any month, the Manufacturer *may* sell the units in excess of 500 to a Person other than the Retailer.

---

24. For a detailed discussion of conditions in an acquisition agreement, *see* Lou Kling & Eileen Nugent, *Negotiated Acquisitions of Companies, Subsidiaries and Divisions* ch. 14 (1st ed. 1992).

25. *See id.* at § 4.02[3], which further discusses this relationship. *See generally id.* at § 14.02[7]. Acquisition agreements generally also provide that as a condition to the buyer's obligation to perform, all of the representations and warranties must have been true on the signing date and must be true on the closing date. This condition often provides an exception for any change in facts that the parties anticipate. *See generally id.* at § 14.02.

> *2*—**Publication of Paperback Edition**. If the Book *earns* net sales in excess of $30 million, the Publisher *may* publish the paperback edition of the Book at any time afterwards.
>
> *3*—**Remedies**. If an Event of Default *occurs and is continuing*, then the Bank *may* accelerate the Loan and foreclose on the Bank's security [i.e., Bob's house] . . . .

Like a condition to an obligation, a condition to discretionary authority allocates risk. For example, Example 3, above, is a provision similar to one that we looked at in Chapter 10 on page 98, when we were trying to understand discretionary authority. Without the condition, the Bank could exercise their remedies at any time. In this case, that would mean accelerating the loan and foreclosing on the house. Of course, Bob would find this risk unacceptable. Bob's risk is significantly reduced by the condition stating that the event of default needs to occur and be continuing before the Bank may foreclose on Bob's house.

VI. CONDITIONS TO DECLARATIONS

Some declarations have substantive consequences only if a condition is satisfied. In the following provision, the full second sentence states the policy. As you can see, that second sentence begins with a condition, and the policy applies only if the condition in that sentence is satisfied.

Both the condition and the declaration should be drafted in the present tense. When drafting the *if* clause, follow the guidelines that were set out earlier in this chapter on page 111. For example, always use a present tense verb.

When drafting the *then* clause, follow the guidelines set out in Chapter 10 on page 113 for how to draft declarations. For example, use a present tense verb.

Here is an example of a declaration that has a substantive consequence only if a condition is satisfied:

> *Example—Condition to a Declaration*
>
> **Anti-assignment**. Neither party may assign its rights under this Agreement. If either party purports to assign its rights under this Agreement, that purported assignment is void.

A condition to a declaration allocates risk like a condition to an obligation and a condition to discretionary authority.

VII. EXERCISES

A. EXERCISE 11A: DRAFTING CONDITIONS

Draft the provisions that are needed for each of the scenarios below. Remember to follow the guidelines from this chapter on conditions, such as putting the provision into the *if / then* format whenever possible and using a present tense verb in the *if* clause.

1. Tom Payne and Georgia Washington are negotiating their prenuptial agreement. Tom has agreed to pay Georgia $100,000 if they divorce before they have been married five years. However, they have agreed that Tom is not obligated to pay Georgia if the couple divorces because Georgia wants to marry someone else.

_____

_____

2. Ralph LP owns all rights in the cartoon character Ralph — a short, eight-year-old boy with glasses for whom life never goes quite right. Ralph LP has agreed to indemnify their licensee, Merchandisers, Inc., if a third-party claims that Merchandisers, Inc., is violating that party's trademark in Ralph. This means that if a third party comes after Merchandisers, Inc. for damages, Ralph LP will pay Merchandisers, Inc. or that third party on behalf of Merchandisers, Inc. for any such damages. However, Ralph LP insists that Ralph LP will be liable only if Ralph LP receives notice from Merchandisers, Inc. no later than ten business days after Merchandisers, Inc. receives notice of the claim from the third party.

_____

_____

3. The Law Firm will not allow Alan Associate to work on client matters until he has been sworn in as an attorney before the Ohio bar.

_____

_____

4. Barbara Rodriguez has hired Carl Contractor to build the addition to her house. Contractor insists that he will not start work on the house until Rodriguez receives the Housing Department's approval.

_____

_____

B. EXERCISE 11B: CORRECT THE DRAFTING ERRORS

Redraft the following provisions to correct the drafting errors. Delete language that is not needed and add language that would be more appropriate. As you redraft, remember to follow best drafting practices, such as keeping verbs together, avoiding legalese, and using the active voice.

1a. Expense Reimbursement. The Company is willing to reimburse the Executive's business expenses in accordance with the Company's regular payroll practices in the instances that the Executive shall have submitted appropriate receipts no later than five business days after the last day of the month in which the Executive shall have incurred them.

_____

_____

1b. Redraft your redraft in 1a using the language that follows as the beginning of the first sentence:
    Expense Reimbursement. To be reimbursed for business expenses that the Executive incurs,

_____

_____

2. Termination. _If_ the Contractor shall have completed construction before the Deadline, _then_ the Owner must pay the Contractor a $5,000 bonus no later than five Business Days after the construction is complete.

_____

_____

3. Termination. If the Retailer shall fail to pay the Manufacturer when Payment is due, the Manufacturer shall be entitled to terminate this Agreement.

_____

_____

CHAPTER TWELVE

Summary of Drafting the Contract Concepts

I. CONTRACT CONCEPTS AND DRAFTING GUIDELINES

The following chart summarizes the material in Chapters 8 through 11. Reading it does not replace reading the chapters. Use it as a handy, quick reference tool.

CONTRACT CONCEPT AND CHAPTER	TOPIC	DRAFTING GUIDANCE
Representations and Warranties (Chapter 8, page 55)	The Language Introducing Representations and Warranties	■ Representations and warranties in a business contract are often paired together instead of used alone. ■ Example: *Party A represents and warrants to Party B as follows:*
	Drafting the Substance: Content and Questions to Ask	■ Ask your client what information they were relying on when they entered into the transaction—information that the other party provided. ■ Consult any previous agreement or list of business issues that the parties have agreed to already. ■ Most contracts that have an entity as a party share a set of foundational representations and warranties. ■ Parties often make parallel or reciprocal representations and warranties, where the same words are used for each party.
	Drafting the Substance: Past or Present Facts	■ The facts in a representation and warranty statement must relate to a state of affairs that exists in the present or existed in the past but not in the future. ■ With respect to facts that presently exist, draft the representation and warranty in the present tense. ■ Do not use *currently* or *presently* in a representation and warranty statement. ■ With respect to facts that occurred in the past, draft the representation and warranty in the past tense or the present perfect tense. ■ Statements with respect to the future should probably be drafted as covenants.

CONTRACT CONCEPT AND CHAPTER	TOPIC	DRAFTING GUIDANCE
	Drafting the Substance: Active or Passive Voice	▪ Generally, draft representations and warranties in the active voice but use the passive voice when the issue is the action rather than the actor. ▪ Example: The parachute has been used five times.
	Risk Allocation: Flat or Qualified Representations and Warranties	▪ Each representation and warranty establishes a standard of liability. ▪ The degree of risk that each party assumes with respect to a statement varies depending on how broadly or narrowly the statement is drafted. ▪ Have your client give qualified representations and warranties instead of flat representations and warranties to reduce their risk. See examples on page 62. ▪ List any exceptions on a disclosure schedule and then refer to the schedule in the representation and warranty.
	Risk Allocation: Knowledge, Materiality, Efforts, and Other Qualifiers	▪ Instead of including a general qualifier like "material" or "best efforts," take the time to be more specific and thoughtful in your drafting and the standards that you are setting. ▪ Use defined terms and definitions in your representations and warranties to further establish standards.

	Drafting Warranties That Stand Alone	▪ Occasionally, but not often, a party might make only a warranty without a representation.
		  ▪ In such cases, it is usually because a party wants another party to warrant that a state of facts will exist in the future, and they will want to be paid appropriate damages if that state of facts does not occur.
		  ▪ Another possibility occurs when a party refuses to represent a "fact" because it is false, but the parties agree that the would-be maker should be liable if the fact is not as stated. The parties can also instead use qualifiers, more specific language, or a promise to indemnify the other party.

Covenants (Chapter 9, page 71)	Drafting the Substance: Content and Questions to Ask	▪ Ask your client what your client and the other parties have promised to do and not do. ▪ Consult any binding or not binding previous agreement or list of business issues that the parties have agreed to already. ▪ Ask and answer in your provisions the following for the business issues in question: who, what, when, where, why, how, and how much. ▪ Make sure that your client is promising something that is entirely in their control so they will be able to meet their obligation.
	Drafting the Substance: Active Versus Passive Voice	▪ Always use the active voice when drafting covenants.

CONTRACT CONCEPT AND CHAPTER	TOPIC	DRAFTING GUIDANCE
	Drafting the Substance: Verbs in Covenants	■ *Shall:* 　■ Use *shall* to indicate a covenant in business contracts. 　■ Always put the name of one of the parties to the agreement as the subject before *shall.* 　　■ Exceptions: (1) do not use *shall* with a form of the verb *to be;* (2) do not use *shall* with a form of the verb *to have;* (3) do not use *shall* if the name of a party comes before *shall* in a clause that establishes a condition or other circumstances under which an event may occur. ■ *Will:* 　■ Consumer contracts use *will* often for covenants and some statutes even mandate the use of *will.* 　■ Use *will* if (1) a provision states a party's opinion, determination, or belief about the future; (2) when the provision states that a party or a nonparty will take action in the future and the nonparty is not the contract party promising to perform a covenant or to whom discretionary authority has been granted; (3) a provision contrasts the present with the future or the past with the future; or (4) if a provision warrants future performance of a good or a future state of facts. ■ However, using *will* and *shall* interchangeably is still not recommended. ■ Use *may* to draft a covenant that begins with a negative subject. ■ Do not state what a party *has a right, is entitled,* or *is permitted to do.* Instead, draft these provisions preferably as covenants with *shall.* ■ Do not use *is obligated, is responsible, warrants,* or *agrees* instead of *shall.*
	Drafting the Substance: Negative Covenants	■ When you are drafting and want a party to promise *not* to do something, use *shall not* after the party's name. ■ If you want two or more parties to promise not to do something, use a negative subject, such as *neither party* or *no party,* and the verb *may* instead of *shall not.* ■ When drafting an exception to an affirmative covenant, you can use *is not obligated to.*
	Drafting the Substance: Covenants Posing as Declarations	■ Test whether a declaration is appropriate by asking whether your client would want to have access to remedies when it comes to that provision. If the answer is *yes*, then redraft the provision as a covenant.
	Risk Allocation in Covenants	■ A drafter can change a covenant significantly by using different degrees of obligation. ■ See examples on pages 87–89. ■ If your client is making the covenant, the degree of obligation should be as weak as possible. The reverse would be true if your client has the right to receive the performance. ■ No matter what, be as clear and specific as possible so that the parties are on the same page on what the standard is and what each party has to do to meet that standard.

CONTRACT CONCEPT AND CHAPTER	TOPIC	DRAFTING GUIDANCE
	Covenants in Acquisition Agreements and Financings	■ The modern acquisition agreement often combines the pre- and post-closing covenants of both parties into one article with no introductory language and where each covenant states the time period and party to which it applies. ■ Another drafting style for covenant articles in these agreements begins the article with an unnumbered introductory paragraph, where a specific party promises to perform obligations from signing to closing. When drafters use this style, they put the post-closing covenants in a separate article.
	How to Deal with Third Parties	■ You cannot bind a third party with a covenant, even if you use *shall* after their name, because they are not a party to the agreement. ■ Use *shall cause* or *shall not permit* when one of the parties to the contract is more responsible for a result, but a third party has to perform in order to achieve that result. Draft the provision in the active voice and state who has the obligation to perform.
Discretionary Authority and Declarations (Chapter 10, page 97)	Drafting: Verb: Use *May* for Discretionary Authority	■ Use *may* to grant a party discretionary authority rather than *has the right to, is entitled to,* or *is permitted.* ■ When using *may* alone does not properly express the parties' intent, draft with both *shall* and *may.* ■ When drafting a provision of discretionary authority that gives a party permission, consider whether the exercise of that permission acts as a condition to the performance of the other party. If so, the correlative obligation must be drafted. ■ When using discretionary authority, always consider whether you should be drafting covenants relating to the same issue. ■ A provision granting discretionary authority to do something cannot prohibit a party from doing anything else, but it can limit the other party's actions.
	Drafting: Discretionary Authority Versus Having a Right	■ Lawyers sometimes negotiate whether an equitable remedy can or should be drafted as a right rather than discretionary authority.
	Drafting: Discretionary Authority Posing as a Declaration	■ A grant of discretionary authority can pose as a declaration. If so, redraft with *may.*

	Drafting: Risk Allocation in Discretionary Authority Provisions	■ If your client will be exercising the discretionary authority:
		  ■ Draft the grant as broadly as possible as to type, matter involved, time, etc. to give your client as much discretionary authority as possible.
		  ■ Draft any condition to the exercise of discretionary authority so it can be easily satisfied.
		■ If the other party will be exercising the discretionary authority:

CONTRACT CONCEPT AND CHAPTER	TOPIC	DRAFTING GUIDANCE
		▪ Narrow the grant of discretionary authority as much as possible as to type, matter involved, time, etc. so the other side has a more limited choice or permission to act. ▪ Draft any condition to the exercise of the discretionary authority so it applies only in the most limited circumstances.

	Drafting Declarations	▪ You can often find declarations in the definitions article of an agreement and in the general provisions article.
		▪ Ask your client whether the parties have agreed to specific facts or policies, such as definitions or policies for the management of the contract.
		▪ To test whether a factor policy should be included as a declaration, ask yourself: Would a party want monetary damages if the legal consequences were not as stated?
		  ▪ If the answer is *no*, then the provision should probably be a declaration.
		  ▪ If the answer is *yes*, then the provision should be drafted as either a representation, warranty, covenant, and/or condition to an obligation.
		▪ Draft declarations using the present tense.
		▪ You determine how much risk your client takes on when you draft and agree to a declaration in a contract, so think about, research, and tailor declarations. For example, do you have a choice over the governing law, and would one state be less risky for your client?

Conditions (Chapter 11, page 107)	Condition to an Obligation	▪ To increase the likelihood that a court will interpret a provision as a condition rather than as a covenant:
		  ▪ State that a provision is a condition,
		  ▪ State the intended consequences of a condition that has not been satisfied,
		  ▪ Use *must* and insert an interpretive provision that *must* signals a condition, and/or
		  ▪ Construct the condition using an *if / then* formulation.
		▪ Try to fit the fact pattern into an *if / then* format.
		▪ In the *if / then* format:
		  ▪ When drafting the *if* clause:
		    ▪ If the client is to be obligated to perform, you may want to include a condition that is hard to satisfy.
		    ▪ If the client has the right to performance, draft a condition with objective, fact-based standards.
		    ▪ Keep in mind that a party's own actions cannot be a condition to its own obligations.
		    ▪ The passage of time cannot be a condition.
		  ▪ When drafting the *then* clause, you should include which party has the obligation to perform, state explicitly what the obligation is, write in the active voice, and avoid negative language.
		  ▪ Verb guidelines:
		    ▪ State the condition in the *if* clause using the present tense.
		    ▪ Do not use *shall* or *must* in the *if* clause.
		    ▪ Use *must* preferably in the *then* clause, but you can use *shall.*

CONTRACT CONCEPT AND CHAPTER	TOPIC	DRAFTING GUIDANCE

		■ Risk allocation:
		  ■ Parties allocate risk by (1) including a condition; (2) choosing to frame a business issue as a condition rather than as a covenant; (3) choosing the standard that establishes the state of facts that must exist before the obligation to perform arises; and (4) deciding whose obligations are subject to the satisfaction of which conditions.
		  ■ Decide whose obligations are subject to the satisfaction of which conditions.

	Conditions in the Conditions Article of an Acquisition or Financial Agreement	■ Conditions articles appear almost exclusively in these types of agreements and generally begin with an unnumbered introductory paragraph that establishes that each condition in the article is a condition to the party's obligation to close on the transaction. ■ Join the verb *must* or *must have* with one or more words that signal different time periods or dates relating to the acquisition or financing. ■ When you have conditions for both parties, make sure to include them in the conditions list for both parties, not just one. ■ Mirror the language of the conditions sections for each party as much as possible. ■ When drafting conditions in a conditions article, omit from that article the consequences of failing to satisfy a specific condition. ■ When considering risk allocation, you want to think about whether you only want a closing condition on the issue or a condition and a covenant relating to the same issue in the different parts of the agreement.

	Condition to Discretionary Authority	■ A party's exercise of discretionary authority may be subject to the satisfaction of one or more conditions.
		■ Use the *if / then* format.
		  ■ For the *if* clause: Follow the guidelines on page 129 — use a present tense verb.
		  ■ For the *then* clause: Follow the guidelines for discretionary authority provisions in Chapter 10 on page 97 — use *may*.

	Conditions to Declarations	■ Some declarations have substantive consequences only if a condition is satisfied.
		■ Use the *if / then* format:
		  ■ For the *if* clause: Follow the guidelines on page 129 — use a present tense verb.
		  ■ For the *then* clause: Follow the guidelines for declarations in Chapter 10 on page 103 — use a present tense verb.

II. EXERCISES

A. EXERCISE 12A: DRAFT PART OF AN AGREEMENT

Polly Producer is the producer of an off-, off-, off-Broadway musical, *Passing the Bar*. It will run from August 1 through September 30 and will be presented at the Williston Theater. She would like you to draft the business terms of an agreement with Serious Scenery, Inc., the owner of the scenery that she would like to rent.

Use only the information in this paragraph and in the following points to draft as much as you can, bringing together everything you have learned about the different contract concepts. Each numbered paragraph should be a new section. Use the following defined terms, as necessary, and do not draft definitions for them: Owner, Producer, Scenery, Theater, and Musical. If you need additional defined terms and definitions, you may pick the best ones possible and use them. The business terms are as follows:

1. Serious Scenery is to deliver the scenery on July 1, 20__.

2. Polly must, of course, return the scenery. She would like not to have to do that until three days after the run concludes.

3. The scenery can be used only in connection with *Passing the Bar*, and at the specific theater discussed.

4. The scenery is not to be altered or added to, although it is OK to make minor repairs and adjustments.

5. Polly must make sure that the scenery is insured at her expense for all loss or damage.

6. Serious Scenery is willing to give assurances that it owns the scenery and has the right to rent it.

B. EXERCISE 12B: CORRECT THE DRAFTING ERRORS

Mark up the following provisions so they use the proper verb forms. Make any other appropriate changes, bringing together everything that you have learned about the different contract concepts. You may need more than one sentence, and you may need to bring in more than one contract concept. Also, there may be different ways to draft them using different contract concepts.

1. **Effects of Termination.** If the transactions that this Agreement contemplates shall not have been consummated on or before July 18, 20__, this Agreement shall terminate on July 18, 20__, and thereafter, neither party shall have any rights or obligations under it, and Buyer will continue to perform all of its obligations under the Confidentiality Agreement.

2. **Publicity.** The parties agree that no publicity release or announcement concerning the transactions contemplated hereby shall be issued by any party without the advance consent of the other, except as such release or announcement may be required by law, in which case the party making the release or announcement shall show the release or announcement in advance to the other party.

3. **Delays.** The Contractor agrees that it shall be accountable for promptly notifying the Owner in writing of any event that may delay completion of the Building. The notice shall explain why the delay has occurred and its estimated duration.

4. **Compliance**. The Tenant must comply in all material respects with any law the violation of which could have a material adverse effect on the Landlord.

5. **Article and Section Headings.** Article and Section headings and the Table of Contents contained in this Agreement shall be for reference purposes only and shall not affect in any way the meaning or interpretation of this Agreement.

6. **Change of Control.** A change in control of the Licensee will constitute a default under this License.

7. **Restrictions on Transfer.** During the term of this Agreement, none of the Shares now owned or hereafter acquired by any of the Stockholders may be transferred unless such transfer of Shares shall be made in accordance with the provisions of this Agreement.

8. **Seller Representations and Warranties.** The Seller represents and warrants to the Buyer the following:

    (i) **Compliance with Applicable Law**. The Seller has complied with, is currently in compliance with, and will be in compliance with on the Closing Date, all laws, rules, and regulations, except for any noncompliance that would not have a material adverse effect on the Seller.

9. **Unacceptable Content**. The Book will contain no matter that invades any person's privacy or that is scandalous, libelous, obscene, or otherwise unlawful.

10. **Notices**. All notices to be effective shall be sent by nationally recognized overnight courier and will be effective when they are received.

A Contract's Parts

CHAPTER THIRTEEN

Overview of a Contract's Parts

I. INTRODUCTION

In Chapters 2 through 7, you learned how to translate a business deal into contract concepts. Then, in Chapters 8 through 12, you learned how to draft each contract concept. This chapter introduces you to the parts of an agreement into which the contract concepts and a business deal are integrated. We start with an overview of a contract as a whole, which will give you some perspective on how the various parts of an agreement work together.

Look at the list of contract parts that follows. They are organized in the order in which they typically appear in an agreement. Although contracts may address radically different topics, their organizations will generally be remarkably similar. The remaining sections in this chapter introduce you to each of these contract parts. Some of these parts would be usually included in the contract in one article with the same name as you see below (e.g., Definitions, General Provisions), while others are parts of the contract that may not include the name below and may cover several articles (e.g., Action Sections, Endgame Provisions).

Parts of an Agreement
- Introductory Provisions
  - Title
  - Preamble
  - Recitals or Background Section
  - Words of Agreement
- **Defined Terms and Definitions**
- **Action Sections**
  - Subject Matter Performance Provision
  - Payment Provisions
  - Duration of Contract (if applicable) (also known as *term*)
  - Action Sections in Acquisitions and Financings (if applicable)
    - Closing and Closing Date (when and where)
    - Closing Deliveries
  - Other Substantive Business Provisions

- Endgame Provisions
- General Provisions
    - ◆ Third Parties (e.g., assignment and delegation, successors and assigns)
    - ◆ Determine What Constitutes a Contract (e.g., severability, amendments, waiver, integration, or merger, counterparts)
    - ◆ Communications (e.g., notice)
    - ◆ Dispute Resolution (e.g., governing law, forum selection, waiver of right to jury trial, alternative dispute resolution)
    - ◆ Risk Allocation (e.g., force majeure)
- Signature Lines
- Schedules and Exhibits

II. INTRODUCTORY PROVISIONS

The **introductory provisions** are composed of the *title, preamble, recitals* or *background section,* and *words of agreement.* They precede the more substantive provisions between the parties and provide the contract's reader with basic information about who the parties are and why they are entering into the agreement.

A. TITLE

Almost all agreements begin with a **title**, the name of the agreement, often based on the subject matter of the agreement, such as *Asset Purchase Agreement, Licensing Agreement,* or *Employment Agreement.* The title is centered on a separate line at the very top of the first page. It is usually in a larger font than the rest of the agreement and boldfaced. However, what is most important about the title in terms of its formatting is that it should be easy to find and read. The name of the agreement in the preamble should be written exactly the same as in the title. If you are putting together several agreements that are similar, or if you are drafting an agreement that is similar to other agreements that your client already has, we recommend that you use the name to differentiate among the various agreements.

B. PREAMBLE

The **preamble** is the first paragraph of the contract; it states the name of the agreement, the parties, and the date that the parties signed the contract. For example:

Example—Preamble

This License Agreement, dated April 17, 20__, is between Hong Licensing Corp., a California corporation ("**Hong**"), and Browne Manufacturing, Inc., an Alabama corporation ("**Browne**").

C. RECITALS OR BACKGROUND SECTION

The **recitals** or **background** section explains the setting of the transaction and why the parties are entering into the contract. They are not enforceable provisions, so they do not provide rights or remedies. You will find in practice that some drafters prefer using the term *recitals,* while others refer to these same provisions taken together as the *background* section. The following background section is from a guaranty, an agreement in which the parent company is guaranteeing the debt of the borrower (a wholly owned subsidiary), so the parent will be responsible for the loan as well if the borrower is not able to meet the loan's requirements under the credit agreement:

Example—Recitals or Background Section

Background

1. The Bank has agreed to lend funds to the Borrower in accordance with the Credit Agreement that the Bank and the Borrower are signing as of the date of this agreement.
2. The Borrower is a wholly owned subsidiary of the Parent.
3. The Bank will lend to the Borrower only if the Parent guarantees the Borrower's debt.
4. The Parent and the Borrower are engaged in related businesses, and the Parent will derive substantial direct and indirect benefit from the Bank's loans to the Borrower.
5. The Parent is willing to guarantee the Borrower's debt.

D. WORDS OF AGREEMENT

The **words of agreement** do what they say: They state for the record that the parties have agreed to the terms of the contract. Historically, these words had a secondary function, which is to recite the contract's consideration. But today that recitation is antiquated and unnecessary in many instances. Lawyers who continue to use the more traditional language often refer to the words of agreement as the **statement of consideration**. Here are three examples of words of agreement, ranging from contemporary to traditional:

Examples—Words of Agreement

Contemporary:

Accordingly, the parties agree as follows:

Mix of Contemporary and Traditional:

Accordingly, in consideration of the mutual promises stated in this Agreement, the parties agree as follows:

Traditional:

NOW, THEREFORE, in consideration of $10 paid in hand and other good and valuable consideration, the receipt of which is hereby acknowledged, the parties hereto hereby agree as follows:

III. DEFINED TERMS AND DEFINITIONS

Although it is not always the case, a list of **defined terms** and their **definitions** often follow the words of agreement. Definitions are used for multiple purposes, including expanding or narrowing the ordinary meaning of a word or phrase. They establish the meaning of particular terms in the agreement, provide consistency for how the parties refer to those terms, and give us a shorthand way of referring to complex concepts (e.g., the example below regarding *Litigation Expense*). By using defined terms, drafters ensure that the same concept is stated the same way throughout an agreement.

As noted in Chapter 10 on page 103, definitions are drafted as declarations. Here is an example of a defined term and its definition drafted as a declaration:

> *Example—Defined Term and Definition*
>
> **"Litigation Expense"** means any expense incurred in connection with asserting, investigating, or defending any claim arising out of or relating to this Agreement, including without limitation, the fees, disbursements, and expenses of attorneys and other professionals.

IV. ACTION SECTIONS

This is a term that you may not necessarily hear from other drafters, but this book refers to the next part of an agreement as the **action sections**.[1] We refer to them as *action sections* because they are *where the action is* from the client's perspective.

In the action sections, the parties

- promise to perform the main subject matter of the contract;
- promise to pay the financial consideration, if any (be it purchase price, rent, or royalties);
- state the term of the contract (if any);
- state the closing date and list the closing deliveries (if an acquisition or financing agreement); and
- include any other substantive business provisions.

For a detailed sample of the action sections of an agreement, see the Website Development Agreement available on the CasebookConnect Resources page and on the Aspen website product page for this book.

The next sections explain some of the most common provisions in action sections, which are subject matter performance, payment, term (referring to the time duration of a contract), and other substantive business provisions. Acquisitions and financing agreements include many of these provisions plus the date the transaction is supposed to close (the closing date) and the list of items that need to be executed and delivered by each party at closing (the closing deliveries).

Most of the provisions in the action sections of agreements are covenants because this is the part of the contract where the parties are promising to perform the more specific requirements of the contract. In addition, you may find at times conditions in the action sections. This is because a drafter may need to provide for different options relating to how the parties are going to perform their obligations, given what may or may not happen in the future.

---

1. Tina Stark coined the phrase *action sections* because no name existed that one could use to refer to these sections collectively.

A. SUBJECT MATTER PERFORMANCE PROVISIONS

The first of the action sections is the **subject matter performance provision**. Most commonly, this is where each side promises to the other that they will perform the main subject matter of the contract.

> *Examples—Subject Matter Performance Provision with Reciprocal Covenants*
>
> **Purchase and Sale.** At the Closing, Sally *shall sell* the house to Bob, and Bob *shall buy* the house from Sally.
>
> **License.** During the Term, the Licensor *shall license* the Trademark to the Manufacturer, and the Manufacturer *shall manufacture and market products* with the Trademark.

These reciprocal executory covenants establish the agreement's primary consideration.[2]

A subject matter performance provision does not always consist of **reciprocal covenants** of future performance. Sometimes it can be a **self-executing provision**, as follows:

> *Example—Subject Matter Performance Provision with Self-Executing Provision*
>
> **Grant of Security Interest.** By signing this Security Agreement, the Borrower grants a security interest in the Assets to the Bank.

In the example above, the main subject matter of the contract is the creation of a security interest that is given to the Bank when the Borrower signs the security agreement (this security interest would give the Bank the right to take over all or part of the assets under certain conditions). The Borrower does not promise to *grant* a security interest. The parties do not *intend* for performance to be in the future. Instead, performance *occurs concurrently* with the borrower's independent act of signing the agreement.

B. PAYMENT PROVISIONS

What is usually the next provision of the action sections sets out the **financial consideration**, such as a purchase price, salary, royalties, or some other type of payment (usually from one party to the other for performing certain obligations).

Practitioners generally draft financial consideration in one of two ways. The first way, demonstrated in Example 1 that follows, states what the financial consideration is and then, in a separate section or sentence, states which party covenants to pay that financial consideration. Therefore, as you can see in Example 1, a declaration is followed by a covenant. The second way of expressing the payment provisions shown in Example 2 combines in *one* statement what the financial consideration is and the covenant to pay it. Therefore, Example 2 is only one covenant.

---

2. Jeff Ferriell, *Understanding Contracts*, 72-73 (2d ed. 2009).

Examples—Financial Consideration Statement

1 — Declaration Followed by a Covenant:

Rent. The Rent for each calendar month of the Term is $700 (the "**Rent**"). The Tenant shall pay the Landlord the Rent for each calendar month no later than the first day of that calendar month.

2 — Only as a Covenant

Royalties. With respect to each calendar month of the Term, the Tenant shall pay the Landlord the rent of $700 no later than the first day of that calendar month (the "**Rent**").

C. DURATION OF CONTRACT PROVISIONS

Another common provision of the action sections states **the term of the contract** — the period of time during which the contract will govern the parties' relationship — which could be over multiple years. Supply agreements, software licensing agreements, and leases are all agreements that commonly have terms.

Not all contracts have terms. Some contracts contemplate a one-time transaction, such as an acquisition, which terminates at the conclusion of that transaction. Lawyers refer to these transactions as **one-off transactions**.

The following examples illustrate two of the possible ways to incorporate a term into the action sections. In Example 1 below, the term is stated as a declaration in a stand-alone provision. In Example 2, the first sentence includes both the reciprocal covenants in the subject matter performance provision and the contract's term. The next sentence is a declaration that states the term's beginning and ending dates.

Examples—Term Provisions

1—Term as a Stand-Alone Declaration:

Term. The term of this Lease is three years and begins on the date of this Agreement and ends at 5:00 PM on the date immediately preceding the third anniversary of the date of this Agreement.

2—Term Integrating Covenants in Subject Matter Performance Provision with Declaration:

Term. The Landlord shall lease the Premises to the Tenant, and the Tenant shall rent the Premises for a term of three years. The term begins on the date of this Agreement and ends at 5:00 PM on the day immediately preceding the third anniversary of the date of this Agreement.

D. CLOSING-RELATED PROVISIONS

Some transactions, but not all, have a closing-related provision. Generally, these are necessary only in acquisitions and financings, where there is a moment when the transaction is finalized, which is the moment when the asset is sold and transferred or the loan is extended. Closing-related provisions in acquisition and financing agreements include details on the **closing date** and on the **closing deliveries**. The closing date is when the transaction will be formally concluded, so the parties would state in this part of the agreement when and where the closing is to take place.

In the closing deliveries' provisions, each party covenants to the other how they will deliver their performance at closing. In an acquisition, the seller usually promises to execute and deliver transfer documents, and the buyer usually promises to deliver the purchase price. Similarly, in a financing agreement, the bank promises to deliver the loan amount to the borrower, and the borrower promises to execute and deliver a note to the bank. The closing deliveries for each party are usually included in the agreement as lists, so that they are easy to refer to and check when preparing for the closing.

E. OTHER SUBSTANTIVE BUSINESS PROVISIONS

In this book, we are including the other substantive business provisions within the action sections, since these provisions are still where the action is. However, other practitioners and commentators may include them as a set of provisions separate from the action sections.

The other substantive business provisions can include any or all of the contract concepts and can be organized in different ways, depending on the agreement. For example, in the House Purchase Agreement (available on the CasebookConnect Resources page and on the Aspen website product page for this book), the other provisions are organized by contract concept. They appear in chronological order on the transaction's timeline. First, the representations and warranties from each party are made at the time of the signing of the agreement. This is followed by covenants from each party that govern the gap period between signing and closing. The final provisions are conditions to provide walk-away rights for each party at closing.

V. ENDGAME PROVISIONS

The **endgame provisions** could be considered part of other substantive business provisions, but they are sufficiently important to many commentators and practitioners to warrant a discussion devoted just to them. These provisions generally are the next-to-last provisions of a contract. They state the business terms that govern the end of the parties' contractual relationship and provide for options if specific events occur, from a party having to pay additional interest and a penalty fee if they are late on a payment to actual termination of the agreement. They require a drafter to determine the different ways that a contract can end and how the contract will deal with each of the scenarios. Because endgame provisions invariably involve money, the parties and their lawyers often intensely negotiate these provisions.

As a generalization, contracts can end happily, unhappily, or in a neutral manner. A joint venture can be successfully concluded, a borrower can fail to pay the principal amount on a loan when due, or a grocer may decide to terminate a contract to do business with a less expensive supplier. Regardless of why an agreement ends, its provisions must address the consequences of the contract's end.

The endgame provisions set out any final payments that need to be made or state any covenants that survive the termination of a contractual relationship that ends happily. For example, an employment agreement might include a confidentiality covenant that continues past the end of the term of the contract.

The endgame provisions will state what constitutes a default, as well as the agreed-on remedies, in the event that the contract should end unhappily. Furthermore, the termination provisions must detail the procedure to terminate the relationship in the event that a contract ends in a neutral manner in which no party is at fault.

Endgame provisions may be drafted as various contract concepts: as a condition to an obligation to perform and the statement of the obligation or as a condition to discretionary authority and the statement of the discretionary authority. Occasionally, they are drafted as conditions to a right and a statement of the right. Here are some examples of endgame provisions incorporating these different contract concepts:

Examples—Endgame Provisions Drafted as Conditions

Condition to an Obligation and the Obligation:

Release of Collateral. After the Borrower has paid all of the outstanding principal and accrued interest, the Bank shall sign any documents necessary to release the Collateral.

Condition to Discretionary Authority and the Discretionary Authority:

Late Submission of Manuscript. If the Author does not submit the Manuscript before November 1, 20__, the publisher may refuse to publish the Book.

Condition to a Right and the Right:

Return of Deposit. If the Tenant does not return the Premises in broom-clean condition, the Landlord has the right to retain the amount of the Deposit equal to the cost of appropriately cleaning the Premises.[3]

In Chapter 11 on page 114, we recommended that you draft provisions as covenants instead of rights and that you do the same when drafting conditions. In other words, that you draft conditions to an obligation and not conditions to a right. However, unlike other provisions, endgame provisions are often drafted as a condition to a right, with the right following the condition. As discussed in Chapter 17 on page 254, parties often do state just a party's rights when stating their entitlement to a remedy.

VI. GENERAL PROVISIONS

The final provisions of an agreement are the **general provisions**, often referred to as the **boilerplate provisions**. These provisions tell the parties how to govern their relationship and administer the contract.

General provisions can be grouped into the following categories: provisions dealing with third parties (assignment and delegation, successors, and assigns), provisions that determine what constitutes the contract (severability, amendments, waiver, integration or merger, and counterparts), provisions regarding communications (notice), dispute resolution provisions (governing law, forum selection, waiver of right to a jury trial, and alternative dispute resolution), and risk allocation provisions (force majeure). Note that not all possible general provisions or even categories are covered in this book, and some of these provisions could be grouped by practitioners and commentators in different categories.

The names *boilerplate provisions* and *general provisions* can mislead drafters because they suggest that the provisions are standardized and in no need of tailoring. Do not treat these provisions in this way; instead, be thoughtful and careful with what you included in this part of the agreement. Each of these provisions raises important business and legal issues that you must address.

---

3. *See* Chapter 17 on page 254 for explanations of why a *right* may be appropriate here rather than *discretionary authority*.

Some general provisions are covenants, while others are declarations, as in the examples that follow:

Examples—General or Boilerplate Provisions

As Covenants:

Assignment and Delegation. The Tenant shall not assign the Tenant's rights or delegate the Tenant's performance under this Lease to any person.

As Declarations:

Successors and Assigns. This Agreement binds and benefits the parties and their respective permitted successors and assigns.

VII. SIGNATURE LINES

A contract concludes, of course, with the parties' **signatures**. Although signatures are not always required to create a contract (e.g., an oral contract), they are good to have in all circumstances because they can provide evidentiary proof about when and how the parties came to an agreement. Generally, all parties who make promises in a particular contract sign that contract. In some contracts, such as in a guaranty agreement, only one party makes promises, so only that party must sign.

VIII. SCHEDULES AND EXHIBITS

Schedules and exhibits are additional sections not within the body of a contract, which means that they do not appear after the preamble or before the signature lines. Nonetheless, they are integral in establishing the parties' rights and duties. Schedules and exhibits tend to be attached to the rest of the contract after the signature pages. The schedules should come first, followed by the exhibits.

Because schedules and exhibits are technically outside the body of the contract, the contract must incorporate them to make them enforceable. It matters how drafters create the link between these items and the primary agreement.[4]

This book focuses primarily on how to use and draft schedules and exhibits. If you are using any other terms to refer to materials added after the signature lines (such as *attachments, appendices, addenda,* and/or *riders*), make sure that you understand well what they mean for the type of agreement and the industry in which you are working and how they will be interpreted by the courts or any governing bodies in the relevant jurisdiction.

---

4. *See United Cal. Bank v. Prudential Ins. Co. of Am.*, 681 P.2d 390, 420 (Ariz. App. 1983) ("While it is not necessary that a contract state specifically that another writing is 'incorporated by this reference herein,' the context in which the reference is made must make clear that the writing is part of the contract.").

IX. EXERCISES

A. EXERCISE 13A: 1ST DRAFT OF CAR PURCHASE AGREEMENT

Draft a car purchase agreement using the facts below incorporating everything that you have learned so far about the six contract concepts and the various parts of the agreement. Use the House Purchase Agreement (available on the CasebookConnect Resources page and the Aspen website) as precedent. Try to use the same formatting and as much content as possible from the House Purchase Agreement. Draft from the buyer's perspective, but in a manner that would be reasonably acceptable to the seller. Here are some additional suggestions for this exercise:

- Focus on the provisions mentioned by the facts below.
- Assume that no statutes apply to the transaction.
- Do not worry about fine-tuning the termination and general provisions since you do not have information on those parts of the agreement now.
- You do not have to draft any relevant exhibits but may reference them.
- Use your common sense: What would make the most sense if you were the client and wanted to buy the car? If you were the buyer, what would you want to make sure you get from the seller, and vice versa?

Facts for 1st Draft of Car Purchase Agreement:

1. The parties are Barbara Balram, the seller, and Tom Rogers, the buyer.
2. The car is a red, 20__ Acura. For the "20__," choose a year in the past that you want and choose a model.
3. The car has been driven almost 26,000 miles.
4. The purchase price is $11,000. The buyer will pay the seller with a certified check.
5. The seller owns the car, and the car is not subject to any liens.
6. The car has been maintained in accordance with the owner's manual and is in good operating condition, normal wear and tear excepted.
7. The date of the agreement is the date that this assignment is due. The closing will take place on the last day of the month that follows the month of the date of the agreement. (For example, if your assignment is due October 15, then the date of the agreement is October 15, and the closing will take place on November 30.)
8. Choose a closing time and location that makes sense.
9. With respect to the period beginning on the day that the agreement is signed and ending on the closing date, the seller promises not to paint the car and not to drive it more than 500 miles. The seller also promises to garage the car and to continue to maintain it.
10. The buyer has to close only if the seller has performed its covenants and if the seller's representations and warranties are true on the date that they were made and on the closing date as if they were made on that date, except to the extent that the agreement contemplates that specific facts might change.

B. EXERCISE 13B: EMPLOYMENT AGREEMENT AND CONTRACT CONCEPTS AND PARTS

Follow the instructions supplied in the following email from Senior Associate to Overworked Junior Associate. For the purposes of this exercise, assume that it is March 1, 20__.

Here are the most important provisions of the contract:

From: Senior Associate

To: Overworked Junior Associate

Date: March 1, 20__

Our client, Healthy Hearts Inc., an immediate care medical facility ("**Healthy Hearts**"), has been conducting an extensive search for a new chief executive officer. Last week, it reached a handshake deal with Adele Administrator ("**Administrator**").

As you know, Corporate Partner went on vacation last week and left me in charge of one of her matters. As I will be conducting the negotiations, I need your assistance in preparing the documents. Please review the deal terms and determine both of the following:

- Which of the following contract concepts best expresses each business term?
  - Representation and warranty
  - Covenant
  - Discretionary authority
  - Declaration
  - Condition
    - Condition to an obligation (ongoing or walk-away?)
    - Condition to discretionary authority
    - Condition to a declaration
- Where in the contract would each of the business terms below go?
  - Introductory provisions (title, preamble, recitals, words of agreement)
  - Defined terms and definitions
  - Action sections (subject matter performance provision, payment provisions, duration of contract, closing/closing date and closing deliveries, other substantive business provisions)
  - Endgame provisions
  - General provisions
  - Signature lines
  - Schedules and exhibits

---

continued on next page >

Several of the business terms require more than one contract concept and may be included in different parts of the contract. It will not help me to tell me that a business term belongs in the action sections or the endgame provisions. What I really need to know is which contract concept to use.

Put your answer on the line that follows each numbered paragraph. Do not worry so much about Paragraph 12. We will deal with that information later in the transaction. We will review your work as soon as you finish.

1. Healthy Hearts agrees to hire Administrator, and Administrator agrees to work for Healthy Hearts.

_____

_____

2. Administrator will be engaged as Chief Executive Officer of Healthy Hearts.

_____

_____

3. Administrator is currently Executive Vice President at Holistic Hospitals Corp. ("**Holistic**") and is party to an Employment Agreement with Holistic that is dated April 1, 20__, and supposedly ends March 31, 20__. Healthy Hearts is very concerned about that agreement. According to Administrator, the terms of the Holistic agreement do not permit her to show it to anyone other than her advisors. Healthy Hearts does not want to tortiously interfere with that agreement. In other words, Healthy Hearts does not want to be a party to a contract that violates the Holistic agreement. Administrator insists that she is free to enter into the employment agreement with Healthy Hearts and that doing so will not breach her employment agreement with Holistic. Please see if you can put language in one provision that will give Healthy Hearts comfort on this point. Specifically:

  (a) Healthy Hearts wants to show that they entered into their employment agreement with Administrator in the good faith belief that they were not causing her to breach her agreement with Holistic Hospitals. As you may recall from law school, a party can defend against a claim of tortious interference by demonstrating that it had no intent to interfere with the other contract. Other than Healthy Hearts self-servingly stating that they entered into the contract with Administrator in the good faith belief that they were not causing her to breach her contract, what could demonstrate our client's good faith?

  (b) Healthy Hearts wants to be able to sue Administrator if the employment agreement with Healthy Hearts in fact causes a breach under her employment agreement with Holistic.

_____

_____

4. The term of employment will be for three years, beginning on April 1, 20__.

_____

_____

5. Healthy Hearts negotiated for the right to terminate Administrator's employment for "cause," in which event Healthy Hearts would pay Administrator her salary through the date of termination, plus reimbursement of any expenses incurred through the date of termination. Healthy Hearts must make such payment on the date of the termination.

---

6. Administrator will be paid $25,000 per month, payable on the first business day of each month.

---

7. During her negotiations with Healthy Hearts, Administrator stated that she received her AB from Brown University in 20__ and her MD from Harvard University in 20__. She also advised Healthy Hearts that she is enrolled in the MBA program at Fordham University and is specializing in Hospital Administration. Healthy Hearts is very "hung up" on credentials and is also concerned about what it calls "résumé fraud." Therefore, Healthy Hearts wants to be able to sue Administrator if she in fact does not have the credentials that she claims. In addition, Healthy Hearts does not want to be obligated under the Employment Agreement if Administrator has not been awarded her MBA by the time her employment under the Employment Agreement is to begin.

---

8. Administrator shall perform all duties that are customary for an officer of a corporation holding the office of Chief Executive Officer.

---

9. During her negotiations with Healthy Hearts, Administrator insisted on two things to which Healthy Hearts agreed:

(a) She wants Healthy Hearts to employ Samuel Samaritan as her Administrative Assistant no later than March 31, 20__. (Healthy Hearts agreed that Administrator would not only have the right to sue if Healthy Hearts failed to employ Samaritan by March 31, 20__, but also the right not to go forward with Healthy Hearts.)

(b) Administrator can back out of the deal if Phil Philanthropic has not contributed $5 million to the Healthy Hearts capital fund-raising program by March 31, 20__.

---

10. Administrator agreed that she would devote her attention and energies on a full-time basis to the business of Healthy Hearts, except for her work at the animal shelter.

---

11. If Healthy Hearts terminates Administrator's employment "without cause," Healthy Hearts must pay Administrator any salary currently payable, plus $100,000, plus reimbursement of any expenses incurred through the date of termination. Healthy Hearts must make such payment on the date of termination.

---

12. Healthy Hearts is incorporated in Michigan, and Administrator lives in Detroit, Michigan.

C. EXERCISE 13C: LICENSING AGREEMENT AND CONTRACT CONCEPTS AND PARTS

Please follow the instructions in the email below.

From: Senior Associate

To: Overworked Junior Associate

Date: April 20, 20__

I really appreciated your help on that last project. As you know by now, the reward for excellent work is more work. . . .

Our client is Ralph Products LP ("**Ralph LP**"). Ralph LP owns all rights in the cartoon character Ralph — a short, eight-year-old with glasses for whom life never goes quite right. For reasons that no one understands, anything with a likeness of Ralph on it sells out immediately. Ralph LP has been making millions by licensing the trademark rights to use this character to different companies who manufacture and then market products bearing Ralph's likeness.

Our client and Merchandisers Extraordinaire, Inc. ("**Merchandisers**"), have agreed to enter into a license agreement with the terms stated in this memorandum. Please tell me

- Which of the following contract concepts best expresses each business term?
    - Representation and warranty
    - Covenant
    - Discretionary authority
    - Declaration
    - Condition
        - Condition to an obligation (ongoing or walk-away?)
        - Condition to discretionary authority
        - Condition to a declaration
- Where in the contract does each of the business terms below go?
    - Introductory provisions (title, preamble, recitals, words of agreement)
    - Defined terms and definitions
    - Action sections (subject matter performance provision, payment provisions, duration of contract, closing/closing date and closing deliveries, other substantive business provisions)

- ◆ Endgame provisions
- ◆ General provisions
- ◆ Signature lines
- ◆ Schedules and exhibits

Write your answer on the lines following the paragraph. Do not worry so much about Paragraph 11. We will deal with that information later.

---

1. Ralph LP will grant Merchandisers a license for caps and t-shirts bearing the Ralph likeness, and Merchandisers will be obligated to market and merchandise them in Maine, New Hampshire, and Vermont.

_____

_____

2. Ralph LP has an ongoing concern about the financial condition of their licensees. They are willing to enter into this agreement only because Merchandisers's most recent financial statements showed substantial financial strength. Ralph LP wants the contract to reflect their reliance on those financial statements. In addition, Ralph LP wants the right to terminate this agreement if Merchandisers's net worth — as at the end of any fiscal year during the term of the contract — drops below $15 million.

_____

_____

3. The agreement will have a three-year licensing term, to begin on the first day of the month after the end of this month. Please assume that we will be able to execute this agreement tomorrow.

_____

_____

4. Merchandisers is to have an obligation to use commercially reasonable efforts to market the Ralph merchandise. If Merchandisers has any unsold merchandise on hand at the time the term ends, Ralph LP will buy that merchandise at its cost.

_____

_____

5. Merchandisers wants some kind of assurance in the contract

(a) that Ralph LP actually owns what they are licensing; and
(b) that during the term of the license, Ralph LP will
  (i) enforce their intellectual property rights against all third parties; and
  (ii) defend their licensees against all intellectual property claims of third parties.

_____

_____

6. The parties have agreed that with respect to each year of the term of the contract, Merchandisers must pay royalties equal to 15% of all net sales.

_____

_____

7. Ralph LP has a reputation for having a high standard when it comes to the quality of their licensees' products. Ralph LP always requires their licensees to submit samples of any item that the licensee intends to manufacture at least 30 days before the item goes into production. Ralph LP then must either accept or reject the item. If Ralph LP approves the item, then Merchandisers must manufacture it. If Ralph LP rejects the sample, they must explain in detail why they did so. After the receipt of the rejection notice, Merchandisers may revise the sample and resubmit it for approval. If Ralph LP approves the revised sample, then Merchandisers must manufacture it.

_____

_____

8. Merchandisers wants Ralph LP to give assurances that Merchandisers is the only one now with the right to sell trademarked caps and t-shirts in their territory and that during the term of the contract Ralph LP will not grant anyone else a competing right.

_____

_____

9. Merchandisers was concerned that its territory was relatively small. Our client agreed to extend the territory to include Delaware and Rhode Island if Merchandisers's sales for the first year of the term exceeded $7 million.

_____

_____

10. Virginia law will govern.

_____

_____

11. Ralph LP is a Virginia limited partnership, and Merchandisers is an Oregon corporation.

_____

_____

D. EXERCISE 13D: WEBSITE DEVELOPMENT AGREEMENT AND CONTRACT CONCEPTS AND PARTS

Through this exercise, you will begin to learn how to read, organize, and identify the different parts of a contract. Plus, you will do the same for the six contract concepts and put together the parts of a contract with the six contract concepts. For this exercise, you will need to review and analyze the Website Development Agreement located on the CasebookConnect Resources page and on the Aspen website product page for this book.

Do the following:

1. Find where each of the contract parts listed are included in the Website Development Agreement and write down the number of that section and/or the specific language in the second column.

2. Find where the relevant contract concepts are included in the same agreement and write down the number of that section and/or the specific language in the second column.

3. The last items in the following table bring together the parts of a contract and the contract concepts. Find those in the agreement as well, and include the section number where found and/or the specific language in the second column.

CONTRACT PART	SECTION NUMBER WHERE FOUND AND / OR SPECIFIC LANGUAGE
Preamble	
Recitals	
Words of Agreement	
Subject Matter Performance Provision. Covenant or self-executing?	
CONTRACT CONCEPT	**SECTION NUMBER WHERE FOUND AND/OR SPECIFIC LANGUAGE**
In the section on fees, a declaration, a covenant, and discretionary authority.	
In Paragraph 5 (other than Paragraph 5.6), three covenants, a condition to discretionary authority, and the related discretionary authority. In Paragraph 5.6, a condition to a declaration and a declaration. (It's tricky.)	
In Paragraph 8, a self-executing provision.	
Representations and warranties.	
CONTRACT PART AND CONTRACT CONCEPT	**SECTION NUMBER WHERE FOUND AND/OR SPECIFIC LANGUAGE**
In the endgame provisions, a condition to discretionary authority and discretionary authority.	

CHAPTER FOURTEEN

Introductory Provisions: Title, Preamble, Recitals, and Words of Agreement

I. INTRODUCTION

The first four parts of a contract, which are the title, preamble, recitals or background, and words of agreement, set the stage for the remainder of the contract. They identify the type of contract, explain its purpose, and state that the parties agree to the provisions that follow. Although they seem simple and easy, if not written accurately, they can bind the wrong party and change the effect of the contract.

When drafting the introductory provisions, you want to use straightforward language with short sentences in a contemporary style, as in Example 1 below. Unfortunately, many drafters continue to draft these introductory provisions in a traditional style, meaning long provisions with a lot of legalese that remind us of language from eighteenth-century England, as in Example 2 below.

> **Example 1—Introductory Provisions in More Contemporary Style**

NONCOMPETITION AGREEMENT

This Noncompetition Agreement, dated March 16, 20__, is between Attorney Staffing Acquisition Co., a Delaware corporation (the "**Company**"), and Maria Rodriguez (the "**Executive**").

Background

1. Attorney Staffing Inc., a Delaware corporation (the "**Seller**"), provides temporary lawyers to law firms in the greater Chicago area.
2. The Seller is selling substantially all of Seller's assets to the Company in accordance with the Asset Acquisition Agreement, dated February 1, 20__ (the "**Acquisition Agreement**").
3. The Executive is the Seller's sole stockholder and President.
4. The Executive has extensive knowledge of the Seller's business, including Seller's client base and pool of temporary lawyers.

---

continued on next page >

5. It is a condition to the consummation of the Acquisition Agreement that the Executive enter into this Noncompetition Agreement.

    Accordingly, in consideration of the mutual promises stated in this Agreement, the parties agree as follows:

Example 2—Introductory Provisions in More Traditional Style

NONCOMPETITION AGREEMENT

THIS NONCOMPETITION AGREEMENT, made the 16th day of March, 20__, by and between ATTORNEY STAFFING ACQUISITION CO., a corporation organized under the laws of Delaware (hereinafter, the "Company"), and MARIA RODRIGUEZ, residing at 21 Melmartin Road, Chicago, Illinois 60606 (hereinafter, the "Executive"),

W I T N E S S E T H:

WHEREAS, Attorney Staffing Inc., a Delaware corporation (hereinafter, the "Seller"), provides temporary lawyers to law firms in the greater Chicago area;

WHEREAS, the Seller is selling substantially all of its assets to the Company in accordance with the Asset Acquisition Agreement, dated the first day of February 20__ (hereinafter, the "Acquisition Agreement");

WHEREAS, the Executive is the sole stockholder of the Seller and its President;

WHEREAS, the Executive has extensive knowledge of the Seller's business, including its client base and pool of temporary lawyers; and

WHEREAS, it is a condition to the consummation of the Acquisition Agreement that the Executive enter into this Noncompetition Agreement;

NOW, THEREFORE, in consideration of the mutual promises herein contained and other good and valuable consideration, the receipt of which is hereby acknowledged, the parties hereto hereby agree:

Note that the provisions are actually part of one long sentence:

"This Noncompetition Agreement . . . witnesseth [the following things]. . . . Now, therefore, . . . the parties hereto hereby agree:"

This format is outdated and can be revised without any change in substance or effect.

In the remainder of this chapter, we will look at how to draft each of these introductory provisions.

II. TITLE

Almost all agreements begin with the title, which is the name of the agreement. The title helps the reader to quickly identify the agreement, often based on the subject matter of the agreement. The name of the agreement is then repeated in the preamble, which is the part that directly follows the title. An agreement's name should describe its subject matter—for example, *Supply Agreement*. Some drafters simply use *Agreement*, but that defeats the purpose of the title and preamble, which are to identify the agreement and differentiate it from others. Such a short, generic agreement name becomes especially problematic if multiple agreements in a transaction are named *Agreement*. In that case, a reader may have to wade through the agreement to learn its subject matter. A short, generic name like this can further frustrate a reader if one agreement refers to another. A cross-reference to the *Agreement* conveys no meaningful information.

The title should be centered at the top of the first page. To make the title obvious and easy to read, its type should be boldfaced and in a larger font than the text in the body of the agreement. Some drafters prefer to make the title all caps and bold, or all caps and not bold. What is important in terms of formatting is that the title be easy to find and read. Also, the name of the agreement should be exactly the same in both the title and preamble. And, for consistency, we recommend that you use the same formatting style in all three places.

A subtitle may be useful in a transaction where the parties sign multiple agreements of the same type, but one party differs in each agreement. For example, this might occur in a financing transaction where multiple subsidiaries guarantee the parent corporation's debt. To make it easier to distinguish among related agreements, drafters may title all of the agreements according to their subject matter and then put below the title the name of the party to that agreement in brackets, as in the example below.

Example—Title with Subtitle

Guaranty
[Subsidiary A]

Guaranty, dated October 15, 20__, by Subsidiary A, an Arkansas corporation (the "**Guarantor**"), in favor of Big Bank, N.A., a national banking corporation (the "**Bank**").

In practice, you will often receive a stack of contracts that all have the exact same title, making it hard to distinguish between them. If possible, we recommend that you avoid using the same title if you are putting together more than one agreement or if you know that you will likely be drafting another one or the company already has similar agreements, and instead find a way of differentiating among them, as demonstrated above.

III. PREAMBLE

The **preamble** is the first paragraph of an agreement, and some drafters refer to it as the **introductory paragraph**. The preamble identifies the agreement by stating the agreement's name and date and the parties entering into the agreement. Example 1 below is a well-drafted contemporary preamble. Many practitioners use this format because it states the preamble as a complete, grammatically correct sentence. Also, using a bold font for the agreement's name and the parties' defined terms, as illustrated below, quickly alerts the reader to the most important information in the preamble.

Example 1—Preamble in More Contemporary Style

This Supply Agreement, dated March 3, 20__, is between Carpetmakers, Inc., an Indiana corporation (the "**Manufacturer**"), and Big Retail Corp., a Florida corporation (the "**Retailer**").

Example 2 demonstrates another way of drafting the preamble. More traditional, yet somewhat contemporary, this version is still the preference of many drafters. It has the same information as in Example 1, but it is no longer a sentence. This book uses both styles to familiarize you with what you will see in practice.

Example 2—Preamble with Mix of Traditional and Contemporary Style

Supply Agreement, dated March 3, 20__, between Carpetmakers, Inc., an Indiana corporation (the "**Manufacturer**"), and Big Retail Corp., a Florida corporation (the "**Retailer**").

The following sections, A through D, provide guidelines for drafting the preamble.

A. NAME OF THE AGREEMENT

Typically, the preamble begins with the name of the agreement. The name should be indented approximately five spaces and is often typed in all capital letters. Some drafters put the title in a bold font. That said, these authors prefer the alternative, more contemporary style in which the agreement's name appears in uppercase and lowercase letters and a bold font in both the title and preamble. The bold font and placing it first suffice to make the title obvious. However, this is all a matter of preference. Here is an example of a preamble with the name in bold:

Example—Preamble

Lease, dated November 14, 20__, between Real Estate, Inc., a Florida corporation (the "**Landlord**"), and Red Shoes LLC, a Texas limited liability company (the "**Tenant**").

B. DATE

In the preamble, drafters can date an agreement in one of two ways:

Examples—Drafting Dates

1 — Date Is the Date That the Agreement Is Signed
    , dated January 6, 20__,

2 — Date Is an "As Of" Date
    , dated *as of* January 1, 20__,

Drafters use the Example 1 format when the parties either reach an agreement on the same day that they sign the agreement or when they reach an agreement before they sign the agreement but do not take action on anything in the agreement until the date they sign.

By contrast, drafters use the Example 2 format when parties want to apply the terms of the agreement starting on the *as of* date, but do not sign their agreement until a later date. For example, if a senior executive begins work on May 23, 20__, without a written contract, the parties will want the agreed-on business terms to be effective as of that date. Accordingly, the employment agreement will be dated *as of May 23, 20__*, even if it is not signed until July 1, 20__. The fact that the effective date and the signing date differ causes no legal problem.[1] That said, and to state what should be self-evident, an *as of* date should never be used to deceive a third party, such as the government, because that would be fraud.[2]

Using an *as of* date can affect the accuracy of representations and warranties and the effective date of covenants. Recall that representations and warranties speak as of the moment in time when they are given.[3] If a contract has an *as of* date, then the representations and warranties speak *as of that date*, not the date when the contract is signed.

Suppose, for example, that on October 15, Bob agreed to buy Sally's car, and on that day, Sally represented and warranted that the fuel tank was one-half full. If the contract is signed October 20 without being effective *as of* October 15, then Sally's representations and warranties should be true as of October 20. However, if this were the case, the representation and warranty with respect to the fuel tank would possibly not be true as of October 20. Fuel may have been used or the tank refilled.

To keep the representation and warranty accurate, the parties could date the contract *as of* the date of their agreement, October 15. However, this is assuming that all representations and warranties are as of that same date. A better strategy would be to date the contract October 20 and update the representations and warranties because that would keep the contract clear and simple. Or, to avoid the parties going to the effort of verifying and updating their representations and warranties five days after they provided that information, they could draft this particular representation and warranty as, "The tank is one-half full as of October 15."

An *as of* date can raise a similar issue with respect to covenants. Specifically, when an *as of* date is used, the parties want the covenants to take effect as of that date rather than on the date when the parties sign the contract. Otherwise, a party could do as they pleased from the agreement date (the *as of* date) until the signing date. So, for example, if Bob and Sally agree that their contract is dated as of October 15, and Sally may drive the car no more than 100 miles before the closing, that covenant must limit Sally's driving beginning on October 15. If, instead, they sign the agreement October 20 without stating that it is *dated as of* October 15, Sally can drive as much as she wants from October 15 to October 20 without breaching her covenant.

When drafting a contract with an *as of* date in the preamble, you should also indicate its actual signing date somewhere in the contract. This might be important for different reasons, such as for tax purposes.

Courts have concluded that dated signatures can create ambiguity as to the contract's effective date.[4] However, many drafters will put a date line under each

---

1. *See Brewer v. Nat'l Sur. Corp.*, 169 F.2d 926, 928 (10th Cir. 1948).
2. *See United States v. Bourgeois*, 950 F.2d 980, 982-983 (5th Cir. 1992).
3. *See* Chapter 3 on page 14.
4. *Am. Cyanamid Co. v. Ring*, 286 S.E.2d 1, 2-3 (Ga. 1982); *Sweetman v. Strescon Indus., Inc.*, 389 A.2d 1319, 1322 (Del. Super. 1978).

signature. This approach is not recommended unless the effective date of the contract is explicitly tied to the date that the last party signs the contract.[5] We recommend a different approach, as explained below in Example 1:

Examples 1—Step-by-Step for Drafting "As Of" Date

Step A — State the "as of" date in the preamble:

Settlement Agreement, dated as of January 5, 20__, between Cartoon Characters LLC, a Pennsylvania limited liability company ("**Cartoon**"), and Specialty Manufacturing, Inc., a Texas corporation ("**Specialty**").

and

Step B — Include effective date provision in the action sections:

Effective Date. The parties executed and delivered this Agreement on February 27, 20__, but this Agreement is effective as of the date stated in the preamble.

and

Step C — State effective date in the concluding paragraph:

To evidence the parties' agreement to this Agreement, the parties have executed and delivered this Agreement *as of the date stated in the preamble.*

Another alternative is to state the *as of* date in the preamble and then state both the *as of* date *and* the signing date in the concluding paragraph, as follows:

Examples 2—Step-by-Step for Drafting "As Of" Date

Step A — State the "as of" date in the preamble:

Settlement Agreement, dated as of January 5, 20__, between Cartoon Characters LLC, a Pennsylvania limited liability company ("**Cartoon**"), and Specialty Manufacturing, Inc., a Texas corporation ("**Specialty**").

and

Step B — State both the "as of" date and the effective date in the concluding language:

To evidence the parties' agreement to this Agreement, the parties have executed and delivered this Agreement *on February 27, 20__, but this Agreement is effective as of the date stated in the preamble.*

Both examples make the intent of the parties clear, which is important, especially if a court ends up reviewing the contract and needs to know the intent of the parties. However, we recommend Example 1 above because of the explicit action section provision—a provision within the body of the contract—as opposed to only including the date in the concluding paragraph.

If the parties decide that they want the agreement to be effective on the date that the last party signs, omit the date from the preamble and include an effective date provision in the action sections that states what factor determines the effective date. In addition, conform the concluding language to reflect this change.

---

5. *See* Chapter 19 on page 298.

If you include a line for the date in the preamble but leave it blank until the date is known, what happens if the date is never inserted or the wrong date is inserted? Better to fill that date in, even if it is right before you sign the agreement.

Some drafters put the effective date provision in the counterparts provision, which is in the general provisions article, but that makes it harder to find. It works, but the action sections and elsewhere in the contract are a better option.

Here is an example of the suggested provisions and signature line that a drafter can use if the agreement's effective date is the date that the last party signs the agreement.

Example—Contract Takes Effect When Last Party Signs the Agreement

[*Preamble*] Settlement Agreement between Cartoon Characters LLC, a Pennsylvania limited liability company ("**Cartoon**"), and Specialty Manufacturing, Inc., a Texas corporation ("**Specialty**").

and

[*Action Sections*] Section 2.1. Effective Date. This Agreement is effective on the date that the last party executes and delivers this Agreement as indicated by the date stated under that party's signature line.

and

[*Concluding Paragraph*] To evidence the parties' agreement to this Agreement, each party has executed and delivered it on the date stated under that party's name, with this Agreement being effective on the date stated in Section 2.1.

and

[*Signature Lines*]
Cartoon Characters LLC
By: _____
    Ann Chin,
    Supervisory Manager
Dated: _____

Special Manufacturing, Inc.
By: _____
    Joseph Garcia,
    Director of Advertising
Dated: _____

In the preamble, do not use a date in the future. If parties want provisions to be effective beginning on a future date, use the signing date in the preamble and include an effective date provision in the action sections. This results in the contract being enforceable on the signing date stated in the preamble but postpones the enforceability of other provisions until the effective date.

Example—Signing Date and Different Effective Date for Action in Future

Effective Date. This Agreement's provisions other than this Section and [*list provisions that should be enforceable on the signing date*] are effective on the third day after the Contractor receives all municipal approvals. This Section and [*the previously listed provisions*] are effective on the date stated in the preamble.

Whether an agreement is dated based on the agreement date or the signing date, drafting the date is straightforward. Separate the date with two commas. Some drafters omit the set of commas, but the better practice is to include them.

Examples—Dates and Commas

1 — Date with Two Commas Before and After the Date Preferred:
..., dated January 6, 20__, ... (signing date)

or

..., dated as of January 1, 20__, ... (*as of* date)

2 — Date with No Commas Before or After the Date Less Preferred:
... dated January 6, 20__ ... (signing date)

or

... dated as of January 1, 20__ ... (*as of* date)

C. PARTIES

After the name of the agreement and the date, the preamble states who the parties are.

Example—Preamble with Parties

This Settlement Agreement, dated as of January 10, 20__, is between Cartoon Characters LLC, a Pennsylvania limited liability company (**"Cartoon"**), and Specialty Manufacturing, Inc., a Texas corporation (**"Specialty"**).

Although some drafters precede the first party's name with *by and between,* the words *by and* are usually unnecessary, so you should omit them.[6]

Some lawyers use *between* if a contract has two parties and *among* if it has three or more. However, *between* is correct whenever two or more parties are in a direct, reciprocal relationship with each other. In contrast, *among* should be used to express a less direct relationship within a group.[7] Using *between* or *among* in the preamble does not affect a contract's substance.[8] Therefore, do not waste negotiating capital on this point.

1. Identifying the Parties

When drafting the preamble, take the time to be sure that you properly identify the parties. Using the wrong name may bind the wrong parties and may even start litigation to determine who the correct party to the contract is.

---

6. *By and between* is a relatively recent innovation — probably early twentieth century, perhaps late nineteenth century. Before then, indentures and other documents used only *between* when stating the parties.

7. *The Oxford English Dictionary* 154-155 (2d ed. 1989); *see also* H. W. Fowler, *A Dictionary of Modern English Usage* 57 (Sir Ernest Gowers ed., 2d ed. 1965).

8. However, the terms *between* and *among* can have different meanings in a contract's substantive provisions outside of this preamble context, so make sure that you understand when each should be used.

If the party is an individual, confirm that you have that person's full legal name, not a shortened version. Some drafters put the parties' names in all capital letters, which is not necessary but a matter of preference.

> ***Drafting Tip:*** Draft the preamble and signature lines at the same time, so you focus on the parties' names in both of these critical places. Include the same information in both places, and make sure that the parties' names are included correctly in both places.

To ascertain an entity's name, check their organizational document—for example, a corporation's certificate of incorporation. That will give you the entity's legal name, including such details as whether a comma precedes *Inc.*

After an entity's name, state what type of entity they are and their jurisdiction of organization, which together are known as their **organizational identity**. Some drafters omit this information, believing it to be inappropriate in a preamble. That may be correct in the context of consumer agreements being drafted in plain English. However, in the context of sophisticated parties entering into a complex commercial agreement, it may be important to include this information here so it's readily available.

Specifically, the jurisdiction of organization may be necessary to identify an entity and to prevent confusion as to which entity is a party to the contract. Although no two entities organized in the same state may have the same name, entities organized in different states may have the same name.

Indeed, some holding companies intentionally give their subsidiaries the same name so that they have the same public persona. For example, ABC Inc., a holding company incorporated in Delaware, may have 49 subsidiaries, each of which is named ABC Inc. and is incorporated in a different state. If the preamble lists ABC Inc. as a party but omits their state of incorporation, a nonparty might not know which ABC Inc. is the party to the agreement. Including an entity's organizational identity avoids any ambiguity.

Here are two examples of an entity's name followed by their organizational identity:

> ### Examples—Identifying a Party
>
> Internet Inc., a Delaware corporation,
>
> Colossal Construction LP, a New York limited partnership,

Note that a comma precedes and follows the organizational identity. Grammar dictates this punctuation because the organizational identity is an **appositive**, which is a word or phrase following a noun that further describes the noun. Note also that neither *corporation* nor *limited partnership* is capitalized. Capitalize these terms only if they are part of an entity's name.

> ### Examples—Capitalization of Entity
>
> ***Incorrect:*** Hong Corporation, a California Corporation,
>
> ***Correct:*** Hong Corporation, a California corporation,

In addition, avoid the old-fashioned, longer version of an entity's organizational identity included below in Example 1. Instead, shorten the appositive as in the previous example and Example 2:

Examples—Entity's Organizational Identity

1—Incorrect, Longer:

Internet Inc., a corporation organized under the laws of the State of Delaware,

2—Correct, Shorter:

Internet Inc., a Delaware corporation,

Including an entity's organizational identity in the preamble is no substitute for including that information in the agreement's representations and warranties. In the representations and warranties, the information becomes part of a substantive provision, giving a party a remedy if the information is incorrect. For example, banks often want this information included as representations and warranties so they know where to file to perfect their security interests in a borrower's assets and they are better protected and can recover damages if anything goes wrong.

Entities sometimes operate through divisions with names that differ from the entity's legal name. A division differs from a subsidiary. A **subsidiary** is a separate legal entity, whereas a division is not. A **division** is merely an organizational tool designed to refer to a group dedicated to a specific purpose. For example, Bushwick Electric Co. might have two divisions: the first, Bushwick Appliances, dedicated to the manufacturing of kitchen appliances; and the second, Bushwick Engines, dedicated to the manufacturing of aircraft engines. As neither Bushwick Appliances nor Bushwick Engines is a legal entity, neither can bind Bushwick Electric Co. Therefore, the divisions should not be listed as parties to the agreement. Instead, the preamble must name Bushwick Electric Co., as should the signature block. If the parties want to refer to the division, the drafter can include that information in the recitals and even give each division a defined term.[9]

When one of the parties is an individual, some drafters state that the party is an individual and give the state where the individual lives:

Example—Individual in Preamble

Maria Rodriguez, an individual residing in Oregon,

This drafting is technically correct because it makes the identifying information parallel to the information about the other party. However, stating that a person is an individual is unnecessary and provides no identifying information. You can omit it. But, if you are a junior team member, you may want to include it in your draft, especially if it is in the precedent that you are using.

If a person's name does not narrow the universe of people to that one person, their address and other information can. The best way to include that information is through the person's representation and warranty as to their name and address. In the past, practitioners have used social security numbers, but it is no longer common practice to use such personal, identifying information in a contract that anyone can see and possibly use without permission. However, in many other countries using the person's individual, government-issued number is required.

Drafters differ on the wisdom of including the parties' addresses in the preamble—especially when a party is an individual. The better practice is to put

---

9. *See* this chapter on page 172 for information about how to create a defined term in recitals.

that information in a representation and warranty, in the notice section, or at the end of the contract. The address should appear either under a party's signature line or in a schedule, but not in the preamble. Omitting the personal address of entities and individuals from the preamble keeps the preamble short and easy to read. It also reduces the likelihood of accidentally including inconsistent addresses.[10]

2. Defined Terms for Parties

We recommend that you create a *defined term* for the parties and include it first in the preamble, which is the usual practice. The defined term should appear in parentheses following the legal name and appropriate identifying information of the party. As in the examples below, the comma should follow, not precede, the defined term in parentheses.

> *Examples—Defined Terms with Comma and Parentheses*
>
> Build Your Dreams, Inc., an Illinois corporation ("**Contractor**"),
>
> April Fernandez, an individual residing in Wisconsin ("**Tenant**"),
>
> Colossal Construction LP, a New York limited partnership ("**Colossal**"),
>
> Samuel William Josephson, an individual residing in Idaho ("**Josephson**"),

Choose a defined term that either relates to the party's role in the transaction or is a shorthand name for the individual or entity. Good shorthand names include an individual's last name and a significant word from an entity's name, as you can see from the examples above. Be careful when choosing a defined term that is role-related, as the term may affect the agreement's interpretation.[11] Capitalize the defined term, bold it, insert quotation marks around it, and then use it capitalized (but in regular font) throughout the agreement to signal that it is a defined term.

Avoid **acronyms** because readers generally find it difficult to remember what the letters stand for. However, if an entity is commonly referred to by an acronym (e.g., IBM), then you may use it.

As a guiding principle in choosing defined terms, ask yourself, "Which will be easier for the audience—names or role-related terms?" If you choose to use role-related terms, avoid using terms like *mortgagor* and *mortgagee* or *lessor* and *lessee*, because only one or two letters distinguish these terms, so drafters can easily include the wrong one. Instead, use the parties' names or other terms that indicate a party's role, such as *bank* and *borrower*, or *landlord* and *tenant*.

When creating defined terms, take into account the number of parties to the agreement. If there are more than two, using role-related defined terms is often a good choice. For example, in a credit agreement, the parties often include the borrower, multiple lending banks, and an agent bank (a bank that acts on behalf of the other banks). In this instance, a reader will probably find it easier to keep track of the parties if the contract uses role-related defined terms.

---

10. *See Gildor v. Optical Solutions, Inc.*, 2006 WL 4782348 at *1-2 (Del. Ch. June 5, 2006).

11. *See In re Taxes, Aiea Dairy, Ltd.*, 380 P.2d 156, 160-161 (Haw. 1963) (finding that the parties' choice of role-related defined terms (*producer* and *distributor*) was evidence that the parties had an agency relationship rather than that of buyer and seller).

Consider whether others will use this agreement as a precedent. If so, role-related terms are preferable, as they will facilitate the drafting of future agreements.

Defined terms for all parties should be parallel. For example, if the first party is *Landlord*, a parallel defined term for the other party would be *Tenant*, but not *Beatrice*. Make sure that you have made a final decision on the defined terms for all parties before you finalize any of them. That way, you know exactly what you will use for each party and will not have to make changes to correct any defined terms in the contract.

Here are some examples of parties' defined terms:

Examples— Parties' Defined Terms

Landlord and Tenant

IBM and General Foods

Josephson and Martinez

If you choose a role-related defined term, you must decide whether the word *the* will precede each and every use of it within the agreement.

Example 1— Defined Term with The

Rent. *The* Tenant shall pay *the* Landlord the Rent no later than the first business day of each month.

Example 2—Defined Term Without The

Rent. *Tenant* shall pay *Landlord* the Rent no later than the first business day of each month.

Both formats are acceptable, although drafters may disagree over which to use. Some drafters omit *the* on the theory that it shortens the agreement. Others reason that the agreement will not be that much longer for including *the* and that its absence is jarring to lay readers. No matter which format you choose, just make sure you use or omit *the* consistently throughout the contract.

If *the* will come before the defined term, insert it *inside* the parentheses, but *before* the open quotation marks. If *the* will *not* precede the defined term, only the defined term should be inside the parentheses.

Examples—Defined Term with or Without the Before Quotation Marks

1—With: (the "**Executive**")

2—Without: ("**Executive**")

Try not to precede the defined term with *hereinafter referred to as*, or anything similar. This is legalese and unnecessary.

> **Examples—Language Before Defined Term**
>
> **Incorrect:** (hereinafter referred to as the "**Executive**")
>
> **Correct:** (the "**Executive**")

Also, do not create two defined terms for a party, such as *IBM* and the *Company*, because that will confuse the reader. Create only one defined term and use only that term to refer to that party throughout the contract.

> **Examples—Creating Only One Defined Term**
>
> *1—Incorrect: Creating Two Defined Terms:*
> ("**IBM**" or the "**Company**")
>
> *2—Correct: Creating Only One Defined Term:*
> ("**IBM**")
>
> *3—Correct: Creating Only One Defined Term:*
> (the "**Company**")

Some drafters do not bold the defined terms in the preamble, but, that is inconsistent with bolding defined terms in a definitions section[12] and in the body of the agreement, when they are first defined within the body of the agreement. As an alternative, some drafters underscore or write defined terms either using all caps or all bold to make a word stand out.

The punctuation at the end of the preamble is a period, regardless of whether you use the sentence or non-sentence format.

The following are examples of complete preambles that use different formatting styles.

> **Examples—Different Ways to Format the Preamble**
>
> *1—With the and Role-Related Names:*
> **This Supply Agreement**, dated October 10, 20__, is between Spikes Inc., a Delaware corporation (the "**Supplier**"), and Bayou Bicycle Manufacturing LP, a Mississippi limited partnership (the "**Purchaser**").
>
> *2—Without the and Role-Related Names:*
> **This Supply Agreement**, dated October 10, 20__, is between Spikes Inc., a Delaware corporation ("**Supplier**"), and Bayou Bicycle Manufacturing LP, a Mississippi limited partnership ("**Purchaser**").
>
> *3—Without the and Real Names:*
> **This Supply Agreement**, dated October 10, 20__, is between Spikes Inc., a Delaware corporation ("**Spikes**"), and Bayou Bicycle Manufacturing LP, a Mississippi limited partnership ("**Bayou**").

---

12. In this book, the author refers to the *definitions section*. Whether the definitions are contained in a section or an article of an agreement, the same rules apply.

4—With the, All Capitalized, and Underlining:

> THIS SUPPLY AGREEMENT, dated October 10, 20__, is between SPIKES INC., a Delaware corporation (the "Supplier"), and BAYOU BICYCLE MANUFACTURING LP, a Mississippi limited partnership (the "Purchaser").

Occasionally, an agreement will have multiple parties in the same role. If so, define each party in the role by name and use an inclusive defined term for all the parties in the same role, as follows in Example 1. As an alternative to listing in the preamble all the parties in the same role, if there are a lot of additional parties, put the information concerning those parties in a schedule and refer to the schedule in the preamble, as in Example 2 below. This last option unclutters the preamble, making it easier to read.

Example 1—Preamble with Multiple Parties in the Same Role Listed in Preamble

> **Shareholders' Agreement**, dated July 18, 20__, between Cuddle Blankets Inc., a Maine corporation (the "**Corporation**"), and Investment Corp., an Ohio corporation ("**Investment**"), Barbara Steckler ("**Steckler**"), Shanice Washington ("**Washington**"), and Andrew Yates ("**Yates**") (Investment, Steckler, Washington, and Yates, individually, a "**Shareholder**" and collectively, the "**Shareholders**").

Example 2—Preamble with Multiple Parties in the Same Role Listed in Schedule

> **Shareholders' Agreement**, dated July 18, 20__, between Cuddle Blankets Inc., a Maine corporation (the "**Corporation**"), and each shareholder listed in **Schedule A**[13] (individually, a "**Shareholder**" and collectively, the "**Shareholders**").

In sophisticated transactions, an entity may play more than one role. For example: A bank may play two roles in a financing transaction: as lender to the borrower and as the agent for the group of banks lending to the borrower.[14] In that event, the preamble must include defined terms that indicate each role that the entity plays.

Example—Preamble with Entity with More than One Role

> New York Bank, a New York banking corporation, as a lender (in that capacity, a "**Lender**")[15] and as administrative agent (in that capacity, the "**Administrative Agent**") . . .

---

13. Many drafters bold references to Schedules and Exhibits, especially the first time they are used. This makes it easier for the reader to determine what other documents need to be read, and easier for the drafter when collating the full agreement.

14. Multiple banks often act together as lenders to one borrower to spread the credit risk.

15. When a credit agreement has multiple lenders, the preamble may not separately list each lender and define it. Instead, the preamble may use the defined term *Lenders* and include a cross-reference to a schedule or the definitions section. In that event, individual banks will be listed in the preamble to the extent they play a secondary role.

Along with using a defined term for each party, some practitioners choose to include the additional defined term *Parties* to be able to refer to the parties collectively in certain provisions of the contract. However, some drafters believe that you do not need this additional defined term and, instead, prefer to use the term *parties* and leave it undefined because *parties* is enough to refer to the parties to the agreement.[16] Also, some drafters think that *signatories* is the better choice if the drafter intends to refer only to those signing the agreement and not to third-party beneficiaries[17] or successors and assigns. *Signatories* explicitly states what the drafter intends, and for this reason, it may seem more clear. The key is to think through whom you are including in whatever defined term you are putting together and to be specific, clear, and consistent with your defined terms and definitions.

D. DEFINING THE AGREEMENT

You may define the agreement being drafted either in the preamble or in the definitions section:

> ### Examples—Definitions of Agreement in Preamble
>
> *In Preamble, Option 1:*
> **Shareholders' Agreement** (this "**Agreement**"), dated as of July 18, 20__, between Cuddle Blankets Inc., a Maine corporation (the "**Corporation**"), and each shareholder listed in **Schedule A** (individually, a "**Shareholder**" and collectively, the "**Shareholders**").
>
> *In Preamble, Option 2:*
> **Shareholders' Agreement** (including all schedules, exhibits, and amendments, this "**Agreement**"), dated as of July 18, 20__, between Cuddle Blankets Inc., a Maine corporation (the "**Corporation**"), and each shareholder listed in **Schedule A** (individually, a "**Shareholder**" and collectively, the "**Shareholders**").
>
> *In Definitions Section:*
> "**Agreement**" means this Shareholders' Agreement and all Schedules and Exhibits, as any one or more is amended from time to time.

Some drafters prefer to define the agreement in the definitions section because it shortens the preamble, especially if the definition includes schedules, exhibits, and amendments. They will do this even if they use the defined term *Agreement* in the recitals or the words of agreement. Although this violates traditional rules relating to the use of defined terms, it is customary and acceptable in the legal community.

If an agreement does not have a definitions section, define the agreement in the preamble. To preclude any dispute as to whether they are part of the agreement, include the schedules and exhibits in the defined term.[18] Also, you will probably want to include a reference to any amendments in the definition of *Agreement*.

---

16. One instance when it might be useful to define *parties* is if there is a state law or regulation that governs the contract addresses the meaning of the word *parties* or a similar term, as can be the case in Nebraska. *See Properties Investment Group v. Applied Communications Inc.*, 495 N.W.2d 483, 489-490 (Neb. 1993) (holding that *party* refers to nonsignatories).

17. *See Props. Inv. Group of Mid-Am. v. Applied Commun. Inc.*, 495 N.W.2d 483 (Neb. 1993) (finding that *parties* included third-party beneficiaries); *see also Bush v. Brunswick Corp.*, 783 S.W.2d 724 (Tex. App. 1990) (finding that *person* included shareholders who were not signatory to a merger agreement).

18. *See* Chapter 20 on page 311.

IV. RECITALS OR BACKGROUND

A. OVERVIEW

As we discussed in Chapter 13 on page 137, the recitals or background section follows the preamble. It describes the setting, what has led up to the contract being drafted, and the purpose of the contract. From this point on in this book, we will mostly use the term *recitals*, but both *recitals* or *background* are acceptable.

Here is an example of the recitals in an escrow agreement, along with the title, preamble, and words of agreement:

> *Example— Title, Preamble, Recitals, and Words of Agreement*

Escrow Agreement

This Escrow Agreement (this **"Escrow Agreement"**), dated July 1, 20__, is between Pretty Pearls, Inc., a Delaware corporation (**"Pearls"**), Bijoux Extraordinaires Co., a New York corporation (**"Bijoux"**), and Big Bank Corp., a New York banking corporation, as escrow agent (the **"Escrow Agent"**).

Recitals

1. Each of Bijoux and Pearls is a general partner in Gems & Jewels, a New York general partnership (the "**Partnership**").
2. Bijoux and Pearls have decided to dissolve the Partnership and have memorialized their decision in the Dissolution Agreement, dated the date of this Agreement (the "**Dissolution Agreement**").
3. In accordance with the Dissolution Agreement,

   (a) Bijoux has executed and delivered to Pearls a certificate, dated the date of this Agreement and attached as **Exhibit A** (the "**Warranty Certificate**"), in which Bijoux makes representations and warranties with respect to specific matters; and

   (b) Bijoux and Pearls have agreed that the Partnership will deposit with the Escrow Agent into the Escrow Account (as defined in Section 2(f)) $250,000 that the Partnership would otherwise pay to Bijoux as a distribution in respect of Bijoux's general partnership interest in the Partnership.

Accordingly, the parties agree as follows:

If this escrow agreement had no recitals, its title would give information as to the agreement's *general* purpose, but not its *specific* purpose. By using recitals, the drafter explains to the reader both the parties' relationship and *why* they have entered into the escrow agreement.

Recitals are particularly useful if the parties want to inform interested third parties about an agreement's purpose.[19] For example, a potential buyer of a company

---

19. *See Ohio Valley Gas, Inc. v. Blackburn*, 445 N.E.2d 1378, 1383 (Ind. App. 4th Dist. 1983).

could be an interested third party because a potential buyer would need to review all of the company's contracts to better understand that company, assess any risks, and determine how to move forward with that company. Recitals are especially helpful when someone is reviewing a lot of documents for a transaction, such as when such a potential buyer is reviewing all of a company's contracts, because the recitals, if drafted correctly, provide a quick summary of the purpose of each document.

Drafters also use recitals to support a contract term that might otherwise be unenforceable. For example, the recitals in a noncompetition agreement may inform the reader that the noncompetition agreement is part of a larger transaction: the sale of a business. That information could tip the balance in favor of enforceability of a more stricter than usual, specific clause in that agreement (because courts are more likely to enforce restraints on a person's ability to work if they arise in the context of an acquisition).[20] Therefore, by including the provision in the recitals, a drafter can explain more of the facts, giving the court a basis on which to ground its decision and enforce the more specific clause.

The recitals are often used by drafters to state explicitly the parties' intent, especially because the courts use the recitals to better understand what the parties intended. Courts often have to look into the intent of the parties when interpreting ambiguous provisions.[21]

Drafters may also use recitals to identify a contract's **consideration**,[22] which is an important element when forming a contract and is what each party is promising to provide in a contract. For example, when a party guarantees another person's debt, the return consideration to the guarantor may not be immediately apparent. In this case, the drafter should specify the consideration in the recitals to dispel any notion that there is only consideration from one party to the other and ensure that both parties are giving and gaining something from the contract.[23] For example:

> *Example—Title, Preamble, Recitals, and Words of Agreement Regarding Consideration*

Guaranty

This Guaranty, dated March 18, 20__, by Handicrafts Corp., a Missouri corporation (the "Guarantor"), in favor of Big Bank Corp., a Missouri banking corporation (the "Lender").

Background

1. Baskets Inc., a Missouri corporation (the "**Borrower**"), and the Lender have entered into a loan agreement, dated March 18, 20__ (the "**Loan Agreement**"), under which the Lender will make loans to the Borrower.

---

continued on next page >

---

20. *See Purchasing Assocs., Inc. v. Weitz*, 196 N.E.2d 245, 247 (N.Y. 1963).
21. *Wood v. Lucy, Lady Duff-Gordon*, 118 N.E. 214 (N.Y. 1917).
22. Consideration is "[s]omething (such as an act, a forbearance, or a return promise) bargained for and received by a promisor from a promisee; that which motivates a person to do something, esp. to engage in a legal act. Consideration, or a substitute such as promissory estoppel, is necessary for an agreement to be enforceable." *Consideration, Black's Law Dictionary* (11th ed. 2019).
23. *See State v. Larsen*, 515 N.W.2d 178, 180-181 (N.D. 1994).

2. The Guarantor owns all of the issued and outstanding shares of the Borrower.
3. The Guarantor and the Borrower are engaged in related businesses, and the Guarantor will derive substantial direct and indirect benefit from the Lender's loans to the Borrower.
4. The Loan Agreement requires as a condition to the making of any loans by the Lender that the Guarantor guarantee the Borrower's obligations under the Loan Agreement.

In consideration of the Lender making loans to the Borrower, the Guarantor agrees as follows:

Recitals are part of a contract in that they are included in the document that is the contract, but they are generally not part of the contract that binds the parties.[24] Therefore, recitals normally do not create enforceable provisions of a contract (like a covenant in another part of the agreement).

It is generally not a good idea to incorporate the recitals to the contract. However, some courts have held that a specific recital provides evidence of the material facts stated.[25] In addition, statutes sometimes apply, making the recitals prima facie or conclusive evidence of the facts stated.[26]

If the parties want to incorporate the recitals into the contract, the parties need to explicitly state that the recitals are enforceable provisions.[27] For example, a drafter may include that the recitals are incorporated to the agreement as if set forth in the body of the agreement and that the recitals constitute material and operative provisions in the agreement.

If the recitals are incorporated into the agreement by reference, they can easily create ambiguity: Who made the representation and warranty? Who made the covenant? Was the incorporated language intended as a covenant or condition? As noted, recitals can be problematic because a court may deem them to be conclusive evidence of the facts stated. Therefore, if you do incorporate the recitals to an agreement, be careful and make sure that the recitals are consistent with the other provisions in the agreement. If the recitals conflict with another provision in the agreement, the following rules of interpretation will usually govern:

> If the recitals are clear and the operative part is ambiguous, the recitals govern the construction. If the recitals are ambiguous and the operative part is clear, the operative part must prevail. If both the recitals and the operative part are clear, but they are inconsistent with each other, the operative part is to be preferred.[28]

Thus, in almost all cases, do not put representations and warranties, covenants, or conditions in the recitals because they probably will not be enforceable. If the

---

24. *See Williams v. Barkley*, 58 N.E. 765, 767 (N.Y. 1900) ("The promise is what the parties agreed to do, and hence is the operative part of the instrument, while the recital states what led up to the promise and gives the inducement for making it"); *see also, e.g., Fugate v. Town of Payson*, 791 P.2d 1092, 1094 (Ariz. App. 1990) ("A recital . . . is not strictly part of the contract.").

25. *Det. Grand Park Corp. v. Turner*, 25 N.W.2d 184, 188-189 (Mich. 1946) ("[P]articular recitals in a contract involving a statement of fact are as a rule to be treated as conclusive evidence of the fact stated, while general recitals may not be."); *see Union Pac. Resources Co. v. Texaco, Inc.*, 882 P.2d 212, 222 (Wyo. 1994).

26. *See Rosenberg v. Smidt*, 727 P.2d 778 (Alaska 1986) (finding recital of compliance with notice requirements to be "'conclusive evidence of compliance.'") (quoting Alaska Stat. Ann. § 34.20.090(c) (1957)).

27. *See In re Taxes, Aiea Dairy Ltd.*, 380 P.2d 156, 163 (Haw. 1963).

28. *Jamison v. Franklin Life Ins. Co.*, 136 P.2d 265, 269 (Ariz. 1943), quoting *Williams v. Barkley*, 58 N.E. 765, 767 (N.Y. 1900), quoting English case law (citations omitted).

following recital were added to the recitals already in an Escrow Agreement (like the one on page 168), a court would probably not enforce what is actually a condition to an obligation.[29]

Example—Incorrect: Recital with Condition to an Obligation

   5. **Release of Funds**. The Escrow Agent shall release funds to Bijoux only if

   (a) Pearls delivers a certificate to the Escrow Agent stating that the Warranty Certificate has no misrepresentations or breaches of warranties; or

   (b) Pearls and Bijoux deliver a certificate to the Escrow Agent stating the amount that the Escrow Agent should release to Bijoux.

Try not to draft the recitals as identical, short, reciprocal statements of the parties. Try a simpler sentence, like the one below, for each party. However, if the Example 2 recital were the only one in the employment agreement, it would be unnecessary, as the title of the agreement would convey the necessary information. The parties would probably want to add more information to the recitals with the specific intent of each party in such an agreement, especially if it were for a unique or important position.

Examples—Recitals Not as Reciprocal Statements

1—Incorrect: Recital as Reciprocal Statement:
   The Company desires to employ the Executive, and the Executive desires to work for the Company.

2—Correct Recital as Simpler Sentence But Needs More Information:
   This Agreement provides for the Company's employment of the Executive.

B. GUIDELINES FOR DRAFTING THE RECITALS

   1. **Do not overuse recitals.** Use them only if they add clarity or specificity to the agreement. Lawyers have a history of writing unnecessarily long and complicated recitals. The practice began in England hundreds of years ago when clients paid their lawyers based on the length of the document.[30]

   2. **Determine the content of the recitals by their purpose.** As with the drafting of anything else, you must determine what you want to accomplish before you write. Consider who the audience is. It may include not only the parties and their lawyers, but perhaps also the parties' shareholders, financial analysts, a judge, and the judge's clerk. For example, some bank loan agreements no longer include recitals because after reading the agreement's title, no one needs to know much more about the background of the agreement. However, if the audience will be wider and the transaction

---

   29. Of course, if the operative provisions of the contract restate or incorporate what is in the recitals, those provisions are enforceable.

   30. David Mellinkoff, *The Language of the Law* 190-191 (Little, Brown & Co. 1963).

is not straightforward, the recitals should be thorough enough to explain the contract's background and the parties' intent.

3. **If the agreement includes recitals, they should tell a story.** They should include a narrative that explains the parties' relationship and the reason for the agreement.

4. **If the background surrounding the agreement is complicated, consider stating the facts in chronological order.** Chronology can often be a helpful organizing principle.

5. **When stating facts in the recitals that relate to the parties' past relationship, make sure that they are accurate.** If they are wrong, they might damage your client's case in a litigation. Courts have held recitals to be conclusive evidence of the material facts stated.[31] Recitals that include more detailed information, rather than recitals with more general information, are more likely to be deemed conclusive evidence of the facts stated.[32]

6. **Do not put operative provisions in the recitals.** Representations and warranties, covenants, and conditions all belong in the *body* of the agreement, *not* in the recital, and *after* the words of agreement. A court probably will not enforce operative provisions that are in the recitals.

7. **Generally, do not put information concerning the purchase price or consideration in the recitals.** But if the consideration's adequacy is unclear, then use the recitals to explain what the consideration is and why it is adequate. For example, look at the recitals for the Guaranty set out earlier in this section. In addition, use recitals to further support a contract term that might otherwise be unenforceable (e.g., a noncompete clause).

8. **Do not incorporate the recitals into the body of the agreement.** It is generally not a good idea to incorporate the recitals into the contract. If the parties want to incorporate the recitals into the contract, the parties need to state explicitly that the recitals are enforceable provisions and must make sure that the recitals are consistent with the other provisions in the agreement.

9. **Draft recitals in a contemporary language and format.**
   (a) Do not introduce recitals with the archaic *Witnesseth*. Instead, either proceed directly from the preamble to the recitals or indicate that the recitals follow by using either the word *Recitals* or *Background*.
   (b) Do not precede each recital with *Whereas*. As with *Witnesseth*, it is outdated. Instead, write one or more well-drafted paragraphs or a series of numbered sentences. Which option to use depends on which format will facilitate the reading of the recitals.

10. **Avoid drafting the recitals as reciprocal statements of the parties.** Include a simple sentence for each of the parties with the specific intent of each party, especially if there are unique or important circumstances.

11. **If you define a term in the recitals, bold the defined term inside quotation marks surrounded by parentheses and precede the defined term with the word *the* if you are doing so for other such terms in the agreement.**

---

31. *See Union Pac. Resources Co. v. Texaco, Inc.*, *supra* n. 25.
32. *See Det. Grand Park Corp. v. Turner*, *supra* n. 25, at 188.

> *Examples—How to Draft Defined Term in Recitals*
>
> (the **"Asset Purchase Agreement"**)
>
> (**"Danowski"**)

12. **Avoid using defined terms in the recitals if they are not defined in the preamble or recitals.** Rarely, it is appropriate to use a defined term in the recitals, even though the definition for that term appears in the definitions section. Do this only if the defined term clearly conveys the definition's substance, and if including the definition in the recitals is awkward. Any defined term used without a definition should cross-reference the location of the definition immediately following the defined term's first use. The cross-reference should be inside a set of parentheses.

Look at the recitals in the introductory provisions of the Escrow Agreement at the beginning of this section on page 168. There, in subsection 3(b), the defined term *Escrow Account* is used. But the defined term and the cross-reference make the recitals messier. At this stage of contract review, the reader does not need to know the exact meaning of the term. Using *escrow agreement*, uncapitalized, conveys just as much information without interrupting the flow of the recitals.[33]

As noted earlier, practitioners commonly violate this rule by using the phrase *this Agreement* in the recitals without a cross-reference to the definitions section.

V. WORDS OF AGREEMENT

The **words of agreement** follow the recitals, and, as we discussed in Chapter 13, they state for the record that the parties have agreed to the terms of the contract. Some drafters refer to them as the **statement of consideration** because this is where traditionally lawyers would include the consideration of the parties to each other. Today, in most instances, the specifics of consideration do not have to be included in the words of agreement.

The words of agreement should be as clear and simple as possible, like the following:

> *Examples—Correct Words of Agreement*
>
> *1—Correct with Less Legalese:*
>   Accordingly, the parties agree as follows:
>
> *2—Correct with More Legalese:*
>   Accordingly, in consideration of the mutual promises stated in this Agreement, the parties agree as follows:

You may still find words of agreement that often long-winded and are full of legalese, but do not use these provisions, if possible. For example:

---

33. The recital in the Website Development Agreement located online on the CasebookConnect Resources Page and the Aspen website uses the undefined term *website,* as it provides sufficient information to the reader for the purpose of the recital. *Website* is then defined in Section 1 so that its subsequent use in the agreement conveys the information provided in its related definition.

> *Examples—Words of Agreement with Legalese*
>
> *3*—NOW, THEREFORE, in consideration of the premises[34] and of the mutual agreements and covenants hereinafter set forth, the Owner and the Contractor hereby agree as follows:
>
> *4*—NOW, THEREFORE, in consideration of $10 paid in hand, and other good and valuable consideration the receipt of which is hereby acknowledged, the parties agree as follows:
>
> *5*—NOW, THEREFORE, in consideration of the mutual representations, warranties, covenants, and agreements, and on the terms and conditions hereinafter set forth, the parties hereto do hereby agree as follows:

Look at Examples 2 through 5 above. Each provision has two parts:

- A recitation of the consideration (e.g., "Accordingly, in consideration of the mutual promises stated in this Agreement").
- A statement that the parties agree to the provisions that follow (e.g., "the parties agree as follows:").

The first part relating to consideration is old-fashioned, and, in most states, it no longer serves a legal purpose, which is why Example 1 above does not include that part.

Without going into too much depth, a drafter cannot turn into consideration something that cannot be consideration. As stated by Professor Farnsworth, "[An] employer cannot transform an unenforceable promise to give an employee a gold watch into an enforceable one simply by reciting, 'In consideration of your past service, I promise. . . .'"[35] Therefore, in most instances the recitation of consideration can be taken out of the words of agreement. However, in some states, a recitation of consideration creates a rebuttable presumption of consideration.[36] Although the presumption is rebuttable, litigators tend to appreciate any advantage. In these states, use similar language to the one in Example 2 and check to make sure that it is the appropriate language for your jurisdiction. Also, a general reference to consideration can be helpful, but stating the precise amount can backfire if it is wrong or ambiguous — unless, of course, there is a strategic reason for including it.

If there is room for doubt in your transaction as to whether the consideration is adequate, draft recitals explaining what the consideration is and tailor the words of agreement to reflect the recitals. Drafters do this regularly with guaranties and options where the return consideration for the guaranty and option is unclear.[37] In this situation, it is also helpful for the words of agreement to reflect the actual consideration.

The second part of the words of agreement, where the parties agree to the provisions that follow, evidences the parties' agreement to the contract provisions that follow. This statement can be quite simple as in Example 1.

---

34. *Premises* is not a typographical error. It means that which came before — that is, the information provided in the recitals.

35. E. Allan Farnsworth, *Farnsworth on Contracts* vol. 1, 157 (3d ed. 2004).

36. *See, e.g., Earl v. St. Louis U.*, 875 S.W.2d 234, 237 (Mo. App. 1994); *Finegan v. Prudential Ins. Co.*, 14 N.E.2d 172, 175-176 (Mass. 1938). In some states, statutes provide that a written instrument is presumptive evidence of consideration. *See* Okla. Stat. tit. 15, § 114 (1996); Idaho Code § 29-104. *See also Farnsworth on Contracts, supra* n. 35, vol. 1, 158, and the cases cited therein.

37. *See* Arthur L. Corbin, *Corbin on Contracts* vol. 2, 84-88 (Joseph M. Perillo & Helen Hadjiyannakis Bender eds., rev. ed., West 1995). In some states, it may also be necessary to recite the consideration in land contracts. *See generally* W. W. Allen, *Necessity and Sufficiency of Statement of Consideration in Contract or Memorandum of Sale of Land, Under Statute of Frauds*, 23 A.L.R.2d 164 (1952).

VI. COVER PAGE AND TABLE OF CONTENTS

Long contracts often have a **cover page** and a **table of contents** that precede the agreement, even though they are not traditionally thought of as the introductory provisions of the contract. The cover page typically states the name of the agreement, the date, and the parties, all centered on the page (both horizontally and vertically). The font should be larger than the regular font. If the regular font size is 12 points, 20 points might be appropriate for the cover page.

Example—Cover Page

Revolving Credit Agreement between
Printing and Graphics Inc.
and
Tribeca Banking N.A.
April 10, 20__

The table of contents, discussed further in Chapter 23, page 354, should immediately follow the cover page and list the agreement's articles, sections, schedules, and exhibits and provide page references for each. Most word-processing programs can create a table of contents automatically with relative ease.

VII. EXERCISES

A. EXERCISE 14A: RULES FOR DRAFTING A PREAMBLE

Review this chapter and create a top ten list of rules for drafting a contemporary preamble. Each rule should be no more than one sentence — no run-on sentences or semicolons.

B. EXERCISE 14B: DRAFT THE PREAMBLE

Return to Exercise 13C, and using the facts in that exercise, draft the preamble to the agreement described in that exercise.

C. EXERCISE 14C: CORRECT DRAFTING ERRORS IN INTRODUCTORY PROVISIONS

Mark up the following introductory provisions so that they follow the guidelines in this chapter.

EXCLUSIVE MANUFACTURING AND SUPPLY AGREEMENT

THIS AGREEMENT made as of April 12, 20_4, by and between THE STEIGER DIVISION OF THE JOHNSON GROUP, INC., a Delaware corporation, ("Steiger") and CREATIVE PARTIES GROUP CORP., a Delaware Corporation, ("CPG").

WITNESSETH:

WHEREAS, CPG designs, promotes, distributes, and sells disposable party goods, including the Products (as hereinafter defined); and

WHEREAS, in accordance with a Sales Agreement between the parties, CPG has concurrently herewith sold to Steiger all of CPG's rights in the machinery and equipment that CPG used to manufacture the Products; and

WHEREAS, Steiger and CPG have determined that they will mutually benefit from an exclusive manufacturing and distribution relationship in accordance with which CPG will use Steiger exclusively to manufacture the Products to CPG's specifications and in accordance with which Steiger will manufacture the Products for sale to CPG.

NOW, THEREFORE, for good and valuable consideration, the receipt and sufficiency of which are hereby acknowledged, Steiger and CPG hereby agree as follows:

D. EXERCISE 14D: DRAFT THE INTRODUCTORY PROVISIONS IN AN INDEMNITY AGREEMENT[38]

This exercise has to do with an indemnity agreement, through which one party (the indemnitor or indemnifier) agrees to cover the losses or damages of another party (the indemnitee).

You, Leslie Lawyer, have received the following email message and must do what your client is asking for in the message. Make sure that you correctly draft the preamble. Remember to include clear, succinct, and useful recitals and use contemporary words of agreement.

Memorandum

To: Leslie Lawyer

From: Brad S. Dennison

Subject: Indemnity Agreement

As you know, I am Vice President in charge of sales for Locomotive Transportation, Inc., a New York corporation ("**Locomotive**"). Three months ago, after negotiations with Rapid Trains Corp., a Massachusetts corporation ("**Rapid**"), Locomotive sold Rapid 2,100 30-ton coal cars — everything that we had in stock. About a week later, Anne Winsom (a new sales representative) met with Coal Transportation, Inc., a New Jersey corporation ("**Coal Transportation**"), and signed a contract with Coal Transportation. That contract committed Locomotive to deliver 300 30-ton coal cars within one week. Obviously, we didn't meet that schedule, as we had no more cars in stock. Coal Transportation sued, alleging breach of contract.

Yesterday, I got a call from Sally Milton, President of Rapid. According to Sally, Rapid would love to purchase an additional 300 cars. As we now have at least that number of cars in stock, I want to do this deal. Of course, Rapid has heard about Coal Transportation's suit against us and is afraid Coal Transportation will sue Rapid for tortious interference. After I told Rapid that Locomotive would indemnify Rapid, Sally agreed that Rapid would do the deal. (I'm not worried about the lawsuit. According to David Fein in your Litigation Department, the damages we may have to pay are minimal. Our profit on the deal will more than cover anything we have to pay to Coal Transportation. Apparently, it purchased the cars from another manufacturer at approximately the same price as our contract price.)

Please draft the preamble, recitals, and the words of agreement for the indemnity agreement. I would like to review the draft as soon as possible. Please be sure that the agreement is effective as of today, no matter when we sign it.

B.S.D.

---

38. This exercise is based on *Hocking Valley Ry. Co. v. Barbour*, 192 N.Y.S. 163 (App. Div. 3d Dept. 1920), *aff'd without op.*, 130 N.E. 909 (N.Y. 1921).

E. EXERCISE 14E: DRAFT THE INTRODUCTORY PROVISIONS IN AN ASSIGNMENT AND ASSUMPTION AGREEMENT

This exercise has to do with an assignment and assumption agreement, which is used to transfer obligations and rights from one party (the assignor) to another party (the assignee).

You, D. Fender, have received the following email message and must do what your client is asking for in the message: draft the introductory provisions of an assignment and assumption agreement. You will need to review both the Purchase Offer and the Escrow Agreement that follow the message to properly do what your client needs and complete this exercise. You can find a sample Assignment and Assumption Agreement on the CasebookConnect Resources page and on the Aspen website product page for this book.

Memorandum

To: D. Fender

From: H. Flighty

Date: August 31, 20___

Re: Purchase of Sam Samson's Icarus I-800

Last evening, while sharing a bottle of Chablis with Sam Samson, I finally agreed to buy his jet for $21 million! The Chablis must have been a better vintage than I thought, because I had no intention of agreeing to a price in excess of $15 million. Nonetheless, I signed a Purchase Offer in my capacity as President of Fly-by-Night Aviation, Inc. ("**Aviation**"). A copy of the Purchase Offer is attached. In my current financial situation, I am simply unable to consummate this transaction. It would, of course, be most embarrassing if I had to admit my current financial issues to Sam.

There is a solution.

I know that Sam's archrival, Rob Robertson, has really wanted Sam's Icarus I-800 for years and that Robertson would be willing to purchase the I-800 for a price in excess of $21 million. I'm sure that I can strike a deal with him under which Aviation will

(a)   assign all of their rights in the Purchase Offer to Robertson's holding company, The Robertson Jet Corp., a Delaware corporation ("**Robertson Jet**"); and

(b)   delegate its performance to Robertson Jet, which would assume Aviation's performance under the Purchase Offer and contemporaneously pay Aviation $1,000,000.

I plan to speak to Robertson about this transaction in the next week or so. When I meet with him, I would like to show him at least part of the Assignment and Assumption.

Therefore, please draft the preamble, recitals, and words of agreement for the Assignment and Assumption Agreement and have it ready for my review as soon as possible. Also, be sure to check whether my company can delegate its duty to execute the promissory note. If there's an issue, write me a one-paragraph explanation of the law and how we can deal with the problem.

H.F.

Purchase Offer Attached

Fly-by-Night Aviation, Inc.
987 West 48th Street
New York, NY 10036

Purchase Offer   August 30, 20__2

    Fly-by-Night Aviation, Inc. ("**Buyer**") hereby offers to purchase the Icarus Aerospace Corporation I-800 aircraft, bearing United States Registration No. N765BW and Manufacturer's Serial No. 8181, equipped with two Rolls-Royce engines, Model No. BR710, Serial Numbers 72725 and 72726 (the "**Aircraft**"), from Supersonic Wings Corp. ("**Seller**") for $21 million, subject to the following terms and conditions:

1. Negotiation and execution of a definitive Aircraft Purchase Agreement satisfactory to both parties.
2. $5 million of the purchase price shall be paid by delivery of Buyer's promissory note to Seller. The note will bear interest at 9% per annum and will be due in a single bullet payment on December 31, 20__8.
3. Aircraft to be delivered with title free and clear of all liens and encumbrances of any nature whatsoever.
4. At Closing, Aircraft to have no more than 2,500 hours total flying time, exclusive of any flying time necessary to deliver the Aircraft to the location specified in Paragraph 5.
5. On the Closing Date, the Aircraft must be at Reagan National Airport in Washington, D.C., or such other reasonable and mutually convenient location as Buyer shall designate.
6. Seller to execute a bill of sale and any other documents necessary to convey good title to the Buyer.
7. Maintenance Agreement, dated as of April 3, 20__0, with Greasemonkeys, Inc., to be assigned by Seller to Buyer. Buyer is to assume all liabilities arising on or after the date of closing.
8. Pilot Agreement, between Ace Pilots, Inc. and Seller, dated as of May 12, 20__1, to be assigned to Buyer. Buyer is to assume only those liabilities that arise on or after the closing date.
9. Closing to occur on November 25, 20__2, at the offices of Workhard & Playlittle LLP, 1133 Avenue of the Americas, New York, New York, or on another date to which the parties agree. If the Closing does not occur on or before November 25, 20__2, because of Buyer's fault, Buyer shall pay Seller a $3 million termination fee.

    On acceptance of this offer, Buyer will cause a deposit of $300,000 to be placed in escrow with Harold C. Astor & Associates, Oklahoma City, Oklahoma (HCA). (The escrow deposit will be governed by the terms of the escrow agreement being entered into by the parties and HCA concurrently with the execution of this Purchase Offer. The Escrow Agreement is attached.) The deposit will be used in partial payment of the purchase price. If the Closing does not occur and Buyer is not at fault, then Buyer is entitled to the return of its deposit, including accrued interest.

Very truly yours,
Fly-by-Night Aviation, Inc.
By: _Horatio Flighty_
Horatio Flighty, President

Accepted by:
Supersonic Wings Corp.
By: _Sam Samson_
Sam Samson, President

Escrow Agreement[39]

Escrow Agreement (this "**Escrow Agreement**"), dated August 30, 20_2, is between Supersonic Wings Corp., a Delaware corporation (the "**Seller**"), Fly-by-Night Aviation, Inc., a New York corporation (the "**Buyer**"), and Harold C. Astor & Associates, an Oklahoma partnership, as escrow agent (in that capacity, the "**Escrow Agent**").

Background

The Seller and the Buyer have executed a Purchase Offer dated August 30, 20_2 (the "**Purchase Offer**"), that provides for the Seller's sale to the Buyer of an Icarus Aerospace Corporation I-800 aircraft. Among other things, the Purchase Offer requires the Buyer to deposit $300,000 in escrow with the Escrow Agent. This Escrow Agreement states the terms relating to the escrow.

The Seller, the Buyer, and the Escrow Agent agree as follows:

1. **Escrow Deposit.** Simultaneously with the execution and delivery of this Escrow Agreement, the Buyer shall deliver $300,000 in immediately available funds to the Escrow Agent. The $300,000 delivered to the Escrow Agent, together with all interest that it earns, is referred to as the "Escrow Amount." Immediately on receipt of the Escrow Amount, the Escrow Agent shall invest it in an interest-bearing money market account at the Bank of Oklahoma City. Afterwards, the Escrow Agent shall hold and dispose of the Escrow Amount as provided in this Escrow Agreement.

2. **Payment of the Escrow Amount.** The Escrow Agent shall dispose of the Escrow Amount in one of the following two ways:

   2.1 **In Accordance with Notice of the Seller and Buyer.** The Escrow Agent shall dispose of the Escrow Amount in the manner instructed in accordance with a notice, substantially in the form of Exhibit A, that both the Seller and the Buyer execute and then deliver to the Escrow Agent.

   2.2 **In Accordance with a Court Order.** The Escrow Agent shall dispose of the Escrow Amount when and in the manner that a court of competent jurisdiction instructs in an order that is final and no longer subject to appeal in the opinion of the Escrow Agent's counsel.

3. **Compensation.** The Escrow Agent's fees for its services under this Escrow Agreement are to be determined in accordance with its publicly announced fee schedule as in effect from time to time. The Seller and the Buyer shall each

   3.1 pay 50% of the Escrow Agent's fees for its services under this Escrow Agreement; and

   3.2 reimburse the Escrow Agent for 50% of the Escrow Agent's reasonable out-of-pocket expenses incurred in providing its services under this Escrow Agreement.

4. **Indemnification.**

   4.1 **Indemnity Obligation.** The Seller and the Buyer, jointly and severally, shall indemnify and defend the Escrow Agent against any loss, liability, obligation, claim, damage, or expense (including, without limitation, reasonable attorneys' fees and expenses) arising from or relating to acting under this Escrow Agreement, unless caused by the Escrow Agent's gross negligence or willful misconduct.

   4.2 **Right of Setoff.** Without limiting the Escrow Agent's other rights and remedies against the Seller and the Buyer, the Escrow Agent may satisfy all or part of the Seller and the Buyer's indemnity obligations under subsection 4.1 by setoff against the Escrow Amount. The Escrow Agent shall promptly notify the Seller and the Buyer of any setoff.

---

39. This Escrow Agreement is based, in part, on an escrow agreement drafted by Alan Shaw from Fordham University School of Law.

5. **Escrow Agent's Role.** The Seller and the Buyer acknowledge that the Escrow Agent is acting solely as a stakeholder and that, in this capacity, it is not the Seller's or the Buyer's agent. The Escrow Agent has no obligations under this Escrow Agreement, except as expressly stated in this Escrow Agreement.

6. **Escrow Agent's Liability.**

   6.1 **Gross Negligence and Intentional Misconduct.** The Escrow Agent is not liable for any loss arising because it acted or refrained from acting in connection with the transactions this Escrow Agreement contemplates, except for any loss arising because of its gross negligence or intentional misconduct.

   6.2 **Advice of Counsel.** The Escrow Agent is not liable for any loss arising because it acted or refrained from acting in connection with the transactions this Escrow Agreement contemplates if it relied in good faith on its counsel's advice.

7. **Resignation and Discharge of the Escrow Agent.**

   7.1 **Resignation.** The Escrow Agent may resign from its duties under this Escrow Agreement by notifying the Seller and the Buyer in writing that it is resigning and stating in that notice the effective date of the resignation.

   7.2 **Discharge.** The parties may discharge the Escrow Agent from its duties under this Escrow Agreement by a written agreement that
   (a) the Seller and the Buyer execute;
   (b) is delivered to the Escrow Agent; and
   (c) states the effective date of the discharge.

   7.3 **Successor Escrow Agent.** If the Escrow Agent resigns or is discharged, the Seller and the Buyer shall jointly and promptly appoint a successor escrow agent. If they are unable to agree, then a court of competent jurisdiction is to appoint the successor escrow agent.

8. **General Provisions.**

   8.1 **Assignment and Delegation.** The Escrow Agent shall not assign its rights or delegate its performance under this Escrow Agreement without the other parties' written consent. The Seller and the Buyer may each assign its rights and delegate its performance under this Escrow Agreement. Any assignment or delegation in violation of this Section is void.

   8.2 **Amendments.** The parties may not amend this Escrow Agreement, except by an agreement that all the parties execute.

   8.3 **Merger.** This Escrow Agreement is the final and exclusive expression of the parties in connection with the transactions this Escrow Agreement contemplates.

Fly-by-Night Aviation, Inc.
By: _____
Horatio Flighty, President

Supersonic Wings Corp.
By: _____
Sam Samson, President

Harold C. Astor & Associates,
a general partnership
(in its capacity as Escrow Agent)
By: _____
Harold C. Astor, General Partner

Exhibit A to Escrow Agreement

Harold C. Astor & Associates
1911 Main Street
Oklahoma City, OK 73110

[Insert date]

Ladies and Gentlemen:

We refer to the Escrow Agreement (the "**Escrow Agreement**"), dated August 30, 20_2, between Supersonic Wings Corp., a Delaware corporation (the "**Seller**"), Fly-by-Night Aviation, Inc., a New York corporation (the "**Buyer**"), and Harold C. Astor & Associates, an Oklahoma partnership, as escrow agent (in that capacity, the "**Escrow Agent**").

Each capitalized term used in this letter without definition has the meaning assigned to it in the Escrow Agreement.

By this letter, the Seller and the Buyer instruct the Escrow Agent to wire transfer in immediately available funds to the Seller's bank account or the Buyer's bank account or to both accounts, based on the information in the chart that follows:[40]

	WIRE TRANSFER AMOUNT	**LOCATION AT WHICH THE FUNDS ARE TO BE IMMEDIATELY AVAILABLE**	**ACCOUNT INFORMATION**
Payment to Seller			
Payment to Buyer			

Very truly yours,

Supersonic Wings Corp.
By: _____
   Title: _____

Fly-by-Night Aviation, Inc.
By: _____
   Title: _____

---

40. Note the use of the chart as a better way of organizing information.

CHAPTER FIFTEEN

Definitions and Defined Terms

I. INTRODUCTION

A **defined term** is a word or a few words that are used consistently throughout a contract to indicate an entity, place, or thing, so that you do not have to repeat the entire formal name and all the characteristics that identify and correspond to that entity, place, or thing. A **definition** of a defined term is that entire formal name and all the characteristics that identify and correspond to that entity, place, or thing. In our example of the house purchase, in the preamble, we would identify the parties to the contract. We would use *Seller* as a defined term, and the definition would be Sally's full name. A list of defined terms and their definitions often follow the words of agreement, but you may find some contracts that do not have a separate definitions section with all the defined terms.

A. DEFINITIONS

In contracts, definitions state the meaning of a defined term and reflect the intended meaning of the term as agreed upon by all parties to the contract. But beyond simply providing the drafter's intended definitions for terms in the contract, definitions are a multi-use tool for avoiding the many legal pitfalls that can result from confusion or ambiguity. Drafters use definitions for various purposes, such as:

1. **To Expand or Limit the "Dictionary Meaning" of Words or Phrases.** For example, the dictionary meaning of *lake* is "a considerable inland body of standing water."[1] But in a contract dealing with the bottling of water from a specific lake, the definition of *lake* might limit its meaning to the specific lake from which water is to be taken for bottling.
2. **To Clarify the Meaning of Words or Phrases.** For example, although Monday, Tuesday, Wednesday, Thursday, and Friday are typically thought of as business days, the parties might want to clarify that if a holiday falls on any of those days, that day is not a *Business Day*.
3. **To Resolve the Meaning of Ambiguous Words or Phrases.** The word *dollar* is a classic example. In a contract between two U.S. companies, we

---

1. *Lake, Merriam-Webster's Dictionary*, https://www.merriam-webster.com/dictionary/lake (last visited on November 13, 2022).

would assume *dollar* would refer to U.S. money. But in a contract between a Canadian and a U.S. company, *dollar* would be ambiguous because it could refer to either Canadian or U.S. dollars. A definition would eliminate this ambiguity by specifying the correct currency.

4. **To Explain Technical Words or Phrases.** For example, *Capitalized Lease* has a specific meaning under the accounting rules. To avoid any doubt as to the meaning of this phrase, the parties might want to spell out the specifics of those rules or refer to them in a definition.[2]

5. **To Express a Specific Concept.** For example, in a loan agreement, the bank might want to limit the borrower's investments to those that are liquid; that is, easily convertible into cash.[3] This is a contract-specific concept. To draft the definition for this concept, the parties might list all the permitted investments in a definition.

6. **To List All Things to Which Words or Phrases Refer.** For example, this might specify only one thing, such as the pledge agreement between a bank and their borrower, or it could specify multiple things, such as all the permitted investments.

7. **To Explain the Meaning of Words or Phrases by Listing Their Most Significant Characteristics.** For example, the dictionary defines *computer* as "a programmable electronic device that can store, retrieve, and process data."[4]

8. **To Set Standards that Affect the Parties' Rights and Obligations.** For example, assume that a stockholders' agreement has a defined term *Affiliate,* and that a contract provision prohibits assignments except to Affiliates. In this context, the defined term *Affiliates* is a standard that is integral to the contract's business purpose. Depending on whether the term is defined broadly or narrowly, the brother of the president of a subsidiary might or might not be included within the scope of the definition. Therefore, you must exercise great care when crafting definitions and think through the consequences of each definition the same way that you would if you were crafting a full provision.

B. DEFINED TERMS

Drafters use defined terms as an easy way of saying the same thing the same way every time they say it. Failure to say the same thing the same way is an open invitation to the parties to the agreement, third parties, and the court to construe two provisions differently. Moreover, without defined terms, drafters would have to repeat the full-blown definition each time a concept was needed in a contract. This would make the agreement long and difficult to read. For instance, compare the following two versions of the same provision. The first version does not use a definition for *storage space,* while the second does.

---

2. *See* this chapter, Guideline 15 of *Guidelines for Drafting All Definitions*, on page 196 for a discussion of the issues relating to referring to materials outside the agreement.

3. A bank would want a borrower's investments to be liquid so that the borrower would always have ready access to cash to pay the loan.

4. *Computer, Merriam-Webster's Dictionary*, https://www.merriam-webster.com/dictionary /computer (last visited on November 13, 2022).

Examples—Provision with and Without a Defined Term and Definition

1—Without:

Condition of Storage Space. When the Tenant takes possession of the 2,500 square feet of storage space shown on the drawing attached to this Lease as Exhibit A, that possession is conclusive evidence that the 2,500 square feet of storage space shown on the drawing attached to this Lease as Exhibit A was in the condition that the Tenant and Landlord agreed on.

2—With:

The Definition: "**Storage Space**" means the 2,500 square feet area shaded in blue in the drawing attached to this Lease as Exhibit A.

The Provision: **Condition of Storage Space**. When the Tenant takes possession of the Storage Space, that possession is conclusive evidence that the Storage Space was in the condition that the Tenant and Landlord agreed on.

Now imagine what Example 1 would be like if Tenant and Landlord had not been defined in the preamble!

II. STRATEGIC CONCERNS IN DEFINING TERMS[5]

You should always consider strategy when defining a term, focusing on keeping your client's interests and goals. As we see in the examples that follow, whether your client is the party performing or not performing makes a difference in how you want to write the definition of *Force Majeure Event*. As detailed further in Chapter 18 on page 289, a force majeure provision provides for what the parties should do in case of unforeseen circumstances (such as earthquakes, wars, and pandemics). Look at the following two definitions:[6]

Examples—Two Different Types of Force Majeure Definitions

1—As a List of Criteria for Determining a Force Majeure Event:

"**Force Majeure Event**" means any act or event, whether foreseen or unforeseen, that meets all three of the following tests:

(a) The act or event prevents a party (the "**Nonperforming Party**"), in whole or in part, from either or both of the following:
   (i) Performing any obligation under this Agreement.
   (ii) Satisfying any condition to any obligation of the other party (the "Performing Party") under this Agreement.
(b) The act or event is beyond the reasonable control of, and not the fault of, the Nonperforming Party.
(c) The Nonperforming Party has been unable to avoid or overcome the act or event by the exercise of due diligence.

---

5. This section draws on class materials from Alan Shaw, formerly from Fordham University School of Law.

6. These definitions are from Nancy F. Persechino, *Force Majeure, in Negotiating and Drafting Contract Boilerplate* Ch.11, 201-202 (Stark et al. eds., ALM Publg. 2003).

Examples—As a List of Specific Events:

> **"Force Majeure Event"** means war, flood, lightning, drought, earthquake, fire, volcanic eruption, landslide, hurricane, cyclone, typhoon, tornado, explosion, civil disturbance, act of God or the public enemy, terrorism, military action, epidemic, famine or plague, shipwreck, action of a court or public authority, or strike.

Which of these definitions will better serve your client depends on whether your client is more likely to be the performing party or the nonperforming party. If your client is more likely to be the nonperforming party, Example 1 will be more helpful if an unfortunate event occurs. Because it lists criteria, Example 1 is elastic, permitting a client to argue that almost any event falls within the definition. By contrast, Example 2 provides a nonperforming party with no flexibility. If an event is not listed, it is not a *force majeure event*—and that is exactly why the party most likely to be the performing party would prefer it. The event's absence from the list results in the nonperforming party being in breach, rather than its performance being excused.

The COVID-19 pandemic demonstrates the impact of different *Force Majeure Event* definitions. COVID-19 prevented many parties to contracts from performing their obligations. If *Force Majeure Event* were defined by a list of criteria, as in Example 1, then the pandemic met the contract's criteria for a Force Majeure Event: Nonperformance would be beyond the reasonable control of and not the fault of the supplier, and the supplier would be unable to overcome the obstacles caused by the pandemic through the exercise of due diligence. On the other hand, if Example 2, which lists specific events, were the definition in a supplier's contract and the supplier were the nonperforming party, then the pandemic would not have been considered a Force Majeure Event in contracts where "pandemic" was not explicitly listed in the definition for Force Majeure Event.

III. PLACEMENT OF DEFINITIONS

A. INTRODUCTION

Most business contracts typically have many defined terms. For this reason, those contracts generally include a separate definitions section or article, where all the defined terms used in the agreement are listed together in alphabetical order. This book generally refers to the section containing defined terms and definitions as the *definitions section.* In some agreements, drafters might alternatively use the phrase *definitions article.* Regardless of what we call them, the same rules apply.

Terms in a definitions section either will be defined fully in the definitions sections or there will be a cite in the definitions section to where you can find the definition *in context.* If you include the complete definition in the definitions section, then you can simply use the defined term throughout the agreement without having to restate the definition anywhere else. If you include a cite in the definitions section and define the term *in context*, the definition would be provided only once somewhere in the agreement, preferably where the term first appears.

On the other hand, short or informal agreements with only a few defined terms often do not include a definitions section and instead exclusively provide definitions for defined terms *in context.* In contract drafting, when we talk about defining a term *in context*, we mean that the definition would be provided only once somewhere in the agreement, preferably where the term first appears. In these short or informal agreements, all the defined terms would be defined in context.

B. DEFINITIONS SECTION

Commentators and drafters disagree as to where the definitions section should go in business contracts. Some lawyers advocate for putting the definitions section immediately after the words of agreement, so that the definitions appear in the beginning pages of an agreement. Others believe that the definitions section should appear as the next-to-last section of an agreement, preceding the contract's general provisions, or in a separate appendix or stand-alone document, particularly if there are multiple agreements that rely on the same set of definitions. Finally, some lawyers think that definitions should appear only *in context*, even if the contract is lengthy and sophisticated. Let's look briefly at the pros and cons of each approach.

1. After the Words of Agreement

The most common approach is to put a complete list of defined terms and their definitions in a separate section or article after the words of agreement. This way, terms used throughout the body of an agreement are at the beginning of the contract, making them easier to find and reminding the parties that definitions often contain deal-critical concepts.

Having all the definitions in one place near the front permits the sophisticated practitioner to skim through them to see how the contract treats specific issues. For example, loan agreements often include financial covenants, such as requiring the borrower to maintain a certain ratio of cash flow to their debt obligations. These financial covenants are generally drafted using defined terms, so by reading the definitions, a practitioner can get a preview of the covenants to come.

2. At the End of the Contract

Some drafters prefer to put the definitions in a separate section at the end of the contract, so as not to hinder a reader who wishes to read the action sections first. These drafters also often believe that having the definitions at the end expedites negotiations because the parties will focus first on the substantive provisions rather than on the definitions.

3. In Appendix or Separate Document

Drafters often put definitions in an appendix or separate document for transactions in which multiple agreements rely on the same definitions. For example, a credit agreement, a security agreement, and a pledge agreement all need terms to refer to the debt outstanding, the agent bank, and the maturity of the loan. If the defined terms are not the same in all three agreements, problems inevitably follow. To ensure that the agreements all use the same defined terms with the same definitions, the parties use an appendix, the defined terms of which are properly incorporated into each agreement.

4. In Context

There are those relatively few drafters who prefer not to include a list of definitions in the agreement. Instead, they define each term in the body of the agreement — generally, but not necessarily, the first time it is used. They believe that this format yields at least three benefits: First, readers gain a better understanding of a defined term by seeing its definition in context. Second, readers do not need to page through the contract in search of the definition section to learn the definition of a term. Third, the definitions section no longer obstructs the reader's path to the business provisions of the action sections, which action sections now directly follow the words of agreement.

Note that defining terms in context exclusively can lead to ambiguity and make the definitions hard to find and identify when used in other parts of the agreement. Typically, the defined term is placed immediately after the language that constitutes the definition, even if it is in the middle of a sentence.[7] This placement can lead to disputes as to how much of the preceding or succeeding[8] language is intended to be included in the definition. Look at the following recital, where ambiguity concerning two definitions led to litigation:

> ### Example—Recital with Definitions in Context That Led to Litigation
>
> WHEREAS, Seller possesses technical information and know-how (the **"Technical Information"**) relating to the production and manufacture of food products which look similar to the thin, crispy crust of *French bread* from which the dough has been removed (the **"Products"**). . . .[9]

In the lawsuit over the meaning of *Products,* the plaintiff argued that the definition of *Products* began with the words *food products,* and that *Products* was not limited to Products produced in accordance with the Technical Information being transferred. The defendant, however, asserted that *Products was* limited to those produced in accordance with the Technical Information. Realistically, it is likely that neither party noticed this issue when drafting the recital. It was a subtlety that both sides missed. However, if the parties had been forced to construct a definition for a definitions section, they would have been much more likely to confront the issue as to how much of the language preceding the word *Products* was included in the definition of that defined term.

If you define terms in context, one possible way to reduce the risk of ambiguity is to put the defined term at the end of the sentence and indicate within parentheses the noun or phrase to which the defined term refers. Yet even when this approach works, it is not always the perfect fix. Sometimes too much information needs to be included inside the parentheses. For example, assume that the recital from the litigated case were rewritten as follows:

> ### Example—Recital with Definitions and Parentheses Indicating Noun or Phrase
>
> WHEREAS, Seller possesses technical information and know-how relating to the production and manufacture of food products which look similar to the thin, crispy crust of *French bread* from which the dough has been removed *(the technical information and know-how, the "Technical Information;" the food products manufactured in accordance with the Technical Information, the "Products"). . . .*

Here, the parenthetical is almost as long as the recital. It is cumbersome and interrupts the flow of the contract. A solution would be to write the recital without any definitions and include them in the definitions section. These definitions would

---

7. *Olympus Ins. Co. v. Aon Benfield, Inc.*, 2012 WL 1072334 at *4, No.11-CV-2607 (D. Minn. Mar. 30, 2012).

8. *Id.* (holding that the defined term is not limited by language following it).

9. *G. Golden Assocs. of Oceanside, Inc. v. Arnold Foods Co., Inc.*, 870 F. Supp. 472, 474 (E.D.N.Y. 1994).

remedy any ambiguity in the recitals, particularly because, as mentioned previously, generally the recitals are not part of the contract that binds the parties.

In most business contracts, while you will find a separate definitions section, a number of the defined terms in that definitions section will still be defined *in context* even though they are also included in the list. As explained in this chapter on page 201 in Guideline 2 of *Guidelines for Drafting the Definitions in Context*, the terms defined in context would be listed in the definitions section with the following or similar language: "*has the meaning assigned to it in Section ___*" or "*is defined in Section ___.*"

Even if a contract includes a definitions section, it is appropriate and often essential to define a particular term *in context* in the following three instances:

- When you cannot easily reorder the words of a provision to turn them into an independent definition and defined term.
- When you use a defined term multiple times, but in only one section.
- When you use a defined term in the monetary provisions and the defined term and its definition can be placed in a subsection by themselves. Defining a term dealing with a monetary provision in context may be important, so that the parties have a clear understanding of the monetary provisions. Including the definitions with the monetary provisions facilitates the reading of some of the agreement's more sophisticated financial provisions. Furthermore, by isolating the definition into its own subsection, the risk of ambiguity is reduced.

5. Conclusion

So, what do you do if you are a junior lawyer and the designated drafter? The real-world answer is that you will probably follow the precedent that you are given or the preferred style of the person for whom you are working. Once you are more experienced, you will have a better sense of what you prefer to do in different circumstances.

As we have seen, there are a variety of approaches to using defined terms and definitions in business contracts. It is important to be aware of the different possibilities so you can choose the right approach for the agreement and transaction in question, which may vary.

IV. GUIDELINES FOR DRAFTING DEFINITIONS AND DEFINED TERMS

A. HOW TO APPROACH DRAFTING THE DEFINITIONS

If you use a *precedent* (another contract for the same type of transaction) to draft the agreement, you will begin your draft with some defined terms and definitions that probably work perfectly well—that is one of the benefits of using a precedent. Of course, you can only be sure that no change is required by reviewing each instance in which the defined term is used, comparing it to the already agreed-upon terms of the current transaction and tailoring the definitions in the precedent accordingly. For example, in a contract for the sale of real property, the definition of *Premises* will need to be changed so it refers to the specific property being sold in your business transaction.

Likewise, you will want to add different or additional defined terms to your contract throughout your negotiation because of your particular transaction. Therefore, even if you have the definitions section at the beginning of the agreement, you may not want to spend a lot of time drafting those definitions until after you begin drafting the latter action sections in the agreement. It often helps to start drafting your action section provisions and worry about the concepts before trying to finalize or fine-tune definitions. In the middle of drafting your action sections, you may come to realize which definitions you need and how to best draft them.

Note that there is no magic number of defined terms and definitions. The next section includes guidelines for how to draft all the definitions in the contract, followed by guidelines for how to draft the definitions included in the definitions section and the definitions in the context of the agreement.

B. GUIDELINES FOR DRAFTING ALL DEFINITIONS

Here are our recommended guidelines for drafting all definitions in a contract:

1. **Create and use only one defined term for each definition and only one definition for each defined term.** Then, use the defined terms exclusively throughout the agreement. Confirm that each defined term's definition is appropriate for each specific context in which it is used. Sometimes, during the drafting process, the meaning of a defined term can become inappropriate, requiring a new concept or an additional defined term.

    Before finalizing a defined term and its definition, check every use of it. Sometimes a definition that works perfectly in three provisions does not work in the fourth. Most word-processing applications can search a document for specific words. This automates the task, making it much easier to complete. If you subsequently decide to change a definition, repeat the search to make sure that each provision still makes sense with the new definition. Drafters often make the mistake of leaving an old defined term in an agreement or not capitalizing a word that they intended to use as a defined term.

2. **Create a defined term only if you are going to use it more than once, and use it each time the definition is appropriate.** Before finalizing an agreement, search for each defined term listed in the definitions to confirm that it is used in the agreement more than once. A defined term that seemed necessary in an early draft may have been deleted from the body of the agreement or its use minimized.

    There is the exception that you may use a defined term only once if its use will enhance a provision's readability. Rarely, including a complicated concept in the middle of a provision interferes with a reader's ability to assimilate the provision's meaning. For example, the definition of termination *For Cause* in an employment agreement would be overwhelming in the middle of the termination provision. In this case, using the defined term of *For Cause*, even though it might be used only once, permits the reader to concentrate on the substance of the provision and then turn to the definition for other specific details. In these circumstances, break down the provision into two subsections. Put the defined term and its definition ("**For Cause**" means ____.) in the first subsection and the substantive provision (The Company may terminate the Employee For Cause.) in the second.[10] Some drafters prefer to reverse the order, especially if the substantive provision is short and the definition long. Good craftsmanship requires that the agreement be internally consistent as to format, so pick one format and use it throughout the agreement. Drafters also

---

10. *See* this chapter, Guideline 1 of *Guidelines for Drafting the Definitions in Context*, on page 201 for an example.

use this approach in credit agreements when a formula requires one or more complex accounting concepts.

3. **Use singular nouns as defined terms, if possible.** Avoid defined terms in the plural and those that are not nouns, such as verbs, whenever you can. Also, after you define a noun, always use it as a noun. Do not use the defined term that you defined as a noun as an adjective or verb with other nouns or other defined terms.

4. **Choose as the defined term words that convey information to the reader about the substance of the definition**. Thus, *Residence* would be a good defined term if the definition were *house, townhouse, apartment, cooperative, houseboat*, and *condominium*. The substance of a definition should not include concepts unrelated to the other concepts in a definition. Thus, the definition of *Residence* should not include office towers.

5. **If a definition varies the usual meaning of a word or phrase, choose a defined term that signals the variation.** For example, a good defined term for an electronic book would be *E-book,* not *Book.*

6. **Do not define a term when the ordinary meaning of the word or phrase expresses the concept.** For example, the following definition of *Resume Performance* is not necessary.

Example—Defined Term Not Needed

"**Resume Performance**" means to restart performance after it was suspended because of a *Force Majeure Event.*

Similarly, as explained in Chapter 14 on page 167, a definition of *Parties* is generally unnecessary for many practitioners.

7. **Write a definition as narrowly as possible so that additional information may be included as part of a substantive provision, such as a representation and warranty covenant or a condition to an obligation.** A party may sue on a representation, warranty, a covenant, or a condition to an obligation, but not on a definition on its own. Therefore, make sure that there are no representations, warranties, covenants, and conditions in your definitions. Furthermore, think carefully how your definitions work with your substantive provisions. Here is an example of a definition that could be more narrowly drafted to better work with the representation and warranty:

Example—Incorrect Narrow Definition for Representation and Warranty

Definition: "**Shares**" means the 1,000 issued and outstanding common shares of the Company, par value $1 per share.

Representation and Warranty: **Shares Outstanding**. The Company has 1,000 issued and outstanding Shares [1,000 issued and outstanding common shares of the Company, par value $1 per share], each of which has a par value of $1 per share.

Because the information as to the number of shares and their par value is included in the definition of *Shares,* a representation and warranty as to the number and par value of the Shares presents the same information twice, explicitly and through the use of the definition of *Shares.* You do not need the information included twice, even though some drafters will draft it like this and not be bothered by the circularity created. However, if the number of issued and outstanding shares and the par value are omitted from the definition of *Shares*, then the representation and warranty works as it should.

Example—Correct Narrow Definition for Representations and Warranties

Definition: "**Shares**" means the Company's common shares.

Representation and Warranty: Shares Outstanding. The Company has issued and outstanding 1,000 Shares [the Company's common shares], each of which has a par value of $1 per share.

---

8. **Avoid definitions that apply to more than one person, place, or thing at one time.** For example, the definition of *Contract* in a share purchase agreement is often intended to apply to the Seller, the Buyer, and the Target. The definition in Example 1 below can be overwhelming. A simpler version in Example 2 applies the definition to a *Person*, thereby applying it to only one person at a time but making the definition generally applicable. Therefore, if you have a defined term that applies to various persons, places, or things, think carefully how to best define it.

Example 1—Acceptable: Definition that Applies to More than One Party

"**Contract**" means any contract, lease, arrangement, commitment, or understanding to which the Seller, the Buyer, or the Target is a party or by which the Seller, the Buyer, or the Target or any of their respective properties may be bound or affected.

Example 2—Recommended: Definition That Applies to More Than One Party

"**Contract**" means, with respect to a Person, any contract, lease, agreement, license, arrangement, commitment, or understanding to which that Person is a party or by which that Person or any of its properties is bound or affected.

---

9. **Once a term is defined, do not repeat any part of the definition when using the defined term.** For example, if a contract includes the following definition of *Shares*, then the phrase "of the Company" should not be included when the defined term *Shares* is used in the substantive provisions that follow:

Examples—Definition and Repeating Information

Definition: "**Shares**" means the issued and outstanding common shares of the Company.

1—Incorrect Because Repeating Information:
A shall deliver 500 Shares *of the Company* to B.

1—Correct Because Not Repeating Information:
A shall deliver 500 Shares to B.

2—Incorrect Because Repeating Information:

Purchase Price. The purchase price of the Car is $11,000 (the "**Purchase Price**"). The Buyer shall pay the Purchase Price of $11,000 to the Seller by certified check.

2—Correct Because Not Repeating Information:

Purchase Price. The purchase price of the Car is $11,000 (the "**Purchase Price**"). The Buyer shall pay the Purchase Price to the Seller by certified check.

10. **Do not create a circular definition; that is, do not define a term by using the same term.** For example, see the following:

Examples—Circular Definitions

Incorrect Because Circular:

"**Subsidiary**" means a subsidiary of the Company.

Correct Because Not Circular:

"**Subsidiary**" means any corporation with respect to which the Borrower owns more than 50% of the ***issued*** and outstanding shares.

Despite the general rule, you may include the defined term in the definition *if* the definition is intended to narrow the general meaning of the term so it applies to a specific instance and there is no better substitution. In the following, for example, *song* is used in the definition for the defined term *Song,* but the definition is narrowed down further to specific Beatles songs and there may not really be a better word for *song*:

Example—Correct Because Narrowing Down Definition

"**Song**" means any song that the Beatles recorded and included on any of their albums.

---

11. **If you want to make sure that a definition includes a particular issue or example, follow the defined term and definition with the verb *includes*.**

Example—When to Use "Includes"

"**Breach**" means _____ and includes a cross-default.[11]

Avoid using *includes* as the verb to introduce a definition because it risks creating an over-inclusive definition. However, you may want to use *includes* to signal specific instances. Before finalizing the definition, analyze whether the definition should also exclude any specific matter.[12]

---

11. A **cross-default** is a default that occurs in the subject agreement because of a default in another agreement. For example, a credit agreement may specify that a default under that agreement occurs if a borrower fails to pay when due any material liability under any other agreement.

12. *See* Chapter 27 on page 426 for a discussion of *including* and *including without limitation.*

Some drafters prefer not to use both *means* and *includes* to introduce a definition. They believe when used together, they create an internally inconsistent definition. *Means* signals that the defined term and the definition are equivalents. Logically, therefore, the definition cannot be expanded. In contrast, *includes* signals that the defined term and the definition are not equivalent because the definition is intended to include matters in addition to those specifically enumerated in the definition. Therefore, using *means* and *includes* together to introduce a definition could result in ambiguity if you include items after *includes* that do not fit the definition. Therefore, if you use *means* and *includes,* make sure that anything you list after *includes* fits the definition after *means* too.

12. **To exclude something that would ordinarily be within the contemplation of a defined term, some drafters follow the defined term and definition with *excludes*, as they do with *includes*.** Avoid using *excludes* as the verb to introduce a definition as follows:

Example—Incorrect Use of "Excludes"

"Telephone" excludes a cellular telephone that does not take photographs.

Note that this definition does not state what a telephone is. It relies on the parties' understanding of this everyday term. The preferable alternative would be to define *telephone* and to follow it in that same sentence with the exclusion as follows:

Example—Correct Use of "Excludes"

"Telephone" means an instrument for reproducing sound at a distance,[13] but excludes cellular telephones that do not take photographs.

---

13. **Include a defined term in the definition of another defined term if one definition builds on another definition.** For example, the following definition is from a website-linking agreement under which one company agrees to include in its website a hyperlink to another company's website.[14]

Example—Use of a Defined Term Within the Definition of Another Defined Term

"Company A Users" means users accessing Company B's Website through the Link.

If the definition of *Company A Users* could not include the defined terms *Company B's Website* and *Link,* then, on eliminating the defined term *Company A Users,* the replacement language would be as follows:

---

13. "[A]n instrument for reproducing sound at a distance" is a quotation from *Telephone, Merriam Webster's Dictionary*, https://www.merriam-webster.com/dictionary/telephone (last accessed Nov. 13, 2022).

14. This definition is based on a definition in Gregory Battersby and Charles W. Grimes eds., *License Agreements: Forms and Checklist* 4-27 (2001).

> ***Example—Definition with Full Definitions of Other Defined Terms***
>
> . . . users accessing [definition of *Company B's Website*] through [definition of the *Link*]

Great care would be required to ensure that the definitions were completely and accurately transferred each time the concept of Company A Users was needed. Any deviation would open the door to a claim that the parties intended the deviation to be a substantive change. In addition, integrating the definitions would make the provision lengthier and more difficult to understand. As drafted, the defined terms nicely signal their meaning, permitting a shorter definition.

Including a defined term in another defined term's definition often effectively shortens and simplifies a definition. But drafters can go overboard. They create unnecessarily complicated definitions that force a reader to hunt through the contract to find all the defined terms necessary to understand a defined term's definition. Also, some drafters may include so many other defined terms in a definition in such an awkward way that it can make the definition hard to understand.

If the defined term that is incorporated into the definition is used only in that definition, follow the exception to Guideline 14, which is next.

14. **Do not define a defined term in another term's definition.** If you do, you will frustrate the poor reader who will search for the definition after reading its defined term later in the contract. The reader will look for the defined term and its definition in the alphabetical list of defined terms, but they will not appear in the expected location — they will be buried in another definition. But which one?

> ***Example—Defined Term Defined Within Another Term***
>
> ***Incorrect:*** "**Royalty Period**" means each calendar quarter in the three-year term that begins on January 1, 20_3 and ends on December 31, 20_5 (the "**Term**").
>
> ***Correct:*** "**Royalty Period**" means each calendar quarter in the Term.
>
> *and*
>
> "**Term**" means the three-year period that begins on January 1, 20_3 and ends on December 31, 20_5.

Some drafters will make an exception when it comes to defining a defined term within a definition if that term is used only in that definition. Then they put the definition in a paragraph immediately after the definition, as follows:

> ***Example—Correct Exception of Defined Term Defined Within Another Term***
>
> For the purposes of the preceding definition of [insert the defined term], "**X**" means . . .

If you use this exception, it may be unnecessary to include the defined term in the alphabetical list of defined terms because the reader will have no reason to look for it there. However, you are still encouraged to include it in the definitions list so you have all definitions in one place.

15. **Be careful when defining a legal term by referring to a source outside the contract if the information in that source can be easily restated in the contract.** A reference to an outside source means that the contract does not stand on its own, making it more difficult for a reader to understand the contract's full implications.

Sometimes, however, it is appropriate to define a term by referring to an outside source. For example, a real estate lease may need to refer to various environmental laws. As restating those laws in the contract would be unwieldy, a cross-reference is appropriate. If the outside legal source changes over time, the definition must indicate whether it is referring to the source as it exists on the day of the agreement's signing or as it exists from time to time (i.e., including past and future amendments). This detail is indispensable because unless otherwise stated, a contract incorporates the law as it exists at the time the contract is signed.[15]

Example—Correct Definition Referring to Outside Source

"**CERCLA**" means the federal Comprehensive Environmental Response, Compensation, and Liability Act of 1980, as amended [as of the date of this Agreement] [from time to time].

Drafters regularly use the phrases *as in effect from time to time* and *as amended from time to time.* Neither phrase is controversial nor a regular source of litigation.[16]

16. **Define an agreement, other than the agreement being drafted, by using the information in the preamble of the agreement being defined: the name of that agreement, its date, and the parties.** Some drafters precede the name of the agreement in the definition with the words *that certain.* Those are **pointing words**, and they make the definition no more specific. Omit them.

Examples—Definitions of Another Agreement

1—Incorrect: Using "That Certain":
"**Credit Agreement**" means *that certain* Credit Agreement, dated April 11, 20__, between the Borrower and the Lender, as amended from time to time.

2—Correct:
"**Credit Agreement**" means the Credit Agreement, dated April 11, 20__, between the Borrower and the Lender, as amended from time to time.

The definition should indicate whether references to the agreement are to the agreement's provisions as they exist on the day of that agreement's signing (Example 1 below) or as they may exist from time to time (Example 2 below).

---

15. *See generally,* Williston, *11 Williston on Contracts* § 30:19 (Richard A. Lord ed., 4th ed. 2000).
16. *See* Chapter 27 on page 423.

Examples—Other Agreement Reference to Date and Time

1—"**Credit Agreement**" means the Credit Agreement, dated April 11, 20__, between the Borrower and the Lender as of the date of its signing.

2—"**Credit Agreement**" means the Credit Agreement, dated April 11, 20__, between the Borrower and the Lender, as amended from time to time.

17. **When working with multiple agreements, make sure that you accurately incorporate by reference the separate definitions list or the definitions from other agreements.** For example, pledge agreements and other security agreements often incorporate by reference the credit agreement's definitions. This saves time and paper and ensures that the definitions in the two agreements are exactly the same and remain in sync.

Example—Incorporating Definitions from Another Agreement

Definitions. Each capitalized term used in this Pledge Agreement without definition has the meaning assigned to it in the Credit Agreement.

However, the definitions of the two agreements will fall out of sync if the Pledge Agreement includes a definition of *Credit Agreement* that freezes it as of the date of signing (the previous Example 1) and if the parties subsequently amend the Credit Agreement's definitions. This disconnect could cause conflicting obligations. To ensure that the two agreements always work in tandem, the Pledge Agreement's definition of the Credit Agreement must refer to that agreement *as it exists from time to time* (the previous Example 2).

A different approach may be appropriate, however, when drafting an acquisition agreement. Then, the buyer may want to freeze the provisions of the seller's contracts so that it knows what is being assigned to it. Accomplishing this business goal requires a two-step process. First, the parties must narrowly define the contracts so their definitions exclude future amendments between the signing of the agreement and the closing date. Second, the seller must promise that it will not amend the contracts between the signing of the agreement and the closing date.

Examples—Definitions of Other Agreements

1—Incorrect Definition:

"**Maintenance Agreement**" means the Maintenance Agreement, dated March 13, 20__, between the Seller and ABC Inc., as amended from time to time.

2—Correct Definition and Provision:

"**Maintenance Agreement**" means the Maintenance Agreement, dated March 13, 20__, between the Seller and ABC Inc., as amended to the date of this Agreement.

Amendments to Contracts. The Seller shall not amend the Maintenance Agreement.

C. GUIDELINES FOR DRAFTING THE DEFINITIONS SECTION

Here are our recommended guidelines for drafting the defined terms and definitions in a definitions section or article:

1. **Introduce the definitions and their defined terms with words similar to the following:**

Examples—Introductory Language in Definitions Section

Definitions and Defined Terms. Each term defined in the preamble and the recitals of this Agreement has its assigned meaning. Each defined term that follows has the meaning assigned to it.

If no terms are defined in the recitals, do not refer to the recitals in this introductory language. Many drafters continue to use the term *recitals* although their agreement uses *background* or includes a paragraph in that part of the agreement that is not titled in any way with *recitals, background,* or anything else. Use the correct term or title that preceded the recitals, if any. If no title preceded the recitals, then you can refer to that section as the preceding introductory paragraph, but it is better to have the title of *recitals* or *background* and use that in the definitions section.

2. **List the defined terms alphabetically.** You do not need to include the relevant next subsection number or letter like (a), (b), or (c) before each term, but you may do so. Getting your word-processing program to stop its automatic lettering may not be worth the trouble.

3. **Include all defined terms in the definitions section, other than terms defined in the preamble and the recitals.** The language used to introduce the list of definitions and their defined terms, described in Guideline 1 above, incorporates the terms defined in the preamble and the recitals.

4. **Use capitalization, bold, and quotation marks to make sure that defined terms stand out.** To create a defined term, capitalize the first letter of each word, other than prepositions or other words that would not be capitalized in a title, put the entire defined term in bold, and surround the defined term with unbolded quotation marks.

Examples—Defined Terms Capitalized, in Bold, with Quotation Marks

"**Mechanical Failure**"

"**Notice of Intent to Terminate**"

Modern drafters prefer boldface for the defined terms. Some drafters continue to underline defined terms rather than use boldface, or they both underline and boldface the defined term. In contrast, some drafters who prefer a plain English style omit the quotation marks.

5. **Follow the defined term with the verb *means*.** *Shall mean* and *shall be* are incorrect, even though you will see these in agreements. *Shall* is the language of obligation, and only parties can be obligated to do something.[17] As the defined term is not promising to do anything, *shall* is wrong.

---

17. *See* Chapter 9 on page 74.

...

> ### Examples—Verb for Definition
>
> **1—Incorrect Verb:** "**Mechanical Failure**" shall mean
>
> **2—Correct Verb:** "**Mechanical Failure**" means

However, unfortunately, note that you may run into a lot of precedent that uses the word *shall* in this way in definitions. Also, if the defined term is plural, the verb is still *means*.

6. **When in the body of a contract, signal that a term is defined by capitalizing it in the same way as was done when the term was defined in the definitions section, but use a regular font.**

> ### Example—Defined Term Capitalized and Regular Font in Contract
>
> **(a) Consequences of a Mechanical Failure.** If a Mechanical Failure occurs, the Owner shall . . .

Be careful. Occasionally, a defined term should not be capitalized because the word or phrase is not intended to signal a definition. For example, drafters generally use *Agreement* as the defined term to refer to the parties' contract. Capitalizing *agreement* would be incorrect, however, in the following representation and warranty:

> ### Example—Incorrect Capitalization of Word Because Not a Defined Term
>
> **Agreements. Schedule 4.12** lists each agreement to which the Borrower is a party.

In this instance, *agreement* refers to contracts between the Borrower and one or more third parties, not the contract between the parties.

7. **Do not cross-reference a defined term used in a definition, even if the defined term and its definition are included later in the definitions section because all the defined terms are alphabetized within the definitions section.** Cross-references are unnecessary because the definitions section's introductory language establishes that the definitions section warehouses the contract's definitions. Therefore, the reader knows where to find a definition—in the alphabetical listing of defined terms.

> ### Examples—Cross-Reference in Definition
>
> *Incorrect:* "**Consent**" means any consent of, approval by, authorization of, notice to, designation of, or filing with, any Person (as defined in this Article 1).
>
> *Correct:* "**Consent**" means any consent of, approval by, authorization of, notice to, designation of, or filing with any Person.

This drafting practice differs from that which a drafter should use when the recitals include a defined term that is not defined in the recitals.[18] Then, a cross-reference becomes essential because it tells the reader where to find the definition. The reader might otherwise not know because the recitals precede the definitions section's introductory language that details the section's content. Using a defined term in the recitals without a definition strays from best practices, and a drafter should resort to it only if they have no viable alternative.

8. **Do not include substantive provisions, such as representations and warranties, covenants, and conditions, in a definition in the definitions section.** Their inclusion may create an ambiguity as to the substantive provision's purpose. For example, consider the following definition of Intellectual Property from an agreement of sale:

Example 2—Incorrect Because Includes Substantive Provisions

"**Intellectual Property**" means patents, copyrights, trade secrets, registered trademarks and service marks, trade names, and Internet domain names, *all of which are to be unencumbered as of the Closing Date.*

Are the italicized words a condition to closing, a preclosing covenant, or both? The proper way to draft the definition would be to omit the italicized words from here and then insert them into the appropriate article or articles of the agreement.

Including substantive provisions in a definition increases the likelihood that a reader will miss the provision when reviewing the contract and that it will be interpreted differently by a court. For example, a reader trying to find all of the conditions to closing in an acquisition agreement will look at the conditions article, not the definitions article. If the reader has a wonderful memory, they may remember that a definition had a substantive provision, but that is only if they remember. It is far better to put the substantive provision where it belongs.

Note that when you are defining a term in context, the definition may be in the middle of the representation and warranty, covenant, or condition.

D. GUIDELINES FOR DRAFTING THE DEFINITIONS IN CONTEXT

Here are guidelines for how to draft defined terms and their definitions in the context of the agreement:

1. **Define the term and then put the defined term immediately after the language that constitutes the definition using (a) parentheses, (b) quotation marks, (c) capital letters, and (d) boldface.** The format is straightforward. Follow the rules for defining parties in the preamble. Capitalize the defined term, surround it with quotation marks, put it in bold, and possibly precede it with "the" if it is a noun other than a person's name and that is the style that you are following. As you may remember from Chapter 14 on page 164 relating to the preamble, using "the" before the noun is a stylistic choice. Then, make sure to put parentheses around the defined term, as follows:

---

18. *See* Chapter 14 on page 173 for more information on recitals.

Example 1—Formatting for In-Context Definitions

Post-decree Sale of the House. Lisa and Edward Boswick shall put their house and property at 496 Maple Avenue, Glen Street, Maryland (the "**House**") on the market no later than 30 days after their divorce decree is final.

As discussed earlier in this chapter, the key to defining terms in context is their proper placement. Be sure to look carefully at any sentence that includes a defined term for any possible ambiguities in its definition. For example, in the previous definition, does the defined term include both the house and the property? If the definition could be ambiguous, consider indicating within the parentheses the noun or phrase to which the defined term refers. Also, consider putting the defined term with an explanatory noun or phrase at the end of the sentence.

Example 2—Formatting for In-Context Definitions Clarifying Which Nouns

Post-decree Sale of the House. Lisa and Edward Boswick shall put their house and property at 496 Maple Avenue, Glen Street, Maryland (the house and the property, the "**House**") on the market no later than 30 days after their divorce decree is final.

Alternatively, to resolve any possible ambiguity and be as clear and efficient as possible, carve the section into subsections and put the definition in the first subsection and the substantive provision in the second subsection. Also, use this format if a defined term is used multiple times but used in only one section. Another possible solution is to move such a defined term and definition to the definitions section, if you have one.

Example—Formatting for In-Context Definitions with Sub-sections

Sale of the House.

(a) **Definition.** "House" means the house and property at 496 Maple Avenue, Glen Street, Maryland.

(b) **Post-decree Sale of the House.** Lisa and Edward Boswick shall put the House on the market no later than 30 days after their divorce decree is final.

---

2. **List alphabetically in the definitions section any term defined in context and cross-reference to the section in which the term is defined.** By including the cross-reference, the reader will be able to find the defined term's definition easily. Here are two examples:

Examples—Defined Term in Context as Listed in Definitions Section

1 — "**Rent**" has the meaning assigned to it in Section 2.2.

2 — "**Rent**" is defined in Section 2.2.

Examples 1 and 2 differ only in style. Example 1 parallels the language in the paragraph introducing the defined terms and their definitions. Example 2 is short and accurate. Either works; what is most important is that the style be consistent throughout the definitions section.

V. OTHER PROVISIONS IN THE DEFINITIONS SECTION

In many sophisticated commercial agreements, the definitions section sometimes has a second part. Often entitled *Interpretive Provisions* or *Other Definitional Provisions*, these provisions are of general applicability. The following is typical:

Example—Interpretative Provisions or Other Definitional Provisions

1.2 Interpretive Provisions. Each term defined in this Agreement has its defined meaning when used in any other Deal Document, unless the term is otherwise defined in that Deal Document. In that event, the term has the meaning that the Deal Document assigns it. *(Prevents ambiguity.)*

(a) References to "Sections," "Exhibits," and "Schedules" are to Sections of, and Exhibits and Schedules to, this Agreement, unless otherwise specifically stated. *(Eliminates references to this Agreement after each reference to a Section, Exhibit, or Schedule. In addition, it expressly acknowledges that the Schedules and Exhibits are part of the Agreement, regardless of whether they are attached.)*[19]

(b) The words "including," "includes," and "include" are deemed to be followed by the words "without limitation." *(Prevents ambiguity by deeming all variations of includes to be nonrestrictive.)*

(c) References to a "Person" include that Person's permitted successors and permitted assigns and, in the case of any governmental Person, the Person succeeding to the relevant functions of that governmental Person. *(Prevents ambiguity in changed circumstances.)*

(d) All references to statutes and related regulations include
   (i) any past and future amendments of those statutes and related regulations; and
   (ii) any successor statutes and related regulations.[20]

(e) All references in this Agreement to "Dollars" or "$" refer to lawful currency of the United States of America. *(This subsection is generally needed only in agreements with non-U.S. parties.)*

(f) When "must" is used in this Agreement, it signals a condition. *(Clarifies drafting and prevents ambiguity.)*

---

19. *See* Chapter 20 on page 311 regarding schedules and exhibits.
20. *See* this chapter, Guideline 15 on page 196 regarding being careful when defining a legal term by referring to a source outside the contract if the information in that source can be easily restated in the contract.

VI. EXERCISES

A. EXERCISE 15A: DEFINITION OF MONETARY PROVISIONS IN LICENSING A GREEMENT

The following is a monetary provision from a license agreement. How much of what precedes the defined term is part of the definition?

>   **Royalties.** The royalties for each calendar month are the amount equal to 2% times Net Sales for that calendar month (the "**Monthly Royalties**").

B. EXERCISE 15B: CHOOSING DEFINITIONS

In choosing between the following definitions, what would you consider?

1. **"Breach"** means a misrepresentation, breach of warranty, and breach of covenant.
2. **"Breach"** includes any breach of warranty or covenant.

C. EXERCISE 15C: PURCHASE PRICE DEFINITION

1. Create a defined term and definition to be included in a definitions section for "purchase price" based on the sentence that follows.
2. Create a defined term and definition in context for the sentence that follows.

The purchase price for the House is $250,000.

D. EXERCISE 15D: DEFINITION FOR TERRITORY IN LICENSE AGREEMENT

Return to the facts for the licensing agreement in Exercise 13C on page 148. Define the territory that Merchandisers will have under the license agreement, as you would include it in the definitions section below. To properly do so, review the provisions that follow. They are the provisions that would use the defined term *Territory*. To test whether your definition works, try replacing the defined term with the definition in each of the provisions. Consider whether more than one defined term is necessary.

>   *Definitions:*
>
>   **"Licensed Products"** means caps and t-shirts bearing the Trademark.
>   **"Term"** has the meaning assigned to it in Section 2.1.
>   **"Territory"** . . . . [Include here your definition.] . . .
>   **"Trademark"** means the pictorial representation of the cartoon character Ralph.
>
>   *Subject Matter Performance Provisions:*
>
>   **2.1 Grant of License.** By signing this Agreement, Ralph LP grants Merchandisers an exclusive

license to manufacture and sell Licensed Products during the period beginning January 1, 20__ and ending on December 31, 20__ (the "Term") in the Territory. [*This is only one side of the subject matter performance provision.*]

Representation and Warranty:

3.1 Other Licenses. Ralph LP has not granted any other license with respect to the Territory for the manufacture and sale of Licensed Products.

Covenants:

4.3 No Other Grants. Ralph LP shall not grant any license to any other Person for the manufacture and sale of Licensed Products with respect to the Territory.

4.4 Licenses in Delaware and Rhode Island. Ralph LP shall terminate or cause to terminate any license that Ralph LP has granted with respect to Delaware and Rhode Island no later than the last day of the Term's first year, but only if Merchandisers may manufacture and sell Licensed Products in the Territory during the Term's second and third years.

E. EXERCISE 15E: DEFINITIONS OF FINANCIAL STATEMENTS IN REPRESENTATIONS AND WARRANTIES

1. Draft a defined term and definition for a definitions section for the financial statements described in the following representation and warranty.
2. Mark up the provision so that the financial statements are defined in context.

Financial Statements. The balance sheet of the Company as of December 31, 20_4, and December 31, 20_3, and the related statements of income, cash flows, and shareholders' equity for each of the two years in the period ended December 31, 20_4, reported on by Debit & Credit LLP, independent accountants, present fairly, in all material respects, the financial position of the Company as of December 31, 20_4, and December 31, 20_3, and the results of its operations and its cash flows for each of the two years in the period ended December 31, 20_4, in conformity with accounting principles generally accepted in the United States of America.

F. EXERCISE 15F: EXCLUSIONS FROM FORCE MAJEURE EVENT DEFINITION

Assume that your client wants to exclude industrywide strikes from the definition of *Force Majeure Event.* How would you redraft this provision?

"**Force Majeure Event**" means any act or event that

(a) prevents the affected party, in whole or in part, from

  (i) performing its obligations under this Agreement or

  (ii) satisfying any conditions required by the other party under this Agreement;

(b) is beyond the reasonable control of and not the fault of the affected party; and

(c) the affected party has been unable to avoid or overcome by the exercise of due diligence, including, without limitation: war, flood, lightning, drought, earthquake, fire, volcanic eruption, landslide, cyclone, typhoon, tornado, explosion, civil disturbance, act of God or the public enemy, epidemic, famine or plague, shipwreck, action of a court or public authority, or strike, work-to-rule action, go-slow or similar labor difficulty, each on an industry-wide, region-wide or nationwide basis.[21]

G. EXERCISE 15G: AIRCRAFT PURCHASE AGREEMENT

Please follow the instructions in the e-mail that follows.

---

21. This definition is from Nancy F. Persechino, *Force Majeure, in Negotiating and Drafting Contract Boilerplate* 201-202 (Tina L. Stark et al. eds., ALM Publg. 2003).

Memorandum

To: D. Fender

From: H. Flighty

Date: September 14, 20_2

Re: Purchase of Aircraft

As it is our responsibility to draft the purchase agreement, we need to get moving on it. To save some money and give you a head start, I wrote some of the contract last night. Please take a look at it. I think I did a pretty good job, but if you find any errors, correct them.

Remember that you have the Purchase Offer if you need it. [Note: The Purchase Offer was included in Exercise 14E on page 178.] One other thing: I used an October 30 date in the preamble because that's the date Samson and I want to sign the agreement.

AIRCRAFT PURCHASE AGREEMENT

AGREEMENT, dated October 30, 20__, by and among Supersonic Wings Corp., a Delaware corporation, (the "**Seller**") and Fly-by-Night Aviation, Inc., a New York corporation having its principal place of business at 987 East 48th Street, New York, New York 10036 ("**Buyer**").

WHEREAS, the Seller desires to sell to Buyer, and Buyer desires to purchase from the Seller, the Aircraft; and

WHEREAS, the Buyer hereby agrees to pay the Seller $23,000,000 in immediately available funds.

NOW, THEREFORE, in consideration of the mutual promises herein set forth and subject to the terms and conditions hereof, the parties agree as follows:

Article 1 — Definitions

1.1 Defined Terms. As used in this Agreement, terms defined in the preamble and recitals of this Agreement have the meanings set forth therein, and the following terms have the meanings set forth below:

"**Agreement**" means this Agreement of Sale and all Schedules and Exhibits hereto, as the same may be amended from time to time.

"**Aircraft**" means the Airframe, equipped with two Rolls-Royce engines Model No. MK611-8 bearing Serial Nos. 72725 and 72726, together with all appliances, avionics, furnishings, and other components, equipment, and property incorporated in or otherwise related to the Airframe or engines.

"**Airframe**" means the Icarus Aerospace Corporation I-800 aircraft, bearing United States Registration No. N765BW and Manufacturer's Serial No. 8181.

"**Assigned Contracts**" means the Maintenance Agreement (as hereafter defined) and the Pilot Agreement (as hereafter defined).

"**Assumed Liabilities**" means, collectively, all liabilities and obligations of the Seller that arise under either (a) the Maintenance Agreement on or after the Closing Date or (b) the Pilot Agreement on or after the date of the Closing.

"**Aviation Fuel**" means the gas or liquid that is used to create power to propel the aircraft. At the time of the Seller's delivery of the Aircraft to Buyer, the fuel gauge of the Aircraft shall register as full.

"**Closing**" means the closing of the sale of the Aircraft contemplated by this Agreement in New York, New York on the Closing Date.

"**Closing Date**" has the meaning specified in Section 2.04(a).

"**Consent**" shall mean any consent of, approval of, authorization of, notice to, or designation, registration, declaration or filing with, any Person.

"**Contract**" shall mean any contract, lease, agreement, license, arrangement, commitment or understanding to which the Buyer or any Seller is a party or by which it or any of its properties or assets may be bound or affected.

"**Engines**" means the two Rolls-Royce engines, Model No. BR710, bearing Serial Nos. 72725 and 72726.

"**Laws**" means all federal, state, local or foreign laws, rules and regulations.

"**Lien**" means any lien, charge, encumbrance, security interest, mortgage, or pledge.

"Maintenance Agreement" means that certain Maintenance Agreement, dated as of April 3, 20X0 between Greasemonkeys, Inc., and Seller, as the same may be amended from time to time.

"**Order**": any judgment, award, order, writ, injunction or decree issued by any federal, state, local or foreign authority, court, tribunal, agency, or other governmental authority, or by any arbitrator, to which any Seller or its assets are subject, or to which the Buyer or its assets are subject, as the case may be.

"**Person**" shall mean any individual, partnership, joint venture, corporation, trust, unincorporated organization, government (and any department or agency thereof) or other entity.

"**Pilot Agreement**" means that certain Pilot Agreement between Seller and Ace Pilots, Inc., dated as of May 12, 20_1, as of the date of this Agreement.

CHAPTER SIXTEEN

Action Sections

I. INTRODUCTION

In this book, we use the phrase **action sections** to refer to those parts of the contract that tell the parties how to perform the principal objective of the contract. Bear in mind that *action sections* is not a legal term of art.

The primary components of the *action sections* are

- The provisions in which the parties agree to perform the main subject matter of the contract
- The financial provisions (generally the payment of money)
- The duration of the contract (such as the term, if any)
- The information on the closing, the closing date, and any closing deliveries (if the transaction is an acquisition or financing)
- The other substantive business provisions

II. SUBJECT MATTER PERFORMANCE PROVISION

The first section of the action sections is always the **subject matter performance provision**. In this provision, the parties promise to accomplish a contract's primary objective.

Imagine that a client receives her dream job offer and that her prospective employer asks her to sign an employment agreement. The primary subject matter of that agreement is her employment. The contract will deal with other significant topics, such as salary, duties, and benefits, but the agreement's primary purpose is to obligate the employer to hire your client and to obligate her to work for the employer. These obligations are the promises that comprise the subject matter performance provision. Similarly, if a client decides to write a book, the primary subject matter of the agreement with the client's publisher is the book's publication. So, in this instance, the subject matter performance provision contains the client's agreement to write the book and the publisher's agreement to publish it. In both instances, these provisions are classic consideration: bargained for, reciprocal, executory promises. The following examples show how these provisions might appear in a contract.

Examples—Performance Provision

1—**Employment**. Subject to the provisions of this Agreement, the Company shall hire the Executive, and the Executive shall work for the Company for the Term.

2—**Agreement to Write and Publish**. Subject to the provisions of this Agreement, the Author shall write a book on seals in the Galapagos Islands, and the Publisher shall publish that book.

Note that both provisions include **reciprocal promises** and are introduced with qualifying language: *Subject to the provisions of this Agreement*. The reciprocal promises reflect the mutuality of the transaction. The qualifying language makes explicit that the reciprocal promises must be read in conjunction with the contract's other provisions. For example, the publisher's promise to publish the book may be subject to a condition—for example, the author must have written a summary and detailed outline that the publisher finds acceptable.

Although the subject matter performance provision often takes the form of mirror image reciprocal promises that reflect the flip sides of a transaction—*hire* and *work for, write* and *publish*—this is not always the case. In some agreements, a party's principal promise cannot be reduced to a few words that can easily be put next to the other party's promise. The return promise may be much more elaborate and require multiple provisions. In addition, the structure of the transaction may not allow the mirror image promises. Thus, in a loan agreement, while the bank promises to lend money, the borrower does not promise to borrow it. Instead, it generally has the discretion to borrow on an as-needed basis. The borrower's reciprocal promise would be its promise to repay the principal with interest. Moreover, other provisions may provide consideration. The entire contract is a bargained-for exchange, and the subject matter performance promises play a unique role.

Although the subject matter performance provisions in many contracts are promises, that is not the case for all contracts. In these contracts, rather than a party promising to perform in the future, the party performs when it signs the contract because of the nature of the words in the contract. The words in the subject matter performance provision constitute the performance. These provisions are **self-executing**. Contract promises that are to be performed in the future are often called **executory promises**. With a self-executing provision, a party does not promise performance. Instead, that performance is achieved through the signing of the contract and the words of the provision. Classic examples are guaranties, waivers, releases, options, and grants of security interests.

Examples—Self-Executing Provisions

1—**Guaranty**. By signing this Guaranty,[1] Conglomerate Corp. guarantees to Big Bank the debt of its subsidiary, Oliveira Manufacturing Inc.

2—**Grant of Security Interest**. By signing this Security Agreement, the Borrower grants the Lender a security interest in the Borrower's assets.

3—**Appointment of Escrow Agent**. By signing this Agreement, the parties appoint Vivienne Kim as Escrow Agent.

---

1. Historically, the words *By signing this [Agreement]* were encapsulated in *X hereby. Hereby* is legalese, and therefore, it is not usually a drafter's first choice, even though it gets quickly to the point.

Finally, the subject matter performance provision of a contract need not contain reciprocal promises or be self-executing. Instead, one party might promise to perform, while the other might perform by signing. This is the case with the Website Development Agreement available on the CasebookConnect Resources page and on the Aspen website product page for this book.

III. PAYMENT PROVISIONS

A. INTRODUCTION

The payment provision of a contract sets forth its financial terms, which practitioners often refer to as the **consideration**. In this section, one party promises to pay the other in exchange for whatever that party has promised to do. In a publishing agreement, the publisher promises to pay the author royalties for the book that the author will write, while, in a lease, the tenant promises to pay the landlord rent in exchange for the use of the leased premises.

Money is not the only form of payment that parties use. They can also pay with other things similar to money such as shares, a promissory note, an assignment of rights, an assumption of liabilities, or any other type of exchange to which they agree. For example, parties could agree to a barter exchange in which one party promises to deliver ten bushels of apples in exchange for five bushels of corn. Similarly, Henry can promise to paint Morris's living room in return for Morris's promise to tutor Henry's son. This section will refer to the different forms of payment, when referred to together, as *payment*.

Every payment provision must state the amount of the payment and include a promise to pay it. You can draft the provision as two sentences or sections, one a declaration stating the amount of the payment, and the other a promise to pay it, which would be a covenant. Alternatively, you can combine the statement of the amount and the promise to pay into a single sentence into only a covenant.

Examples—Payment Provisions as One or Two Contract Concepts

1—Declaration and Covenant:

   Rent. The rent is $2,500 per month (the "**Rent**"). With respect to each month of the Lease, the Tenant shall pay the Landlord the Rent no later than the first day of that month. *(Two sentences: the first is a declaration and the second is a covenant.)*

2—Only Covenant:

   Fee. The Owner shall pay the Contractor a $35,000 fee for renovating the House, $10,000 contemporaneously with the signing of this Agreement and $25,000 no later than three days after the Contractor completes the renovation. *(A single sentence, including the amounts to be paid and the obligation to pay them.)*

B. GUIDELINES FOR PAYMENT PROVISIONS

When drafting payment provisions, keep the following guidelines in mind:

1. ***Follow the cash***[2] and make sure that the payment provisions answer the questions of *who* is paying *what* to *whom*, *when*, *why*, and *how*. Make

---

2. The phrase *follow the cash* is the mantra of Donald Schapiro, a former partner at Chadbourne & Parke.

certain that you **keep track of all the money in the transaction: Who has the money? What triggers the payment? Is there a deposit? Who is entitled to the** deposit when the contract ends? Are multiple payments being made to one or more parties?

State clearly the *type* and *amount* of the payment to answer the *what* question. For example:

Examples—Payment Provisions with Type and Amount

Purchase Price. The purchase price is $40 million.

Rent. The monthly rent is $2,500.

Purchase Price. The purchase price is 20,000 shares of the Company's Class A Common Stock.

If the transaction involves international parties, state the currency in which payment is to be made. If you have several payments made at different times, you may want to create a chart that lists each payment and how it is to be made.

As noted earlier, payment is typically money, shares, or promissory notes, but it can also be an assignment of rights or an assumption of liabilities. If a party assigns their rights, they transfer to a third person their right to the other party's performance. Imagine that Colossal Construction Corp. owes Tong's Machinery LLC $100,000, but the payment is not due until year-end. If Tong's Machinery needs cash immediately, they can assign to their bank, Big Bank, their right to payment from Colossal Construction. In exchange, Big Bank will pay Tong's Machinery a discounted amount (say, $90,000). The consideration is the assignment of the right to payment and the return payment of $90,000. Big Bank earns a $10,000 profit when Colossal Construction pays Big Bank the $100,000 originally owed to Tong's Machinery LLC.

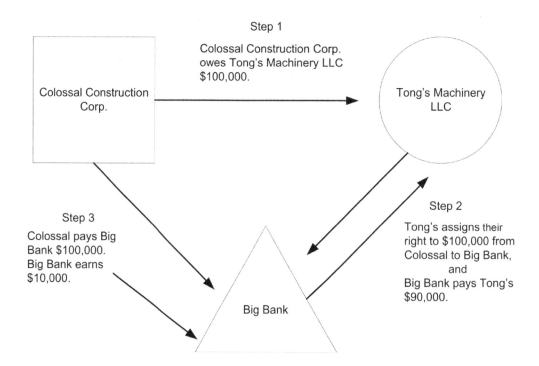

An assumption of liabilities is the converse of an assignment of rights. In this situation, a third party takes on a party's duty to perform. To see how this works, we will first look at a transaction without an assumption, and then we will compare it to the same transaction, but with an assumption.

Imagine that Darnell Winston purchased Blackacre last year for $80,000 and paid $50,000 with his own money and the remaining $30,000 with money that he borrowed from a bank. After completing the purchase, Darnell has a $30,000 liability, the amount he owes to the bank. Because the real estate market is hot, Darnell decides a year later to sell Blackacre for $100,000 to Phyllis Wright. If Phyllis pays Darnell $100,000, Darnell must use $30,000 of that amount to repay the bank. After that payment, he has $70,000 in cash. But to determine his profit, his cash out-of-pocket investment of $50,000 must be subtracted from the $70,000, giving him a profit of $20,000.

Darnell's cash from Phyllis	$100,000
Darnell's cash repayment to the bank	($30,000)
Darnell's cash after repayment to the bank	$ 70,000
Darnell's cash out-of-pocket cost for the initial investment	($50,000)
Darnell's cash profit	$ 20,000

Alternatively, if the bank agrees, Phyllis could assume (become legally obligated to pay) Darnell's $30,000 liability to the bank, which means that Phyllis could take over Darnell's obligation to pay the $30,000 loan. If she does so, her total out-of-pocket cost does not change; the recipients change. Phyllis will still pay $100,000, but she will pay $30,000 to the bank as a loan repayment, either immediately or on a future date. In addition, Phyllis must pay Darnell $70,000. That amount is, of course, what he would have netted if Phyllis had paid him $100,000 and he then paid the bank $30,000. But does Darnell end up in the same position as before with a $20,000 cash profit? Yes. To determine his cash profit, his cash out-of-pocket cost for the initial investment is subtracted from the cash he received.

Darnell's cash from Phyllis	$ 70,000
Darnell's cash out-of-pocket cost for the initial investment	($50,000)
Darnell's cash profit	$ 20,000

So, whether the payment is $100,000 in cash, or $70,000 in cash plus the assumption of $30,000 in debt, both parties end up in essentially the same financial position.[3]

2. **State *who* is paying *what* to *whom* in the active voice.**

Examples—Payment Provisions with Who, What, and To Whom

Payment of Rent. With respect to each month of the Term, the Tenant shall pay the Rent to the Landlord.

---

3. In the real world, a buyer is in a slightly different financial position if they assume a seller's liabilities to third parties. First, a buyer may not have to pay the seller's liabilities immediately. Instead, the buyer may be able to pay them over time, either in accordance with the seller's agreements with the third parties or in accordance with an arrangement that they can negotiate. This delayed payment could be a substantial advantage to a buyer. Second, a buyer could also negotiate with the third parties to reduce the amount to be paid, thus obtaining a discount. Third, a buyer may have to pay interest that they would not have had to pay if they had paid the full amount owed.

Some drafters violate this rule by providing that a payee has a right to payment. Although this is technically correct as every obligation to perform includes a right to that performance, better drafting is to state who has the obligation to perform, which is what would need to be proven in a litigation that alleged breach of performance.

Do not use different types of wording or indirect language when drafting the obligation to pay. State explicitly that *X shall pay Y.*

Examples—Obligations Stated Explicitly

Incorrect: **Fee.** The Producer is responsible for paying the Screenwriter $6,000 for the Script.

Correct: **Fee.** The Producer shall pay the Screenwriter $6,000 for the Script.

---

3. **State explicitly and clearly *when* the consideration is payable.**

Example—Payment Provisions with When Consideration is Payable

Rent. With respect to each month of the Term, the Tenant shall pay the Rent to the Landlord *no later than the fifth day of that month.*

---

4. **If a contract term creates any stub periods, provide for appropriate payments.** Think through the consequences of a term starting on a date other than January 1. The contract might require a specially calculated payment to deal with the stub period. A **stub period** is a period less than a calendar year that occurs when a contract term either begins after January 1 or ends before December 31 of a calendar year. For example, if an executive begins work on September 15, the midyear start date creates two stub periods. The first occurs in the first year of the contract term. It begins on September 15 and ends on December 31. The second stub period occurs in the contract's final year. It begins on January 1 and ends on September 14, the last day of the contract term. In both instances, if the executive is entitled to a bonus based on the company's performance for each calendar year, the parties might need to provide special rules to calculate the bonus for the stub periods.[4]

   Also, consider what timing issues are created if the contract term does not match up with the fiscal year[5] or quarters. For example, if a license agreement term begins on March 15, are payments to be made

   - at the end of every three months based on a term beginning on March 15 (i.e., June 14, September 14, December 14, and March 14) or
   - at the end of each calendar quarter (i.e., March 31, June 30, September 30, and December 31)?

5. **Consider also whether any payment should be accelerated or delayed.** Loan agreements often require mandatory prepayments of principal if the borrower sells equity securities, borrows more money, or sells substantially all of its assets.

---

4. *See* Chapter 25 on page 383 regarding avoiding ambiguity in the measurement of dates and time in contracts.

5. A company's fiscal year is the one-year period that the company uses to determine their annual revenues, etc. Often, the fiscal year is a calendar year, but that does not hold true for all entities in all industries.

6. **State *how* a party is to pay money: personal check, company check, cashier's check, certified check, online payment, or wire transfer of immediately available funds.**

Example—Type of Payment

Rent. With respect to each month of the Term, the Tenant shall pay the Rent to the Landlord *by certified check* no later than the fifth day of that month.

The form of payment determines when a recipient has access to the money and reflects an allocation of risk between the parties. Some forms of payment are more risky for a recipient than others. The most risky are personal checks and company checks. When a party pays by such checks, the recipient does not have immediate access to the funds. They must first deposit the check at their bank, and that bank must technically receive payment from the paying party's bank. The delay that this process entails creates a credit risk: The paying party might not have money in their account at the time that payment is required. Thus, even if the recipient has performed, they might not get paid. Despite this risk, many recipients are willing to accept a personal or company check. For example, internet service providers, telephone companies, and electric utilities all accept their customer's personal checks—although most would prefer an online payment.

Less risky for a payee are cashier's checks (also known as *bank checks*) and certified checks. A cashier's check is a check that a bank issues from its own account. It is the bank's promise to pay the recipient.[6] The paying party applies to their bank for a cashier's check, at which time the bank takes the money from that party's account and issues their own check payable to the order of the recipient. Therefore, when a recipient accepts a cashier's check as payment, they no longer take a risk as to the paying party's creditworthiness. Instead, their credit risk hinges on the bank's creditworthiness. Although the recipient's credit risk is significantly reduced, they still do not have access to the funds until the business day after the banking day on which the cashier's check was deposited.[7] In addition, the check is subject to final clearing and reversal if it is dishonored because of fraud or some other issue.

A certified check is a check as to which a bank has set aside sufficient funds from the paying party's account to ensure full payment of the check. The bank *certifies* the check by having an authorized employee sign the check.[8] Again, while the recipient has reduced their credit risk, the funds are not available until the business day after the banking day on which the certified check was deposited.[9] In addition, the bank can take back their payment if they discover that the check was fraudulently issued.

Parties often use certified checks or cashier's checks when the parties know the payment amount several days before the transaction, the amount is relatively large, and the recipient wants to reduce their credit risk. Car dealers often insist on one of these forms of payment.

---

6. 12 C.F.R. § 229.2(i) (2006).
7. 12 C.F.R. § 229.10(c)(v) (2003).
8. 12 C.F.R. § 229.2(j) (2006).
9. 12 C.F.R. § 229.10(c)(v) (2003).

In complex, sophisticated transactions with significant sums at risk, many recipients refuse to take any risk of nonpayment and, in addition, they want immediate access to the money for investment or other purposes. In these transactions, the paying party can wire-transfer immediately available funds from their bank account to the recipient's.[10] The recipient need not make a deposit because the wire transfer accomplishes that, and the funds do not need to clear because the funds transferred were immediately available. Although wire transfers can be made through different systems,[11] generally the parties use a system that the Federal Reserve System (Fed) maintains.[12] Parties may refer to it as a Fed funds transfer.

If a wire transfer involves multinational parties or parties located in different cities, determine where the funds are to be sent and the currency for payment. Are funds being transferred to an account in New York City, Detroit, or Tokyo? Funds immediately available in New York City are not immediately available in Tokyo because of the difference in time zones and processes. An obligation to pay by a Fed funds transfer is generally along the following lines:

Example— Wire Transfer Instructions

Payment of Purchase Price. The Buyer shall pay the Seller the Purchase Price by wire transfer of [immediately available funds] [funds immediately available in Chicago] [immediately available funds in pound sterling]. The Seller shall notify the Buyer of the bank account into which the funds are to be transferred no later than two business days before the Closing Date.

Some drafters provide that the paying party must pay the consideration in *cash*. Avoid doing this. **Cash** is currency (bills and coins), and the parties probably do not intend for the paying party to arrive with stacks of dollar bills. Although some courts have interpreted *cash* to mean immediately available funds,[13] other courts have held that *cash* means currency.[14] While using the word *cash* is unlikely to cause a problem, when drafting, be clearer and say what you mean.

7. **If money is payable for more than one reason, the terms for each payment should conform to this section's guidelines**. For example, if a company is obligated to pay an executive both a salary and a bonus, create separate payment sections for each payment, and then in each section, state the appropriate amount, when the payment is due, and other requirements. Treating the two types of payments separately will help you analyze the possibly different business issues associated with each of the payments. For example, under what circumstances is the bonus paid? Is it paid if the company terminates the executive for cause?

---

10. 12 C.F.R. § 229.2(ll) ("Wire transfer means an unconditional order to a bank to pay a fixed or determinable amount of money to a beneficiary on receipt or on a day stated in the order, that is transmitted by electronic or other means through Fedwire, the Clearing House Interbank Payments System, other similar network, between banks, or on the books of a bank.").

11. *Id.*

12. *See generally Fedwire Funds Servs.*, http://www.federalreserve.gov/paymentsystems /fedfunds_about.htm (accessed November 13, 2022).

13. *Upchurch v. Chaney*, 635 S.E.2d 124, 125 (Ga. 2006) (holding that in context of a judicial sale cash meant immediately available funds).

14. *Nance v. Schoonover*, 521 P.2d 896, 897 (Utah 1974) (holding that parties intended cash to mean currency).

8. **Use defined terms in your payment provisions.** Some drafters put defined terms relating to the payment of consideration in the payment provision, as this is often the only place they are used. Also, many drafters like defining the defined terms related to payment in context within the payment provisions so that the parties, courts, or any other third parties know right away what those defined terms clearly mean. Some drafters may define any needed terms in the definitions section or in a separate subsection devoted exclusively to the payment term being defined. No matter which option you choose for each defined term, you want to make the defined terms and payment provisions as clear as possible and avoid any ambiguity because they are extremely important to the parties and the transaction. Here are some examples:

Examples—Payment Provisions with Defined Terms

A — **Purchase Price**. The Buyer shall pay the Seller $100,000 for the House by

(a) paying the Seller $50,000 at Closing by wire transfer of immediately available funds; and

(b) executing and delivering at Closing the Buyer's promissory note in the principal amount of $50,000, substantially in the form of **Exhibit B** (the "**Note**").

B — **Purchase Price**. The purchase price for the Premises is $2,000,000 (the "**Purchase Price**"). The Buyer shall pay the Purchase Price to the Seller as follows:

(a) $500,000 by certified check concurrently with the execution and delivery of this Agreement (the "**Down Payment**"); and

(b) 1,500,000 by wire transfer at Closing (the "**Closing Payment**").

---

9. **Calculate any amounts that can be calculated before signing, if possible, rather than including a mathematical formula.** For example, if possible, state the amount that each party is to be paid, rather than stating that each party is to be paid its allocable share. This explicit statement of amount should reduce the likelihood of a dispute because the parties will check the calculations before signing the agreement. Do not state the formula and the results of the formula. You will create ambiguity if the calculation does not line up with the formula.

If a party will be using more than one form of payment to more than one party, create a chart that specifies the type and amount of payment payable to each party. For example:

Examples—More than One Form of Payment and/or Party

Acceptable: **Consideration**. The Purchase Price is $100 million in immediately available funds, $25 million in subordinated debt, and 5 million Class A Shares, each Shareholder to be paid that Shareholder's allocable share.

Recommended: **Consideration**. The Purchase Price is $100 million in immediately available funds, $25 million in subordinated debt, and 5 million Class A Shares, payable to each Shareholder as follows:

	IMMEDIATELY AVAILABLE FUNDS	SUBORDINATED DEBT	EQUITY
Shareholder A	$20 million	$5 million	1 million Class A Shares
Shareholder B	$70 million	$17.5 million	3.5 million Class A Shares
Shareholder C	$10 million	$2.5 million	.5 million Class A Shares

10. **If payment is based on a formula, state the formula accurately.** While a formula may appear simple at first, it often requires sophisticated drafting, especially if tax or accounting issues are implicated.[15]

IV. DURATION OF CONTRACT

Some contracts relate to a specific transaction, such as the sale of Blackacre. Although it may take time for the parties to consummate this transaction, their contract has a limited time horizon. Some lawyers refer to these transactions as **one-off deals**. However, in other contracts, the parties anticipate a relationship that will span an extended time period. Their contract will govern their relationship for an agreed-on number of years—that is, a specific **term**. Leases and license agreements are examples of contracts that have terms.

When drafting a contract for a term of years, the beginning and ending dates of the term must be clear. The easiest way to accomplish this is to state the term's beginning and ending dates.[16] You may do this either by drafting a stand-alone section or by incorporating the dates into the subject matter performance provision. In either case, drafters often define *Term* in context in the action sections.[17]

Examples—Term Provisions

1—Term as a Stand-Alone Section:

    Term. This Agreement's term begins on January 1, 20_5 and ends on December 31, 20_7 (the "**Term**").

2—Term Incorporated into a Subject Matter Performance Provision:

    Term. Subject to the provisions of this Agreement, the Supplier shall supply the Manufacturer with the Materials listed in **Exhibit A**, and the Purchaser shall purchase those Materials, during a three-year term beginning on January 1, 20_5 and ending on December 31, 20_7 (the "**Term**").

If you are drafting a precedent for use in multiple transactions, you may want a contract that requires minimal changes each time it is used. In this case, key the

---

15. For more information on tax and accounting issues, *see* Chapter 26 on page 403, "Drafting Numbers and Financial Provisions" and Chapter 30 on page 459, "Adding Value to the Deal."

16. Unfortunately, provisions dealing with dates are often full of ambiguity. *See* Chapter 25 on page 383, which discusses how to avoid ambiguity when drafting contract provisions that include time periods.

17. If you define "Term" in context in the action sections, remember to include it in the contract's alphabetical listing of defined terms, along with a cross-reference to the section where you define it.

beginning of the term to the date when the parties sign the contract. The ending date then keys off the anniversary date[18] of the contract's signing.

Example—Beginning of Term Keyed to Date Parties Sign

Term. This Agreement's term begins on the date that the parties execute and deliver this Agreement and ends at 5:00 PM [on the day preceding the third anniversary] [on the third anniversary] of the date the parties execute and deliver this Agreement (the "**Term**").

A contract need not state the specific date on which a term begins. Instead, the contract can provide that the first day of the term coincides with a future event. Here, the parties distinguish the creation of a binding contract from the first day of the term. That is, although a binding contract comes into existence on the date that the parties sign the contract, the term does not begin until a later date, when a specified event occurs. For example, a lease term may begin on the first day of the month after the month during which a tenant pays its deposit.

When drafting the ending date of the contract, some drafters provide for the contract's early termination in the action sections to connect with the endgame provisions that come later in the agreement. Here is such an example:

Example—Early Termination Language in Term Provision

Term. The Agreement's term begins on the date that the parties execute and deliver this Agreement and ends at 5:00 PM on the day preceding the third anniversary of the day the parties execute and deliver this Agreement (the "**Term**"), *unless sooner terminated in accordance with the provisions of this Agreement.*

Other drafters believe that the additional language is not necessary. However, the advantage of the language is that it signals the parties' intent by explicitly recognizing that the term could prematurely end. To complete the circle, the endgame provisions, especially the termination provisions, should include language such as the following:

Example—Early Termination Language in Termination Provision

Termination for Cause. The Company may terminate the Executive's employment for Cause before the end of the Term.

When drafting contracts with a term, discuss with the client whether the contract should include an **evergreen provision,** which automatically renews a contract's term. When drafting an evergreen provision, consider the following issues:

- Does the term automatically renew unless one party notifies the other that it is terminating the contract?
- Does the term automatically end unless a party exercises its option to renew?
- Does each party have the authority to renew?
- How long should the renewal period be: the same length of time as the original period, or shorter?

---

18. Referring to the anniversary date is preferable because of its precision. On the other hand, references to years can be ambiguous. *See* Chapter 25 on page 385 for more information on this topic.

The following is an example of an evergreen provision:[19]

Example— Evergreen Provision Regarding Renewal of Term

Term. This Agreement's term begins on January 1, 20_5 and ends on December 31, 20_7. This Agreement automatically renews for successive one-year terms, unless either party exercises its option to terminate this Agreement. (The initial three-year period and each successive one-year renewal, a "**Term**.") To exercise its option to terminate the Agreement at the end of the then-existing Term, a party must deliver a written notice of termination to the other party that is received no later than 30 days before the last day of the then-existing Term.

When drafting an evergreen provision, do not provide that the parties will agree on a price increase at the time of a renewal. Agreements to agree are unenforceable.[20] Instead, provide a contractual mechanism for determining the amount of the increase (e.g., a stated percentage increase or a percentage increase tied to cost-of-living increases). If the parties want to be able to negotiate the increase at the end of a term, the contract can require the parties to negotiate in good faith. However, counsel should advise the parties that if they do not reach an agreement, the renewal right may be unenforceable.[21]

Careless drafting of evergreen provisions can easily lead to problems. Consider the following provision, which generated a lawsuit:

Example— Bad Evergreen Provision

Term. This Agreement continues in force for a period of five years from the date it is made, and thereafter for successive five-year terms, unless and until terminated by one-year prior notice in writing by either party.

The *unless* clause at the end of the sentence was the problem. Did the discretionary authority apply only to its immediate antecedent (the successive five-year terms) or also to the initial term? Two sentences rather than a comma would have made all the difference, as follows:

Example— Better Evergreen Provision

Term. This Agreement continues in force for a period of five years from the date it is made. After the initial term, the Agreement continues in force for successive five-year terms, unless and until terminated by one-year prior notice in writing by either party.[22]

---

19. For an excellent discussion of the term "provisions," *see* David C. Burgess, *Duration of the Agreement, in Drafting Business Contracts: Principles, Techniques, and Forms* ch. 6 (Cal. CEB 1994).

20. *Joseph Martin, Jr., Delicatessen, Inc. v. Schumacher*, 417 N.E.2d 541, 543-544 (N.Y. 1981).

21. *Id.* at 544.

22. *See* Chapter 25 on page 377 for more information on ambiguities from sentence structure.

V. ACTION SECTIONS IN ACQUISITIONS AND FINANCINGS

The action sections of an acquisition or financing agreement can be quite complex because of the payments and the deliveries relating to the transfer of title or the loan. On the CasebookConnect Resources page and on the Aspen website product page for this book, you will find an exemplar of the action sections of an asset purchase agreement. It includes notes and comments, and you may use it as a precedent.

These types of agreements will have in their action sections the subject matter performance provision and detailed payment provisions. These transactions do not have a term since they are one-off transactions. Instead, these agreements will include information on the closing, closing date, and closing deliverables.

A. CLOSINGS AND CLOSING DATES IN ACQUISITIONS AND FINANCINGS

Recall from Chapter 4 on page 29 that a closing is the consummation of a transaction at which time the parties exchange financial consideration. It is the final step in actuating certain transactions. Usually, closings are necessary only in acquisitions and financings—both are one-off transactions where the parties sign multiple documents and exchange significant sums, and the relationship generally terminates at closing. In the context of the Sally and Bob house sale described in Part A, the closing will occur when Sally delivers the deed (which conveys the property) and Bob pays the purchase price. In a financing, the closing occurs when the bank funds the loan and the borrower signs the note.[23]

Most transactions do not require a closing. For example, the Website Development Agreement (located on the CasebookConnect Resources page and on the Aspen website product page for this book) does not require a closing, and neither does a trademark licensing agreement. Similarly, no closing is necessary in most leasing transactions. Generally, the parties must just sign the lease and the tenant pay the deposit. The parties need not even get together to sign the lease. They can exchange signature pages by PDFs attached to e-mails. Hard copies of the signatures can be exchanged by regular postal service mail or special courier like FedEx, but the parties may not insist on that.

If the transaction will have a closing, the contract should state its place, date, and time. The statement of the time should take into account where the parties are located because they might be in different time zones. If they are in the same time zone, a reference to "local time" is sufficient. If they are in different time zones, refer to the time at the location where the closing is to be held. In addition, when drafting that provision, consider whether the closing date should be fixed or whether it should be determined by the happening of an event. For example, the closing date in the following Example 2 ties into the date that the parties receive all the consents to their transaction. The closing date provision should be drafted in the present tense as a declaration. It reflects the parties' policy decision as to the closing's date, time, and location. The parties are not obligated to close because this provision is in the agreement. Rather, the provision states when and where the parties have agreed that they will appear—if they hold a closing.

---

23. In a financing, the loan is the consummation of the lending part of the transaction. The parties continue to have a relationship because the borrower has the use of the loan for a specified time period and covenants to do certain things so long as the loan is outstanding.

Examples—Closing and Closing Date Provisions

1—In the Definitions Article:

"**Closing**" means the consummation of the transactions that this Agreement contemplates.

"**Closing Date**" means the date stated as such in Section 3.1.

1—In the Action Sections:

Section 3.1 Closing. The Closing is to occur on December 22, 20_2, beginning at 9:00 AM local time (the date and time, the "**Closing Date**"). It is to take place at the offices of Workhard & Playlittle LLP, 1180 Avenue of the Americas, New York, New York.

2 — In the Definitions Article:

"**Closing**" means the consummation of the transactions that this Agreement contemplates.

"**Closing Date**" means the date and time determined in accordance with Section 3.1.

2 — In the Action Sections:

Section 3.1 Closing. The Closing is to occur on the third business day after the parties receive the last of the consents listed in **Schedule 3.7**. It is to take place at the offices of Workhard & Playlittle LLP, 8000 Sears Tower, Chicago, Illinois, at 10:00 AM Chicago time (the date and time of the Closing, the "**Closing Date**").[24]

If the contract provides for a specific closing date, determine with your client whether the parties must close on that date. If so, consider a time-of-the-essence clause, but be sure that you and your client understand the consequences of that provision in your jurisdiction. If time is *not* of the essence, provide that the parties may jointly postpone the closing date. It is awkward to need an amendment or a waiver if documenting the transaction takes longer than expected. Many deals have what are referred to as **rolling closing dates**. For example, the parties agree to close, say, on March 15, but the documentation is not ready then, so the parties postpone day by day until they are ready to close.

If the agreement permits postponements, consider whether the contract should include a **drop-dead date** — a date after which the parties may no longer postpone the closing. A drop-dead date might be appropriate, for instance, in an acquisition that needs to close before year-end so that the seller can include the income in its year-end financial statements. A drop-dead date might also be appropriate in the purchase and sale of a house, if a seller has another buyer waiting in the wings. The following provision provides for a rolling closing date with a drop-dead date:

Example—Closing with Drop-Dead Date

Closing. The Closing is to take place on June 15, 20__ at 10:00 AM local time or on another date and time as to which the parties agree, but in no event later than June 30, 20__ (the date and time of the Closing, the "**Closing Date**"). The Closing is to be held at the offices of Workhard & Playlittle LLP, 200 Peachtree Street, Atlanta, Georgia.

---

24. The location of the defined term in this paragraph is tricky. It includes not only the time in the immediately preceding sentence, but also the date in the first sentence. To avoid ambiguity, the parenthetical creating the defined term expressly indicates that both the date and time are components of the definition.

If a contract includes a drop-dead date, include endgame provisions that provide for the contract's termination and that spell out the consequences of a failure to close. You may put this endgame information in the action sections or in the endgame provisions discussed in Chapter 17 on page 229.

B. CLOSING DELIVERIES IN ACQUISITIONS AND FINANCINGS

The phrase **closing deliveries** has both a narrow and a broad meaning. Its narrow meaning arises in the context of an acquisition or a financing agreement and refers to the exchange of documents and consideration necessary to consummate the transaction. Thus, in a sale of assets, the seller's closing deliveries are primarily the assets themselves and the documents or other items that the seller has to provide in order to convey the assets being sold. Each type of asset needs its own conveyancing document. **A bill of sale** is a document that conveys most assets.[25] **An assignment agreement** is used to convey rights under a contract, while **a deed** conveys title to a property like Blackacre. The buyer's closing deliveries are the delivery of the purchase price (whether immediately available funds, a promissory note, or shares of the buyer) and, if appropriate, **an assumption of liabilities agreement**, if the buyer is assuming certain liabilities of the seller or the business.

Deal lawyers also use **closing deliveries** in a broader sense in acquisitions and financings to refer to all the documents that a party delivers at closing. These documents include bring-down certificates,[26] incumbency certificates (confirming the officers of the entity, etc.), certified resolutions, and opinion letters.

Where the closing deliveries are listed depends on what is being delivered. In an acquisition agreement, the action sections will include a closing delivery section in which the buyer and seller obligate themselves to exchange the documents and consideration necessary to consummate the transaction. These are the *closing deliveries* as that term is used in its narrow sense — the documents and payments necessary to consummate the transaction. The following closing delivery section excerpt comes from an acquisition agreement. As you read the provision, note the italicized language that establishes the standard as to the form of the conveyancing document. The more specific the standard is, the more favorable it is to the Buyer because it reduces the risk that the conveyancing document will fail or otherwise not be satisfactory to the Buyer.

---

25. See the CasebookConnect Resources page and the Aspen website product page for this book for examples of conveying documents, such as a bill of sale and an assignment and assumption agreement.

26. Lou R. Kling & Eileen T. Nugent, *Negotiated Acquisitions of Companies, Subsidiaries, and Divisions* vol. 2, § 14.02 [5].

Examples—Closing Deliveries Provision

Closing Deliveries.

(a) **Seller's Deliveries.** At the Closing, the Seller shall execute and deliver to the Buyer the following:

   (i) **A bill of sale** for the Purchased Assets.

   (ii) An assignment of each real property lease under which the Seller is lessee, *each assignment to be satisfactory to the Buyer*.

   (iii) Assignments for all funds on deposit with banks or other Persons that are Purchased Assets, *each assignment to be reasonably satisfactory to the Buyer*.

   (iv) A general warranty deed for each real property interest owned by the Seller, *drafted in the manner customarily used in commercial transactions in the place where the real property is located*.

   (v) Assignments for each Assigned Contract, each to be *substantially in the form of Exhibit C*.

As to the other closing deliveries (*closing deliveries* as used in its broader sense), some are included in the action sections and others in the conditions article. Where a closing delivery is listed has contractual consequences. If the delivery is listed in the action sections, a party covenants to deliver the document. Any failure to deliver it breaches the agreement, entitling the other party to damages. In addition, the other party would have a walk-away right because, in an acquisition agreement, a condition to closing is the performance of every covenant to be performed *on or before the Closing Date*—and that would include the delivery obligations in the action sections. The contractual consequences differ, however, if the closing delivery is listed only in the conditions article. Then, the buyer's sole remedy is a walk-away right.

In deciding where to list a closing delivery, determine whether the party responsible for the delivery has control over their delivery. If the party can control their delivery, list the closing delivery in the action sections. In this event, the delivering party accepts the risk of breaching their covenant to deliver the document. If the party cannot control the delivery, list it as a condition to closing, so that a walk-away right is the other party's only remedy.

For example, drafters always carefully provide that the delivery of a legal opinion is a condition to closing, not an action section covenant. This protects the parties because they cannot control whether their lawyers will deliver the opinion. A peculiarity in the transaction's structure or a new court opinion can make a specific opinion difficult, if not impossible, to give. By listing the delivery of the opinion in the conditions article, an opinion's non-delivery creates only a walk-away right — not a right to damages.

In contrast, deliveries that properly appear in the action sections include certified resolutions of a party and agreements that the delivering party must sign — for example, a noncompetition agreement. Parties can control whether they sign and deliver these types of documents.

VI. OTHER SUBSTANTIVE BUSINESS PROVISIONS

Apart from the specific provisions already discussed above, the parties may include other substantive business provisions in the action sections of an agreement. As mentioned in Chapter 13 on page 141, in this book, we are including the other substantive business provisions within the action sections, since these provisions are still where the action is. However, other practitioners and commentators may include them as a set of provisions separate from the action sections in a category by themselves.

These other substantive business provisions can include any or all of the contract concepts and can be organized in different ways, depending on the type of agreement that you are doing. We discussed briefly in Chapter 13 on page 141 how the House Purchase Agreement (located on the CasebookConnect Resources page and on the Aspen website product page for this book) has the other substantive business provisions organized by contract concept (representations and warranties, covenants, conditions), technically also in the chronological order of the transaction.

Other agreements may use the same contract concepts for this section but organize them in different ways. For example, the Website Development Agreement (located on the CasebookConnect Resources page and on the Aspen website product page for this book) is organized primarily by subject matter, instead of so directly by contract concept. In that agreement, only the parties' representations and warranties are set out expressly by contract concept and appear toward the end of the agreement. Their location at the end reflects their relative lack of importance in this agreement compared to other subject matters such as effective date, fees, additional payments, provision of services, ownership, warranties, representations and warranties, and development credit.

VII. EXERCISES

A. EXERCISE 16A: IDENTIFYING ACTION SECTIONS IN AN ESCROW AGREEMENT

Which are the action sections in the Escrow Agreement included in Exercise 14E on page 178?

B. EXERCISE 16B: DRAFTING THE TERM PROVISION

Arthur Wright ("**Wright**"), a quarterback for the San Jose Dragons (the "**Dragons**"), has hired Davis Reynolds ("**Reynolds**") to represent him in contract negotiations with the Dragons. (This kind of contract is known as a **representation agreement**.) The parties have agreed that the representation will begin on the day that their contract is signed and is to continue during the term of any contract that Reynolds negotiates with the Dragons until either party gives notice of termination. Termination of the representation is effective on the 20th day after a party receives notice of termination.

Draft the term provision for the representation agreement between Wright and Reynolds. You may want to create a defined term and definition for Wright's contract with the Dragons to make your provision easier to read.

C. EXERCISE 16C: DRAFTING ACTION SECTIONS IN A LICENSING AGREEMENT

Draft the action sections of the trademark licensing agreement in Exercise 13C on page 148. Remember that the territory may change, so the action sections will need to provide the appropriate provisions.

D. EXERCISE 16D: CORRECTING DRAFTING ERRORS IN ACTION SECTIONS

Below are two versions of the same provision based on the facts that follow. Do the following:

1. Find and correct the drafting errors in Version (a).
2. Correct the drafting error in Section 3.1(a)(ii)(B) in Version (b).
3. Redraft all these provisions to make them clearer based on everything that you have learned in this chapter.

Facts

- Assume that it is October 18, 20_6. Your client, the employer, is entering into an agreement on this day for the employment of an executive.
- The executive is to begin work on January 1, 20_7. The last day of the employment term is December 31, 20_9.
- The salary is at a rate of $85,000 per year for the first year. The company will pay the employee every two weeks. The salary will increase each year over the previous year's salary by at least 7½%. The increase takes effect on January 1 of each year.

- The executive is entitled to a bonus of $15,000 each year. The bonus will be paid on December 31, 20_7, December 31, 20_8, and December 31, 20_9.
- The company will pay the executive with its company check.

Version (a)

From the definitions section:

"**Employment Term**" means the three-year period beginning on January 1, 20_7, and ending on December 31, 20_9.

From the action sections:

3.1 Salary. For the first year of the Employment Term, the Company shall pay the Executive a salary of $85,000 (the "**Base Salary**") in biweekly installments of $3,269.23. Beginning on the first anniversary of this Agreement and on each subsequent anniversary during the Employment Term, the Base Salary of the Executive increases by an amount not less than 7½% of the preceding year's Base Salary.

3.2 Bonus. In addition to the Base Salary, with respect to each year that the Executive is employed under this Agreement, the Company shall pay the Executive a $15,000 bonus (the "**Bonus**") on the last day of that year.

Version (b)

From the definitions section:

"**Employment Term**" means the three-year period beginning on January 1, 20_7, and ending on December 31, 20_9.

From the action sections:

3.1 Compensation

(a) **Salary.** During the Employment Term, the Company shall pay the Executive a salary in an amount computed as follows (the "**Salary**"):

(i) With respect to the first year of the Employment Term, the Salary is $85,000.

(ii) With respect to each year of the Employment Term, other than the first year of the Employment Term, the Salary is the amount equal to the *sum* of

continued on next page >

(A) the Salary for the immediately preceding year *plus*

(B) an amount equal to 7½% of the Salary for the immediately preceding year or such greater amount as the Company determines in its sole discretion. [The Company shall pay the Executive the Salary for each year in the Employment Term in equal, biweekly installments.]

(b) **Bonus**. During the Employment Term, the Company shall pay the Executive a $15,000 bonus (the "**Bonus**") no later than the last day of each year of the Employment Term.

E. EXERCISE 16E: DRAFTING ACTION SECTIONS IN AN AIRCRAFT PURCHASE AGREEMENT

To: Portia Porter

From: Sam Samson

Date: September 22, 20_2

Re: Sale of Aircraft

While we can't take over the drafting of the whole agreement, I convinced Flighty to let us draft the action sections. I told him that it would save him money. That guy is so cheap, he said yes immediately. Of course, the real reason I want you to do the drafting is that I don't trust Flighty. He is just a little too "sharp."

You may recall that several years ago his company bought a helicopter from Rich Lefkowitz's company. The purchase price was to be paid partially in cash and the rest in notes. In addition, as part of the business deal, Flighty was supposed to personally guarantee his company's notes. As I heard the story, he signed the guaranty and then took it off the table while the money was being wired. It wasn't until Lefkowitz threatened to sue for fraud that Flighty delivered the guaranty. What a bum.

I would appreciate your getting me the draft of the action sections as soon as possible. You probably know this, but to draft those provisions, you will need information from the Purchase Offer and the Escrow Agreement [See Exercise 14E on page 178 for these documents.] and a few defined terms from the first draft of the Aircraft Purchase Agreement. [See Exercise 15G on page 205 for this document. Also, see the example of the action sections in an acquisition agreement online on the CasebookConnect Resources page and on the Aspen website product page for this book.] Thanks.

CHAPTER SEVENTEEN

Drafting the Endgame Provisions

I. INTRODUCTION

A contract may change or end for countless reasons, which could be neutral, friendly, or unfriendly. For example, a contract could end because of the decision to shift to a less expensive supplier, the successful conclusion of a joint venture, the end of a lease term, the consummation of a transaction, the sale of a partnership interest, the breach of an agreement, or the death of a party. The provisions in a contract that relate to how a contract may possibly end and what happens before, as, and after it ends are called the **endgame provisions.**

This book uses the term *endgame provisions* instead of *termination provisions,*[1] but note that in practice, you will find drafters that refer to these as *termination provisions.* However, *endgame* is a more appropriate term because, first, it echoes the language that we often use at the time of drafting of the contract, when trying to anticipate and plan for possible endgame scenarios (situations in which the parties would want to exit from the relationship or in which there would be significant challenges to the relationship). Second and, more important, endgame provisions contemplate a broader range of provisions than termination provisions. Endgame provisions include not only *termination*, *default*, and *remedy* provisions, but also *exit strategies* for any party, as well as provisions to tie up loose ends in successful transactions.

Keep in mind that in some transactions, you will have to think of possible significant changes in the relationship because of the nature of the work, particularly in a project with different phases. However, in most transactions, you will see that if there are possible significant changes, the parties will want the option to terminate. Therefore, the drafters and clients may be more centered on termination language. Regardless, we encourage you to think of other possible changes that are realistic but may not trigger termination, and what the possible consequences could be.

When drafting a contract, you should try to foresee how the parties could possibly breach a part of the contract and whether or not the breach should result in the

---

1. Some contracts distinguish between termination and expiration. Specifically, a contract terminates if it ends prematurely because a specified event occurs. In contrast, a contract expires on the last day of its term. UCC § 2-106 U.L.A. § 2-106 (2013) distinguishes termination from cancellation. Here, termination occurs when a party ends a contract other than for breach, while cancellation occurs when a party ends a contract because of a breach. *Termination* is not used in either of its technical senses in this chapter. Instead, it refers to the end of a contract for any reason.

termination of that contract. For example, it's not unheard of for a borrower to be late in paying the interest that is due on a specific date. As a short-term solution, a bank may agree to a **grace period**, a short period of time during which the borrower may pay and forestall a formal breach. Of course, the bank exacts a price for their gracious extension of the payment date—the borrower must pay a higher rate of interest. If the grace period ends without the borrower having paid as required, the borrower would then be in breach and the bank would have the right to exercise its remedies. In this example, the endgame provisions in the contract between the bank and the borrower would include the provisions relating to the grace period and the higher rate of interest, as well as the termination provisions relating to an actual breach (if the borrower does not pay after the grace period) that gives the bank the chance to terminate the contract, take any other action under the contract, and pursue any contractual and common law remedies.

Note that there is a close relationship between the endgame and general provisions covered in Chapter 18 on page 263. In fact, there are a number of provisions that could be included in the general provisions article but could be also considered an endgame provision and vice versa. An example of such a provision is the *force majeure* clause, which provides for what the parties should do in case of unforeseen circumstances (such as earthquakes, wars, and pandemics) and is covered in more detail in Chapter 18 on page 289.

In addition, in acquisitions and financings, there is a unique, important relationship between the conditions article and the termination article in the agreement. You can explore that relationship in more detail by reviewing the information on this topic provided online at CasebookConnect's Resources page and on the Aspen website product page for this book.

II. THINKING THROUGH ENDGAME PROVISIONS BEFORE DRAFTING

Deal lawyers find endgame provisions difficult to negotiate and draft. They often require tailoring to refine them to make them deal-appropriate. While clients may not read an entire contract, they sometimes devote considerable time and effort (**transaction costs**) to these provisions. They are the go-to provisions when the parties have disputes—which frequently involve money, something about which clients are sensitive. Thus, these provisions can typically be difficult to know how to approach and draft, and unfortunately, they can be a source of litigation.[2]

To figure out the possible endgame scenarios and solutions during the negotiation process, you need to take the initiative to think through the problem and exercise your creativity to develop a workable solution. A drafter with the skills to do this can add value to the deal, as we discuss in more detail in Chapter 30 on page 469.

In general, a drafter should consider the following six points when drafting endgame provisions:

1. The events triggering a possible termination of the agreement or a significant change in the relationship between the parties.
2. The contractual consequences (both monetary and nonmonetary) of receipt of notice of termination or any such events.

---

2. *See generally United Rentals, Inc. v. RAM Holdings, Inc.*, 937 A.2d 810 (Del. Ch. 2007) (dueling endgame provisions resulted in protracted litigation, with court finding that one of the drafters was not a forthright negotiator).

3. The date the contract terminates or significantly changes, which may depend on the type of event and its contractual consequences.
4. Whether a party is entitled to any common law remedies.
5. Whether any specific contract provisions survive the contract's termination or how other contract provisions may be affected with a change in the relationship. [The answers to these questions can also sometimes be found in the general provisions.]
6. Dispute resolution provisions. [These can be also often found instead in the general provisions.]

As a drafter, you should stay up to date on any type of developments that may affect your transactions, especially when it comes to endgame provisions and general provisions. For example, the COVID-19 pandemic brought about supply chain interruptions, sudden drops in sales in some industries, extensive layoffs (which were later followed by new waves of hiring), and the temporary or permanent closure of various businesses (especially businesses that depended on large gatherings of people). Millions of contracts around the world were affected because the parties could no longer perform, and many parties ended up having to alter their relationship and/or engaging in serious disputes.

The COVID period highlights more than ever how important endgame and general provisions are, even though they are usually at the end of the agreement and are sometimes not negotiated or thought through in any way. For example, there were contracts being disputed during the COVID-19 pandemic that did not even have a *force majeure* provision. In addition, there were agreements that did contain a *force majeure* provision but still left many open questions on whether a pandemic and/or any of its effects would be covered under that provision. This book does not go through specific recommendations on *force majeure* or related provisions but stresses the need to be up to date with issues in this area that may emerge in the future.

III. LOCATION OF THE ENDGAME PROVISIONS

The beginning of the contract has the parties' plan for a successful transaction or relationship. The conclusion of that relationship, whether good or bad, is addressed at the end of the contract. This order reflects the chronology of a transaction.

Drafters generally place endgame provisions toward the end of the contract in a single section or article to make them easy to find. However, occasionally, as previously mentioned, parts of the endgame provisions may be included in the general provisions article, which is usually the last article right before the signature lines. In addition, drafters sometimes integrate endgame terms with substantive business provisions in the action sections or other parts of the agreement.

The following example is a provision from a distribution and licensing agreement.[3] The licensor licenses software ("Product") to the distributor. The distributor pays royalties to the licensor for each product sold. This provision authorizes the licensor to audit the distributor's accounting records to ensure that the distributor is paying the licensor the proper amount in royalties based on the sales figures. This provision

---

3. Bitrix, Inc., *Distribution and Licensing Agreement,* http://www.bitrixsoft.com/partners /agreement.html (accessed November 13, 2022; provision can be found at Section 5.5, Right to Audit; Understated Statements). Note that this provision could be tabulated and better organized to make it easier to read.

includes the grounds and method of termination in the event that the distributor's underpayment exceeds a certain amount.

Example — Endgame Integrated with Substantive Business Provisions

5.5 Right to Audit; Understated Payments. Licensor or its designated agent may, at Licensor's sole expense (except as provided herein), upon 10 days advance written notice to Distributor during Distributor's business hours examine and/or audit the books and records of Distributor which relate to payments due and Products distributed under this Agreement. Licensor shall not have access to any of Distributor's records beyond those necessary to complete any audit contemplated under this Section 5.5. If any examination or audit should reveal that the License Fees to Licensor under this Agreement for any period was [*sic*] understated in any Sales Report, then Distributor shall pay to Licensor immediately upon demand the amount understated and any penalty fee due with respect thereto. If any examination or audit discloses an understatement in any Sales Report of five percent (5%) or more, Distributor shall also reimburse Licensor for any and all costs and expenses connected with the examination or audit (including without limitation, reasonable accountants' and attorney's [sic] fees). In the event that any examination or audit discloses . . . an understatement in any Sales Report of ten percent (10%) or more, Distributor shall also pay to Licensor as an underpayment penalty an amount equal to the amount of the underpayment. In the event any of the understatement of ten percent (10%) or more is determined to be intentional, Licensor may at its option terminate this Agreement immediately upon written notice to Distributor. The foregoing remedies shall be in addition to any other remedies Licensor may have hereunder. No provision of this Section 5.5 shall be construed as limiting or restricting any Licensor's rights or remedies provided elsewhere in this Agreement or by law.

Although Section 5.5 above is a stand-alone provision, the agreement's termination article, which is part of the endgame provisions, cross-references Section 5.5 when listing the grounds for termination. This aids the reader who has turned to the back of the contract to find the endgame provisions in their usual location.

Example — Termination Provision Cross-Referencing Endgame Integrated with Substantive Business Provisions

Termination. The Parties may terminate this Agreement as provided in the subsections of this section:
[Intentionally omitted.]

    (a) Licensor may terminate this Agreement as provided in Section 4.2 and 5.5 hereof . . .

An endgame provision that is commonly found outside the endgame section is the walk-away right that arises from a failure to satisfy a condition to closing in an acquisition or a financing agreement. The language introducing the conditions article states this remedy but is not usually as explicit as it could be. For example:

> ### *Example — Endgame Integrated with Conditions Article in Acquisition*
>
> **Conditions**. Each of the following conditions must have been satisfied or waived before the Buyer is obligated to close the transactions that this Agreement contemplates.

This language means that if the conditions in the list that follows are not met or are waived by the Buyer, then the Buyer may walk away from the deal.

For a more detailed discussion of the role of conditions in endgame provisions in acquisition agreements, see Chapter 6 on page 45 and Chapter 11 on page 116.

IV. HOW TO APPROACH DRAFTING THE ENDGAME PROVISIONS

Endgame provisions are a series of *if / then* propositions, so they are usually composed of *conditions* (which you learned about in Chapter 6 on page 39 and focused on *drafting* in Chapter 11 on page 107).

This is a good way to approach drafting endgame conditions:

- If this good event happens, then this is the consequence.
- If this bad event happens, then this is the consequence.

Therefore, when developing the endgame provisions, you will want to ask yourself: *What if? What if* the author wants to publish other books under a pseudonym? *What if* the parent company files for bankruptcy? *What if* a natural disaster, war, or pandemic prevents delivery of time-critical construction material? *What if* a competitor wants to open a store in the same shopping mall? *What if* the play closes and two months later the producer wants to reopen in the same city, but at a different theater?

Lawyers often excel at asking *what if*? Their training instills the need to test assumptions and to discover and expose risk. But the transaction costs of addressing every *what if* question are high. As a counselor, you must help your client assess the *what if* questions to determine whether addressing them is worth the time and money. The answer may well depend on the risk analysis discussed in Chapter 30 on page 463. U.S. lawyers tend to want to address most issues. This tendency stems partly from our common law system that does not have a set of rules to address common business issues, as in civil law countries.[4]

While the consequences differ from contract to contract based on the parties' business concerns, endgame conditions generally fall into one of three categories, as all conditions do:

- An obligation to perform:
  - *"If* ____, *then* the Borrower shall pay default interest."
- A grant of discretionary authority.
  - *"If* ____, *then* the Bank may foreclose."

---

4. Barbara J. Beveridge, *Legal English — How It Developed and Why It Is Not Appropriate for International Commercial Contracts*, 6 (Sept. 13-15, 2000), included in *The Development of Legal Language: Papers from an International Symposium at the University of Lapland* ("[W]e do not have general code provisions governing the matters between the parties. Because of this everything must be dealt with in the contract itself. One problem that arises from this is that the drafter must include wording which will deal with every situation and cover off every possible contingency that could happen in the future.").

- A declaration:
  - "*If* _____, *then* the contract terminates on a party's delegation of its performance without the other party's consent."

The organization of endgame provisions depends on the contract. If they deal with defaults (something has gone wrong), two schemes are common. The first puts a list of the offending events into one section and the consequences into another. Credit agreements and employment agreements often follow this scheme, as these types of agreements often have default provisions primarily relating to only one party (the borrower and the employee are the only ones who may be found to be in default of the agreement).

The second scheme creates an endgame or termination article that has separate sections for each party's defaults. If the consequences of both parties' defaults are the same, an additional section can detail the remedies. Otherwise, each party's section should be broken into subsections, with either the first subsection listing the defaults and the second listing the consequences, or just one set of subsections where each level down includes a description of the event and the consequences of each default (grouped by the type of default). Remember that these organizational schemes may not be appropriate for all contracts and are merely guidelines.

If the endgame provisions are not related to defaults (a friendly endgame), create separate sections or articles as needed to address specific business issues. For example, acquisition agreements sometimes have provisions that apply after the transaction has been successfully consummated, such as covenants requiring that the seller change its name post-closing and covenants not to compete. You may want to detail in those specific sections covering the post-closing covenants what the parties would need to do if something goes wrong.

A more specific organizational scheme that may apply in many situations creates individual sections to address each of the six major issues that endgame provisions should address:

1. The events triggering a possible termination of the agreement or a significant change in the relationship between the parties
2. The contractual consequences (both monetary and nonmonetary) of receipt of notice of termination or any other significant change
3. The date that the contract terminates or changes, which may depend on the type of event and its contractual consequences
4. Whether common law rights survive the contract's termination or the significant change in the relationship
5. Whether any specific contract provisions survive the contract's termination or how other contract provisions may be affected with a change in the relationship
6. Dispute resolution provisions

Here is an example of a termination provision from a movie distribution agreement:

Example — Endgame Provision from Movie Distribution Agreement

17. **Termination**

17.1 **Grounds for Termination.**

(a) **Discretionary Authority to Send Notice of Intent to Terminate.** The Distributor may send a notice stating that it has grounds for termination and that it intends to terminate this Agreement (a "**Notice of Intent to Terminate**") in accordance with this Section 17 if any one or more of the following events has occurred and is continuing.

(i) The Movie Owner made any misrepresentation under this Agreement.

(ii) The Movie Owner breached any material covenant under this Agreement that cannot be cured.

(iii) The Movie Owner breached any material covenant under this Agreement that can be cured, and it failed to cure that breach before the 16th calendar day after receiving the Distributor's Notice of Intent to Terminate.

(iv) The Movie Owner becomes insolvent or fails to pay any of its debts when due.

(v) A petition under any bankruptcy or insolvency law is filed by or against the Movie Owner.

(vi) The security interest that the Movie Owner granted to the Distributor in the Collateral ceases to be enforceable or perfected.

(b) **Notice of Intent to Terminate.** The Distributor shall include in the Notice of Intent to Terminate

(i) a statement of all amounts owed;

(ii) the amount of any setoff to be taken under Section 17.4; and

(iii) a statement of all obligations due.

17.2 **Movie Owner's Obligations Arising from Receipt of Notice of Intent to Terminate.** If the Distributor sends a Notice of Intent to Terminate under Section 17.1,

(a) then no later than five business days after receiving that notice, the Movie Owner shall pay the Distributor by wire transfer of immediately available funds an amount equal to

(i) the Distributor's out-of-pocket costs incurred in connection with the Picture *plus*

(ii) the Advance or any portion of the Advance that the Distributor paid to the Movie Owner *minus*

(iii) the amount of any setoff that the Distributor takes in accordance with Section 17.4, as stated in the Notice of Intent to Terminate; and

(b) the Movie Owner shall perform all obligations under this Agreement that the Distributor declares due.

continued on next page >

17.3 **Specific Performance.** The Distributor may specifically enforce the Movie Owner's obligations under Section 17.2.

17.4 **Setoff.** Without limiting any other remedies available to the Distributor under this Agreement or at law, the Distributor may set off against any amount it is obligated to pay under this Agreement to the Movie Owner, sums in the Distributor's possession that are reasonably sufficient to secure the Distributor from and against the Movie Owner's liabilities or the Movie Owner's breach of any of its obligations under this Agreement.

17.5 **Cumulative Remedies.** In addition to any rights and remedies stated in this Agreement, the Distributor may exercise all of its rights at law or equity, including without limitation, its rights and remedies in and to the Collateral.

17.6 **Effective Date of Termination.** If the Distributor delivers a Notice of Intent to Terminate under Section 17.1, then termination is effective when the Distributor has both received payment of all money due under Section 17.2(a) and the Movie Owner has performed all its obligations to be performed in accordance with Section 17.2(b).

17.7 **Survival of Common Law Rights and Obligations.** All rights in law and equity and all obligations arising from any ground for termination stated in Section 17.1 survive this Agreement's termination.

V. NOTICE RELATING TO ENDGAME PROVISIONS

If one party has done something to activate a particular endgame provision, such as a possible termination, the contract should include provisions that require the parties to give each other notice about that event.

If it is in the context of a possible termination, this notice is usually referred to as **notice of termination** or **termination notice.** These terms can be misleading, however, because they may suggest that the mere receipt of the notice ends the contract, which is not true. Receipt of notice might terminate an agreement, but it just as easily might not. The notice might instead trigger *contractual consequences* that the parties must address before the agreement actually ends.

Often, but not always, when contracts use these terms, they mean notices that *provide information regarding possible termination* or that *trigger the exercise of remedies*, not notices that necessarily terminate an agreement. If the drafting world were perfect, drafters might substitute the term *notice of termination* with more specific language, such as *Termination Event Notice, Notice of Intent to Terminate, or Notice of Intent to Exercise Remedies.*

What should these notices contain, and what effect should they have on the contract—and for whom—when the notices are sent or received?

They should be transaction specific. As the drafter, you should take the time to include in detail what a notice should contain and what are the effects of that notice and any possible subsequent step afterward by each party, including the possible remedies at each step. Also, remember to think about carefully and coordinate how the notice provisions in the endgame provisions work with other provisions in the agreement, such as the notice provision in the general provisions article, covered in more detail in Chapter 18 on page 279. For example, some termination provisions state that all notices given under the provision must be in writing, but that language is redundant if the agreement's general provision on notices already requires notices to be in writing.

Because termination notices have substantial consequences, drafters should insist that they be effective only on receipt and be sent by national courier or delivered personally. Drafters are each day more and more comfortable with e-mail delivery, which is quicker and more efficient. Consider using more advanced options than a simple e-mail message to ensure that the relevant parties receive and open the message. Bottom line, the recipient should not be able to dispute the date of receipt, and the sender should have certainty of receipt. That date may well be a factor in determining other time periods and deadlines.[5]

VI. DIFFERENT TYPES OF ENDGAME

As noted, a contract may significantly change or end for multiple reasons: some neutral, some friendly, and some unfriendly. At the outset, a drafter must determine the **grounds** (also known as the **breaches, defaults,** or **triggering events**), which are those events that will bring the endgame provisions into play and possibly end the agreement.

However, specific contract provisions like the following often survive any type of termination:

- Noncompetition obligations (e.g., in connection with an acquisition or an employment agreement).
- Confidentiality obligations (e.g., in connection with a termination of employment or a joint venture).
- Further assurance obligations (e.g., in connection with an acquisition).

The sections that follow explore what we call *neutral, friendly,* and *unfriendly* changes or terminations (these are not terms necessarily used in legal practice), including their definitions, examples, issues relating to notice for each one, and possible consequences after each type of change or termination.

A. NEUTRAL ENDGAME

1. What Is a Neutral Change or Termination?

Neutral terminations provide the parties the ability to change or discontinue their relationship without blaming one party or the other or finding anyone responsible of doing something wrong. Sometimes all parties agree that one party may exit the

---

5. Notice provisions are risk allocation provisions. If a notice were effective when sent, or a stated number of days after deposit with the U.S. Postal Service, the intended recipient could be at risk that the sender has rights against the recipient about which the recipient does not yet know.

relationship subject to specific terms, as in the following example, where the grocer might want to use the ability to terminate if it finds a superior supplier from which it can purchase better-quality produce:

> ### Example — Neutral Termination from a Supply Agreement
>
> **Termination**. The Grocer may terminate this Agreement at any time by notifying the Supplier of termination and by paying all outstanding accounts. Termination occurs on the date that the last of these two requirements are satisfied: i) the Supplier receives the notice of termination, and ii) the Supplier receives payments sufficient to satisfy all outstanding accounts.

In the context of an acquisition or financing, a neutral termination would be good to include if the drafter can anticipate either party failing to satisfy a condition through no fault of their own. For example, let's say that a seller cannot obtain a required consent from the government or another third party. With a neutral termination provision that addresses this contingency, the contract would end and the parties walk away without common law rights or remedies (no direct rights to pursue in court) — a neutral ending.

Neutral terminations can also occur if a contract explicitly provides that the parties may agree to terminate at any time or at specific times, as follows:

> ### Example — Neutral Termination in Writing at Any Time
>
> **Termination by Written Agreement**. The parties may terminate this Agreement at any time by written agreement of both parties.

The provision in this last example is really not needed since the parties may agree to terminate the agreement at any time anyway if they both agree, under the common law. Nonetheless, parties include these provisions to state their intent and to notify third parties of that intent. These provisions are typically simple, like the one above. The future seems the appropriate time to negotiate the consequences of terminating the contract, given that the parties are agreeing that, if they agree, they can terminate the agreement in the future. If they cannot agree in the future, then termination by agreement is not going to happen.

2. Termination Notice and Date

If a party receives a notice of termination, other provisions of the contract may be triggered and there may be additional consequences. Let's go back to one of the examples in the previous section:

> ### Example — Neutral Termination from a Supply Agreement
>
> **Termination**. The Grocer may terminate this Agreement at any time by notifying the Supplier of termination and by payment of all outstanding accounts. Termination occurs on the date that the last of these two requirements are satisfied: i) the Supplier receives the notice of termination, and ii) the Supplier receives payments sufficient to satisfy all outstanding accounts.

If the grocer were able to terminate the agreement merely by sending notice, the supplier might need to argue for the money due to them. If the contract has terminated, where is the contractual obligation to pay? The supplier might well find a way to recover their money, but why make work for the litigators and extra expenses for the parties? Therefore, the receipt of the notice of termination should not trigger the agreement's termination before the grocer has performed their obligation to pay all outstanding accounts. Termination should depend on the grocer first performing this payment obligation. When the grocer does, then the contract terminates.

Neutral termination scenarios may also include contractual provisions that tie up loose ends. For example, in a construction contract, the owner might need to end the project because financing has disappeared. The contractor is not at fault, but the parties must address the monetary consequences of the termination as follows:

Example — Neutral Termination from a Construction Agreement

Owner's Termination of Contractor Without Cause. If the Owner terminates this Agreement, except for Cause, the Owner shall pay the Contractor for all completed construction work on the Project and for all proven loss or expense in connection with the Project's construction. On the date of the Contractor's receipt of payment in full, this Agreement terminates, and neither party has any other rights or remedies against the other.

---

3. Survival of Rights, Obligations, and Provisions

Parties often include a clause in neutral terminations that addresses the rights and obligations of the parties going forward. This clause is usually toward the end of the section, after the agreement has already described the type of termination, notice issues, and steps that the parties must take, as follows:

Example — Neutral Termination from a Supply Agreement

Termination. The Grocer may terminate this Agreement at any time by notifying the Supplier of termination and by payment of all outstanding accounts. Termination occurs on the date that the last of these two requirements are satisfied: i) the Supplier receives the notice of termination, and ii) the Supplier receives payments sufficient to satisfy all outstanding accounts. *On termination, neither party has any rights or remedies against the other party.*

By definition, the neutral termination is without fault of a party, so neither party has any right or incentive to pursue remedies. As to the survival of specific contractual provisions, that depends on the transaction and provision. For example, as mentioned earlier, confidentiality provisions often survive any type of termination, including neutral ones.

B. FRIENDLY ENDGAME

1. What Is a Friendly Change or Termination?

The classic friendly change or termination results from the successful consummation of a transaction, completion of a project or a portion of it, or the conclusion of a multi-year term relationship. For example, a friendly termination is when parties close an acquisition, the developer completes the website, or a lease term ends.

2. Termination Notice and Date

Friendly changes or terminations sometimes require a notice from one party to the other, but generally they do not. If a tenant has a three-year lease term, the parties know when the term ends. A party generally does not need to give notice unless a statute requires one or the contract provides for renewal terms. Nonetheless, parties still need to articulate the parties' contractual obligations at the end of the term, and the contract does not usually immediately terminate. The success of the contract triggers these final contractual obligations, and the contract does not terminate until those final obligations are performed. Therefore, although a trademark *license* may terminate at the end of a three-year term, parties may need to perform post-term obligations before the *agreement* terminates.

Once you determine what constitutes a friendly change or termination, you and your client must decide the *contractual consequences*. They usually fall into one of three categories. Here are some examples for each category:

- Obligations that return the parties to their status quo before the contract.
  - On payment in full of their loan, a bank is obligated to release the collateral they hold and to execute any documents necessary to reflect their release of the collateral.
  - A landlord is obligated to return a security deposit in connection with the termination of a lease.
  - A tenant is obligated to return the premises to the landlord in broom-clean condition.
- Contractual performances necessary to tie up loose ends.
  - Fulfillment of monetary obligations (e.g., a licensee's final, post-term payment to their licensor; an employer is obligated to reimburse an executive for travel expenses).
- Exit strategies.
  - Becoming a publicly traded company.
  - Take-out financing (e.g., long-term lenders take over the debt of a lender that provided construction financing).
  - Buyouts (e.g., shareholders purchasing another shareholder's equity interest).

3. Survival of Rights, Obligations, and Provisions

In a friendly change or termination, the parties are usually not arguing over misrepresentations or breaches of warranties or covenants, so the common law causes of action usually serve no function in such a termination. Furthermore, the parties can also anticipate most friendly changes or terminations and include contractual remedies for them in the agreement. Also, certain contractual provisions may survive depending on the transaction and provision.

C. UNFRIENDLY ENDGAME

Clients do not always want to discuss or negotiate the endgame provisions that address unfriendly changes or terminations, because when they are negotiating a contract, they usually anticipate a successful working relationship. You must ensure that your client understands the consequences of the business transaction succeeding or failing. Some clients contend that these provisions are unnecessary because the principals will work it out based on the strong personal relationship that they have developed. That works until the person on the other side whom you negotiated with changes jobs or changes their mind about the relationship or transaction.

1. What Is an Unfriendly Change or Termination?

In the context of unfriendly changes or terminations, drafters often use the terms **grounds, breaches**, **defaults,** and **triggering events**. Grounds for termination and triggering events mean exactly what they describe. *Breaches* is often used as an umbrella term for any misrepresentations, breaches of warranties, and breaches of covenants, which are grounds for termination that are related to the contract. On the other hand, some practitioners use *grounds* and *defaults* as broader terms that include breaches as a subset.

A ground for termination or default does not have to be related to the contract. For example, death, bankruptcy, merger, and change of control of a company are common *grounds for termination* that are not *breaches* because they are not related to the violation of other provisions in the contract.

Another example of a ground for termination or a default that may not be directly in the contract is a **cross-default,** which arises under one agreement because a party is in default under another agreement.

When reflecting on what events might entitle your client to remedies, consider what non-contract-related events (grounds or defaults) could affect the parties sufficiently to warrant grounds for termination or a remedy. (This analysis requires an understanding of business, the client's business, the industry, and the specific transaction in question.)

Also, because there can be different interpretations of these terms (*grounds, defaults, breaches, triggering events,* etc.), make sure that you know what your team and client really mean, depending on which terms they use.

Drafters usually approach the listing of unfriendly events in two possible ways. First, you could list the possible breaches of the contract—a quick, easy approach. Here are examples of such a provision in an agreement between two parties:

Examples—Unfriendly Termination Provisions Listing Only Breaches

1—**Termination**. A party may terminate this Agreement by written notice to the other party in the event of the other party's misrepresentation, breach of warranty, or breach of covenant. In that event, the parties have the rights and remedies provided at law and at equity.

2—**Termination**. This Software License terminates without notice on the first day the Licensee breaches the terms of this Software License. The Software License's termination does not preclude the Font Owner from suing the Licensee for damages for breach of the Software License.

In the second approach, the parties want to extend the contract's grounds for termination or possible default beyond the common law causes of action, so the lawyers have a bit more work to do. They must think through not only the consequences of a contract breach, but also what else could affect the parties' relationship. For example, if a pharmaceutical company hires a sales representative, they expect that the person will generate a certain sales volume. If the person does not, the client's expectations are frustrated, and the client will want the right to terminate the contract to cut their losses. This analysis requires more than looking at a specific provision and determining how it works. You must understand and lay out clearly the *mechanics* of how the parties will work together and what could destabilize that relationship, plus what will happen when that relationship is struggling.

Again, the question when developing endgame provisions is: *What if*? As part of this *what if* exercise, think through what circumstances could frustrate your client's assumptions and expectations.[6]

Finally, when analyzing what events should result in a termination, analyze whether those events should be the same for both parties. They do not need to be. A credit agreement is an extreme example of how termination events differ. Those agreements will have an entire article devoted to the borrower's defaults but will be silent with respect to the lender's defaults.

2. Termination Notice and Date

Unlike neutral and friendly terminations, if a party has grounds for an unfriendly termination or remedy, that party must usually notify the party who allegedly breached the contract or did not perform as they were required to in order to continue the contract. To prevent ambiguity and provide adequate communication and resolution between the parties, you should draft notice provisions that explicitly include:

- Grounds for termination and contract provisions that give the nonbreaching party the right to send the notice of termination.
- Contract provisions that trigger monetary or other contractual obligations, if any.
- Details with respect to the payment of money (who, what, when, where, how, and how much).
- Whether the notice terminates the agreement on receipt.
- The date the agreement terminates if either or both parties must first satisfy specific conditions to the termination.
- Whether any common law rights and obligations survive termination.
- Whether specific contractual provisions survive termination.

Also, as mentioned previously, agreements do not generally terminate on receipt of a termination notice and have no other contractual consequences. But they can terminate in just that way—sometimes in unfriendly terminations. In an acquisition, if a seller fails to satisfy a condition to closing, the buyer has a walk-away right. If the seller has not made any misrepresentations or breached any warranties or covenants, then the buyer has no other rights against the seller. For a detailed discussion of this endgame scenario, see the discussion on endgame provisions in acquisition agreements online at CasebookConnect and on the Aspen website.

---

6. This analysis was suggested by Alan Shaw, formerly from Fordham University School of Law.

3. Consequences After Event of Possible Termination

With respect to an unfriendly termination, what happens after a party receives a termination notice may vary depending on many factors, including the grounds for termination and whether the contract has provided for contractual consequences — monetary or specific enforcement. The consequences of a default are as varied as the contracts themselves. For example, the parties may decide to give a party who allegedly breaches the contract the opportunity to fix the problem.

In legal terms, the first issue to think about is: "Should the contract include a grace period and the opportunity to cure?"

a) Grace Period and Opportunity to Cure

As mentioned previously, a **grace period** is a predetermined amount of time past the occurrence of a default when the breaching party has the **opportunity to cure** the default — that is, they may do what they should have done in the first place (prior to defaulting). This will stop the non-defaulting party from pursuing any remedies.

Generally, for the grace period to begin, the non-defaulting party notifies the defaulting party of the breach, but sometimes the cure period begins without formal notice.

Credit agreements often permit a borrower a grace period during which the borrower can cure a default. For example, a credit agreement may grant a borrower a five-day grace period to cure a breach arising from a failure to comply with an affirmative covenant (e.g., an obligation to deliver financial statements no later than the third business day of each month). If the borrower provides the financial statements within the grace period, it is as if the default had never occurred. The bank is *gracious* because it recognizes that the borrower may have breached the covenant without meaning to do so.[7]

Here is a classic termination provision, unedited from the original, that provides for a cure and could be used in a credit agreement or any other type of agreement, with slight modifications:[8]

> *Example — Unfriendly Termination Provision with a Cure*
>
> **Termination.** If either Party believes that the other Party is in material breach of this Agreement . . . , then the non-breaching Party may deliver notice of such breach to the other Party. In such notice, the non-breaching Party will identify the actions or conduct that it wishes such Party to take for an acceptable and prompt cure of such breach (or will otherwise state its good faith belief that such breach is incurable); provided, however, that such identified actions or conduct will not be binding upon the other Party with respect to the actions that it may need to take to cure such breach. If the breach is curable, the allegedly breaching Party will have ninety (90) days to either cure such breach (except to the extent such breach involves

---

7. Sandra Stern, *Structuring and Drafting Commercial Loan Agreements* vol. 1, 8.01[2], 8-2–8-3 (rev. ed., A.S. Pratt 2012).

8. Sec. Exch. Comm'n, *License and Co-Development Agreement by and between Genzyme Corporation and Isis Pharmaceuticals, Inc.,* http://www.sec.gov/Archives/edgar/data/732485/000104746908009073/a2186974zex-10_7.htm (accessed November 13, 2022).

the failure to make a payment when due, which breach must be cured within thirty (30) days following such notice) or, if a cure cannot be reasonably effected within such ninety (90) day period, to deliver to the non-breaching Party a plan for curing such breach which is reasonably sufficient to effect a cure within a reasonable period. If the breaching Party fails to (a) cure such breach within the ninety (90) day or thirty (30) day period, as applicable, or (b) use Commercially Reasonable Efforts to carry out the plan and cure the breach, the non-breaching Party may terminate this Agreement by providing written notice to the breaching Party.

If a credit agreement provides for notice of a default, a grace period, or both, the agreement may definitionally distinguish between a **default** and an **event of default**. In that case, a default can be a ground for termination before the grace period ends, but with the possibility of a cure still pending. If the grace period ends without a cure, the *default* would then generally ripen into an *event of default*, entitling the non-defaulting party to exercise their remedies.

Examples — Default and Event of Default Definitions in an Agreement

"**Default**" means any of the events specified in Section . . . , whether or not any requirement for the giving of notice, the lapse of time, or both has [sic] been satisfied.[9]

"**Event of Default**" means any of the events specified in Section . . . , provided that any requirement for the giving of notice, the lapse of time, or both has been satisfied.[10]

Be careful because some practitioners could use the terms *default* and *event of default* in a different sequence and assign different meanings to these terms. For example, they may first use the term *event of default*, which would lead eventually to a *default*.

Remember that even though we are using the term *default* to present these issues, the event that permits a termination or remedy may not be termed a default. Instead, the contract may simply state the specific events that permit termination or remedy without categorizing them as defaults. Or, the contract may use a different term, such as *cause*, to describe what are still, essentially, defaults. For example, in an employment agreement, the term *cause* is often used to describe the conditions under which the employer has a right to terminate the contract or pursue remedies.

Apart from or along with grace and cure periods, parties can sometimes devise other ways of transforming defaults into non-defaults. For example, some credit agreements constrain a bank's exercise of remedies by requiring that a default must *have occurred* and *be continuing* at the time the bank is to exercise their remedies. That is, while a borrower may well have been in breach, a bank loses its discretionary authority to exercise their remedies if a borrower cures the breach, so that the

---

9. *Id.* at 8-4.
10. *Id.*

breach is no longer continuing or ongoing. Banks are not huge fans of this borrower-friendly language.[11] They often want the right to exercise their remedies, worrying that a breach, even if cured, is a sign of worse things to come.

Note that contracts regularly require a representation and warranty stipulating that no event exists which, with notice and a lapse of time, will constitute a default. Parties often insist on this representation and warranty because it factors heavily into their risk assessment. If notice has been given to a party under one transaction, the counterparty has fair warning that something is not right already. It's an early warning system.

Note that not all defaults can be cured. For example, the death of a chief operating officer is final and hard to address.

b) Price Adjustments

When first analyzing how a contract should treat a specific ground for termination, the parties should address whether they can do anything to remedy the situation that is not simply immediately terminating. What remedy will provide both parties with the economics they need, yet leave the contractual relationship intact? For example, in a long-term supply contract, the supplier might give a discount for a late delivery.

The following is an unedited provision from an international supply agreement which combines a grace period with a price adjustment in the event that the seller is delayed in providing the goods to the buyer:[12]

> ### Example — Price Adjustment Provision If Delayed Delivery
>
> **Price Adjustment**. In case of delayed delivery except for force majecure [sic] cases, the Seller shall pay to the Buyer for every week of delay a penalty amounting to 0.5% of the total value of the goods whose delivery has been delayed. Any fractional part of a week is to be considered a full week. The total amount of penalty shall not, however, exceed 5% of the total value of the goods involved in late delivery. The Seller grants a grace period of four weeks from the delivery date before penalties shall be applied.

Clients may forgive many glitches, but drafting the monetary payment provisions incorrectly is not one of them. It's critical to *follow the cash*. This means that you must understand and track all the monetary consequences, including the reason for each payment and its source, as well as each adjustment. When drafting these provisions, general promises to pay are not enough.

As with the consideration payments in the action sections, a promise to pay money must answer the following questions: *Who is obligated to pay what to whom? When and how are they obligated to pay it?* See Chapter 16 on page 211 for more information on how to best draft payment provisions.

---

11. Stern, n. 7, at 8.02, 8-5.

12. Sec. Exch. Comm'n, *Contract between Shanghai Ja Solar Technology Co., Ltd. and Roth & Rau AG*, http://www.sec.gov/Archives/edgar/data/1385598/000119312507009458/dex1012.htm (last accessed Nov. 13, 2022).

c) Default Interest

Some types of agreements have relatively standard economic remedies provisions. For example, in financing agreements, a borrower's default usually gives the lender the right to receive **default interest**—a higher rate of interest than the borrower was paying the lender before the default. So, for example, if a borrower is paying X% interest on a promissory note, the default rate might be X% plus 2%.

d) Liquidated Damages

Liquidated damages are "[a]n amount contractually stipulated as a reasonable estimation of actual damages to be recovered by one party if the other party breaches. If the parties to a contract have properly agreed on liquidated damages, the sum fixed is the measure of damages for a breach, whether it exceeds or falls short of the actual damages."[13]

Liquidated damages can be a useful remedy when the parties anticipate that the actual damages from a breach would be difficult to measure, and they wish to predetermine what would be a reasonable amount for specific breaches. Drafters can fashion these provisions to be transaction specific, but be careful. Drafters risk that a court could find the liquidated damages provision to be an unenforceable penalty. Before drafting such a provision, review how the courts in your state interpret these provisions.

Here is an example of a transaction-specific liquidated damages provision. Assume that an apartment owner wants to renovate. To do so in some cities, she must enter into a contract not only with the contractor, but also with the entity that owns her apartment building (the "**Building**" below). In the excerpt from the construction contract between the owner and contractor that follows, the contractor promises the owner that the contractor will pay the building a stated sum per day for each day past the contractually imposed construction deadline. In a separate agreement, the apartment owner promises the building that they will cause the contractor to pay the building. Apartment building managers often demand these types of payments to incentivize contractors to finish on schedule, to minimize disruption in the building and to those living in the apartments:

Example — Liquidated Damages Provision in Construction Agreement

Delayed Completion. If the Contractor fails to complete Construction on or before April 30, 20__, the Contractor shall pay $1,000 per day to the Apartment Building until the Construction is completed. After May 30, 20__, the sum increases to $2,000 per day, until the Contractor completes Construction, including the last day of Construction.[14]

---

13. *See Liquidated Damages, Black's Law Dictionary* (11th ed. 2019).
14. Some practitioners may draft aggressive liquidated damages provisions, similar to this one, but litigators could later argue, and certain courts could find, that these are penalties that are not enforceable, instead of liquidated damages provisions in the agreement that should be enforced. Therefore, the parties need to make sure that they know how they measured these damages and that they are reasonable enough to not be deemed a penalty in the relevant jurisdiction.

The parties may liquidate or pay damages for breaches of some provisions in the contract, but not all. Usually, the provisions covered by liquidated damages are those addressing the key performance obligations. Here is a sample liquidated damages clause appearing in a manufacturing agreement for the production of chlorine. This provision applies only to a specific default, terminating the agreement before the end of the term:

Example — Liquidated Damages Provision Tied to a Specific Default

Liquidated Damages. If the Buyer terminates this Agreement before the end of the Term, then

   (a) the Buyer shall pay the Manufacturer $50,000 as liquidated damages and not as a penalty; and

   (b) the remedy stated in this Section is the exclusive remedy if the Buyer terminates this Agreement before the end of the Term.

If this is the only liquidated damages provision included in the contract, any default other than an early termination would have to be remedied through a common law claim for breach, not through liquidated damages. The manufacturer probably included this liquidated damage clause because they believed that their losses from an early termination by the buyer could not be calculated with reasonable certainty. However, they presumably believed that an appropriate remedy could be determined for other types of defaults, such as where the buyer fails to pay amounts that they owe on time. Note that the above provision specifies that liquidated damages are an exclusive remedy for an early termination of the agreement *by the buyer*.

In acquisitions, liquidated damages could look like a **termination fee**, also known as a **breakup fee**. A termination fee serves to compensate the potential buyer for specific costs and efforts, such as due diligence expenses, legal and advisory fees, and the opportunity cost of potentially forgoing other transactions. If the seller walks away from the deal for specific reasons, the seller will have to pay the termination fee to the potential buyer. A **reverse termination fee**, also known as a **reverse breakup fee,** is the same concept, but with the potential buyer compensating the seller, if the potential buyer walks away from the deal.

e) Limitations on Liability

The parties often negotiate and set out **limitations on liability** provisions, which limit a party's or all parties' exposure to damages in the case that a party breaches the contract. Parties include limits of liability provisions in contracts to cap their potential financial exposure and provide predictability in the event of a breach or other adverse contractual event. For example, when negotiating a merger, one company may bargain to stipulate a maximum amount of damages in potential lawsuits that the company would pay after the merger, therefore *limiting their liability*. This provision details the allocation of the risk of economic loss in the event that the contemplated transaction is not fully executed and is enforceable.[15]

---

15. *Negrete v. Citibank, N.A.*, 187 F. Supp. 3d 454, 469 (S.D.N.Y. 2016).

When you are drafting these provisions, you will want to think about and clearly lay out which types of damages are covered. Make sure you consider direct and indirect damages.[16] Also, be clear about how much of the damages each party will be responsible for and how those damages will be calculated. Usually, the amount of the damages or limitation on liability is tied to the total amount of the contract, insurance coverage, another agreed upon amount, or a combination of such factors.

Here is an example of a limitations of liability provision:

> ### Example — Limitations on Liability Provisions
>
> *Definition of Excluded Claims:*
>
> **"Excluded Claims"** means a party's breach of its confidentiality obligations; breaches of its data privacy obligations or data security obligations; indemnification obligations; failure to comply with Applicable Law; or fraud, gross negligence, willful misconduct, or criminal acts.
>
> *Actual Provisions:*
>
> **Unrecoverable Damages.** Except for damages that arise from Excluded Claims, to the maximum extent permitted by Applicable Law, neither party is liable to the other party for any incidental damages, indirect damages, or loss of profits; or breach-of-contract damages that the breaching party could not reasonably have foreseen at the time of breach.
>
> **Limitation of Liability.** Except for damages that arise from Excluded Claims, for which liability is unlimited, the total aggregate liability of Supplier, and the total aggregate liability of Company, in each case for claims asserted in connection with this Agreement, regardless of the form of action or the theory of liability, is limited to the greater of [insert figure]; and the total fees paid and payable to Supplier in this Agreement during the 60-month period preceding the last act or omissions giving rise to the liability.

Note that when you are drafting these provisions, if you end up having to go to a court, many courts distinguish between foreseeable and unforeseeable damages, and unforeseeable damages are probably not recoverable. Some courts have not enforced these provisions when the provision is unconscionable or ambiguous, the intentions of one party or multiple parties are not clearly stated or expressed, one party has a greater level of sophistication or unequal bargaining power, and statute or public policy exists that prohibits the provision's enforcement.[17] Therefore, to ensure that your limitations on liability provisions are enforced, make them clear, conspicuous, reasonable, and unambiguous.[18]

Make sure that you coordinate any limitation of liability provision in your contract with your indemnity and other related provisions because the limitation of liability provision could be interpreted as limiting the other provisions as well.

---

16. *Despatch Oven Co. v. Rauenhorst*, 229 Minn. 436, 444 (Minn. 1949) (stating that direct "damages resulting in the usual course of things"), *aff'd by Far E. Aluminium Works Co. v. Viracon, Inc.*, 27 F.4th 1361, 1365 (8th Cir. 2022).

17. Parties should expect limitations on liability to be enforced unless these limitations are contrary to public policy by intending to shield one party from intentional fraud. *Abry P'rs V, L.P. v. F & W Acq. LLC*, 891 A.2d 1032 (Del. Ch. 2006).

18. For a more detailed discussion on limitations of liability, how they work, and the rationale behind them, *see* David Tollen's *Tech Contracts Handbook: Cloud Computing Agreements, Software Licenses, and Other IT Contracts for Lawyers and Businesspeople*, 195 (3d ed. ABA-IPL 2021).

f) Indemnities

When Party A promises to pay for the loss for which Party B is financially responsible, Party A **indemnifies** Party B. The **indemnity**[19] allocates risk between the parties. The contract shifts the risk of loss from the **indemnitee** (the party who is compensated for the loss) to the **indemnitor** (the party who will be paying for the loss, also known as the **indemnifier**) because the indemnitor promises to make the indemnitee whole for any loss that the indemnitee sustains. "[I]ndemnities make sense when one party faces a significant risk of getting sued by a third party, thanks to its deal with the other party-and that other party stands in a better position to address the risk."[20]

Using insurance as an example, when you purchase an insurance policy, the insurance company is agreeing to indemnify you, or cover your losses, up to the policy limits, for the types of risks specified in the policy. If you suffer a covered loss, such as damage to your car in an accident, the automobile insurance company will step in and compensate you, either by paying for repairs or providing financial compensation, fulfilling their indemnification obligation.

Here is a simple example of an indemnity provision:

> *Example — Indemnity Provision in Licensing Agreement*
>
> **Indemnity.** The Company shall indemnify and defend[21] the Licensee against all losses and liabilities arising from third-party claims that the Software infringes any ownership rights of third parties.

Drafters commonly use sophisticated indemnity provisions in acquisition agreements as an exclusive contractual remedy to replace the common law remedies. Buyers may prefer indemnities, among other reasons, because they expand the scope of losses for which the seller is responsible. For example, in the United States, each party must pay their own litigation expenses. An indemnity can change this common law rule by adding to the matters indemnified: *the Buyer's cost and expenses in enforcing this indemnity, including reasonable attorneys' fees and expenses.*

Sellers also seek indemnities because they can impose contractual limits on damages (known as **caps**) and shorten otherwise lengthy statutes of limitation. A full review of acquisition indemnities is beyond the scope of this book.[22]

Outside the acquisition context, drafters use indemnities in a multitude of transactions — for example, to indemnify licensees against claims of copyright infringement.[23] For example, in software agreements, an intellectual property indemnity is provided by a software company to protect users against potential infringements of third-party intellectual property rights. Since the user has no control over the software's intellectual property compliance and the company is uniquely positioned to prevent infringement, this indemnity acts as a shield, protecting the user from related claims and liabilities.

---

19. Indemnity is a "duty to make good any loss, damage, or liability incurred by another." *Indemnity, Black's Law Dictionary* (11th ed. 2019).

20. Tollen, n. 18, at 240.

21. See subsequent comments in this section on page 252 about the use of *defend.*

22. For a full treatment of the subject, *see* Morton A. Pierce & Michael C. Hefter, Indemnities, in *Negotiating and Drafting Contract Boilerplate* 243 (Stark et al. eds., 2003).

23. *Id.* at 248.

There are many possible mechanisms that the parties can use when it comes to indemnities inside and outside of the acquisition context. Some of the most common include the following:

INDEMNITY MECHANISM	DEFINITION	EXAMPLE
Cap	▪ A contractual limit on damages set out by the parties in the contract, which will be the maximum amount for which a party will be liable.	▪ If the cap is $10,000 in a contract, the party liable will only be liable up to $10,000 in damages. If there were $12,000 in damages, that party will not be liable for the additional $2,000.
Basket or Deductible	▪ If there is a basket, a party is not liable to the other party until the costs exceed a stated threshold. Once the costs reach the stated threshold, all costs over the threshold must be paid by the indemnitor. ▪ Baskets are also known as deductibles. In addition, there are different types of baskets and deductibles. For example, if the contract provides for a tipping basket, then the indemnitor has to pay not just costs over the threshold amount, but also the costs below the threshold amount. ▪ Apart from including a basket, a contract can provide for a *mini-basket* that goes with the basket. Then, claims must reach a particular minimum amount before they can even count toward the basket.	▪ If the basket or deductible is $30,000 in a contract, then the indemnitee will not be indemnified until the costs reach that amount. If the indemnitee has costs of $20,000, that will not be enough. However, if the indemnitee has costs of $100,000, the indemnitor will then cover costs and the amount will depend on the type of basket it is. If it is a tipping basket, the indemnitor will have to cover the whole $100,000.
Carve-Outs	▪ These are items excluded from indemnification provisions or situations in which a party would not have to indemnify the other party.	▪ Common carve-outs include fraud and intentional misconduct.
Materiality Scrape	▪ This type of provision, most common in acquisition agreements, sets out that in the context of indemnification, any materiality qualifiers (for example, in the representations and warranties) will be scraped and will not be considered.[24]	▪ In a contract, this provision may read as follows: ▪ "Materiality Scrape. For purposes of the indemnity contained in Section X and Section Y, all qualifications and limitations set forth in the parties' representations and warranties as to 'materiality,' 'Material Adverse Effect,' and words of similar import shall be disregarded in determining whether there shall have been any inaccuracy in or breach of any representations and warranties in this Agreement and the Losses arising therefrom."[25]

24. Tyler B. Dempsey, *Seller Beware: Potential Pitfalls and Unintended Consequences of the "Materiality Scrape,"* DocPlayer, https://docplayer.net/42120978-Seller-beware-potential-pitfalls-and-unintended-consequences-of-the-materiality-scrape-by-tyler-b-dempsey.html (last visited Aug. 10, 2023).

25. *See* further examples of Materiality Scrapes at *Materiality Scrapes,* Law Insider, available at https://www.lawinsider.com/clause/materiality-scrape (last accessed Jan. 1, 2023).

INDEMNITY MECHANISM	DEFINITION	EXAMPLE
Limiting Representations & Warranties	▪ Representations and warranties may contain **extra-contractual disclaimers**, which disclaim all representations and warranties not set forth in written agreements.[26]	▪ An example of an extra-contractual disclosure from an asset purchase agreement is the following: ▪ "Except as expressly set forth [herein], Sellers make no representation or warranty, express or implied, at law or in equity, in respect of any of its assets (including, without limitation, the Acquired Assets), or operations, including, without limitation, with respect to the merchantability or fitness for any particular purpose. Buyer hereby acknowledges and agrees that, except to the extent specifically set forth [herein], Buyer is purchasing the Acquired Assets 'as-is, where-is.' Without limiting the generality of the foregoing, Seller makes no representation or warranty regarding any assets other than the Acquired Assets or any liabilities other than the Assumed Liabilities, and none shall be implied at law or in equity."[27]
Representations and Warranty Insurance	▪ This insurance protects a party against unknown breaches of the representations and warranties in a contract.[28]	▪ Typically, the insurance underwriter will charge a premium to the policyholder, and the policy is typically 10% of the acquisition purchase price. The key issues of payment for insurance may also be negotiated between buyer and seller.[29]

You will have to work closely with your client to understand the business, the industry, and their preferences when determining what will be appropriate to draft regarding indemnity.

Common issues to consider when drafting indemnity provisions include the following:

▪ What triggers the indemnity?
▪ Who is on the hook for the indemnity? Is it just Party X or also its parent company?
▪ Is notice a condition to the obligation to indemnify or merely a contractual promise to provide notice?
▪ What kinds of losses are indemnified against — expectation damages, consequential damages, incidental damages, attorneys' fees?
▪ For how long is the indemnity available?
▪ Is the indemnity capped?
▪ Must the indemnitee sustain a minimum loss before the indemnitor has an obligation to indemnify?

---

26. Steven M. Haas, *Contracting Around Fraud Under Delaware Law,* 10 Del. L. Rev 49 (2008).

27. Steve Haas, *Exclusive Remedy Clauses and Extra-Contractual Disclaimers,* Deallawyers .com (May 2, 2008), available at https://www.deallawyers.com/blog/2008/05/exclusive-remedy-clauses -and-extra-contractual-disclaimers.html (last accessed Jan. 1, 2023).

28. Randy A. Bridgeman, *Representation and Warranty Insurance: A Primer on Its Uses and Features,* 2014 WL 7666069 (2015).

29. Richard Harroch, *A Guide to M&A Representations and Warranties Insurance in Mergers and Acquisitions,* Forbes (Jan. 23, 2019), available at https://www.forbes.com/sites/allbusiness/2019/01/23 /guide-mergers-acquisitions-representations-warranties-insurance/?sh=1e7f483167f3.

An important issue that the drafter must also address is whether the indemnitor will defend (and pay to defend) the indemnitee. The common law does not include defense as part of the indemnity, so drafters must explicitly provide for it. If an obligation to defend is included, issues include the following:

- Is there a duty to defend or just to pay costs?
- Who controls the defense (that is, the legal strategy)?
- May the indemnitee participate with its own counsel if it pays for the counsel?
- Does the indemnitee need to approve any settlement?

If your client wants a short contract with a short, one-sentence indemnity, include *defend* along with *indemnify*. Otherwise, address these issues carefully and at length because substantial money is at stake.

g) Setoff Provisions

A **setoff provision** allows Party A, who rightfully possesses Party B's money for one reason, to use that money to pay itself (Party A) amounts Party B owes Party A for another reason.

Banks regularly include a setoff provision in their credit agreements. For example, if a borrower owes money to a bank and has money on deposit with the bank, the bank may take the borrower's money on deposit and pay itself all or part of the principal amount of the loan. So if a borrower owes a bank $10,000 and has deposited $3,000 with the bank, the bank may set off the $3,000 against the $10,000 and reduce the borrower's outstanding principal to $7,000.

Setoffs are also common in leases. Typical provisions state that the landlord may set off against the security deposit (an amount the tenant originally paid to the landlord at the beginning of the lease) any money that the tenant owes the landlord for damage to the apartment.

The following is a setoff provision from an escrow agreement:[30]

> ### Example — Setoff Provision in Escrow Agreement
>
> **Right of Setoff.** Without limiting the Escrow Agent's other rights and remedies against the Seller and the Buyer, the Escrow Agent may satisfy all or part of the Seller and the Buyer's indemnity obligations under Section 4 by setoff against the Escrow Amount. The Escrow Agent shall promptly notify the Seller and the Buyer of any setoff.

h) Self-Help

Some parties believe that if something needs doing and is not getting done, they might as well do it themselves. Therefore, such parties will include a provision where, if the other party is not able to meet certain obligations, they can do it themselves so they no longer need to wait around for the other party to do it.

---

30. The original bank example discussing setoff provisions can be found in Chapter 24 on page 368.

Here is a self-help provision from a construction contract, where, if the contractor is not able to meet its obligations, the owner can take over again and do what they need to do to meet them:

Example — Self-Help Provision in Construction Agreement

Owner's Right to Perform Contractor's Obligations. If the Contractor persistently fails to perform any of its obligations under this Agreement, the Owner may

(a) give the Contractor five days' written notice of its failure to perform and the Owner's intent to perform the Contractor's obligations; and

(b) perform any one or more of the Contractor's obligations if five days after the Contractor's receipt of this notice the Contractor continues to fail to perform any of its obligations under this Agreement.

The Contract Sum is reduced by the Owner's cost of performing the Contractor's obligations.

As with many remedy provisions, this provision is not limited to just one fix—just having the self-help provision. The parties have combined it with an economic remedy to compensate the owner. The provision could be written to provide for the contractor to begin work again if certain requirements are met, or for the contract to terminate after a particular period of time or under certain circumstances. The parties decide what the provision should provide.

Here's another self-help provision adapted from a theater license agreement,[31] which is again paired with economic consequences:

Example — Self-Help Provision in Theater License Agreement

Restoration of Theater.

(a) **Theater Owner's Rights**. If the Production Company does not remove its equipment and property before the end of 24 hours after the last performance,
  (i) the Production Company is deemed to have abandoned its equipment and property (collectively, the "**Property**");
  (ii) title to the Property passes immediately to the Theater Owner, but regardless of title to the Property, the Theater Owner may dispose of the Property as it sees fit, inclusive of the right (but not the obligation) to remove or store the Property, or to do both.
(b) **Production Company's Monetary Obligations**. The Production Company shall pay the Theater Owner for
  (i) all damages the Theater Owner sustains because the Production Company failed to timely vacate the Theater; and
  (ii) all expenses incurred in doing any one or more of the following: removing, disposing, and storing the Property.

---

31. This provision is based on a contract in Thomas D. Selz et al., 5 Ent. L. 3d: Leg. Concepts & Bus. Pracs. app. D-13, § 18 (West July 2012) (available at http://web2.westlaw.com/find/default.wl?cite=UU(Ib7ce5de7265a11ddabcef8d187e8c05a)&sr=TC&rs=WLW13.04&pbc=DA010192&vr=2.0&rp=%2ffind%2fdefault.wl&sv=Split&fn=_top&findtype=l&mt=Westlaw&db=200165) (last accessed Nov. 13, 2022).

i) Equitable Remedies

Equitable remedies are usually non-monetary remedies, "such as an injunction or specific performance,[32] obtained when available legal remedies, usually monetary damages, cannot adequately redress the injury."[33]

The enforceability of provisions entitling a party to injunctive relief or specific performance and what type remains questionable. Parties cannot force a court to grant injunctive relief or specific performance since it is an equitable remedy that only a court can impose. Parties cannot compel a court to issue an order to enforce a contract provision if that provision gives discretion to the court for its enforcement. That said, evidence suggests that these provisions may influence a court's findings when determining the parties' intent.[34]

As a general matter, this also means that parties cannot change the standard for equitable relief by an agreement: damages must be inadequate.[35] However, if the parties include a right to equitable relief, including injunctive relief and specific performance, stating facts in the agreement that justify this relief may be helpful.[36]

Confidentiality agreements often provide injunctive relief for the party whose confidential information is at risk. They do so as a way of limiting unauthorized disclosures. The following provision is common and tries to justify its claim for injunctive relief by explaining why monetary damages are insufficient:

Example — Injunctive Relief Provision in a Confidentiality Agreement

Injunctive Relief. Because of the unique nature of the Confidential Information and the Research, the Executive acknowledges that

(a) the Company will suffer irreparable harm if the Executive breaches any one or more of his obligations stated in Paragraphs 1 through 5 of this Agreement;

(b) monetary damages will be inadequate to compensate the Company for any breach; and

(c) the Company is entitled to injunctive relief to enforce the terms of Paragraphs 1 through 5, in addition to any other remedies available to it at law or in equity.

Sales of real property also often include provisions for specific enforcement of the sale, such as the following:

---

32. An injunction is "a court order commanding or preventing an action." *See Injunction, Black's Law Dictionary* (11th ed. 2019). Specific performance is "A court-ordered remedy that requires precise fulfillment of a legal or contractual obligation when monetary damages are inappropriate or inadequate." *See Specific Performance, Black's Law Dictionary* (11th ed. 2019).

33. *See Equitable Remedy, Black's Law Dictionary* (11th ed. 2019).

34. For a more detailed discussion of this issue and case citations, *see* Edward Yorio, *Contract Enforcement: Specific Performance and Injunctions* §§ 19.2-19.3 (Little, Brown & Co. 1989); *see generally* Frederick A. Brodie & Nathan R. Smith, *The False Promises of Injunction Clauses,* 189 Managing Intell. Prop. 92 (May 2009) (available at https://www.pillsburylaw.com/images/content/2/4 /v2/2458/0A2CEF551BAAB8AC5609A63540231EA3.pdf).

35. *Restatement (Second) of Contracts* § 359 cmt. a (1981).

36. For an excellent discussion of this issue and case citations, *see* Edward Yorio, *Contract Enforcement: Specific Performance and Injunctions* §§ 19.2–19.3 (Aspen Law & Business 1989).

> *Example — Specific Performance Provision in a Real Estate Purchase Agreement*
>
> **Purchaser's Remedies**. The Purchaser may enforce specific performance of this Agreement against the Seller, if the Seller intentionally refuses to sell the Property and if the Purchaser is not in breach. In connection with that enforcement, the Seller shall pay the Purchaser's costs and expenses, including reasonable attorneys' fees.

4. Survival of Rights, Obligations, and Provisions: Cumulative and Exclusive Remedies

Whether common law rights and obligations survive will depend on the alternative remedies that the parties have negotiated and whether they are **cumulative** or **exclusive**. When drafting contracts that provide remedies beyond the common law remedies, drafters must address whether the contractual remedies are exclusive and replace the common law remedies or whether the contractual remedies are merely one of the options. If the contractual remedies are exclusive, then usually no common law rights and obligations survive. If they are cumulative, then usually the common law rights and obligations survive.

Liquidated damages provisions are generally exclusive, but not always. When they are exclusive, parties typically explicitly say so. However, the exclusive remedy, like the one in the example that follows, can come with a caveat. The equitable remedy of rescission may still be available if one of the parties has committed fraud.[37]

> *Example — Remedies in Contract Are Exclusive Remedies*
>
> **Indemnity as Exclusive Remedy**. The remedies of the parties stated in this Article 10 are exclusive and preclude either party's assertion of any other rights that party may have under the Purchase Agreement, applicable law, or otherwise.

When a liquidated provision is not exclusive, the other remedies under the common law are said to be **cumulative**. Contracts generally also make the availability of cumulative remedies explicit in a contract. Here are some examples:

> *Examples — Cumulative Remedies Provisions*
>
> *1*—**Cumulative Remedies**. The remedies stated in this Section are cumulative and in addition to all other remedies available under this Agreement, at law, and in equity.
>
> *2*—**Cumulative Remedies**. The rights and remedies of the parties under this Article are nonexclusive and are in addition to all other remedies available to the parties at law or in equity.

---

37. *Abry Partners V, L.P. v. F & W Acq. LLC*, 891 A.2d 1032 (Del. Ch. 2006).

Cumulative provisions undermine the theoretical framework for a liquidated damages provision, which is based on the inability to calculate damages with reasonable certainty at a later time but the need for transactional certainty as to the dollar amount of monetary risk. Common law claims are arguably inconsistent, since they may give a party two bites at the apple when one (the contractual remedy) should often be enough.

As to specific contract provisions surviving, you must look at each agreement to determine whether a transaction-specific provision should survive and make it clear.

VII. TERMINATION CHART

The following is an endgame chart, a way to organize information regarding endgame provisions. It does not cover every point, but it is often a good way to begin. Some of the exercises that follow will show you how these charts can help you.

TERMINATION CHART

GROUND FOR TERMINATION	MONETARY CONSEQUENCES OF RECEIPT OF NOTICE OF TERMINATION	OTHER CONTRACTUAL CONSEQUENCES OF RECEIPT OF NOTICE OF TERMINATION	DATE OF CONTRACT TERMINATION	SURVIVAL OF COMMON LAW CAUSES OF ACTION	SURVIVAL OF OTHER CONTRACT PROVISIONS

VIII. EXERCISES

A. EXERCISE 17A: TERMINATION CHART FOR ASSISTED-LIVING FACILITY CONTRACT

Bertha Ellsworth ("**Ellsworth**") has come to you for help figuring out the possible endgame scenarios in a contract, and you have learned the following information:

- Ellsworth has decided to live in an assisted-living facility that is associated with a charitable institution. Concurrent with entering the facility, Ellsworth is donating $25,000 to the charity. She must also pay a monthly fee.
- The facility has a two-month probationary period, during which Ellsworth can decide if she wants to remain in the facility for the long term. If Ellsworth leaves before the two-month probationary period ends, the charity will return the $25,000 donation. If she leaves afterward, the charity may keep the donation.
- The contract must also contemplate Ellsworth's death and what happens to the donation in that event.

To help Ellsworth and figure out the possible grounds for termination and consequences in this contract, do the following:

1. Fill in the left column of the following chart to reflect all the circumstances (grounds for termination) for which the monetary consequences must be determined.
2. Complete the right column by writing whether the donation is kept or returned in each instance.

GROUNDS FOR TERMINATION	MONETARY CONSEQUENCES (DONATION KEPT OR RETURNED?)

B. EXERCISE 17B: TERMINATION CHART FOR EMPLOYMENT AGREEMENT

You represent Healthy Hearts, Inc. ("**Healthy Hearts**"), and they have decided to hire Adele Administrator ("**Administrator**"). Healthy Hearts will pay her an annual salary at a rate of $100,000, plus a discretionary bonus. In addition, Healthy Hearts will reimburse Administrator for documented business expenses. The parties have agreed on four termination events: failure to perform up to standards, misrepresentations as to previous experience, disability, and death.

To figure out the possible grounds for termination and consequences in this contract, do the following:

1. In the chart that follows, complete the far-left column by listing each ground for termination.
2. Because Healthy Hearts is obligated to pay Administrator for three reasons, the contract must address the three monetary consequences for each ground of termination. In the first row, replace the bracketed instructions with each of the three types of payments that Administrator receives.
3. Complete the endgame chart as best as you can for your client by using common sense and listing the possibilities or most likely possibility for each ground for termination and type of payment.

FOLLOW THE CASH — TRACKING PAYMENT TYPES AND SOURCES

GROUNDS FOR TERMINATION	MONETARY CONSEQUENCES RELATING TO [INSERT TYPE OF PAYMENT]	MONETARY CONSEQUENCES RELATING TO [INSERT TYPE OF PAYMENT]	MONETARY CONSEQUENCES RELATING TO [INSERT TYPE OF PAYMENT]
Ground 1 for Termination			
Ground 2 for Termination			
Ground 3 for Termination			
Ground 4 for Termination			

C. EXERCISE 17C: TERMINATION CHART FOR AN ACQUISITION AGREEMENT

Here are some facts relating to the grounds for termination in an acquisition agreement:

1. Concurrently with the execution and delivery of the acquisition agreement, the Buyer pays the Seller a $100,000 deposit.
2. The acquisition agreement has a confidentiality provision which by its terms applies regardless whether the transaction closes.
3. For this exercise, the acquisition agreement has the following grounds for termination:
   (a) The Seller may terminate because the Buyer made a misrepresentation.
   (b) The Buyer may terminate because the Seller made a misrepresentation.
   (c) The Buyer may terminate if a condition to their obligation to close is not satisfied.
4. The parties agree that liquidated damages based on the amount of the deposit make sense if the Buyer makes a misrepresentation and that is why the transaction does not close.
5. Assume that the transaction does not close and that the indemnification provisions do not apply.

Complete the endgame chart as best you can by using common sense and listing the possibilities or the most likely possibility for each ground for termination and type of payment.

FULL ENDGAME CHART FOR A SIMPLE ACQUISITION

GROUND FOR TERMINATION	MONETARY CONSEQUENCES RELATING TO THE DEPOSIT (KEEP OR RETURN?)	OTHER CONTRACTUAL CONSEQUENCE OF RECEIPT OF NOTICE OF INTENT TO TERMINATE (DO THE FACTS PROVIDE FOR ANY?)	DATE CONTRACT TERMINATES (DOES IT VARY DEPENDING ON THE FACTS?)	SURVIVAL OF COMMON LAW CAUSES OF ACTION (IF THE CONTRACT PROVIDES FOR LIQUIDATED DAMAGES, SHOULD THE COMMON LAW CAUSES OF ACTION SURVIVE?)	SURVIVAL OF OTHER CONTRACT PROVISIONS (WHAT PROVISION IS A CANDIDATE FOR SURVIVAL?)
Seller may terminate if Buyer's representation was false					
Buyer may terminate if Seller's representation was false					
Buyer may terminate if a condition to the Buyer's obligation to close is not satisfied					

D. EXERCISE 17D: CURE PROVISION

The following cure provision does not address an issue that it should address. What is it?

Termination. If either Party believes that the other Party is in material breach of this Agreement . . . , then the non-breaching Party may deliver notice of such breach to the other Party. In such notice, the non-breaching Party will identify the actions or conduct that it wishes such Party to take for an acceptable and prompt cure of such breach (or will otherwise state its good faith belief that such breach is incurable); provided, however, that such identified actions or conduct will not be binding upon the other Party with respect to the actions that it may need to take to cure such breach. If the breach is curable, the allegedly breaching Party will have ninety (90) days to either cure such breach (except to the extent such breach involves the failure to make a payment when due, which breach must be cured within thirty (30) days following such notice) or, if a cure cannot be reasonably effected within such ninety (90)-day period, to deliver to the non-breaching Party a plan for curing such breach which is reasonably sufficient to effect a cure within a reasonable period. If the breaching Party fails to (a) cure such breach within the ninety (90)-day or thirty (30)-day period, as applicable, or (b) use Commercially Reasonable Efforts to carry out the plan and cure the breach, the non-breaching Party may terminate this Agreement by providing written notice to the breaching Party.

E. EXERCISE 17E: LICENSE AGREEMENT ENDGAME PROVISIONS

Draft the endgame provisions for Exercise 13C on page 148. What is missing from your provisions—both from a drafting and a business perspective? Review one or two precedents to help you answer the question in the previous sentence. Use the following defined terms and definitions to help with your drafting:

> "**License**" means the license Ralph LP grants in Section 2.1.
> "**Licensed Products**" means caps and t-shirts bearing the Trademark.
> "**Term**" has the meaning assigned to it in Section 2.1.
> "**Trademark**" means a pictorial representation of the cartoon character Ralph.

F. EXERCISE 17F: AIRCRAFT PURCHASE AGREEMENT ENDGAME PROVISIONS

Draft the endgame provisions of the Aircraft Purchase Agreement. Use the information from the Purchase Offer and the Escrow Agreement, found in Exercise 14E on page 178, and the defined terms that were included in the Aircraft Purchase Agreement excerpt in Exercise 15G on page 205.

G. EXERCISE 17G: EMPLOYMENT AGREEMENT ENDGAME QUESTIONS

Read the following excerpt from an employment agreement and then answer the questions that follow:

Excerpt from an Employment Agreement

10. **Termination.** The Executive's employment terminates before the termination date stated in Article 2 as follows:

  10.1 **Death or Disability.** If the Executive dies or becomes permanently disabled, this Agreement terminates effective at the end of the calendar month during which his death occurs or when his disability becomes permanent.

  10.2 **Cause.** If a majority of the disinterested directors of the Company's board of directors vote to remove the Executive from his duties for Cause, this Agreement terminates and the Executive ceases to be an officer of the Company effective on the date specified by the directors. For purposes of this Agreement, "Cause" means the occurrence of any one or more of the following events:

    10.2.1 The Executive has been convicted of or pleaded guilty or no contest to

      10.2.1.1 any misdemeanor reflecting unfavorably on the Company; or

      10.2.1.2 any felony offense.

    10.2.2 The Executive has committed fraud or embezzlement, that determination to be made by a majority of the disinterested directors of the Company's board of directors in their reasonable judgment.

    10.2.3 A majority of the disinterested directors of the Company's board of directors has determined in their reasonable judgment that

      10.2.3.1 the Executive has breached one or more of his fiduciary duties to the Company or has made an intentional misrepresentation to the Company; and

      10.2.3.2 the breach or misrepresentation has had or is likely to have a material adverse effect on the Company's business operations or financial condition.

    10.2.4 The Executive has failed to obey a specific written direction from the board of directors consistent with this Agreement and the Executive's duties under this Agreement.

    10.2.5 After written notice and a 30-day cure period, the Executive has materially neglected or failed to satisfactorily discharge any of his duties or responsibilities, that determination to be made by a majority of the disinterested directors of the Company's board of directors in their reasonable judgment.

Questions

1. Section 10.1 provides for termination on death or permanent disability. While death is relatively certain, the Company and Executive might dispute whether the Executive's disability has become permanent. If you represented the Executive, what substantive changes could you recommend that would provide greater certainty as to when a disability would become permanent?

2. Why are fraud and embezzlement treated differently from misdemeanors and felonies that require conviction?

3. Does subsection 10.2.3 adequately protect the Company if the Executive makes misrepresentations or breaches his fiduciary duties? What if he lied on his résumé? Will this lead to a material adverse effect on the Company's financial condition?

4. If you represented the Executive, what change could you ask for in subsection 10.2.4 that would provide your client with greater protection? Use the other subsections as a guide.

5. Assume that the Company pays the Executive an annual salary and a guaranteed bonus of $10,000, and reimburses his expenses. The guaranteed bonus increases each year by 5 percent on a compounded basis. If you represented the Company, what would you suggest that the Company pay the Executive upon termination for each of the scenarios in the excerpt? (The answer does not have to include precise dollar amounts, but just be conceptual.) What would you recommend if you represented the Executive?

CHAPTER EIGHTEEN

Drafting the General Provisions

I. INTRODUCTION[1]

The **general provisions,** also known as the **boilerplate provisions**, are usually at the end of the contract, usually after or combined with the endgame provisions and under the heading of *Miscellaneous* or *General Provisions*, giving the impression that these provisions are an afterthought or should remain the same from contract to contract. For this reason, drafters often do not take the time to think about how they should be tailored to the parties and transaction in question. These provisions supply a road map that tells the parties how to govern their relationship and administer the contract.

The terms *general* and *boilerplate* suggest standardized provisions that can be used in all circumstances. But, in practice, you will regularly find key business issues hidden within these provisions, which can get you into trouble if you do not redraft them, as many unfortunate drafters and clients have discovered, especially with *force majeure* during the COVID-19 pandemic. For example, they may not have thought through about which governing law might be more advantageous for their side when it came to enforcing a *force majeure* provision. Therefore, take the time to review the general provisions in a contract carefully and make all necessary changes.

Furthermore, if the parties are executing multiple agreements as part of a single transaction, make sure that the general provisions are the same in each agreement. For example, when a party borrows money, the parties involved may sign multiple contracts—not only a credit agreement, but also a security agreement and a pledge agreement. All of these contracts should use the *same general provisions*. Any differences between the general provisions in those three agreements could result in confusion and challenges should any problems arise.

Each section that follows discusses one of the general provisions and includes examples of the relevant provisions. General provisions can be grouped into the following categories: provisions dealing with third parties (assignment and delegation, successors, and assigns), provisions that determine what constitutes the contract (severability, amendments, waiver, integration or merger, and counterparts),

---

1. Parts of this chapter are based on a chapter in *Negotiating and Drafting Contract Boilerplate* (Stark et al. eds., ALM Publg. 2003) ("Negotiating and Drafting Contract Boilerplate"). We thank each of the authors for their contributions to *Negotiating and Drafting Contract Boilerplate* and to this book.

provisions regarding communications (notice), dispute resolution provisions (governing law, forum selection, waiver of right to a jury trial, and alternative dispute resolution), and risk allocation provisions (force majeure). Therefore, these provisions are included in the following sections of this chapter in this order.

Note that not all possible general provisions or even categories are covered in this chapter, and some of these provisions could be grouped by practitioners and commentators in different categories. For example, the confidentiality provisions examined in Chapter 17 on pages 248-254 could be general provisions included in the communications provisions, even though they are not covered separately here in more depth. Another possible category too of general provisions is interpretive provisions, discussed in Chapter 15 on page 202, Chapter 22 on page 332, Chapter 25 on page 390, and Chapter 27 on page 429, which could include provisions that address captions, headings, numbers, and gender. Furthermore, as mentioned previously, a number of the general provisions covered here can also be considered endgame provisions, such as *alternative dispute resolution* and *force majeure*; and several of the endgame provisions covered in Chapter 17, such as *indemnities*, could be included in the general provisions.

By learning the business and legal implications of the general provisions that follow, you will know when and how to modify them accordingly.

II. ASSIGNMENT AND DELEGATION[2]

The **assignment and delegation provision** is one of the general provisions that you will most often need to tailor to the needs of the parties or the terms of the contract. When you do, you must deal with both assignments and delegations, not just assignments. You have to account for whether the benefits of a contract can be assigned and, if so, to whom and under what circumstances; and you have to determine whether the parties will be allowed to delegate their duties, and, if so, to whom and under what circumstances. Many provisions in precedents do not even mention delegation, but this is incorrect. Here is an example of a provision that addresses both:

Example—Assignment and Delegation Provision

Section 10.3. Assignment and Delegation. No party may assign any right or delegate any performance under this Agreement. All assignments of rights are prohibited, whether they are voluntary or involuntary, by merger, consolidation, dissolution, operation of law, or any other manner. A purported assignment or purported delegation in breach of this Section 10.3 is void.

A. THE BASICS OF ASSIGNMENTS AND DELEGATIONS

Recall from Chapter 4 on page 25 that the flip side of every obligation is a right. For example, if Leslie has an obligation to pay Ibrahim $100, Ibrahim has a right to be paid $100. An assignment is a transfer of that right to a third party. If Ibrahim transfers that right of payment to Mark, that would make Ibrahim the **assignor** and Mark the **assignee,** and Leslie would be the **nonassigning party**.

---

2. This section is based on Tina L. Stark, Assignment and Delegation, in *Negotiating and Drafting Contract Boilerplate* ch. 3.

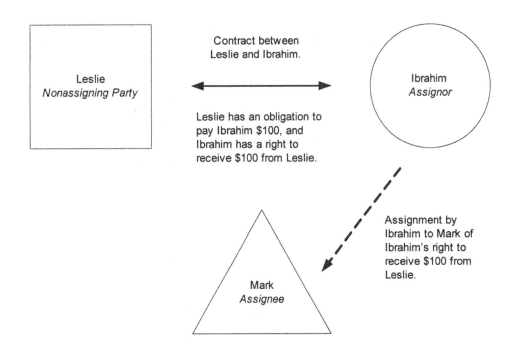

Once Ibrahim assigns his rights to Mark, he no longer has a right to Leslie's performance. Instead, Mark has that right, and Leslie has a duty to perform in Mark's favor.[3]

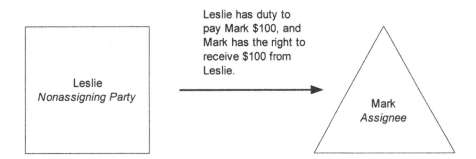

Note that the arrow goes in only one direction: Mark has no duty to perform in favor of Leslie, as Ibrahim did not delegate to Mark his duty to deliver the paper to Leslie. Ibrahim only assigned to Mark his right to receive $100 from Leslie. This leads us to delegations.

A party **delegates their performance** when they appoint someone else to perform instead.[4] The party who delegates their performance is the **delegating party**. The person to whom they delegate their performance is the **delegate**, and the other party to the original contract is the **nondelegating party**. However, delegation of a duty does not discharge the delegating party's performance obligation. Rather,

---

3. *See Pac. E. Corp. v. Gulf Life Holding Co.*, 902 S.W.2d 946, 958-959 (Tenn. App. 1995) (citing Samuel Williston, *A Treatise on the Law of Contracts* vol. 3, § 433 (3d ed., Baker, Voorhis & Co. 1960) and *Restatement (Second) of Contracts* §§ 280 cmt. e (1979)).

4. *See Proriver, Inc. v. Red River Grill, LLC*, 83 F.Supp. 2d 42, 50 n. 14 (D.D.C. 1999).

the delegating party remains secondarily liable.[5] Were it otherwise, the delegating party could effectively eliminate their performance obligation by delegating it to someone unable to perform.

Not all duties are *delegable*. If a duty is personal in nature or requires the delegating party's unique skills, the would-be delegating party cannot delegate.[6] For example, a Grammy-award-winning artist could not delegate their duty to perform at Madison Square Garden to your professor.

Assume that Ibrahim has a right to the $100, but only if he delivers two boxes of multipurpose paper to Leslie. Now Ibrahim has not only a right, but also a duty to perform. A delegation would consist of Ibrahim delegating to Mark the former's duty to deliver the paper to Leslie.

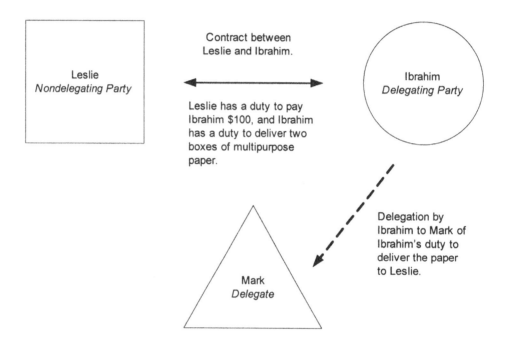

Delegation alone does not bind a delegate to perform in favor of the nondelegating party. If it did, anyone could become obligated to perform anything even though that person had not agreed to do so. Thus, the delegate must agree with the delegating party that they will perform in favor of the nondelegating party. They must *assume* the delegating party's duties to the nondelegating party.[7] When they do so, the nondelegating party becomes a third-party beneficiary of that assumption. For example, among the nondelegable duties is a party's obligation to execute a promissory note.[8] That duty would become delegable, however, if the delegate were willing and able to tender cash to the nondelegating party at the time of the delegation.[9,10]

---

5. *Lonsdale v. Chesterfield*, 662 P.2d 385, 388 (Wash. 1983).

6. *In re Schick*, 235 B.R. 318, 323 (Bankr. S.D.N.Y. 1999).

7. *Lumsden v. Roth*, 291 P.2d 88, 89-90 (Cal. App. 1955).

8. *See* Joseph M. Perillo, *Calamari and Perillo on Contracts* 631 (5th ed., West 2009).

9. *Id.*

10. Parties can also create a performance obligation through a novation. *See First Am. Com. Co. v. Wash. Mut. Sav. Bank*, 743 P.2d 1193, 1195 (Utah 1987) (stating that the "essential element of a novation is the discharge of one of the parties to a contract and the acceptance of a new performer by the other party as a substitute for the first original party.").

When Mark, a willing delegate, assumes Ibrahim's duty to Leslie, Mark becomes obligated to deliver to Leslie the two boxes of multipurpose paper. And because the flip side of every obligation is a right, Leslie has a right to Mark's performance: the delivery of the multipurpose paper. Leslie becomes the third-party beneficiary of Mark's assumption of Ibrahim's duty.

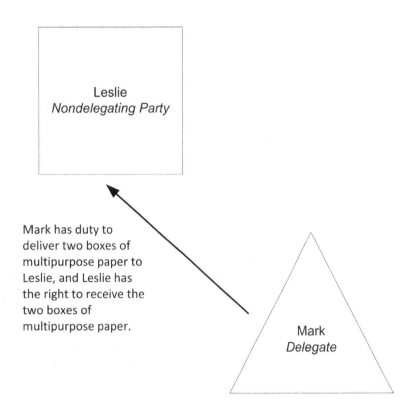

Mark has duty to deliver two boxes of multipurpose paper to Leslie, and Leslie has the right to receive the two boxes of multipurpose paper.

B. ANTI-ASSIGNMENT PROVISIONS

An **anti-assignment provision** prohibits a party from assigning their rights under a contract. This type of provision can be tailored for specific parties, rights, and possible assignees. Parties insert these provisions to prevent assignments that would materially change the nonassigning party's duties or materially increase the nonassigning party's risks.[11] In one line of cases, for example, the anti-assignment provisions were held enforceable because the nonassigning party would lose certain tax benefits, if an assignment were allowed.[12] In addition, some parties pair anti-assignment provisions with anti-delegation provisions to ensure that they need to deal with only one party—the one with whom they originally contracted.

An anti-assignment provision must be carefully drafted in detail to make it enforceable. However, even then, often the provision is still not enforceable. There are two reasons for this. First, for commercial transactions, the provisions of the Uniform Commercial Code (the "**UCC**") render ineffective any anti-assignment

---

11. *See Restatement (Second) of Contracts* § 317(2)(a) (1981).
12. *See, e.g., Grieve v. Gen. Am. Life Ins. Co.*, 58 F. Supp. 2d 319, 323 (D. Vt. 1999).

provisions subject to the UCC.[13] So, no matter how careful you are, the provision will be ineffective. Second, even if the UCC is inapplicable, courts are hostile to these provisions and judges may determine these provisions to be unenforceable[14] on the basis that they restrain commerce.[15]

To prohibit a transfer of rights, you should draft the anti-assignment provision to prohibit *an assignment of rights under the agreement*. If the provision prohibits only *the assignment of the agreement*, courts generally interpret the provision as an anti-delegation provision. Both the UCC and the *Restatement (Second) of Contracts* specifically provide canons of interpretation to that effect.[16]

Courts dislike anti-assignment provisions and, therefore, as a policy matter, construe them narrowly.[17] In making their decisions, courts determine whether the parties intended an anti-assignment provision or an anti-delegation provision.

To create an anti-assignment provision that renders an assignment void, you must take away not only the right to assign, but also the power to assign.[18] To do this, a contract must prohibit the assignment of rights under the contract and declare that any purported assignment is void.[19] You do not need to add *null* or *of no further force and effect,* terms synonymous with *void*. Using *void* is enough.

Finally, in drafting an anti-assignment provision, *be specific*. Courts narrowly construe the meaning of the verb *assign*. For example, if you want to prohibit assignments by merger, or by operation of law, you should explicitly prohibit these types of assignments because a general prohibition on assignments would not include them.[20] Indeed, do not rely on *general* anti-assignment language if the parties agree that only a *specific* assignment is prohibited. If the parties want to prohibit *all* mergers, consider defining *merger* by stating that the term refers to *any* merger, regardless of which party survives.

---

13. *See* UCC § 2-210(2), U.L.A. UCC § 2-210(2) (2004); UCC §§ 9-406–9-409, U.L.A. UCC §§ 9-406–9-409 (2002).

14. Calamari & Perillo, *supra* n. 8, at 709 (stating that the cases "have tended to find that the particular provision before the court was not drafted with sufficient clarity to accomplish its purpose of prohibiting assignment. They have often emasculated the provision by holding it to be merely a promise not to assign.").

15. *See Segal v. Greater Valley Terminal Corp.*, 199 A.2d 48, 50 (N.J. Super. App. Div. 1964). The following is an example of how an anti-assignment provision can impede commerce. Assume that Rancher Rob sells Stockyard Sue ten heads of cattle for $500 and that the contract provides that Stockyard Sue can pay Rancher Rob at a later date. Assume further that before the payment date, Rancher Rob needs cash to make an investment. One way that Rancher Rob can fund that investment is to assign his $500 account receivable to Credit Bank. In exchange, Credit Bank would pay Rancher Rob a discounted amount (say, $450). The benefit of this assignment is that it gives Rancher Rob access to funds that he would not otherwise have. Thus, the assignment permits a new commercial venture. That venture is not possible, however, if Rancher Rob's contract with Stockyard Sue has an enforceable anti-assignment provision.

16. UCC § 2-210(4), U.L.A. UCC § 2-210(4) (2004); *Restatement (Second) of Contracts* § 322(1) (1981).

17. *Rumbin v. Utica Mut. Ins. Co.*, 757 A.2d 526, 531 (Conn. 2000).

18. *Bel-Ray Co., Inc. v. Chemrite (Pty) Ltd.*, 181 F.3d 435, 442 (3d Cir. 1999).

19. *Pravin Bankers Assocs., Ltd. v. Banco Pop. del Peru*, 109 F.3d 850, 856 (2d Cir. 1997).

20. *Dodier Realty & Inv. Co. v. St. Louis Nat'l Baseball Club, Inc.*, 238 S.W.2d 321, 325 (Mo. 1951).

You may also want to explicitly prohibit a **change of control**.[21] For example, a change of control may occur if a shareholder sells more than 50 percent of a company's shares to another person. Parties worry about such a change because a new person controlling the other party can dramatically change the parties' relationship. To prohibit a change of control, provide either that a change of control is deemed an assignment for purposes of the anti-assignment provision or that a change of control is a default. In addition, consider whether the agreement should define change of control.

C. ANTI-DELEGATION PROVISIONS

Unlike anti-assignment provisions, **anti-delegation provisions** are generally enforceable[22] and may be drafted in a straightforward manner by stating that neither party may delegate performance.[23] Just as with an anti-assignment provision, include a declaration that any purported delegation in violation of the parties' agreement is void.

If the parties desire an anti-delegation provision but wish to permit a specific delegation, consider whether the right to delegate should be subject to any conditions. A common condition requires the delegate to be creditworthy. In addition, drafters often require the delegate to assume, in writing, the delegating party's performance obligations. If you represent a client that is likely to be the delegating party, secure an agreement in which the delegating party is deemed released from their performance obligations on the signing of the delegation documents. Otherwise, they remain secondarily liable.

III. SUCCESSORS AND ASSIGNS[24]

The **successors and assigns provision** is a staple of commercial contracts. Although inserted almost routinely, its function and effect are rarely understood and some practitioners do not think they are worthwhile to include. It is sometimes confused with the assignment and delegation provision, but that provision addresses whether the contract permits assignments and delegations. By contrast, the successors and assigns provision addresses the *consequences* of an assignment and delegation. That is, it assumes that an assignment and delegation have occurred, and addresses how that occurrence affects those involved.

> *Example—Successors and Assigns Provision*
>
> **Successors and Assigns.** This Agreement binds and benefits the parties and their respective permitted successors and assigns.[25]

---

21. *Segal v. Greater Valley Terminal Corp.*, *supra* n. 15.

22. *See* UCC § 2-210(1), U.L.A. UCC § 2-210(1) (2004); *Restatement (Second) of Contracts* § 318(1) (1981).

23. *Performance* is a better word choice than *duty* because performance is broader, encompassing not only duties, but also conditions. *Restatement (Second) of Contracts* § 319(1) (1981).

24. This section is based on Tina L. Stark, Successors and Assigns, in *Negotiating and Drafting Contract Boilerplate*.

25. An alternative provision can be found in this chapter on page 271.

Courts differ as to this provision's purpose and effect.[26] To understand successors and assigns provisions better, some additional detail on the law of assignments and delegation is helpful.

As noted previously, when a party assigns their rights under a contract to a third party, the nonassigning party becomes bound to perform for the benefit of the assignee.[27] But an assignment confers *only the benefits of the rights being assigned*, not any performance obligations.[28] The assignee is only an assignee, not an assignee and a delegate. Acceptance of the assignment does not create performance obligations.

However, an assignee may also be a delegate. If a party simultaneously assigns their rights and delegates their performance, the assignee becomes a delegate in assuming the delegating party's duties to the nondelegating party.[29] Unfortunately, assignments are often ambiguous and do not always clearly state whether the assignor is simultaneously delegating its performance or not.[30] In these cases, the courts look to whether the assignee assumed their assignor's performance.[31] If they did, then the court will also find a delegation.[32] Unfortunately, no consensus exists in the courts as to whether an assumption must be express or whether an implied assumption is also permissible.[33]

The *Restatement (Second) of Contracts* and the UCC provide that broad, general words of assignment constitute not only an assignment, but also a delegation.[34] So, for example, an assignment *of all my rights under the contract* would be both an assignment and a delegation, even though the delegation was unstated and the assumption was implied. Some courts have created an exception if evidence demonstrates that the parties intended something different, such as when an assignment is a grant of a security interest. Other courts hold that assumptions must be express.[35]

We return now to the successors and assigns provision. The courts have interpreted the successors and assigns provision in different ways. Although some

---

26. *See* nn. 36-40 on pages 271-272.

27. *See Pac. E. Corp. v. Gulf Life Holding Co., supra* n. 3.

28. *See Petals Factory Outlet of Del., Inc. v. EWH & Assocs.*, 600 A.2d 1170, 1174 (Md. Spec. App. 1992).

29. *Lumsden v. Roth, supra* n. 10; *see* John Edward Murray, Jr., *Murray on Contracts* §§ 136[A][2], 139 (5th ed., Matthew Bender & Co., Inc. 2011); E. Allan Farnsworth, *Farnsworth on Contracts* vol. 3, § 11.10, 129 (3d ed., Aspen Publishers 2004).

30. Arthur L. Corbin et al., *Corbin on Contracts* vol. 9, § 47.6 (Joseph M. Perillo ed., rev. ed., West Publg. Co. 2007).

31. *See generally* Murray, *supra* n. 29, at § 141[E].

32. *Id.*

33. *See Meighan v. Watts Constr. Co.*, 475 So. 2d 829, 833 (Ala. 1985) (stating that the law "in most states" requires an express assumption (citing *Rose v. Vulcan Materials Co.*, 194 S.E.2d 521, 533 (N.C. 1973))); *but see Nofziger Commun., Inc. v. Birks*, 757 F. Supp. 80, 82, 85 (D.D.C. 1991) ("[A]lthough some jurisdictions seem to have accepted the express assumption rule as one of general applicability, [it is not the general rule]. . . . [A] review of the law in other jurisdictions reveals that many jurisdictions have applied the express assumption rule only in a few narrow situations [the sale of land and assumption of liability for past breaches].").

34. *Restatement (Second) of Contracts* § 328(1) (1981); UCC §§ 2-210(4), U.L.A. UCC § 2-210(4) (2004).

35. *See Bluebonnet Warehouse Coop. v. Bankers Trust Co.*, 89 F.3d 292, 297 (6th Cir. 1996); *see also Restatement (Second) of Contracts* § 328(1) (1981); UCC § 2-210(4), U.L.A. UCC § 2-210(4) (2004).

courts have held that it binds an assignee,[36] others have held that it does not.[37] Some courts have held that the successor and assigns provision demonstrates that the parties intended contract rights to be assignable.[38] And other courts have held that it is evidence that a nondelegable duty is delegable.[39] One case even holds that the provision constituted evidence that a preliminary agreement was a binding contract.[40]

In the face of all these different holdings, you rely on this provision at your own risk. The recommended approach is to draft a provision that says exactly what the parties intend, such as:

Example—Recommended and More Explicit Successors and Assigns Provision

X.X Successors and Assigns.

(a) **The Nonassigning Party's Performance Obligations.** If there is an assignment, the nonassigning party is deemed to have agreed to perform in favor of the assignee.

(b) **The Assignee's Performance Obligations.** If there is an assignment,

    (i) a contemporaneous delegation is deemed to have occurred, and

    (ii) the assignee is deemed to have assumed the assignor's performance obligations in favor of the nonassigning party (except if in either instance there is evidence to the contrary).

(c) **Assignability of Rights and Delegability of Performance.** This Section X.X does not address, directly or indirectly, whether

    (i) rights under this Agreement are assignable or

    (ii) performance under this Agreement is delegable.

Section [insert here the number for the anti-assignment provision] addresses these matters.

(d) **Definitions.** For purposes of this Section X.X,

    (i) "**assignment**" means any assignment, whether voluntary or involuntary, by merger, consolidation, dissolution, operation of law or any other manner;

    (ii) "**assignee**" means any successor or assign of the assignor;

    (iii) "**a change of control**" is deemed an assignment of rights; and

    (iv) "**merger**" refers to any merger in which a party participates, regardless of whether it is the surviving or disappearing party.

---

36. *See Mehul's Inv. Corp. v. ABC Advisors, Inc.*, 130 F.Supp. 2d 700, 706 (D. Md. 2001) (stating that because the contract included a successors and assigns provision, the parties contemplated that they might assign their rights "and that their assigns and successors would be bound by the contract.").

37. *See Kneberg v. H.L. Green Co., Inc.*, 89 F.2d 100, 103-104 (7th Cir. 1937), and the cases cited therein.

38. *See Baum v. Rock*, 108 P.2d 230, 234 (Col. 1940) ("The courts generally have held that a contract which otherwise might not be assignable, is made so by the insertion therein of a provision binding the assigns of the parties. We follow this rule.").

39. *See Davis v. Basalt Rock Co.*, 237 P.2d 338, 343 (Cal. Dist. App. 1952) (holding that performance could not be delegated despite a recital of "assignability" in the successors and assigns provision as that provision was not "absolutely determinative," and nothing that "the intention of the parties must be gathered from a consideration of the terms and entire tenor of the contract.") (quoting *Montgomery v. De Picot*, 96 P. 305, 307 (Cal. 1908)).

40. *See Plastone Plastic Co. v. Whitman-Webb Realty Co.*, 176 So. 2d 27, 28-29 (Ala. 1965) (Although the successors and assigns provision made no reference to binding the parties, the contract

By clarifying the parties' obligations under an assignment and expressly stating that a delegation occurs concurrently with assignment, this proposed provision solves the problem presented by the common law and better serves the purpose of the successors and assigns provision.

If you do use a more traditional and simple version, include the word *permitted* before *successors and assigns*. That should prevent a party from successfully arguing that the successors and assigns provision allows assignments and delegations.

Example—Using Permitted

This Agreement binds and benefits the parties and their respective *permitted* successors and assigns.

When the words *successors* and *assigns* are used together, *assigns* denotes a party to whom a voluntary transfer of rights has been made.[41] *Successor* does not usually mean *assignee*. Instead, the classic definition of a *successor* is a corporation that by merger, consolidation, or other legal succession has been transferred rights and has assumed the performance obligations of another corporation.[42]

IV. SEVERABILITY[43]

Courts will not enforce obligations arising out of illegal agreements.[44] However, a contract that contains one illegal provision may also contain legal, enforceable provisions. In these situations, a refusal to enforce the entire contract might prove unduly harsh. Instead, courts often strike the offending provisions and allow the rest of the agreement to stay in force.[45]

The purpose of a **severability provision** is to express the parties' intent that a court enforce the valid provisions of a contract, even if it finds a provision to be illegal or unenforceable. Usually, the provision is similar to the following:

Example 1—Severability Provision

Severability. If any provision of this Agreement is determined to be illegal or unenforceable, the remaining provisions of this Agreement remain in full force, if the essential provisions of this Agreement for each party remain legal and enforceable.

---

was found to be "binding upon the original parties[.]") (citing *Tex. Co. v. Birmingham S. College*, 194 So. 192 (Ala. 1940)); *but see Normandy Place Assocs. v. Beyer*, 1988 WL 35311 at *1 (Ohio App. 2d Dist. Mar. 16, 1988) (referring to the successors and assigns provision as evidence that a preliminary agreement was a binding contract).

41. *See S. Patrician Assocs. v. Int'l Fid. Ins. Co.*, 381 S.E.2d 98, 99 (Ga. App. 1989).

42. *See Enchanted Ests. Community Ass'n, Inc. v. Timberlake Improvement Dist.*, 832 S.W.2d 800, 802 (Tex. App.—Houston [1st Dist.] 1992) ("As applied to corporations, 'successor' does not normally mean an assignee . . . .") (*citing Int'l Ass'n of Machinists, Lodge No. 6 v. Falstaff Brewing Corp.*, 328 S.W.2d 778, 781 (Tex. App.—Houston 1959)).

43. This section is based on C. James Levin & Avery R. Brown, Severability, in *Negotiating and Drafting Contract Boilerplate* ch. 17.

44. *See generally* Richard A. Lord, *Williston on Contracts* vol. 6, § 13.25, 831-837 (4th ed., West 2009) (discussing traditional blue-pencil rule).

45. *See Rogers v. Wolfson*, 763 S.W.2d 922, 924 (Tex. App. Dallas 1989), *cert. denied*, (Tex. Feb. 13, 1989) (holding that clearly severable provision will not render entire contract invalid).

> ### Example 2—Severability Provision
>
> **Severability.** If any provision of this Agreement is illegal or unenforceable, that provision is severed from this Agreement and the other provisions remain in force.

Unfortunately, these provisions rarely reflect the parties' actual intent. For example, imagine a noncompete agreement that requires an employer to pay an employee $3 million, in return for which the employee agrees not to compete anywhere in the world for ten years. Imagine further that the court holds that the noncompete is overly broad and unenforceable. With a severability provision like Example 1 or 2, the noncompete would be severed, but the payment obligation would remain. The likelihood that this would accomplish the parties' intent is low. More likely, they intended that the provisions that were not severed would remain in effect only if the essential provisions of the agreement for each party remained binding and enforceable.

While Examples 1 and 2 may not preclude *all* intent-related issues, at least they explicitly express that the parties cannot do without some provisions. In addition, they give the parties the opportunity to argue which provisions are essential in the context of any later dispute.

Under the traditional **blue-pencil rule**, a court will delete portions of an otherwise unenforceable provision if the deleted portions can be clearly—and grammatically—separated from the remainder of the provision (i.e., if the provision will still be grammatically correct after the offending terms have been deleted). For example, an overbroad covenant forbidding future employment in Connecticut could not be reduced to cover one county in a blue-pencil jurisdiction.[46] By contrast, that result could be reached if the covenant had separately listed each county in Connecticut. Then a court could salvage the noncompete by deleting specific counties until the list was no longer overbroad. States that have adopted the blue-pencil approach include Connecticut, Indiana, and North Carolina.[47]

The *Restatement (Second) of Contracts* has rejected the blue-pencil approach in favor of the more flexible **rule of reasonableness**.[48] Under this rule, a court may reform an unenforceable provision to the extent reasonable under the circumstances and then enforce it as so reformed.[49] States that have adopted this approach include Delaware, Florida, New Jersey, New York, Pennsylvania, and Tennessee.[50] Courts have sought to limit the risk of overreaching that this approach might entail by requiring proof that the offending provisions were drafted in good faith and in accordance with standards of fair dealing.[51]

Keep one other thing in mind when drafting severability provisions: The way that you draft the provision should reflect whether the governing law is that of a

---

46. *See Beit v. Beit*, 63 A.2d 161, 166 (Conn. 1948) (covenant unenforceable where parties intended the covenant to apply to a certain county, not a severable portion of it).

47. *See id.* at 165-166; *College Life Ins. Co. of Am. v. Austin*, 466 N.E.2d 738, 744 (Ind. App. 1st Dist. 1984); *Whittaker Gen. Med. Corp. v. David*, 379 S.E. 2d 824, 828 (N.C. 1989).

48. *Restatement (Second) of Contracts* § 184 (1979).

49. *Id.*

50. *See Knowles-Zeswitz Music, Inc. v. Cara*, 260 A.2d 171, 175 (Del. Ch. 1969); *Dorminy v. Frank B. Hall & Co.*, 464 So. 2d 154, 157 (Fla. 5th Dist. App. 1985); *Solari Indus., Inc. v. Malady*, 264 A.2d 53, 57 (N.J. 1970); *Karpinski v. Ingrasci*, 268 N.E.2d 751, 754-755 (N.Y. 1971); *Sidco Paper Co. v. Aaron*, 351 A.2d 250, 254-255 (Pa. 1976); *C. Adjustment Bureau v. Ingram*, 678 S.W.2d 28, 37 (Tenn. 1984).

51. *See* Lord, *supra* n. 44, at § 13.26, 853-854; Farnsworth, *supra* n. 29, at § 5.8, 347; *C. Adjustment Bureau v. Ingram, supra* n. 50 (noting that credible evidence that a contract is "deliberately" unreasonable and oppressive will render it invalid).

state that follows the blue-pencil rule[52] or that of a state that follows the **rule of reasonableness**.[53]

V. AMENDMENTS[54]

Amendment provisions outline how the parties may amend the agreement in the future. Here are some examples of provisions relating to amendments to the contract:

Examples 1—Amendment Provisions

Amendments. The parties may amend this Agreement only by signing a written agreement that identifies itself as an amendment to this Agreement.

Amendments. To amend this Agreement, all parties must sign a written agreement that identifies itself as an amendment. [If these conditions are not satisfied, the purported amendment is not effective.]

For more on amending contracts, see Chapter 34 on page 527.

A. ENFORCEABILITY OF THESE PROVISIONS

The **no oral amendments provision** is a classic general provision—always present, rarely negotiated. This provision would not allow the parties to make changes to the written contract by a verbal agreement, but it is generally unenforceable under the common law. In a Texas case, the court stated that a written contract "is of no higher legal degree than an oral one, and either may vary or discharge the other."[55] Similarly, in a New York case, Judge Cardozo said:

> Those who make a contract may unmake it. The clause which forbids a change, may be changed like any other. . . . What is executed by one act is restored by another. . . . Whenever two [persons] contract, no limitation self-imposed can destroy their power to contract again.[56]

To bring greater predictability to contractual relations, some states have enacted laws providing that no oral amendment provisions are enforceable.[57] However, the courts have undermined these statutory provisions by finding that parties can modify the underlying agreement by an executed (completed) oral amendment, a course of conduct, or estoppel.[58]

A nationwide solution has also been attempted through UCC § 2-209(2), which provides that *no oral amendment* provisions are enforceable in contracts.[59] Unfortunately, this solution is limited in scope to contracts subject to UCC Article 2 and is not bulletproof. Specifically, under UCC § 2-209(4), a purported amendment

---

52. *See generally* Lord, *supra* n. 44, at § 13.25, 831-837 (discussing traditional blue-pencil rule).

53. *See generally Restatement (Second) of Contracts* § 184 (1979).

54. This section is based on Brian A. Haskel, General Provisions, in *Negotiating and Drafting Contract Boilerplate* ch. 16.

55. *Mar-Lan Indus., Inc. v. Nelson*, 635 S.W.2d 853, 855 (Tex. App. El Paso 1982).

56. *Beatty v. Guggenheim Exploration Co.*, 122 N.E. 378, 381 (N.Y. 1919).

57. *See, e.g.*, Cal. Civ. Code § 1698 (2012); N.Y. Gen. Oblig. Law § 15-301 (2013).

58. *See Wechsler v. Hunt Health Sys., Ltd.*, 186 F. Supp. 2d 402 (S.D.N.Y. 2002); *S. Fed. Sav. & Loan Ass'n of Ga. v. 21-26 E. 105th St. Assocs.*, 145 B.R. 375, 380 (S.D.N.Y. 1991) ("Under certain conditions . . . a written agreement which provides that it cannot be modified except by a writing, can be modified by a course of conduct or actual performance.") (internal citations omitted).

59. UCC § 2-209(2) states:

that does not satisfy the requirements of the statute of frauds can operate as a waiver of the no oral amendments provision.[60] The rationale is that the course of performance during the term of the contract either represents a waiver or is relevant in determining whether a particular act affects the agreement's meaning. In essence, UCC § 2-209(4) codifies the estoppel theory, under which courts have enforced oral amendments despite contractual prohibitions against them.

With all these obstacles to an enforceable *no oral amendments* provision, the obvious question is whether it makes sense to try to include one. The answer is *yes*. These provisions evidence the parties' agreement and their intent at the time that the contract was signed. Many parties use them as guideposts for their actions during the life of the contract. If a dispute arises as to whether a purported amendment is enforceable, these provisions set the starting point for a court's analysis because they reflect the parties' understanding when they made their agreement.

B. DRAFTING THE NO ORAL AMENDMENTS PROVISION

Although most agreements use a variation of *amend* in the provision, parties often refer to the provision by an acronym: **NOM**, which stands for **no oral modification**.

The *no oral amendments* provision can be very simple. A typical provision can be written giving the parties discretionary authority (*may*) to amend the provision only by a signed, written agreement. Alternatively, the provision can be stated as a declaration.

You may tailor the provision by specifying who must sign on behalf of each party. You may also include as a condition to the enforceability of the amendment that each party must deliver to the other a board resolution authorizing the amendment. Also, consider including language that requires the amendment to identify itself as an amendment to the agreement. This can be helpful in New York, for instance, where the state's highest court held that the minutes of a board of directors' meeting, signed by the corporate secretary, were a sufficient writing to constitute the execution of an amendment.[61]

VI. WAIVER[62]

A **waiver provision** details the process that a party must take to waive a provision in the agreement. Here is an example of a provision stating that any waiver by a party relating to an issue in the contract must be in writing and signed by the party who probably stands most to lose from the waiver:

> *Example—Waiver Must Be in Writing and Signed by the Parties*
>
> **No Oral Waiver.** No purported waiver is effective as a waiver unless it is in writing by signed by the party against whom the waiver is sought to be enforced.

A signed agreement which excludes modification or rescission except by a signed writing cannot be otherwise modified or rescinded, but except as between merchants such a requirement on a form supplied by the merchant must be separately signed by the other party.

"Between merchants" is interpreted to mean between sophisticated parties. *Wis. Knife Workers v. Nat'l Metal Crafters*, 781 F.2d 1280, 1284 (7th Cir. 1986).

60. UCC § 2-209(4) states: "Although an attempt at modification or rescission does not satisfy the requirements of subsection (2) or (3) it can operate as a waiver."

61. *DFI Commun., Inc. v. Greenberg*, 394 N.Y.S.2d 586, 589-590 (N.Y. 1977).

62. This section is based on Tina L. Stark, Successors and Assigns, in *Negotiating and Drafting Contract Boilerplate*.

Practitioners and judges often describe a **waiver** as the intentional relinquishment of a known right.[63] However, many commentators take issue with this definition. They note that the doctrine of waiver typically applies to the waiver of a condition, not a right.[64] Thus, the doctrine applies when a party (called the *obligor*) agrees to perform their obligations under the contract even though the condition to those obligations has not been satisfied. However, the doctrine of waiver often only applies to immaterial conditions.[65]

To see how a waiver of a condition works, suppose that a lender agrees to lend $1 million to a borrower. Suppose that the lender's duty to lend the money is conditioned on the borrower's lawyer giving the lender a legal opinion about the absence of any litigation against the borrower. If the borrower's lawyer does not deliver this legal opinion, the lender has no duty to lend the money. But what if the borrower's lawyer refuses to give this legal opinion? While the lender has no duty to make the loan because the condition to its duty is not satisfied, it could decide that the litigation does not pose a significant risk to the lender. Thus, the lender could decide to waive that condition.

A waiver may be established expressly, as in the example in this section. However, a waiver also may be inferred from the obligor's conduct. For example, a waiver is effective where the obligor performs their duty even though they are aware, or should be aware, that a condition to their performance has not been fulfilled.[66] Further, where the obligor has a duty to object to the obligee's failure to fulfill a condition, silence also may constitute a waiver.[67] The language in the example attempts to state that waivers are only the first kind—an express promise, which is in a writing signed by the obligor.

However, these *no oral waiver* provisions—much like the *no oral amendments* provision—do not necessarily preclude a waiver. Instead, the decision is a question of fact in light of the circumstances, including the existence of an anti-waiver provision.[68] In making these determinations, courts look to the parties' words and deeds after the execution of the contract. Nonetheless, some courts have enforced provisions requiring waivers to be in writing.[69]

In analyzing issues regarding waiver, it is important to keep in mind that commentators and courts frequently use the word *waiver* to mean different things. To avoid confusion, commentators prefer to confine the use of the term to waiver of *nonmaterial conditions*, but they also recognize that the word is one that has an indefinite connotation.[70] For example, lawyers often apply the concept of waiver to duties too.

When applied to a duty, a waiver refers to a party's *voluntary relinquishment of their right to sue the other party for breach* under the contract. By viewing a waiver as applying to duties as well, a lawyer worries that if a client waives a right to sue for breach in one instance, the other party will view that as a permanent waiver, so they will never have to perform that duty in the future. To address this concern, lawyers sometimes include the following language in a no-waiver provision:

63. *See generally Restatement (Second) of Contracts* § 84 cmt b (1979).

64. *See, e.g.,* Lord, *Williston on Contracts* § 39:14 at 564 (4th ed. 2000); 8 McCauliff, *Corbin on Contracts,* § 40.1 at 514 (Perillo, ed., rev. ed. 1999).

65. *See Restatement (Second) of Contracts* § 84 (1979).

66. Lord, *Williston on Contracts* § 39:31 at 637-642 (4th ed. 2000); 8 McCauliff, *Corbin on Contracts,* § 40.4 at 533-540 (Perillo, ed., rev. ed. 1999).

67. Lord, *Williston on Contracts* § 39:35 at 653-654 (4th ed. 2000).

68. *See Winslow v. Dillard Department Stores Inc.,* 849 S.W.2d 862, 864 (Ct. App. Tex. 1993) ("Essentially, our view is that, while a nonwaiver provision may be some evidence of a party's nonwaiver, that provision, like any other contractual provision, may be waived.").

69. *See, e.g., Tillquist v. Ford Motor Credit Co.,* 714 F. Supp. 607, 612 (D. Conn. 1989); *National Payment Data Systems, Inc. v. Meridican Bank,* 212 F.3d 849, 855 (3d. Cir. 2000).

70. II Farnsworth, *Farnsworth on Contracts* § 8.5 at 425-426 2d ed. 1998).

> *Example—More Limiting Waiver*
>
> **No Waiver**. A waiver made in writing on one occasion is effective
>
> (a) only for the instance of non-performance of a duty specified in the written waiver, and
>
> (b) only for the benefit of the party to whom it is given,
>
> and does not waive the party's right to enforce that duty in any future instance not specified in the written waiver, or against any other Person.

VII. INTEGRATION OR MERGER[71]

An **integration provision**, sometimes called a **merger provision**[72] or a **zipper clause**, is "[a] contractual provision stating that the contract represents the parties' complete and final agreement and supersedes all informal understandings and oral agreements relating to the subject matter of the contract."[73] Here is an example of such a provision:

> *Example—Integration or Merger Provision*
>
> **Integration**. This Agreement constitutes the final, exclusive agreement between the parties on the matters contained in this Agreement. All earlier and contemporaneous negotiations and agreements between the parties on the matters contained in this Agreement are expressly merged into and superseded by this Agreement.

If there is no integration provision, courts will examine all the relevant facts and circumstances to determine whether it is a final and exclusive expression of the parties' agreement.[74] A writing that is a final expression of the parties' agreement is said to be **partially integrated**, while a writing that is both a final and exclusive expression of the parties' agreement is said to be **fully integrated**.

Including a *merger provision* in your agreement is the best way to ensure that parol evidence cannot be used to supplement the contract. Under the **parol evidence rule**,[75] if a writing is integrated, whether fully or partially, a term that contradicts the existing writing cannot be admitted into evidence.[76] If the writing is partially integrated,

---

71. This section is based on Ronald B. Risdon & William A. Escobar, Merger, in *Negotiating and Drafting Contract Boilerplate* ch. 18.

72. Merger is a real estate concept. Any covenants in the pre-closing documents not included in a deed are merged and superseded by the deed. Other transactions have not, historically, relied on this concept. Documents transferring ownership had no purpose other than the conveyance. However, the term "merger" has been adopted by many in contract drafting to refer to this concept not just in real estate transactions, but also in other business transactions.

73. *See Merger Clause and Integration Clause, Black's Law Dictionary* (11th ed. 2019).

74. *In re William Rakestraw Co.*, 450 F.2d 6 (9th Cir. 1971) (applying California law).

75. *See Parol Evidence Rule, Black's Law Dictionary* (11th ed. 2019) ("The common-law principle that a writing intended by the parties to be a final embodiment of their agreement cannot be modified by evidence of earlier or contemporaneous agreements that might add to, vary, or contradict the writing. This rule usu. operates to prevent a party from introducing extrinsic evidence of negotiations that occurred before or while the agreement was being reduced to its final written form.").

76. Farnsworth, *supra* n. 29, at vol. 2, § 7.3, 226 (quoting *Restatement (Second) of Contracts* § 215 (1981)).

evidence of prior negotiations and agreements is admissible to supplement the writing, but not to contradict it.[77] If the agreement is partially integrated, it is not the exclusive statement of the parties' agreement. Therefore, consistent provisions can supplement it. But if the writing is fully integrated (final and exclusive), generally, not even evidence of an additional consistent term is admissible.

Despite these rules, parol evidence is always admissible to explain an ambiguous contract term.[78] In addition, courts generally permit a party to introduce parol evidence that the other party fraudulently induced them to enter into the contract. A number of courts have prohibited the introduction of this evidence if the allegedly defrauded party disclaimed reliance in the contract on the representation that it now claims was the basis of the fraud.[79]

When drafting an integration provision, describe the agreement being signed as *final and exclusive* to signal that the parties intend the agreement to be fully integrated. Also, state the consequences of the agreement being final and exclusive — namely, that all prior negotiations and agreements are superseded by (i.e., merged into) the agreement being signed. If the agreement being signed does not supersede an existing agreement, such as a confidentiality agreement, state the exception.

If the parties are signing multiple agreements at the same time, use a defined term to refer to all the agreements — for example, use *Transaction Documents*. The merger provision should then state that those documents together constitute the final and exclusive agreement of the parties. Be sure that each of the other agreements being executed includes a merger provision that is exactly the same as the one in the primary agreement.

VIII. COUNTERPARTS[80]

A **counterpart** is a duplicate original that parties sign. Drafters use counterparts to expedite transactions when not all the parties attend the agreement's signing and to create multiple originals so that each party can have a fully executed original. A **counterpart** *provision* ensures that, even if there are multiple copies of the original, there is only one agreement between the parties. Here is an example of a counterparts provision:

> *Example—Counterparts Provision*
>
> **Counterparts.** The parties may execute this Agreement in one or more counterparts, each of which is an original, and all of which constitute only one agreement between the parties.

Historically, the rationale for using multiple counterparts was as an antifraud measure for contracts. The use of counterparts originated in real property conveyancing in England,[81] but it is less relevant today with the development of technologies making it easier to produce and transmit copies of documents.

---

77. *Id.*

78. *Id.* (quoting *Restatement (Second) of Contracts* § 216(1) (1981)).

79. *See e.g., Consarc Corp. v. Marine Midland Bank, N.A.*, 996 F.2d 568 (2d Cir. 1993) (applying New York law).

80. *See Abry Partners V, L.P. v. F & W Acq. LLC*, 891 A.2d 1032, 1059 (Del. Ch. 2006); *Danann Realty Corp. v. Harris*, 5 N.Y.2d 317 (N.Y. 1959).

81. This section is based on Frances Kulka Browne, Counterparts, in *Negotiating and Drafting Contract Boilerplate* ch. 19; *see also* Chapter 19 on page 306 for details concerning the signing of counterparts.

The typical counterparts provision in a modern contract provides that the parties may execute the contract in one or more counterparts. This is usually interpreted in two ways. First, the provision permits each party to sign separate counterparts, which, when collated, together constitute a fully executed original. Second, the provision allows for there to be multiple originals, each of which is signed by all the parties. In this event, each party leaves the signing with a single document that is a fully executed original. Some drafters prefer to spell out each of the two possibilities.

A well-drafted counterparts provision also states that the counterparts *constitute only one agreement*. This means that each party makes only one set of promises even though the parties may have executed multiple counterparts, creating multiple, fully executed originals. That is, neither party promises to do something as many times as it has executed counterparts.

IX. NOTICE[82]

Nearly every contract has a notice provision, which allocates the risk of a notice's nonreceipt. A well-drafted notice provision should state the ways by which a party may give notice, and it should do more than simply list the addresses to which parties should send their notices. Here is an example of a notice provision:

Example—Notice Provision

Section XX. Notice.

(a) **Requirement of a Writing; Permitted Methods of Delivery.** Each party giving or making any notice, request, demand, or other communication (each, a "**Notice**") in accordance with this Agreement shall give the Notice in writing and use one of the following methods of delivery, each of which for purposes of this Agreement is a writing:
   (i) Hand delivery by courier.
   (ii) Registered or Certified Mail (in each case, return receipt requested and postage prepaid).
   (iii) Internationally-recognized overnight courier (with all fees prepaid).
   (iv) E-mail.
(b) Addressees and Addresses. Any party giving a Notice shall address the Notice to the appropriate person at the receiving party (the "Addressee") at the address listed below:
   (i) If to [Name of party]: [Name of person and/or title]
       [Address Line #1]
       [Address Line #2]
       E-mail: [E-mail Address]

---

82. This section is based on Steven R. Berger, Notices, *Negotiating and Drafting Contract Boilerplate* ch. 15.

> (ii) If to [Name of party]: [Name of person and/or title]
> [Address Line #1]
> [Address Line #2]
> E-mail: [E-mail Address]
>
> (c) **Effectiveness of a Notice.** Except as provided elsewhere in this Agreement, a Notice is effective only if the party giving the Notice has complied with subsections (a) and (b) and if the Addressee has received the Notice.

Notice provisions used to focus on when the sender sent notice, such as: "A notice is effective three days after its deposit in a U.S. Postal Service mailbox." This meant that even if the notice was lost, the sender of the notice had rights against the recipient three days after mailing. The risk of nonreceipt was on the recipient. As this led to inequitable results, many parties now insist that the risk of nonreceipt should be on the sender. To do so, notice must be effective only on its receipt.

Typically, a provision permits notices to be given in writing by in-person delivery, by overnight courier, or by e-mail. The sender can easily monitor these delivery methods to determine whether the other party has received the notice. Many notice provisions no longer permit delivery by U.S. Postal Service first-class mail because of its unreliability. If the parties insist on delivery through the U.S. Postal Service, a common compromise is delivery by certified or registered mail. The benefit of these two forms of delivery is that a sender can request a return receipt.[83] The delivery of notice by e-mail has become more common, but some drafters still have some hesitation and would prefer a hard copy notice to be delivered of some important document to avoid any technological issues.

In drafting a notice provision, consider whether counsel should receive a copy of the notice. If so, the contract will need to address whether the notice should be effective only *after both the party and their counsel receive it*, or whether it should be effective only *upon receipt by the contract party, regardless of when counsel receives it*. Which of these two approaches to take depends on the rationale for requiring notice to counsel.

For example, if the purpose of the copy is to merely keep counsel up to date on the transaction's status, then arguably the notice's effective date should be unaffected by the date counsel receives it.

Alternatively, the copy to counsel could be a way of assuring that the party to the contract heeds the substantive message of the notice. The counsel may be more attentive to the client's business affairs than the client. Along similar lines, requiring a copy of notice to counsel can be a way of assuring the one giving notice that the receiving party's counsel will explain its importance to their client and encourage them to take any necessary action.

In either event, failing to give notice to counsel, should probably not affect the effective date of the notice to the client.

Finally, sending a copy to counsel may be an attempt to eliminate the risk of a failed notice if an individual corporate officer ceases to be with the organization—in that case, counsel can make sure that the appropriate party at the client receives the notice.

---

83. "Return receipt service provides a mailer with evidence of delivery (to whom the mail was delivered and date of deliver), along with information about the recipient's actual delivery address." U.S. Postal Serv., *Domestic Mail Manual* § 5.2.1, http://pe.usps.com/text/dmm300/503.htm#_top (accessed November 18, 2022).

To avoid confusion as to the meaning of the commonly used phrase *with a copy to:* in a notice provision, attorneys should take one of two approaches:

1. Where counsel should receive the notice at the same time as the client, the drafter should list counsel as a separate addressee in the notice provision, without the label "copy to:."
2. If the copy is a courtesy copy only, then the language of the notice provision should make this clear, as in the example that follows.

> *Example—Possible Notice Language for Copy to Counsel*
>
> The party sending the Notice shall also send an informational copy of each Notice to counsel for the Addressee as follows:
>
> [insert contact information for counsel here]
>
> The sender's failure to deliver an informational copy of a Notice to counsel does not constitute a breach of this Agreement or affect the effectiveness of the Notice.

If the notice provision indicates that the parties' addresses are set out on the signature page, then the counsel's address should be set out *in the notice provision itself*, as counsel is not a party to the agreement and will not be signing on the signature page. However, as discussed previously, we recommend including all addresses, even the parties', in the *notice provision*, not in the preamble or signature page, so that, for this and other reasons, they are easy to find and all in one place.

Additional points to consider when drafting a notice provision include:

- Is delivery of the notice a covenant or condition or both?
- If a copy of a notice is to be sent to a person other than a party, is that party's receipt required for the notice to be effective?
- Should the addressee be a specific person or the corporate title of the person in charge of the transaction?
- If the parties to the agreement are companies or other organized entities instead of individuals, how do you take into account what would happen if someone were to leave that entity?
- What accommodation, if any, needs to be made for international deliveries?
- How will you coordinate the notice provision in the general provisions with the other provisions in the agreement relating to providing notice, such as the notice of termination provisions discussed in Chapter 17 on page 236?

X. GOVERNING LAW[84]

A **governing law provision,** also known as a **choice of law provision**, establishes the law that governs a dispute arising from an agreement. In the absence of a governing law provision, common law conflict of laws principles govern. In that event, the governing law is that of the state with the most significant relationship to the transaction.[85] In a litigation matter, the parties may disagree about which state that

---

84. This section is based on Brad S. Karp & Shelly L. Friedland, *Governing Law and Forum Selection,* in *Negotiating and Drafting Contract Boilerplate* ch. 6.

85. *See Intercontinental Plan., Ltd. v. Daystrom, Inc.*, 248 N.E.2d 576, 582 (N.Y. 1969); *Restatement (Second) of Conflicts* § 188 (1971).

is, particularly when the law in one state favors one party. By choosing the governing law when drafting the contract, the parties may forestall a dispute on this issue.

Example—Governing Law Provision

Governing Law. The laws of [insert state name] (without giving effect to its conflicts of law principles) govern all matters arising under and relating to this Agreement, including torts.

Courts routinely enforce these provisions unless the chosen state has no substantial relationship to the parties or transaction, or in cases where the application of the law would violate the public policy of a state with a greater interest.[86]

When choosing which state's law should govern, consider several factors. First, evaluate whether the law of the jurisdiction under consideration is well developed and predictable in the area that your agreement covers. For example, Delaware and New York both have well-developed and predictable bodies of contract law in specific types of transactions, making an agreement's interpretation more predictable than might be true in other jurisdictions for those specific types of transactions. In addition, evaluate whether the particular body of state law is hostile or friendly to the type of client and the subject matter being represented. For example, while California courts have upheld significant punitive damages awards for bad faith denials of insurance coverage, New York courts, as a general matter, rarely make such awards.[87] Therefore, if you are representing an insurance company, you may prefer New York, but you would have to also take a closer look at all the jurisdictions that may be involved in case another jurisdiction could have a claim over the matter.

When drafting a governing law provision, pay attention to the language defining the scope of the provision. Despite the plain meaning of the words, the following provision is not as broad in scope as it seems to be:

Example—Incorrect Governing Law Provision Because Not as Broad

The laws of Kentucky govern all matters arising under this Agreement.

As drafted, the provision excludes torts and other claims.[88] One way to bring those claims within the provision's embrace is to add the phrase *or relating to*. Courts have stated that the phrase extends the scope of the governing law clause to

---

86. *See, e.g., Elgar v. Elgar*, 679 A.2d 937, 943 (Conn. 1996); *see Restatement (Second) of Conflicts* § 187 (1971); *see generally* Symeon C. Symeonides, *Choice of Law in the American Courts in 1996: Tenth Annual Survey*, 45 Am. J. Comp. L. 447, 488 (1997).

87. *Compare Delos v. Farmers Group, Inc.*, 155 Cal. Rptr. 843, 857 (App. 4th Dist. 1979), *with Rocanova v. Eq. Life Assurance Soc'y of the U.S.*, 634 N.E.2d 940, 944 (N.Y. 1994).

88. *See, e.g., Shelley v. Trafalgar House Pub. Ltd. Co.*, 918 F. Supp. 515, 521-522 (D.P.R. 1996) (Where the provision indicated that "this letter shall be subject to and construed in accordance with the laws of the State of New York," the provision did not apply to the tort claim.); *Caton v. Leach Corp.*, 896 F.2d 939, 943 (5th Cir. 1990) (finding that claims of tort, breach of duty of good faith, and fair dealing and claims for restitution were not included in the parties' narrow choice of law clause, which stated that "[t]his Agreement shall be construed under the laws of the State of California."); *Gloucester Holding Corp. v. U.S. Tape and Sticky Prods., LLC*, 832 A.2d 116, 122, 123-125 (Del. Ch. 2003) (holding that torts and statutory claims were outside the embrace of a governing law provision stating the agreement "shall be construed, interpreted and the rights of the parties determined in accordance with the laws of the State of Delaware . . . .").

matters beyond the specific contract.[89] This option may be startling because it uses a couplet. Generally, couplets should be banished from contracts as legalese.[90] Here, however, the couplet has meaning.

Alternatively, some drafters expressly state that the governing law will cover matters relating to torts by adding *including torts* immediately after *all matters*.

Example—Recommended Governing Law Provision Because Broader

The laws of Kentucky govern all matters arising under this Agreement, including torts.

Although this addition broadens the coverage to include tort claims, it is narrower than the phrase *arising out of or relating to,* which can even allow future oral agreements related to the contract to be considered.[91] Not covering torts one way or the other often leads to litigation.[92]

In many commercial transactions, the parties wish New York or Delaware law to govern, even though the transaction has no relationship with either state. This can be done if the amount of the transaction meets statutory thresholds set forth in New York and Delaware law.[93] If you go this route, pair the New York or Delaware governing law provision with a New York or Delaware *choice of forum provision* so that the litigation is in a forum that will enforce the governing law provision.[94] Be careful to check the dollar threshold for whatever state you are using because the amount required for the choice of forum provision may exceed that for a governing law provision.[95]

Some choice of law provisions deal with **renvoi,** French for *return* or *send back.* It occurs when one state's conflict of law principles require that a second state's principles be used, but that second state's principles require that the first state's principles be used. This referral from one state's principles to another and back to the first creates an endless cycle of return.

To break this cycle, some lawyers qualify the governing law provisions with the clause *without regard to its conflict of law principles*. See the provision introducing this section on page 282. In reality, this clause is unnecessary, as the law of the chosen state typically excludes its choice of law rules;[96] but the clause is commonly found in contracts nonetheless.

---

89. *See Turtur v. Rothschild Registry Int'l, Inc.*, 26 F.3d 304, 309 (2d Cir. 1994) (holding that a governing law provision was broad enough to cover torts when the agreement covered any controversy "arising out of or relating to" that agreement); *Caton v. Leach Corp.*, 896 F.2d 939, 943 (5th Cir. 1990) (comparing the contract's narrow clause that did "not address the entirety of parties' relationship" to broader clause that included "arising from or relating in any way.").

90. *See* F. Reed Dickerson, *The Fundamentals of Legal Drafting* 208 (2d ed., Little, Brown & Co. 1986).

91. *See ePresence, Inc. v. Evolve Software, Inc.*, 190 F.Supp. 2d 159, 162-163 (D. Mass. 2002) (construing California choice of law clause to include a subsequent and independent oral contract where the clause stated that it governed "[the] Agreement and all matters arising out of or relating to [the] Agreement. . . .").

92. *Abry Partners V, L.P. v. F & W Acq. LLC*, 891 A.2d 1032, 1059 (Del. Ch. 2006).

93. Del. Code Ann. tit. 6, § 2708(c) (2013); N.Y. Gen. Oblig. Law § 5-1401(1) (2013).

94. *See* Del. Code Ann. tit. 6, § 2708(b) (2013); N.Y. Gen. Oblig. Law § 5-1402 (2013); *but see Nutracea v. Langley Park Invs. PLC*, 2007 WL 135699 at *3 (E.D. Cal. Jan. 16, 2007). Although no California court has explicitly overruled *Nutracea*, in 2010 the Federal District Court for Massachusetts held that *Nutracea*'s holding was "no longer supported by the weight of law." *Huffington v. Carlyle Group*, 685 F. Supp. 2d 239, 244 (D. Mass. 2010).

95. For example, New York requires a $250,000 threshold for New York law to be governing law and a $1 million threshold for New York to be the forum. N.Y. Gen. Oblig. Law §§ 5-1401–5-1402 (2013). California requires a $250,000 threshold for California law to be governing law. Cal. Civ. Code § 1646.5 (2013). California also requires a $1 million threshold for California to be the forum. Cal. Civ. Proc. Code § 410.40 (2013).

96. *See Restatement (Second) of Conflict of Laws* § 187 cmt. h (1971) ("The reference [to the laws of a particular state], in the absence of a contrary indication of intention, is to the 'local law' of the

XI. FORUM SELECTION[97]

A **forum selection provision** designates, by agreement of the parties, one or more courts to adjudicate a dispute between the parties. In essence, the parties agree that a court will have personal jurisdiction over the parties with respect to disputes relating to the contract.[98]

Forum selection provisions are either **exclusive** (also known as **mandatory**) or **permissive** (also known as **nonexclusive** or **consensual**). In an exclusive forum selection provision, the parties designate one forum as the only jurisdiction where a plaintiff may bring suit. In a permissive forum selection provision, although the parties consent to jurisdiction in the identified forum, a plaintiff may bring an action elsewhere.

Forum selection provisions are generally enforceable.[99] However, a party may be able to void a forum selection provision on the grounds that the provision is unreasonable or against public policy.[100] For example, assume that a contract has a mandatory choice of forum provision that has stated that all suits are to be brought in Texas. A Louisiana court might be willing to void this provision and permit the suit to be brought in Louisiana if enforcing the Texas choice of forum provision would result in a Texas court decision that violated an important Louisiana public policy. In that event, the Louisiana court would hold that the importance of Louisiana's public policy would defeat the parties' intent.

A. FACTORS IN CHOOSING A FORUM

Before a drafter can decide which forum to include in the parties' contract, the drafter should confirm that the contracting parties want to litigate their dispute in court and not resort to alternative dispute resolution mechanisms, as discussed in more detail in this chapter on page 288. If the parties agree to address any disputes in court, the drafter should analyze which court would best serve their client's interests should litigation be necessary. Lawyers often consider factors such as geographic convenience of litigating in various jurisdictions (lawyers often prefer their client to have the *home court advantage*), whether the court will exercise jurisdiction over the parties, the caseload of the courts, and the personality of the courts. As part of a decision-making process, the drafter should also consider the differences between state and federal courts.

---

chosen state and not to that state's 'law,' which means the totality of its law including its choice-of-law rules. When they choose the state which is to furnish the law governing the validity of their contract, the parties almost certainly have the 'local law,' rather than the 'law,' of that state in mind (*compare* § 186, cmt. b). To apply the 'law' of the chosen state would introduce the uncertainties of choice of law into the proceedings and would serve to defeat the basic objectives, namely those of certainty and predictability, which the choice-of-law provision was designed to achieve."); *see also* Donald W. Glazer, Scott T. FitzGibbon & Steven O. Weise, *Glazer and FitzGibbon on Legal Opinions: Drafting, Interpreting, and Supporting Closing Opinions in Business Transactions* § 9.12.1 n. 2 (Aspen Publishers 2001).

97. This section is based on Tina L. Stark, Successors and Assigns, in *Negotiating and Drafting Contract Boilerplate.*

98. Corporations sometimes include mandatory forum selection provisions in their respective corporate charters or bylaws. These provisions require shareholders to bring any internal corporate claims against the corporation's officers, directors, and other shareholders in the state of incorporation. States typically uphold these forum selection provisions. *See, e.g.,* Del. Gen. Corp. L. § 115 (2021); *Drulias v. 1st Century Bancshares, Inc.*, 30 Cal. App. 5th 696 (Cal. Ct. App. 6th Dist. 2018) (upholding an exclusive forum selection bylaw choosing Delaware as the exclusive forum).

99. A few states still refuse to enforce any forum selection provisions, while others limit enforcement to specific types of contracts. *See, e.g.,* CA LAB § 925 (prohibiting an employer from requiring an employee to adjudicate a dispute outside of California if that employee primarily lives and works in California). For states that holds forum selection provisions are void, *see* Idaho Code § 29-110 (2020); Mont. Code Ann. § 28-2-708 (2019).

100. *See, e.g., Handoush v. Lease Fin. Grp., LLC*, 254 Cal. Rptr. 3d 461 (Cal. Ct. App. 2019).

B. DRAFTING THE FORUM SELECTION PROVISION

As noted earlier, there are two types of forum selection provisions: permissive and mandatory. This section explains how to draft each of these types of provisions.

1. Permissive

The following is a classic permissive forum selection provision in which subsections (a) and (b) serve different purposes.

Example—Classic Permissive Forum Selection Provision

1.1 Forum Selection.

(a) Any party bringing a legal action or proceeding[101] against any other party arising out of or relating to this Agreement[102] or the transactions it contemplates may bring the legal action or proceeding in the United States District Court for the Northern District of Illinois or in any court of the State of Illinois sitting in Chicago.

(b) For the purpose of all legal actions and proceedings arising out of or relating to this Agreement, each party to this Agreement submits to the nonexclusive jurisdiction of

(i) the United States District Court for the Northern District of Illinois and its appellate courts, and

(ii) any court of the State of Illinois sitting in Chicago and its appellate courts.

Subsection (a) establishes the discretionary authority of one party, as against the other, to commence a proceeding in a particular state or federal court. This subsection focuses on on the rights of the parties as potential plaintiffs. The provision appropriately uses *may* to signal that a party has the power to choose which jurisdiction in which to sue. The provision does not prohibit either party from bringing a suit elsewhere, but it also does not prohibit a party from contesting any forum other than the one stated.

Subsection (b) flips the provision's perspective, turning the focus to the parties' roles as potential defendants. Specifically, each party forfeits their right as a defendant to contest the court's personal jurisdiction over them, except to the extent that there is *insufficiency of process*.

The combined effect of the two subsections above (assuming appropriate service of process and a waiver of venue provision) is to box the parties into at least one jurisdiction in which they may litigate a dispute.

---

101. Some states such as New York distinguish between an action and a proceeding.

102. Recall from the discussion under the *Governing Law* section above that some courts have found the phrase *arising under or relating to* as implying a broader application than the phrase *arising under*. The drafter should use the same language in choice of law and forum selection provisions, as well as in venue waiver provisions.

2. Exclusive

The following is a typical *exclusive* (mandatory) forum selection provision:

Example—Typical Exclusive Forum Selection Provision

1.2 Choice of Forum

(a) Any party bringing a legal action or proceeding against any other party arising out of or relating to this Agreement or the transactions it contemplates shall bring the legal action or proceeding in either the United States District Court for the Northern District of Illinois, or in any court of the State of Illinois sitting in Chicago.

(b) For the purpose of all legal actions and proceedings arising out of or relating to this Agreement or the transactions it contemplates, each party to this Agreement consents to the exclusive jurisdiction of
  (i) the United States District Court for the Northern District of Illinois and its appellate courts, and
  (ii) any court of the State of Illinois sitting in Chicago and its appellate courts.

(c) Each party agrees that the exclusive choice of forum set forth in this Section does not prohibit the enforcement of any judgment obtained in that forum or any other appropriate forum.

As with the nonexclusive form selection provision, each subsection (a), (b), and (c) serves a different purpose. Subsection (a) focuses on the parties in their capacity as plaintiffs, while subsection (b) focuses on their roles as defendants. The purpose of subsection (c) is to preclude a defendant from arguing that subsection (b) renders unenforceable a judgment obtained against the defendant in another jurisdiction.

The term *shall* in subsection (a) indicates that each party has an obligation to bring all actions in the specified jurisdiction. However, the use of *shall* is not sufficient, as some courts nonetheless view these provisions as permissible. Therefore, in subsection (b), use the word *exclusive* to indicate that the parties consent to the exclusive jurisdiction of the courts set out in subsection (a).

While most forum selection provision are binding on both parties, occasionally a provision limits only one party. For example, in the banking context, loan agreements sometimes compel borrowers to bring all actions in specific jurisdictions, but they place no such restrictions on the bank. Courts have enforced these unilateral provisions in other contexts as well[103]—provided that there is no indication that one party lacked sufficient bargaining power or the provision was not freely negotiated.

---

103. Unilateral provisions also may arise in contracts between contractors and property owners. *See, e.g., Karl Koch Erecting Co., Inc. v. N.Y. Conv. Ctr. Dev. Corp.*, 838 F.2d 656, 658 (2d Cir. 1988) (applying New York law, upholding contract requiring contractor to sue in New York State court in New York County, but not similarly restricting property owner).

XII. WAIVER OF RIGHT TO A JURY TRIAL[104]

The United States Constitution, as well as many state constitutions, guarantee the right to a jury trial.[105] In most states, a party may waive this right.[106] But before inserting a waiver of jury trial provision into a contract, first consider whether a waiver benefits your client. If your client is a large, commercial corporation, a waiver of jury trial provision might be a good idea since jury members often dislike large, commercial corporations and/or see them as having deep pockets.[107] Here is an example of such a provision:

Example—Waiver of Right to a Jury Trial

XIII. [Section number XX—usually the last section of the agreement]. **Waiver of Right to a Jury Trial**. Each party knowingly, voluntarily, and intentionally waives its right to a trial by jury in any legal proceeding arising out of or relating to this Agreement and the transactions it contemplates. This waiver applies to any legal proceeding, whether sounding in contract, tort, or otherwise. Each party acknowledges that it has received the advice of competent counsel.

Because the right to a jury trial is a constitutional right, courts disfavor a waiver of this right and require that a waiver be *knowing, intentional, and voluntary*.[108] The key, of course, is to draft the waiver in such a way that a court will reach the "appropriate" conclusion. The following drafting guidelines are derived from the case law:

Guidelines for Drafting a Waiver of the Right to a Jury Trial

1. Put the waiver of jury trial provision as the last of the general provisions, so that it immediately precedes the signature lines.[109]
2. Make the provision prominent by putting it in a bold font and in a font size that is larger than that used in the rest of the contract.[110]

---

104. This section is based on Lauren Reiter Brody & Frances Kulka Browne, Waiver of Jury Trial, in *Negotiating and Drafting Contract Boilerplate* ch. 7.

105. U.S. Const. amend. VI; Cal. Const. art. 1, § 16; Mass. Const. Part the First, art. 12; N.Y. Const. art. 1, § 2; Neb. Const. art. 1, § 6.

106. *But see* Ga. Code Ann. § 9-11-38 (2013); Mont. Code Ann. § 28-2-708 (2011).

107. David T. Rusoff, *Contractual Jury Waivers: Their Use in Reducing Lender Liability*, 110 Banking L. J. 4, 5 (1993).

108. *See Conn. Nat'l Bank v. Smith*, 826 F. Supp. 57, 59 (D.R.I. 1993).

109. *See In re Reggie Packing Co.*, 671 F. Supp. 571, 574 (N.D. Ill. 1987) (enforcing jury waiver where "the waiver clause is located at the end of a paragraph, just two inches above the parties' signatures").

110. *See Luis Acosta, Inc. v. Citibank, N.A.*, 920 F. Supp. 15, 19 (D.P.R. 1996) (ordering jury trial where "the waiver clause is not in boldface and is buried at the end of the contract"). You may also consider putting the provision in all capital letters. Although some commentators believe that a provision using all capital letters is difficult to read, courts have nonetheless suggested that the all-capital-letters format is an acceptable way to make the waiver of jury trial provision prominent.

3. Use a caption that indicates that the right to a jury trial is being waived.[111]
4. List the provision in the table of contents, using a caption that indicates the right to a jury trial is being waived.[112]
5. Draft the provision so that it applies to all parties.[113]
6. Especially if the other party is a natural person,

   (a) require that person to initial the provision,[114]
   (b) include a statement that the waiver is knowing, voluntary, and intentional,[115]
   (c) require that person to acknowledge that their lawyer explained the provision,[116] and
   (d) require that person's lawyer to sign a form stating that they have explained the provision and its ramifications to their client.[117]

XIII. ALTERNATIVE DISPUTE RESOLUTION

As mentioned previously in this chapter on page 284, the parties have to decide first whether they will want to litigate any contract disputes or rely on an alternative dispute resolution mechanism like arbitration or mediation. The parties could also agree to a series of meetings to discuss the issue, elevating the level of the individuals representing each side as the meetings continue.

If the parties agree *not* to resolve their contractual disputes through litigation and instead use an alternative dispute resolution mechanism like arbitration or mediation, the dispute resolution provisions should still include governing law, forum selection, and service of process provisions. Other provisions to consider are a waiver of venue objections, a waiver of the right to a jury trial,[118] and a provision requiring the losing party to pay the prevailing party's attorneys' fees and other expenses. The last is often difficult to obtain.

If the parties agree to arbitrate their disputes, the provisions with respect to the arbitration can be short (a simple statement of the agreement to arbitrate) or detailed. A detailed provision will specify, among other things:

- The disputes to be arbitrated
- The rules that will govern the arbitration

---

111. *Smyly v. Hyundai Motor Am.*, 762 F. Supp. 428, 430 (D. Mass. 1991) (enforcing an agreement that "plainly set out the jury waiver [and] foretold it in capital letters in an introductory table of contents").
112. *Id.*
113. *See, e.g., U.S. v. Mt. Village Co.*, 424 F. Supp. 822, 825 (D. Mass. 1976).
114. *Coop. Fin. Ass'n, Inc. v. Garst*, 871 F. Supp. 1168, 1172 n. 2 (N.D. Iowa 1995) (recommending that parties initial clause to demonstrate that it was reviewed).
115. *Bank of Bos. Conn. v. Rusconi*, 1994 WL 506622 at *1 (Conn. Super. Sept. 6, 1994); *cf. In re Pate*, 198 B.R. 841, 843 (Bankr. S.D. Ga. 1996) (upholding contractual waiver of jury trial and preference for arbitration because contract reflected parties' understanding of the nature of the right relinquished).
116. *See* Robert H. MacKinnon & Nathan M. Eisler, Drafting Lending Documents to Avoid Lender Liability Claims, in *Lender Liability Litigation 1990: Recent Developments* 27, 49 (PLI Course Handbook Series No. 551, 1990).
117. It has also been suggested that an acknowledgment should describe the counseling provided, including, for example, that the party agreeing to the waiver was told that it was under no compulsion to execute the waiver, that the party exercised independent judgment to act, and that it acted of its free will, without duress, coercion, or compulsion. *See id.* at 43; *cf. Ricker v. U.S.*, 417 F. Supp. 133, 140 (D. Me. 1976) (holding elderly couple's waiver of right to notice and hearing in a mortgage agreement was unenforceable because "[n]o attorney was advising them, and at no time did anyone explain to them that by signing the mortgage they were waiving rights to notice and hearing.").
118. Although a waiver of the right to a jury trial is enforceable in most states, some states prohibit a waiver. *See, e.g.,* Mont. Code Ann. § 28-2-708 (2011).

- The location of the arbitration
- The governing law
- The qualifications of the arbitrators
- The method of choosing the arbitrators
- The payments of expenses relating to the arbitration
- The finality of the arbitration

XIV. FORCE MAJEURE

As we previously discussed in more detail in Chapter 17 on page 230, a *force majeure* provision provides for what the parties should do in case of unforeseen circumstances or situations out of their control (such as earthquakes, wars, and pandemics). *Force majeure* and other similar provisions, like alternative dispute resolution, are both endgame and general provisions. These provisions are often included in the general provisions article at the end of the agreement.

The COVID-19 pandemic and the litigation that has ensued from those disruptions highlighted and elevated the importance of *force majeure* provisions. One of the issues that came up with *force majeure* was that many agreements included epidemics[119] and endemics[120] in the definition of *force majeure event*, but they did not include the term *pandemics*.[121] Therefore, many parties struggled to determine whether COVID-19 qualified as an epidemic, an endemic, or both, and whether, thus, it was included in their definition of *force majeure event*.

In part because of all the issues raised by COVID-19, drafters now are extremely careful with these provisions and take the time to think through and carefully draft these clauses. Many drafters take the time to change their precedent immediately, especially when it comes to these provisions, when a new court decision comes out on a related matter. Drafters may allow the other party to terminate due to a force majeure event, but, often, you will see provisions stating that any delay in performance is not a breach, so long as the non-performing party is using reasonable efforts to mitigate the effects of the non-performance and gives notice, as in the following provision:

Example—Force Majeure Provision

Force Majeure. Any delay in a party's performance under this Agreement that is caused by fire, flood, earthquake, elements of nature or acts of God, pandemics, wars, terrorist acts, site-specific terrorist threats, riots, civil disorders, rebellions or revolutions, or any other similar

---

119. *Epidemic, Merriam-Webster's Dictionary,* https://www.merriam-webster.com/dictionary /epidemic (last visited on August 16, 2023) ("an outbreak of disease that spreads quickly and affects many individuals at the same time").

120. *Endemic, Merriam-Webster's Dictionary,* https://www.merriam-webster.com/dictionary /endemic (last visited on October 31, 2023) ("a disease or outbreak of disease that is typically present in a particular region or population").

121. *Pandemic, Merriam-Webster's Dictionary,* https://www.merriam-webster.com/dictionary /pandemic (last visited on August 16, 2023) ("an outbreak of a disease that occurs over a wide geographic area (such as multiple countries or continents) and typically affects a significant proportion of the population").

cause beyond the reasonable control of that party, is not a breach of this Agreement for so long as those conditions exist and that party continues to use reasonable efforts to mitigate its effects. Each party shall give the other party prompt notice of (i) the occurrence of an alleged force majeure event and (ii) a good-faith estimate of its anticipated duration.

However, keep in mind with *force majeure* and other risk allocation provisions in the general provisions or in the endgame provisions that we can try to anticipate issues as much as possible, but we do not know everything and cannot predict what is going to happen. We can only do what we can with the knowledge and experience that we have at the time, and new issues will always come up. When they do, we will deal as best we can with them.

XV. EXERCISES

A. EXERCISE 18A: ASSIGNMENT PROVISION

1. The following provision is intended as an anti-assignment provision. How would you rewrite it to fulfill the parties' intent and to otherwise improve the drafting?
2. If your client has plans to restructure and, as part of that plan, will assign this Agreement to an affiliate, what change would you suggest?

> **Assignment.** This Agreement may not be assigned by either party without the
>
> prior written consent of the other.

B. EXERCISE 18B: SUCCESSORS AND ASSIGNS PROVISION

1. Answer the following questions:

   a. From a business perspective, what are the parties trying to accomplish in the provision in 2 below?

   b. In the first sentence, to what does the word "respective" refer?

   c. The first sentence uses the words "assign or transfer." The second sentence uses the words "sell, assign, transfer, or grant." Should "sell" and "grant" be deleted from the second sentence?

   d. Does the provision preclude the Company from delegating its obligations under the Agreement?

   e. If the Company were to negotiate the prior consent exception, what additional language could it ask for that might make it more likely that the Bank would consent?

2. Rewrite the provision to correct drafting errors, including formatting.

> **Successors and Assigns.** This Agreement shall be binding on and inure to the
>
> benefit of the Company, the Bank, all future holders of the Note and their respective
>
> successors and assigns, except that the Company may not assign or transfer any
>
> of its rights under this Agreement without the prior written consent of the Bank. The
>
> Company acknowledges that the Bank may at any time sell, assign, transfer, or
>
> grant participations in the Loan to other financial institutions (a "**Transferee**"). The
>
> Company agrees that each Transferee may exercise all rights of payment (including

rights of setoff) with respect to the portion of such loans held by it as fully as if such

Transferee were the direct holder thereof.

C. EXERCISE 18C: SEVERABILITY PROVISION

Rewrite the following provision to improve its drafting.

In the event that any provision of this Agreement shall be rendered illegal or

unenforceable for any reason, the same shall not affect the validity of the remainder

of this Agreement.

D. EXERCISE 18D: AMENDMENTS AND WAIVERS PROVISION

1. Rewrite the following provision to improve its drafting. Are "change," "waiver," "discharge," and "termination" redundant and legalese?
2. Answer the following questions: Are "modify," "change," and "amend" redundant and legalese? What cardinal rule of good drafting does the provision violate? How could the heading be improved?

Amendments and Waivers. Neither this Agreement, the Note, nor any terms

hereof or thereof may be changed, waived, discharged, or terminated unless such

change, waiver, or discharge is in writing signed by the Company and the Bank.

E. EXERCISE 18E: INTEGRATION OR MERGER PROVISION

1. Rewrite the following provision so that it is well drafted.
2. What drafting change would you make if the transaction also included an Employment Agreement?

Entire Agreement. This Agreement, together with the Confidentiality

Agreement and the other instruments delivered in connection herewith, embody the

entire agreement and understanding of the parties hereto and supersede any prior

agreement or understanding between the parties with respect to the subject matter

of this Agreement.

F. EXERCISE 18F: COUNTERPARTS PROVISIONS

1. Assume that you drafted an employment agreement that is effective on December 15 and permits the parties to sign different counterparts of the agreement. What language would you need to include in the counterparts provision to create

certainty as to the agreement's effective date where the parties will be signing in early November?

2. Rewrite the following provision to improve its drafting.

Counterparts. This Agreement may be executed in one or more counterparts,

each of which shall be deemed an original, but all of which togher shall constitute

one and the same document.

G. EXERCISE 18G: NOTICE AND RECEIPT

Revise this notice provision so it does not condition a notice's effectiveness on counsel's receipt of the notice.

A party desiring to change its address for notice must give the other party

notice of the change in accordance with the notice requirements of this Agreement;

the notice of the change must be marked for the attention of the other party's legal

counsel, and for the avoidance of doubt is not effective unless it is so marked.

H. EXERCISE 18H: NOTICE BY E-MAIL

Find a notice provision precedent that addresses the delivery of notices by e-mail.

CHAPTER NINETEEN

Drafting Signatures

I. INTRODUCTION

With a few exceptions,[1] creation of a contract requires neither a writing nor a signature.[2] Instead, contract formation generally requires offer, acceptance, consideration, and mutual assent to the agreement's essential terms.[3] But the drafter must make sure that the signature lines are correct if the parties want a written contract to memorialize their contract and intend that signatures evidence their agreement. Attention to detail is essential.

The formal name for the language that introduces the signature blocks (which we will discuss in Section V of this chapter) is the **testimonium clause**. This book refers to that clause as the **concluding paragraph**. The following is typical:

> ### Example — Language Introducing the Signature Blocks
>
> In Witness Whereof, the parties have executed and delivered this Agreement on the date hereof.

This chapter will first address the meaning of *executed* and *delivered,* and then the benefits of a more contemporary approach than the example above. We end the chapter with a discussion of e-signatures, the drafting of signature blocks, and a variety of issues related to signature pages.

II. EXECUTION AND DELIVERY

A. DEFINITIONS

Parties have repeatedly litigated the meanings of the terms **executed** and **delivered**, and whether both of these actions are necessary to create an enforceable contract. The case law is complicated.

---

1. Among the exceptions are contracts subject to the statute of frauds. *See, e.g.,* N.M. Stat. § 55 2-201 (2003).
2. *See, e.g., Schaller Tel. Co. v. Golden Sky Sys., Inc.*, 298 F.3d 736, 743 (8th Cir. 2002).
3. *See, e.g., Fant v. Champion Aviation, Inc.*, 689 So. 2d 32, 37 (Ala. 1997).

Older, but not overruled, cases distinguish the verb *to execute* from the verb *to sign*.[4] *To sign* means to affix one's name in one's own handwriting, while *to execute* is broader and connotes affixing a signature either in one's own handwriting or through a representative. Other cases use the verbs synonymously.[5] Statutes can also be determinative. The Uniform Commercial Code (UCC) provides that a signature includes the signing by a person's authorized representative.[6]

In some instances, cases distinguish execution from delivery,[7] while others interpret *execution* more broadly to include both execution and delivery.[8] When the terms are differentiated, *delivery* means the exchange of signed copies of the agreement.[9]

B. DELIVERY AND CONTRACT FORMATION

Delivery is not generally required for an agreement to be effective[10] except for a few documents, such as deeds,[11] contracts under seal,[12] negotiable instruments,[13] and documents of title.[14] That said, the law in several states is that delivery is required.[15] Moreover, if parties intend that delivery should be an element of formation, courts will effectuate that intent.[16] Similarly, if they intend that signing is sufficient, courts will effectuate that intent.[17]

In sophisticated commercial transactions with closings, parties generally intend that the agreements that are to be signed at the closing be both signed and delivered. As a closing is not certain until the parties successfully complete their negotiations, the signed agreements on the closing table (or exchanged electronically) must remain ineffective until the actual closing. To do this, delivery becomes an additional element of the agreements' formation, and delivery is postponed until the parties agree that they are ready to close. Then they exchange consideration and deliver the agreements. Although many transactions rely on this type of arrangement, it is not always memorialized in writing. It is an unstated understanding.

You can directly address the issue of the parties' intent with respect to delivery by stating in the contract when it becomes effective: on signing, or on signing and delivery.

---

4. *Wamesit Nat'l Bank v. Merriam*, 96 A. 740, 741 (Me. 1916).
5. *Elliott v. Merchants' Bank & Trust Co.*, 132 P. 280, 281 (Cal. App. 1913).
6. UCC § 3-401.
7. *See Brown Bros. Lumber Co. v. Preston Mill Co.*, 145 P. 964, 966-967 (Wash. 1915).
8. *See Nodland v. Chirpich*, 240 N.W.2d 513, 517 (Minn. 1976) ("Delivery is ordinarily an essential element of the execution of a written contract."); *Hayes v. Ammon*, 90 A.D. 604 (App. Div. 1904).
9. *See Am. Fam. Mut. Ins. Co. v. Zavala*, 302 F. Supp. 2d 1108, 1117 (D. Ariz. 2003) ("Generally, it is the delivery of an executed document, not the mere signing of the document, that creates a binding contract.").
10. *See In re Roman Crest Fruit, Inc.*, 35 B.R. 939, 944-945 (Bankr. S.D.N.Y. 1983).
11. *See Herr v. Bard*, 50 A.2d 280, 281 (Pa. 1947).
12. *See Restatement (Second) of Contracts* § 95 (1981). Some states still recognize the vitality of a seal and its consequences, although most states have abolished seals or the distinction between sealed and unsealed agreements. *See* Eric Mills Holmes, *Corbin on Contracts* vol. 3, § 10.18 (Perillo ed., rev. ed. 1996).
13. UCC § 3-201 (2004).
14. UCC § 7-501 (2005).
15. *See Nodland, supra* n. 8; *Am. Fam. Mut. Ins., supra* n. 9.
16. *See Schwartz v. Greenberg*, 107 N.E.2d 65, 67 (N.Y. 1952); *Midwest Mfg. Holding, L.L.C. v. Donnelly Corp.*, 1998 WL 59500 at *5 (N.D. Ill. Feb. 6, 1998).
17. *See Bohlen Indus. of N. Am., Inc. v. Flint Oil & Gas, Inc.*, 483 N.Y.S.2d 529, 530 (4th Dept. App. Div. 1984).

Requiring both elements, signing and delivery, presents the parties with an additional hurdle to contract formation. However, you may want to require delivery as an element of contract formation. For example, parties can change their minds after signing, so requiring delivery gives them the opportunity to do so. Also, by requiring delivery, every involved party is more likely to have a full copy of the executed agreement.

Contract formation is also an issue when parties sign agreements in counterparts.

III. THE CONCLUDING PARAGRAPH

The concluding paragraph generally resembles the following:

> *Example — Less Preferable Concluding Paragraph Because of Legalese*
>
> In Witness Whereof, the parties hereto have executed and delivered this Agreement on the date hereof.

This language is full of legalese, which is technically unnecessary. However, it shows that the parties have intentionally signed the agreement, and it reminds the parties that they have agreed to bind themselves to the agreement.[18] Here is a more contemporary version:

> *Example — Better Concluding Paragraph Because of Less Legalese*
>
> To evidence the parties' agreement to this Agreement, the parties have executed and delivered this Agreement on the date set forth in the preamble.

This version retains both *executed* and *delivered* to reflect the historical distinction between the terms. You could replace *executed* with the simpler and more contemporary *signed*, which continues to recognize the historical distinction between *executed* and *delivered* but further modernizes the concluding paragraph. However, make this change *only* if you change all the contract's provisions that use *executed* or a form of *executed* and if you know your state's case law. For example, many contracts include a representation and warranty that a party has the power and authority to execute, deliver, and perform the agreement. Legal opinions and other transaction-related documents may also need to be changed. Be careful. Not saying the same thing in the same way can cause problems.[19]

The proposed concluding paragraph assumes that the parties wish to retain the historical distinction between *execution* and *delivery*. If they do not, use just *executed* or just *signed*. If you use *signed*, again be sure to conform the contract's other provisions. However, some case law does give *execute* a broad meaning that encompasses *delivery*.[20] Therefore, you should confirm the interpretation of *execute* under the contract's governing law.

---

18. *See* Lon L. Fuller, *Consideration and Form*, 41 Colum. L. Rev. 799, 800 (1941).

19. *See* Chapter 25 on page 380 for more information on ambiguity and saying the same thing in the same way.

20. *See Hayes v. Ammon*, *supra* n. 8.

The concluding paragraph also deals with the date of signing and delivery. The proposed language refers to execution and delivery *on* the date set forth in the preamble.[21]

When the parties sign the agreement in counterparts on different dates, the contract must reflect the different signing and effective dates. The usual options for effectiveness are *the date that the last party executes and delivers the agreement or on delivery of one executed counterpart from each party to the other parties.*[22] Do not rely on a provision that merely states that the provision can be executed in counterparts.[23] Instead, in the action sections, state specifically what constitutes effectiveness.

Examples — Drafting Effective Date

1 — *Effective When Each Party Delivers Executed Agreement:*
Effective Date. This Agreement is effective when each party has delivered to each other party one executed counterpart of this Agreement.
2 — *Effective on Date Last Party Executes and Delivers Agreement:*
Effective Date. This Agreement is effective on the date that the last party executes and delivers this Agreement to the other party.

In both instances, the concluding paragraph and the signature line must be tailored to fit the facts:

Example — Concluding Paragraph and Signature Line

To evidence the parties' agreement to this Agreement, each party has executed and delivered it *on* the *date* indicated under that party's signature.

FURNITURE BY FRANCES, INC.

By: *Frank Rabb*
Frances Rabb, President

Dated: 4-13-20XX

LARGE CORPORATION, CORP.
By: _____
Rufio Lawrence, Director of Purchasing

Dated: _____

You can take one of three approaches to the date in the preamble when effectiveness is tied to the date that the last party signs. First, the preamble could

---

21. *See* Chapter 14 on page 156 for a discussion of *as of* dates, Chapter 16 on page 218 for a discussion of effective dates in contracts for a term of years, and Chapter 18 on page 278 and this chapter in Section V.B on page 306 for a discussion of effective dates with respect to contracts executed in counterparts.

22. *Bohlen Indus. of N. Am., Inc. v. Flint Oil & Gas Co., Inc.*, *supra* n. 17 (provision stating that contract could be signed in counterparts was "merely for procedural purposes"; delivery was not necessary when subsequent provision states that the agreement was not effective until all had signed). If effectiveness is tied into delivery, confirm in the notice section the contractual mechanism for determining delivery dates.

23. *Id.*

omit any reference to date, and the effective date would be that stated in the provision within the body of the agreement. Second, once you know the date of the last signature (and therefore, the *as of* effective date), you could insert it in a blank left in the preamble for the *as of* date. However, be careful and keep in mind that there could be significant problems if the wrong date is inserted or if the blank is not filled in. Third, the first sentence of the preamble could omit a date and add a second sentence to state the effective date. In that event, you would omit the effective date provision in the action sections to preclude any possible differences in how the effective date is stated. A difference could create ambiguity. Here is an example:

> ### *Example — Preamble with Separate Sentence on Effective Date*
>
> **This Settlement Agreement** (this "**Agreement**") is between Cartoon Characters LLC, a Pennsylvania limited liability company ("**Cartoon**"), and Specialty Manufacturing, Inc., a Texas corporation ("**Specialty**"). This Agreement is effective on the date that the last party executes and delivers this Agreement to the other party.

The most important point to make here is that the agreement must be internally consistent. The preamble, the action sections' effective date provision, the counterparts provision, and the concluding provision must all work together.

IV. DRAFTING THE SIGNATURE BLOCKS

A. THE BASICS

The **signature block** for an individual or entity is the signature line and surrounding text, which usually includes the name of the party and the name and title of a person signing on behalf of that party. Drafting the signature block for an entity can be more difficult than it may seem. Before drafting the signature blocks, make sure that you have the correct name of the person or entity signing. If the party is an individual, *confirm that you have that individual's full legal name* rather than a nickname or professional name.

Companies sometimes do not operate under their legal name but instead use a trade name. Using the trade name could result in making the individual signing personally liable.[24] Because the potential for mistakes is high, *check the organizational documents of each party to confirm the details of each name, including any commas and where they go.* Then *confirm that the name in the preamble is the same as the name in the signature block.*[25] Next, *check an entity's organizational documents and bylaws* to find out who has authority to bind the entity, whether a vote of the entity's board of directors is required to approve the transaction, and whether more than one signature is necessary. Sometimes two or more signatures are required for a particular kind of contract, such as a loan, or if the contract involves more than a certain amount of money. In addition, statutes may have signature requirements for particular entities or contracts.[26] Finally, *obtain an incumbency certificate* —a document that states the name and title of each officer

---

24. *See Lachmann v. Houston Chronicle Publg. Co.*, 375 S.W.2d 783, 784-786 (Tex. Civ. App. 1964).

25. *See Boudreau v. Gentile*, 646 F. Supp. 2d 1016, 1022 (N.D. Ill. 2009) (different names in preamble and signature led to inference of fraud).

26. *See, e.g.,* 765 ILCS 115/0.01.

or person authorized to sign the contract for the other party, along with each person's specimen signature. With this information, some member of your client's legal team can confirm that the signature and other information of the signatories accord with the information in the incumbency certificate.

Assuming that the entity is a corporation, the corporate secretary should certify the incumbency certificate by signing it.[27] In addition, a second person should certify the portion of the incumbency certificate that relates to the corporate secretary. Absent the second signatory, the corporate secretary would be self-certifying—which is not a time-honored security measure.

Signature blocks are typically placed on the right half of a page. If more than one person is signing, the signatures should be stacked one above the other, as in the following example of two typical signature lines properly placed on the page:

Example — Signature Block

Tanya Williams
Tanya Williams

Rochester Realty Corp.
By: *James Tao*
James Tao, President

Some drafters precede each signature block with the defined term that best describes the role of each party. Typically, when this is done, the defined term appears in bold and all capital letters. Theoretically, this formatting helps visually distinguish a party's role from its name. The name also appears in bold, but only the first letter of each word is capitalized. However, many contemporary commercial drafters do not like using all capitals. Drafters seeking an alternative to all caps can consider increasing the font size of the type used for the party's role. The amount of the increase depends on the font used in the contract, but probably at least two points. The change in font size also provides visual differentiation, as follows:

Example — Signature Block

TENANT
Tanya Williams
Tanya Williams

LANDLORD
Rochester Realty Corp.

By: *James Tao*
James Tao, President

---

27. If the entity is not a corporation, check whether other approval is necessary, as appropriate for the type of entity.

B. DRAFTING THE SIGNATURE BLOCK OF AN INDIVIDUAL

The signature line for an individual is easy to draft: It is a line with the individual's name typed directly under it. The individual then "signs on the dotted line." Here is an example:

Example — Signature Block for Individual

John Hancock

C. DRAFTING THE SIGNATURE BLOCK OF A CORPORATION

The signature block for a corporation must reflect that the person signing *is acting in a representative capacity*.[28] You should do this in three steps:

Step 1. Put the name of the corporation on a separate line to indicate what entity is represented by the person signing the contract.[29]

Step 2. Four lines down from the corporation's name, insert the line on which the officer will sign and precede it with *By*. The use of *By* signals that the entity is acting through its agent.[30]

Step 3. Immediately beneath the line on which the officer will sign, put the officer's name and title. This establishes who the agent is and their representative capacity.[31]

Failure to draft the signature line in this way could result in personal liability for the officer.[32]

In what follows, Example 1 shows what the signature block would look like if the drafter had all the information relating to the officer at the time of drafting. Although that is optimal, it is not always possible.

Example 2 shows an alternative that you can use when you do not have the details of the person who will be signing. If you draft the signature block as in Example 2, include any information that you know ahead of time, and then fill in the blanks when the parties sign.

---

28. *See Stewart Coach Indus., Inc. v. Moore*, 512 F. Supp. 879, 884 (D. Ohio 1981); *see generally* S. C. Vass, *Personal Liability of One Who Signs or Indorses Without Qualification Commercial Paper of Corporation*, 82 A.L.R.2d 424 (1962).

29. *See 780 L.L.C. v. DiPrima*, 611 N.W.2d 637, 644-645 (Neb. App. 2000).

30. *See Restatement (Third) of Agency* § 6.01 cmt. d(1) (2006) (stating that a contract may indicate the representative capacity of an agent in multiple ways, including "statements of: (1) the principal's name followed by the agent's name preceded by a preposition such as 'by' or 'per' . . . "); *see also id.* cmt. d(2) (stating that "[T]the basic principles discussed in Comment (d)(1) are applicable when a principal is an organization, such as a corporation or limited-liability company. An organizational executive does not become subject to personal liability on a contract as a consequence of executing a document in the executive's organizational capacity . . ."); *but see Bristow v. Adm'r of Isaac Erwin*, 1851 WL 3552 at *1 (La. 1851) (finding that agency was implied by the circumstances, though noting that it would have been "more proper" if "by" or "per" had been used).

31. *See Agric. Bond & Credit Corp. v. Courtenay Farmers' Coop. Ass'n*, 251 N.W. 881, 887-888 (N.D. 1933).

32. *See Bissonnette v. Keyes*, 64 N.E.2d 926, 927 (Mass. 1946) (failure to include corporate name resulted in personal liability for agent, even though "agent" followed the agent's name).

Examples — Signature Blocks of Corporations

1 — With Corporation Information Already:

Sweat & Toil, Inc.

By: _Elizabeth N Workhorse_ _____
Elizabeth N. Workhorse, Vice President

2 — Blank to Be Filled:

Sweat & Toil, Inc.

By: _____
Name:
Title:

D. DRAFTING THE SIGNATURE BLOCKS OF A GENERAL PARTNERSHIP, A LIMITED PARTNERSHIP, AND A LIMITED LIABILITY PARTNERSHIP

In the same way that a corporation's signature line must reflect that the corporation acts through their officers, a partnership's signature block must reflect that the partnership acts through their general partners. *By*, therefore, precedes the signature line. If the general partner is an individual, use the following format:

Example 1 — Signature Block of General Partnership

Sweat & Toil Partners, a general partnership

By: _Elizabeth N Workhorse_ _____
Elizabeth N. Workhorse, General Partner

In Example 1 above, the name of the entity does not disclose what type of partnership they are (general or limited). Therefore, the typical practice is to identify the type of entity; here, a general partnership. Identifying Elizabeth N. Workhorse may be unnecessary because it may be obvious. In addition, identifying Elizabeth as a general partner is not needed because all partners in a general partnership are general partners. However, you still may want to explicitly include this information to make it clear.

If the general partner is a corporation, then you must add an additional layer to the signature block. The signature block must reflect that the partnership is acting through their general partner, a corporation, which is in turn acting through their officer. Some drafters reflect the relative relationship between the partnership and the corporate partner by indenting the information five spaces with respect to the corporate officer as follows in Example 2:

Example 2 — Signature Block of Limited Partnership

Sweat & Toil LP, a limited partnership
By: Sweat Inc., General Partner

By: _Elizabeth N Workhorse_ _____
Elizabeth N. Workhorse, Vice President

Many personal service businesses, such as law firms and accounting firms, are organized as **limited liability partnerships** (**LLPs**). A proper signature block for an LLP uses the following format:

Example 3 — Signature Block of Limited Liability Partnership

Sweat & Toil LLP, a limited liability partnership

By: _Elizabeth N Workhorse_
Elizabeth N. Workhorse, Partner

For LLPs, a law firm's signature line may follow the signer's name with the title *partner* rather than *general partner*. If the signature line uses *partner* rather than *general partner*, the other party to the contract relies on the apparent authority of the person holding himself out as a partner. The cure for any concern regarding apparent authority is to ask for a copy of the partnership agreement (which law firms rarely share) or any other official, certifying document, and then to make sure that the partner signing is duly authorized to act on behalf of the partnership in that transaction. This capacity issue is usually more important in the context of commercial dealings with the LLP (e.g., bank loans, leases, and major commercial contracts) than in professional dealings with the LLP (e.g., opinions, pleadings, confidentiality agreements, and formal advice to clients).

E. DRAFTING THE SIGNATURE BLOCKS OF A LIMITED LIABILITY COMPANY

A **limited liability company** (**LLC**) may be managed by their members or by managers.[33] In each case, the signature block must reflect who manages the LLC.

Example 1 — Signature Block of Limited Liability Company

Sweat & Toil, LLC

By: _Elizabeth N Workhorse_
Elizabeth N. Workhorse, Member

Example 2 — Signature Block of Limited Liability Company

Sweat & Toil, LLC

By: _Elizabeth N Workhorse_
Elizabeth N. Workhorse, Managing Director

F. DRAFTING OFFICERS' CERTIFICATES

Officers or managers of entities often sign certificates—statements that a particular fact is true. The following are common certificates:

---

33. Del. Code Ann. tit. 6, § 18-402.

- A certificate of incumbency certifying which persons hold which offices and providing a specimen signature for each such person.
- A certificate as to stockholders' and directors' resolutions, certifying that they were duly adopted and are still in effect.
- A certificate with respect to a copy of the organizational documents (e.g., certificate of incorporation, the bylaws, or both), certifying the accuracy of the attached copy.

For these certificates, the officer, not the entity, is the signatory. The rationale is that the officer is signing based on personal knowledge. The signature block reflects the officer's different role:

Example — Signature Block of Officers' Certificates

_____

Alex Glover, Secretary

In acquisitions and financings, officers are often asked to sign a **bring-down certificate**—a document certifying two things: first, that the representations and warranties made at signing are true at closing; and second, that all covenants to be performed on or before closing have been performed. Officers sometimes resist signing these certificates because they fear personal liability. The parties can address this issue in multiple ways, one of which is to have the corporation, rather than the officer, sign the certificate. Should the parties agree to this solution, use a standard corporation signature block.[34]

V. MODE OF EXECUTION

Generally, if in person at a formal signing, most parties use a pen to sign an agreement, but anything that makes a mark and is identifiable to a party usually suffices.[35] The following sections discuss e-signatures and execution in counterparts.

A. E-SIGNATURES

Lawyers are now called on to electronically draft contracts that become legally binding.[36] These documents present a modern spin on the classic evidentiary problem of authentication. In today's world, what constitutes a valid *e-signature,* and what safeguards ensure its authenticity?

---

34. For a detailed discussion of officers' certificates, *see* Lou Kling & Eileen Nugent, *Negotiated Acquisitions of Companies, Subsidiaries and Divisions* vol. 2 § 14.02[5] (Law Journal Press 1992).

35. *Haywood Sec., Inc. v. Ehrlich,* 149 P.3d 738, 740 (Ariz. 2007) (quoting from its earlier decision, the court stated that "[t]he signature may be written by hand, or printed, or stamped, or typewritten, or engraved, or photographed, or cut from one instrument and attached to another. . . . [I]t has been held that it is immaterial with what kind of an instrument a signature is made."); *Salt Lake City v. Hanson,* 425 P.2d 773, 774 (Utah 1967) (stating that "[w]hile one's signature is usually made writing his name, the same purpose can be accomplished by placing any writing, indicia or symbol *which the signer chooses to adopt and use as his signature and by which it may be proved: e.g., by finger or thumb prints, by a cross or other mark* . . .").

36. *See generally* Richard A. Lord, *A Primer on Electronic Contracting and Transactions in North Carolina,* 30 Campbell L. Rev. 7 (Fall 2007).

In the United States, the enforceability of e-signatures is principally governed by two pieces of legislation: the federal Electronic Signatures in Global and National Commerce Act (**E-Sign Act**),[37] and the Uniform Electronic Transactions Act (**UETA**),[38] a uniform state law adopted in some form by all states, except for New York. A provision of the E-Sign Act allows UETA to supersede the E-Sign Act, but only if a state enacts the uniform law in the form recommended by the National Conference of Commissioners on Uniform State Laws.[39]

UETA's stated purpose is "to remove barriers to electronic commerce by validating and effectuating electronic records and signatures."[40] It then defines an e-signature as "an electronic sound, symbol, or process attached to or logically associated with a record and executed or adopted by a person with the intent to sign the record."[41] Digital signatures are often created with a program that can encrypt and decrypt data, such as DocuSign, Adobe Sign, HelloSign, or PandaDoc.[42] This capability allows a digital signature to be attributable to a specific person and to authenticate a document.[43] However, electronic signatures may also include signatures in electronic messages, a text message in response, and clicking on a message stating that you agree.

Internationally, different legislative bodies have developed their own laws, such as the European Union's Electronic Commerce Directive.[44] In addition, the United Nations Commission on International Trade has issued model legislation addressing electronic signatures.[45]

If you need to create an electronic signature, be sure to research the law in the relevant jurisdictions, as it is evolving. Make sure that you know which statutory framework and jurisdictions govern, so you know better what steps to take when gathering and releasing your client's and other parties' signatures. For example, you want to make sure that the signatures are effective and have formed a contract. Also, you want to know when the contract is deemed formed — when your client signs, when the last party signs (if this is the case, make sure to have a method for finding this out and having it documented), when the signatures are officially exchanged, or whether the parties sign under differing circumstances. Most parties sign an agreement with the assumption that their signature does not go into effect and the contract is not formed until all the parties have signed. In addition, you will have to think about which software is most appropriate for gathering your client's and/or the parties' signatures, and whether the software complies with the laws and regulations of the relevant jurisdictions. A detailed discussion of how to create e-signatures is beyond the scope of this book.[46]

---

37. The Electronic Signatures in Global and National Commerce Act, 15 U.S.C. §§ 7001-7031.

38. Unif. Elecs. Transactions Act (UETA) §§ 1-21 (2002).

39. 15 U.S.C. § 7002(a).

40. UETA, *supra* n. 38, Prefatory Note, U.L.A. Elec. Trans., Prefatory Note.

41. *Id.* at § 2(8).

42. F. Lawrence Street, Mark P. Grant & Sandra Sheets Gardiner, *Law of the Internet* § 1.05 (Michie 2009); Larry N. Zimmerman, *2021 ABA Techshow*, 90 J. Kan. B. Ass'n 18 (2021).

43. Julian S. Millstein, Jeffrey D. Neuberger & Jeffrey P. Weingart, *Doing Business on the Internet: Forms and Analysis* § 8.05[1] (Law Journal Press 1997).

44. Council Directive 2000/31/EC, O.J. (L 178) 1-16, Directive on electronic commerce (available at http://eur-lex.europa.eu/LexUriServ/LexUriServ.do?uri=CELEX:32000L0031:EN:NOT, last accessed Nov. 21, 2022).

45. UNCITRAL Model Law on Electronic Signatures (2001) (https://uncitral.un.org/sites/uncitral.un.org/files/media-documents/uncitral/en/ml-elecsig-e.pdf , last accessed Nov. 21, 2022).

46. *See generally* Street et al., *supra* n. 42; Millstein et al., *supra* n. 43.

B. COUNTERPARTS[47]

As discussed previously, parties do not always convene to sign an agreement.[48] In these circumstances, lawyers often arrange for each party to sign a separate, duplicate original—**a counterpart**. Once each party has signed its counterpart, the lawyer assembles the signature pages of all of the parties to produce a fully executed, original counterpart agreement.

Parties also use counterparts to create multiple originals, so each party to a transaction has their own fully executed original. To do this, each party signs as many counterparts as the number of parties. So, if there are eight parties, each party signs eight counterparts.

C. STAND-ALONE SIGNATURE PAGES

Often, drafters create signature pages without text from the agreement. Generally, they do this to resolve a logistical problem. It permits a party who cannot attend a closing to sign in advance while the lawyers continue to draft the agreement. It also creates signatures to be gathered if the transaction is going to have a virtual closing. The party's lawyer then holds the signature pages until the closing and, at that time, attaches them to the final version of the agreement.[49]

While convenient, this practice involves risk. First, the parties may dispute whether the signed pages constituted execution and delivery of the contract or whether they were a mere logistical convenience.[50] Second, a drafter risks a malpractice claim. A client could allege that the lawyer had no authority to attach the signature pages because they never would have assented to the final version of the agreement had they known and understood the terms. To prevent such a claim, send your client the final text and get their approval of any last-minute changes.

VI. CREATING SIGNATURES AND BINDING AGREEMENTS THROUGH ELECTRONIC CORRESPONDENCE

As contracts are increasingly negotiated through e-mail and even text messages, courts are increasingly finding that parties can create or modify a binding agreement through these communications.[51] Unless the parties explicitly convey in their negotiations that their agreement is conditioned on the formal execution of a written

---

47. *See* Chapter 18 on page 278 for a more detailed discussion of counterparts provisions in contracts.

48. *Id.*

49. *Chariot Group, Inc. v. Am. Acq. Partners, L.P.*, 751 F. Supp. 1144, 1151 (S.D.N.Y. 1990) (no contract existed where the one party signed the signature pages for convenience only, the pages remained in the custody of that party's attorney, and the pages were never delivered to the other party).

50. *See Midwest Mfg. Holding, L.L.C. v. Donnelly Corp.*, 1998 WL 59500 at *4 (N.D. Ill. Feb. 6, 1998).

51. *See, e.g., Nusbaum v. E-Lo Sportswear LLC*, No. 17-cv-3646 (KBF), 2017 WL 5991787, at *4 (S.D.N.Y. Dec. 1, 2017) (reasoning that a series of e-mails formed a binding employment contract, even though they "did not qualify as a signed writing" because they "demonstrate[d] a 'meeting of the minds' on essential terms"); *CX Dig. Media, Inc. v. Smoking Everywhere, Inc.*, No. 17-cv-3646 (KBF), 2011 WL 1102782, at *11 (S.D. Fla. Mar. 23, 2011) (noting "the instant-message conversation and the parties' conduct surrounding it provide specific and direct evidence the parties agreed to modify the [agreement]").

contract,[52] they may bind themselves through statements made in e-mails or instant messages.[53] Courts have also held that informal electronic communications can satisfy the writing and signature requirements of the statute of frauds, in some cases even when the communication did not end with the sender's typed name.[54] To minimize the risk that these electronic negotiations create a binding agreement before both parties are willing, attorneys and principals should consider adding language to their e-mails that no contract is formed despite any statements made in the e-mails, and no party will be bound until the principals sign a final written agreement.[55] Disclaimers like this are never a cure-all, though. The most prudent approach is to avoid including statements in e-mails or text messages that may be construed as a final agreement to key terms.

VII. ANTIFRAUD MECHANISMS

As signatures can create an enforceable contract, their misuse can create a contract that at least one party did not intend. You can address this potential fraud in several ways.

Although stand-alone signature pages can be helpful logistically, they also create the possibility of fraud. For example, a person could attach them to a different document.[56] If all the parties can attend a signing, format the agreement so that the signature lines are on the same page as the final provisions or at least begin on that page. If the signature lines naturally fall on a separate page, stop the text of the agreement about halfway down the previous page, space down several lines, and insert in bold letters "**INTENTIONALLY LEFT BLANK**" or draw an X through the blank space. Then, on the following page of the agreement, conclude the text of the agreement and add the signature lines.

Alternatively, some drafters insert a special footer into the signature pages that identifies, usually in brackets, the agreement's title and its date from the preamble. That way, if the signature pages get separated from the rest of the agreement, the footer indicates which agreement they belong with. With this approach, you do not need to insert a page number or any contractual provisions on the signature page.

As another antifraud mechanism, the parties should initial each subsequent change to an agreement. Doing so can be used to demonstrate the parties' agreement to the change.[57] In addition, the parties could initial each page of the agreement if a client worries that the other side might replace a page with one that included *nonagreed to* provisions. As initialing every page of a long agreement can be

---

52. *See Sarissa Capital Domestic Fund LP v. Innoviva, Inc.*, C.A. No. 2017-0309-JRS, 2017 WL 6209597, at *22 (Del. Ch. Dec. 8, 2017) (holding that parties agreed to the essential terms of a settlement agreement through a series of phone calls and e-mails circulating a draft of a written settlement agreement, despite a statement in the draft that the agreement would "become effective" only when the signature pages were "signed by each of the Parties and delivered to the other Party").

53. *See, e.g., Cloud Corp v. Hasbro*, 314 F.3d 289 (7th Cir 2002).

54. *See Cloud Corp. v. Hasbro, supra* n. 53; *Int'l Casings Grp. v. Premium Standard Farms, Inc.*, 358 F. Supp. 2d 863, 873 (W.D. Mo. 2005).

55. Similar disclaimers might state that nothing in the e-mail constitutes an electronic signature, assent to a final agreement, or assent to conduct the transaction electronically. *See* D.C. Toedt III, *Why My E-mail Signature Block Says What It Does About Electronic Signatures, On Contracts Blog* (May 29, 2015), https://www.oncontracts.com/email-signature-agreement-disclaimer/ (last accessed Nov. 21, 2022).

56. *See Winston v. Mediafare Ent. Corp.*, 777 F.2d 78, 79-80, 83 (2d Cir. 1985).

57. *GBF Eng'r, Inc. v. John*, No. 09-CV-11367, 2010 WL 3342260 at *10 (E.D. Mich. Aug. 25, 2010) (initialing changes manifested assent to them); *Lerman v. Rock City Bar & Grille, Inc.*, No. 09-CV-2444, 2010 WL 2044865 at *4 (N.D. Ohio May 21, 2010) (absence of initials raises question of fact as to whether the parties agreed on the change).

burdensome, it is not common practice. Therefore, reserve this procedure for the appropriate situations (e.g., separation agreements and settlement agreements with respect to contentious litigation).

Although parties do not typically initial every page in significant commercial transactions in the United States, parties in some foreign jurisdictions almost always do it. Accordingly, be sure to check local custom and practice.

VIII. INITIALING OTHER THAN AS AN ANTIFRAUD MECHANISM

Parties occasionally initial a contract not as an antifraud mechanism, but to indicate that they have read and understood a provision. For example, a lawyer sometimes requires a party to initial a jury waiver provision.[58] The lawyer can then use the initials as evidence that the waiver was *knowing, voluntary, and intentional* — the standard that courts insist be met before enforcing a waiver.[59]

IX. ACKNOWLEDGMENTS AND APOSTILLES

An **acknowledgment** is a party's formal declaration before an authorized public official, generally a notary public, that they voluntarily executed an agreement.[60] In some states, it authenticates an agreement,[61] while in others it makes the agreement effective.[62] An acknowledgment is only obligatory when a statute requires one, as in connection with real estate conveyances and mortgages. Because the laws with respect to acknowledgments differ from state to state, check the law in your jurisdiction. If an acknowledgment is required, it follows the signature lines. It may also be on a separate page attached to the agreement.

If a contract is with a non-U.S. party, the contract may require an **apostille**, a legal certification similar to a notarization. In the apostille, generally, a public official from the non-U.S. jurisdiction certifies that the contract is authentic in that official's jurisdiction. Under the Hague Apostille Convention, any member-country of the convention can issue an apostille to certify the authenticity of agreements made in that jurisdiction. In the United States, which is a party to the convention, the secretary of state of a particular state or the U.S. Department of State can issue apostilles for agreements made in the United States.

---

58. *See Coop. Fin. Ass'n v. Garst*, 871 F. Supp. 1168, 1172, n. 2 (N.D. Iowa 1995).
59. *See K.M.C. Co. v. Irving Trust Co.*, 757 F.2d 752, 755-756 (6th Cir. 1985).
60. *Est. of Burleson*, 210 S.E.2d 114 (N.C. App. 1974).
61. *Webster Bank v. Flanagan*, 725 A.2d 975, 980 (Conn. App. 1999).
62. *Lewis v. Herrera*, 85 P. 245, 246 (Ariz. 1906).

X. EXERCISES

A. EXERCISE 19A: DRAFTING SIGNATURE LINES

1. It took Marley McDonough five years to save enough money to incorporate a business. Yesterday, McDonough's lawyer filed the necessary paperwork. McDonough is now the sole shareholder, director, and officer (president, of course) of McDonough Enterprises Inc. Today, McDonough is at D'Argent Bank to open the business's bank account. In addition, McDonough has decided to move all of her personal accounts to D'Argent. The bank has asked McDonough to sign two signature cards, one for the personal accounts and the other for the business.

    Draft the following two signature lines. Do not worry about placement on the page.

    a. Marley McDonough's signature line.

    _____

    _____

    _____

    _____

    b. McDonough Enterprises Inc.'s signature line.

    _____

    _____

    _____

    _____

2. A lawyer-friend convinced McDonough that a corporation is not really the best entity for doing business. So McDonough has instructed her lawyer to create a second entity, an LLC. McDonough has decided not to dissolve the corporation for sentimental reasons. McDonough, of course, will be the sole member and manager of McDonough Enterprises LLC.

    Draft the signature line for the LLC.

    _____

    _____

    _____

    _____

3. Avery Springs and her best friend, Jake Lisko, have decided to form a limited partnership to pursue their passion, space exploration. Their business will design and manufacture space probes. The partnership's name is Springs and Lisko LP.

  Draft the business's signature line, providing lines for both Springs and Lisko.

_____

_____

_____

_____

4. Nathan Nocturne is managing director of Nocturne LLC, a manager-managed LLC. Nocturne LLC is the general partner of Nocturne Luminescence LP, which is in turn the general partner of Nitelite LP.

  Draft the signature line for Nitelite LP.

_____

_____

_____

_____

CHAPTER TWENTY

Drafting Schedules and Exhibits

I. INTRODUCTION

Although some drafters use the terms *schedules* and *exhibits* interchangeably, they have different purposes. Parties typically use **schedules** (also known as **disclosure schedules**) to disclose information that would otherwise be in representations and warranties. **Exhibits** are agreements or other documents that the parties want to treat as part of the contract.

Schedules and exhibits are additional materials that are not within the body of the contract but are nonetheless part of the contract. Schedules and exhibits generally gain their status as part of an agreement by being *referred to* in the agreement or in the interpretive section of the definition article, but not being explicitly in the contract. Under common law, if the reference is specific enough, then a more explicit incorporation is not necessary.[1]

In practice, drafters generally do not define schedules and exhibits separately, but these terms often appear with their first letters capitalized where they are referred to in the contract. That said, by referring to them in the definition of *Agreement* or in the interpretive section, you can forestall any technical argument that the schedules or exhibits are not part of the agreement.

---

1. *See United Cal. Bank v. Prudential Ins. Co. of Am.*, 681 P.2d 390, 420 (Ariz. App.1983) ("While it is not necessary that a contract state specifically that another writing is 'incorporated by this reference herein,' the context in which the reference is made must make clear that the writing is part of the contract."); *see also New Park Assoc., LLC v. Blardo*, 906 A.2d 720, 725 (Conn. App. 2006) (stating that "the language of the contract clearly and unambiguously refers to A205 as part of the contract."); *see CJS Contracts* § 402, Separate writings—Incorporation by reference (Westlaw, database updated June 2013) ("A reference to another document must be clear and unequivocal, and the terms of the incorporated document must be known or easily available to the parties. . . . [A] mere reference to another document is not sufficient to incorporate that other document into a contract; the writing to which reference is made must be described in such terms that its identity may be ascertained beyond reasonable doubt."); *but see Rosenblum v. Travelbyus.com Ltd.*, 299 F.3d 657, 664-665 (7th Cir. 2002) ("There is no doubt that the Acquisition Agreement refers to the Employment Agreement, but there is no 'intention to incorporate the document and make it a part of the contract' on the face of the Acquisition Agreement itself. (citations omitted). Indeed, Article 1.4 is not an incorporation clause at all; rather, it is a merger clause.").

> ### Example—Agreement Definition with Schedules and Exhibits
>
> **"Agreement"** means this Power Purchase Agreement and the Schedules and Exhibits to it, each as amended from time to time.

This definition intentionally does not state that the schedules and exhibits are *attached*. Sometimes these documents are so large that attaching them becomes unwieldy. As drafted, this definition prevents any technical problems of interpretation that might arise because the documents are not physically or electronically attached to the agreement.[2]

Note that some contracts use the terms *attachments, appendices, addenda,* and/or *riders* to refer to materials added after the signature lines. Be aware of what these terms mean for the type of agreement and industry that you are working in and how these materials will be interpreted by the courts or any relevant governing bodies in the jurisdiction that applies.

II. SCHEDULES

Sometimes the schedules contain additional information that supplements a party's representations and warranties, while other times, schedules list exceptions to representations and warranties.[3]

> ### Examples—Two Different Types of Schedules
>
> *1—With Additional Information:*
> **Material Contracts. Schedule 3.10** lists all the material contracts to which the Borrower is a party.
>
> *2—With Exceptions:*
> **Defaults.** Except as stated in **Schedule 3.18**, the Borrower is not in default under any agreement.[4]

Properly or improperly scheduling information directly affects liability under an agreement. If a borrower fails to schedule a material contract to which they are a party, they will have misrepresented the facts, subjecting themselves to liability.[5] Therefore, you must carefully prepare schedules and verify them with the client.

Parties put information into schedules for several reasons, including the following:

---

2. *See United Cal. Bank v. Prudential Ins. Co. of Am., supra* n. 1, at 420 ("While the parties recognize that physical attachment is not necessary *if* the document to be incorporated is *clearly and unambiguously* incorporated by reference, there was no such clear and unambiguous incorporation by reference in this case.") (emphasis in original).

3. Lou R. Kling & Eileen T. Nugent, *Negotiated Acquisitions of Companies, Subsidiaries and Divisions* vol. 2, § 10.01 (Law Journal Press 1992, 2012).

4. *See* Chapter 27 on page 420 for more information on exceptions. It is common practice to begin representations and warranties with the exception stated first: "Except as specified in Schedule 3.18, ..."

5. *See Gildor v. Optical Solutions, Inc.,* 2006 WL 4782348 (Del. Ch. June 5, 2006) (drafter's failure to prepare and annex schedule with stockholders' addresses resulted in defendant sending insufficient notice under the stockholders' agreement).

1. To unclutter the agreement and make the agreement easier to read.
2. To simplify the logistics of preparing the agreement.

The lawyers responsible for drafting the schedules are not necessarily the lawyers who draft the agreement. For example, a bank's lawyers invariably draft the loan agreement, but the borrower and their counsel compile and draft the schedules used to expand or qualify the borrower's representations and warranties. Having the schedules in a separate word-processing document simplifies the drafting process.

When drafting an agreement, you usually want to provide for a schedule only if you know that you will need it. If only one or two short items are to be listed, include them in the representation and warranty. Readers quickly become frustrated if they keep turning to schedules that provide little or no information. However, often, precedent includes particular schedules. Instead of deleting the schedules that may not be relevant to that transaction, parties will leave the schedules and any such references in the agreement and simply include the schedule with "None" on that page. In these cases, it can be safer to do this so you do not mistakenly erase relevant cross-references, and so the provisions in the agreement keep working together in the same way. Also, if there is any change in a schedule that had *None* listed, the schedule can be simply edited to include the new information.

Each schedule in a contract is identified by a number, which is usually the section number of the provision that requires the schedule. So, if Section 4.12 requires the seller to disclose all litigations, the list of litigations will appear in Schedule 4.12.

Drafters often bold schedule references the first time that they are used to visually alert the reader to the existence of a schedule: **Schedule 4.12**. This also serves as a reminder to the drafter to prepare the schedule.

Putting together a disclosure schedule can be a sophisticated task. Before finalizing any schedules, make sure that you assess the business and legal issues and deal with each appropriately.[6]

III. EXHIBITS

By attaching specific forms as exhibits at the contract's signing, the parties establish a *standard* as to the content of the agreements and documents that they are planning to use or sign at a future date. For example, when a loan agreement is signed, it includes *as exhibits* a form for each of the following: the promissory note, the security agreement, the pledge agreement, and the opinion that borrower's counsel must deliver. These forms are exactly what the parties will sign at closing. All that needs to be done at closing to turn the exhibits into agreements is to delete the title *Exhibit,* date the document, and have the parties sign them. With luck, these exhibits, which all parties have reviewed and agreed to in advance, will preclude any negotiation or dispute at the closing as to their substance.

Exhibits of unsigned documents and agreements are often first referenced in the definitions article:

Example — Exhibit Definition

"Pledge Agreement" means the Pledge Agreement by the Borrower in favor of the Bank, *substantially in the form of Exhibit F*.

6. *See generally* Kling & Nugent, *supra* n. 3, Ch. 10.

Drafters include the italicized language above (but not in italics) to handle the possibility that the Pledge Agreement might differ slightly from the exhibit. This could occur either because the parties must complete blanks in the form, such as the date, or because the parties agree to a minor change.

As indicated, parties may also include as an exhibit an agreement that has been previously signed. Parties often do this if the agreement directly relates to the agreement's purpose. For example, the parties might attach to an assignment and assumption agreement a copy of the contract being assigned. Again, the rationale is to prevent a dispute (in this instance, which contract is being assigned).

In the United States, parties would not generally attach as an exhibit a letter of intent or confidentiality agreement signed before the signing of the main agreement. Outside the United States, customs differ, so be aware of local practices in other countries.

Occasionally, parties also use exhibits to display technical information or to demonstrate how a mathematical formula works.[7] The sample computations act as a form of legislative history that the parties or a court can use to resolve disputes.

Exhibits are generally given sequential letters or numbers based on the order in which they appear in an agreement, such as Exhibit A, Exhibit B, and Exhibit C, or Exhibit 1, Exhibit 2, and Exhibit 3. To facilitate keeping track of the exhibits, some drafters bold the references to them the first time they are used: **Exhibit A**.

---

7. *See* Chapter 26 on page 403 for more information on drafting numbers and financial provisions.

CHAPTER TWENTY-ONE

Summary of a Contract's Parts

The following chart summarizes the material in Chapters 14 through 20. Reading it does not replace reading the chapters. Use it as a handy, quick reference tool.

CONTRACT PARTS	DEFINITION	TOPIC	DRAFTING GUIDANCE
TITLE Introductory Provisions — (Chapter 14, page 155)	▪ A **title** is the name of the agreement.	Title	▪ An agreement's name should describe its subject matter. ▪ The title should be centered at the top of the first page with the type boldfaced and a larger font than the text in the body of the agreement. ▪ The name of the agreement should be exactly the same in both the title and preamble. ▪ A subtitle may be useful in a transaction where the parties sign multiple agreements of the same type, but one party differs in each agreement.
PREAMBLE Introductory Provisions — (Chapter 14, page 155)	▪ The **preamble** is the first paragraph of the contract, also known as the *introductory paragraph*. ▪ The preamble states the name of the agreement, the parties, and the date when the parties signed the contract.	Name of the Agreement Date	▪ The name should be indented approximately five spaces and is often typed in all capital letters and/or bolded. ▪ Date can be drafted in one of two ways: (1) date is the date when the agreement is signed, or (2) date is an *as of* date. ▪ When drafting a contract with an *as of* date in the preamble, you should also indicate its actual signing date somewhere in the contract. ▪ Do not put a date line under each signature unless the effective date of the contract is explicitly tied to the date that the last party signs the contract. ▪ An *as of* date can be drafted under one of two approaches: (1) by stating the *as of* date in the preamble, including effective date provision in the action sections, and stating the effective date in the concluding paragraph; or (2) by stating the *as of* date in the preamble and stating both the *as of* date and the effective date in the conclusion language. ▪ If the parties decide that they want the agreement to be effective on the date that the last party signs, omit the date from the preamble and include an effective date provision in the action sections that states what factor determines the effective date.

CONTRACT PARTS	DEFINITION	TOPIC	DRAFTING GUIDANCE
			▪ In the preamble, do not use a future date. If parties want provisions to be effective beginning on a future date, use the signing date in the preamble and include an effective date provision in the action sections.
		Parties	▪ You do not need the words *by and between* preceding the first party's name, *between* is enough. *Among* is used to express a less direct relationship, but it does not affect the contract's substance. ▪ Draft the person or the entity's full legal name. ▪ After an entity's name, state what type of entity it is and its jurisdiction of organization. ▪ A comma precedes and follows the organizational identity (e.g., a Delaware corporation,). ▪ If a person's full legal name does not narrow the universe of people to that one person, their address and other information can. The best way to include that information is through the person's representation and warranty as to name and address.
		Defined Terms for Parties	▪ The defined term should appear in parentheses, in quotes, capitalized, and boldfaced, following the legal name and appropriate identifying information of the party. The comma should follow, not precede, the defined term in parentheses. ▪ Choose a defined term that either relates to the party's role in the transaction or is a shorthand name for the individual or entity. Use it capitalized (but in regular font) throughout the agreement to signal that it is a defined term. ▪ Avoid acronyms because readers generally find it difficult to remember what the letters stand for. ▪ When creating defined terms, take into account the number of parties to the agreement. If there are more than two, using role-related defined terms is often a good choice. ▪ Consider whether others will use this agreement as a precedent. If so, role-related terms are preferable, as they will facilitate the drafting of future agreements. ▪ Defined terms for all parties should be parallel. ▪ Do not create two defined terms for a party. ▪ The punctuation at the end of the preamble is a period, regardless of whether you use the sentence or non-sentence format.

CONTRACT PARTS	DEFINITION	TOPIC	DRAFTING GUIDANCE
			■ Occasionally, an agreement will have multiple parties in the same role. If so, define each party in the role by name and use an inclusive defined term for all the parties in the same role. As an alternative to listing in the preamble all the parties in the same role, if there are a lot of additional parties, put the information concerning those parties in a schedule and refer to the schedule in the preamble. ■ If an entity plays more than one role, the preamble must include defined terms that indicate each role that the entity plays.
		Defining the Agreement	■ Define the agreement being drafted either in the preamble or in the definitions section. ■ To preclude any dispute as to whether they are part of the agreement, include the schedules and exhibits in the defined term.
RECITALS OR BACKGROUND SECTION Introductory Provisions — (Chapter 14, page 168)	■ The recitals or background section explains the setting of the transaction and why the parties are entering into the contract.	Recitals or Background Section	■ Recitals are useful if the parties want to inform interested third parties about an agreement's purpose. They are also used to support a contract term that might otherwise be unenforceable, to explicitly state the parties' intent, or to identify a contract's consideration. ■ Recitals are generally not part of the contract that binds the parties. Therefore, they do not create enforceable provisions of a contract. If the parties want to incorporate the recitals into the contract (which is usually not recommended), the parties need to explicitly state that the recitals are enforceable provisions.
		Guidelines for Drafting the Recitals	■ Do not overuse recitals. Use them only if they add clarity or specificity to the agreement. ■ Determine the content of the recitals by their purpose. ■ If the agreement includes recitals, they should tell a story. ■ If the background surrounding the agreement is complicated, consider stating the facts in chronological order. ■ When stating facts in the recitals that relate to the parties' past relationship, make sure that they are accurate. ■ Do not put operative provisions in the recitals. Do not put representations and warranties, covenants, or conditions in the recitals because they probably will not be enforceable.

CONTRACT PARTS	DEFINITION	TOPIC	DRAFTING GUIDANCE
			■ Generally, do not put information concerning the purchase price or consideration in the recitals. But if the consideration's adequacy is unclear, then use the recitals to explain what the consideration is and why it is adequate. ■ Do not incorporate the recitals into the body of the agreement. ■ Draft recitals in a contemporary language and format. Do not introduce recitals with the archaic *Witnesseth.* Instead, either proceed directly from the preamble to the recitals or indicate that the recitals follow by using either the word *Recitals* or *Background.* Do not precede each recital with *Whereas.* Instead, write one or more well-drafted paragraphs or a series of numbered sentences. ■ Avoid drafting the recitals as reciprocal statements of the parties. Include a simple sentence for each of the parties with the specific intent of each party, especially if there are unique or important circumstances. ■ If you define a term in the recitals, bold the defined term inside quotation marks surrounded by parentheses and precede the defined term with the word *the* if you are doing so for other such terms in the agreement. ■ Avoid using defined terms in the recitals if they are not defined in the preamble or recitals.
WORDS OF AGREEMENT Introductory Provisions — (Chapter 14, page 173)	■ The words of agreement state for the record that the parties have agreed to the terms of the contract. ■ Also referred to as the *statement of consideration.*	Words of Agreement	■ The words of agreement should be as clear and simple as possible. ■ If there is room for doubt in your transaction as to whether the consideration is adequate, draft recitals explaining what the consideration is and tailor the words of agreement to reflect the recitals. ■ Draft in a contemporary format, if possible, with no legalese.
DEFINED TERMS AND DEFINITIONS (Chapter 15, page 183)	■ A defined term is a word or a few words that are used consistently throughout a contract to indicate an entity, place, or thing, so that you do not have to repeat the entire formal name and all the characteristics that identify and correspond to that entity, place, or thing.	Guidelines for Drafting All Definitions	■ Create and use only one defined term for each definition and only one definition for each defined term. Then use the defined terms exclusively throughout the agreement. ■ Create a defined term only if you are going to use it more than once, and use it each time the definition is appropriate. ■ Use singular nouns as defined terms, if possible. ■ Choose as the defined term words that convey information to the reader about the substance of the definition. ■ If a definition varies the usual meaning of a word or phrase, choose a defined term that signals the variation. ■ Do not define a term when the ordinary meaning of the word or phrase expresses the concept.

CONTRACT PARTS	DEFINITION	TOPIC	DRAFTING GUIDANCE
	■ A definition of a defined term is that entire formal name and all the characteristics that identify and correspond to that entity, place, or thing. ■ Defined terms and definitions are used for multiple purposes, including expanding or narrowing the ordinary meaning of a word or phrase, establishing the meaning of particular terms in the agreement, providing consistency for how the parties refer to those terms, and giving a shorthand way of referring to complex concepts.		■ Write a definition as narrowly as possible so that additional information may be included as part of a substantive provision, such as a representation and warranty or a covenant. ■ Avoid definitions that apply to more than one person, place, or thing at one time. ■ Once a term is defined, do not repeat any part of the definition when using the defined term. ■ Do not create a circular definition; that is, do not define a term by using the same term. ■ If you want to make sure a definition includes a particular issue or example, follow the defined term and definition with the verb *includes*. ■ To exclude something that would ordinarily be within the contemplation of a defined term, some drafters follow the defined term and definition with *excludes*, as they do with *includes*. ■ Include a defined term in the definition of another defined term if one definition builds on another definition. ■ Do not define a defined term in another term's definition. ■ Be careful when defining a legal term by referring to a source outside the contract if the information in that source can be easily restated in the contract. ■ Define an agreement, other than the agreement being drafted, by using the information in the preamble of the agreement being defined: the name of that agreement, its date, and the parties. ■ When working with multiple agreements, make sure that you accurately incorporate by reference the separate definitions list or the definitions from other agreements.
	■ Definitions can be included in a definitions section (after the words of agreement, at the end of the contract, in a separate document) and/or in the context of the agreement.	Guidelines for Drafting the Definitions Section	■ Introduce the definitions and their defined terms first in the definitions section with an introductory sentence or sentences, including references to the preamble and recitals if there are terms defined in those sections. ■ List the defined terms alphabetically. ■ Include all defined terms in the definitions section, other than terms defined in the preamble and the recitals. ■ Use capitalization, bold, and quotation marks to make sure that defined terms stand out. ■ Follow the defined term with the verb *means*. ■ When in the body of a contract, signal that a term is defined by capitalizing it in the same way as was done when the term was defined in the definitions section, but use a regular font. ■ Do not cross-reference a defined term used in a definition, even if the defined term and its definition are included later in the definitions section because all the defined terms are alphabetized within the definitions section. ■ Do not include substantive provisions, such as representations and warranties, covenants, and conditions, in a definition in the definitions section.

CONTRACT PARTS	DEFINITION	TOPIC	DRAFTING GUIDANCE
		Guidelines for Drafting the Definitions in Context	▪ Define the term and then put the defined term immediately after the language that constitutes the definition using (a) parentheses, (b) quotation marks, (c) capital letters, and (d) boldface. ▪ List alphabetically in the definitions section any term defined in context and cross-reference to the section in which the term is defined.
ACTION SECTIONS — SUBJECT MATTER PERFORMANCE PROVISION (Chapter 16, page 209)	▪ The subject matter performance provision is where each side promises to the other that they will perform the main subject matter of the contract.	Subject Matter Performance Provision	▪ Usually, these provisions are mirror image, reciprocal promises from the parties about their future performance, but sometimes one party's promises may be more elaborate. ▪ Sometimes it can be a self-executing provision.
ACTION SECTIONS — PAYMENT PROVISIONS (Chapter 16, page 211)	▪ The payment provisions set out the financial consideration, such as a purchase price, salary, royalties, or some other type of payment. ▪ It can be drafted in one of two ways: (1) stating what the financial consideration is, and then in a separate section or sentence, stating which party covenants to pay that financial consideration; or (2) combining in one statement what the financial consideration is and the covenant to pay it.	Guidelines for Drafting Payment Provisions	▪ Follow the *cash* and make sure that the payment provisions answer the questions of *who* is paying *what* to *whom, when, why*, and *how*. ▪ State *who* is paying *what* to *whom* in the active voice. ▪ State explicitly and clearly *when* the consideration is payable. ▪ If a contract term creates any stub periods, provide for appropriate payments. ▪ Consider also whether any payment should be accelerated or delayed. ▪ State *how* a party is to pay money: personal check, company check, cashier's check, certified check, online payment, or wire transfer of immediately available funds. ▪ If money is payable for more than one reason, the terms for each payment should conform to this section's guidelines. ▪ Use defined terms in your payment provisions. ▪ Calculate any amounts that can be calculated before signing, if possible, rather than including a mathematical formula. ▪ If payment is based on a formula, state the formula accurately.
ACTION SECTIONS — DURATION OF CONTRACT (if applicable) (Chapter 16, page 218)	▪ The duration or term of a contract is the period of time during which the contract will govern the parties' relationship, which could be over multiple years.	Terms	▪ Terms can be drafted in two ways: (1) stating the term as a declaration in a stand-alone provision; or (2) including both the reciprocal covenants in the subject matter performance provision and the contract's term in the first sentence. The next sentence states the term's beginning and ending dates. ▪ When drafting a contract for a term of years, the beginning and ending dates of the term must be clear. ▪ If you are drafting a precedent for use in multiple transactions, key the beginning of the term to the date when the parties sign the contract. The ending date then keys off the anniversary date of the contract's signing.

CONTRACT PARTS	DEFINITION	TOPIC	DRAFTING GUIDANCE
	■ Not all contracts have terms. Contracts contemplating one-off transactions terminate at the conclusion of that transaction.		■ When drafting contracts with a term, discuss with the client whether the contract should include an evergreen provision, which automatically renews the contract. ■ When drafting an evergreen provision, do not provide that the parties will agree on a price increase at the time of a renewal. Agreements to agree are unenforceable. Instead, provide a contractual mechanism for determining the amount of the increase.
ACTION SECTIONS — ACQUISITIONS & FINANCINGS — CLOSING AND CLOSING DATE (if applicable) (Chapter 16, page 221)	■ The closing date is when the transaction will be formally concluded, so the parties would state in this part of the agreement when and where the closing is to take place. ■ Closing-related relations are necessary only in acquisitions and financings, where there is a moment when the transaction is finalized, which is the moment when the asset is sold and transferred or the loan is extended.	Closing and Closing Date	■ If the transaction will have a closing, the contract should state its place, date, and time. The statement of the time should take into account where the parties are located because they might be in different time zones. ■ Consider whether the closing date should be fixed or whether it should be determined by the happening of an event. ■ If the contract provides for a specific closing date, determine with your client whether the parties must close on that date. If so, consider a time-of-the-essence clause, but be sure that you and your client understand the consequences of that provision in your jurisdiction. If time is not of the essence, provide that the parties may jointly postpone the closing date. ■ If the agreement permits postponements, consider whether the contract should include a drop-dead date—a date after which the parties may no longer postpone the closing. If a contract includes a drop-dead date, include endgame provisions that provide for the contract's termination and that spell out the consequences of a failure to close.
ACTION SECTIONS — ACQUISITIONS & FINANCINGS — CLOSING DELIVERIES (if applicable) (Chapter 16, page 223)	■ In the closing deliveries' provisions, each party covenants to the other how they will deliver their performance at closing.	Closing Deliveries	■ In an acquisition, the seller usually promises to execute and deliver transfer documents, and the buyer usually promises to deliver the purchase price. Similarly, in a financing agreement, the bank promises to deliver the loan amount to the borrower, and the borrower promises to execute and deliver a note to the bank. ■ The closing deliveries for each party are usually included in the agreement as lists, so that they are easy to refer to and check when preparing for the closing. ■ In deciding where to list a closing delivery, determine whether the party responsible for the delivery has control over its delivery. If the party can control its delivery, list the closing delivery in the action sections. If the party cannot control the delivery, list it as a condition to closing, so that a walk-away right is the other party's only remedy.

CONTRACT PARTS	DEFINITION	TOPIC	DRAFTING GUIDANCE
ACTION SECTIONS — OTHER SUBSTANTIVE BUSINESS PROVISIONS (Chapter 16, page 225)	■ Apart from the specific provisions discussed above, the parties may include other substantive business provisions in the action sections of an agreement.	Other Sub-stantive Business Provisions	■ Other practitioners and commentators may include other substantive business provisions as a set of provisions separate from the action sections in a category by themselves. ■ These other substantive business provisions can include any or all of the contract concepts and can be organized in different ways (e.g., by contract concept and by party, by subject matter, or in chronological order), depending on the type of agreement that you are doing.
ENDGAME PROVISIONS (Chapter 17, page 229)	■ The endgame provisions state the business terms that govern the end of the parties' contractual relationship. They require a drafter to determine the different ways that a contract can end and how the contract will deal with each of the scenarios. ■ In practice, many drafters may refer to these as "termination provisions."	Endgame Provisions	■ A drafter should consider the following six points when drafting endgame provisions: ■ The events triggering a possible termination of the agreement or a significant change in the relationship between the parties ■ The contractual consequences (both monetary and nonmonetary) of receipt of notice of termination or any such events ■ The date when the contract terminates or changes, which may depend on the type of event and its contractual consequences ■ Whether a party is entitled to any common law remedies ■ Whether any specific contract provisions survive the contract's termination or how other contract provisions may be affected with a change in the relationship ■ Dispute resolution provisions ■ The endgame provisions set out any final payments that need to be made or state any covenants that survive the termination of a contractual relationship that ends happily. ■ Drafters generally place endgame provisions at the end of the contract in a single section or article or as part of the general provisions to make them easy to find. In addition, drafters sometimes integrate some endgame provisions with the action sections or other parts of the agreement. ■ Endgame provisions are a series of *if / then* propositions, so they are usually composed of conditions. ■ A good approach to drafting them: If this good / bad event happens, then this is the consequence. Ask yourself: *What if?* ■ Be specific about what a notice should contain, when it is deemed to be effective (e.g., only on receipt and by national courier), and what are the effects of that notice. ■ The endgame provisions in this chapter are divided into three categories: neutral, friendly, and unfriendly. ■ A neutral change or termination allows the parties to shift or discontinue their relationship without blaming a party or anyone doing anything wrong. ■ A friendly termination results from the successful consummation of a whole or part of a transaction. Sometimes they require notice and you want to provide for anything that needs to be done.

CONTRACT PARTS	DEFINITION	TOPIC	DRAFTING GUIDANCE
			▪ An unfriendly change or termination is the result of a transaction or part of a transaction failing or not succeeding as well as it might have. Drafters often use the terms *grounds for termination, breaches, defaults,* and *triggering events. Grounds, defaults,* and *triggering events* tend to be used as broader terms that include breaches as a subset. There are many possible consequences for unfriendly changes or terminations, including a grace and cure period, price adjustments, liquidated damages, limitations on liability, indemnities (see chart with examples on p. 250), setoff provisions, self-help provisions, and equitable remedies. ▪ See the sample chart on p. 256 to help you organize your endgame provisions.
GENERAL PROVISIONS (Chapter 18, page 263)	▪ General provisions tell the parties how to govern their relationship and administer the contract. ▪ Often referred to as *boilerplate provisions.*	General Provisions	▪ General provisions can be generally grouped into the following categories: provisions dealing with third parties (assignment and delegation, successors and assigns), provisions that determine what constitutes the contract (severability, amendments, waiver, integration or merger, counterparts), provisions regarding communications (notice), dispute resolution provisions (governing law, forum selection, waiver of right to a jury trial, alternative dispute resolution), and risk allocation provisions (*force majeure*). Therefore, these provisions are included in the following sections of this chapter in this order. ▪ If the parties are executing multiple agreements as part of a single transaction, make sure that the general provisions are the same in each agreement.
		Assign- ment and Delegation	▪ When drafting the assignment and delegation provision, you must deal with both assignments and delegations, not just assignments. ▪ To prohibit a transfer of rights, you should draft the anti-assignment provision to prohibit *an assignment of rights under the agreement.* If the provision prohibits only *the assignment of the agreement,* courts generally interpret the provision as an anti-delegation provision. ▪ To create an anti-assignment provision that renders an assignment void, you must take away not only the right to assign, but also the power to assign. To do this, a contract must prohibit the assignment of rights under the contract and declare that any purported assignment is void.
		Successors and Assigns	▪ The successors and assigns provision addresses the *consequences* of an assignment and delegation. That is, it assumes an assignment and delegation have occurred, and addresses how that occurrence affects those involved.

CONTRACT PARTS	DEFINITION	TOPIC	DRAFTING GUIDANCE
		Severability	▪ The way that you draft the severability provision should reflect whether the governing law is that of a state that follows the blue-pencil rule (a court will delete portions of an otherwise unenforceable provision if the deleted portions can be clearly—and grammatically—separated from the remainder of the provision) or that of a state that follows the rule of reasonableness (a court may reform an unenforceable provision to the extent reasonable under the circumstances and then enforce it as so reformed).
		Amendments	▪ Amendment provisions outline how the parties may amend the agreement in the future.
		Waiver	▪ A waiver provision details the process that a party must take to waive a provision in the agreement.
		Integration or Merger	▪ An integration provision is sometimes called a *merger provision* or a *zipper clause* is "[a] contractual provision stating that the contract represents the parties' complete and final agreement and supersedes all informal understandings and oral agreements relating to the subject matter of the contract."[1] ▪ When drafting an integration provision, describe the agreement being signed as *final and exclusive* to signal that the parties intend the agreement to be fully integrated. Also, state the consequences of the agreement being final and exclusive: that all prior negotiations and agreements are superseded by (merged into) the agreement being signed. If the agreement being signed does not supersede an existing agreement, such as a confidentiality agreement, state the exception.
		Counterparts	▪ A counterpart is a duplicate original that parties sign. Drafters use counterparts to expedite transactions when not all the parties attend the agreement's signing and to create multiple originals so that each party can have a fully executed original. A *counterpart provision* ensures that, even if there are multiple copies of the original, there is only one agreement between the parties.
		Notice	▪ Nearly every contract has a notice provision, which allocates the risk of a notice's nonreceipt. A well-drafted notice provision should state the ways by which a party may give notice, and it should do more than simply list the addresses to which parties should send their notices. ▪ In drafting a notice provision, consider whether counsel should receive a copy of the notice. If so, the contract will need to address whether the notice should be effective *only after both the party and its counsel receive it,* or whether *it should be effective only upon receipt by the contract party, regardless of when counsel receives it.*

---

1. *See Merger Clause and Integration Clause, Black's Law Dictionary* (11th ed. 2019).

CONTRACT PARTS	DEFINITION	TOPIC	DRAFTING GUIDANCE
		Governing Law	■ A governing law provision, also known as a *choice of law provision*, establishes the law that governs a dispute arising from an agreement. ■ When choosing which state's law should govern, consider several factors. First, evaluate whether the law of the jurisdiction under consideration is well developed and predictable in the area that your agreement covers. In addition, evaluate whether the particular body of state law is hostile or friendly to the type of client and the subject matter being represented. Also, pay attention to the language defining the scope of the provision (e.g., including tort claims arising out of or relating to the agreement).
		Forum Selection	■ A forum selection provision designates, by agreement of the parties, one or more courts to adjudicate a dispute between the parties. ■ Forum selection provisions are either exclusive (also known as *mandatory*) or permissive (also known as *nonexclusive* or *consensual*). In an *exclusive* forum selection provision, the parties designate one forum as the only jurisdiction where a plaintiff may bring suit. In a *permissive* forum selection provision, although the parties consent to jurisdiction in the identified forum, a plaintiff may bring an action elsewhere.

		Waiver of Right to a Jury Trial	■ The United States Constitution and many state constitutions guarantee the right to a jury trial, and this provision allows parties to waive this right.
			■ Put the waiver of jury trial provision as the last of the general provisions, so that it immediately precedes the signature lines.
			■ Make the provision prominent by putting it in a bold font and in a larger type size than that used in the rest of the contract.
			■ Use a caption that indicates that the right to a jury trial is being waived.
			■ List the provision in the table of contents, using a caption that indicates the right to a jury trial is being waived.
			■ Draft the provision so that it applies to all parties.
			■ Especially if the other party is a natural person,
			  ■ require that person to initial the provision,
			  ■ include a statement that the waiver is knowing, voluntary, and intentional,
			  ■ require that person to acknowledge that her lawyer explained the provision, and
			  ■ require that person's lawyer to sign a form stating that he has explained the provision and its ramifications to his client.

CONTRACT PARTS	DEFINITION	TOPIC	DRAFTING GUIDANCE

		Alternative Dispute Resolution	▪ The parties have to decide first whether they will want to litigate any contract disputes or rely on an alternative dispute resolution mechanism like arbitration or mediation.
			▪ A detailed provision will specify, among other things:
			  ▪ The disputes to be arbitrated
			  ▪ The rules that will govern the arbitration
			  ▪ The location of the arbitration
			  ▪ The governing law
			  ▪ The qualifications of the arbitrators
			  ▪ The method of choosing the arbitrators
			  ▪ The payments of expenses relating to the arbitration
			  ▪ The finality of the arbitration

		Force Majeure	▪ A *force majeure* provision provides for what the parties should do in case of unforeseen circumstances or situations out of their control (such as earthquakes, wars, and pandemics). ▪ In part because of all the issues raised by COVID-19, drafters now are extremely careful with these provisions and take the time to think through and carefully draft these clauses. Many drafters take the time to change their precedent immediately, especially when it comes to these provisions, when a new court decision comes out on a related matter. ▪ Drafters may allow the other party to terminate due to a *force majeure event*, but often, you will see provisions stating that any delay in performance is not a breach, so long as the non-performing party is using reasonable efforts to mitigate the effects of the non-performance and gives notice.
SIGNATURE LINES (Chapter 19, page 295)	▪ A contract concludes with the parties' signatures. ▪ Generally, all parties who make promises in a particular contract sign that contract. In some contracts, such as in a guaranty agreement, only one party makes promises, so only that party must sign.	Signature Lines	▪ Do not rely on a provision that merely states that the provision can be executed in counterparts. Instead, in the action sections, state specifically what constitutes effectiveness. ▪ You can take one of three approaches to the date in the preamble when effectiveness is tied to the date the last party signs. First, the preamble could omit any reference to date, and the effective date would be that stated in the provision within the body of the agreement. Second, once you know the date of the last signature (and therefore, the *as of* effective date), you could insert it in a blank left in the preamble for the *as of* date. Third, the first sentence of the preamble could omit a date and a second sentence be added stating the effective date. In that event, you would omit the effective date provision in the action sections to preclude any possible differences in how the effective date is stated. ▪ Signature blocks are typically placed on the right half of a page. If more than one person is signing, they should be stacked one above the other. ▪ The signature block for a corporation must reflect that the person signing *is acting in a representative capacity.*

CONTRACT PARTS	DEFINITION	TOPIC	DRAFTING GUIDANCE
			■ A partnership's signature block must reflect that the partnership acts through its general partners. *By*, therefore, precedes the signature line. For limited liability partnerships, the signature line uses *partner* rather than *general partner*.
			■ Limited liability companies may be managed by their members or managers, and the signature block must reflect who manages it.
			■ Officers or managers of entities often sign certificates, statements that a particular fact is true.
			■ Generally, if in person, most parties use a pen to sign an agreement, but anything that makes a mark and is identifiable to a party usually is enough.
			■ Electronic signatures may include signatures in electronic messages, a text message in response, and clicking on a message stating that you agree. If you need to create an electronic signature, be sure to research the law in the relevant jurisdiction, as it is evolving. Make sure you know which statutory framework and jurisdictions govern, so that you know better what steps to take when gathering and releasing your client's and other parties' signatures (e.g., make sure that signatures are effective and form a contract).
			■ Courts are increasingly finding that parties can create or modify a binding agreement through email, text messages, and other forms of communications, so be clear about these issues.
			■ Often, drafters create signature pages without text from the agreement to get early and hold the signature pages until the parties have reached an agreement.
SCHEDULES AND EXHIBITS (Chapter 20, page 311)	■ Parties typically use schedules (also known as "disclosure schedules") to disclose information that would otherwise be in representations and warranties. ■ Exhibits are agreements or other documents that the parties want to treat as being part of the contract.	Drafting Schedules and Exhibits	■ Schedules and exhibits are additional materials that are not within the body of the contract but are nonetheless part of the contract. Schedules and exhibits generally gain their status as part of an agreement by being *referred to* in the agreement or in the interpretive section of the definition article, but not by being explicitly in the contract.
			■ In practice, drafters generally do not separately define schedules and exhibits, but these terms often appear with their first letters capitalized where they are referred to in the contract. That said, by referring to them in the definition of *Agreement* or in the interpretive section, you can forestall any technical argument that the schedules or exhibits are not part of the agreement.
			■ Schedules and exhibits tend to be attached to the rest of the contract after the signature pages. The schedules should come first, followed by the exhibits.
			■ Each schedule in a contract is identified by a number, usually the section number of the provision that requires the schedule.

CONTRACT PARTS	DEFINITION	TOPIC	DRAFTING GUIDANCE
			■ When drafting an agreement, you usually want to provide a schedule only if you know that you will need it. If only one or two short items are to be listed, include them in the representation and warranty. ■ Exhibits are generally given sequential numbers or letters based on the order in which they appear in an agreement, such as Exhibit A, Exhibit B, and Exhibit C, or Exhibit 1, Exhibit 2, and Exhibit 3. ■ Note that some contracts use the terms *attachments*, *appendices*, *addenda*, and/or *riders* to refer to materials added after the signature lines. Be aware of what these terms mean for the type of agreement and industry that you are working in and how these materials will be interpreted by the courts or any relevant governing bodies in the jurisdiction that applies.

Drafting Clearly and Unambiguously

CHAPTER TWENTY-TWO

Legalese

I. INTRODUCTION

Legalese annoys almost anyone who reads contracts—whether it is a client, third party, lawyer, or judge. Obscure words and phrases from the past clutter provisions and make them difficult to understand.

Commentators have not liked legalese for centuries, but legalese remained the norm until 1975 when Citibank lawyers rewrote their consumer promissory note.[1] These lawyers did more than revise the bank's contracts. They reconceived how consumer contracts should be written. They eliminated legalese from their revised note and focused on presenting each provision clearly with everyday language, plus organized the contract into different sections with headings.[2] In addition, they improved the contracts' appearances by using white space and easily readable fonts. They also turned full-page sentences into short, clear sentences and adopted a more informal tone, making the contracts less intimidating. Together, these changes resulted in a new style of contract drafting, known as **plain English**.

As previously discussed, the benefits of plain English drafting are so apparent and appealing that some states have mandated by statute that plain English be used in consumer contracts.[3] No such laws have been passed with respect to sophisticated commercial contracts, but, over time, drafters have incorporated some plain English concepts into their contracts, such as by eliminating a lot of legalese.[4]

In this chapter and in Chapters 23, 24, and 25, you will learn how to replace legalese with ordinary words, format provisions to make complicated material easier to assimilate, and redraft long, dense sentences into shorter, simpler ones.

---

1. *See* Carl Felsenfeld, *Plain English Movement, The Plain English Movement: Panel Discussion*, 6 Can. Bus. L.J. 409 (1981-1982).

2. *Id.* at 411.

3. *See, e.g.,* N.Y. Gen. Oblig. Law § 5-702 (2020).

4. However, federal regulations do mandate the use of plain English principles in a prospectus. 17 C.F.R. § 230.421 (2022).

II. FORMAL AND ARCHAIC WORDS

Legalese creeps into contracts in several ways. One of the most common is the use of formal, archaic words, such as the following:[5]

> above (as an adjective)
> abovementioned
> aforementioned
> aforesaid
> before-mentioned
> henceforth
> hereby
> herein
> hereinafter
> hereinbefore
> hereof
> hereto
> herewith
> said (as a substitute for "the," "that," or "those")
> same (as a substitute for "it," "he," "him," etc.)
> such (as a substitute for "the," "that," or "those")
> thereof
> therewith
> whatsoever
> whensoever
> whereof
> wheresoever
> whosoever
> within-named
> witnesseth

Some drafters complain that some of these terms are actually helpful and should be used. However, in almost all instances, acceptable alternatives are available and preferable to make the contract more straightforward and less ambiguous.

For example, drafters often use *hereof*, *hereto*, and similar words to indicate the section, schedule, or exhibit to which a provision is referring is to the section, schedule, or exhibit being read. To eliminate these words easily, include an interpretive provision, either in the definitions section or with the general provisions, such as the following.[6]

Example—Interpretive Provision

Internal References. Unless otherwise stated, references to Sections, subsections, Schedules, and Exhibits are to Sections, subsections, Schedules, and Exhibits of this Agreement.

---

5. *See* F. Reed Dickerson, *The Fundamentals of Legal Drafting* 207 (2d ed., Little, Brown & Co. 1986).

6. Interpretive provisions are also discussed in Chapter 15 on page 202, Chapter 18 on page 264, Chapter 22 on page 332, Chapter 25 on page 390, and Chapter 27 on page 429.

Hereby is also easily replaced. Replace it with the thing to which *hereby* is referring.

> ### Example—Replace "Hereby"
>
> ***Incorrect:*** **Waiver of Right to a Jury Trial**. Each party waives its right to a jury trial with respect to the transactions contemplated *hereby*.
>
> ***Correct:*** **Waiver of Right to a Jury Trial**. Each party waives its right to a jury trial with respect to the transactions [*contemplated by this Agreement*] [*that this Agreement contemplates*] [*in this Agreement*].

The second bracketed phrase is better as it changes the phrase from the passive to the active voice, and the third bracketed phrase may be the best because it's simpler and more straightforward.

Thereof can often be replaced with *its*. An even better option is to determine what *thereof* refers to and then create a prepositional phrase beginning with *of* and ending with the thing to which *thereof* refers:

> ### Examples—Replace "Thereof"
>
> ***Incorrect:*** **Escrow Fund**. The Escrow Fund shall be held by the Escrow Agent under the Escrow Agreement pursuant to the terms *thereof*.
>
> ***Correct:*** **Escrow Fund**. The Escrow Agent shall hold the Escrow Funds under the Escrow Agreement pursuant to its terms.
>
> ***Recommended:*** **Escrow Fund**. The Escrow Agent shall hold the Escrow Funds pursuant to [*the terms of the Escrow Agreement*] [*the Escrow Agreement's terms*].

The correct and recommended examples above also change the sentence from the passive to the active voice, which is preferable. Look also at this additional example of how to eliminate *thereof*:

> ### Example—Replace "Thereof"
>
> ***Incorrect:*** Without limiting the generality *thereof* . . .
>
> ***Correct:*** Without limiting the generality of the preceding sentence . . .

Said and *such* are words that refer to something previously stated. Replace them with *a*, *that*, *the*, or *those*.

> ### Example—Replace "Said" and "Such" with "A," "That," "The," or "Those"
>
> ***Incorrect:*** **Bonus**. With respect to each year of the Term, the Company shall pay the Executive a bonus equal to 10% of [*such*] [*said*] year's Net Profits, except that the Company is not obligated to pay [*such*] [*said*] bonus with respect to any year of the Term in which Net Profits are less than $1 million.

> ***Correct:* Bonus**. With respect to each year of the Term, the Company shall pay the Executive a bonus equal to 10% of *that* year's Net Profits, except that the Company is not obligated to pay *the* bonus with respect to any year of the Term in which Net Profits are less than $1 million.

Drafters should not use formal words that refer to something else in the provision because they can create ambiguity as to what nouns they refer to, whether in that same provision or throughout the contract. For example, *hereunder* is a common word used in this way that is usually problematic and can easily create ambiguity. A version of the provision in the examples below was litigated.[7] An important issue in the complaint was whether *hereunder* referred to Section 12.2 or to the entire agreement. The court ruled that the provision's scope was narrow and limited to issues under Section 12.2.[8]

Example—Replace "Hereunder"

Incorrect: Despite anything to the contrary stated in this Section 12.2, each party may institute judicial proceedings against the other party to enforce the instituting party's rights *hereunder* through specific performance, injunction, or similar equitable relief.

Correct: Despite anything to the contrary stated in this Section 12.2, each party may institute judicial proceedings against the other party to enforce the instituting party's rights [*under this Section 12.2*] or [*under this Agreement*] through specific performance, injunction, or similar equitable relief.

Note that it is more to common to find legalese in longer, commercial agreements between more sophisticated parties and in precedents that drafters have been using for a long time. It takes time and great effort to update all your precedents to eliminate legalese and improve it in many other ways, so there are many drafters who intend to do it but are so busy they do not get a chance to do so.

Finally, it is also very common to see *Whereas* introducing each sentence of the recitals or background section. While many lawyers seek to eliminate legalese in the rest of the agreement, they feel they need *Whereas* in that part of the contract to properly start each sentence and signal the true intent of the parties.

III. COUPLETS AND TRIPLETS

Contracts are often full of couplets and triplets that are redundant. A classic example is *null and void.* Drafters are often afraid to simplify these couplets and triplets by using only one word, worried that any deletion will result in an unknown, disastrously substantive change. Usually, there is no reason to fear that this will happen, so

---

7. *Medicis Pharm. Corp. v. Anacor Pharms., Inc.,* No. 8095-VCP, 2013 WL 4509652, at *2 (Del. Ch. Aug. 12, 2013).

8. *See id.*; *see also Chase v. Columbia Nat. Corp.,* 832 F. Supp. 654, 661 (S.D.N.Y. 1993) ("Columbia's argument that 'herein' refers only to Section 11 is untenable. 'Herein' and 'hereof' are used throughout the document to refer to the entire Agreement . . .").

drafters should take the time to thoughtfully simplify their precedents and eliminate unnecessary couplets and triplets.

The use of couplets and triplets reflects the evolution of the English language.[9] After the Normans invaded England in 1066, French slowly became the language used in English courts and contracts. The English came to resent the use of French and began eventually once again to use English for legal matters. As the use of "law French" began to wane, English lawyers were faced with a recurring problem. When they went to translate a French legal term into an English legal term, they were often unsure whether the English word had the same connotation. The solution was obvious: Use both the French and the English word. For example, *free and clear* is actually a combination of the Old English word *free* and the French word *clair*.[10] Here are a few other examples:[11]

■ Acknowledge and confess	Old English and Old French
■ Breaking and entering	Old English and French
■ Goods and chattel	Old English and Old French
■ Right, title, and interest	Old English, Old English, and French

In addition to this practice of joining French and English synonyms, the English often used more than one word when one would have been sufficient.[12] Here are a few common examples of synonyms that were used and may have not been necessary:

■ To have and to hold
■ Aid and abet
■ Part and parcel
■ Rest, residue, and remainder

The bottom line is that most couplets and triplets reflect our linguistic heritage, not legal distinctions. Therefore, they should be pared down to one word — unless the drafter intends a substantive difference, as in the phrase *represent and warrant*.

The following is a list of word combinations that should not be used.[13] Instead, use only one of these words; which one would depend on the law of your jurisdiction.

All and every	Each and every
Alter or change	Final and conclusive
Any and all	For and in behalf of
Amend, modify, or change	Full force and effect
Bind and obligate	Furnish and supply
By and between	Kind and character
By and with	Known and described as
Convey, transfer, and set over	Made and entered into
Covenant and agree	Means and includes
Due and owing	Null and of no effect
Each and all	Null and void

---

9. *See* David Mellinkoff, *The Language of the Law* ch. 9 (Little, Brown & Co. 1963).

10. *See Kohlbrand v. Ranieri*, 823 N.E.2d 76, 78 (Ohio Ct. App. 2004), for a taste of a judge's displeasure with the parties litigating the meaning of the couplet *free and clear*.

11. *See* Mellinkoff *supra* n. 9, at 121-122.

12. *See* Mellinkoff *supra* n. 9, at 42-46 and 120-122.

13. Dickerson, *supra* n. 5, at 208.

Over and above   Sole and exclusive
Perform and discharge   Suffer or permit
Relieve and discharge   Then and in that event
Remise, release, and forever   True and correct
    quitclaim (except in states where   Type and kind
    required by statute)   Understood and agreed

IV. PRETENTIOUS AND VERBOSE EXPRESSIONS

Look closely at the lists that follow. The words in the *Don't Use* column are either pretentious or verbose. Replace them, as appropriate, with the words in the *Use* column.[14]

DON'T USE	USE
Above	[refer to the specific provision]
Attains the age of	Becomes . . . years old
At the time	When
Below	[refer to the specific provision]
By means of	By
By reason of	By, because of
Cease	Stop
Commence	Begin
Consequence	Result
Contiguous to	Next to
Dated as of even date hereof	Dated the date of this Agreement
Does not operate to	Does not
During such time as	During
During the course of	During
Effectuate	Carry out
Endeavor (verb)	Try
Enter into a contract with	Contract with
For the duration of	During
For the purpose of holding	To hold
For the reason that	Because
Forthwith	Immediately
In case	If
In cases in which	When, where (use "whenever" or "wherever" only when needed to emphasize the exhaustive or recurring applicability of the rule)
In lieu of	Instead of, in place of
Inquire	Ask
Institute	Begin, start

DON'T USE	USE
In the event that	If
Is able to	Can
Is authorized	May
Is binding upon	Binds
Is unable to	Cannot
Loan (as a verb)	Lend
Mutually agree	Agree
Necessitate	Require
Notwithstanding anything to the contrary in this Agreement	Despite any other provision in this Agreement
Notwithstanding the foregoing	Despite the previous [sentence]
Party of the first part	[the party's name]
Prior to	Before
Provision of law	Law
Purchase (as a verb)	Buy
Suffer (in the sense of *permit*)	Permit
Sufficient number of	Enough
Until such time as	Until
Utilize, employ (in the sense of "use")	Use

V. EXERCISES

A. EXERCISE 22A: ELIMINATE THE LEGALESE

Mark up the following provisions from different types of agreements to eliminate the legalese. If appropriate, make other drafting changes that improve the provisions.

1. Definition of Cause. For purposes hereof, *Cause* with respect to the termination of any Shareholder's employment has the meaning set forth in said Shareholder's employment agreement with the Company.

2. Term. The term of this Agreement commences as of the date set forth in Section 8.6 hereof.

3. Delivery of Financial Statements. No later than 90 days after the end of each fiscal year, the Borrower shall provide the Bank a copy of the Borrower's year-end financial statements. Such financial statements shall be certified by the Borrower's chief financial officer to fairly present the financial condition of the Borrower.

4. Release. Except as herein to the contrary provided, each party releases, remises, and forever discharges the other from any and all actions, suits, debts, claims, and obligations whatsoever, both in law and equity, that either of them ever had, now has, or may hereafter have, against the other by reason of any matter, cause, or thing to the date of the execution of this Agreement.[15]

5. Waiver. In the event of the failure of the Borrower aforesaid to comply with the terms of the aforementioned Note, the undersigned Guarantor waives notice of acceptance of this Guaranty, diligence, presentment, notice of dishonor, demand for payment, any and all notices of whatever kind or nature, and the exhaustion of legal remedies available to the holder of said Note.

6. Lease. The Lessor leases to the Lessee, and the Lessee leases from the Lessor, all the machinery, equipment, and other property described in

    (a) the schedule executed by the parties concurrently herewith; and

    (b) any schedule hereafter executed by the parties hereto.

All said machinery, equipment, and other property described in all said schedules are hereinafter collectively called the "equipment," and all said schedules are hereinafter collectively called the "schedules."

7. Compliance with Communications Act. The Merger's consummation does not violate the Communications Act or the rules and regulations promulgated thereunder.

---

15. This provision is based on a general release in Gary N. Skoloff, Richard H. Singer, Jr. & Ronald L. Brown, *Drafting Prenuptial Agreements* VII-61 (Aspen 2003).

CHAPTER TWENTY-THREE

Clarity Through Format

I. INTRODUCTION

Imagine if this book had no page numbers, no paragraphs separating ideas, and no chapters; instead, from start to finish, it was all one long, continuous, dense block of words. Daunting — it would be a nightmare to read. But the publisher has spent considerable money and effort to enhance the book's clarity through format. In this same way, lawyers enhance their contracts' clarity through format.

In the remainder of this chapter, you will learn formatting techniques that will improve the clarity of the contracts you draft.

II. SECTIONS AND SUBSECTIONS

One of the easiest ways of formatting a contract is to use sections and subsections. By using a greater number of shorter sections, you make a contract easier to read.

Look at the following provision from a joint venture agreement, which states the procedure for appointing officers and indemnifies the officers:

> *Example — Provision Without Subsections*
>
> **9.3 Officers of the Joint Venture**. The Managing Venturer shall appoint the chief executive officer, chief financial officer, and other officers of the Joint Venture. The officers are to perform those duties and have those responsibilities that the Managing Venturer assigns to them. The Non-Managing Venturer must approve the appointment and replacement of the chief executive officer and shall not unreasonably withhold or delay its approval. The Managing Venturer may appoint one or more officers of either Venturer to be an officer of the Joint Venture, but only if that officer intends to devote substantially full time to the Joint Venture. If that officer fails to devote substantially full time to the Joint Venture, the Managing Venturer shall terminate that officer's employment. The Managing Venturer may determine, in its sole discretion, the benefits to be offered to any officer appointed in accordance with this subsection. The Joint Venture shall indemnify and defend each officer of the Joint Venture against all

claims, losses, damages and liabilities, including reasonable attorneys' fees, relating to any act or failure to act by that officer, but only if the officer's act or failure to act was in good faith and, in both cases, in a manner that officer reasonably believed to be in, or not opposed to, the Joint Venture's best interests; or if the officer relied on the opinion or advice of competent legal counsel. Any indemnity under this Section is to be paid from the Joint Venture's assets, and no Venturer has any individual liability on account of the indemnity under this Section 9.3.

No doubt, this provision was difficult to read and follow. Did you even finish reading it? Provisions drafted like this make it harder to carefully analyze and comment on a contract. What follows is the same provision, but formatted. No other changes have been made. It is now much easier to read because it has been broken into multiple subsections. Each subsection is separated from the next by white space, and each subsection has a heading to signal its substance. It is still long and not as interesting as a best-selling novel, but it is better than before.

Example — Provision with Subsections

9.3 The Joint Venture's Officers.

9.3.1 Appointment of Officers. The Managing Venturer shall appoint the chief executive officer, chief financial officer, and other officers of the Joint Venture. The officers are to perform those duties and have those responsibilities that the Managing Venturer assigns to them.

9.3.2 Approval of Chief Executive Officer's Appointment. The Non-Managing Venturer must approve the appointment and replacement of the chief executive officer and shall not unreasonably withhold or delay its approval.

9.3.3 Appointment of a Venturer's Officer. The Managing Venturer may appoint one or more officers of either Venturer to be an officer of the Joint Venture, but only if that officer intends to devote substantially full time to the Joint Venture. If that officer fails to devote substantially full time to the Joint Venture, the Managing Venturer shall terminate that officer's employment. The Managing Venturer may determine, in its sole discretion, the benefits to be offered to any officer appointed in accordance with this subsection.

9.3.4 Indemnity of Officers. The Joint Venture shall indemnify and defend each officer of the Joint Venture against all claims, losses, damages and liabilities, including reasonable attorneys' fees, relating to any act or failure to act by that officer, but only if

(a) the officer's act or failure to act was in good faith and, in both cases, in a manner that the officer reasonably believed to be in, or not opposed to, the Joint Venture's best interests; or

(b) the officer relied on the opinion or advice of competent legal counsel.

9.3.5 Source of Funds. Any indemnity under this Section 9.3 is to be paid from the Joint Venture's assets, and no Venturer has any individual liability on account of the indemnity under this Section.

III. TABULATION

A. DEFINITION AND WHEN TO USE TABULATION

Look again at the *Provision with Subsections* in Section II of this chapter. In that provision, a long sentence is broken into two additional subsections, each of which is grammatically independent of the other. They are conceptually related, which is why they are under the same section. Subsections can also be used to join two or more related sentences. This reduces the length of the contract and aids the reader by showing how the sentences are related. In both cases, each subsection is indented and separated from the other by white space. This type of formatting is known as **tabulation** and takes its name from the use of the *Tab* key on the keyboard, which is used to indent the tabulated material.

The following example from a noncompetition agreement shows how tabulation can be used to join two related sentences.

Examples — Using Tabulation to Join Two Related Sentences

Untabulated Sentences:

Noncompetition. For a one-year period after the Term, the Executive shall not employ any person who was an employee during the Term. In addition, during that period, the Executive shall not interfere with the relationship between the Company and any of its employees.

Tabulated Sentence:

Noncompetition. For a one-year period after the Term, the Executive

    (a) shall not employ any person who was an employee during the Term; and

    (b) shall not interfere with the relationship between the Company and any of its employees.

The next example shows a long, untabulated sentence from a construction contract[1] and the same sentence but tabulated.

Examples — Using Tabulation to Join Two Related Sentences

Untabulated Sentence:

Contractor's Right to Terminate. The Contractor may terminate this Agreement for cause if work is stopped for 30 days or more through no fault of the Contractor or because of a court order, if the Architect unjustifiably refuses to approve a payment request, or if the Owner refuses to pay a payment request that the Architect approved.

---

1. This provision is based on a provision from Stanley P. Sklar & Gregory R. Andre, Design and Construction Contracts, in *Commercial Contracts: Strategies for Drafting and Negotiating* vol. 2, ch. 29, 29-85 (Morton Moskin ed., Aspen Publishers 2006).

Tabulated Sentence:

> **Contractor's Right to Terminate**. The Contractor may terminate this Agreement for cause if
>
> (a) work stops for 30 days or more through no fault of the Contractor or because of a court order;
> (b) the Architect unjustifiably refuses to approve a payment request; or
> (c) the Owner refuses to pay a payment request that the Architect approved.

Deciding when to use tabulation is a judgment call. If you are deciding whether to join two or more sentences through tabulation, the subject matter of the sentences should be related. For example, if both sentences relate to the rights of a bank on their borrower's default, tabulation is probably appropriate. If the subject matter is not related, create separate sections and insert them in the appropriate place in the contract. If you are deciding whether to break one sentence into a tabulated format, any sentence with a compound or a series is a candidate. For these purposes, a **compound** refers to two items in a sentence joined by *and* or *or*. A **series** refers to three or more items in a sentence joined by *and* or *or*.

A drafter should also consider the length and complexity of a sentence. Any sentence that is already a candidate becomes a stronger candidate if it is three lines or longer—the **three-line rule,** discussed in Chapter 24 on page 362. The ultimate deciding factor is whether tabulation makes it easier for a reader to assimilate the information. So, if you have a long sentence with *and* and *or*, you should probably tabulate it.

Do not tabulate a provision simply because it includes a series of items. The example below should not have been tabulated since it is short and easy to understand in its untabulated state. In addition, avoid including concluding language at the end of your provision that applies to each tabulated subsection. See the incorrect example below that has *this Agreement* at the end and which the drafter meant to apply to every item above it.

> ### Examples—Sentences That Should Not Be Tabulated
>
> *Correct to Include Untabulated Sentence:*
>
> > **Corporate Power and Authority**. The Licensor has full corporate power and authority to execute, deliver, and perform this Agreement.
>
> *Incorrect to Include Tabulated Sentence:*
>
> > **Corporate Power and Authority**. The Licensor has full corporate power and authority to
> >
> > (a) execute,
> > (b) deliver, and
> > (c) perform
> >
> > this Agreement.

If you find yourself having to include concluding language, check to see whether you should even tabulate the provision at all. If you still do need to tabulate the provision, redraft the provision so that the concluding language is included in the introductory language, as we have done with the examples below:

> *Examples—Redraft to Remove Concluding Language*
>
> *Incorrect with Concluding Language:*
>
> **Employee Sanctions**. Each time an Employee
>
> (a) is absent from work for an unexcused reason,
> (b) takes a coffee break longer than 15 minutes, or
> (c) smokes a cigarette in a designated no-smoking area,
>
> that Employee loses one vacation day.
>
> *Correct with Concluding Language Incorporated into Introductory Language:*
>
> **Employee Sanctions**. An Employee loses one vacation day each time an Employee
>
> (a) is absent from work for an unexcused reason,
> (b) takes a coffee break longer than 15 minutes, or
> (c) smokes a cigarette in a designated no-smoking area.

B. GUIDELINES FOR BOTH SENTENCE AND LIST FORMAT TABULATION

Follow these guidelines when tabulating any type of provision, whether it is one in the sentence format or in the list format, which are explained in further detail in Guideline 1.

1. Guideline 1: Choose the Right Format for Tabulation

There are primarily two formats for tabulation: the sentence format and the list format. In the **sentence format,** each tabulated subsection creates a full sentence when joined with the introductory language. In the **list format**, the introductory language is a complete sentence, and each tabulated subsection is part of a list. A strong clue that a list format is appropriate is if the introductory language includes some form of the word follow. Note also that each tabulated subsection can also be referred to as an **enumerated item.**

Up to this point, the examples illustrating tabulation have been in the sentence format. The following example of tabulation uses the list format:

> *Example—Tabulation Using List Format*
>
> **Events of Default**. Each of the following events is an Event of Default:
>
> (a) The Borrower has failed to pay interest when due.
> (b) The Borrower has failed to pay principal when due.
> (c) Any representation or warranty of the Borrower stated in Article 3 was false when made.
> (d) The Borrower has breached any covenant in Article 4.

Sometimes, with a little editing, you can draft a provision using either the list format or the sentence format. Look at Example 1 below, which is drafted using the sentence format. Then see Example 2 below, which is Example 1 revised to the list format. Also, note as you compare the examples below that your punctuation will vary depending on which format you choose. This will be explained further in the guidelines that follow for each specific type of tabulation, whether the sentence format or the list format.

Examples — Tabulation Using Sentence or List Format

1 — Tabulation Using Sentence Format:

Employee Sanctions. An Employee loses one vacation day each time an Employee

    (a) is absent from work for an unexcused reason,

    (b) takes a coffee break longer than 15 minutes, or

    (c) smokes a cigarette in a designated no-smoking area.

2 — Tabulation Using List Format:

Employee Sanctions. An Employee loses one vacation day each time the Employee does any one of the following:

    (a) The Employee is absent from work for an unexcused reason.

    (b) The Employee takes a coffee break longer than 15 minutes.

    (c) The Employee smokes a cigarette in a designated no-smoking area.

---

2. Guideline 2: Use Parallel Drafting

Use **parallel drafting** to construct the tabulated sentences, which means that the grammatical structure of each of the tabulated sentences should be the same.[2] You can check your tabulation for parallel drafting in either the sentence or list format by making sure that each of the tabulated subsections begins in the same way (e.g., a verb in the present tense, as in Example 1 below). It is possible that what follows is similar for each tabulated subsection, but there can also be some variation, as in Example 1 below, which is acceptable.

In addition, to check parallel drafting in the sentence format, you can join the language that introduces the tabulated subsections and the language of each subsection so that the introductory language creates a coherent, grammatically correct sentence when joined with each enumerated item. Consider the tabulated provisions that follow, which use parallel drafting. You can test this by joining the introductory language to each of the subsections and creating separate sentences.

Examples — Parallel Drafting

1 — Tabulated Sentence in Sentence Format:[3]

Developer's Representations and Warranties. The Developer represents and warrants that the Software

    (a) is unique and original;

    (b) is clear of any claims or encumbrances; and

    (c) does not infringe on the rights of any third parties.

---

2. *See* Chapter 24 on page 365 for a more detailed discussion of parallel drafting.

3. The provision is from Gregory J. Battersby & Charles W. Grimes eds., *License Agreements: Forms and Checklists* 4-27 (Aspen Publishers 2003).

1 — Untabulated Sentences to Check Parallel Drafting:

- The Developer represents and warrants that the Software is unique and original.
- The Developer represents and warrants that the Software is clear of any claims or encumbrances.
- The Developer represents and warrants that the Software does not infringe on the rights of any third parties.

2 — Tabulated Sentence:

Employee Sanctions. An Employee loses one vacation day each time an Employee

    (a) is absent from work for an unexcused reason,
    (b) takes a coffee break longer than 15 minutes, or
    (c) smokes a cigarette in a designated no-smoking area.

2 — Untabulated Sentences to Check Parallel Drafting:

- An Employee loses one vacation day each time an Employee is absent from work for an unexcused reason.
- An Employee loses one vacation day each time an Employee takes a coffee break longer than 15 minutes.
- An Employee loses one vacation day each time an Employee smokes a cigarette in a designated no-smoking area.

The following tabulated sentence does not use parallel drafting. Why?

Example — Incorrect Parallel Drafting

Landlord's Rights on Termination. If this Lease terminates because of a default by the Tenant, the Landlord may

    (a) enter the Premises immediately by any legal proceeding; and
    (b) has the right to evict any person on the Premises.

The problem is with subsection (b). When joined with the introductory language, it creates an incoherent sentence. The problem is clear when the tabulation is removed, as follows:

Example — Incorrect Parallel Drafting

Landlord's Rights on Termination. If this Lease terminates because of a default of the Tenant, the Landlord *may has the right to* evict any person on the Premises.

To fix the tabulated sentence so that it uses parallel drafting and makes sense, drop the words *has the right to* from subsection (b) and do not separate the verb *may* from the other verbs, as will be discussed next in Section C. Keeping verbs together will also help ensure that you tabulate provisions correctly. Here is the final provision correctly tabulated:

Example — Correct Parallel Drafting

> **Landlord's Rights on Termination**. If this Lease terminates because of a default by the Tenant, the Landlord
>
> (a) may enter the Premises immediately by any legal proceeding; and
> (b) may evict any person on the Premises.

C. GUIDELINES FOR SENTENCE FORMAT TABULATION

If you are thinking of tabulating a provision using the sentence format, use the following guidelines:

1. **Use the sentence format for tabulation when the introductory language and the tabulated subsections form a complete, grammatical sentence.**
2. **Include in the introductory language all the words common to each tabulated subsection.** In doing so, make sure that you do the following:
   - Do not separate an article (e.g., *the*, *a*, or *an*) from the noun that it precedes. Doing so makes the reading of the tabulated subsections awkward.
   - Consider not separating *to* from the rest of the infinitive form of verbs (e.g., *to see*, *to walk*, *to draft*) and keeping all verbs together (e.g., *may enter* and *may evict*, as in the last correct provision in Section B).
   - Draft a negative covenant (*shall not*) so that *shall not* is included in each enumerated item, not with the introductory language. This stylistic change makes it easier to read such a covenant and reminds the reader that the provision prohibits the acts in each subsection.
3. **Punctuate the introductory language as you would do if the sentence were untabulated.** If you would not put punctuation after the last word in the introductory language if the sentence were untabulated, then do not use any punctuation when the sentence is tabulated. But if the introductory language would end with a comma if the sentence were untabulated, then that comma should remain when the sentence is tabulated.
4. **Begin each tabulated subsection with a lowercase letter.** We do this because each subsection is the continuation of a sentence.
5. **End each tabulated subsection with whatever punctuation would be used if the sentence were untabulated.** Often, this will mean that you will end each subsection with a semicolon, so that each tabulated subsection results in a complete sentence when combined with the introductory language. To determine the punctuation, join the introductory language with each subsection to see what punctuation is appropriate. Then, insert *and* or *or* as appropriate after the punctuation (e.g., semicolon) of the next-to-last subsection. Note that if you are drafting a provision using punctuation just as you would in a complete sentence and you follow grammatical rules, this will mean that in simple tabulated lists, you only need to use commas and you do not need to use semicolons. While this would be the correct way to draft, some drafters prefer using semicolons at the end of each tabulated item, even in a simple list. What is important is to be consistent throughout your agreement and follow the precedent that you are using when drafting or tabulating a new provision.

End the last tabulated subsection with a period. Again, we recommend that you do not include concluding language at the end of your provision that applies to all the tabulated subsections. However, if there is no way to avoid having concluding language, make sure you begin the concluding language at the left margin, so it has the same margin as the introductory language, and end the concluding language with a period.

Examples 1 and 2 below show us how to apply the guidelines above. Example 1 is a classic example of a provision tabulated using the sentence format: All the common words are in the introductory language; that language does not conclude with any punctuation; and each subsection, other than the last, ends with a semicolon. Example 2 is a variation of Example 1. It differs in that the introductory language ends with a comma because that language is a prepositional phrase that would end with a comma if the sentence were untabulated. In addition, although *the* is common to both subsections, it is omitted from the introductory language, as articles should be kept with their nouns.

Example 1 — Provision Tabulated Using Sentence Format

Architect's Obligations. The Architect

    (a) shall consult with the Owner at least once a week; and

    (b) shall deliver to the Owner an accounting of expenses incurred each month in connection with the Project, no later than five business days after the end of each month.

Example 2 — Provision Tabulated Using Sentence Format

Force Majeure Event. If a *Force Majeure Event* occurs,

    (a) the Contractor shall advise the Owner of its existence as soon as possible after its occurrence; and

    (b) the Contractor's obligation to perform is suspended until the *Force Majeure Event* ends.

D. GUIDELINES FOR LIST FORMAT TABULATION

If you need to tabulate a provision using the list format, use the following guidelines:

1. **Draft the introductory language so that it includes the phrase *as follows* or *the following* or otherwise incorporates that concept and end it with a colon.**
2. **Draft the introductory language, if appropriate, so that it signals whether the items in each tabulated subsection are cumulative or alternative.** The following examples show how introductory language can signal whether the items in each tabulated subsection are cumulative or alternative.

Examples — Introductory Language That Signals Cumulative or Alternative Items

Signals Alternative Items:

    Termination. The Company may terminate the Executive for any one or more of the following reasons:

    Notice. When the Company sends a notice, the Company shall use one of the following methods, but the Company may choose which one:

Signals Cumulative Items:

    Duties. During the Term, the Executive shall perform all of the following duties:

3. **Begin each tabulated subsection with a capital letter and end it with a period.**
4. **Do not put *and* or *or* after the next-to-last subsection.**

Here is another example of the list format tabulation incorporating the guidelines above:

Example — Tabulation Using List Format

    Events of Default. Each of the following events is an Event of Default:

    (a) The Borrower has failed to pay interest when due.

    (b) The Borrower has failed to pay principal when due.

    (c) Any representation or warranty of the Borrower stated in Article 3 was false when made.

    (d) The Borrower has breached any covenant in Article 4.

E. MULTILEVEL TABULATION

Some sentences are sufficiently complex that they require more than one level of tabulation, which we refer to as **multilevel tabulation**. If so, follow the numbering system for the sublevels as set out in Section IV on page 350. The following termination provision is in both untabulated and tabulated formats. The tabulated version has two levels of subsections.

Examples — Multilevel Tabulation

Untabulated Provision:

    9.1 Termination. Either party may terminate this Agreement if the other party breaches any covenant in this Agreement, but only if that breach remains uncured for 30 days after written notice of it to the breaching party, and as a result of that breach, the nonbreaching party cannot substantially realize the benefits that it would have realized from this Agreement absent that breach, or if the other party files a petition for bankruptcy in any court pursuant to any statute of the United States or any state.

Tabulated Provision:
> **9.1 Termination**. Either party may terminate this Agreement if the other party
>
>   (a) breaches any covenant in this Agreement, but only if
>   (i) that breach remains uncured for 30 days after written notice of it to the breaching party and
>   (ii) as a result of that breach, the nonbreaching party cannot substantially realize the benefits that it would have realized from this Agreement absent that breach;
>
>   **or**
>
>   (b) files a petition for bankruptcy in any court pursuant to any statute of the United States or any state.

When drafting a multilevel tabulated sentence, indent each subordinate level five more spaces than the previous level so the reader can see the subordinate relationship between one level and the next. In establishing the relative relationship between the levels, make each subsection parallel with its subordinate subsection to prevent a confusing or ambiguous provision.

Subsection (i) in the *Tabulated Provision* of the example above does not end with a semicolon because the end of the clause is at the end of subsection (ii). Finally, note the placement of the bolded *or*. Although some drafters would place this *or* after the semicolon in subsection (ii), others put it on its own line at the same indentation of the subsections that it joins, so that it can provide a useful visual clue as to how the levels relate to each other.

F. DOUBLE TABULATION

Double tabulation occurs in a sentence that has two or more independent sets of subsections at the same level. In the following representation and warranty from a loan agreement, the double tabulation occurs because subsections (i) and (ii) are not subsections of either subsection (a) or (b). Subsections (i) and (ii) are not labeled (c) and (d) because that would mislead the reader, since it would suggest that the introductory language that applies to subsections (a) and (b) also applies to subsections (i) and (ii).

Example — Double Tabulation
> **3.11 Leases. Schedule 3.11** lists each lease to which the Borrower is a party. With respect to each lease listed in **Schedule 3.11**,
>
>   (a) no default has occurred and is continuing, and
>   (b) no event has occurred and is continuing which, with notice or lapse of time or both, would constitute a default on the part of the Borrower,
>
> *except* for those defaults and events of default, if any, that
>
>   (i) are not material in character, amount, or extent; and
>   (ii) do not, severally or in the aggregate, materially detract from the value of or materially interfere with the present use of the property subject to the lease.

As this example demonstrates, double tabulation is awkward and possibly confusing. You should avoid double tabulation as much as possible. Instead, break the provision into two or more sentences, as has been done in the following redraft:

Example — Avoiding Double Tabulation by Breaking Down the Provision

3.11. Leases

    (a) **Borrower's Leases. Schedule 3.11(A)** lists each lease to which the Borrower is a party.

    (b) **Defaults. Schedule 3.11(B)** lists each lease to which the Borrower is a party and where either

        (i) a default has occurred and is continuing; or

        (ii) an event has occurred and is continuing which, with notice or lapse of time or both, would constitute a default by the Borrower.

    (c) **Materiality of Defaults**. The defaults and events listed in **Schedule 3.11(B)**

        (i) are not material in character, amount, or extent; and

        (ii) do not, severally or in the aggregate, materially detract from the value or materially interfere with the present use of the property subject to the lease.

IV. NUMBERING SYSTEMS

In the same way that a brief or a memorandum can be organized into main ideas and subsidiary ideas, so can a contract. To reflect the different organizational levels in a contract, use a simple, easy-to-read numbering system. Most firms have templates for numbering systems, as do most word-processing programs. The key is to use an outline format, white space, indentations, and other formatting options to show the relative relationship between the provisions and make the contract easy to read. You will find in this section more information on three common numbering systems. You will find these three numbering systems used throughout this book in the different examples.

A. NUMBERING SYSTEM 1

Here is what this first numbering system looks like:

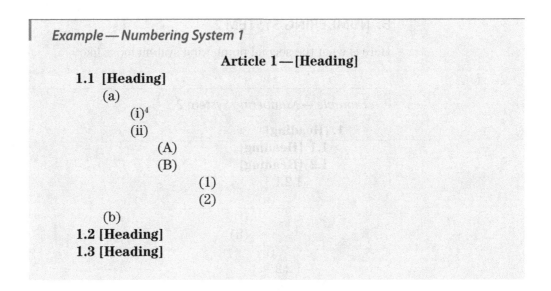

Example—Numbering System 1

Article 1—[Heading]

1.1 [Heading]
    (a)
        (i)[4]
        (ii)
            (A)
            (B)
                (1)
                (2)
    (b)
1.2 [Heading]
1.3 [Heading]

This is one of the most common numbering systems. The agreement is divided into articles, each article comprising a set of related provisions. The House Purchase Agreement, which you can find on the CasebookConnect Resources page and at www.aspenpublishing.com, uses this numbering system. So, for example, Article 3 states the Seller's representations and warranties, and Article 4 states the Buyer's representations and warranties.

Each article number and its title are bolded and centered. Although many drafters number the articles using Roman numerals, you should use Arabic numerals because they are easier for a reader to understand. Do not put a period at the end of the title of the article.

As you can see from the outline of this system in the previous example, each article is broken into sections (1.1, 1.2, etc.) and then subsections ((a), (b), etc.). Each section number is in bold and is not followed by a period. Each section has a bold heading followed by a period in regular font. The word *Section* does not need to precede a section's number, although many lawyers do include it. They feel that the slightly longer heading helps the reader find a specific section. Drafters using a more contemporary style omit *Section*. The provision is in the regular font and immediately follows the period after the heading unless the section has only subsections.

The formatting of subsections resembles the formatting of sections, although the subsection referent ((a), (b), etc.) is not in bold. If a subsection includes one or more sentences, it should have its own heading, as should every other subsection at that level. But if the subsections are part of a tabulation, do not use a heading. Instead, follow the punctuation guidelines for tabulation previously discussed in this chapter.

All subsections at the same level should be indented relative to the indentation of the section or subsection that precedes it, which visually shows the reader the logical relationship between the contract's parts. Each level is indented five more spaces than the previous sublevel.

In the same way that an outline must have a subsection 2 if it has a subsection 1, a contract must have at least two subsections at each level.

---

4. Drafters sometimes refer to this level as *one in the hole* or *romanette*, followed by the appropriate number (e.g., *romanette one*).

B. NUMBERING SYSTEM 2

Here is what the second numbering system looks like:

Example — Numbering System 2

1. [Heading]
  1.1 [Heading]
  1.2 [Heading]
    1.2.1
        (a)
                (i)
                (ii)
        (b)
    1.2.2
  1.3 [Heading]

The first level in the example above (1.) is the equivalent of an article in *Numbering System 1*. Typically, the only text is a heading, but drafters sometimes begin the provision immediately after the heading.

The guidelines with respect to headings and fonts are the same for both formats. Only the numbering and margins differ.

Some drafters prefer the precision of this numbering system. Specifically, it helps a reader who flips through a contract looking for a particular provision. Rather than a page having merely a series of subsection referents (e.g., (a), (b), and (c)), each referent tells the reader a provision's location relative to the contract's other provisions (e.g., 1.2.2).

Some drafters modify this numbering system using lettered and numbered subsections after the third level, concerned that subsequent numbered referents (e.g., 1.2.2.5.7) become long and harder to follow.

C. NUMBERING SYSTEM 3

Here is what the third numbering system looks like:

Example — Numbering System 3

1. [Heading]
    (a)
            (i)
            (ii)
                    (A)
                    (B)
                        (1)
                        (2)
    (b)

Some contracts are relatively short and do not require articles. For these contracts, the provisions can be set up as a series of numbered sections, each section having a bolded heading. If no subsections are required, the text of the provision immediately follows the heading.

Some drafters refer to provisions using this numbering system as paragraphs and subparagraphs, which is a perfectly acceptable alternative.

V. HEADINGS

Integral to any numbering scheme are the headings that identify for the reader the substance of the provision. Readers often flip through contracts looking for a specific provision. Headings that accurately relate a provision's substance facilitate a reader's review.

When choosing a heading, take care that it accurately describes the provision's contents. Drafters often include in their contracts a general provision stating that headings do not affect the contract's construction or interpretation. Do not rely on such a provision though, and be careful when selecting your headings.

Headings are sometimes too short. Consider the provision in the example that follows from an agreement between a publisher and an author. Although the heading *Copies* is descriptive, it could be more so. By changing the name to *Free Copies*, adding just one more word, the heading becomes more informative.

Examples — Length of Headings

Too Short:

Copies. No later than ten days before the Book's publication, the Publisher shall provide the Author with five free copies of the Book.

Recommended Because More Informative:

Free Copies. No later than ten days before the Book's publication, the Publisher shall provide the Author with five free copies of the Book.

Headings can also be too long, trying to encapsulate too much of a provision. Generally, if the heading must list more than two topics to be accurate, divide the provision into two or more sections. If the heading has multiple topics, separate them with a semicolon.

Example — Heading with Multiple Topics

Free Print Copies; E-book Access. No later than ten days before the Book's publication, the Publisher shall provide the Author with five free print copies of the Book and access to the Book's E-book version.

VI. TABLE OF CONTENTS

A table of contents, previously discussed in Chapter 14 on page 175, is particularly handy in long contracts because it permits a reader to find a specific provision quickly. Generally, a sophisticated word-processing program can automatically create a table of contents if you use automatic numbering.

VII. TYPOGRAPHY

Contracts are long and difficult to read. Anything that makes them easier to read is worth doing. Font is one of the factors in the mix, but which font should you select? Typographers classify fonts into two types: **serif** and **sans serif**. A serif font has extra small lines at the ends of the horizontal and vertical strokes of a letter.

Example — Serif Font

The dog wagged its tail.

Sans serif fonts are simpler; they do not have the extra small lines. (*Sans* is French for "without.")

Example — Sans Serif Font

The dog wagged its tail.

The accepted wisdom has long been that serif fonts, such as Times New Roman, are easier to read. But multiple studies have questioned whether that is correct.[5] Indeed, some studies suggest that the easiest font to read is the one with which the reader is most familiar.[6]

The development of computers and new devices have added an additional layer of complexity to the mix. The issue is no longer simply which font facilitates reading

---

5. *See* Alex Poole, *Which Are More Legible: Serif or Sans Serif Typefaces?*, http://alexpoole .info/blog/which-are-more-legible-serif-or-sans-serif-typefaces (last updated March 2012; accessed April 30, 2023) (explaining the rationale for each of serif and sans serif fonts and reviewing the literature comparing the two fonts); *see also* Ruth Anne Robbins, *Painting with Print: Incorporating Concepts of Typographic and Layout Design into the Text of Legal Writing Documents,* 2 J. Ass'n Leg. Writing Dirs. 108, 119-120 (2010).

6. Poole, *supra* n. 5.

a *printed* document. Lawyers must take into account that they now draft and review contracts mostly on their computers and different devices. Therefore, lawyers must really consider which fonts facilitate reading documents on different types of electronic devices, such as laptops, tablets, and phones.

Beginning with the Windows XP version of its operating system, Microsoft has offered a new font-rendering software technology, ClearType, which makes text on LCD screens sharper and easier to read.[7] To take advantage of this technology, Microsoft has created new fonts.[8] Several of these fonts are also intended to be easily read in print. Microsoft offers two of these fonts as default fonts: Cambria (a serif font)[9] and Calibri (a sans serif font).[10]

Here are examples of both:

Examples — Cambria and Calibri Fonts

Cambria:

This Confidentiality Agreement, dated March 1, 20___, is between Wonder Drugs, Inc., a Delaware corporation ("Wonder Drugs"), and Still Viable Venture Capital Fund LP, a Delaware limited partnership ("VC Fund").

[Other provisions intentionally omitted.]

19.2 Definition of Confidential Information. "Confidential Information" means all information that Wonder Drugs discloses to VC Fund that is in

(a) tangible form and clearly labeled as confidential when disclosed; or

(b) non-tangible form and that is both

(i) identified as confidential when disclosed and

(ii) summarized and designated as confidential in a written memorandum delivered to VC Fund no later than 10 business days after the information was first disclosed.

19.3 Confidentiality Period. VC Fund shall hold in confidence and shall not disclose any Confidential Information for a period of five years, beginning on the date this Agreement is executed and delivered and ending on the day immediately preceding the fifth anniversary of its execution and delivery.

---

7. Microsoft Corp., *Microsoft ClearType Overview,* https://learn.microsoft.com/en-us/typography/cleartype/ (last updated Jun. 9, 2022).

8. Microsoft commissioned these fonts from designers and engineers. *See* Microsoft, *ClearType Font Collection,* https://learn.microsoft.com/en-us/typography/cleartype/clear-type-font-collection (accessed April 30, 2023).

9. Microsoft, *Cambria Font List,* https://docs.microsoft.com/en-us/typography/font-list/cambria (accessed September 4, 2022).

10. Microsoft, *Calibri Font List,* https://docs.microsoft.com/en-us/typography/font-list/calibri (accessed September 4, 2022).

Calibri:

This Confidentiality Agreement, dated March 1, 20____, is between Wonder Drugs, Inc., a Delaware corporation ("Wonder Drugs"), and Still Viable Venture Capital Fund LP, a Delaware limited partnership ("VC Fund").

[Other provisions intentionally omitted.]

19.2   Definition of Confidential Information. "Confidential Information" means all information that Wonder Drugs discloses to VC Fund that is in

19.2.1   tangible form and clearly labeled as confidential when disclosed; or

19.2.2   non-tangible form and that is both

(a)   identified as confidential when disclosed and

(b)   summarized and designated as confidential in a written memorandum delivered to VC Fund no later than 10 business days after the information was first disclosed.

19.3   Confidentiality Period. VC Fund shall hold in confidence and shall not disclose any Confidential Information for a period of five years, beginning on the date this Agreement is executed and delivered and ending on the day immediately preceding the fifth anniversary of its execution and delivery.

Microsoft and other technology companies, like Apple, will continue to develop new fonts with their programs, as well as to improve on the fonts already available. You may have a favorite font that you prefer to use in your contracts across electronic devices, or you may have to go with the font used as precedent from your side or the other side.

VIII. EXERCISES

A. Exercise 23A: Only Tabulate

Tabulate the following provision so that it is easier to read and understand. Do not change anything else.

6.1 Audit by Licensor. With respect to each Royalty Period, the Licensor may cause an independent accounting firm to audit or review all the Licensee's books and records and to issue a report pertaining to the Royalties earned in that Royalty Period. The Licensor shall give the Licensee reasonable prior written notice of the audit or review. The Licensee shall make its books and records available to the Licensor during normal business hours. If the Licensor wants to object to the Licensee's determination of Royalties for a Royalty Period, it must deliver to the Licensee a statement describing its objections not later than 60 days after the Licensor receives the applicable report obtained. Each party shall use reasonable efforts to resolve the Licensor's objections. If the parties do not resolve all objections on or before the 30th day after the Licensee received the statement of the Licensor's objections, the parties shall promptly submit those objections for resolution to an independent accounting firm acceptable to both parties. If the parties cannot agree on an independent accounting firm, the parties shall select a "big-four" accounting firm by lot. Each party may eliminate one firm by objecting to it in writing. The determination of the independent accounting firm selected in accordance with this provision is conclusive and binding on the parties. The following provisions apply with respect to each audit or review pursuant to this Section 6.1: If an audit or review as finally determined pursuant to this Section 6.1 determines that the Licensee has underpaid Royalties for a Reporting Period, the Licensee shall promptly pay to the Licensor the amount equal to the Royalties owing *minus* the Royalties paid *plus* interest of 10% per year on that amount, accruing from and including the date on which that amount was due to, but excluding, the date on which that amount is paid. If an audit or review as finally determined pursuant to this Section 6.1 determines that the Licensee has overpaid Royalties for a Reporting

Period, the Licensor shall promptly pay to the Licensee the amount equal to the Royalties paid *minus* the

Royalties owing. With respect to each audit and review conducted in accordance with this Section 6.1, the

Licensor shall pay the fees of the independent accounting firm that conducted that audit or review and the

fees of any other independent accounting firm selected in accordance with this Section 6.1. Despite the

immediately preceding sentence, if the audit or review, as finally determined, determines that the Royalties for

the applicable Reporting Period are understated by 2% or more, then the Licensee shall pay the fees of the

independent accounting firm that audited or reviewed the Licensee's books and records and the fees of any

other independent accounting firm selected in accordance with this Section 6.1.

B. EXERCISE 23B: CORRECT DRAFTING ERRORS

Mark up the following provision to correct any drafting errors and make the
provision easier to read.

Covenants of the Borrower. From and after the Effective Date and through the end of the Lending

Term, the Borrower hereby agrees to

(a) provide the Lender with fiscal year-end financial statements no later than

60 days after the end of each fiscal year; and

(b) the insurance currently in place will continue throughout the term of the Agreement.

C. EXERCISE 23C: TABULATE AND CORRECT DRAFTING ERRORS

Tabulate each of the following provisions and correct any drafting errors.

1. Termination of Agreement. On the termination or expiration of this Franchise Agreement, the

Franchisee shall immediately cease to operate the Franchised Business. The Franchisee further

covenants that it will no longer represent to the public that it is a franchisee of the Franchisor.[11]

---

11. This provision is based on a provision from Andrew J. Sherman, Franchise Agreements, in
Commercial Contracts: Strategies for Drafting and Negotiating vol. 2, ch. 21, 21-58 (Morton Moskin
ed., Aspen Publishers 2006).

2. Limitations on Dividends, etc. No dividend or other distribution or payment shall be declared, paid, or made by the Seller in respect of shares of its capital stock. No purchase, redemption, or other acquisition shall be made, directly or indirectly, by the Seller of any outstanding shares of its capital stock.

3. Use of Premises. The Tenant shall use and occupy the Premises for the purposes of a sandwich café, and the Tenant's use of the space will be for the sale of quality food for consumption on or off the Premises or for take-out or for delivery, for the operation of catering services and for the sale of nonalcoholic beverages for consumption on or off the Premises or for take-out or delivery.

4. Each of the Parties warrants and represents for itself that each has been represented by legal counsel of their own choice in the negotiation and joint preparation of this Agreement, has received advice from legal counsel in connection with this Agreement and is fully aware of this Agreement's provisions and legal effect, that all agreements and understandings between the Parties are embodied and expressed in this Agreement, and that each of the Parties enters into this Agreement freely, without coercion, and based on each of the Parties' own judgment and not in reliance on any representations or promises made by any of the other Parties, apart from those expressly set forth in this Agreement.[12]

---

12. This provision is excerpted from CD Form 7, Settlement Agreement with Detailed Provisions Dealing with Potential Claims-by-Non-Settling Entities, in *Settlements Agreements in Commercial Disputes: Negotiating, Drafting & Enforcement,* vol. 1 (Richard A. Rosen ed., Aspen 2003).

CHAPTER TWENTY-FOUR

Clarity Through Sentence Structure

I. INTRODUCTION

Chapter 23 examined how an agreement's formatting can affect its clarity. In this chapter, we examine how an individual sentence's organization can affect its clarity.

II. SENTENCE CORE

A. KEEP THE CORE TOGETHER

Every sentence has core words: the subject, verb, and object. These words convey a sentence's critical information. In the sentence "Bob ate a sandwich," *Bob* is the subject, *ate* is the verb, and *sandwich* is the object. A writer could expand the sentence by telling the reader the kind of sandwich and when Bob ate it, but the core words have conveyed the sentence's essence.

To facilitate a reader's understanding of a sentence, keep the core words next to each other. If they are separated, a reader must work harder to process a sentence's information. This is especially so when the subject is separated from the verb. Instead of reading all the core information at once, a reader must put the core information on hold while wading through the noncore information. By the time the reader reaches the remainder of the core words, the thread of the sentence may be lost.

In the provision that follows, identify the core words of the sentence. Notice how the *if* clause inserted in the middle of the core words interrupts the sentence's flow in the incorrect example.

Examples—Keeping Core Words Together

Incorrect: **Revised Architectural Plans.** The Architect shall, if the Owner agrees to pay the Architect's additional fee in accordance with Section 2.2, revise the Final Plans for the House.

Correct: **Revised Architectural Plans**. If the Owner agrees to pay the Architect's additional fee in accordance with Section 2.2, the Architect shall revise the Final Plans for the House.

B. REDUCE THE NUMBER OF WORDS BEFORE THE CORE WORDS

A sentence's core words should be as close to the beginning of a sentence as possible. If they are not, the reader becomes overburdened with the ancillary information that precedes them. By reducing the number of words preceding the core words, a reader can more readily absorb all the information in the sentence.

Drafters sometimes have problems adhering to this rule because they begin a sentence with a long introductory clause that precedes the sentence's core words, such as in Example 1 that follows. In that example, the sequence of clauses makes logical sense because it establishes an *if/then* relationship. If x condition exists, then y consequence follows. The sequence reflects the temporal order in which the events must occur. But because the core information comes so late in the sentence, the reader has difficulty assimilating the sentence's information. The solution is to flip the clauses' sequence, which we see in Example 2. The provision becomes even clearer in Example 3, though, when the rearranged sentence structure is tabulated.

> *Examples—Sentence Beginning with Long Introductory Clause*
>
> *1—Acceptable but Not as Good Because of Long Introductory Clause:*
> **Bankruptcy**. If a party makes a general assignment of all or substantially all of its assets for the benefit of creditors, or applies for, consents to, or acquiesces in, the appointment of a receiver, trustee, custodian, or liquidator for its business or all or substantially all of its assets, the other party may immediately terminate this Agreement by sending written notice.
>
> *2—Recommended and Better After Flipping the Sequence of the Clauses:*
> **Bankruptcy**. A party may immediately terminate this Agreement on written notice, if the other party makes a general assignment of all or substantially all its assets for the benefit of creditors, or applies for, consents to, or acquiesces in, the appointment of a receiver, trustee, custodian, or liquidator for its business or all or substantially all of its assets.
>
> *3—Best After Switching the Sequence of the Clauses and with Tabulation:*
> **Bankruptcy**. A party may immediately terminate this Agreement on written notice if the other party
>
> (a) makes a general assignment of all or substantially all its assets for the benefit of creditors; or
> (b) applies for, consents to, or acquiesces in, the appointment of a receiver, trustee, custodian, or liquidator for its business or all or substantially all its assets.

III. DRAFT IN SHORT SENTENCES

In Chapter 23 on page 342, you learned one aspect of the **three-line rule**: Any sentence longer than three lines is a good candidate for tabulation if it includes a compound or a series. A variation on the three-line rule is that any sentence longer than three lines is also a candidate for being recast as two or more sentences. As with tabulation, the shorter sentences facilitate a reader's processing of a sentence's substance.

The following incorrect example comes from a lease. Compare it to the corrected version and note how much easier the corrected one is to read.

> **Examples — Drafting in Short Sentences**
>
> *Acceptable but Not as Good Because of Long Sentences:*
> **Termination on Fire or Casualty**. If a fire or other casualty destroys the Building, the Landlord may terminate the Lease by notifying the Tenant in writing, and then, all Base Rent and Additional Rent due under this Lease ceases as of the date of the casualty, and the Tenant shall remove its trade fixtures and personal property from the Premises no later than 35 calendar days after it receives the Landlord's termination notice, whereupon both parties are released from all further obligations under this Lease, except for any obligations previously incurred.
>
> *Recommended Because of Shorter Sentences:*
> **Termination on Fire or Casualty**. If a fire or other casualty destroys the Building, the Landlord may terminate the Lease by notifying the Tenant in writing. In that event, all Base Rent and Additional Rent due under this Lease cease as of the date of the casualty. The Tenant shall remove its trade fixtures and personal property from the Premises no later than 35 calendar days after it receives the Landlord's termination notice. On completion of that removal, both parties are released from all further obligations under this Lease, except for any obligations previously incurred.

IV. SHORT BEFORE LONG

A. PUT SHORT PHRASES BEFORE LONG PHRASES

Often a drafter may choose the order in which two or more phrases appear in a sentence. Generally, you should put the short phrase first. Again, this helps the reader process information faster and more effectively by reducing what must be remembered before the second phrase appears. Look at Examples 1 and 2 below and notice where the italicized language, which is the shorter phrase, appears in each. While Examples 1 and 2 are both grammatically correct, Example 2 is preferable. In its new location in Example 2, the italicized language is easier to understand and remember. The provision can be improved further by tabulating it, as we see in Example 3.

> **Examples—Putting Short Phrase First in a Sentence**
>
> *1—Acceptable but Not as Good:*
> **Maintenance of the Building**. The Landlord shall maintain the Building's Common Areas, including lobbies, stairs, elevators, corridors, and restrooms, the windows in the Building, the mechanical, plumbing, and electrical equipment serving the Building, and the structure of the Building *in reasonably good order and condition.*[1]

---

1. This provision is based on a provision from Mark A. Senn, *Commercial Real Estate Leases: Preparation, Negotiation, and Forms*, 17-2 (6th ed., Wolters Kluwer 2018).

2—Preferable:

Maintenance of the Building. The Landlord shall maintain *in reasonably good order and condition* the Building's Common Areas, including lobbies, stairs, elevators, corridors, and restrooms, the windows in the Building, the mechanical, plumbing, and electrical equipment serving the Building, and the structure of the Building.

3—Best with Tabulation:

Maintenance of the Building. The Landlord shall maintain *in reasonably good order and condition*

   (a) the Building's Common Areas, including lobbies, stairs, elevators, corridors, and restrooms;
   (b) the windows in the Building;
   (c) the mechanical, plumbing, and electrical equipment serving the Building; and
   (d) the structure of the Building.

B. MAKE THE SHORT PHRASE THE SUBJECT IN A DECLARATION

Some declarations are drafted as if the verb is a mathematical equal sign, making the language before and after equal. Definitions are an example:

> *Example — Declaration with Two Equal Parts*
>
> **"Alphabet"** means the letters *a through z*.

Thus, *alphabet* equals the letters *a* through *z*. If this type of sentence occurs outside of the definitions section, putting the shorter phrase before the verb generally facilitates a reader's comprehension, as we do with the shorter phrase of *the indemnity stated in Article 10* in the example that follows:

> *Examples—Putting Shorter Phrase Before Verb*
>
> *1—Correct but Not as Good:*
>
> **Exclusive Remedy**. After the Closing, a party's sole remedy with respect to any claim (including any torts claim) relating to this Agreement and the Transaction Documents is *the indemnity stated in Article 10*.
>
> *2—Recommended:*
>
> **Exclusive Remedy**. After the Closing, *the indemnity stated in Article 10* is a party's sole remedy with respect to any claim (including any torts claim) relating to this Agreement and the Transaction Documents.

V. WORD CHOICE AFFECTING SENTENCE STRUCTURE

A. USE THE ACTIVE VOICE

This book has discussed the preference in drafting for using the active voice in various chapters, including in Chapter 8 on page 60, and in Chapter 9 on page 73.

Assuming that using the active voice does not change the meaning of a provision, using the active voice will enhance the readability of almost any provision. Of course, when working under pressure, your focus may well not be on the active versus the passive voice, but most word-processing programs can provide assistance. If you can, activate a setting that will alert you whenever a sentence is crafted in the passive voice.

The arbitration provision that follows has two clauses in the passive voice, both the statement of the condition to the declaration and the declaration:

Examples—Passive Voice and Active Voice

1—Incorrect Because of Passive Voice:

Arbitration. In the event any controversy arising under this Agreement *shall not have been resolved by* informal negotiations by 30 days after any party requests such negotiations, the controversy *shall be resolved by* binding arbitration governed by the rules of the American Arbitration Association. This redraft not only restates the provision in the active voice but also cures multiple other drafting errors.

2—Correct Because of Active Voice:

Arbitration. If the parties *do not resolve* a controversy arising under this Agreement by informal negotiations on or before 30 days after a party requests those negotiations, the parties *are to resolve* the controversy by binding arbitration under the rules of the American Arbitration Association.

B. USE PARALLEL DRAFTING

In Chapter 23 on page 344, you learned about parallel drafting in connection with tabulating a single sentence. Parallel drafting also applies to multiple sentences dealing with similar subject matter. To be parallel, the grammatical structure of each of those sentences must be the same. Fixing parallel structure sometimes also requires that you redraft the provisions so that they say the same thing in the same way.

Here are two provisions from an employment agreement that are not parallel, as well as a revision that fixes the problem. The caption dealing with death in the corrected version has been revised so that the two captions also parallel each other. As with any two provisions, either could be redrafted to make it parallel to the other. Here, the *if* clauses are relatively short, so they can be at the beginning of each sentence.

Examples—Parallel Drafting

1—Not as Good Because Not Parallel:

Disability During Employment. The compensation payable to the Executive is reduced by 50% if the Executive is disabled for more than six months.

Death Benefits. If the Executive dies during the Term, the Company shall pay the Executive's estate the Executive's salary through the date of his death.

2—Recommended Because Parallel:

Disability During Employment. If the Executive is disabled for more than six months during the Term, the Company shall pay to the Executive the Executive's salary reduced by 50%.

Death During Employment. If the Executive dies during the Term, the Company shall pay to the Executive's estate the Executive's salary through the date of his death.

C. USE THE POSSESSIVE

Many lawyers shy away from using a noun's possessive form, but its use shortens a sentence, making it easier to read while doing no harm to its substance, as in the examples below:

Examples—Using Possessive Form

1—Acceptable:

Confidentiality. During and after the term *of this Agreement*, each party shall protect the secrecy of the Confidential Information *of the other party*. All Confidential Information remains the exclusive property *of the disclosing party*. *(33 words)*

2—Recommended:

Confidentiality. During and after this *Agreement's* term, each party shall protect *the other party's* Confidential Information. All Confidential Information remains *the disclosing party's* exclusive property. *(24 words)*

D. AVOID NOMINALIZATION

The **nominalization** of a word is the conversion of a verb into a phrase that includes the noun form of the verb. When you have a choice between using a verb or a noun phrase that includes a nominalization, choose the verb. Using the verb makes the sentence shorter and more direct. Here are two examples:

Examples—Using Verb Instead of Nominalization

1a—Incorrect: On the *expiration* of the term of this Agreement . . .

1b—Correct: When this Agreement *expires* . . . .

1c—Correct and Recommended Because Simpler: When this Agreement *ends*. . . .

2a—Incorrect: A party shall give the other party a *notification* . . . .

2b—Correct: A party shall *notify* the other party . . . .

2c—Correct and Recommended Because More Specific by Defining Notice: A party shall *send Notice to* the other party . . . .

Common nominalizations and their verb forms and possible alternatives include the following:

NOMINALIZATIONS	VERB
Administration	Administer, manage
Alteration	Alter, change
Application	Apply
Compensation	Compensate, pay
Consideration	Consider
Contribution	Contribute, pay
Notification	Notify
Payment	Pay
Submission	Submit
Violation	Violate

E. AVOID USING *THERE IS* AND *THERE ARE*

You can often eliminate *there is* and *there are* from a sentence, which makes it tighter. Look for the sentence's core meaning and use those words to create a new subject and verb.

> ### Examples—Eliminating "There Is" and "There Are"
>
> *1—Acceptable:*
>   **Litigation**. There is no litigation pending or threatened against the Licensor with respect to the Trademark.
>
> *2—Recommended:*
>   **Litigation**. No litigation is pending or threatened against the Licensor with respect to the Trademark.

VI. EXERCISES

A. EXERCISE 24A: CORRECT DRAFTING ERRORS

Mark up each of these provisions to create clarity through sentence structure, given what you have learned so far. If appropriate, make other drafting changes that improve the provision.

1. ***Agreement*** means this Manufacturing Agreement, as it may from time to time be amended.

2. **Updating of Disclosure Schedules**. The Seller shall, in the event of any omission or misstatement in the Disclosure Schedules, or any change in the underlying facts with respect to any matter disclosed in the Disclosure Schedules, amend and update the Disclosure Schedules so that they are at all times true and correct.

3. **Reproduction of Documents**. This Agreement and all documents relating thereto, including, without limitation, (a) consents, waivers, and modifications that may hereafter be executed, (b) documents received by the Lender on the Closing Date (except the Notes themselves), and (c) financial statements, certificates, and other information previously or hereafter furnished to the Lender, may be reproduced by the Lender by any process, and the Lender may destroy any original document so reproduced.

4. **Share Ownership**. On the transfer of the certificate or certificates evidencing the Shares owned by each Seller to the Buyer, each Seller will have transferred good and valid title to the Shares to the Buyer, free and clear of all Liens.

5. **Increase to Contract Price**. If the Contractor is required to pay or bear the burden of any new federal, state, or local tax, or of any rate increase of an existing tax (except a tax on net profits) taking effect after May 30, 20__, the Contract Price increases by the amount of the new tax or the increased tax resulting from the rate increase.[2]

---

2. This provision is based on a provision in Glower W. Jones, *Alternative Clauses to Standard Construction Contracts* 455 (2d ed., Aspen 1998).

3. This provision is from a bank loan agreement. It describes when a bank has a setoff right. It provides that if a borrower owes money to the bank and has money on deposit with the bank, the bank may use the money on deposit to reduce the principal amount of the loan. For example, if a borrower owes a bank $10,000 and has $3,000 on deposit with the bank, the bank may *set off* the $3,000 against the $10,000 and reduce the borrower's outstanding principal to $7,000. For more on setoff provisions, *see* Chapter 17 on page 252.

6. **Setoff.**[3] In addition to any rights and remedies of the Bank provided by law, the Bank shall have the right, without prior notice to the Company, any such notice being expressly waived by the Company to the extent permitted by applicable law, on the filing of a petition under any of the provisions of the federal Bankruptcy Act or amendments thereto, by or against; the making of an assignment for the benefit of creditors by; the application for the appointment, or the appointment, of any receiver of, or of any of the property of; the issuance of any execution against any of the property of; the issuance of a subpoena or order, in supplementary proceedings, against or with respect to any of the property of or the issuance of a warrant of attachment against any of the property of; the Company, to set off and apply against any indebtedness, whether matured or unmatured, of the Company to the Bank, any amount owing from the Bank to the Company, at or at any time after, the happening of any of the abovementioned events, and the aforesaid right of setoff may be exercised by the Bank against the Company or against any trustee in bankruptcy, debtor in possession, assignee for the benefit of creditors, receiver or execution, judgment or attachment creditor of the Company, or against anyone else claiming through or against the Company or such trustee in bankruptcy, debtor in possession, assignee for the benefit of creditors, receiver, or execution, judgment or attachment creditor, notwithstanding the fact that such right of set off shall not have been exercised by the Bank prior to the making, filing or issuance, or service on the Bank of, or of notice of, any such petition; assignment for the benefit of creditors; appointment or application for the appointment of a receiver; or issuance or execution of a subpoena, order or warrant.

7. **Force Majeure Event.** Upon the occurrence of a Force Majeure Event, if the Completion Date is delayed, the parties shall engage in good faith negotiations to obtain an equitable adjustment in the Completion Date. Negotiations shall begin no later than two business days after the Completion Date.

8. **Use of Partnership Assets.** The General Partner shall not use, and hereby specifically agrees not to use, directly or indirectly, the assets of this Partnership for any purpose other than conducting the business of the Partnership, for the sole and exclusive benefit of the Partners.

CHAPTER TWENTY-FIVE

Ambiguity

I. INTRODUCTION

In the context of contract drafting, **ambiguity** refers to the possibility that a word or provision in a contract can be interpreted in two or more possible ways. You should always aim to draft clearly to avoid any ambiguity, since ambiguity can lead to conflict and be expensive. If parties dispute the meaning of a provision, they must either renegotiate it or litigate. In either event, clients pay attorneys' fees and bear the cost of time not spent on more productive matters and incur the economic risks of the costs involved in the transaction. In the remainder of this chapter, you will learn the common causes of ambiguity and how to avoid them.[1]

II. AMBIGUITY AND VAGUENESS

A. TYPES OF AMBIGUITY

Imagine a contract between a Canadian manufacturer of ski equipment and a U.S. retailer that provides for payment of $10,000 on the retailer's receipt of the merchandise. But what kind of dollars—U.S. or Canadian? This type of ambiguity, which arises when a word has multiple dictionary meanings, is known as **semantic ambiguity**.[2]

The two other types of ambiguity are **syntactic** and **contextual ambiguity**. **Syntactic ambiguity** occurs when it is unclear what a word or phrase refers to or modifies. In the following example, it is unclear whether each seller is obligated to sell their shares to the buyer, or whether the sellers are obligated to sell their jointly owned shares to the buyer.

---

1. For a more in-depth discussion on the law of contract interpretation, *see* Steven J. Burton, *Elements of Contract Interpretation* (Oxford U. Press 2009).

2. Words that are spelled the same but have multiple dictionary meanings are called **homonyms.** Homonyms do not necessarily create ambiguity, since often the intended meaning is revealed by context. For example: "If the bear escapes, the owner shall bear the cost." F. Reed Dickerson, *Materials on Legal Drafting* 55 (West Publ'g Co. 1981).

> *Example—Syntactic Ambiguity*
>
> **Sale of Shares**. The Sellers shall sell their Shares to the Buyer.

Contextual ambiguity occurs when two provisions are inconsistent. The two provisions can be in the same agreement or different agreements. The following example is more obvious than most ambiguities, but it demonstrates the point:

> *Examples—Contextual Ambiguity*
>
> **Section 3.4 Landlord's Obligations**. The Landlord shall maintain and make any necessary repairs at any time and for any reason in the Apartment and the Building.
>
> **Section 5.3 Tenant's Obligations**. The Tenant shall maintain the Apartment and all public areas in the Building in good order and condition and shall repair any damages the Tenant causes to any fixtures or any equipment.

It does not matter whether you can name the three types of ambiguity. What matters is developing a sensitivity to ambiguities so that you do not draft them, and so that you can recognize and resolve them.

B. VAGUENESS DISTINGUISHED FROM AMBIGUITY

Vagueness is not the same as ambiguity. A word or a phrase is **vague** if its meaning varies depending on the context or if its parameters are not plainly delineated. For example, *reasonable* is vague. What is reasonable in one context may be wholly unreasonable in another. The word *blue* is also vague, because it could be anything from robin's-egg blue to midnight blue.[3]

In his contract-drafting treatise, Reed Dickerson distinguishes ambiguity from vagueness:

> Language can be ambiguous without being vague. If in a mortgage, for example, it is not clear whether the word *he* in a particular provision refers to the mortgagor or the mortgagee, the reference is ambiguous without being in the slightest degree vague or imprecise. Conversely, language can be vague without being ambiguous. An example is the written word "red."[4]

Vagueness is inherently neither good nor bad. It depends on what concept best expresses the parties' agreement and on what best protects your client or advances their interests. Assume that you represent a senior executive in the negotiation of their employment agreement with a large, privately held company. The company's first draft of the employment agreement states that they will lend the executive "$500,000 at 3.5% per year for the purchase of a house in Manhattan." *House* is problematic, because it is too specific. Manhattan has very few houses. It has

---

3. *See* F. Reed Dickerson, *The Fundamentals of Legal Drafting* 39 n. 3 (2d ed., Little, Brown & Co. 1986).

4. *Id.* at 40.

cooperatives, condominiums, apartments, townhouses, and lofts. While *house* might be perfectly appropriate in most parts of the country, in Manhattan, a vaguer, more inclusive term such as *residence* or *home* is more appropriate.[5]

Drafters sometimes choose to go with language that is vague, especially if they do not have a lot of time to draft a contract. There is a cost of money and time to negotiating and drafting more precise language, so you will have to make the judgment call at times of whether to slow things down to draft things more precisely or draft some provisions somewhat vaguely. No matter what, make sure to draft important provisions as specifically and precisely as possible. For example, if you have a services agreement, you should negotiate and draft the specific services that one party is providing to the other, just as you would include the exact amount and timing of payment for those services, who would be paid by whom, etc.

III. AMBIGUITIES FROM *AND* AND *OR*

Provisions that include *and*, *or*, or *and* and *or* often create ambiguity. Sections A through C that follow explain the confusion that these simple, short words can create.[6]

A. THE MEANING OF *AND* AND *OR*

Grammar rules often state that *and* is **conjunctive** and inclusive,[7] meaning that it joins two or more things, and that *or* is **disjunctive**, meaning that it establishes alternatives between two or more things.[8] Look at the following two sentences:

> ### Examples—Conjunctive "And" and Disjunctive "Or"
>
> ***Conjunctive* and:** Fred likes cake *and* cookies.
>
> ***Disjunctive* or:** Samantha may have a dog *or* a cat as a pet.

The first sentence uses *and* in its traditional role, conjunctively, to signal that Fred likes both cake and cookies. The second sentence uses *or* in its traditional role, disjunctively, to signal that Samantha may have only one pet—either a dog or a cat. This is the exclusive use of *or*. But contract drafting is rarely so simple. Both *and* and *or* can be used in ways that your English teacher never mentioned.

In addition to being used disjunctively, *or* can signal that matters that seem to be exclusive alternatives may also exist concurrently, creating a third alternative or changing the standard from alternatives to a single cumulative standard.[9] If *or* is only disjunctive in the incorrect example below, the Tenant can sue for damages if the Landlord either makes a misrepresentation or breaches a covenant. But what

---

5. *See* Albert Choi & George Triantis, *Strategic Vagueness in Contract Design: The Case of Corporate Acquisitions,* 119 Yale L. J. 848 (2010) (discussing why a vague material adverse change provision in an acquisition agreement may be superior to a more precise provision).

6. *See* Maurice B. Kirk, *Legal Drafting: The Ambiguity of "And" and "Or,"* 2 Tex. Tech. L. Rev. 235 (1970-1971).

7. *The New Oxford American Dictionary* 57 (Erin McKean ed., 3d ed., Oxford U. Press 2010); *see also Ace Cash Express, Inc., v. Silverman,* 2004 WL 101684 at *3 (Tex. App. Jan. 23, 2004).

8. *The New Oxford American Dictionary, supra* n.7, at 1232; *see also Perkins & Will v. Sec. Ins. Co. of Hartford,* 579 N.E.2d 1122, 1126 (Ill. App. 4th Dist. 1991).

9. *Vinograd v. Travelers' Protective Ass'n of Am.,* 258 N.W. 787, 788-789 (Wis. 1935).

happens if the Landlord does both? Has the Tenant lost all their remedies? That makes no business sense. Instead, the parties probably intended that if the Landlord both misrepresented and breached, the Tenant would have two causes of action, and could pursue all their remedies. This interpretation results in three alternatives, instead of two, that will give rise to remedies: (1) a misrepresentation, (2) a breach of covenant, and (3) a misrepresentation and a breach of covenant. The correct examples 1 through 3 that follow reflect the parties' actual intent:

Examples—Using "Or"

   Incorrect—**Default**. If the Landlord makes a misrepresentation or breaches a covenant, then the Tenant may pursue all remedies to which they are entitled under the law.

   Correct 1—**Default**. If the Landlord makes a misrepresentation, breaches a covenant, or makes a misrepresentation and breaches a covenant, then the Tenant may pursue all remedies to which they are entitled under the law.

   Correct 2—**Default**. The Tenant may pursue all remedies to which they are entitled under the law if the Landlord does one or both of the following:

   (a) Makes a misrepresentation.
   (b) Breaches a covenant.

   Correct 3—**Default**. The Tenant may pursue all remedies to which they are entitled under the law if the Landlord does one of the following:

   (a) Makes a misrepresentation.
   (b) Breaches a covenant.
   (c) Makes a misrepresentation and breaches a covenant.

This use of *or* is known as the **inclusive** use.[10] Some contracts include an interpretive provision that any use of *or* is inclusive rather than exclusive. As some contract provisions do use *or* in its exclusive sense, such an interpretive provision could cause problems within an agreement. Furthermore, adding the phrase *unless the context otherwise requires* may render the interpretive provision void. Unless well drafted, one side could contend that the context otherwise required it. Instead, scrutinize each use of *or* and draft the provision so it says what you intend. One easy way to indicate the exclusive sense of *or* is to use *either* in conjunction with *or*:

Example—Using "Either" in Conjunction with "Or"

   Purchase Price Payment. The Buyer shall pay the Seller *either* $8.6 million in immediately available funds on the Closing Date *or* $10 million in immediately available funds on the third anniversary of the Closing Date.

---

10. *Shaw v. Nat'l Union Fire Ins. Co. of Pitt.*, 605 F.3d 1250, 1254 n.8 (11th Cir. 2010).

Although *and* is often used conjunctively, it can have the same meaning as the inclusive *or*.[11] In the following example, both provisions permit the Contractor to paint the house using employees, subcontractors, or both employees and subcontractors.

Examples—"And" with Same Meaning as "Or"

1—**Painters**. The Contractor may use its employees or subcontractors to paint the House.

2—**Painters**. The Contractor may use its employees and subcontractors to paint the House.

Finally, courts will interpret *and* to mean *or* and vice versa if necessary to implement the parties' intent.[12] Given the inherent ambiguity of *and* and *or*, look carefully at each use of these words to determine whether a provision requires tailoring to clarify the parties' intent.

B. *AND* AND *OR* IN THE SAME SENTENCE

When *and* and *or* appear in the same sentence to join items in a series, their joint presence almost always creates ambiguity. To demonstrate how the ambiguity arises, we will work with the following provision:

Example—"And" and "Or" in the Same Sentence

Incorrect: **Registration for Litigation Clinic**. A student may register for the Litigation Clinic only if that student has taken Evidence or Advanced Civil Procedure and is a third-year student.

This incorrect example has three standards: the taking of Evidence, the taking of Advanced Civil Procedure, and being a third-year law student. The ambiguity in this incorrect example stems from the different ways in which the standards can be combined. Looking at the alternatives as mathematical symbols can be helpful.

- A = The taking of Evidence
- B = The taking of Advanced Civil Procedure
- C = Being a third-year student

Using the letter equivalents, the provision, as drafted, can be restated as follows:

- A or B and C

Now, using parentheses to establish the relationship between the letter equivalents, here are the two possibilities:

---

11. *Id.* at 1254 (citing Kirk, *Legal Drafting: The Ambiguity of "And" and "Or,"* 238 (citing Dickerson, *The Fundamentals of Legal Drafting* 77).

12. *Noell v. Am. Design Inc., Profit Sharing Plan*, 764 F.2d 827, 833-834 (11th Cir. 1985) (citing *Dumont v. U.S.*, 98 U.S. 142, 143 (1878)).

> *Examples—"And" and "Or" in the Same Sentence*
>
> *Correct 1:*
>
> *(A or B) and C* = The student must have taken either Evidence or Advanced Civil Procedure and, in addition, must be a third-year student.
>
> *Correct 2:*
>
> *A or (B and C)* = The student must have taken Evidence, or, as an alternative, must have taken Advanced Civil Procedure and must be a third-year student.

Tabulation easily cures an ambiguity arising from *and* and *or* appearing in the same sentence by showing the relative relationship between the sentence's parts. Note that in the correct example 1 below, subsections (a) and (b) establish a cumulative standard, while, in the correct example 2, subsections (a) and (b) establish alternative standards.

> *Examples—"And" and "Or" in the Same Sentence*
>
> *Correct 1:*
>
> **Registration for Litigation Clinic**. A student may register for the Litigation Clinic only if that student
>
> (a) has taken either Evidence or Advanced Civil Procedure
>
> and
>
> (b) is a third-year student.[13]
>
> *Correct 2:*
>
> **Registration for Litigation Clinic**. A student may register for the Litigation Clinic only if that student
>
> (a) has taken Evidence
>
> or
>
> (b) has taken Advanced Civil Procedure and is a third-year student.

C. AND/OR

When used in a contract, *and/or* is usually intended to mean *either Choice 1 or Choice 2 or, if not either one of those choices, then both Choice 1 and Choice 2 concurrently*. Judges and commentators do not recommend using *and/or* in your drafting.[14] This phrase repeatedly causes problems for the parties and anyone else involved with the contract. Look at the following language from an employment contract:[15]

---

13. An alternative redraft is the following:

Only third-year students who have taken either Evidence or Civil Procedure may register for the Litigation Clinic.

However, some readers may find this version more difficult to understand because of the long *who* clause that separates *students* from *may*.

14. *See* Kirk, *Legal Drafting: The Ambiguity of "And" and "Or", supra* n.6, at 235.

15. This language paraphrases the contract language at issue in *Hicks v. Haight*, 11 N.Y.S.2d 912 (N.Y. Sup. Ct. 1939).

> *Example—"And/Or"*
>
> The Company shall hire the Executive to act as president *and/or* general manager.

The sentence has at least three possible meanings, all mutually exclusive, based on context.

1. The Company shall hire the Executive to act only in the capacity of president.
2. The Company shall hire the Executive to act only in the capacity of general manager.
3. The Company shall hire the Executive to act as both the president and the general manager.

The case from which this language derives presented a fourth meaning: that the executive was the company's chief executive officer because he was hired to act as both the president and general manager.[16]

Although *and/or* may seem to be a harmless, useful, shorthand solution to a drafting challenge, its long-term risks outweigh the short-term benefits. Don't use it.

IV. AMBIGUITIES FROM SENTENCE STRUCTURE

A. MODIFIERS OF ITEMS IN A COMPOUND OR SERIES

Whenever a modifier follows a compound or a series, ambiguity may be created. The issue is whether the qualifier modifies each item in the compound or series or only the closest item. (The use of *and* or *or* does not directly cause the ambiguity in this instance, but that use to create the compound or the series is a prerequisite. Again, the presence of one or both of these words should signal potential ambiguity.) The grammatical rule that is applied in these situations is known as **the rule of the last antecedent**. According to this rule, the qualifier qualifies the noun or phrase that immediately precedes it.[17]

In the incorrect example that follows of a representation and warranty, note that the qualifier *to the Borrower's knowledge* follows *pending or threatened*. This provision's meaning differs significantly depending on whether the knowledge qualifier modifies both *pending* and *threatened* or only *threatened*. Usually, a bank insists that a borrower make a flat representation and warranty with respect to pending litigation. A bank will argue that the borrower should know what litigation is pending and, if they do not know, then they should perform the necessary due diligence so that they can give an unqualified representation and warranty. In contrast, a bank will usually accept a knowledge qualifier with respect to threatened litigation. A bank recognizes that a borrower might not know that a third party has been injured and is threatening to sue. Therefore, to make the representation and warranty reflect the agreed-on risk allocation, *to the Borrower's knowledge* needs to be moved so that it follows the *or* and immediately precedes *threatened,* as in the correct example

---

16. *Id.* at 914.
17. *See In re Enron Creditors Recovery Corp.*, 380 B.R. 307, 319-323 (Bankr. S.D.N.Y. 2008) (The rule of the last antecedent "provides that, where no contrary intention appears, a limiting clause or phrase should ordinarily be read as modifying only the noun or phrase that it immediately follows.") (citing Norman J. Singer & J. D. Shambie Singer, *Sutherland Statutes and Statutory Construction* vol. 2A, § 47:33 (7th ed., Thomson/West 2007)).

below. However, note that in many transactions, to better protect themselves, if your client is the borrower, they will probably prefer that the knowledge qualifier apply to both pending and threatened litigation.

> ### Examples—Modifier in a Compound or Series
>
> *Incorrect:* **Litigation**. No litigation against the Borrower is pending or threatened to the Borrower's knowledge.
>
> *Correct:* **Litigation**. No litigation against the Borrower is pending or, to the Borrower's knowledge, threatened.

B. MULTIPLE ADJECTIVES

Ambiguity can arise if two or more adjectives or adjectival phrases modify the same noun. (Once again, *and* will probably be involved in causing the ambiguity.) Do the adjectives describe two required characteristics of a particular thing, or do they describe two kinds of things? To test which it is, ask whether the sentence could be redrafted as two separate sentences. If yes, the adjectives signal two kinds of things.

For example, the phrase *charitable and educational institutions* is ambiguous in the incorrect example that follows.[18] The issue is how the two adjectives, *charitable* and *educational*, relate to each other and to the noun *institutions*. The phrase may contemplate institutions that are both charitable and educational, which we see in the correct example 1. In the correct example 1, we see that the provision means for one thing to have two characteristics, so the adjectives are *cumulative*. This is the typical interpretation of a string of adjectives modifying a noun.[19]

> ### Examples—Multiple Adjectives
>
> *Incorrect:* **Identity of Donee**. The Trust may donate funds only to charitable and educational institutions.
>
> *Correct 1:* **Identity of Donee**. The Trust may donate funds only to an institution that is both charitable and educational.

Alternatively, the provision could contemplate two different kinds of institutions: charitable institutions and educational institutions. This could be demonstrated by drafting the provision in different ways, as we see in the correct examples 2 below. However, note that the language in the correct example 2B is preferable because of the use of the limiting word *only*. Finally, a third possibility in meaning exists, as we see in the correct example 3 below. The Trust could have authority to donate funds to three kinds of institutions: (1) charitable institutions, (2) educational institutions, and (3) institutions that are both charitable and educational.

---

18. *See* Dickerson, *The Fundamentals of Legal Drafting, supra* n. 3, at 110.
19. *Id.*

> *Examples—Multiple Adjectives*
>
> **Correct 2, Option A: Identity of Donee**. The Trust may donate funds to charitable institutions, and the Trust may donate funds to educational institutions.
>
> **Correct 2, Option B: Identity of Donee**. The Trust may donate funds only to an institution that is either charitable or educational.
>
> **Correct 3: Identity of the Donee**. The only institutions to which the Trust may donate funds are the following:
>
> (a) Institutions that are charitable only or educational only.
> (b) Institutions that are both charitable and educational.

Therefore, when using multiple adjectives, repeat the nouns as necessary to create clarity and use tabulation to simplify and clarify your provisions.

C. SENTENCE ENDING WITH A *BECAUSE* CLAUSE

Sentences that end with a *because* clause are often ambiguous. As explained by Reed Dickerson:

> A terminal "because" clause is often ambiguous in that it is not clear whether the clause applies to the entire statement or merely to the phrase immediately preceding. For example, in the sentence, "The union may not rescind the contract because of hardship," it may not be clear whether the draftsman intends to say, "The union may not rescind the contract, because to do so would cause hardship," or "The union may not rescind the contract, using hardship as the justification."[20]

Therefore, when faced with such ambiguity, redraft the sentence to clarify the intent.

D. SUCCESSIVE PREPOSITIONAL PHRASES

Ambiguity can occur when one prepositional phrase immediately follows another. In such a case, the provision generally does not indicate whether the second prepositional phrase modifies only the immediately preceding prepositional phrase or the preceding prepositional phrase and that which came before it. For example, the following sentence is ambiguous in the absence of any other context. Specifically, does the second prepositional phrase, *in New York,* modify *cooperative apartment, owner of a cooperative apartment,* or both? Once you know the answer, you can easily rewrite the provision for whichever meaning you want it to have. See correct examples 1 and 2 that follow for different meanings. Note that you may have to include more words to better clarify the meaning of the provision.

> *Examples—Prepositional Phrases That Follow Each Other*
>
> **Incorrect: Entitlement to Tax Rebates**. Every owner of a cooperative apartment in New York is entitled to a tax rebate.

---

20. *Id.* at 103.

> ***Correct 1:* Entitlement to Tax Rebates.** Every owner of a cooperative apartment who owns a cooperative apartment located in New York is entitled to a tax rebate.
>
> ***Correct 2:* Entitlement to Tax Rebates.** A Person is entitled to a tax rebate if the Person is a resident of New York and the Person's cooperative apartment is located in New York.

Although the redraft cured the ambiguity caused by the successive prepositional phrases, a second ambiguity remains: the use of *New York*. That could refer to New York State, New York City (which includes its five boroughs), or Manhattan (one of the five boroughs).

V. SAY THE SAME THING IN THE SAME WAY

Practically every word or phrase in a contract establishes a standard, and by changing a few words, a drafter can change that standard. Must a party take an action in *no later than three days*, *reasonably promptly*, or *as soon as practicable*? Each of these time frames represents a different standard. By changing the standard, you change the time frame in which a party must perform their obligation. Therefore, by choosing between the standards, the parties allocate risk by making it more or less likely that the party with the obligation will breach the standard.

Because a change of a word can change the meaning of a contract provision, a cardinal principle of good drafting is to **say the same thing in the same way**. If you do not, a court may hold that the difference in wording is substantive, even if sloppy drafting caused it.[21] Here is a lawyer's nightmare:

You are drafting the purchase agreement in connection with your client's purchase of a chain of gyms. During a negotiation, you agreed to add a knowledge qualifier to four of the Seller's representations and warranties. When redrafting the contract, you use the phrase *to the knowledge of each of the Seller's officers* in the first three representations and warranties, but in the fourth, you use *to the knowledge of each of the Seller's executive officers*. The fourth is a more lenient standard from the Seller's perspective because the Seller is liable for the knowledge of a smaller group of people. In the real world, this could occur accidentally (but inexcusably) because you copied and pasted the fourth representation and warranty from another contract and failed to notice the different knowledge qualifier. Of course, if you chose this more lenient standard for the fourth one, then that would be OK because you did so intentionally. Even though we have discussed being consistent and using the same standards throughout your agreements, there will be times where you may intentionally choose a different standard for a particular provision because of a difference in a business issue.

---

21. *See Int'l Fid. Ins. Co. v. Co. of Rockland*, 98 F. Supp. 2d 400, 412 (S.D.N.Y. 2000) (stating that "sophisticated lawyers . . . must be presumed to know how to use parallel construction and identical wording to impart identical meaning when they intend to do so, and how to use different words and construction to establish distinctions in meaning."); *see also Pac. First Bank v. New Morgan Park Corp.*, 876 P.2d 761, 767-768 (Or. 1994) (determining that a lease intentionally did not require a landlord to be reasonable when rejecting a tenant's transfer of the lease but required any rejection of a sublease to be reasonable).

Now, the disaster. Post-closing, your client discovers that the fourth representation and warranty is materially false, and that one of the Seller's officers knew it at the time of the contract's signing. Outraged, your client tells you to draft the complaint and to claim $100,000 in damages. You are now in a most unfortunate predicament. The fourth representation and warranty, as drafted, stated that none of the Seller's *executive* officers knew that the representation and warranty was false. That representation and warranty is, in fact, true. It was a lower-level officer who knew of the falsity. Therefore, your client has no cause of action against the Seller. If you had used the same qualifier in all four representations and warranties (*to the knowledge of each of the Seller's officers*), the representation and warranty would have been false, and your client would have had a viable cause of action.

Saying the same thing in the same way, but in different parts of the agreement, is a skill that you must develop to be a successful drafter. In the following sections, we will look at some of the more common examples of when drafters apply the *say the same thing the same way* principle throughout different agreements.

A. ISSUES IN ACQUISITION AND CREDIT AGREEMENTS: REPRESENTATIONS AND WARRANTIES VS. COVENANTS

Within acquisition agreements, representations and warranties on the one hand, and covenants on the other, often deal with the same subject matter. For example, in the representation and warranty that follows with respect to property, plant, and equipment, a seller states the current condition of those assets. Then, in the covenants, the seller promises how they will maintain those assets from signing to closing. If the standards in the representations and warranties and the covenants differ, a seller could be obligated to upgrade the condition of the assets. A parallel issue arises in a credit agreement in which a borrower often makes representations and warranties on a topic that is also a subject of a borrower covenant.

Look at the following provisions from the perspective of the seller and determine what modifications you would ask the buyer for and why.

> ### Example—Provisions from the Perspective of the Seller
>
> #### The Seller's Representation and Warranty:
> **4.12 Condition of Property**. Except as set forth in **Schedule 4.12**, the Seller's property, plant, and equipment are in customary operating condition, subject only to ordinary wear and tear.
>
> #### The Seller's Covenant:
> **5.10 Maintenance of Properties, etc**. The Seller shall maintain all of their properties in good order, reasonable wear and tear excepted.

As a close read of these provisions reveals, the standard for upkeep differs from the representation and warranty to the covenant, but unless there are other extenuating circumstances, these standards should read the same. Also, the representation and warranty is vague. The reader does not know whether *customary operating condition* means poor or good condition. It may not be clear to the parties what is meant by that term, or there could be a difference in opinion between the parties as to what is meant by *customary operating condition*. Furthermore, in these circumstances, an aggressive buyer might reasonably argue that the covenant obligates the seller to upgrade the condition of the properties to good order, reasonable wear and tear excepted.

B. SIMILAR PROVISIONS IN MORE THAN ONE AGREEMENT

Just as different standards in representations and warranties and covenants can create a problem, different standards in different agreements can create a problem. The classic scenario occurs when a buyer purchases all the outstanding shares of a target company and borrows money to fund this acquisition. In the acquisition agreement, the seller makes representations and warranties to the buyer. In the financing agreement, the buyer turns into the borrower, who makes representations and warranties to the lender about the target company. (The bank wants these representations because the bank's risk is as to the target company.) Although the representations and warranties in the two agreements will be similar, they may not be the same. For example, compare the following representations and warranties from an acquisition agreement and a financing agreement:

> *Examples—Representations and Warranties in Acquisition and Financing Agreements*
>
> *The Seller's Representation and Warranty to the Buyer:*
>   **Condition of Property**. The Seller's equipment and machinery are in the condition that industry standards require.
>
> *The Borrower's Representation and Warranty to the Lender:*
>   **Property, Plant, and Equipment**. All of the Target's property, plant, and equipment are in good order, reasonable wear excepted.

If the buyer/borrower believes that the two standards materially differ and the financing agreement standard is tougher, then the buyer/borrower must decide whether they have enough facts to make a truthful statement to the lender. If they do not, the buyer/borrower has four options. First, they can ask the seller to change their representation and warranty so that it mirrors the one that the buyer/borrower must give in the financing agreement. Second, they can ask the lender to change their representation and warranty so that it mirrors the one the buyer/borrower receives in the purchase agreement. Third, they can ask the lender for some other change in the representation and warranty, such as a qualification. Fourth, they can leave the representation and warranty unchanged, but only after performing additional due diligence so that they can truthfully make the representation and warranty.

The same issue can arise when memorializing a transaction requires multiple contracts. For example, if two agreements in an integrated transaction unintentionally had different governing law provisions, imagine the repercussions. To prevent such mistakes, always take the time to conform all the general provisions in each of a transaction's agreements.

C. CONTRACT PROVISIONS AND DOCUMENTS BASED ON STATUTORY PROVISIONS

Contract provisions and documents are sometimes based on statutory provisions. For example, a certificate of incorporation reflects the requirements of the statute authorizing the formation of corporations. Although most drafters use a treatise form as the basis of a certificate of incorporation, that form, when it was first created, was based on the statute.

When creating a provision or a document based on a statute, repeat the words of the statute: Say exactly what the statute says. Although a difference between the two may not cause a difference in substance, it could.[22] And if it does, it may prevent your firm from opining that the document meets the statute's requirements. Think of it as sanctioned plagiarism. To draft the document, you must copy and paste the statute into your document. Then change only what is necessary to tailor the document to your transaction.

The following example shows a provision from a certificate of incorporation based on the statutory provision:

Example—Provision Based on Statutory Provision

Delaware General Corporation Law § 102 (a)(3) (Statute Regarding Contents of Certificate of Incorporation):

The certificate of incorporation shall set forth . . . [t]he nature of the business to be conducted or promoted. It shall be sufficient to state, either alone or with other businesses or purposes, that *the purpose of the corporation is to engage in any lawful act or activity for which corporations may be organized under the General Corporation Law of Delaware* . . .

Statement of Purpose in the Corporation's Certificate of Incorporation:

The purpose of the Corporation is to engage in any lawful act or activity for which corporations may be organized under the General Corporation Law of Delaware.

VI. DATES, TIME, AND AGE

Drafters regularly cause ambiguities by the ways in which they express dates, age, and time. One can get rid of these ambiguities from an agreement by being aware of them and being more specific.

A. DATES

Misuse of prepositions causes many ambiguities with respect to dates. Common problem prepositions are *by, within, between, from,* and *until,* as in the following examples.

For example, the use of *by* in incorrect example 1 raises the issue of whether November 14 or November 15 is the last day on which the Manufacturer may submit the sample.[23] To prevent ambiguities in provisions with dates, state the beginning and ending dates and, if appropriate, specify the time with each date. As an alternative, use one of the following, as in correct example 1 below: before, on or before, after, on or after, *or* no later than. Although each of the three alternatives in correct example 1 cures the ambiguity, clients often prefer the first and second alternatives, as they state the last permissible date for submission. On the other hand, the third alternative requires a client to determine (even if rather easily) the deadline of November 15, 20__.

---

22. *See* Vincent L. Teahan, *Why Don't Our Clients Like Their Wills?,* 69 N.Y. St. B. J. 26, 30 (1997) (stating that "the lawyer has to hold a mirror to the language of the GST statute and its regulations" for a particular tax exemption to apply to a will).

23. *Phoenix Newspapers v. Molera,* 27 P.3d 814, 819 (Ariz. Ct. App. 2001) ("The word 'by' when used before a date certain may mean 'before a certain date,' but it just as readily may mean 'on or before a certain date.'")

Examples—Preventing Ambiguities in Provisions with Dates

1—Incorrect—By [a Stated Date]:

Samples. The Manufacturer shall submit a sample *by* November 15, 20__.

1—Correct—By [a Stated Date]:

Samples. The Manufacturer shall submit a sample

- *no later than* November 15, 20__.
- *on or before* November 15, 20__.
- *before* November 16, 20__.

Now, let's look at the use of *within* in the incorrect example 2 below. There, it is unclear whether the 30 days precedes or follows the Closing, or both. Most likely, it is a pre-closing covenant, so the drafter probably intended for it to state 30 days before the Closing. Determining which alternative from the correct example 2 to include in the contract requires a review of relevant statutes and knowing the business transaction. In addition, it is unclear from the incorrect example 2 whether the 30 days includes the day of the Closing.[24] In either alternative included in the correct example 2 below, the 30-day period excludes the day of the Closing, so you would also want to make sure that this is your intention.

Examples—Preventing Ambiguities in Provisions with Dates

2—Incorrect—Within [X Days Of]:

Notice to the EPA. The Buyer shall notify the Environmental Protection Agency of the sale *within* 30 days of the Closing.

2—Correct—Within [X Days Of]:

Notice to the EPA. The Buyer shall notify the Environmental Protection Agency of the sale

- no later than 30 days before the Closing.
- no later than 30 days after the Closing.

The incorrect example 3 below demonstrates a common problem that comes up with the use of *between*. The ambiguity in the incorrect example 3 is whether the dates are bookends surrounding the dates on which a party may tender bids, or whether the dates are also dates on which a party may tender bids.[25] The inclusion of the time on each of the two days in the correct example 3 avoids any issues as to how early or late in the day a potential buyer may tender a bid.

---

24. *See Reifke v. State*, 31 A.D.2d 67, 70 (N.Y. App. Div. 1968) ("[T]he word 'within' fixes the limit beyond which action cannot be taken, but does not fix the first point of time at which action shall be taken. It prescribes the end, not the beginning; it means 'not longer in time than' or 'not later than.'"); *Glenn v. Garrett*, 84 S.W.2d 515, 516 (Tex. Civ. App. 1935) ("The word 'within,' used relative to time, has been 'defined variously as meaning: any time before; at or before; at the end of; before the expiration of; not beyond; not exceeding; not later than.'"); *Kramek v. Stewart*, 648 S.W.2d 399, 401 (Tex. App. 1983) ("The term 'within' has numerous definitions including 'not later than,' 'anytime before,' and 'before the expiration of.'").

25. *Atkins v. Boylston Fire & Marine Ins. Co.*, 46 Mass. 439, 440 (Mass. 1843) ("[Between] . . . has various meanings . . . . The most common use of the word is to denote an intermediate space of time or place.").

> **Examples—Preventing Ambiguities in Provisions with Dates**
>
> *3—Incorrect—Between [Date 1] and [Date 2]:*
>
> **Tender of Bids**. A potential buyer may tender bids for the Target *between* November 1, 20__, and November 15, 20__.
>
> *3—Correct—Between [Date 1] and [Date 2]:*
>
> **Tender of Bids**. A potential buyer may tender bids for the Target beginning on November 1, 20__, at 9:00 a.m. and ending on November 15, 20__, at 5:00 p.m.

As the incorrect example 4 below shows, the use of *from* and *until* can create the same ambiguity as *between*: Are the stated dates also dates on which a party may tender bids, or are they bookends?[26] Since *from* and *until* create the same ambiguities as *between*, the same cure works, as we can see in the correct example 4.

> **Examples—Preventing Ambiguities in Provisions with Dates**
>
> *4—Incorrect—From [Date 1] Until [Date 2]:*
>
> **Tender of Bids**. A potential buyer may tender bids for the Target *from* November 1, 20__, *until* November 15, 20__.
>
> *4—Correct—From [Date 1] Until [Date 2]*
>
> **Tender of Bids**. A potential buyer may tender bids for the Target beginning on November 1, 20__, at 9:00 a.m. and ending on November 15, 20__, at 5:00 p.m.

B. TIME

Time ambiguities fall into two broad categories: the measurement of a time period and the statement of the time of day.

1. Measurement of Periods

Parties often need to refer to time periods—for example, the length of a loan or the number of days' notice to be given. The best alternative is to use exact dates, but that is not always possible. Notice provisions operate in the future, and no one knows when the provisions will come into play. In addition, precedents regularly try to limit the number of blanks to be filled in by expressing time periods in words.

a. Years

To avoid any ambiguity, follow these rules **when measuring years**:

- Use the concept of an anniversary date.

---

26. *See Hecht v. Powell*, 240 Ill. App. 124, 130 (Ill. App. 1st Dist. 1926) ("Strictly etymologically, [until] is a word of exclusion, but as commonly used, it is just as likely to be used in an inclusive as an exclusive sense."); *Fetters v. Des Moines*, 149 N.W.2d 815, 818 (Iowa 1967) ("The words 'from' and 'to' when used with respect to measurement of time have no fixed or specific meaning. Standing alone they are ambiguous and equivocal."), *overruled in part on other grounds by, Mease v. Fox*, 200 N.W.2d 791 (Iowa 1972); *Conway v. Smith Mercantile Co.*, 44 P. 940, 940 (Wyo. 1896) ("The word 'until' may either, in a contract or a law, have an inclusive or exclusive meaning, according to the subject to which it

- Refer to calendar years only to refer to the period from and including January 1 through December 31 of the same year.[27]
- Check for the consequences of leap years.
- Confirm that a future date is a Business Day by using a perpetual calendar or provide that the event must occur on the next Business Day.

Here are some examples:

> **Examples—Measuring Years**
>
> *1*—**Due Date**. The Note is due on May 6, 20__.
>
> *2*—**Due Date**. The Note is due on the day immediately preceding the fifth anniversary of its issuance, except if that day is not a Business Day, then it is due on the next Business Day.

Be careful when you use a term that already signifies a particular time period relating to years or any other measure of time, such as biannual or biennial. For example, these two terms do not mean the same thing, though drafters use them interchangeably. Dictionaries define *biannual* as "occurring twice a year," and *biennial* as occurring "once every two years,"[28] Although many courts properly interpret these terms, the confusion concerning the proper interpretation can lead to problems. Contract dispute cases discuss provisions where drafters referencing a biannual occurrence intended to denote an event that happened *once every two years,*[29] or *every other year.*[30]

A drafter need not remember which is which, as she can always check. The key is to remember that there is a problem. Here is an instance where the drafter might find it helpful to include an example to clarify intent in the relevant phrase:

> **Examples—Including an Example to Clarify Intent**
>
> *1*—*X should be biennial; for example in 2018 and in 2020.*
>
> *2*—*X should be biannual, meaning twice each year; for example, two times in 2018.*

---

is applied, the nature of the transaction which it specifies, and the connection in which it is used, and this rule extends to the correlatives of the word.").

27. *See Draper v. Wellmark, Inc.*, 478 F. Supp. 2d 1101, 1108 (N.D. Iowa 2007) ("The term 'calendar year' has been construed in several cases, though not without exception to indicate the period from January 1 to December 31, inclusive.") (citing E. L. Strobin, *What 12-Month Period Constitutes "Year" or "Calendar Year" as Used in Public Enactment, Contract, or Other Written Instrument,* 5 A.L.R.3d 584, § 4[d] (1966)). Failure to do so can create ambiguity. *See also Gottesman & Co., Inc. v. Int'l Tel. & Telegraph Corp.*, 477 N.Y.S.2d 139, 140 (N.Y. App. Div. 1st Dept. 1984) (The meaning of "full years of operation" was interpreted by one party to mean the full calendar year from January 1 to December 31 and by the other party to mean successive twelve-month periods.).

28. *See, e.g., Suquamish Tribe v. Central Puget Sound Growth Management Hearings Board,* 743, 755 n.13 (Wash. App., 2010) (court and parties used the phrase *biennial review* for a review occurring once every two years, and expressly contrasted it to a *biannual review*, which occurs twice a year) (citing *Webster's Third New Internat'l Dictionary* 213, 211 (2002)).

29. *Brockmeier v. Greater Dayton Regional Transit Authority,* 2013 WL 4647139 at *6 n.5 (No. 3:12CV327, S.D. Ohio, Aug. 29, 2013) ("The word 'biannual' is defined [by Merriam Webster] as 'occurring twice a year' . . . . Nevertheless, the medical certification cards carried by the bus drivers normally expired after two years. . . . Therefore, the word 'biannual,' as used in the collective bargaining agreement, appears to mean 'once every two years' rather than twice a year.").

30. *Northgate Towers Associates v. Charter Tp. of Royal Oak,* 214 Mich. App. 501, 505 (1995) (defendant's ordinance, which required payment of an inspection fee on both a biannual and biennial basis, was unconstitutionally vague; no interpretation of the conflicting ordinance resolutions could "bring them into harmony"), *vacated in part on other grounds,* 453 Mich. 962 (1996).

The drafter can also use neither word and, instead use either the phrase *twice yearly* or *once every other year.*

Example—Using Alternative Phrase for Clarity

  X will occur twice a year.

---

b. Months

When measuring months, determine which of the following possibilities the parties intend and draft accordingly:

- Calendar months, meaning from the first day of a named month through its last day.
- 30-day periods, beginning on any day.[31]
- The period beginning on a specific date and ending on the day in the next month which numerically corresponds to the day in the starting month *minus* 1 (March 18, 20__, through April 17, 20__).[32]

Ambiguity can easily arise when using months as the standard of measurement. In ordinary speak, the meaning of a calendar month is clear: from the first day of the month through the last day—May 1 through May 31. In contracts, the expected meaning is not necessarily the meaning that a court will attribute to the phrase. Moreover, certain types of contracts have conventions that determine the meaning of *month*, such that a month is a period from a day in the calendar month to the corresponding numerical day of the next month (not the corresponding numerical day, *minus* 1).[33] When weighing what language to use, look at whether changing the reference from a number of months to a number of days clarifies an ambiguity or makes the provision easier to draft. Some examples follow. Note that examples 1, 2, and 3 may be difficult to calculate because you may not find out the exact dates when all the parties sign the lease. Therefore, you may not get a specific date for when the lease started and when it should end, or, at the very least, it will be difficult to figure out. Example 4 sets out the specific period from the beginning, so it is easier for the parties to know the term, which is an important provision in a lease.

Examples—Measuring Months

  1—Difficult: **Term.** The term of this Lease is *six calendar months.* If the parties sign this Lease on the first day of a calendar month, then the term begins on that date, and the month in which the Lease is signed is the first calendar month. If the parties do not sign this Lease on the first day of

---

31. *Mercer v. Aetna Life Ins. Co.*, 593 P.2d 23, 24-25 (Kan. App. 1979) ("While the term 'calendar month' means a month as designated in the calendar, without regard to the number of days it may contain, 'thirty days' and 'one month' are not synonymous terms and do not necessarily nor ordinarily mean the same periods of time.").

32. *Ruan Transport Corp. of Neb. v. R. B. "Dick" Wilson, Inc. of Neb.*, 79 N.W.2d 575, 577 (Neb. 1956) ("The term calendar month, whether employed in statutes or contracts, and not appearing to have been used in a different sense, denotes a period terminating with the day of the succeeding month numerically corresponding to the day of its beginning, less one. If there be no corresponding day of the succeeding month, it terminates with the last day thereof.").

33. For the definition of *interest period, see* Prac. L. Co., *Loan Agreement: Borrowing Mechanics,* http://us.practicallaw.com; search "loan agreement: borrowing mechanics" (accessed May 4, 2023).

a calendar month, then the term begins on the first day of the next calendar month, which is then the first calendar month of the term. In either event, the term ends at 5:00 p.m. on the last day of the sixth calendar month of the term.

2—Difficult: **Term**. The term of this Lease is *six months*. The first day of the term is the date that the parties sign this Lease. If that date is

(a) the first day of a calendar month, the term ends at 5:00 p.m. on the last day of the sixth calendar month of the term; and

(b) not the first day of a calendar month, the term ends at 5:00 p.m. in the sixth month following the month in which the parties signed this Lease, on the day of the month numerically corresponding to the day on which the parties signed this Lease, *minus* 1.

3—Difficult: **Term**. The term of this Lease is 180 days, beginning on the date that the parties sign this Lease and ending at 5:00 p.m. on the 180th day.

4—Best: **Term**. The term of this Lease begins on March 14, 20__ and ends on September 13, 20__.

c. Weeks

When measuring weeks, determine which one of the following possibilities the parties intend:

- The seven-day period beginning on Sunday and ending on Saturday.[34]
- The seven-day period beginning on a specific day and ending one day before the same day in the following week (Wednesday through Tuesday).
- The five-day period beginning on Monday and ending on Friday.

Also, think through the effect of holidays and look at whether changing the reference from a number of weeks to a number of days clarifies an ambiguity or makes the provision easier to draft. Compare the following provisions:

Examples—Measuring Weeks

*1—***Beginning of Production**. The Manufacturer shall begin production of the Item no later than two weeks after the Retailer approves the Item. The two-week period begins on the day after the Manufacturer's receipt of the Retailer's approval and ends at 5:00 p.m. on the last day of the two-week period.

*2—***Beginning of Production**. The Manufacturer shall begin production of the Item no later than 9:00 a.m. on the 14th day after the Manufacturer's receipt of the Retailer's approval. The 14-day period includes weekends and holidays.

---

34. *Syversen v. Saffer*, 140 N.Y.S.2d 774, 778 (Sup. Ct. 1955) (noting that calendar week "is a definite period of time, commencing on Sunday and ending on Saturday") (citing *In re Wright's Will*, 171 N.Y.S. 123, 124 (App. Div. 4th Dept. 1918)), *aff'd*, 150 N.Y.S.2d 551 (App. Div. 2d Dept. 1956).

d. Days

When measuring days, determine the following:

- Which is the first day and which is the last.
- Whether days should be limited to business days.
- Whether a time of day should be specified.

In making these determinations, parties often rely on statutes,[35] interpretive provisions, and definitions. For example, when a mathematical formula includes the number of days in a time period, an interpretive provision can prevent disputes by resolving which are the first and last days of the period.[36] The following provision is from a credit agreement:

> *Example—Measuring Days*
>
> **Determining the Number of Days of Interest Accrual.** When calculating the amount of interest owed, the number of days as to which interest accrues includes the first day of a period but excludes the last day of that period.

e. Business Day

Similarly, to avoid disputes as to whether weekends and holidays are part of a time period, parties often define *Business Day* to distinguish it from other days. Parties typically rely on commercial bank closures to define the standard for what is not a business day. These definitions usually use local bank holidays as their starting point because a bank holiday in Hawaii might not be a bank holiday in Nebraska. Make sure that it is clear to which provisions *Business Day* will apply and not apply in your contract. For example, in a financing agreement, interest still accrue every day, not just on a *Business Day*, while notice provisions may incorporate *Business Day*. See the examples that follow for a definition of *Business Day* and how it is used in a provision.

> *Examples—Defining Business Day*
>
> *Definition: Business Day* means a day other than a Saturday, Sunday, or other day on which commercial banks in [insert location] are authorized or required by law to close.
>
> *Not as Good:* **Response to Notice of Arbitration.** If a party gives the other party a Notice of Arbitration, the other party shall respond no later than *five days* after the date of its receipt of the Notice of Arbitration.

---

35. *See, e.g.,* Cal. Civ. Code § 10 (1872) (stating that time is "computed by excluding the first day and including the last"); Ind. Code § 34-7-5-1 (1998) (stating that time "shall be computed by excluding the first day and including the last."); N.Y. Gen. Constr. Law § 20 (1988) (stating that "[t]he day from which any specified period of time is reckoned shall be excluded in making the reckoning").

36. A day is ordinarily considered a calendar day, but in construing an agreement the court must factor in the intention of the parties. *U.S. v. Sargent-Tyee Co.*, 376 F. Supp. 1375, 1376 (E.D. Wash. 1974) (stating that the term "days" as used in the contract at issue referred to "days of the ordinary 5-day work week during which the Bell 205 helicopter was available to the defendant").

> ***Better Because More Specific*: Response to Notice of Arbitration**. If a party gives the other party a Notice of Arbitration, the other party shall respond no later than *five Business Days* after the date of its receipt of the Notice of Arbitration.

f. Interpretive Provisions

If a time period keys off the date of a notice's receipt, parties often include the following two interpretive provisions in the general provisions' notice section:[37]

Examples—If Time Period and Notice Interpretive Provisions

> **Date of Receipt**. If a party receives a notice on a day that is not a Business Day or after 5:00 p.m. on a Business Day, the notice is deemed received at 9:00 a.m. on the next Business Day.

> **Rejection or Nondelivery**. If a party rejects a notice, or the notice cannot otherwise be delivered in accordance with this Agreement, then the notice is deemed received on the notice's rejection or the inability to deliver the notice.

---

2. Time of Day

When stating the time of day as of when something should be determined, state whether it is *AM* or *PM*. Do not use 12:00 AM or 12:00 PM, as they can be ambiguous.[38] To deal with which day midnight belongs to, write either 11:59 PM or 12:01 AM. If the two-minute differential matters (which it generally does not), write 11:59:59 PM or 12:00:01 AM.

3. Using *If/Then* Formulations to Draft Conditions

When drafting a condition using an *if/then* formulation, an ambiguity can be created if the *if* clause includes a time or date, as in the incorrect example below. Since *before 5:00 PM. on any day* immediately precedes *then*, the Landlord could argue that the Tenant owes the Additional Rent on the day that the Landlord provides the Additional Air-conditioning. The correct example eliminates the ambiguity by deleting *then* and stating how to determine the time of payment, although it is only a general statement:

Examples—A Condition Where If Clause Includes a Time or Date

> *Incorrect:* **Additional Air-conditioning**. If the Landlord provides Additional Air-conditioning before 5:00 PM on any day, then the Tenant shall pay Additional Rent as computed in accordance with **Exhibit C**.

---

37. Interpretive provisions are also discussed in Chapter 15 on page 202, Chapter 18 on page 264, Chapter 22 on page 332, Chapter 25 on page 390, and Chapter 27 on page 429.
38. *See State v. Hart*, 530 A.2d 332, 333-334 (N.J. Super. App. Div. 1987) (noting the inconsistency of New Jersey opinions deciding the meaning of 12:00 PM); *see also Warshaw v. Atlanta*, 299 S.E.2d 552, 554 (Ga. 1983) (finding that zoning ordinance's use of *12:00 PM* referred to midnight).

> *Correct:* **Additional Air-conditioning**. If the Landlord provides Additional Air-conditioning on any day, the Tenant shall pay Additional Rent in accordance with the provisions of this Agreement, including **Exhibit C.**

C. AGE

When referring to a person's age, do one of the following, as in the Examples 1 and 2 below:

- State the age as of which a right begins.
- Refer to the *celebration* of a particular birthday.

Examples—Referring to a Person's Age

1—**Authority of Officers**. Only a corporate officer who is 21 or older may bind a party.

2—**Drinking Age**. Only a person who has celebrated that person's 21st birthday may drink alcoholic beverages.

VII. PLURALS

Using the plural form of nouns or possessives can easily create ambiguity. Whenever possible, contracts should be drafted using singular nouns and singular possessives.[39] This applies to nouns that are the subject of the sentence and those used elsewhere, such as defined terms.

Look at the three circles below and notice how they intersect with each other. Imagine that Circle A represents the knowledge of Seller A, that Circle B represents the knowledge of Seller B, and that Circle C represents the knowledge of Seller C.

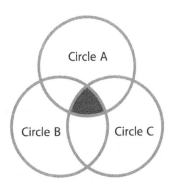

Now assume that the Buyer has drafted the incorrect example below as a representation and warranty for the Sellers. To determine whether the representation and warranty is true, we would need to know what constitutes the Sellers' knowledge.

---

39. *See BP Amoco Chem. Co. v. Flint Hills Resources LLC*, 600 F. Supp. 2d 976, 982 (N.D. Ill. 2009) (finding that the use of the plural noun, *production units,* was "ambiguous as to whether the parties intended the representation to refer to the simultaneous or individual production capacity of the three units").

A reasonable argument could be made that the Sellers' knowledge is not the aggregate knowledge of the Sellers, as represented by the aggregate area of the three circles. Instead, it is only the knowledge that all three Sellers share, as represented by the shaded area where the three circles intersect. To prevent this latter interpretation, the knowledge qualifier must be rewritten as in the correct example below to clarify that the Buyer is asking about the knowledge of each Seller.

Examples—Use Singular Nouns and Possessives

Incorrect: **Defaults**. To the Sellers' knowledge, the Target is not in material default under any contract.

Correct: **Defaults**. To each Seller's knowledge, the Target is not in material default under any contract.

Below is another example of ambiguity caused by plurals. In the incorrect example, it is unclear whether each shareholder must exchange only that shareholder's shares or whether the shareholders must also exchange the shares that they own jointly. The revised provision contemplates that some shares might be jointly owned, but by fewer than all the shareholders.

Examples—Use Singular Nouns and Possessives

Incorrect: **Exchange of Shares**. On December 31, 20__, the Shareholders shall exchange their preferred shares for common shares.

Correct: **Exchange of Shares**. On December 31, 20__, each Shareholder shall exchange for common shares all of the preferred shares that Shareholder owns, whether individually or jointly with one or more other Shareholders.

In the next incorrect example, the ambiguity is whether the schedule must list agreements to which not all of the Sellers are a party. The revision refers to *each* agreement but could have referred to *all* agreements or *every* agreement without creating any ambiguity, but that is not always the case. *Each* is preferable because it distinguishes separately all of the contracts, limiting the possibility of ambiguity. As in the correct example, try to always draft in the singular.

Examples—Using "Each" to Avoid Ambiguity

Incorrect: **Agreements. Schedule 3.6** lists and describes all agreements to which the Sellers are a party.

Correct: **Agreements**. With respect to each Seller, **Schedule 3.6** lists and describes each agreement to which that Seller is a party.

Ambiguity can also arise when parties are listed individually but joined by *and*. For example, see how in the incorrect example below the ambiguity is whether each Borrower is obligated to notify the Bank or whether the Borrowers must act jointly. The provision can be redrafted as either correct example 1 or 2.

> **Example—Ambiguity When Parties Listed Individually Are Joined by "And"**
>
> **Incorrect:** **Notice of Borrowing Amount.** Borrower A and Borrower B shall notify the Bank of the Borrowing Amount at least three days before the Borrowing Date.

> **Examples—Ambiguity When Parties Are Listed Individually but Joined by "And"**
>
> **Correct—1:** **Notice of Borrowing Amount.** Borrower A and Borrower B shall each notify the Bank of the Borrowing Amount at least three Business Days before the Borrowing Date.
>
> **Correct—2:** **Notice of Borrowing Amount.** Borrower A and Borrower B shall jointly notify the Bank of the Borrowing Amount at least three Business Days before the Borrowing Date.

VIII. PROVISOS

A **proviso** is "[i]n drafting, a provision that begins with the words *provided that* and supplies a condition, exception, or addition."[40] Drafters use provisos for three purposes:

1. To state a condition.
2. To state an exception to a rule.
3. To add additional material.

All these uses might suggest that provisos are an indispensable drafting tool. They are not. Instead, the multiplicity of purposes creates serious problems for a drafter because of their potential for ambiguity — as in the incorrect example below. The proviso in this incorrect example has two possible meanings. First, Mrs. Nowicki's previous disclosure of her assets could be a condition to Mr. Nowicki's obligation to disclose his assets (a condition to an obligation and the obligation). Second, the proviso could merely be signaling an additional covenant — a covenant that Mrs. Nowicki is also obligated to disclose her assets.[41] With two alternative meanings that are mutually exclusive, the proviso creates a classic ambiguity. You can see two possible ways to redraft the provision in the correct examples 1 and 2.

> **Examples—Provisos with Potential Ambiguity**
>
> **Incorrect:** **Disclosure of Assets.** Mr. Nowicki shall disclose all of his assets to Mrs. Nowicki, *provided* that Mrs. Nowicki discloses all of her assets to Mr. Nowicki.

---

40. *Proviso, Black's Law Dictionary* (11th ed. 2019).
41. *Hohenberg Bros. Co. v. George E. Gibbons & Co.*, 537 S.W.2d 1, 3 (Tex. 1976) (stating that "in the absence of such a limiting clause, whether a certain contractual provision is a condition, rather than a promise, must be gathered from the contract as a w0hole and from the intent of the parties").

> ***Correct—1:*** If Mrs. Nowicki discloses all of her assets to Mr. Nowicki, Mr. Nowicki shall disclose all of his assets to Mrs. Nowicki. *(Condition to an obligation and the obligation.)*

> ***Correct—2:*** Mr. Nowicki shall disclose all of his assets to Mrs. Nowicki, and Mrs. Nowicki shall disclose all of her assets to Mr. Nowicki. *(Reciprocal covenants.)*

Finally, provisos can create an interpretive nightmare because when you see one, there is usually another. This results from the usual back-and-forth of negotiation. First, the drafter crafts a provision, believing that it memorializes the parties' agreement. The other party readily agrees—with one proviso. The drafter then acknowledges that the proviso seems right, except for one issue that can be cured—with another proviso. This can keep going until the provision has three or even four provisos. The accumulation of provisos exacerbates the difficulty of analyzing the provision. The reader gets lost trying to puzzle out what each proviso means (condition, exception, or additional material) and how each proviso relates to the others and to the main provision.

In drafting contemporary commercial agreements, try not to use provisos. They may have been a staple of commercial drafting for centuries, but they can be confusing and difficult to interpret.

When faced with a provision that typically might be handled with a proviso, do the following:

1. Determine whether you need the proviso or whether you can address the drafting issue in a different way.
2. If you do need the proviso, determine the proviso's purpose (stating a condition, stating an exception, or adding additional material).
3. Redraft the proviso, but use the alternative, appropriate language depending on your purpose:
   - To state a condition, use *if/then*, *must*, or *it is a condition that*. Consider adding an interpretive provision, particularly if you use *must*.[42]
   - To state an exception to a rule, use *except that*, *but*, or *however*.
   - To add material, use a new sentence or subsection or a connective such as *furthermore* or *and*.
4. If a provision has more than one proviso, determine how each one relates to the other and to the main purpose of the provision. Then, use formatting to establish how they relate to each other. Depending on the provision, tabulation, multiple sentences, multiple sections, or multiple subsections may be appropriate.

The following are examples of improperly drafted provisos and appropriate redrafts:

Examples—Proviso as a Condition

> ***Incorrect:*** **Change Order**. The Owner may change the bathroom tile, *provided that* the new tile does not cost more than the original tile.

> ***Correct:*** **Change Order**. The Owner may change the bathroom tile, if the new tile does not cost more than the original tile.

---

42. See Chapter 11 on page 110.

> ### Examples—Proviso as Exception to a Rule
>
> **_Incorrect:_ Consents.** The Contractor shall obtain all Consents; _provided, however_, the Owner shall obtain the Community Board's Consent.
>
> **_Correct:_ Consents.** The Contractor shall obtain all Consents, _except_ that the Owner shall obtain the Community Board's Consent.

When drafters used typewriters, they underscored _provided_, _provided that_, and _provided, however_, to highlight the proviso. The contemporary equivalent is to italicize _except,_ as in the correct example above.

> ### Example—Proviso as Additional Material
>
> **_Incorrect:_ Consents.** The Contractor shall obtain the Consent of the Housing Department _provided, however_, the Contractor shall also obtain the Community Board's Consent.
>
> **_Correct:_ Consents.** The Contractor shall obtain the Consent of both the Housing Department and the Community Board.

IX. EXERCISES

A. EXERCISE 25A: PLACEMENT CHANGES THE MEANING

Analyze how the meaning of the following sentence changes depending on where in the sentence *only* is placed. Write a brief explanation of how the meaning changes for each example.

> Subsidiary A leased five new computers.

1. Only Subsidiary A leased five new computers.

2. Subsidiary A only leased five new computers.

3. Subsidiary A leased only five new computers.

B. EXERCISE 25B: IDENTIFY AND REDRAFT AMBIGUITIES

1. In the provision below, two words are vague and one phrase is ambiguous. What are they? Mark up the provision to resolve the ambiguity.

> **Assignment**. Neither party may assign any right under this Agreement to any Person without the prior written consent of the other party. Manufacturer consents, without any further consent being required, to the assignment by Purchaser to any affiliate of Purchaser that is as creditworthy as Purchaser.

2. Mark up the following provision to clarify the ambiguities and to correct any drafting errors.

> **Compliance with Applicable Law.** The Borrower has complied with all Laws and is currently in compliance with all Laws, except for any noncompliance which would not have a material adverse effect on the Borrower.

3. Mark up the following provision to clarify the ambiguities and to correct any drafting errors.

> **Conditions to Closing.** The Buyer's obligation to perform is subject to the fulfillment of each of the following conditions: The representations and warranties of the Seller must be true on and as of the Closing Date with the same force and effect as if made on the Closing Date. The Seller must have complied with the

covenants to be complied with by the Closing Date. The Seller must have delivered

to the Buyer a certificate to the foregoing effect.

4. The following provision comes from a website development agreement. Determine how *and* and *or* are used in it and whether their use creates any ambiguities. Mark up the provision to clarify any ambiguities.

> **Third-party Content.** The Developer shall use commercially reasonable efforts to secure for the Client the broadest possible rights to any third-party content that the Developer incorporates into the Website. The Developer may either purchase the third-party content or license it. Any use of third-party content is subject to the Client's final approval. The Client shall pay all costs or fees for third-party content, either by directly paying the third party or by reimbursing the Developer, after receiving appropriate documentation.

5. Mark up the following provisions to correct the drafting errors. The provisions create a substantive business issue. What is it?

Article 5 — Landlord's Covenants

Throughout the term of the Lease, the Landlord agrees as follows:

[Provisions Intentionally Omitted]

5.4 Alterations. The Landlord shall not unreasonably withhold permission from the Tenant in determining whether the Tenant may proceed with making alterations to the Premises.

Article 6 — Tenant's Covenants

Throughout the Lease Term, the Tenant agrees as follows:

[Provisions Intentionally Omitted]

6.6 Alterations. The Tenant shall not make any changes or alterations to the Premises without the Landlord's prior written consent.

6. Mark up the following sentence from an employment agreement to correct the ambiguity and any other drafting errors. Assume that the Closing Date is not January 1, 20__, and that the parties intend a term based on the number of days in a calendar year.

> **Term.** This Agreement and the employment hereunder shall commence on the Closing Date (as such term shall be defined in the Purchase Agreement) and shall continue in effect for a period of five calendar years from such Closing Date.

7. Mark up the following provisions to clarify the ambiguities and correct any other drafting errors.

> **(a) Due Date.** The Note is due one year from its date of issuance. Interest is to be computed on the basis of a 360-day year.

> **(b) Interest Accrual.** Interest accrues on the Note from the date of the Note's issuance until the Prepayment Date.

> **(c) Acceptance of Bids.** Seller shall accept all bids (for the purchase of Blackacre) delivered to its offices between April 3, 20__, and April 16, 20__.

> **(d) Trust.** Never trust anyone over 30.

> **(e) Expiration of Option.** This option expires at 12:00 midnight Tuesday, July 9, 20__.

8. Mark up the following provision to eliminate the provisos and to correct any other drafting errors.

> **Nonsolicitation.** During the Noncompetition Period, Wagner shall not employ or seek to employ any employee of Sugarcane Corp.; provided, however, Wagner may employ or seek to employ Mark Bender, provided that Wagner first notifies Sugarcane Corp. in writing at least 10 days prior to contacting him with respect to any such employment; provided further, that this provision does not apply to the employment of any hourly employee.

9. Mark up the following provision to clarify the ambiguity.

> **Allocation of Losses.** Losses shall be borne by the General Partner and the Limited
>
> Partners in equal shares.

10. Find the ambiguity in the following sentence, and then rewrite it twice to show two different possibilities.

> The Buyer shall pay for the House to be inspected by an engineer within 10 days of signing the contract.

11. Review the following provision and explain: How could ambiguity be avoided by using the list format instead of the sentence format? Redraft the provision using the list format to eliminate the ambiguity. You may want to look at the Guidelines for List Format Tabulation in Chapter 23 on page 347.

> **Contractor's Right to Terminate**. The Contractor may terminate this Agreement for cause if
>
> (a) work stops for 30 days or more through no fault of the Contractor or because of a court order;
>
> (b) the Architect unjustifiably refuses to approve a payment request; or
>
> (c) the Owner refuses to pay a payment request that the Architect approved.

C. EXERCISE 25C: UNIVERSITY COLLECTIVE BARGAINING AGREEMENT[43]

Big Ten University (Big Ten) entered into a collective bargaining agreement with the Local Union (the Local Union) on January 1, 20__.

1. As drafted, do the following provisions require Big Ten to contribute to the Welfare Fund and the Employees' Pension Fund on behalf of each probationary employee? What do you think was the parties' intent?

2. Redraft the provisions to clarify that the agreement does not require a contribution with respect to any probationary employee.

---

43. This exercise is based on *In re Teamsters Indus. Employees Welfare Fund*, 989 F.2d 132 (3d Cir. 1993).

4.4 New Employees. New employees may be disciplined or discharged with or without cause for a trial period of sixty days. New employees must become members of the Local Union by the sixty-first day of their employment, at which time they shall be deemed to be regular employees covered by this Agreement and entitled to all health and retirement benefits of this Agreement. Trial period employees will sometimes be referred to as probationary employees.

[Provisions Intentionally Omitted]

10.1 Contributions to Benefit Funds. Big Ten will contribute to the Employees' Welfare Fund and the Employees' Pension Fund on behalf of each employee.

D. EXERCISE 25D: A MERGER AND STATUTORY PROVISIONS

Memorandum

To: Andrew McKenzie

From: Sasha Petrov

Our client, Coffee & Cream Corp. (**"Coffee"**), owns a chain of high-end, company-operated retail stores that sell and serve coffee. They are merging with Tea for Two, Inc. (**"Tea"**), a similar chain of stores, but one that sells and serves tea. The parties signed the Merger Agreement on April 18, 20__. Tea agreed to merge into Coffee, making Coffee the surviving corporation.

Both Tea and Coffee are Delaware corporations. Between now and the Closing, which will be on June 1, 20__, each of the parties will submit the Merger Agreement to its stockholders in accordance with the requirements of Section 251 of the Delaware General Corporation Law. Instead of filing and recording the Merger Agreement as required by Section 251(c), Coffee has decided to file a certificate of merger as permitted by Section 251(c). Please draft the Certificate of Merger. Attached as Exhibit A are the relevant statutory provisions. In your draft, you may assume that each of the constituent corporations will comply with all of the statutory provisions relating to mergers and that there will be no amendments or changes to the certificate of incorporation of Coffee. Coffee's principal place of business is located at 445 Tenth Avenue, New York, New York 10022.

The President of Coffee is Carla Cappuccino, and the President of Tea is Larry Lipton.

Exhibit A

Delaware General Corporation Law § 251(c)

The agreement required by subsection (b) of this section shall be submitted to the stockholders of each constituent corporation at an annual or special meeting for the purpose of acting on the agreement. Due notice of the time, place, and purpose of the meeting shall be mailed to each holder of stock, whether voting or nonvoting, of the corporation at the stockholder's address as it appears on the records of the corporation, at least 20 days prior to the date of the meeting. The notice shall contain a copy of the agreement or a brief summary thereof, as the directors shall deem advisable. At the meeting, the agreement shall be considered and a vote taken for its adoption or rejection. If a majority of the outstanding stock of the corporation entitled to vote thereon shall be voted for the adoption of the agreement, that fact shall be certified on the agreement by the secretary or assistant secretary of the corporation. If the agreement shall be so adopted and certified by each constituent corporation, it shall then be filed and shall become effective, in accordance with § 103 of this title. In lieu of filing the agreement of merger or consolidation required by this section, the surviving or resulting corporation may file a certificate of merger or consolidation, executed in accordance with § 103 of this title, which states:

(1) The name and state of incorporation of each of the constituent corporations;

(2) That an agreement of merger or consolidation has been approved, adopted, certified, executed, and acknowledged by each of the constituent corporations in accordance with this section;

(3) The name of the surviving or resulting corporation;

(4) In the case of a merger, such amendments or changes in the certificate of incorporation of the surviving corporation as are desired to be effected by the merger, or, if no such amendments or changes are desired, a statement that the certificate of incorporation of the surviving corporation shall be its certificate of incorporation;

(5) In the case of a consolidation, that the certificate of incorporation of the resulting corporation shall be as set forth in an attachment to the certificate;

(6) That the executed agreement of consolidation or merger is on file at an office of the surviving corporation, stating the address thereof; and

(7) That a copy of the agreement of consolidation or merger will be furnished by the surviving corporation, on request and without cost, to any stockholder of any constituent corporation.

Delaware General Corporation Law § 103

(a)   Whenever any instrument is to be filed with the Secretary of State or in accordance with this section or chapter, such instrument shall be executed as follows:

    (1)   The certificate of incorporation, and any other instrument to be filed before the election of the initial board of directors if the initial directors were not named in the certificate of incorporation, shall be signed by the incorporator or incorporators (or, in the case of any such other instrument, such incorporator's or incorporators' successors and assigns). If any incorporator is not available by reason of death, incapacity, unknown address, or refusal or neglect to act, then any such other instrument may be signed, with the same effect as if such incorporator had signed it, by any person for whom or on whose behalf such incorporator, in executing the certificate of incorporation, was acting directly or indirectly as employee or agent, provided that such other instrument shall state that such incorporator is not available and the reason therefor, that such incorporator in executing the certificate of incorporation was acting directly or indirectly as employee or agent for or on behalf of such person, and that such person's signature on such instrument is otherwise authorized and not wrongful.

    (2)   All other instruments shall be signed:

        (a)   By any authorized officer of the corporation; or

        (b)   If it shall appear from the instrument that there are no such officers, then by a majority of the directors or by such directors as may be designated by the board; or

        (c)   If it shall appear from the instrument that there are no such officers or directors, then by the holders of record, or such of them as may be designated by the holders of record, of a majority of all outstanding shares of stock; or

        (d)   By the holders of record of all outstanding shares of stock.

CHAPTER TWENTY-SIX

Drafting Numbers and Financial Provisions

I. INTRODUCTION

Clients may forgive many things, but getting monetary provisions wrong is not one of them. To draft them properly, you will often need to understand not just the business deal, but also other issues, such as financial accounting practices, tax law, and other relevant areas of law (e.g., labor and employment laws when drafting vacation pay provisions). Therefore, drafting these provisions is generally a collaborative effort involving the client's accountants and tax advisors. You should bring these specialists into the process as early as possible so any business issues related to the monetary provisions can be resolved as soon as possible.

This chapter teaches you how to draft numbers and mathematical formulas used in agreements. In addition, the final section discusses how to draft provisions involving financial statement concepts and practices.

II. HOW TO DRAFT PROVISIONS USING NUMBERS

Historically, drafters have written numbers both in words and Arabic numerals (e.g., 1, 2, 3), but this unnecessary duplication can make a contract more difficult to read. You should write the numbers one through ten in words and the numbers higher than ten in Arabic numerals. However, if the first word of a sentence begins with a number and other numbers are in the sentence, write out all the numbers in words.

> *Examples — Drafting Numbers Only in Arabic Numerals*
>
> *Incorrect:* **Samples**. The Licensee shall deliver to the Licensor a sample of any Product that it wants to manufacture at least thirty (30) days before manufacturing is to begin.
>
> *Correct:* **Samples**. The Licensee shall deliver to the Licensor a sample of any Product that it wants to manufacture at least 30 days before manufacturing is to begin.

Although many drafters have stopped drafting numbers in both words and Arabic numerals, they continue to draft dollar amounts both ways. Instead, generally, only Arabic numerals should be used.

Examples — Draft Dollar Amounts Only in Arabic Numerals

Incorrect: **Payment of Rent**. The Tenant shall pay the Landlord Ten Thousand Dollars ($10,000.00) for each calendar month of the Term, no later than the third Business Day of that calendar month of the Term.

Correct: **Payment of Rent**. The Tenant shall pay the Landlord $10,000 for each calendar month of the Term, no later than the third Business Day of that calendar month of the Term.

Some drafters prefer to include numbers in both words and Arabic numerals, especially monetary amounts, because they believe that the words act as a safety net in the event of error, such as a number unintentionally added or transposed. There is a statutory canon of construction that addresses this issue, which provides that if the words and numbers differ, the words are to be given effect.[1] But what happens if the number is correct but the words are not (as in *60* versus *six*)?[2] The better approach is to *draft currency amounts using only numerals*, and to *carefully proofread* what you have written. Some drafters who generally use only numerals make an exception for promissory notes and mortgages, using both numerals and words for these documents. But, as case law demonstrates, the danger remains.[3]

You can easily reduce the likelihood of miswriting dollar or other currency amounts when using numerals by omitting the last two digits of any dollar amount that has no cents. Write $345,286, rather than $345,286.00. Some drafters believe that, for dollar amounts greater than $1 million, you should express the millions or billions of dollars in words if the last three numbers of the dollar amount are all zeros. This means you would write $103.255 million, rather than $103,255,000. However, other drafters believe the opposite is true, and that $103,255,000 is clearer than $103.255 million and that you are less likely to make a mistake writing out the entire number.

Whether a number should be rounded and how that should be done depend on context and convention. Dollar amounts in publicly disclosed information are adjusted upward or downward to the nearest whole number. Payment amounts are sometimes rounded to the nearest whole number. If not, they are generally rounded to two decimal points. Here is a rounding provision from a credit agreement.

Example — Rounding Provision from a Credit Agreement

Rounding. Any financial ratio that the Borrower is required to maintain in accordance with this Agreement is to be calculated by

---

1. U.C.C. § 3-114, U.L.A. § 3-114 (2004) states: "If an instrument contains contradictory terms, typewritten terms prevail over printed terms, handwritten terms prevail over both, and words prevail over numbers."

2. *See Yates v. Com. Bank & Trust Co.*, 432 So. 2d 725, 726 (Fla. 3d DCA 1983) ($10,075 vs. Ten hundred seventy-five dollars [$1,075]).

3. *See also Charles R. Tipps Family Trust v. PB Commercial LLC*, 459 S.W.3d 147, 154-155 (Tex. App. 2015) ("The parties to this appeal entered into a residential loan agreement and guaranty for the principal amount of "ONE MILLION SEVEN THOUSAND AND NO/100 ($1,700,000.00) DOLLARS").

> (a) dividing the first appropriate component by the second appropriate component;
>
> (b) carrying the result to one place more than the number of places by which the ratio is expressed in this Agreement; and
>
> (c) rounding the result up or down (with a rounding up if there is no nearest number).

Subsection (c) addresses the possibility that the numeral in the last decimal place is "5," which is, of course, equidistant between the highest and the lowest numbers. To prevent a dispute in this situation, the contract provides a default rule: round up.

III. HOW TO DRAFT MATHEMATICAL FORMULAS

Mathematical calculations are commonplace in contracts. Parties often calculate royalties, cost-of-living adjustments, bonuses, purchase price adjustments, profit and loss allocations, earnouts (provisions that allow a party to earn money in the future if certain goals are met), mandatory prepayments, clawbacks (a provision that allows one party to recover money it has already paid), interest rate changes, currency exchange rates, financial covenants, and more. Drafting these provisions requires *an understanding of the business purpose of the formula*, as well as the ability to express mathematical concepts and calculations clearly.

A. BASIC MATHEMATICAL OPERATIONS

A formula begins with the four basic mathematical operations: addition, subtraction, multiplication, and division. Signal these operations by using mathematical terms to avoid any ambiguity that might arise from the use of common expressions. For example, the mathematical operation expressed as *six over two* can be interpreted in two ways. If a court interprets it to signal subtraction, the result is four. But *six over two* could also signal a ratio, the numerator of which is six and the denominator of which is two. If that is how a court interprets the language, the result would be three, not four. See the examples that follow on how to express mathematical operations. Note that some drafters use *result* rather than *sum, difference, product,* or *quotient,* but these last four terms are probably better because they are more specific.

Examples — Using Mathematical Terms to Avoid Ambiguity

Addition: The *sum* of (a) _____ *plus* (b) _____
Subtraction: The *difference* of (a) _____ *minus* (b) _____
Multiplication: The *product* of (a) _____ *times* (b) _____
Division: The *quotient* of (a) _____ *divided by* (b) _____

In addition to the four basic mathematical operations, you may need to express a fraction or a percentage. For example, an executive fired without cause might be entitled to a percentage of a previously agreed-on bonus. Although the contract could refer to a prorated percentage of the bonus, the following language is more precise, which reduces the likelihood of a dispute as to the calculation:

Examples — Using Mathematical Terms to Express Fraction or Percentage

Ratio — Expressed as a Fraction:
the fraction, the numerator of which is _____ and the denominator of which is _____

Ratio — Expressed as a Percentage:
the fraction, expressed as a percentage, the numerator of which is ____ and the denominator of which is _____

When writing a formula, bold or italicize the mathematical terms. The emphasis makes it easier for a reader to follow the mathematical operations. Do not put a comma before a mathematical term, as in the following example:

Examples — Bolding or Italicizing the Mathematical Terms in a Formula

Incorrect: **Purchase Price.** The Buyer shall pay the Seller the Purchase Price, which is the amount equal to

(a) $100,000, plus
(b) the Adjusted Net Worth.

Correct: **Purchase Price.** The Buyer shall pay the Seller the Purchase Price, which is the sum of

(a) $100,000 *plus*
(b) the Adjusted Net Worth.

B. THE ORDER OF MATHEMATICAL OPERATIONS

If calculating a result requires more than one mathematical operation, indicate the order in which the operations are to occur by using parentheses. A change in the order could change the result, so be careful what order you put the operations in and where you put the parentheses. For example:

Examples — Use Parentheses to Indicate Order of Mathematical Operations

Formula —	$6 + 3 \div 3$
1 —	$(6 + 3) \div 3$
	$= 9 \div 3 = 3$
2 —	$6 + (3 \div 3)$
	$= 6 + 1 = 7$

If you do not use parentheses and the contract has no other instructions, the answer would be determined by using the default mathematical order of operations: multiplication, division, addition, and subtraction. Example 2 above would be the correct answer because division precedes addition in the order of operations.

As discussed in the next section, tabulation is a great way to indicate the order in which mathematical operations are to be calculated, as it shows the relative relationship among the operations.

C. DRAFTING A FORMULA

You can draft a formula in three ways:

1. **Using an algebraic equation.** This method defines each component of a formula and then specifies the operations and their order using mathematical notation.
2. **Using narration and tabulation.** This method expresses the algebraic equation in words. It describes each component of the formula and each mathematical operation in sequence.
3. **Using the narrative cookbook approach.** This method directs the reader to perform mathematical operations in the correct sequence.[4] The narrative cookbook approach is probably the least well known of the methods to state financial formulas but the easiest to draft and follow.

Here is a fact pattern with the formula drafted using each of the methods. Let's say that A, B, C, and D wish to enter into a shareholders' agreement, but they would like to see one provision before you draft the entire agreement. They want the agreement to provide that if any shareholder wants to sell that shareholder's shares to a third party, that shareholder must first offer the shares to the other shareholders. This is known as **a right of first refusal**, although the shareholders do not know or use the term. The shareholders are not terribly good at explaining how to determine the number of shares each non-selling shareholder could buy. Instead, they give the following example: Assume that the corporation has 50 shares issued and outstanding and that A wants to sell the 10 shares that A owns. B, who owns 20 shares, could purchase 50% of those 10 shares because B owns 50% of the shares not being sold.

Before trying to draft any formula, a drafter should analyze what business issues are behind the clients' goals. That understanding may well facilitate the drafting. Here, the original shareholders want to maintain control. The non-selling shareholders want to perpetuate their control by owning all of the outstanding shares. That means allocating all the shares being sold among the non-selling shareholders. Stated from a different mathematical perspective, 100% of the shares being sold must be allocated. The issue then becomes who gets what percentage of the shares.

The example in the fact pattern now guides the drafter in creating the formula that will calculate the percentage and number of shares. The calculation begins by knowing the number of shares being sold. Each non-selling shareholder owns a percentage of those shares. It is that percentage that determines the number of shares that each non-selling shareholder is entitled to buy. If a non-selling shareholder owns 40% of the shares not being sold, that shareholder is entitled to buy 40% of the shares being sold.

With this background and analysis, you can begin to draft. To draft a formula, break down the financial business deal into its components, determine the mathematical operation for each component, and then state the formula using one of three methods: algebraic equation, narration and tabulation, or the narrative cookbook approach.

---

4. *See* F. Reed Dickerson, *The Fundamentals of Legal Drafting* 202 (2d ed., Little, Brown & Co. 1986).

No matter which method you end up including in the contract, some drafters will advise you to always draft the formula using an algebraic equation first, even if you do not end up including that in the contract. It may help you test your understanding of the formula. If you cannot draft it as an algebraic equation, you will probably also have a difficult time drafting using either of the narrative methods, as each one expresses the equation in words. If you cannot draft the formula, it is possible that the parties have not clearly articulated their intent, so you may need to go back to them to get more information.

See how each of these three methods works as you read through the following examples for the fact pattern that we just discussed regarding a right of first refusal involving a shareholder selling their shares:

Examples — Formula Drafted in Three Ways

Example 1 — Using Algebraic Equations

4.1 Right of First Refusal. [Intentionally Omitted]

4.2 Calculation of the Number of Shares to Be Purchased

(a) **Definitions**. For the purpose of this Section, each of the following terms has the meaning assigned to it:

   (i) **"A"** means the number of shares owned by the non-selling shareholder entitled to purchase shares and with respect to whom the calculation is being made.

   (ii) **"B"** means the aggregate number of shares that all the non-selling shareholders own, whether individually or jointly.

   (iii) **"C"** means the number of shares that the selling shareholder is selling.

   (iv) **"D"** means the number of shares that may be purchased by the non-selling shareholder entitled to purchase shares and with respect to whom the calculation is being made.

Section 2.2 Formula. The formula for calculating the number of shares a non-selling shareholder may purchase is as follows:

$$\frac{A}{B} \times C = D$$

Example 2A — Using Narration and Tabulation

4.1 Right of First Refusal. [Intentionally Omitted]

4.2 Calculation of the Number of Shares to Be Purchased. A non-selling shareholder may purchase the number of shares equal to the product of

(a) the number of shares it owns *divided by* the aggregate number of shares that the non-selling shareholders own, whether individually or jointly

times

(b) the number of shares that the selling shareholder is selling.

Example 2B — Using Narration and Tabulation

4.2 Calculation of the Number of Shares to Be Purchased. A non-selling shareholder may purchase the number of shares equal to

(a) the fraction, the *numerator* of which is the number of shares that the non-selling shareholder owns and the *denominator* of which is the aggregate number of shares that the non-selling shareholders own, whether individually or jointly

times

(b) the number of shares that the selling shareholder is selling.

Example 3A — Using the Narrative Cookbook Approach

4.1 Right of First Refusal. [Intentionally Omitted]

4.2 Calculation of the Number of Shares to Be Purchased. A non-selling shareholder may purchase the number of shares determined as follows:

(a) *Divide* the number of shares that the non-selling shareholder owns by the aggregate number of shares that the non-selling shareholders own, whether individually or jointly (the "**Proportionate Entitlement**").

(b) *Multiply* the Proportionate Entitlement *times* the number of shares that the selling shareholder is selling.

Example 3B — Using the Narrative Cookbook Approach

4.2 Calculation of the Number of Shares to Be Purchased. A non-selling shareholder may purchase the number of shares determined as follows:

(a) *Divide* the number of shares that the non-selling shareholder owns by the aggregate number of shares that the non-selling shareholders own, whether individually or jointly.

(b) *Multiply* the quotient determined in accordance with subsection (a) *times* the number of shares that the selling shareholder is selling.

Note that Example 3A above includes a defined term even though the general rule is to not create a defined term if it is to be used only once. It is a judgment call whether creating the defined term in subsection (a) facilitates the understanding of the formula as stated in subsection (b). Remember that the cookbook approach is probably the easiest for readers to understand, although most contracts would probably be drafted using the narrative and tabulation approach.

After drafting the formula, review it with the client and have the client approve it. Reviewing it means more than merely sending the contract provision to the client. Also, send multiple examples of how the formula works, including examples demonstrating what could happen in unusual circumstances (e.g., somehow the calculation results in a negative number). Save the client's approval and file it in the appropriate place. If you speak with the client, write a memo to the file memorializing your discussion or send the client an e-mail confirming the conversation. These contemporaneous documents may help you if the client ever claims that they did not approve the formula. Do the same if any other experts prepared and/or reviewed the formula — include those experts in the correspondence and make sure to keep a copy of all the correspondence.

Once the client approves the formula, with the client's permission, send it and the examples of the formula's application to the other side. If the other side agrees with what you have drafted and the examples, consider including those examples as an exhibit in the contract. If they are included, the parties and the court will be able to refer to those examples — as a type of "legislative history" — when later determining the parties' intent.[5]

IV. USING A CHART

At times, you may want to use a chart or spreadsheet in a contract to make the agreement between the parties more visual and easier to understand. For example, a wholesaler may decrease the price per unit if the retailer's purchases increase to a specific benchmark number. So if the retailer buys fewer than 1,000 units, the wholesaler's price per unit is $15. But if the retailer buys 1,000 or more units, the wholesaler may decrease its price to $12 per unit. If the parties negotiate multiple benchmarks and cost changes, a drafter may more easily record the business deal in writing by using a chart or spreadsheet. This is known as a cost structure, pricing, or fees on a **sliding scale**. Here is the business deal between the wholesaler and retailer drafted in chart form:

Example 1 — Correct Way to Use a Chart with Numbers to Represent a Sliding Cost Scale Structure

Price per Unit	Number of Units to Be Purchased
$15	1 to and including 999
$12	1,000 to and including 2,999
$10	3,000 and above

When drafting a sliding scale cost structure with a chart, as in Example 1 above, each layer of cost (e.g., the second row in example 1) must unambiguously state the fewest number of units (i.e., 1,000) and the largest number of units (i.e., 2,999) to which that cost applies. The largest number of units is the benchmark number. In stating the number of units associated with the next layer of costs, the smallest number of units is 1 more than the benchmark number (i.e., 3,000).

Example 2 below illustrates the problem that may arise if the chart memorializes the cost structure differently.

---

5. *See* Howard Darmstadter, *Precision's Counterfeit: The Failures of Complex Documents, and Some Suggested Remedies,* 66 Bus. Law. 61, 73-82 (Nov. 2010).

Example 2 — Incorrect Way to Use a Chart to Represent a Sliding Scale Cost Structure

Price per Unit	Number of Units Being Purchased
$15	1 to 999
$12	1,000 to 2,999
$10	Above 3,000

The first two rows of Example 2 are adequately, if imperfectly, drafted. The last row is problematic. How much do 3,000 units cost? As drafted, no dollar amount is associated with that number of units.

V. HOW TO DRAFT PROVISIONS INVOLVING FINANCIAL STATEMENT CONCEPTS

If you have not taken an accounting course, the following discussion may be difficult to understand. Nonetheless, by reading it, you should have at least the following takeaway: Drafting provisions using financial statement concepts can be tricky.

Many contract provisions that require calculations use accounting concepts and practices. For example, a publisher will pay an author based on a book's **net sales**[6] (an accounting concept), and a bank will have the right to declare a default if a company's **net worth**[7] (another accounting concept) falls below an agreed-on dollar amount. You cannot draft those provisions without understanding those concepts. A mini-course in accounting concepts is beyond the scope of this book, but this section will address the role that standard corporate accounting plays in drafting provisions using financial concepts.

GAAP is the acronym for **generally accepted accounting principles**. The principles and practices codified in GAAP guide the preparation of a company's financial statements and how they maintain their books and records. All public companies, as Securities and Exchange Commission (SEC) registrants, are required to report their results using GAAP, and many private companies do so, because their lenders or shareholders require it. This agreed-on set of principles and methods benefits users of financial statements by making companies comparable to one another and more transparent to a variety of users. GAAP is a "common language" for communicating financial results.

GAAP does not establish just one method of accounting to which all companies must adhere. GAAP is like a six-lane highway. Multiple optional methods for some items coexist. Some methods allowed under GAAP are very conservative (the far-right lane), while others are very aggressive (the far-left lane). Companies may choose which lane to drive in. They may even "change lanes" from time to time. These choices determine a company's financial reporting "personality"—some are consistently aggressive, while others are consistently conservative.[8]

---

6. **Net sales** is gross sales (the total sales of a company) minus returns, discounts, or allowances.

7. **Net worth** is often used synonymously with **equity** in describing the value of the owners' interest in a business. Both terms describe the amount equal to the sum of a business's assets minus the sum of its liabilities.

8. Companies with conservative reporting practices tend to report lower rates of income, assets, and equity than their more aggressive peers do but are considered to have *high-quality* earnings.

Many unsophisticated drafters react with a knee-jerk response to drafting provisions involving accounting issues: They require all calculations to be made in accordance with GAAP. Unfortunately, that approach may mire the client in some unfortunate trap or deprive the client of a contractual advantage that a more thoughtful analysis could have created.

Among the points to consider are the following:

- GAAP is an evolving set of principles and practices. What is accepted and practiced today may not be tomorrow — or over the term of the contract.
- GAAP allows different accounting treatments for the same event.
- A non-GAAP principle or calculation may better protect your client.

A. GAAP AS AN EVOLVING STANDARD

GAAP is an evolving set of practices, one that tries to stay relevant in a changing commercial environment. Thus, new disclosures of financial information and new methods of accounting for transactions and events are constantly being mandated.[9] As many, if not most, calculations required by an agreement are not made on the date of signing, contractual provisions dealing with GAAP-based calculations must contemplate the consequences of changes in GAAP. The types of provisions in which this issue arises include purchase price adjustments, contingent earnouts, financial covenants in loan agreements, and buy-sell agreements in partnership and stockholder agreements.

Parties can address the fact that GAAP evolves over time in several ways. First, parties can ignore the changes. In this case, the parties would provide for *calculations to be made in accordance with GAAP as in effect as of the date of this Agreement.* Many parties, especially borrowers, prefer this formulation.[10] It provides certainty. The borrower knows what GAAP is and how it is applied in the contract as of the contract date, and that it can comply with the financial covenants. While this may provide the borrower with a business advantage, it does have a disadvantage: the borrower's record keeping becomes more onerous. Specifically, their records for reporting to the SEC and others must comply with whatever version of GAAP is currently in effect. In addition, they must keep whatever records are necessary to compute the financial covenants in accordance with GAAP as it existed on the date when the parties signed the contract.

As an alternative, the parties can provide that the calculations be made *in accordance with GAAP [as in effect from time to time] [as in effect on the calculation date]* — that is, whatever the evolving GAAP is on the calculation date.[11] While this method avoids the record keeping issue, it creates a different problem for borrowers: they must be able to comply with financial covenants based on a future version of GAAP that they neither know nor control.

Although these uncertainties may generate angst for borrowers, the borrower's *friendly* banker may not be similarly bothered. While the lender cannot be certain

---

9. For example, GAAP has evolved to recognize the fair value of some assets, such as securities and intellectual property. **Fair value** is what an asset is worth (as defined) in the marketplace (as defined). This recognition of fair value departs from GAAP's long-standing focus on **historical cost** — what a company paid for an asset. Another relatively recent addition to GAAP is the expensing of the **cost of stock options**.

10. *See* Sandra S. Stern, *Structuring and Drafting Commercial Loan Agreements* ¶7.01[3], A.S. Pratt & Sons (2010).

11. *Id.*

how GAAP may change, the change in GAAP may require a more conservative presentation of the borrower's financial position — a result that appeals, of course, to a banker's conservative nature. This issue's resolution depends on multiple factors, but many borrowers accede to lenders' provisions because of the latter's superior bargaining power.

Other alternatives for resolving the issue of which GAAP to use include the following:

- With respect to a proposed change in a generally accepted accounting principle, the parties may agree during their original negotiations how the change, once implemented, will affect the agreement's calculations. This depends, to some degree, on anticipating what changes may occur in GAAP.

- The parties may agree to negotiate in good faith the contractual consequences of any change in GAAP that materially affects any calculation in the agreement. Be careful with this provision. It is only an agreement to negotiate. The parties may not reach an agreement. To deal with this possibility, some agreements provide that if the negotiations fail, the change in GAAP will not be implemented automatically.

B. GAAP'S AUTHORIZATION OF ALTERNATIVE METHODS

GAAP's flexibility in permitting users to choose among alternative acceptable methods can help or harm your client, depending on whom you represent.

Imagine that a borrower's loan agreement requires them to earn a minimum level of net income, as determined in accordance with GAAP. Unfortunately, our hypothetical borrower has had a dismal year, and it seems likely that they will breach the minimum net income covenant.

The borrower's chief financial officer (**CFO**) has, however, carefully reviewed the loan agreement and has hit on an idea to boost the bottom line for purposes of covenant compliance: By changing the method that they use to account for sales, the borrower can now *recognize* (or book) sufficient revenues[12] to allow the borrower to meet the income test. Although the borrower's chief executive officer (**CEO**) professes concern that this method differs from the one that the borrower has been using, the CFO reassures the CEO that the change presents no problem. ("It's just a small, perfectly acceptable 'lane change,'" he explains.) He reminds the CEO that GAAP does not mandate a particular method to recognize revenue but instead permits users to choose among allowable alternatives. Moreover, the loan agreement gave the company this flexibility by not prohibiting changes in GAAP methods to create compliance with the financial covenants.

Of course, most lenders are sufficiently sophisticated to avoid this type of manipulation. Thus, their standard form agreements invariably require that the GAAP methods to be used to calculate covenant compliance must be consistent with the borrower's past practice or that the practices used in calculating compliance are the same ones used in reporting the borrower's results to other entities (like

---

12. Accountants use the term *revenue recognition* to describe the rules for determining when (or if) a sale has taken place. If a company has not met the rules' requirements, it cannot "recognize" (include) the additional revenue on its income statement. For example, a company may be using a "completed contract" method for recognizing revenue on a long-term contract. Under this approach, the company books the "sale" only when the contract is completed. By "changing lanes" to a percentage of completion method, the company could recognize some income in the current period. "Lane changes" make auditors and lenders nervous, especially when they result in higher income.

the Securities Exchange Commission). However, lenders do not always insist that the requirement be applied to all methods in all instances. Sometimes, a lender may permit a borrower to deviate from past practice and use an alternative GAAP method for a particular calculation.

For example, some companies value their inventory on a LIFO[13] basis. Assuming that inflation is causing the price of inventory to increase, LIFO reduces a company's net income and income taxes by maximizing its reported cost of sales. It also simultaneously minimizes the reported value of the company's inventory.[14] This minimization is in many instances irrelevant. It can, however, be a distinct disadvantage. For example, a lower reported value of inventory may limit the amount that a company can borrow under its loan agreement. In this situation, the borrower will probably want to report a higher inventory number to increase the amount that it can borrow. Often, a borrower can achieve this goal by negotiating for the right to revalue its inventory using the FIFO method[15] — but only to calculate the amount that it can borrow.

C. NON-GAAP ALTERNATIVES

In the same way that parties may need to replace one accepted accounting method with another to reflect the true economic substance of a transaction, sometimes parties need to use a non-GAAP method in valuing an asset or making a calculation. Imagine that the buyer of a business has agreed to pay the seller "the book value of its assets," as stated on its balance sheet, plus $100,000. Included among these assets is a building that the seller has owned for 20 years. As GAAP requires buildings to be depreciated, the building's low book value may not reflect its market value. In this instance, the seller could reasonably insist that the building be valued at its fair market value for the purposes of this transaction, even though that does not accord with GAAP.

VI. PROVISIONS USING BALANCE SHEET ACCOUNTS

Typical provisions that rely on calculations based on balance sheet accounts include the following:

- Purchase price adjustment provisions keyed into changes in net worth or **working capital**[16]
- Financial covenants requiring borrowers to maintain minimum net worth, working capital, or current ratio
- Borrowing base formulas

---

13. **LIFO** is an acronym meaning *last in, first out*. It assumes that the most recent inventory items that the company manufactured or bought for resale are the first ones sold. Typically, when a company reports inventory on the LIFO basis, it reports higher costs for its sales of goods and, therefore, lower profits compared to alternative methods.

14. This may not be the case with respect to a product new to the market. In this case, rather than the cost of the product increasing over time to reflect inflation, the price may fall because of increased manufacturing efficiencies and the debugging of the product.

15. **FIFO** is an acronym meaning for *first in, first out*. It assumes that the first inventory items that the company manufactured or bought for resale are the first ones sold.

16. **Working capital** describes the assets a firm uses in its operations. It is shorthand for the result of the following calculation: the sum of a company's current assets (cash, accounts receivable, and inventory) minus the sum of its current liabilities (accounts payable, notes payable, and current portion of long-term debt). It is a measure of short-term liquidity because the only assets included in the calculation are those that can typically be converted to cash quickly. Working capital is what is left over if it is assumed that all current assets are used to pay all current liabilities.

When negotiating the accounting-related provisions in any of these contexts, a lawyer and client must track through the balance sheet and think through on a line item basis whether any one or more of the accounts requires special treatment. For example, the purchase price in some acquisition agreements is based on the seller's reported or book net worth, which in turn is based on the seller's total reported assets and its total reported liabilities. Thus, the value attributed to each asset and each liability directly impacts the purchase price.

When you represent a seller in such a case, think through which assets on the balance sheet do not reflect that asset's true fair market value. Because GAAP is generally conservative, it tends toward understating assets. For that reason, parties may prefer to value assets using something other than GAAP. As noted before, buildings can be revalued to their fair market value. Other assets that may not be reflected at their actual values are an assembled workforce, a patent portfolio, favorable leases, a catalog of creative works, trade secrets, and goodwill. Most of these intangible assets, when created internally, are typically carried at a value of zero, in accordance with GAAP.

While sellers want to maximize price, buyers fear being left to handle unforeseen liabilities and claims. Therefore, they seek to ensure that the net worth calculation accurately reflects all the company's liabilities — not only those on the balance sheet, but also those that GAAP does not require a company to report. Significant areas of concern include the following:

- Pending litigation
- Environmental cleanup liabilities
- Guaranties
- Purchase obligations
- Unfunded pension obligations

If you represent a buyer, consider dealing with these contingent liabilities by establishing a reserve, even though GAAP would not require one.[17] Of course, the parties must work through the specifics of such an approach collaboratively with their lawyers and accountants.

VII. PROVISIONS USING REVENUE AND EARNINGS CONCEPTS

Revenues and earnings formulas appear in a wide variety of agreements, including:

- Purchase price provisions in acquisition agreements
- Compensation provisions in employment agreements
- Royalty provisions in license and franchise agreements
- Buyout provisions in partnership and stockholder agreements
- Profit and loss sharing provisions in joint ventures or partnerships

In these situations, the amount being paid or received can be significantly affected by the accounting choices made in the documents. To make certain that the documents reflect the intended economics, the formulas need to be crafted carefully.

A salient concern for parties is who controls the accounting. If your client controls it, then, generally, a bottom-line, profits-based formula is best. If your client

---

17. Other possibilities include an indemnity, a holdback, insurance, or a purchase limited to the target's assets.

does not control the accounting, the superior alternative is a top-line, revenue-based formula.[18]

The theory behind this dichotomy is that the party lacking control (say, the seller) risks the bottom line being artificially reduced — either by the inclusion of expenses that might be allowable under GAAP, but not reflective of the transaction's true economics, or by the acceleration of some expenses. Alternatively, if a formula is tied to gross revenues (the "top line"), rather than net profits, the party who controls the accounting has much less leeway in manipulating the payment due. Obviously, if you represent the party with control, the ability to *refine* the bottom line has a certain attraction.

If you represent the party without control and are unsuccessful in negotiating a revenue-based formula, all is not lost. Prophylactic countermeasures can be negotiated. Specifically, negotiate covenants limiting the types of expenses and the amount of each expense included in net income. The goal is to reduce the other side's flexibility as much as possible, putting your client in a position as close to a revenue-based formula as possible.

For example, a seller who is negotiating a contingent payout in connection with an acquisition might argue that the impairment[19] of any goodwill created in connection with the acquisition should be an excluded expense. Analytically, this item arises wholly because of the acquisition, and therefore it could be argued that it distorts the real earnings picture. From the seller's perspective, any other expenses new to the business (e.g., additional overhead) would also be fair game for exclusion. Finally, consider including language that requires the accounting to be consistent with previous years, thus precluding artificial expense or revenue recognition in selected periods.

Obviously, if you represent the buyer, resist any attempt to restrict your client's flexibility. Your client now owns the business, and they should have the ability to run it, including the accounting.

---

18. Parties negotiating an earnout inevitably must address this issue.

19. Accountants use the term *impairment* to describe the decline in value of intangibles like goodwill and customer lists. The amount of the decline can be a highly subjective determination. New management of a purchased business regularly writes off (takes as an expense) assets like goodwill to reduce post-acquisition income immediately after transaction. This act makes income higher in the long term because the write-offs were already taken in the first year after the transaction. Management prefers the higher income in the future because that is probably when their shares vest or their employment contracts are renewed.

VIII. EXERCISES

A. Exercise 26A: Improve a Purchaser's Payment Provision

Redraft the following provision to make it one sentence, use appropriate mathematical language, correct the drafting errors, and make it easier to understand.

Purchaser's Payments. The Purchaser covenants that the Purchaser shall pay the Seller the difference between the Purchase Price and the amount of any loan obtained by the Purchaser from a Lending Institution.

The Purchaser also covenants that the Purchaser will pay all costs in connection with the closing as required by the Lending Institution.

B. Exercise 26B: Right of First Refusal

Shareholders A, B, C, and D wish to enter into a shareholders' agreement, but they would like to see one provision before you draft the entire agreement. They want the agreement to provide that if any shareholder wants to sell shares to a third party, that shareholder must first offer the shares to the other shareholders. This is known as a **right of first refusal**. The shareholders were not terribly good at explaining how to determine the number of shares each nonselling shareholder could buy. Instead, they gave the following example:

Assume that the corporation has 50 shares issued and outstanding, and that A wants to sell the ten shares she owns. B, who owns 20 shares, could purchase 50% of those ten shares because B owns 50% of the shares not being sold. Draft the formula for determining the number of shares that each nonselling shareholder may purchase when a shareholder is selling all the shares they own.

Use the method that you think will make it the easiest for the reader to understand the provision's purpose and how it functions (algebraic equation, narration and tabulation, or the narrative cookbook approach).

C. Exercise 26C: Payment Provision in Representation Agreement

Arthur Wright, a quarterback for the San Jose Dragons, has hired Davis Reynolds to represent him in contract negotiations with the Dragons and in connection with product endorsements. (This kind of contract is known as a **representation agreement**.) The parties have agreed that Wright will pay Reynolds the amount that is the greater of Reynolds's standard hourly rate for the type of services that Reynolds provides under their agreement multiplied by the hours spent on providing the services and 15% of the gross amount of all monies received by Wright or on his behalf from contracts that Reynolds negotiated. The parties have already negotiated the definition of *Services*, so don't worry about that — feel free to use *Services* as a defined term. They're the standard services for this type of representation agreements.

Reynolds has asked you to draft the payment provision and to let him know of any questions with respect to the provision.

D. Exercise 26D: Draft Sliding Scale Cost Structure and Alternative Fee Structure Provisions

1. Robin and Reese have always wanted to be entrepreneurs. They decided last month that they finally have saved enough for the equity investment in their business — Recherché, a consignment store for gently used clothes.

   Robin and Reese have written up what Recherché will pay consignors (individuals who bring their gently used clothes to sell them at the store), if their clothes sell. Robin and Reese are asking you to review their draft and to fix any errors. They also tell you that clarity is to prevail.

   Pay to Consignors. You receive 62% of the selling price for items that sell for $999 and below, 75% for

   items that sell for $1,000 and 80% for items that sell $5,000 and above.

2. Recherché has been in business for three years now. Unfortunately, Jake Raditz has sued Recherché, claiming damages relating to a concussion from his fall in the store. Robin and Reese have once again come to you.

   You have offered Recherché an alternative fee structure for your services. Specifically, rather than charging Recherché for the full amount of your billed time, you offered to invoice Recherché 70% of your billed time and to cap your fees at 70% of your billed time if Recherché had to pay damages. You also asked for an upside to the fee arrangement. You proposed that Recherché pay you an amount equal to 120% of your billed time if the plaintiff had no recovery.

   Please draft the provision for this alternative fee structure so you can include it in the agreement that you will give to Robin and Reese to sign for this new matter.

CHAPTER TWENTY-SEVEN

Other Drafting Considerations

I. GENDER-NEUTRAL DRAFTING

When drafting a contract, try not to use pronouns. Instead, replace the pronouns with the defined terms used to refer to the relevant party or parties, so that you are clearer and do not create any ambiguity.

Examples — Replace Pronouns with Defined Terms

> *Incorrect:* **Shareholder Eligibility**. To be eligible to vote for the members of the Board of Directors, a Shareholder shall submit *his, her, or its proxy* no later than 5:00 p.m., May 18, 20___.

> *Correct:* **Shareholder Eligibility**. To be eligible to vote for the members of the Board of Directors, a Shareholder shall submit *that Shareholder's proxy* no later than 5:00 p.m., May 18, 20___.

As an alternative, delete unnecessary pronouns.

Examples — Delete Unnecessary Pronouns

> *Incorrect:* **Transfer of Shares**. A Shareholder proposing to transfer *his, her,* or *its* Shares . . .

> *Correct:* **Transfer of Shares**. A Shareholder proposing *to transfer Shares* . . .

If individuals are not parties to an agreement, gender-neutral drafting issues still arise if any of the contract's provisions refer to individuals. For example, references to *firemen, policemen,* and *workmen* are no longer appropriate. Contract provisions should use gender-neutral terms, such as *firefighters, police officers,* and *workers*.

II. THE CASCADE EFFECT

The **cascade effect** occurs when the drafting of a business term in one provision requires a change in, or the addition of, a second business term. A simple example: Assume that you are drafting an employment agreement that requires your client, the company, to pay their executive an annual salary of $100,000. The contract also includes an endgame provision that obligates your client to pay the executive their salary through their last day of employment if the company terminates them for cause. Now assume that after the first round of negotiations, the client agrees to pay the executive a $10,000 annual bonus. Here is where the cascade effect kicks in. You will need to make two changes. First, you will need to change the compensation provision in the payment section of the action sections to provide for the bonus. Second, you will need a new endgame provision that spells out how much of the bonus, if any, the client will pay if they fire the executive for cause. One change causes another. The cascade effect plays a significant role in the review of a contract.

III. EXCEPTIONS

When drafting or reviewing an agreement, a lawyer must carefully analyze each provision to determine whether it should apply in all circumstances. When it does not—and it often does not—the contract must provide for an exception.

A. HOW TO SIGNAL AN EXCEPTION

Exceptions are signaled in several ways: *except, except as otherwise provided, other than, unless,* and *provided.* All these signals, other than *provided* and derivations of *provided,* such as *provided, however,* are acceptable. *Provided* can have multiple meanings that create the possibility of ambiguity, as discussed in the Provisos section of Chapter 25 on page 393.

B. PLACEMENT OF THE EXCEPTION

As a general rule, when drafting a provision that includes an exception, put the rule first, and then the exception. If the order is reversed, the provision often becomes more difficult to understand because the reader does not have the context to understand the exception. In addition, with a long exception, the reader has too much information to remember before getting to the provision's main point. Here is an example of an exception before the rule. Note that the concluding language at the end of the tabulation should also be a red flag and should indicate to you that you should be redrafting the provision so that there is no concluding language:

Examples—Put the Rule Before the Exception

Incorrect—Because Exception Is Before the Rule:

Enforceability. Except to the extent that enforcement is limited by

(a) applicable bankruptcy, insolvency, reorganization, moratorium, or other similar laws affecting creditors' rights generally, or

(b) general equitable principles, regardless of whether the issue of enforceability is considered in a proceeding in equity or at law, this Agreement is the Publisher's legal, valid, and binding obligation, enforceable against the Publisher in accordance with its terms.

Correct — Because Rule Is Before the Exception:

Enforceability. This Agreement is the Publisher's legal, valid, and binding obligation, enforceable against the Publisher in accordance with its terms, except to the extent that enforcement is limited by

(a) applicable bankruptcy, insolvency, reorganization, moratorium, or other similar laws affecting creditors' rights generally; or

(b) general equitable principles, regardless of whether the issue of enforceability is considered in a proceeding in equity or at law.

Although you should generally put the exception at the end of a provision, it may work better at the beginning of a provision if it is short and quickly alerts the reader to the exception, or if it provides helpful context. Following are some examples of acceptable provisions with preferred options.

Examples — Exception at the Beginning if Short or Provides Context

1—Acceptable: **Investments**. Except for a $400,000 investment in a subsidiary, the Borrower shall not make any investments.

1—Preferred: **Investments**. The Borrower shall not make any investments, except for a $400,000 investment in a subsidiary.

2—Acceptable: **Litigation**. Except as stated in **Schedule 3.15**, the Seller is not a party to any pending or, to its knowledge, threatened litigation.

2—Preferred: **Litigation**. The Seller is not a party to any pending or, to its knowledge, threatened litigation, except as stated in **Schedule 3.15.**

If a provision and its exception result in a long sentence, consider breaking it down into subsections. Put the general rule in the first subsection and the exception in the next. The captions for the subsections should signal their content: *General Rule* and *Exception.*

Example — General Rule and Exception in Subsections

Duty of Nondisclosure.[1]

(a) **General Rule**. The Executive shall not disclose any item of Confidential Information in any form to any Person.

(b) **Exception**. Despite subsection (a), the Executive may disclose Confidential Information to any one or more of the following Persons:

    (i) A member, manager, or agent of the LLC.

    (ii) A person to whom the LLC has authorized the Executive to make disclosure.

---

1. This provision is based on a provision in John M. Cunningham, *Drafting Limited Liability Company Operating Agreements Form* 17, § 7.1 (Aspen Publishers 2006).

If a rule and its exception are in separate sentences or subsections, their relationship should be explicitly stated in one of the two sentences or subsections, with language such as the following:

Examples — Language to State Exception

1 — Except as set forth in the next [sentence] [subsection], [state the general rule].

2 — Despite the previous [sentence] [subsection], [state the exception].

Do not use *foregoing* instead of a specific reference because it can be ambiguous. Also, if the provision were rewritten without subsections and captions, the sentence with the general rule could contain the reference to the exception, as in the following provision.

Example — Sentence with the General Rule Containing the Reference to the Exception

Duty of Nondisclosure. The Executive shall not disclose any item of Confidential Information in any form to any Person, except in accordance with the remainder of this Section X. The Executive may disclose Confidential Information to any one or more of the following Persons:

(a) A member, manager, or agent of the LLC.
(b) A person to whom the LLC has authorized the Executive to make disclosure.

Putting an exception at the end of a provision or a sentence may create ambiguity if the exception follows a compound or a series. It may be unclear whether the exception modifies only the word or phrase immediately adjacent to it, or whether it modifies each of the items in the compound or the series.[2] To cure any potential ambiguity, draft the exception so that it specifically applies to each item in the compound or series. Alternatively, tabulate the compound or the series and put the exception in the lead-in language. In the provision that follows, the ambiguity is whether the exception, including its reasonableness requirement, applies only to subletting.

Examples — Curing Ambiguity When Exception Follows Compound or Series

Incorrect: **Assignments and Sublets**. The Tenant shall not assign the Tenant's rights under this Lease or sublet the Apartment, except with the Landlord's prior written consent.

Correct 1: **Assignments and Sublets**. The Tenant shall not assign the Tenant's rights under this Lease or sublet the Apartment, except in either instance with the Landlord's prior written consent.

---

2. *See* Chapter 25 on page 377 for a discussion of how modifiers following a compound or series can create ambiguity.

> ***Correct 2:*** **Assignments and Sublets**. Except with the Landlord's prior written consent, the Tenant
>
> > (a) shall not assign its rights under this Lease or
> > (b) shall not sublet the Apartment.

Drafters sometimes put exceptions both at the beginning of a sentence and at the end. Generally, this reflects the drafter's thinking process. She knows about one exception as she begins drafting the provision, but then has a brilliant insight and puts another exception at the end. Instead, put all the exceptions together at the end of the sentence and, if necessary to enhance clarity, tabulate them.

> ***Examples — Put All Exceptions Together at End of the Sentence***
>
> ***Incorrect:*** **Assignments and Sublets**. Except as permitted by Section 4.7, the Tenant shall not assign the Tenant's rights under this Lease or sublet the Apartment, except with the prior written consent of the Landlord.
>
> ***Correct:*** **Assignments and Sublets**. The Tenant shall not assign the Tenant's rights under this Lease or sublet the Apartment, except that the Tenant may do either in each of the following circumstances:
>
> > (a) As permitted by Section 4.7.
> > (b) With the Landlord's prior written consent.

C. EXCEPT AS OTHERWISE PROVIDED

The phrase *except as otherwise provided* signals an exception. However, the exception, is not in the provision, but elsewhere in the contract. The two provisions are related but are not together.

Some drafters specify where the other provision is, but others do not. Those who do not are often concerned with the need for the cross-reference to be updated if any numbering changes or want the flexibility to argue later that the contract includes more than one exception — even if the parties contemplated only one at the time of drafting, but you don't know what the circumstances will be in the future. When you draft, include the cross-reference so that the intent of the parties is clear, and they know what to do specifically going forward. Also, if you discover multiple cross-references to the same section, it may mean that you need to reorganize the contract and put related provisions together.

IV. OTHER COMMON WORDS AND PHRASES

A. *AS IN EFFECT FROM TIME TO TIME* AND *FROM TIME TO TIME*

Drafters regularly use the phrases *as in effect from time to time* and *as amended from time to time* in similar ways. Neither phrase is controversial nor a regular source of litigation. They signal that something is to occur at an unscheduled time and that the something may occur more than once without limit.[3]

B. AS THE CASE MAY BE

Use *as the case may be* to establish that two or more items create alternative relationships when joined with two or more other items in the same sentence. If A occurs, then B occurs, *or* if C occurs, then D occurs. The relationships are alternative, not concurrent. As you can see in the example that follows, the correlations are between *net income* and *credited* and then, separately, between *net loss* and *charged*.

Example — Using "As the Case May Be" to Create Alternative Relationships

Allocation of Income and Losses. All *net income* or *net loss* allocated to a Partner in accordance with the terms of this Article 6 is to be *credited* or *charged*, as the case may be, to that Partner's capital account.

Some drafters use *as the case may be* to clarify that *or* in a sentence is being used in its exclusive sense. Typically, the additional language is not needed because there are not two or more sets being correlated.

Examples — "As the Case May Be" Not Needed to Clarify "Or"

Incorrect: **Death and Retirement Benefits.** The Partnership shall pay the amount calculated in accordance with **Exhibit A** in 60 equal monthly installments, beginning on the first day of the month following the month in which the Partner died or retired, *as the case may be.*

Correct: **Death and Retirement Benefits.** The Partnership shall pay the amount calculated in accordance with **Exhibit A** in 60 equal monthly installments, beginning on the first day of the month following the month in which the Partner died or retired.

---

3. *See, e.g., Union Constr. Co., Inc. v. Beneficial Standard Mortg. Inv.*, 610 P.2d 67 (Ariz. Ct. App. 1980) (holding that a consent-to-extension provision authorizing extensions "from time to time" permitted multiple extensions of time); *Rogers v. W. Riverside 350-Inch Water Co.*, 124 P. 447, 450 (Cal. Ct. App. 1912) (holding that "[t]he words 'from time to time,' as used in the contract, were intended by the parties to apply to and mean the successive irrigation seasons, which may or may not be coextensive with the year"); *Bay Nat'l Bank & Trust Co. v. Mason*, 349 So. 2d 810 (Fla. Dist. Ct. App. 1977) (holding that language permitting two notes to be extended "from time to time without notice . . ." must be held to mean the parties consented in advance to additional extensions of the notes without further notice); *TMG Life Ins. Co. v. Ashner*, 898 P.2d 1145, 1155-1156 (Kan. Ct. App. 1995) (holding that the phrase "from time to time" means "as occasion may arise," "at intervals," "now and then occasionally," and that use of the phrase "from time to time" in a guaranty did not give the lender the "right to enforce the guaranty at one time to the exclusion of another").

C. *CONTINUALLY* AND *CONTINUOUSLY*

Continually can mean either without interruption or repeated in the same way.[4] In contrast, **continuously** means without interruption.[5]

Examples — "Continually" versus "Continuously"

> *Continually:* The Contractor shall install on each floor of the Building a fire alarm that beeps continually [repeatedly] at the statutorily-prescribed decibel level.
>
> *Continuously:* The Contractor shall install on each floor of the Building a fire alarm that blares continuously [without stop] at the statutorily-prescribed decibel level.

Be careful when using these words and other words like them. Do not rely on these words and their meaning being obvious, especially when you use *continually,* since there are two possible meanings.

D. DEEM

Use *deem* or *deemed* sparingly to turn something contrary to reality into a contractual reality. *Deem* creates the fiction that something is true, even though it is not. In most instances, instead of using *deem,* you should be more direct and specific about the matter or standard, as in the examples that follow, where instead of *deem,* the provision specifies more clearly who, what, when, where, and so on.

Examples — Use "Deem" Sparingly and Instead Be Specific

> *Incorrect:* **Notice**. A notice *is deemed effectively given* only if the notice is in writing and the intended recipient receives the notice.
>
> *Correct 1:* **Notice**. A party gives an effective notice only if the notice is in writing and the intended recipient receives the notice.
>
> *Correct 2:* Notice. Any notice or instruction received after 5:00 p.m. on a Business Day or on a day that is not a Business Day is *deemed* received at 9:00 a.m. on the next Business Day.

E. NOT TO BE DEEMED TO BE

Not be deemed to be is not interchangeable with the phrase *be deemed not to be.* These phrases have different meanings. *Not be deemed to be* <u>negates</u> a deemed rule, whereas *be deemed not to be* <u>creates</u> a deemed rule. Therefore, rewrite any such provision to start with *deemed not to be.*

For example, if you want to make clear that a certain action will not be considered *material*, then do not write: [*Action*] *will not be deemed to be material.* The action

---

4. *Continually, Merriam-Webster Dictionary,* https://www.merriam-webster.com/dictionary/continually (last visited May 24, 2023) ("in a continual manner: without stopping or interruption") ("in a constantly repeated manner: over and over.")

5. *Id.* ("in a continuous manner: without interruption").

could still *in fact* be material. Instead, write: [*Action*] *will be deemed not to be material.*[6]

F. GUARANTY

A **guaranty** is one person's promise to pay another person's debt.[7] Traditionally, writers and dictionaries spelled the singular noun with a *y* at the end, as in *guaranty*, and the plural noun by deleting the *y* and inserting *ies*, as in *guaranties*. Here is an example of a correctly used guaranty provision:

Example — Using Guaranty

Condition to Lending. As a condition to lending to the Borrower, the Bank must have received the Parent's guaranty of the Borrower's debt under the Loan Agreement.

To distinguish the noun and the verb, writers and dictionaries spelled the two forms of the root word differently. The verb ended with a double *e*, *guarantee*.[8] Over time, writers began to spell the noun with a double *e* as well. Even though different spellings are permissible, to be clear in your drafting maintain a difference in your spelling of the noun and verb form, and be intentional and consistent with which one you are using and how, as the example below shows:

Example — "Guarantee" versus "Guaranty"

Condition to Lending. As a condition to lending to the Borrower, the Parent must have guaranteed the Borrower's debt under the Loan Agreement by executing and delivering a guaranty substantially in the form of **Exhibit C**.

G. *INCLUDE* AND *INCLUDING*

Drafters tend to like using the words *include* and *including* often. Furthermore, some drafters believe that *including* should always be accompanied by a qualifying phrase — either *including without limitation* or *including but not limited to*. Other drafters think that those phrases are not needed since *including* already takes the limiting and qualifying issue into account. However, there are several different lines of case law relating to the words *include* and *including* that can affect how

---

6. Vincent R. Martorana, *Foundational Concepts in Drafting Contracts: What Most Attorneys Fail to Consider* 2012, Ch. 1, §IIIC (2012).

7. Guaranty, *Black's Law Dictionary* (11th ed. 2019) ("A promise to answer for the payment of some debt, or the performance of some duty, in case of the failure of another who is liable in the first instance").

8. *Guarantee, Black's Law Dictionary* (11th ed. 2019) ("The assurance that a contract or legal act will be duly carried out").

your provision is interpreted. Here are just some of them explained, but keep in mind that case law can vary by jurisdiction.[9]

1. *Including* Is Restrictive

In the first line of cases, courts hold that *including* is restrictive, that the enumerated items after *including* compose all the items that relate to the noun preceding *including*.[10] Consider the following definition from a statute. In construing it, the court held that *shall include* was restrictive and that air transportation companies were not included within the embrace of the defined term *transportation company*.

Example — Including *Is Restrictive*

[T]he term "transportation company" shall include any company . . . owning, leasing or operating for hire a railroad, street railway, canal, steamboat line, and also any freight car company, car corporation, or company . . . in any way engaged in such business as a common carrier over a route acquired . . . under the right of eminent domain.[11]

---

2. *Including* Is a Term of Enlargement

In the second line of cases, the courts hold that *include* is a term of enlargement, meaning that the enumerated items that follow *include* expand the meaning of the noun or phrase that precedes *include*.[12] For example, the meaning of *use of the automobile* would typically be limited to acts involving movement of the automobile. But an insurance policy expanded the meaning of that phrase when it defined *use* to include loading and unloading.[13]

3. *Include* Signals That Illustrations Follow

In the third line of cases, the courts hold that *include* signals that the enumerated items that follow are illustrations of the general principle exemplified in the noun that precedes *include*.[14] For example, in a contract between a utility company and a consumer, the contract provided that the sewerage lines would "include those located

---

9. Indeed, the cases themselves acknowledge the ambiguity of the term. *See, e.g., Auer v. Cmmw.*, 621 S.E.2d 140, 144-45 (Va. App. 2005) ("Generally speaking, the word 'include' implies that the provided list of parts or components is not exhaustive and, thus, not exclusive. . . . However, the word 'include' is also commonly used in a restrictive, limiting sense. . . . Used in this limiting sense, the term typically introduces an exhaustive list of all of the components or members that make up the whole. . . . Thus, when a statute uses the word 'include' in this restrictive, limiting sense to define a term, it sets forth the entire definition, and no other elements or items are includable. . . . Because the word 'include' is susceptible to more than one meaning and because it is not immediately clear from the word's context which meaning is meant to apply . . . we conclude that the statute's provision . . . is ambiguous.") (interpreting a statute).

10. *See In re Est. of Meyer*, 668 N.E.2d 263 (Ind. App. 1996) (interpreting a will).

11. *See In re C. Airlines, Inc.*, 185 P.2d 919, 923-925 (Okla. 1947) (interpreting a statute).

12. *See State ex rel. Nixon v. Estes*, 108 S.W.3d 795, 800 (Mo. App. W. Dist. 2003) ("While the plain meaning of the word 'include' may vary according to its context in a statute, it is ordinarily used as a term of enlargement, rather than a term of limitation.") (interpreting a statute).

13. *See Pac. Automobile Ins. Co. v. Com. Cas. Ins. Co. of N.Y.*, 161 P.2d 423, 427-428 (Utah 1945) (interpreting a contract).

14. *See Fed. Land Bank of St. Paul v. Bismarck Lumber Co.*, 314 U.S. 95, 99-100 (1941) (interpreting a statute); *DIRECTV, Inc. v. Crespin*, 2007 WL 779232 at *3 (10th Cir. 2007) (interpreting a statute); *Pottsburgh Utils., Inc. v. Daugharty*, 309 So. 2d 199, 201-202 (Fla. 1st Dist. App. 1975) (interpreting a contract).

within the boundaries of the Consumer's property." The court held that the consumer was responsible for the construction and maintenance of sewerage lines outside its property boundaries, noting that "shall include . . . connotes simply an illustrative application of the general principle."[15]

4. What Should You Use?

With a mix of case law, you must assess the risk in using *include* or *including*. Will the judge decide that *include* has a restrictive, an expansive, or an illustrative meaning? Since most drafters are risk averse, they choose the more conservative route and include a qualifying phrase — either *including without limitation* or *including but not limited to*.

In making this decision, a drafter could reasonably take into account the efficacy of the qualifying phrases. That is, do they work? The answer is that mostly they do. When interpreting these qualifiers, courts generally acknowledge their significance in turning the enumerated items that follow the qualifier into a nonexclusive list.[16] Indeed, one court, which held that *including* had a restrictive meaning, indicated that the result would have differed had the parties included "but not in limitation of the foregoing."[17] Another court indicated that the qualifying phrase supported their decision that *includes* had an illustrative or expansive connotation.[18] Not surprisingly,

---

15. *Pottsburgh Utils., Inc. v. Daugharty, supra* n.10, at 201 (interpreting a contract).

16. *See People v. Clark-Van Brunt*, 205 Cal. Rptr. 144, 149 (Super. App. Dept. 1984) (stating that, "The clear import of the phrase 'but is not limited to' signifies that the Legislature intended the definition of 'drug paraphernalia' to be expansive and flexible. Thus the expressly enumerated items are simply exemplary of those items which may constitute 'drug paraphernalia' rather than delineating the parameters of the subject.") (interpreting a statute); *McCabe v. Comm'r, Ind. Dept. of Ins.*, 949 N.E.2d 816, 819-821 (Ind. 2011) ("'[M]ay include but are not limited to' . . . is a standard expression designating the permissive inclusion of an open-ended class of items not to be limited by designation of specific items that follow." The court noted that in the context of this case, certain decisions might "restrain the outer limits" of the qualifying phrase.) (interpreting a statute); *In re Forfeiture of $5,264*, 439 N.W.2d 246, 255 (Mich. 1989) ("Contrary to the interpretation of the Court of Appeals in Ewing Road, we do not view the proviso, 'including, but not limited to,' to be one of limitation. Rather, we believe the phrase connotes an illustrative listing, one purposefully capable of enlargement.") (interpreting a statute); *In re Est. of Littlejohn*, 698 N.W.2d 923, 926 (N.D. 2005) ("The words 'includes, but are not limited to' ordinarily includes a partial and non-exclusive list.") (interpreting a power of attorney); *but see Shelby Co. State Bank v. Van Diest Supply Co.*, 303 F.3d 832, 837-838 (7th Cir. 2002) (This case held that "including but not limited to" modified the phrase that preceded it ("all inventory") by restricting it to what followed the "including but not limited to." The contested language was the collateral description in a UCC financing statement drafted by a supplier of goods, Van Diest. A third-party creditor, a bank, argued that the collateral was limited to inventory that Van Diest sold to its purchaser, as suggested by the language following "including but not limited to." Van Diest argued that it had a security interest in all the inventory, not just what it sold. The court found both interpretations reasonable and that the security description was ambiguous. In reaching its decision that the only collateral was the inventory sold to the purchaser, the court first called the listing of items "bizarre" when the broad phrase "all inventory" preceded "including but not limited to." Then, in the same paragraph, it noted that there were "use[s] for descriptive clauses of inclusion, so as to make clear the kind of entities that ought to be included." It concluded its decision as follows: "The most compelling reason to construe the language of this agreement against Van Diest [the supplier] is the fact that it was Van Diest that drafted the security agreement, and that the language of that agreement plays an important part for third-party creditors [that is, the bank].") (citation omitted). The case's facts make it somewhat anomalous and, therefore, weak authority for the proposition that the additional qualifying language is not reliable.

17. *In re Est. of Meyer, supra* n.6, at 265 ("If he had intended to use the word 'including' as a term of enlargement rather than a term of limitation, [the deceased] could have modified 'including' with the phrase 'but not in limitation of the foregoing.'") (interpreting a will).

18. *Jackson v. Concord Co.*, 253 A.2d 793, 800 (N.J. 1969) ("We have earlier held, in analogous interpretation situations under this act, that terms like 'include' are words of enlargement and not of limitation and that examples specified thereafter are merely illustrative . . . This is especially so where the word 'including' is followed by the phrase 'but not limited to'") (citations omitted; interpreting a statute);

some cases also find that a qualifying phrase is unnecessary to turn *including* into an expansive term.[19]

5. Be Consistent in Your Use of *Include* and *Including*

Remember to *say the same thing in the same way*, as we discussed in Chapter 25 on page 380, even if doing so may seem redundant and clunky. For example, if you use a qualifying phrase with *including*, use that same phrase each time you use *including* in the contract. An interpretive provision placed in either the definitions article or with the miscellaneous provisions can also help solve any issues, in case you miss one or there are any doubts going forward.[20]

Example — Interpretive Provision for Include, Includes, *and* Including

The words *include*, *includes*, and *including* are deemed to be followed by the words *without limitation*.

---

6. *Without Limiting the Generality*

If a sentence's grammatical structure does not permit you to add *include* or *including* immediately after the statement of the general concept, you should end the sentence and begin a new sentence with the phrase *without limiting the generality of the preceding [section, sentence]*, as in the following example:

Example — Beginning the Sentence with "Without Limiting the Generality"

Duties. The Company shall employ the Performer as a broadcast anchor for sports programming on the Station. In this capacity, the Performer shall render those services that the Company requires, subject to its direction,

---

see also St. Paul Mercury Ins. Co. v. Lexington Ins. Co., 78 F.3d 202, 206-207 (5th Cir. 1996) (stating that "'including' . . . "is generally given an expansive reading, even without the additional if not redundant language of 'without limitation.'") (interpreting a contract); *Leach v. State*, 170 S.W.3d 669, 672-673 (Tex. App. — Fort Worth 2005) (acknowledging the expansive scope of "but not limited to" in another statute, but stating that that use did not limit the expansive scope of "including" in the statute being interpreted, the court having earlier noted that the Code Construction Act explicitly gave "including" an expansive meaning) (interpreting a statute); *cf. Horse Cave State Bank v. Nolin Prod. Credit Ass'n*, 672 S.W.2d 66, 66-67 (Ky. App. 1984) (In this case, the court had to determine whether the description in a U.C.C. financing statement sufficiently described the collateral. The court relied on an earlier case in stating that "farm machinery," without more, did not give third parties the ability to readily identify the collateral from its description. The court held that the listing of specific machinery after an including but not limited to clause described the collateral sufficiently. Here is the provision at issue: "all farm machindry [*sic*], including but not limited to tractor, plow and disc . . . plus all property similar to that listed . . . .") (interpreting a UCC financing statement).

19. *St. Paul Mercury Ins. Co. v. Lexington Ins. Co.*, *supra* n.14, at 206-207; *People v. Perry*, 864 N.E.2d 196, 208-209 (Ill. 2007) (The court first notes, "[t]he legislature has on many occasions used the phrases 'including but not limited to' or 'includes but is not limited to' to indicate that the list that follows is intended to be illustrative rather than exhaustive. An electronic search of the Illinois Compiled Statutes reveals 1,749 statutes using the phrase 'including but not limited to' and 249 containing the phrase 'includes but is not limited to.'" It then adds that, even in the absence of the qualifying phrases, "includes" should be given its plain and ordinary meaning — that the enumerated items that follow are illustrative, not exclusive).

20. Interpretive provisions are also discussed in Chapter 15 on page 202, Chapter 18 on page 264, Chapter 22 on page 332, and Chapter 27 on page 429.

control, rules, and regulations. *Without limiting the generality* of the preceding sentence, the Performer's services include

(a) preparing for, rehearsing, delivering, and performing on the Station's programs, whether live or recorded;
(b) operating all kinds of technical equipment; and
(c) writing, producing, and directing programs on which the Performer is to appear.

If *including* had been inserted after *regulations*, then *including* may appear to refer to *regulations*, which is its immediate antecedent.

The phrase *without limiting the generality of the preceding [section, sentence]* is a contemporary alternative to *without limiting the generality of the foregoing*. Do not use the traditional formulation with *the foregoing*. In addition to being legalese, it can cause ambiguity because *the foregoing* does not specify to what it refers; it could be referring to one or more sentences or sections.

H. *NOTWITHSTANDING ANYTHING TO THE CONTRARY*

The phrase *notwithstanding anything to the contrary in this Agreement* signals to a reader that this one provision overrides any of the others. No matter what those other provisions say, this provision supersedes them. This phrase may also be used in a more limited way: *notwithstanding anything to the contrary in Section X*.

Be careful when you use this phrase, especially if the contract uses it more than once. If the two instances contradict each other, ambiguity will result. Ambiguity can even result if it is used only once,[21] so make sure that you know the implications of the phrase and that you need to use it. A contemporary alternative to *notwithstanding anything to the contrary in this Agreement* is *despite any other provision of this Agreement.*

I. *REGARDLESS OF WHETHER OR NOT* AND *WHETHER*

If a sentence contains the phrase *regardless of whether or not*, the phrase *regardless of* is generally not needed since its meaning is included in the meaning of *whether or not*. If you are not sure which phrase is correct, write two versions of the sentence. The first version would include the full, longer phrase, and the second would be the same, but with the phrase *regardless of* deleted. Then, compare and ask yourself whether the phrase *regardless of* was necessary to convey meaning and whether it added any meaning.

Examples — Replacing Regardless of Whether or Not with Whether or Not

> *Incorrect:* **Obligation to Mow.** Cooper shall mow the lawn, *regardless of whether or not* Cooper is studying for the bar.

> *Correct:* **Obligation to Mow.** Cooper shall mow the lawn, *whether or not* Cooper is studying for the bar.

---

21. *See United Rentals, Inc. v. RAM Holdings, Inc.*, 937 A.2d 810 (Del. Ch. 2007) (Poor drafting and the use of notwithstanding anything to the contrary resulted in ambiguity as to which provision trumped which other provision.).

Along the same lines, a drafter should decide whether they can shorten the phrase *whether or not* to the core word *whether*. You can do this often, but it can vary depending on the context and what is included in the rest of the provision.

J. *RESPECTIVELY*

Use *respectively* to establish that two or more items create concurrent relationships when joined with two or more other items in the same sentence: If A, B, and C occur, then D, E, and F are true, respectively. A relates to D; B relates to E; and C relates to F, all at the same time.

> ### *Examples — Using Respectively to Create Concurrent Relationships*
>
> *1*—**Election of Directors**. The Group A Shareholders and the Group B Shareholders shall cast their votes for Group A Directors and Group B Directors, *respectively*.
>
> *2*—**Maximum Borrowings**. Subsidiary A, Subsidiary B, and Subsidiary C may borrow a maximum of $2 million, $4.5 million, and $8 million, *respectively*.

As an alternative, the information in Example 2 above could be displayed in a chart with introductory language, which might make it easier for the reader to understand.

> ### *Example — Using a Chart to Display the Correlations*
>
> **Maximum Borrowings**. Each Subsidiary may borrow at a maximum the dollar amount adjacent to each Subsidiary's name in the chart below.
>
> | Subsidiary | Maximum Borrowing |
> | --- | --- |
> | Subsidiary A | $2 million |
> | Subsidiary B | $4.5 million |
> | Subsidiary C | $8 million |

K. *SUBJECT TO* AND *NOTWITHSTANDING*

Subject to and *notwithstanding* are not synonyms. *Notwithstanding* is always part of a provision that takes precedence over what other provisions the clause refers to. *Subject to* should not be used to supersede another provision and has more subtle connotations. Drafters should use *subject to* to signal that the referenced provision *modifies*, but does not trump, the provision that contains the *subject to* clause. *Subject to* connotes that a provision is conditional or dependent on something.

> *Examples — Using Notwithstanding or Subject To to Refer to a Provision*
>
>   **Notwithstanding:** *Notwithstanding* the requirements outlined in the previous section, the lesee will notify the lessor immediately of the following issues. . . .
>
>   **Subject To:** *Subject to* the requirements mentioned in Section 11, the title will be delivered. . . .

According to Scalia and Garner, "[n]otwithstanding performs a function opposite that of subject to. A dependent phrase that begins with notwithstanding indicates that the main clause that it introduces or follows derogates from the provision to which it refers."[22] *Notwithstanding* is a *superordinating* or *trump* term, therefore, when it is used in reference to a prior provision and the clause that it introduces is not limited by the prior provision referenced.[23] *Subject to* may simply add or subtract from the provision.

V. SOME CANONS OF CONSTRUCTION

Canons of construction are rules or guidelines that judges use to help them interpret a legal, written document such as a contract or statute. There are many canons of construction, but here we introduce just some of the more common ones: *ejusdem generis*, *expression unius est exclusion alterius*, and *contra proferentem*.

A. EJUSDEM GENERIS

Ejusdem generis is a Latin phrase that means "of the same kind or class." Courts apply this canon of construction where a list of specific items concludes with general language intended to expand that list. In determining how that list should be expanded, courts limit the breadth of the general language by finding that it embraces only other items of the same kind or class as those already listed. The preceding specific words limit the scope of the general language.

A classic application of *ejusdem generis* arises in the context of a *force majeure* definition. For example:

> *Example — Ejusdem Generis Application to Force Majeure Provision*
>
>   **"*Force Majeure* Event"** means storm, flood, washout, tsunami, lightning, drought, earthquake, volcanic eruption, landslide, cyclone, typhoon, tornado, or any other event beyond a party's control.

Although the concluding language of "any other event beyond a party's control" is broad, a court would likely look at the characteristics of the specific events preceding that language to determine what other events would be within its scope. As the listed events are all natural catastrophes, a court, relying on *ejusdem generis*, could reasonably find that a hurricane fits within the general language, but a war or the COVID-19 pandemic does not. This may or may not be what the parties intended.

---

    22. Antonin Scalia & Bryan Garner, *Reading Law: The Interpretation of Legal Texts* (Eagan, MN: West, 2012), 126.

    23. *Id.*

Parties can attempt to overcome the application of *ejusdem generis* by stating that it does not apply.

B. EXPRESSIO UNIUS EST EXCLUSIO ALTERIUS

Expressio unius est exclusio alterius is another Latin phrase, which means "the expression of one thing excludes the other."[24] When used as a canon of construction, it limits a provision to what it states expressly.

Suppose, for example, that a contract obligates the tenant to pay for specific repairs, as follows.

> *Example — Expressio Unius Est Exclusio Alterius Application to Lease*
>
> **Tenant Repairs.** The Tenant shall repair and pay for the cost of repair of the walls, ceilings, light fixtures, plumbing work, pipes, and fixtures.[25]

Were the landlord to argue that the tenant was also obligated to repair the roof, the tenant could rebut that argument by contending that the provision's failure to mention the roof meant that it was excluded: The expression of one thing excludes the other.

C. CONTRA PROFERENTEM

Another classic rule of construction is ***contra proferentem***: a contract should be construed against the party who drafted it.[26] The rationale is that the drafter is better able to prevent ambiguity. Although this rule of construction makes sense when parties have unequal bargaining power, it loses force when a contract is between sophisticated commercial parties that are each represented by counsel.[27] To rebut the presumption, the drafting parties can include a provision specifically stating that *contra proferentem* does not apply. Each contract may have such a provision drafted in its own way, but here is an example:

---

24. *See generally* Clifton Williams, *Expressio Unius Est Exclusio Alterius*, 15 Marq. L. Rev. 191 (1931).

25. This example is based on the contract provision in *Zbarazer Realty Co. v. Brandstein*, 113 N.Y.S. 1078, 1079 (App. Div. 1909).

26. *See Diversified Energy, Inc. v. Tenn. Valley Auth.*, 223 F.3d 328, 339 (6th Cir. 2000); *S. Energy Homes, Inc. v. Washington*, 774 So. 2d 505, 513 (Ala. 2000); David Horton, *Flipping the Script: Contra Proferentem and Standard Form Contracts*, 80 U. Co. L. Rev. 431 (2008) (arguing for a strict application of *contra proferentem* in standard form contracts); *see also Restatement (Second) Contracts* § 206 (1981) ("In choosing among the reasonable meanings of a promise or agreement or a term thereof, that meaning is generally preferred which operates against the party who supplies the words or from whom a writing otherwise proceeds.").

27. *See Dawn Equip. Co. v. Micro-Trak Sys., Inc.*, 186 F.3d 981, 989 n. 3 (7th Cir. 1999); *see also Restatement (Second) Contracts* § 206, Reporter's Note to cmt. a (1981) (doctrine "has less force when the other party . . . is particularly knowledgeable"); Meredith R. Miller, *Contract Law, Party Sophistication and the New Formalism*, 75 Mo. L. Rev. 493, 504 (2010).

Example — Provision Stating That Contra Proferentem Does Not Apply

11. **Construction of Contract.**

   11.1 Acknowledgments. Each party acknowledges that it

   (a) is a sophisticated commercial party and that it participated in negotiating this Agreement, and

   (b) has been represented by counsel of its choice who either participated in the drafting of this Agreement or had ample opportunity to review and comment on it.

   11.2 *Contra Proferentem.* Accordingly, neither party is presumptively entitled to have the contract construed against the other party in accordance with the canon of construction known as *contra proferentem*. It does not apply to this Agreement.

VI. EXERCISES

A. Exercise 27A: Employment Agreement Between Vera Ward and Scuba Vacations, Inc.

The following provision comes from an employment agreement between Vera Ward and Scuba Vacations, Inc.

> **Benefits and Office.** The Company shall provide Ward with the Company's full range of health and insurance benefits and shall provide her with an office suite similar to the one she had at her previous employer.

1. Given what you have learned in this chapter, mark it up so that it applies only to Ward.
2. What changes would you make so that it could be used in any employment agreement and you could use it going forward as a precedent for any employment agreement?
3. If you were Vera Ward, would you prefer version one or two above, and why?

B. Exercise 27B: Correct Drafting Errors

Mark up the following provisions to correct the drafting errors.

1. **Assignments.** Except for delegations to affiliates, the Contractor shall not assign its performance under this Agreement to any Person, other than Hughes Contracting Corp.

2. **Severability.** If any provision of this Agreement is deemed by the final decree of a court to be unenforceable, the enforceability of the remaining provisions is unimpaired.

3. **Consents.** Other than the approval of the Seller's shareholders, the Seller is not required to obtain any consent or approval or give any notice in connection with the execution and delivery of this Agreement or the consummation of the transactions contemplated hereby, except for notification to and consents and approvals from the persons listed in **Exhibit D**.

CHAPTER TWENTY-EIGHT

Deconstructing Complex Provisions

I. THE SIX-STEP PROCESS

In the previous chapters, you learned multiple skills that will help you write clear and unambiguous provisions. Often, provisions are so dense that you cannot be sure of their substantive effect. To understand them, you need to take them apart, reorganize them, and clean up the language. Only then can you find the ambiguities and incorrect statements in the business deal.

Deconstructing these provisions can be intimidating, but by deconstructing a provision in steps, the process becomes manageable. This chapter describes a six-step process for deconstructing — and reconstructing — complex provisions. You already know five of the six steps, so learning the process should be relatively easy. As the chapter explains each of the steps, it will deconstruct a provision so you can see the process being applied.

Here are the six steps:

1. Explicate.
2. Create clarity through format.
3. Create clarity through sentence structure.
4. Clarify ambiguities.
5. Root out legalese and clean up the language.
6. Check substance.

We will now look at each of them in turn.

A. EXPLICATE

When you **explicate** a provision, you break it down into its component parts. Then you can look at each sentence, clause, and modifier to see how each relates to the other.

Before explicating a provision, copy, paste, and save it into a new document. Then, begin breaking down the provision by separating each sentence from the others and having each sentence start on a different line. Number each of the sentences. If you have long sentences, you may also need to break them down by pressing Enter before any introductory prepositional clause so that it appears on its own line. Also, find each compound and series, move each item to a line by itself, and indent it. As your skill in explicating improves, you may decide not to tabulate every item in a compound or series, but prefer to do it in the beginning. Show the relationship of the items in the compound or series to the preceding language by indenting each item, just as you would if you were formatting or tabulating. If a word or phrase qualifies the compound or series, put it on a separate line. Finally, put each proviso and exception on a separate line.

Here is a provision before and after explication:

Example 1A—Explicate the Provision

Before: **Maintenance and Location.** The Lessee shall, at its own expense, maintain the Equipment in good operating condition and repair and protect the Equipment from deterioration other than normal wear and tear. Lessee shall not make any modification, alteration, or addition to the Equipment without the prior written consent of the Lessor, which shall not be unreasonably withheld, provided that no consent is required for engineering changes recommended by and made by the manufacturer; and shall keep the Equipment at the location shown in the Schedule, and shall not remove the Equipment without the prior written consent of Lessor. The Lessee shall, during the term of this Lease, at the Lessee's own cost, enter into and maintain in force a contract with the manufacturer or other acceptable maintenance company, covering the maintenance of the Equipment.

Example 1B—Explicate the Provision

After: **Maintenance and Location.**

1. The Lessee shall, at its own expense, maintain the Equipment in good operating condition and repair and protect the Equipment from deterioration other than normal wear and tear.
2. Lessee shall not make any modification, alteration, or addition to the Equipment without the prior written consent of the Lessor, which shall not be unreasonably withheld, provided that no consent is required for engineering changes recommended by and made by the manufacturer; shall keep the Equipment at the location shown in the Schedule, and shall not remove the Equipment without the prior written consent of Lessor.
3. The Lessee shall, during the term of this Lease, at its own cost, enter into and maintain in force a contract with the manufacturer or other acceptable maintenance company, covering the maintenance of the Equipment.

B. CREATE CLARITY THROUGH FORMAT

Once you explicate a provision, it becomes relatively easy to format. First, look at each sentence and decide whether the subject matter of another sentence is sufficiently related that the sentences should be combined to create a section or joined into one tabulated sentence. In addition, look at each sentence to decide whether it deals with only one subject. If it does not, then two sentences or sections may be appropriate. Then look at each indented item from a compound or series and decide whether it should be a subsection or joined with the rest of the sentence. If any indented items are preceded or followed by a qualifier, keep the qualifier on a separate line. Later, you will decide whether its placement creates ambiguity. For now, though, we will strictly adhere to the order of the six-step process. But as you become more proficient, you may decide to perform multiple steps simultaneously.

Applying this analysis to our example, we see that sentences 1 and 3 above both deal with maintenance of the equipment. So the redraft will put them together in one section. The second sentence, however, covers two unrelated topics: changes to the Equipment and location of the Equipment. Thus, two sections should be created from this sentence.

Now we will look at the indented items for each sentence and decide whether they should become subsections. The first sentence has two levels of indentation. The words *good operating condition* and *repair* should be rejoined with the preceding language. They both qualify *Equipment*, which precedes them in the sentence, and they are short, with no potential for ambiguity. Deciding whether to keep the remaining tabbed items as subsections is more difficult. Because the qualifier *other than normal wear and tear* follows the tabbed items, it creates ambiguity: Does the language qualify each of the tabbed items or only the second? Thus, you can see that even though we are not yet at the step of clarifying ambiguities, we still see them come up as we are determining how to format the provision. Here, the drafter must make a decision regarding what *other than normal wear and tear* qualifies. For the purposes of this example, we are going to say that it simply qualifies the second of the tabbed items, so we will keep it on the same line with that one. However, note that if you wanted *other than normal wear and tear* to qualify both subsections, you would have to move it to the lead-in language and make any necessary changes.

In the second sentence, *modification, alteration*, and *addition* need not be tabulated, as they are short. As for the other two indented items, we earlier decided that they should be in their own section. However, they are long enough that they should be tabulated in that new section. The last line, *without the prior written consent of the Lessor,* makes substantive sense only as an exception to the prohibition that precedes it. Therefore, the prohibition and the exception can be joined.

In the third sentence, neither set of indented items needs to be drafted as subsections, although that may be revisited when the sentence is moved to become a part of the first section.

Here is the reformatted provision using Numbering System 1, discussed in more detail in Chapter 23 on page 350:

Example 2A—Reformatted Creating Clarity Through Format

7.1 Maintenance. The Lessee shall, at its own expense,

(a) maintain the Equipment in good operating condition and repair and
(b) protect the Equipment from deterioration, other than normal wear and tear.

The Lessee shall, during the term of this Lease, at its own cost, enter into and maintain in force a contract with the manufacturer or other acceptable maintenance company, covering the maintenance of the Equipment.

7.2 Alterations and Additions. Lessee shall not make any modification, alteration, or addition to the Equipment without the prior written consent of the Lessor, which shall not be unreasonably withheld, provided that no consent is required for engineering changes recommended by and made by the manufacturer.

7.3 Equipment's Location. The Lessee shall

(a) keep the Equipment at the location shown in the Schedule and
(b) not remove the Equipment without the prior written consent of Lessor.

Note that Section 7.1 can be further improved when it comes to formatting by breaking it down into more subsections and using list format tabulation. In Example 2B below, you will notice that the introductory language in 7.1(a) includes *the following* and signals that the items in each tabulated subsection are cumulative, as the Guidelines for List Format Tabulation note in Chapter 23 on page 347. Furthermore, the verbs *shall* and *do* are kept together. Also note, in Example 2B, we break Section 7.3 into two subsections, with a full sentence in each. With only *The Lessee* as your introductory language, it makes more sense to include it in each subsection as the subject of each sentence, which will make it much easier for the reader to follow.

Here is the reformatted provision with these additional formatting changes:

Example 2B—Reformatted Creating Clarity Through Format

7.1 Maintenance.

(a) The Lessee shall, at its own expense, do both of the following:
   (i) The Lessee shall maintain the Equipment in good operating condition and repair.
   (ii) The Lessee shall protect the Equipment from deterioration, other than normal wear and tear.
(b) The Lessee shall, during the term of this Lease, at the Lessee's own cost, enter into and maintain in force a contract with the manufacturer or other acceptable maintenance company, covering the maintenance of the Equipment.

7.2 Alterations and Additions. Lessee shall not make any modification, alteration, or addition to the Equipment without the prior written consent of the Lessor, which shall not be unreasonably withheld, provided that no consent is required for engineering changes recommended by and made by the manufacturer.

7.3 Equipment's Location.

(a) The Lessee shall keep the Equipment at the location shown in the Schedule.
(b) The Lessee shall not remove the Equipment without the prior written consent of Lessor.

C. CREATE CLARITY THROUGH SENTENCE STRUCTURE

To create clarity through sentence structure, apply the rules that you learned in Chapter 24 as well as other rules that you have learned that deal with sentence structure. For example, redraft nominalizations, place exceptions after the general rule, use the active voice, use defined terms, and use possessives.

Let's look at each of the sections of the Example 2B provision. In Section 7.1(a), *at its own expense* appears in the middle of the verb, violating the rule that a sentence's core words should be kept together. That can be corrected by moving that phrase to the beginning or end of that introductory language. In this case, we will move it to the beginning. Section 7.1(b) has the same issue, and the words *shall enter into and maintain in force* should be kept together. In addition, *during the term of this Lease* is not needed. That phrase can be deleted. The remainder of the sentence is wordy and should be made more concise.

Section 7.2 violates the three-line rule. This fix is easy. The *proviso* can be turned into its own sentence and rewritten to omit *provided.* In the new first sentence, three changes must be made. First, the nominalizations *modification, alteration,* and *addition* must be changed to their verb forms. Second, *without the prior written consent of the Lessor* must be redrafted so that it uses the possessive. Third, *which shall not be unreasonably withheld* must be changed from the passive to the active voice. In addition, *recommended by and made by the manufacturer* must be changed from the passive to the active voice.

In Section 7.3(b), *without the prior written consent of the Lessor* must be changed so that it uses the possessive form of *Lessor.*

Here is the redraft after making changes to create clarity through sentence structure:

Example 3—Redrafting for Clarity Through Better Sentence Structure

7.1 Maintenance.

(a) At its own expense, the Lessee shall do both of the following:
   (i) The Lessee shall maintain the Equipment in good operating condition and repair.
   (ii) The Lessee shall protect the Equipment from deterioration, other than normal wear and tear.
(b) At its own cost, the Lessee shall enter into and maintain in force a contract with the manufacturer or other acceptable maintenance company.

7.2 Alterations and Additions. Lessee shall not modify, alter, or add to the Equipment without the Lessor's prior written consent, which the Lessor shall not unreasonably withhold. Despite the previous sentence, no consent is required for engineering changes that the manufacturer recommends and makes.

7.3 Equipment's Location.

(a) The Lessee shall keep the Equipment at the location shown in the Schedule.
(b) The Lessee shall not remove the Equipment without Lessor's prior written consent.

D. CLARIFY AMBIGUITIES

There are various issues relating to ambiguity that need to be addressed in Example 3:

- Section 7.1(a) and (b) seem inconsistent with each other. Section 7.1(a) requires the Lessee to maintain the Equipment, while Section 7.1(b) requires the Lessee to enter into a maintenance agreement so that someone else can maintain the equipment. One way to reconcile the two would be to state that the covenant in (b) is in furtherance of the one in (a).

- Section 7.1(a) and (b) do not *say the same thing in the same way*. Section 7.1(a) uses the phrase *at its own expense*, while the second sentence uses the phrase *at its own cost.* You would have to make the decision of which one to use, depending on a number of factors, such as how you are using *expense* and *cost* in the rest of the agreement, what your client prefers, and what is common industry language. In this case, we will use *expense* going forward.

- An additional issue with not *saying the same thing in the same way* arises when we compare Section 7.2 to Section 7.3. Section 7.2 provides that the Lessor shall not unreasonably withhold their consent, while Section 7.3 does not have that limitation on the Lessor's granting of their consent. Before deciding on this redraft, you would need to consult with your client to find out whether a difference was intended.

- Section 7.3(a) refers to a schedule. To avoid any confusion, you should be more specific and state *in Schedule 7.3(a)* and include this schedule at the end of the agreement, along with the other schedules.

Here is the redraft after making changes to clarify ambiguities:

Example 4—Redrafting to Clarify Ambiguities

7.1 Maintenance.

(a) At its own expense, the Lessee shall do both of the following:
  (i) The Lessee shall maintain the Equipment in good operating condition and repair.
  (ii) The Lessee shall protect the Equipment from deterioration, other than normal wear and tear.
(b) At its own expense and in furtherance of its obligations in Section 7.1(a), the Lessee shall enter into and maintain in force a contract with the manufacturer or other acceptable maintenance company.

7.2 Alterations and Additions. Lessee shall not modify, alter, or add to the Equipment without the Lessor's prior written consent, which the Lessor shall not unreasonably withhold. Despite the previous sentence, no consent is required for engineering changes that the manufacturer recommends and makes.

7.3 Equipment's Location.

(a) The Lessee shall keep the Equipment at the location shown in **Schedule 7.3(a)**.

(b) The Lessee shall not remove the Equipment without the Lessor's prior written consent[, which Lessor shall not unreasonably withhold].

E. ROOT OUT LEGALESE AND CLEAN UP THE LANGUAGE

When performing this step, eliminate as much legalese as possible. In addition, clean up any language problems that you have not already fixed.

This sample provision did not have much legalese. The only triplet in the provision is found in Section 7.2: *modify, alter, or add. Modify* and *alter* are synonyms, but *add* arguably is not. If the original equipment is left unchanged, but a new piece of equipment is added to it, that addition, in this business, might not be considered an alteration.

The provision's defined terms, *Lessor* and *Lessee*, are problematic. As discussed in Chapter 14 on page 163 regarding definitions, many readers find it difficult to read contracts with defined terms ending in *or* and *ee*. Alternative defined terms might be *Owner* and *Renter*. If the owner regularly leases equipment, it might nonetheless prefer to retain the traditional defined terms. In either event, the article *the* does not always precede *Lessor* and *Lessee*. The rewrite must use—or not use—*the* consistently. In this case, we have added *the* in front of *Lessee* (now *Renter*) at the beginning of Section 7.2, and in front of *Lessor* (now *Owner*) at the end of Section 7.3(b).

To further clarify the provision and be consistent in your use of defined terms, change the two instances of *At its own expense* in Section 7.1(a) and (b) to *At the Renter's expense*. Also, change *its obligations* in Section 7.1(b) to *the Renter's obligations*. Note that there are drafters that would not stop here and would continue to break down these phrases to make sure that they are drafted in the active voice, such as *The Renter shall pay for ___*.

Also, both Sections 7.2 and 7.3 provide for *prior written consent*. If the general provision on notices requires notices to be in writing, then *written* should be deleted.

> *Example 5—Replacing Lessor and Lessee with Owner and Renter and Cleaning up the Language*
>
> **7.1 Maintenance.**
>
> (a) At the Renter's own expense, the Renter shall do both of the following:
>> (i) The Renter shall maintain the Equipment in good operating condition and repair.
>>
>> (ii) The Renter shall protect the Equipment from deterioration, other than normal wear and tear.
>
> (b) At the Renter's own expense and in furtherance of the Renter's obligations in Section 7.1(a), the Renter shall enter into and maintain in force a contract with the manufacturer or other acceptable maintenance company.
>
> **7.2 Alterations and Additions.** The Renter shall not alter or add to the Equipment without the Owner's prior written consent, which the Owner shall not unreasonably withhold. Despite the previous sentence, no consent is required for engineering changes that the manufacturer recommends and makes.
>
> **7.3 Equipment's Location.**
>
> (a) The Renter shall keep the Equipment at the location shown in **Schedule 7.3(a)**.
>
> (b) The Renter shall not remove the Equipment without the Owner's prior written consent[, which the Owner shall not unreasonably withhold].

F. CHECK SUBSTANCE

Checking substance is the final step of the six-step process. At this stage, you must step back and look at the redrafted provision and confirm that it accurately states the business deal. You may have discovered earlier in the process that the provision was incorrect. Correcting it when you discover an error makes sense. That way, the other changes can work with the new substance. Also, use this step as an opportunity to see if anything else in the provision must be changed. Some changes do not fall neatly into one of the steps, but they must still be made.

For our purposes, we will assume that the provision conforms with the business deal. One point that might be raised with the client is a standards issue. Section 7.1(b) ends with the statement that the maintenance company must be *acceptable*. Presumably, that means *acceptable to the Owner.* If representing the Renter, you might suggest changing that standard to *reasonably acceptable.* At the very least, you would want to clarify this standard.

II. EXERCISES

A. Exercise 28A: Deconstruct Provisions with the Six-Step Process

Apply the six-step process to the following provisions:

1. **Assignment.** No assignment or delegation of the rights, duties, or obligations of this Agreement shall be made by either party except as provided herein without the express written approval of a duly authorized representative of the other party; provided, however, that the Company may assign any or all of its rights and obligations hereunder to a wholly owned subsidiary of the Company; and provided further that the Company may delegate certain of its duties hereunder to ABC Healthcare Systems, Inc.

2. **Use of Mark on Invoices, etc.** The use of the Mark by Licensee on invoices, order forms, stationery, and related material and in advertising in telephone or other directory listings is permitted only upon Licensor's prior written approval of the format in which the Mark is to be so used, the juxtaposition of the Mark with other words and phrases, and the content of the copy prior to the initial such use of the Mark and prior to any material change therein, which approval shall not be unreasonably withheld and shall be granted or denied within ten (10) business days of the submission of such format; provided, however, that such use of the Mark is only in conjunction with the sale of Licensed Items pursuant to this Agreement and further provided that should Licensor require a change in such format due to a revision, change, or modification by Licensor of the Mark, Licensor shall provide Licensee with reasonable notice of any such change or modification of the Mark in order to afford Licensee a reasonable period of time to revise and substitute invoices, order forms, stationery or other material reflecting the new Mark and shall permit Licensee to use, until the earlier of six months or depletion, such existing invoices, order forms, stationery, or other material without objection.

CHAPTER TWENTY-NINE

Summary of Drafting Clearly and Unambiguously

The following chart summarizes the material in Chapters 22 through 28. Reading it does not replace reading the chapters. Use it as a handy, quick reference tool.

CHAPTER	TOPIC	DRAFTING GUIDANCE
Chapter 22: Legalese (page 331)	Introduction	▪ Legalese remained the norm until 1975, when Citibank lawyers rewrote their consumer promissory note and reconceived how consumer contracts should be written. ▪ These changes led to a new style of contract drafting, known as "plain English." ▪ Some states even mandate by statute that plain English be used in consumer contracts.
	Formal and Archaic Words	▪ Do not use formal and archaic words, like "hereunder" and those listed on page 332. ▪ Use acceptable alternatives to make the contract more straightforward and less ambiguous. ▪ Consider including an interpretive provision in the definitions section or with the general provisions, like the one on page 332. ▪ It is more common to find legalese in longer, commercial agreements between more sophisticated parties and in precedents that drafters have been using for a long time. ▪ It is also very common to see "Whereas" introducing each sentence of the recitals or background section.
	Couplets and Triplets	▪ Contracts are often full of couplets and triplets that are redundant. ▪ Most couplets and triplets reflect our linguistic heritage and not legal distinctions. ▪ See examples of triplets and couplets not to use on pages 335 to 336.

CHAPTER	TOPIC	DRAFTING GUIDANCE
	Pretentious and Verbose Expressions	▪ See pages 336 to 337 for examples of expressions you should not use and of suggested replacements for them.
Chapter 23: Clarity Through Format (page 339)	Sections and Subsections	▪ By using a greater number of shorter sections, a contract becomes easier to read. ▪ Consider separating each subsection from the next with white space and adding a heading to each subsection to signal its substance.

	Tabulation	▪ Tabulation is a type of formatting where a long sentence is broken into two or more additional subsections that are conceptually related.
		▪ Tabulation reduces the length of the contract and aids the reader by showing more clearly how the items are related.
		▪ Each subsection is indented and separated from the other by white space.
		▪ To be able to use tabulation, the subject matter of the sentences should be related.
		▪ Usually, the following are good candidates for tabulation:
		  ▪ Any sentence with a compound or a series is a candidate for tabulation.
		  ▪ Any sentence that is three lines or longer—the **three-line rule.**
		▪ Do not tabulate simply because there is a series.
		▪ Avoid concluding language at the end of your provision that applies to each tabulated section.

	Guidelines for Both Sentence and List Format Tabulation	1. Choose the right format for tabulation.
		  ▪ In the **sentence format,** each tabulated subsection creates a full sentence when joined with the introductory language.
		  ▪ In the **list format**, the introductory language is a complete sentence, and each tabulated subsection is part of a list. A strong clue that a list format is appropriate is if the introductory language includes some form of the word follow.
		2. Use parallel drafting.
		  ▪ This means that the grammatical structure of each of the tabulated sentences should be the same so that each tabulated subsection begins in the same way (e.g., a verb in the present tense) and continues with similar items.
		  ▪ In the sentence format, you can check by joining the introductory language and the language of each subsection to create a coherent, grammatically correct sentence.

CHAPTER	TOPIC	DRAFTING GUIDANCE
	Guidelines for Sentence Format Tabulation	■ Use the sentence format for tabulation when the introductory language and the tabulated subsections form a complete, grammatical sentence. ■ Include in the introductory language all the words common to each tabulated subsection. ■ Punctuate the introductory language as you would if the sentence were untabulated. ■ Begin each tabulated subsection with a lowercase letter. ■ End each tabulated subsection with whatever punctuation would be used if the sentence were untabulated. ■ See examples on page 347.
	Guidelines for List Format Tabulation	■ Draft the introductory language so that it includes the phrase *as follows* or *the following* or otherwise incorporates that concept and end it with a colon. ■ Draft the introductory language, if appropriate, so that it signals whether the items in each tabulated subsection are cumulative or alternative. ■ Begin each tabulated subsection with a capital letter and end it with a period. ■ Do not put *and* or *or* after the next-to-last subsection. ■ See examples on page 348.

	Multilevel and Double Tabulation	■ Some sentences are sufficiently complex that they require more than one level of tabulation, which we refer to as **multilevel tabulation**.
		  ■ When drafting a multilevel tabulated sentence, indent each subordinate level five more spaces than the previous level so that the reader can see the subordinate relationship between one level and the next.
		  ■ In establishing the relative relationship between the levels, make each subsection parallel with its subordinate subsection to prevent a confusing or ambiguous provision.
		■ **Double tabulation** occurs in a sentence that has two or more independent sets of subsections at the same level. You should avoid using it, and, instead, further break down the provision.

	Numbering Systems	■ Use a simple, easy-to-read numbering system with an outline format. ■ Three common numbering systems are discussed in this section. See examples starting on page 351.
	Headings, Table of Contents, and Typography	■ Use headings that accurately describe the provisions' contents to make your contract easier to read. ■ Create a table of contents for long contracts to find provisions more easily. ■ Typographers classify fonts into two types: **serif** and **sans serif**. A serif font has extra small lines at the ends of the horizontal and vertical strokes of a letter, while sans serif fonts are simpler without the small lines.

CHAPTER	TOPIC	DRAFTING GUIDANCE
Chapter 24: Clarity Through Sentence Structure (page 361)	Sentence Core	■ Every sentence has core words: the subject, verb, and object. ■ Keep the core words next to each other. ■ Reduce the number of words before the core words.
	Draft in Short Sentences and Short Before Long	■ Any sentence longer than three lines may need to be redrafted into two or more sentences. ■ Put short phrases before long phrases. ■ Put the short phrase as the subject in a declaration.
	Word Choice Affecting Sentence Structure	■ Use the active voice. ■ Use parallel drafting. ■ Use the possessive. ■ Avoid the nominalization of a word, which is the conversion of a verb into a phrase that includes the noun form of the verb. For example, use *expires* and *notifies* (the verbs) instead of *expiration* and *notification* (the nominalizations). ■ Avoid using *there is* and *there are*.

Chapter 25: Ambiguity (page 371)	Ambiguity and Vagueness	■ **Ambiguity** refers to the possibility of a word or provision in a contract being interpreted in two or more possible ways.
		■ You should always draft clearly and avoid any ambiguity, since ambiguity can lead to conflict and be expensive.
		■ Types of ambiguity:
		  ■ **Semantic ambiguity** arises because a word has multiple dictionary meanings.
		  ■ **Syntactic ambiguity** occurs when it is unclear what a word or phrase refers to or modifies.
		  ■ **Contextual ambiguity** occurs when two provisions are inconsistent.
		■ A word or a phrase is **vague** if its meaning varies depending on the context or if its parameters are not plainly delineated. For example, *reasonable* is vague; what is reasonable in one context may be wholly unreasonable in another.
		■ Vagueness is neither inherently good nor bad. It depends on what concept best expresses the parties' agreement and on what best protects your client or advances his interests.
		■ Drafters sometimes choose to go with language that is vague, especially if they do not have a lot of time to draft a contract.
		■ No matter what, make sure to draft important provisions as specifically and precisely as possible.

	Ambiguities from *And* and *Or*	■ Provisions that include *and*, *or*, or *and* and *or* often create ambiguity. ■ *Or* can be used **disjunctively** (meaning you have a choice between two or more items) or **inclusively** (meaning you do not have to choose between one or the other and the items exist concurrently).

CHAPTER	TOPIC	DRAFTING GUIDANCE
		■ *And* can be used **conjunctively** (meaning that it joins two or more things) or can have the same meaning as the inclusive *or*. ■ Using *and* and *or* in the same sentence can easily create ambiguities, but you can use tabulation to clarify the provision. ■ Do not use *and/or* in your drafting because it has usually several possible meanings.
	Ambiguities from Sentence Structure	■ Whenever a modifier (e.g., an adjective or prepositional phrase describing something else) follows a compound or a series, an ambiguity may be created because there is an issue of whether the qualifier modifies each item in the compound or series or only the closest item. The grammatical rule that is applied in these situations is known as **the rule of the last antecedent**. According to this rule, the qualifier qualifies the noun or phrase that immediately precedes it. ■ Ambiguity can arise if two or more adjectives or adjectival phrases modify the same noun. Therefore, when using multiple adjectives, repeat the nouns as necessary to create clarity and use tabulation to simplify and clarify your provisions. ■ Sentences that end with a *because* clause are often ambiguous, so redraft the sentence to clarify the intent. ■ Ambiguity can occur when one prepositional phrase immediately follows another because it is not clear whether the second prepositional phrase modifies only the immediately preceding prepositional phrase or the preceding prepositional phrase and that which came before it, so redraft the provision.

	Say the Same Thing in the Same Way	■ Because a change of a word can change the meaning of a contract provision, a cardinal principle of good drafting is to **say the same thing in the same way**. If you do not, a court may hold that the difference in wording is substantive, even if sloppy drafting caused it. Here are some examples:
		  ■ In acquisition and financing agreements, representations and warranties and covenants often deal with the same subject matter and the standards should probably be the same or there should be a clear reason why they are not.
		  ■ If there is more than one agreement involved in a transaction, they should probably have the same standards.
		  ■ When creating a provision or a document based on a statute, say exactly what the statute says.

CHAPTER	TOPIC	DRAFTING GUIDANCE
	Dates, Time, and Age	■ When measuring years: ■ Use the concept of an anniversary date. ■ Refer to calendar years only if from and including January 1 to December 31 of the same year. ■ Check for the consequences of leap years. ■ Confirm that a future date is a Business Day or provide that the event must occur on the next Business Day. ■ When measuring months, determine whether parties intend calendar months, 30-day periods beginning on any day, or a period beginning on a specific date and ending on the day in the next month minus 1. ■ When measuring weeks, determine whether the parties intend a seven-day period beginning Sunday to Saturday, a seven-day period beginning on a specific day, or a five-day period from Monday to Friday. ■ When measuring days, determine which are the first and last days, whether days are limited to business days, whether a time of day should be specified. ■ Think through holidays, consider adding interpretive provisions, and possibly define Business Day. ■ When stating time of day, include AM or PM and do not use 12:00 AM or PM (e.g., use 11:59 PM or 12:01 AM). ■ When referring to a person's age, state the age as of which a right begins or refer to the celebration of a particular birthday.
	Plurals and Provisos	■ Whenever possible, contracts should be drafted using singular nouns and singular possessives. ■ A **proviso** is "[i]n drafting, a provision that begins with the words *provided that* and supplies a condition, exception, or addition."[1] ■ Try not to use provisos. ■ When faced with a provision that typically might be handled with a proviso, do the following: 1. Determine whether you need the proviso or whether you can address the drafting issue in a different way. 2. If you do need the proviso, determine the proviso's purpose (stating a condition, stating an exception, or adding additional material). 3. Redraft the proviso, but use the alternative, appropriate language depending on your purpose: ■ To state a condition, use *if/then*, *must*, or *it is a condition that*. Consider adding an interpretive provision, particularly if you use *must*. ■ To state an exception to a rule, use *except that*, *but*, or *however*.

---

1. *Proviso, Black's Law Dictionary* (11th ed. 2019).

CHAPTER	TOPIC	DRAFTING GUIDANCE
		▪ To add additional material, use a new sentence or subsection or a connective such as *furthermore* or *and*. 4. If a provision has more than one proviso, determine how each one relates to the other and to the main purpose of the provision. Then use formatting to establish how they relate to each other. Depending on the provision, tabulation, multiple sentences, multiple sections, or multiple subsections may be appropriate.
Chapter 26: Drafting Numbers and Financial Provisions (page 403)	How to Draft Provisions Using Numbers	▪ You should write the numbers one through ten in words and the numbers higher than ten in Arabic numerals (e.g., 11, 338). ▪ Many drafters have stopped drafting numbers in both words and Arabic numerals, but they continue to draft dollar amounts both ways. ▪ The better approach is to *draft currency amounts using only numerals* and to proofread what you have written. ▪ Omit the last two digits of any currency amount that has no cents.
	How to Draft Mathematical Formulas, Using a Chart	▪ Signal the four basic mathematical operation (addition, subtraction, multiplication, and division), fractions, and percentages by using mathematical terms to avoid any ambiguity that might arise from the use of common expressions. ▪ If calculating a result requires more than one mathematical operation, indicate the order in which the operations are to occur by using parentheses. ▪ You can draft a formula in three ways (see examples from pages 408 to 409): 1. **Using an algebraic equation.** This method defines each component of a formula and then specifies the operations and their order using mathematical notation. 2. **Using narration and tabulation.** This method expresses the algebraic equation in words and describes each component of the formula and each mathematical operation in sequence. 3. **Using the narrative cookbook approach.** This method directs the reader to perform mathematical operations in the correct sequence.[2] The narrative cookbook approach is probably the least well known of the methods to state financial formulas but the easiest to draft and follow. ▪ At times, you may want to use a chart or spreadsheet in a contract to make the agreement between the parties more visual and easier to understand (e.g. sliding scale cost structure).

---

2. *See* F. Reed Dickerson, *The Fundamentals of Legal Drafting* 202 (2d ed., Little, Brown & Co. 1986).

CHAPTER	TOPIC	DRAFTING GUIDANCE
	How to Draft Provisions Involving Financial Statement Concepts	■ Many contract provisions that require calculations use accounting concepts and practices. ■ GAAP is the acronym for **generally accepted accounting principles**. The principles and practices codified in GAAP guide the preparation of a company's financial statements and how it maintains its books and records. All public companies, as Securities and Exchange Commission (SEC) registrants, are required to report their results using GAAP, and many private companies do so because their lenders or shareholders require it. This agreed-on set of principles and methods benefits users of financial statements by making companies comparable to one another and more transparent to a variety of users. GAAP is a "common language" for communicating financial results. ■ GAAP is an evolving set of principles and practices. ■ GAAP allows different accounting treatments for the same event. GAAP's flexibility in permitting users to choose among alternative acceptable methods can help or harm your client, depending on whom you represent. ■ A non-GAAP principle or calculation may better protect your client. ■ When negotiating the accounting-related provisions in a context that relies on calculations based on balance sheet accounts, a lawyer and client must track through the balance sheet and think through on a line item basis whether any one or more of the accounts requires special treatment. ■ Revenues and earnings formulas appear in a wide variety of agreements (e.g., purchase price provision in acquisition agreement, compensation provision in employment agreement). The amount being paid or received can be significantly affected by the accounting choices made in the documents and who controls the accounting. Draft carefully.
Chapter 27: Other Drafting Considerations (page 419)	Gender-Neutral Drafting and The Cascade Effect	■ Do not use pronouns—instead, replace the pronouns with the defined terms used to refer to the relevant party or parties. ■ Contract provisions should use gender-neutral terms, such as *firefighters*, *police officers*, and *workers*. ■ The **cascade effect** occurs when the drafting of a business term in one provision requires a change in, or the addition of, a second business term.

CHAPTER	TOPIC	DRAFTING GUIDANCE
	Exceptions	■ Exceptions are signaled in several ways: *except*, *except as otherwise provided*, *other than*, *unless*, and *provided*. All these signals, other than *provided* and derivations of *provided*, such as *provided, however*, are acceptable. ■ As a general rule, when drafting a provision that includes an exception, put the rule first, and then the exception. ■ Although you should generally put the exception at the end of a provision, it may work better at the beginning of a provision if it is short and quickly alerts the reader to the exception or it provides helpful context. ■ If a provision and its exception result in a long sentence, consider breaking it into subsections. Put the general rule in the first subsection and the exception in the next. The captions for the subsections should signal their content: *General Rule* and *Exception*. ■ If a rule and its exception are in separate sentences or subsections, their relationship should be explicitly stated in one of the two sentences or subsections. ■ As often as possible, put all the exceptions together at the end of the sentence and, if necessary to enhance clarity, tabulate them. ■ The phrase *except as otherwise* provided signals an exception elsewhere in the contract.
	Other Common Words and Phrases	■ See this section for how to best use different related words and phrases, such as: *as in effect from time to time* and *as amended from time to time*; *as the case may be*; *continually and continuously*; *deem* and *not to be deemed to be*; *guaranty* and *guarantee*; *include* and *including*; *notwithstanding anything to the contrary*; *regardless of whether or not* and *whether*; *respectively*; *subject to*; and *notwithstanding*. ■ Drafters tend to like using the words *include* and *including* often. There are several different lines of case law relating to the words *include* and *including* that can affect how your provision is interpreted. For example, *including* can be restrictive or can be a term of enlargement, and *include* can signal that illustrations follow. So be more specific and consistent when you draft using such words, and consider adding an interpretive provision.

CHAPTER	TOPIC	DRAFTING GUIDANCE
	Some Canons of Construction	■ **Canons of construction** are rules or guidelines that judges use to help them interpret a legal, written document, such as a contract or statute. ■ There are many canons of construction, but here, we introduce just some of the more common ones: *ejusdem generis*, *expression unius est exclusion alterius*, and *contra proferentem*. ■ ***Ejusdem generis*** is a Latin phrase that means "of the same kind or class." Courts apply this canon of construction where a list of specific items concludes with general language intended to expand that list. In determining how that list should be expanded, courts limit the breadth of the general language by finding that it embraces only other items of the same kind or class as those already listed. The preceding specific words limit the scope of the general language. ■ ***Expressio unius est exclusio alterius*** is another Latin phrase, which means "the expression of one thing excludes the other."[3] When used as a canon of construction, it limits a provision to what it states expressly. ■ ***Contra proferentem*** states that a contract should be construed against the party who drafted it.
Chapter 28: Deconstructing Complex Provisions (page 437)	The Six-Step Process	■ Often, provisions are so dense that you cannot be sure of their substantive effect. To understand them, you need to take them apart, reorganize them, and clean up the language. ■ Deconstruct a provision using the six steps: 1. **Explicate:** Break down the provision by separating each sentence and phrase and start each one on a different line. 2. **Create clarity through format:** Use tabulation, break down sentences into subsections, and other actions. 3. **Create clarity through sentence structure:** Keep core words together, redraft nominalizations, place exceptions after the general rule, use active voice, use defined terms, use possessives, and other actions. 4. **Clarify ambiguities:** Reconcile inconsistent provisions, check your modifiers, say the same thing the same way, and other actions. 5. **Root out legalese and clean up the language:** Eliminate formal and archaic words, take out unnecessary couplets and triplets, improve formatting, check your defined terms, and other actions. 6. **Check substance:** Step back and look at the redrafted provision and confirm that it accurately states the business deal.

---

3. *See generally* Clifton Williams, *Expressio Unius Est Exclusio Alterius,* 15 Marq. L. Rev. 191 (1931).

Putting a Contract Together and Important Considerations

CHAPTER THIRTY

Adding Value to the Deal

I. INTRODUCTION

Drafting contracts is more than translating the business deal into contract concepts; making sure that you include each part (e.g., preamble, recitals, words of agreement, action sections); and writing clear, unambiguous contract provisions. Drafting requires one to understand the transaction from a client's business perspective and to add value to the deal. **Understanding the contract from the client's perspective** means knowing what the client wants to achieve and the risks that they want to avoid. **Adding value to the deal** means finding and resolving business issues that need to be addressed between the parties to ensure the best possible relationship between them and create the best possible outcomes for your client.

In an informal survey, partners were asked how they identified business issues that needed to be addressed. We found that partners learned by experience how to spot these business issues. The following are some of the responses from partners:

- "Identifying business issues requires a sixth sense."
- "A business issue is any issue you find that the client should resolve."
- "I know one when I see one."

Although you will find no substitute for experience, this chapter proposes a framework that will help you learn how more experienced practitioners think, so that you can better identify business issues and add value to future transactions in which you are involved from the beginning.

In Chapter 2, we discussed how you must learn and understand the key business terms that are important to your client and those to which the parties have already agreed. We have already talked in Parts A, B, and C about how you must look at each specific issue agreed to—the terms of the deal—and use the contract concepts to translate them into contract language in all the different parts of the contract. Now, we need to go one step further. To identify business issues that are not yet obvious and that you may still need to address, you will need to analyze the following five areas:

- Money
- Risk
- Control
- Standards
- Endgame

The subsequent sections of this chapter discuss each of these areas, show how they manifest themselves in transactions, and share how you can add value. At the end, you can work through a series of exercises in which you have to apply this framework and examine each of these five areas in the context of specific provisions to which the parties have agreed. You will see that by focusing on these five areas and applying them to specific agreed-upon points from the clients, you will be able to identify even more business issues that you will need to address and draft better provisions that anticipate some of the possible problems that could arise. This framework with the five areas will help you get started, but, with experience, you will be able to better identify business issues and add more value to transactions.

II. MONEY

The first area that we will look at to identify business issues and add value is money. Generally, money is important in a transaction, whether it is an amount to be paid or received, the timing of payments, credit risk, issues relating to payment formulas, transaction expenses, and accounting and tax issues. Note that endgame scenarios also usually involve money, which will be discussed further in Section VI of this chapter, on page 469.

As we discussed in Chapter 16 on page 211, whenever you draft a provision dealing with the payment of money in any part of the contract, you should always answer the following questions: *who, what, when, where, why, how,* and *how much?* You already easily add value to any transaction by making sure that the answers to these questions are clear in your provision. Therefore, include the answers to these questions in every provision having to do with money and be specific about the answer to each of these in your drafting.

In the subsections that follow, you will learn of other ways to add value when thinking through and drafting provisions dealing with money.

A. AMOUNT TO BE PAID OR RECEIVED

Usually, the first money issue to consider is whether a client is entitled to receive more money or to pay less. Although clients generally negotiate and agree on the amount, lawyers can often add value because of their deal-specific expertise or experience with similar transactions. For example, perhaps your client, a major bank, wants to purchase a corporate jet. The client's expertise is finance, not the purchase and sale of airplanes, which is your specialty. If the client consults you before they negotiate the purchase price of the plane, you may be able to add value by explaining that the plane's proposed purchase price exceeds current market value because of the excess number of planes on the market.

In addition, you may be able to identify other types of consideration in the transaction, whether monetary or not, due to your experience with similar types of transactions. For example, buyers and sellers may value a seller's business differently. This is especially true for a new business. The seller is sure that their company has great value and the potential to be a leader in an important future market, and the buyer certainly hopes so, but they question the seller's valuation because the business has no track record of profitability. To bridge the difference in valuation, whether you represent the seller or the buyer, you may suggest that the buyer can pay the seller an amount at closing and additional payments in the future, if certain goals are met. The parties will determine the amount paid in the future based on a formula tied to the business's performance after the acquisition, which is known as an **earnout**.[1] Therefore, as you determine the amount to be paid or received in a transaction going forward, consider whether any of the payment should be contingent, as in the case of an earnout, and try to identify other types of consideration, whether monetary or not.

B. TIMING OF PAYMENTS

Apart from analyzing the amount to be paid, think through any issues with respect to the timing of the payments. Clients usually want to pay later but receive money sooner. The reason for this is **the time value of money**,[2] which is an important concept in finance that money is worth more now rather than later. The longer a client has the money, the longer that money can be invested and earning more money. Also, the money may buy less in the future due to inflation, and you are not sure that you are going to get the money until you actually get it since something could happen beforehand.

If your client must pay the other party, ask whether they can spread out the payments over time or whether the other party will give your client a discount for immediate payment. If the other side must pay your client, negotiate for receipt of the payment as soon as possible. If the other side objects, find out from your client whether they could benefit from an immediate but smaller payment. For example, if the client receives the funds immediately, they may be able to invest in a new deal.

C. CREDIT RISK

Credit risk is always a business issue when the other party is obligated to pay your client in the future. Although the other party may have a lot of cash when the parties make their deal, they may be less strong when payment is due. Therefore, whenever your client has agreed to receive a delayed payment, consider whether the risk of a payment default is significant. If it is, then negotiate a mechanism to secure the payment, as discussed in more detail in Section III.C, Methods to Mitigate Risk of this chapter.

D. ISSUES RELATING TO PAYMENT FORMULAS

Parties often use a formula to determine a contract's consideration. For example, formulas are used to calculate the following:

- Compensation provisions in employment agreements (e.g., salary, commission, and other contingent payments)
- Royalty provisions in license and franchise agreements
- Buyout provisions in partnership and stockholder agreements
- Purchase price adjustment provisions in acquisition agreements

When reviewing a formula, begin by analyzing whether the formula is neutral or whether it favors your client or the other party in some way.

The case of *Buchwald v. Paramount Pictures Corp.* is a good example of a flawed formula for one of the parties in the transaction, but presumably ideal for the other party.[3] In that transaction, Alain Bernheim, the producer of *Coming*

---

1. For a more detailed discussion of earnouts, *see* Lou R. Kling & Eileen T. Nugent, *Negotiated Acquisitions of Companies, Subsidiaries and Divisions* vol. 2, § 17.01 (Law Journal Press 1992).

2. For a more detailed discussion of the time value of money, *see* Terry Lloyd, Present Value Concepts and Applications, in *Accounting for Lawyers 1996: Using Financial Data in Legal Practice* 257 (PLI Course Handbook Series No. B-965, 1996).

3. *See Buchwald v. Paramount Pictures Corp.*, 1990 WL 357611 (Cal. Super. Jan. 8, 1990); *see also* Pierce O'Donnell & Dennis McDougal, *Fatal Subtraction: The Inside Story of Buchwald v. Paramount*, appendix B (Doubleday 1992).

to America, agreed that Paramount would pay him a percentage of the movie's net profits, in addition to a modest upfront fee. Bernheim expected the movie to be a success and anticipated that he could earn much more money by receiving a percentage of net profits rather than a one-time upfront fee.

The movie was a huge hit, and Bernheim was thrilled. Unfortunately, that happiness was short-lived: The studio reported that they lost money on the movie and Bernheim was entitled to no additional money. The problem stemmed from the way the studio accounted for the movie's expenses. The studio included as expenses not only the direct expenses of the movie, but also some of the studio's overhead expenses. Thus, Bernheim would have been far better off receiving a percentage of the movie's gross revenues—before any expenses were deducted. Alternatively, Bernheim and the studio could have agreed on how net profits would be calculated and which expenses would be deducted from gross profits to calculate the net profits.

Assuming that your client and the other party have agreed on a formula for calculating the payment amount, confirm that the formula is properly stated. Is any aspect or variable in the formula ambiguous? Is the formula as a whole ambiguous in any way? Be as specific as possible in drafting a formula.

Some of the most common drafting errors occur when crafting a formula, as previously discussed in Chapter 26 on page 403. To make certain that a formula works as intended, run multiple hypotheticals to see what answers are obtained when numbers are plugged into the formula. Be sure to include in the hypotheticals numbers far outside the range that the client expects. Calculations sometimes result in negative amounts, and the parties need to address what happens in that circumstance.

After running the numbers, send the hypotheticals to your client and other experts involved to make sure that they understand how the formula will work, both when the transaction succeeds and when it fails. (Clients do not like surprises.) Once your client approves the formula and hypotheticals, send them to the other side for their review and approval. With luck, this process will identify any differences at a time when they can be more easily discussed and resolved. As the final step in this process, with the approval of the clients, you may want to add the hypotheticals as an exhibit to the contract so they can better set forth and give examples of the parties' understanding of the formula at the time of contracting.

E. TRANSACTION EXPENSES

Parties do not always address the allocation of transaction expenses—especially at the preliminary stages of negotiation. Since these expenses sometimes can become larger than expected, you and your client should think through whether each party should pay their own expenses or whether the expenses should be shifted from one party to the other from the beginning or at a particular point in the transaction. Then you should make sure that you and/or your client has the discussion with the other side about the transaction expenses.

F. ACCOUNTING AND TAX ISSUES

The accounting and tax issues in a contract can be quite sophisticated. These issues may determine the structure of the transaction, and sometimes even whether the transaction can be done. If you do not have the background to address these issues, you *must* obtain the assistance of a qualified practitioner. For a more detailed discussion of accounting-related drafting issues, see Chapter 26 on page 411.

III. RISK

A. TYPES OF RISK

The second area that we will look at to identify business issues and add value is risk. As we have previously discussed, representations and warranties (Chapter 3) covenants (Chapter 4), and conditions (Chapter 6) are all risk allocation mechanisms.

In addition, risk can manifest itself in multiple other ways in a transaction, the following being just a few types of risk. First, with a contract, there is the possibility of your client having to deal with tort liability. Examples of tort liability include fraudulent inducement (being persuaded to sign an agreement because of fraudulent statements from the other side), product liability (the legal liability if a consumer is harmed by a product, if a product sold to consumers is involved), and tortious interference with a contract (when someone tries to interfere with a contract between you and another party).

Second, the provisions can create contract law risk. For example, a noncompetition provision could be unenforceable. Third, a contract can create statutory liability, such as liability under the securities laws. Fourth, credit risk can be inherent in the transaction, as discussed previously in this chapter. Finally, every transaction carries some kind of litigation risk, including inconsistencies in the facts and the law and the uncertainties of judges and juries.

B. EVALUATING THE RISK

Lawyers are terrific at identifying risks in a transaction. Law school is focused on preparing future lawyers to spot issues. However, if that is all you do as a drafter, you may end some deals before they have the chance to take off.

Determining the risks only begins a drafter's risk analysis. Next, the drafter must assess the probability that the risk will occur. In addition, they should try to quantify the risk and do a risk/reward analysis but note that they may need the client's assistance to complete such an analysis because they may not have all the business information they need. With this information, though, the client can evaluate the risk more completely and determine whether they want to take on all the risk, some of it, or none of it. For example, the client may decide not to elevate the matter to a business issue that needs to be discussed with the other side because they believe that the risk will probably not occur and the financial consequences would be relatively small. In that case, depending on the possible consequences from that issue, the client may be taking on the risk directly.

Alternatively, the client could decide that the benefits of the transaction do not justify the risk, even with a low probability of occurrence. In such a case, the client will want to bring up with the other side possible ways of offsetting the risk, such as by including a limitation on liability provision (see Chapter 17 on page 247) or an indemnification provision (see Chapter 32 on page 503), by restructuring the transaction, or by walking away from the deal.

Whether a risk develops into a business issue that needs to be raised or addressed in the contract in some way often depends on a client's willingness in general to take on risk. How comfortable is the client with taking risk? Is the client an entrepreneur ready to roll the dice, or is it a small, local bank willing to assume only minimal risks? That can sometimes already be an indication of what your client will want, but always make sure to check in with them on issues of risk.

C. METHODS TO MITIGATE RISK

Your reputation as a dealmaker often depends on your ability to resolve risk issues creatively. Although a transaction may require an innovative solution, you can often rely on the techniques discussed in this section: a third party taking a security interest (e.g., as co-obligor or guarantor), escrow agreements, indemnity agreements, letters of credit, insurance, or deal-specific methods.

1. Security Interest

If credit risk is the concern, one party can take a security interest in the other party's assets. If you use this technique, determine which assets are the most valuable and which will be the easiest to liquidate. Be sure that the security interest applies to these assets. As an alternative (or additional) technique for reducing credit risk, a third party's credit can be added to the credit of the party with the payment obligation. Typically, the third party will agree to serve either as a **co-obligor** (an additional party that must fulfill the obligations of one of the parties to the contract if not fulfilled) or as a **guarantor** (an additional party that guarantees to pay the amount owed by one of the parties in the contract). Of course, this additional party must be creditworthy.

2. Escrow Agreements

Escrows are another technique that parties use to lessen credit risk. To create an escrow, the parties deposit cash or other property with a neutral third party, who agrees to release it only in accordance with the terms of the escrow agreement. You can find out more about escrow agreements, including their use and some of the most important business issues dealing with them on the CasebookConnect Resources page and at www.aspenpublishing.com. We also saw an example of an escrow agreement in Chapter 14 on page 180.

3. Indemnity Agreements

In an indemnity agreement, as discussed in Chapter 17 on page 249, one party promises to pay the other party for certain losses, even if the indemnified party did not cause the loss. For example, when a lateral partner joins a firm, the firm generally indemnifies the lateral partner against any existing malpractice claims.

4. Letters of Credit

In a letter of credit transaction, a bank substitutes their credit for that of another party's credit. For example, imagine that a manufacturer in Italy wants to sell goods to a small company in New York but will not do so unless they can be assured of payment. To provide this assurance, the buyer arranges for a letter of credit under which a bank will pay the manufacturer on the fulfillment of certain conditions.

Typically, the conditions require that the manufacturer deliver documents to the bank indicating that the proper goods are being shipped. However, the bank does not undertake to inspect the goods; they *only* examine documents.[4] If the buyer wants an inspection of the goods, the buyer must arrange for a third party to inspect the goods and issue a certificate that the inspected goods were the proper items in the appropriate condition.

---

4. A letter of credit is sometimes referred to as a **documentary letter of credit**, because a bank will look only at documents.

After all the parties have agreed to the conditions, the bank issues their letter of credit in favor of the manufacturer. The letter of credit is the bank's promise to pay the manufacturer on their presentation to the bank of the appropriate documents. Thus, the bank substitutes their credit for the buyer's. The buyer reimburses the bank after the bank pays the manufacturer.

5. Insurance

Parties also use insurance to reduce risk. Companies generally purchase multiple kinds of insurance, such as

- General liability insurance
- Directors' and officers' insurance
- Health insurance
- Environmental insurance
- Business interruption insurance

In reviewing a counterparty's insurance coverage, learning that a party has insurance is insufficient.[5] You must know, among other things, the following:

- What constitutes an event of loss and the number of events covered
- What is excluded from the policy
- Whether there are any specific additional policies for a particular risk (e.g., key person insurance, through which an employer can receive a death benefit if that employee passes away)
- The **deductible** (the amount that the insured must pay before the insurer is liable)
- The insurer's maximum obligation
- Whether the maximum obligation has been reduced by earlier payments
- Whether the insurer is creditworthy (Can the insurer pay up?)

6. Deal-Specific Methods

As noted, parties sometimes need to rely on deal-specific methods to reduce risk. For example, the parties could reduce a buyer's risk by changing a stock acquisition to an asset acquisition. The risk is reduced because of the different structure. In an asset acquisition, a buyer chooses which assets they will buy and chooses which liabilities they will assume. If the buyer does not specifically assume a liability, that liability remains with the seller. So if the seller had significant litigation liabilities, the buyer could choose not to assume those liabilities. In contrast, in a stock acquisition, no assets are assigned or liabilities assumed. Instead, the shareholders of the target sell their shares to the buyer, who becomes the new shareholder. Nothing happens to the business. Thus, any liability of the target continues to be that target's liability. Only the target shareholders have changed, and they are the ones who are now owners of the company.

7. Opinion Letters

In some transactions, a party may ask for **an opinion letter** on a specific legal issue relating to the transaction from the other side's lawyer, even though the other side's lawyer is not their lawyer. The ethical rules that all lawyers must follow state that

---

5. For example, in a due diligence investigation, do not rely solely on a party's representations and warranties. Also, obtain a copy of the insurance policy directly from the insurer.

lawyers owe duties to their clients, including the duties of loyalty and confidentiality.[6] All jurisdictions agree on a lawyer having to provide these duties to their clients, even though there are differences from state to state on the types and degrees of duties.[7] In some circumstances, a lawyer can be found to owe a duty to a third party, someone that is not a client.[8] This can be the case with opinion letters, where the lawyer authoring the opinion letter may owe duties to the other party receiving the opinion letter, as well as to their own client.[9]

Opinion letters act as a risk reduction mechanism, in part because if the lawyer authoring the opinion letter is wrong, the party that is the recipient of the opinion may seek damages from the lawyer authoring the opinion.[10] These potential money damages would offset any loss and, thus, reduce the risk involved in the transaction. However, it's still not so easy to take that risk since this would probably involve filing a lawsuit and engaging in litigation, which is costly and time consuming.

Furthermore, the lawyer giving the opinion letter is not usually strictly liable.[11] They usually need to have been negligent in preparing the opinion letter.[12] For example, imagine that a bank wants a borrower's lawyer to provide an opinion letter stating, among other things, that the borrower was duly formed as a corporation, the loan has been properly authorized by the borrower, the borrower's participation in the transaction will not violate any laws, and the bank's remedies are enforceable. By rendering these opinions to the bank, the borrower's lawyer becomes liable to the bank for damages if the opinion was wrong and the lawyer was negligent.[13]

Lawyers do not like giving opinion letters, and they negotiate relentlessly to limit their scope. Lawyers do not want to be liable to a third party on issues that they cannot fully control. So if you are helping a senior lawyer prepare a legal opinion, do not be surprised when that lawyer is especially cautious with their wording and extremely thorough when reviewing the related due diligence.[14] Also, it will be important in these circumstances to make sure that your client has provided you with accurate background factual information and that you have done your own due diligence.

Most transactions do not require a legal opinion. You will see them most frequently in sophisticated financings. Although they were once more common in acquisitions, that is no longer the case.

IV. CONTROL

In analyzing control when you are trying to figure out how to add value in a transaction, the first question must be whether having control is good or bad from your client's perspective, and what implications control has on them and the transaction. For example, limited partners are entitled to limited liability because they exercise no control over the limited partnership. In this context, lack of control is good. However,

---

6. *Model Rules of Prof'l Conduct R.* 1.6, 1.7 (2013).

7. For more information on professional responsibility issues, *see* Chapter 35.

8. *Gordon v. Ervin Cohen & Jessup LLP*, 305 Cal. Rptr. 3d 53 (Cal. Ct. App. 2023) ("the lawyer's duty—and the concomitant right to sue for legal malpractice—can extend to nonclients, but only if the client's intent to benefit the nonclient is 'clear,' 'certain' and 'undisputed.'").

9. *See Greycas, Inc. v. Proud*, 826 F.2d 1560 (7th Cir. 1987).

10. *See Dean Foods Co. v. Pappathanasi*, No. 012595BLS (Mass. Cmmw. Dec. 3, 2004).

11. *See Greycas, Inc. v. Proud*, 826 F.2d 1560 (7th Cir. 1987).

12. *Id.*

13. *See Allen v. Steele*, 252 P.3d 476 (Colo. 2011).

14. Part of drafting opinion letters is finding backup evidence for each opinion given, which is a form of due diligence.

limited partners do not generally want to give up to the general partner all control over their investment. They want the ability to protect their investment. Thus, the limited partners will seek as much control as the general partner will tolerate and as much control as the limited partners can have without becoming general partners under the relevant state law. Thus, the issue of control can be complicated for limited partners.

Control is always an issue when your client is subject to risk. Indeed, whenever your client worries about risk, ask yourself how the agreement can diminish or control the risk. For example, control and risk business issues often coexist when negotiating and drafting covenants. When you are drafting your client's covenants, with respect to each promise that your client makes, you will have to determine whether your client can control and ensure the outcome. If not, your client is gambling when they agree to the covenant because they could end up in breach through no fault of their own. To protect your client, negotiate a covenant that reduces the risk by changing the degree of obligation, as discussed in more detail in Chapter 9 on page 87. For example, a party may not want to promise that they will obtain an environmental permit because they cannot control the agency's decision. However, that party may be willing to promise that they will prepare and submit the necessary papers by a certain date and that they will enter into good faith negotiations with the agency.

When thinking about control issues, think through which party is in control, whether that is the correct party, or whether control should be shared, and if so, how. Imagine that two companies have entered into a joint venture to build a skyscraper. Should one party decide (i.e., control) who the subcontractors will be? If the decisions are to be made jointly, how will the parties break a deadlock?

Once controls are in place, they do not need to remain at the same level throughout a relationship. For example, after first making a loan, a bank may justifiably insist that the agreement prohibits the borrower from making any capital expenditures. The bank has made the loan for working capital purposes and does not want the loan proceeds sidelined into fixed assets not immediately involved in producing profits. However, the bank may be willing to moderate this restriction once the borrower has repaid an agreed-on percentage of the principal.

Parties can also increase control. Preferred shareholders often negotiate for an increase in control. Generally, they have no voting rights, but, for example, if the parties agree, they could earn the right to have one or more board members, if the company fails to pay dividends for three consecutive quarters.

V. STANDARDS

Next, we will look at standards to identify business issues and add value. Almost every word or phrase in a contract establishes a standard. For example, every representation and warranty establishes a standard of liability. If the standard is not met, the recipient of the representation and warranty may sue the maker. By changing a word or a phrase in a representation and warranty, the standard changes. Are the property, the plant, and the equipment in *good repair, customary repair,* or *in compliance with statutory standards*? Covenants and conditions are also standards, as is every adjective (*good* repair) and adverb (*promptly* deliver). Definitions are also standards. For example, how a financial ratio is defined determines the standard to be incorporated into a loan covenant. Thus, each time that a definition changes, so do a party's rights and duties.

The time or duration of an event, an action, the agreement, or anything else can also be a standard. For example, you can include in a contract that a party must provide notice to the other party by a certain time (e.g., within three business days, with a definition for *Business Days*). Also, you can limit the duration of an employment agreement by having a term provision that states that the agreement is for four years and is automatically renewed for an additional year if no party sends notice to terminate by 30 days before the end of the term. Finally, you can set up a process that includes a timeline of when different parties have to take different steps, such as in a purchase agreement where there are actions that each party must take between signing and closing.

Once you determine what the standard is for a particular issue, determine whether the standard favors your client, and, if not, how it can be modified. Note that this issue of standards ties directly into the issues of risk and control that we previously discussed. Depending on the standard, your client may have more or less risk and more or less control.

Some drafters insist that vague standards are inherently wrong.[15] That is incorrect. While vagueness may invite a dispute over a standard in the future, sometimes it is the only way to bridge different positions or to provide a party with flexibility. Vagueness is the drafter's equivalent of the reasonable person standard. For example, if a *force majeure* event occurs, how quickly must the nonperforming party tell the other party of the occurrence? Immediately? Within 24 hours? What if the nonperforming party is cut off from all communication because of the *force majeure* event? Under those circumstances, the 24-hour cutoff is unreasonable. More equitable would be *as soon as feasible*.

Although vague standards may sometimes further a transaction, they can also disadvantage a client, depending on the business deal. As noted earlier, sometimes a seller of a business will agree to an earnout, a payment in the future if certain goals are met. To memorialize this arrangement, the purchase agreement will state the formula for determining the income on which the earnout is based. Imagine if that formula merely states that *revenues minus expenses equals income.* In that case, the vagueness of the standard *expenses* would permit the buyer to decrease the income by deducting inappropriate expenses. Therefore, do not start drafting with a preconceived notion that vagueness is good or bad. Instead, each time that a provision establishes a vague standard, analyze whether it helps your client or whether a more specific, concrete standard would improve the client's position.

When you contemplate negotiating a change in a standard, think through the business risk of asking for that change. If your client has limited negotiating leverage, a request for a change will focus the other party's attention on that standard and could result in an even more stringent standard.

You and your client must also consider who should decide whether a standard has been met. Sometimes a party decides. For example, a landlord and tenant could agree that the tenant may assign the lease to a third party, but *only if the landlord grants consent in their sole discretion.*

If the parties disagree as to whether a standard has been met, they have several options. Sometimes, but not always, contracts address the consequences of breaching a standard in endgame provisions, as discussed in the following section and in Chapter 17 on page 229. The parties may also be able to adjudicate the matter in court or arbitrate or mediate their disagreement. Alternatively, they may be able to appoint an individual with subject matter expertise to resolve any disputes outside a proceeding. In sophisticated construction agreements, owners and contractors sometimes appoint a third-party engineer to settle any differences in a timely manner — sometimes in just a few days.

---

15. For a more detailed discussion of vagueness, *see* Chapter 28 on page 372.

VI. ENDGAME

Finally, we need to think about endgame scenarios to identify business issues and add value as money. As previously discussed in Chapter 17 on page 229, a contract may significantly change or end for countless reasons, which could be neutral, friendly, or unfriendly. A borrower can repay the loan or default, a joint venture can conclude successfully or fail, and an acquisition can close or fail to be consummated. No matter which way a contract ends, the parties will have issues to address. The parties must try to anticipate the different options going forward and think through the consequences. To figure out the possible endgame scenarios and solutions, you need the initiative to think of the problems that could come up and the creativity and thoughtfulness to develop workable solutions. Then you need to be able to draft simple, clear provisions to reflect these in the contract. A drafter who can do this adds great value to the deal.

Note that, usually, endgame issues involve money, the first area that we discussed in this chapter. Therefore, when drafting endgame provisions, think through what the monetary consequences of the contract's end should be. Follow the cash. For example, when a real estate lease term ends, consider what should happen to the tenant's deposit: The landlord should be required to return it, but they should be able to offset against it any costs incurred because of the tenant damaging the apartment. Remember that monetary endgame issues also include whether the prevailing party in a litigation should be contractually entitled to recover their attorneys' fees and other litigation expenses.[16]

Before turning to the exercises in this chapter, you may want to skim Chapter 17 and its discussion of the business issues that endgame provisions raise. These critical provisions deserve more of your attention at this time, particularly because this is an area that may be hard to grasp when you begin drafting. You will probably develop further your ability to anticipate issues and draft endgame provisions as you move forward in your career.

---

16. Usually, under the common law, each litigant is responsible for their own attorneys' fees. However, the parties can agree that the losing party (whether plaintiff or defendant) must pay the prevailing party's attorneys' fees.

VII. EXERCISES

A. Exercise 30A: Add Value to a Broker Agreement

Review the short letter agreement between a broker and an owner of an apartment in this Exercise. The agreement raises multiple business issues that we need to be sure are addressed. To identify and further analyze what those issues are using the five areas outlined in this chapter, use the Exercise 30A Chart that accompanies this Exercise.

The chart is composed of a horizontal x-axis and a vertical y-axis. Along the x-axis, each in a separate column, are the five areas of the framework: money, risk, control, standards, and endgame. Going down the y-axis, you will find each sentence of the letter of agreement, each in a different row. To complete the chart, determine with respect to each sentence if that sentence affects each area and write out what the business issues would be within that area. Thus, with respect to the first sentence, you will first consider if that sentence raises any money issues. If so, note all the money issues that are raised in that appropriate box. Then, consider whether the sentence raises any risk issues, and, if so, note them all in the appropriate box. Follow the same procedure with respect to each of the other three areas, and then with respect to each of the other sentences. Note, not every sentence will involve every area, but a sentence may involve two or more areas.

Mr. Robert Best
Best Brokerage, Inc.
200 Real Estate Way
Burgeoning City, WY 82646

Dear Mr. Best:

This letter sets forth the agreement between Best Brokerage, Inc. (**"Best"**), and the undersigned.

By signing this letter, I grant Best the exclusive right to act as broker for the sale of my apartment for a three-month period (the **"Brokerage Period"**) beginning the day you countersign this letter agreement. I will pay Best a commission of 5% of the sales price of the apartment, if during the Brokerage Period the apartment is sold to someone other than someone I have already identified as a prospective purchaser.

On the signing of this letter agreement, I will give you a set of keys to my apartment. You promise to give me sufficient notice before bringing any prospective purchaser to the apartment. If any prospective purchaser damages my apartment or its furnishings in any way, Best agrees to indemnify me in full for the cost of replacement or repair.

If this letter correctly sets forth our agreement, please countersign this letter.

Sincerely yours,

Oren Oglethorpe
_____
Oren Oglethorpe, Owner

AGREED:
BEST BROKERAGE, INC.
By: _____
Robert Best, President

EXERCISE 30A CHART

TERM OF THE DEAL	MONEY	RISK	CONTROL	STANDARDS	ENDGAME
By signing this letter, I grant Best the exclusive right to act as broker for the sale of my apartment for a three-month period (the "Brokerage Period") beginning the day you countersign this letter agreement.					
I will pay Best a commission of 5% of the sales price of the apartment if during the Brokerage Period the apartment is sold to someone other than someone I have already identified as a prospective purchaser.					
On the signing of this letter agreement, I will give you a set of keys to my apartment.					
You promise to give me sufficient notice before bringing any prospective purchaser to the apartment.					
If any prospective purchaser damages my apartment or its furnishings in any way, Best agrees to indemnify me in full for the cost of replacement or repair.					

B. Exercise 30B: Add Value to a Licensing Agreement

You have received the following email from a partner at your firm. Follow their instructions and use the chart that follows the email to analyze the terms of this deal, think of business issues, and add value. To complete the chart, determine with respect to each sentence if that sentence affects each area (money, risk, control, standards, and endgame) and write out what the business issues would be within that area. Not every sentence involves every area, but a sentence may involve two or more areas. For more information on how to best fill out the chart, review the instructions for Exercise 30A.

To: Alice Associate

From: Peter Partner

Our client is Ralph Products LP ("**Ralph LP**"). Ralph LP owns all rights in the cartoon character Ralph — a short eight-year-old with glasses for whom life never goes quite right. Ralph LP has been making millions by licensing the character to different companies who manufacture and then market products bearing Ralph's likeness.

Earlier today, Ralph Randolph, the president of Ralph LP, called to tell me that he and Merchandisers Extraordinaire, Inc. ("**Merchandisers**"), had agreed to the main terms of a license agreement with respect to Ralph merchandise. Randolph asked me whether I could foresee any business or legal issues with respect to the manner in which the parties had structured the royalty payments.

I understand that aspect of the deal as follows: With respect to each year of the contract term, Merchandisers must pay royalties equal to 15% of all gross sales under $7 million; 10% with respect to sales that equal or exceed $7 million; but in no event less than an aggregate of $600,000 per year. In addition, Ralph LP will have the right to terminate the contract if Merchandisers' net worth is less than $10 million as of the end of their fiscal year.

As you know, I am on my way to Paris, so I do not have time to analyze these terms now. Please think them through and be prepared to explain the issues to me when I land and call you. As you analyze these terms, try to focus on the following important areas: money, risk, control, standards, and endgame.

EXERCISE 30B CHART

TERM OF THE DEAL	MONEY	RISK	CONTROL	STANDARDS	ENDGAME
With respect to each year of the contract term, Merchandisers must pay royalties equal to 15% of all gross sales under $7 million; 10% with respect to sales that equal or exceed $7 million; but in no event less than an aggregate of $600,000 per year.					
In addition, Ralph LP will have the right to terminate the contract if Merchandisers' net worth is less than $10 million as of the end of their fiscal year.					

C. Exercise 30C: Add Value to a Partnership Agreement

You have received the following email from a partner at your firm. Follow their instructions and use the chart that follows the email to analyze the terms of this deal, think of business issues, and add value. To complete the chart, determine with respect to each sentence if that sentence affects each area (money, risk, control, standards, and endgame) and write out what the business issues would be within that area. Not every sentence involves every area, but a sentence may involve two or more areas. For more information on how to best fill out the chart, review the earlier instructions for Exercise 30A.

To: Leo Pard

From: Ty Gere

Subject: Clark Partnership Agreement

    Two siblings, Margo and Bob Clark, have asked us to consider their plan to form a general partnership for their new business: High End Foods (**"HEF"**). HEF intends to manufacture and market a line of freshly cooked, high-end, filling meals. HEF will sell the meals directly to specialty food stores. The Clarks are confident that the business will do well. Their secret ingredient is a genetically engineered food supplement that makes you feel full — even though the amount consumed is relatively small. The inventor of the ingredient is their cousin Roberta, who has given them the go-ahead to use the ingredient in the business.

    The Clarks intend to capitalize the business with $100,000. Margo will contribute $75,000, and Bob will contribute $25,000. Bob has significant experience in the prepared foods industry, having just completed a three-year stint as executive vice president of the company that is the industry leader — even though they focus mostly on frozen foods. The plan is that Bob will run the business on a day-to-day basis, and Margo will be in charge of advertising and back-office operations. Bob hopes that the new business will keep Margo's mind off her recent illness. He confided that the long-term prognosis is not good.

    The business deal with respect to profits is that the first $75,000 goes to Margo, while the next $25,000 in cash that is distributed is Bob's. Thereafter, the money is split 50-50.

    Please provide me with a list of the business issues that I should raise with the Clarks at my meeting with them later today. It would be helpful if you outlined the issues using the framework that we recently discussed, which covers money, risk, control, standards, and endgame.

EXERCISE 30C CHART

TERM OF THE DEAL	MONEY	RISK	CONTROL	STANDARDS	ENDGAME
Two siblings, Margo and Bob Clark, have asked us to consider their plan to form a general partnership for their new business: High End Foods ("HEF"). HEF intends to manufacture and market a line of freshly cooked, high-end, filling meals. HEF will sell the meals directly to specialty food stores. The Clarks are confident that the business will do well.					
Their secret ingredient is a genetically engineered food supplement that makes you feel full—even though the amount consumed is relatively small. The inventor of the ingredient is their cousin Roberta, who has given them the go-ahead to use the ingredient in the business.					
The Clarks intend to capitalize the business with $100,000. Margo will contribute $75,000, and Bob will contribute $25,000.					
Bob has significant experience in the prepared foods industry, having just completed a three-year stint as executive vice president of the company that is the industry leader—even though they focus mostly on frozen foods. The plan is that Bob will run the business on a day-to-day basis.					
Margo will be in charge of advertising and back-office operations. Bob hopes that the new business will keep Margo's mind off her recent illness. He confided that the long-term prognosis is not good.					
The business deal with respect to profits is that the first $75,000 goes to Margo, while the next $25,000 in cash that is distributed is Bob's. Thereafter, the money is split 50-50.					

D. Exercise 30D: Add Value to an Acquisition

You have received the following email from a partner at your firm. Follow their instructions and use the chart that follows the email to analyze the terms of this deal, think of business issues, and add value. To complete the chart, determine with respect to each sentence if that sentence affects each area (money, risk, control, standards, and endgame) and write out what the business issues would be within that area. Not every sentence involves every area, but a sentence may involve two or more areas. For more information on how to best fill out the chart, review the instructions for Exercise 30A.

To: Developing Associate

From: Proud Partner

Our client is a member of the acquisition committee of a London venture capital fund. What follows is a preliminary report from one of the fund's analysts. Please review the report to determine the business issues that might arise if the fund decides to acquire the target. I will need your list of business issues as quickly as possible. Please break down the issues into the five areas that we identified: money, risk, control, standards, and endgame.

* * * *

1. Wonder Drugs Limited ("**Wonder Drugs**") is a privately held British company specializing in biotechnology. Their primary product is Getbetter, a drug that the founder created to help his son who is afflicted with a rare disease. Because the number of patients with the disease is relatively small, Getbetter has never been particularly profitable despite its effectiveness. Wonder Drugs manufactures only 100,000 doses of the medicine a year. To make matters worse, Wonder Drugs' patent on Getbetter ends December 31 of this year. With the loss of the patent, other companies may begin to manufacture a generic version of Getbetter. If they do, Getbetter's marginal profitability could turn into a loss. As of December 31 of this past year, 40% of the assets of Wonder Drugs consisted of inventory in Getbetter.

2. Despite the issues mentioned in paragraph 1, we believe that Wonder Drugs is a strong acquisition candidate. They have a possible bestseller in a drug that they have been working on for ten years. Feelbetter is an antidepressant for children, which in clinical trials has proved quite effective in relieving the symptoms of depression. Management of Wonder Drugs projects that they could sell over 30 million doses each year. However, antidepressants for children are controversial. Research in England and the United States has demonstrated that some antidepressants increase the likelihood that some children will commit suicide.

3. Although the French regulatory authorities have approved Feelbetter, other countries have not. Wonder Drugs believes that Feelbetter will be profitable only if it can be sold in the Commonwealth and the United States. Accordingly, these approvals are key. Wonder Drugs expects these approvals before the end of this year. Final approval of the patent is also expected around the same time.

continued on next page >

4. The ownership structure of Wonder Drugs is relatively simple. Dr. Niles Smith, the founder of the company, owns 60% of the company's shares. (He has an excellent reputation within the biomedical community.) Various members of his family own the remainder of the shares. Dr. Smith is now 65 and wants to sell his business as part of his estate plan. He has requested that the transaction be structured as a stock sale to minimize the taxes that he and the other shareholders must pay. Dr. Smith believes that he can persuade all the other members of his family to sell their respective shares. His only concern is whether his oldest daughter will sell. They have not spoken in five years, and he is concerned that she might refuse to sell just to be difficult.

5. Dr. Smith has told us that once the sale is complete, he does not want to have any post-closing liabilities to the buyer. He told us that he needed the full amount of the purchase price to fund a trust for his son and to pay for some other activities that he is contemplating as part of his retirement. Dr. Smith is refusing to give any representations and warranties on the efficacy or safety of Getbetter and Feelbetter. He said that those were the buyer's risks. However, he has offered to permit us to review all of the research on Getbetter and Feelbetter. (That is, we can do all the due diligence we want.) In addition, he and his assistant would meet as often as needed with representatives of the buyer (for example, their scientists).

6. Dr. Smith is the chief executive at Wonder Drugs and their primary researcher. He is brilliant and has done a fine job managing the company. However, he has told us that he does not want to work for Wonder Drugs after their sale. He has never worked for anyone and doesn't want to start that now. But a few years ago, as part of a succession plan, Dr. Smith hired Sara Jones as his research assistant. She has top-notch scientific credentials and has been instrumental in bringing Feelbetter through their regulatory trials. To induce Sara to join Wonder Drugs, the company granted her options to purchase 1,000 shares of Wonder Drugs at a price of £100 per share, the options to vest on receipt of the English and American regulatory approvals.

7. Our purchase price discussions with Wonder Drugs have been difficult. Dr. Smith has been insisting on a very high per-share price relative to what the company earns on Getbetter and what they may earn once their patent lapses. He insists the company will generate huge income once Feelbetter receives their regulatory approvals, and he wants the price to reflect the projected income. While it is our hope that the new drug will make the company hugely profitable, the new medicine has no track record. The high level of projected income is completely speculative. In addition, we feel that the price has to factor in the possibility of litigation, should the antidepressant cause suicides — despite the results of the drug's current trials. We will continue to negotiate the purchase price with Dr. Smith.

8. The company's financial records are adequate for a privately held company. We have no reason to believe that there is any fraud. But the company has been using a small accounting firm. Bringing in a big-name accounting firm may be expensive, but it's an essential element for our exit strategy.

9. Wonder Drugs has been selling Getbetter through pharmaceutical distributors. Those distributors then sell the medicine to hospitals and pharmacies. One of these distributors has not paid Wonder Drugs in six months and owes the company £200,000, over 10% of last year's revenues.

10. The production facility machinery was state of the art when Wonder Drugs purchased it 10 years ago. This machinery can last 20 years if it is well maintained. Dr. Smith told us that Wonder Drugs has been negotiating to purchase new machinery for the production of Feelbetter.

EXERCISE 30D CHART

TERM OF THE DEAL	MONEY	RISK	CONTROL	STANDARDS	ENDGAME	OTHER
Paragraph 1 Seller's Issues						
Paragraph 1 Buyer's Issues						
Paragraph 2 Seller's Issues						
Paragraph 2 Buyer's Issues						
Paragraph 3 Seller's Issues						

TERM OF THE DEAL	MONEY	RISK	CONTROL	STANDARDS	ENDGAME	OTHER
Paragraph 3 Buyer's Issues						
Paragraph 4 Seller's Issues						
Paragraph 4 Buyer's Issues						
Paragraph 5 Seller's Issues						
Paragraph 5 Buyer's Issues						

continued on next page >

TERM OF THE DEAL	MONEY	RISK	CONTROL	STANDARDS	ENDGAME	OTHER
Paragraph 6 Seller's Issues						
Paragraph 6 Buyer's Issues						
Paragraph 7 Seller's Issues						
Paragraph 7 Buyer's Issues						
Paragraph 8 Seller's Issues						

TERM OF THE DEAL	MONEY	RISK	CONTROL	STANDARDS	ENDGAME	OTHER
Paragraph 8 Buyer's Issues						
Paragraph 9 Seller's Issues						
Paragraph 9 Buyer's Issues						
Paragraph 10 Seller's Issues						
Paragraph 10 Buyer's Issues						

CHAPTER THIRTY-ONE

Organizing a Contract and Its Provisions

I. INTRODUCTION

A well-written contract has an organizational framework that makes it easy to read. A contract is easy to read if the reader knows where to look for a provision and understands how the contract's provisions relate to each other. By arranging the provisions in a "meaningful sequence,"[1] a drafter reduces the reader's work.

There is no single way to organize a contract. Drafters can organize a contract with the same deal terms in different ways. If an approach makes the contract easier to read, then it is usually a good approach. Nonetheless, over time, through customs and practice, we have standardized how we organize some types of contracts. An acquisition agreement is a good example. If you were to look at a dozen precedents from a dozen different firms, their organization would be almost exactly the same. In instances like this, using the accepted organization makes the agreement easier to read because the reader already knows what to expect where. Changing the organization requires the reader to hunt for a provision that is not in its usual place, a frustrating and time-wasting experience. In addition, a client would probably refuse to pay for the time spent reorganizing a contract if you have precedent with which to start.

In practice, you will draft very few contracts from scratch. Instead, you will use a precedent—either one from your firm or one that you find in a secondary resource. Someone else will have already spent the time to impose order and organize the contract's provisions. You may want to fine-tune that organization, but most of your organizational responsibilities will be limited to inserting new provisions in the appropriate place and organizing individual provisions. These tasks will still be important, and the readers of your contract will appreciate you taking the time to do this carefully and thoughtfully.

In this chapter, we will cover how contracts are organized at both a macro and a micro level. The macro level is the organization of the contract as a whole: What are the beginning, middle, and ending provisions? Micro-level organization refers to the organization of the individual provisions—no matter where in the contract they are.

---

1. Alan Siegel, Language Follows Logic: Practical Lessons in Legal Drafting, remarks made at Conference of Experts in Clear Legal Drafting, National Center for Administrative Justice, Washington, D.C., June 2, 1978, in F. Reed Dickerson, *Materials on Legal Drafting* 150 (West 1981).

Section II focuses on the organization of a contract at the macro level and the typical organization of an overall contract. Section III discusses the micro-level organization of individual provisions and the different approaches you can take.

II. ORGANIZING A CONTRACT AT THE MACRO LEVEL

In Part C, we outlined the typical structure of a contract and discussed each part of the contract in depth. At the macro level, the organization of contracts rarely differs, so, again, here is the overall structure of most contracts:

Outline of Typical Contract Structure
- Introductory Provisions
  - Title
  - Preamble
  - Recitals or Background Section
  - Words of Agreement
- Defined Terms and Definitions
- Action Sections
  - Subject Matter Performance Provision
  - Payment Provisions
  - Duration of Contract (if applicable) (also known as *term*)
  - Action Sections in Acquisitions and Financings (if applicable)
    - Closing and Closing Date (when and where)
    - Closing Deliveries
  - Other Substantive Business Provisions
- Endgame Provisions
- General Provisions
  - Third Parties (e.g., assignment and delegation, successors and assigns)
  - Determine What Constitutes a Contract (e.g., severability, amendments waiver, integration or merger, counterparts)
  - Communications (e.g., notice)
  - Dispute Resolution (e.g., governing law, forum selection, waiver of right to jury trial, alternative dispute resolution)
  - Risk Allocation (e.g., force majeure)
- Signature Lines
- Schedules and Exhibits

As we have discussed, virtually all contracts begin with the introductory provisions that we discussed in Chapter 14 the title, preamble, recitals (or background), and words of agreement — in that order. Exceptions exist, of course. For example, drafters sometimes omit recitals because they may not be needed for the particular contract. After the introductory provisions, we usually find a list of definitions, as we discussed in Chapter 15 even though some drafters may not include a definitions list or may place the definitions list in another part of the contract, like at the end.

After the definitions, the next provisions are almost always the action sections that are most common to all contracts, and their order is, again, fairly standard: Typically, the subject matter performance provision appears first, followed by the provision setting forth the payment, whether monetary or otherwise. Then come the provisions relating to the agreement's term; date, time, and place of closing; and the closing deliveries (in each instance, if appropriate for the transaction).

Within the action sections, you may have additional business provisions that set out the parties' representations and warranties, covenants, conditions, discretionary authority, and declarations. The organization of these business provisions varies from contract to contract, but there are similarities within specific types of contracts (e.g., licensing agreements will often include similar provisions in a similar order). You can review more regarding the action sections in Chapter 16. Note, as we also discussed in that chapter, some drafters prefer to consider these additional business provisions as a separate part of the contract from the action sections.

After the action sections, you will find the endgame provisions. These provisions sometimes adhere to a common organizational scheme: first, the defaults; then, the remedies; and finally, termination. This order mimics the events in the business world: defaults occur, and then a party seeks remedies.[2]

After the endgame provisions are the general provisions, the final provisions of a contract. Some drafters insert these provisions without giving any thought to the order in which they should appear (but, one hopes, with some thought as to their substance). Nonetheless, you can organize these provisions by grouping them by subject matter, as you can see from the outline above: provisions relating to third parties, provisions determining what constitutes a contract, communication provisions, dispute resolution provisions, and risk allocation provisions. In some agreements, a general provision can also be an endgame provision and may be of particular importance — for example, the indemnity provision or the *force majeure* provision. In that case, break the provision out and give it its own article or section, separate from the general provisions, as appropriate.

Case law suggests that a contract's last provision should be the waiver of a right to jury trial.[3] Although courts will enforce a jury waiver, they do so reluctantly and insist that a waiver be knowing, voluntary, and intentional.[4] In deciding whether this standard has been met, courts look at whether the provision was conspicuous, making it more likely that the waiving party read it. Putting the jury waiver provision last is one way of making it conspicuous.

Of course, the contract ends with the parties' signatures, followed by schedules and exhibits, if relevant.

III. ORGANIZING PROVISIONS AT THE MICRO LEVEL

When you are organizing individual provisions in a contract at the micro level, you can use one of the following primary organizing principles:

- Subject Matter
- Relative Importance
- Chronology
- Party
- Contract Concepts

---

2. For a more detailed discussion of the organization and drafting of endgame provisions, *see* Chapter 17.

3. *See Reggie Packing Co. v. Lazere Fin. Corp. (In re Reggie Packing Co.)*, 671 F. Supp. 571, 572 (N.D. Ill. 1987).

4. For a detailed discussion of the provision waiving jury trial, *see* Chapter 18, Section XII.

Most contracts use more than one of these principles. For example, a contract can use one of these organizing principles as the primary organizing principle for a set of provisions and one or more of the others as subsidiary principles.[5] On the other hand, a contract could use one of these organizing principles for a set of provisions in one part of the contract and a different organizing principle for a different set of provisions in another part of the contract. Note that these organizing principles can also be used to organize a contract at the macro level, if needed.

The next subsections explain each of the organizing principles, and the example at the end shows you how they can all come into play at different points of your organization process and how you can use different organizing principles at the same time.

A simple test to determine whether an agreement's organization works is looking at the number of cross-references in the agreement. Sometimes you cannot avoid having a cross-reference, which means one provision referring to a different provision in the contract. For example, there may be two provisions that must be read together; one provision may override another provision in limited circumstances; or a second provision may describe, trigger, or limit a first provision. However, if you see multiple cross-references that relate to the same topic in your agreement, consider reorganizing those concepts in the contract or creating a new section to deal with that topic. Putting those related provisions in one place together may make it easier for the reader.

A. SUBJECT MATTER

Organizing a contract's business provisions by subject matter is the most common way to put together a contract. The process resembles the process used when organizing an outline for a brief or a memorandum. For those documents, a writer first determines the main points and the subsidiary points, and then orders them to create a cohesive and persuasive document. Before settling on the final organizational scheme, the writer may try several different ones.

The parallel process in contract drafting begins with the drafter grouping together business terms on the same or similar topics and creating subject matter groups. These groups will become provisions that must be further organized, often using one or more of the organizing principles that follow, like *relative importance* or *chronology*, discussed next.

B. RELATIVE IMPORTANCE

You always want to think about which provisions are most important and place them, if possible, at the top of a section so they are immediately visible and are read first. In determining the relative importance of provisions, consider, among other things, how important that provision is to your client and whether the parties will need to refer to that provision frequently (more important) or infrequently (less important).

In addition, generally, the statement of a rule should precede its exception[6] to facilitate understanding of the exception. Knowing what the rule is puts the exception

---

5. In *The Fundamentals of Legal Drafting,* F. Reed Dickerson discusses how to use division, classification, and sequence as tools to create a contract's organization — or "architecture," to use his terminology. F. Reed Dickerson, *The Fundamentals of Legal Drafting* 81-91 (2d ed., Little, Brown & Co. 1986). But Dickerson himself had reservations about the utility of these tools: "All the composition books tell you to make an outline, but none that I have seen gives an adequate account of how it should be conceptualized. I tried to remedy the situation in chapter 5 of *The Fundamentals of Legal Drafting,* but I'm afraid that I left the reader awash in a sea of abstraction." F. Reed Dickerson, *Materials on Legal Drafting* 103 (West 1981) (quoting F. Reed Dickerson, *Legal Drafting: Writing as Thinking, or, Talk-Back from Your Draft and How to Exploit It,* 29 J. Leg. Educ. 373, 374 (1978)).

6. For a more detailed discussion of how to draft exceptions, *see* Chapter 27 on page 420.

in context. Also, put provisions that are broader and more comprehensive first, and place the more specific provisions on that same subject matter afterward.

C. CHRONOLOGY

Drafters can use chronology to organize provisions, especially in situations where one party's actions depend on the occurrence—or nonoccurrence—of the other party's actions. For example, suppose that a licensor must approve a sample of a trademarked product before the licensee may manufacture it. A well-drafted provision will need to provide a timetable for the approval process: When must the licensee submit a sample of the product? How soon afterward must the licensor respond, and by when does the licensee need to address the licensor's response? Putting these provisions in chronological order provides the reader with an easy road map to follow.

D. PARTY

Modern contracts are not usually organized so that all the provisions relating to one party go before all the provisions relating to the second party. Instead, organization by party is often a secondary level of organization. For example, in an indemnity agreement, each party usually indemnifies the other party against certain risks. Although a drafter could craft the indemnity so that each party indemnifies the other in one section, often the drafter creates separate sections for each party's indemnification obligation. On the other hand, generally, the remaining provisions of an indemnity agreement are organized by subject matter.

E. CONTRACT CONCEPTS

Contract concepts rarely provide the overarching organizational scheme of a contract's provisions. Acquisition and financing agreements are the exception, as you can see in the House Purchase Agreement (located on the CasebookConnect Resources page and at www.aspenpublishing.com). Nonetheless, a drafter will sometimes use a contract concept to organize part of a contract that is otherwise organized by subject matter. For example, drafters often appropriately put all of a party's representations and warranties in one section, as was done in Section 10 of the Website Development Agreement (also located on the Casebook Connect Resources page and at www.aspenpublishing.com).

F. EXAMPLE

To make these organizing principles concrete, imagine that your client is a chain of stores that sells everything from groceries to clothing and has a photo department (similar to Target or Walmart). Your client is contracting with a photo-finishing lab for their few customers who do not use digital cameras. Your client informs you that the parties have agreed to the following business terms (in no particular order):

1. The lab will develop and print the photographs that each store's customers have dropped off for developing.
2. For nondigital photographs, the lab must use developer manufactured by Chelsea Photo Chemicals, which is located in New York, New York.
3. The lab must pick up film from each store every day, but not until after 5:00 PM.
4. The lab must provide a first-quality product.
5. The lab must return the finished photographs no later than noon the day after it picks up the film.

6. For nondigital photographs, the lab must use fixer manufactured by Berkshire Photo Materials, which is located in Egremont, Massachusetts.

7. All photographs are to be printed on Axon photographic paper with a matte finish unless a customer specifies otherwise.

8. If a customer drops off more than ten rolls of film at a store on any day, the lab may return the photographs developed from that film later than noon the day after it picks up the film, but no later than 5:00 PM.

To organize these eight business terms, first organize them by *subject matter*. This means that you will group together the business terms on the same or similar topics and create subject matter groups. In this case, four points relate to the quality of the product and the materials to be used (numbers 2, 4, 6, and 7); three relate to pickups and deliveries (numbers 3, 5, and 8); and one (number 1) is part of the subject matter performance provision.

Next, you will need to determine in which order these groups should appear, so we need to think about *relative importance*. The first decision — an easy one — is to put the subject matter performance provision first in the action sections, since it's the overarching, broadest provision on the topic.

After this, you must decide which of the remaining provisions should go next: the provisions dealing with pickups and deliveries or the ones dealing with the product's quality. Timing may be the more important business term because of its primacy in the store's marketing efforts. However, a drafter could decide that quality is more important because without it, timing does not matter. You would probably need to learn more information and to better understand the business and your client's interests to make the final decision. Based on the facts available, both analyses seem reasonable and either order would be acceptable.

After deciding the general order of these two groups of provisions, you have to organize the provisions within each group. With respect to the provisions on pickups and deliveries, how could you order them to help a reader understand them? Using the *chronology* organizing principle and, thus, putting them in chronological order is one obvious possibility. In addition, bringing in the *relative importance* principle again, the general rule as to the delivery of the photographs by noon should come before the exception that permits delivery after noon but no later than 5:00 PM of that same day. Here is a possible draft of the provisions we have discussed. Note how the formatting (e.g., bold, headings, tabulation) makes it clearer and easier to read:

Example — Organizing Individual Provisions on Pickups and Deliveries

"Delivery Day" means, with respect to each roll of film, the day after the day that the Lab picks up that roll of film from a Store.

Schedule of Pickups and Deliveries.

(a) **Pickups.**
   (i) The Lab shall pick up from each Store every day all rolls of film that the Store's customers have deposited with that Store; and
   (ii) The Lab shall make that pickup after 5:00 PM local time at each Store.

(b) **Deliveries.**
   (i) **General Rule.** With respect to each roll of film picked up from each Store, the Lab shall return to that Store the photographs

> developed from that roll no later than noon of that roll's Delivery
> Day.
>
> (ii) **Exception.** Despite subsection (i), if a customer of a Store
> deposits more than ten rolls of film on any one day,
>
> (A) the Lab may return the photographs developed from those
> rolls to that Store later than noon of those rolls' Delivery
> Day, but
>
> (B) the Lab shall return them no later than 5:00 PM of those
> rolls' Delivery Day.

Next, you must analyze and organize the provisions dealing with the quality of the photographs and the purchase of the materials. You must first decide whether the lab's obligation to deliver first-quality photographs should be drafted as one section or two—one for the general obligation as to quality and the other as to the lab's obligation to use specific products. As the obligation to deliver a quality product is short, it can be combined easily with its related business terms. Again, see how formatting in the following example is used to enhance the provision's clarity:

Example—Organizing Provisions on the Quality of the Photographs and the Purchase of the Materials

Quality of the Finished Photographs. The Lab shall print first-quality photographs. Without limiting the generality of the preceding sentence,

(a) the Lab shall use, for all nondigital photographs,

(i) developer manufactured by Chelsea Photo Chemicals, located in New York, New York and

(ii) fixer manufactured by Berkshire Photo Materials, located in Egremont, Massachusetts;

and

(b) the Lab shall print all photographs on Axon photographic paper with a matte finish unless a customer specifies a different finish.

This provision has two levels of micro-organization, both of which rely on *chronology*. The substance of subsection (a) appears before subsection (b), as the lab must use the chemicals to develop the photographs before it prints them. Subsections (a)(i) and (ii) list developer first and fixer second, as developer is the first chemical used in the developing process.

IV. ORGANIZATION OF ACQUISITION AGREEMENTS

Acquisition agreements are interesting from an organizational perspective because their organization is multilayered and uses all the organizing principles. As you can see in the House Purchase Agreement (located on the CasebookConnect Resources page and at www.aspenpublishing.com), the overarching organizational principle is the *contract concepts*. In the action sections, after the subject matter performance provision, the agreement's provisions appear in the following order: representations and warranties, then covenants, and finally conditions. The contract concept provisions appear in this order to reflect the *chronology* of the transaction. The parties represent and warrant to each other on the signing date, covenant with respect to the gap period between signing and closing, and establish conditions to the closing on the closing date.

Each set of contract concept provisions is suborganized first by *party*. The seller's provisions come before the buyer's provisions. Finally, each party's provisions are organized by *subject matter*. As a matter of common practice, these provisions are not necessarily organized by *relative importance*. If they were, the seller's representations and warranties with respect to the financial statements would appear first because they are of the utmost importance to the buyer—who determines the purchase price based on them. Instead, the representations and warranties first establish that the party exists as a legal entity, that it has the authority to enter into the transaction, and that the contract is legal, binding, and enforceable.

The end of the action sections of an acquisition agreement includes the articles establishing the conditions to closing, which continue to be organized by *party* and then usually by *subject matter*. After the action sections, the agreement concludes with the endgame provisions (e.g., termination, indemnities, change of name, and noncompete) and the general provisions.

V. EXERCISES

A. Exercise 31A: Organizing an Escrow Agreement

Determine the organizational schemes of the provisions in the Escrow Agreement discussed in Section IV.A of Chapter 14. Which provisions, if any, are organized by the following: subject matter, relative importance, chronology, party, and contract concepts?

B. Exercise 31B: Organizing an Employment Agreement

The provisions in the list on the following page regularly appear in employment agreements. They are not in the order in which they would appear in a contract. Reorder the list so the provisions are in an appropriate order.

1. No oral amendments.   _____

2. Anti-assignment provision.   _____

3. Bonus.   _____

4. Change of control of the Employer. (What happens to the Executive on a change of control of the Employer: forced retirement, bonus to keep on working, nothing?)   _____

5. Death and disability (financial and contractual ramifications of death or disability).   _____

6. Duties (a description of the Executive's responsibilities).   _____

7. Effects of the termination of the Executive's employment.   _____

8. The Executive represents and warrants that entering into this employment agreement does not violate any other agreement to which the Executive is a party.   _____

9. The Employer agrees to employ the Executive, and the Executive agrees to work for the Employer.   _____

10. Merger (all prior writings and negotiations are merged into this contract; sometimes referred to as the "integration provision").   _____

11. Expense account.   _____

12. Extent of service (e.g., full time or part time).   _____

13. Governing law.   _____

14. Waiver of jury trial.   _____

15. Insurance and other employee benefits.   _____

16. Notices.   _____

17. Salary.   _____

18. Severability.   _____

19. Successors and assigns.   _____

20. Term of contract: three years.   _____

21. Termination for cause.   _____

22. Working facilities (windowed, corner office, or cubicle?).   _____

CHAPTER THIRTY-TWO

The Drafting Process

I. INTRODUCTION

Drafting a contract requires much more than pulling out precedents that you may have used before and changing the names and the dates. As we have discussed, the drafting process is sophisticated, requiring you to integrate your knowledge of business, the business deal, the client's business, the law, and your writing skills. This task is not easy, and it is more time-consuming than expected, but it is rewarding.

This chapter often describes the ideal drafting process—what you would do with unlimited time and financial resources. You will rarely have the luxury of being able to follow this process step by step. Instead, you will take shortcuts and find your own way of doing things depending on the transaction, client, and limitations. However, by understanding the different possibilities and steps available, you can create a process that works for you and your client in your transactions going forward.

II. AGREEING TO THE BUSINESS TERMS

As we discussed in Chapter 2, most contracts begin with the parties agreeing to do a deal, which may be as common as the purchase and sale of a house or as exceptional as a multibillion-dollar joint venture. In a transaction, the parties generally negotiate the key business terms, including price.[1] Once they have done so, each party contacts their lawyers. One of the lawyers will probably draw up a list of the key business terms to which all parties have agreed. Then, the parties will review and confirm those key business terms. However, note that there are transactions that may not be handled directly by the lawyers because they are smaller and, thus, may be handled by non-lawyers, such as the negotiation of one of many small vendor contracts at a corporation.

At this point in the deal, the parties may decide to enter into a more formal written agreement, such as a **letter of intent**, **term sheet**, or **memorandum of understanding**. All three of these options have the following in common: (1) they

---

1. Other scenarios are possible. Sometimes a client will meet with a lawyer at the very beginning of a deal, and the lawyer, with other experts, will help the client structure and negotiate the transaction's material terms.

include the key business terms that the parties have agreed to for that transaction; (2) they could be binding or nonbinding, depending on what the parties decide; and (3) they would be preliminary to the parties doing their due diligence and agreeing to a more final business contract. Note that, while letters of intent, term sheets, and memoranda of understanding are common, they are not required in a transaction, so there are many transactions that do not include one.

A letter of intent and a memorandum of understanding are usually signed by both parties and more often can have binding terms, while a term sheet is not usually signed by the parties and is more of a simple list of key business terms that is generally not binding. Since the letter of intent and the memorandum of understanding are signed legal documents, the parties may have to disclose them to comply with state and federal laws, especially if any of them are publicly traded companies. In business transactions with individuals, corporations, limited liability companies (LLCs), and similar entities, you may see the use of letters of intent and term sheets more often, while you will experience the use of a memorandum of understanding more often with local, state, and federal governmental entities and in international relations.

When properly used, these instruments save the parties time and money. By forcing the parties to think about the transaction's details early, with luck, the parties will discover any deal breakers or other roadblocks to completing the transaction.

The list of business terms in these three instruments can be quite short or very detailed, covering almost everything that would appear in a signed agreement. Which approach is chosen depends on how the parties intend to use the document.

Some parties use the letter of intent, term sheet, or memorandum of understanding as a mini-agreement, intending to be bound but also intending to memorialize the deal more fully in a traditional agreement after that. Other parties use these instruments as a nonbinding, general statement of interest in a transaction on the listed terms. In this context, the letter of intent, term sheet, or memorandum of understanding is the basis of future negotiations rather than the final expression of the negotiations. Nonetheless, the parties may choose to include binding terms with respect to confidentiality, payment of expenses, and the obligation to negotiate in good faith.

If you do not properly draft the letter of intent, term sheet, or memorandum of understanding, you can run into serious problems at this point in the negotiation process. One party could claim that the instrument bound the parties to the transaction or that a particular provision was binding, while the other may claim that the instrument was merely a preliminary statement of interest—or that even though some provisions were binding, that particular provision was not binding. To prevent this, the drafters must clarify the letter of intent's purpose and make sure it is clear which provisions are binding and not binding. If the parties intend for the entire instrument to be nonbinding, it should state clearly that the parties have significant, substantive business issues to negotiate, and that the transaction is not binding until memorialized in a definitive, written agreement.

Because letters of intent and memoranda of understanding can be binding more often than term sheets, there is more extensive case law on them in most jurisdictions. Most of the case law revolves around whether an instrument or a provision was binding or not binding. Therefore, if you negotiate letters of intent, term sheets, or memoranda of understanding, you should make sure that you are very familiar with the case law and how to best make clear what is binding and not binding.

III. DETERMINING WHO DRAFTS THE CONTRACT

Before drafting begins, the parties and their lawyers must decide who will draft the contract. Often, though, no one really discusses this issue. Instead, custom and negotiating leverage determine who takes the lead and whose precedent is used. For example, the lender's lawyers always draft the credit agreement and any ancillary agreements, the employer's lawyers always draft the employment agreement, and the publisher's lawyers always draft the book contract. They are risking their money and often have more power, so they set the ground rules—subject to negotiation.

If custom does not dictate who drafts the contract, and, if the other side gives you the opportunity to draft the contract, take it—not because the billings will be greater, but because your client will gain a strategic advantage if you control the agreement and the drafting process. Specifically, as you begin to incorporate the agreed-on business terms into the contract, you will face many issues that the parties did not discuss. For example, should a representation and warranty be flat or qualified, and, if qualified, how? Because you are drafting the contract, you and your client can decide each of these issues to your client's advantage, without violating any ethical limitations. You are not changing the deal. You are addressing matters not previously negotiated.

Depending on her caliber, the drafter on the other side may not question any of the provisions that you craft, giving your client a win at no cost. If she does spot an issue, she can ask for a change and negotiate. Although any redraft may tilt the provision toward the other side, the ultimate provision may still be more favorable to your client than if the other side had produced the first draft.

Drafting the contract also means that you may be able to control the deal's pace. If your client is eager to close the transaction, you can turn around drafts quickly and hope that the other side does the same. But if they want to slow the pace, you can take your time drafting and distributing the first draft or revisions.

IV. LEARNING ABOUT A TRANSACTION

Generally, you will learn about a transaction when a client or supervisor calls you or sends you an e-mail. Although your responsibilities are similar in each situation, they are not the same. This section will first discuss your responsibilities if you are dealing directly with the client, and then if you are dealing with a supervising lawyer.

A. LEARNING ABOUT A TRANSACTION FROM A CLIENT

When a client calls and announces a new transaction, listen carefully to the details. He will probably start by giving you the headlines: *We are hiring a new Executive Vice President, Antoine Johnson. He will be starting June 15th, and we are going to pay him $150,000 per year.*

Although these are certainly important facts, they are not all the facts that you will need to write the contract. If you have been practicing for several years and you specialize in employment law, you may be able to rattle off ten questions without any further research. But if that is not the case, ask the questions that you can think of and then suggest a meeting to discuss the transaction in more detail. Before ending the call, ask the client to bring to the meeting any relevant documents, including any deal memos, letter of intent, correspondence, previous contracts, and notes.

A follow-up meeting in person or online is generally better than a follow-up phone call. At a meeting, the conversations tend to be more wide-ranging, and you are more likely to gain a thorough understanding of the deal and the client's goals. However, the reality is that parties conduct a great deal of business by phone and e-mail.

To prepare for the client meeting, create a checklist of the questions that you want to ask. The checklist should cover all the business terms to be incorporated into the agreement. If you are working at a firm, the firm or your department may have a checklist for each type of transaction that they regularly handle. You can add to this checklist (or create your own) by reviewing agreements from prior transactions with this client or other clients. If you are creating your own checklist, always look at more than one agreement so you review as wide a variety of provisions as possible. Also, look at forms in treatises, continuing legal education materials, and industry association materials. In addition, you can find agreements online, but take care that they come from reputable sources, so that you can have confidence in their quality. Sometimes checklists are even organized and prepared following a precedent, so that it is easier to draft the agreement and you can get the answers you need quickly.

As part of your preparation for the meeting, draw a diagram of the transaction. If you are drafting a simple lease, the diagram will probably not be of much help. But, with a more sophisticated transaction with multiple parties and mini-transactions, the visual may help you see how these mini-transactions fit together. For example, imagine that your client, a bank, intends to lend $100 million to a corporation. Because the borrower has had some financial trouble in the past, the borrower has agreed to grant a security interest in their assets to the bank. In addition, each of the borrower's two subsidiaries will guarantee the borrower's debt and back up the borrower's guaranty by granting a security interest in their assets. This may sound complex, but it is actually a relatively simple transaction.

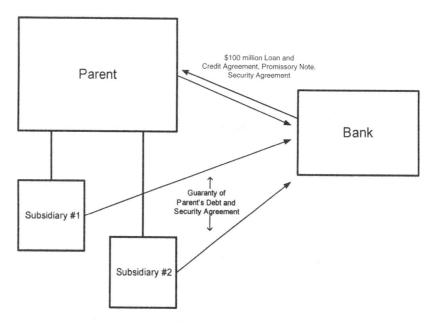

At the client meeting, begin by getting an overview of the transaction and the client's attitude toward it. If the client is eager to discuss the details of the transaction, then bypass the preliminary, overview discussion or integrate it into the discussion of deal points.

Assuming that you begin with a general discussion about the transaction, some of the questions that you might ask are as follows:

- What is the reason for the transaction?
- What are the client's business goals and expectations?
- What would constitute a big win?
- What does the client want to avoid?
- What are the hot-button issues and the deal breakers?
- Is the transaction necessary to the company's survival?
- Is timing a factor? Is time of the essence?

- Do the parties have a previous business relationship? If so, are they parties to any other agreements that will affect the new transaction?
- Is the price a bargain, is it steep, and how was it determined?
- Is it a good deal but one that the client will pass up if the other side is unreasonable or inflexible?
- Which party has negotiating leverage, and what is it?
- How much risk is the client willing to take in different areas?

Knowing the answers to these questions will help you to be more than a simple writer. Your advice will be more strategic, and you will be better able to draft a contract that serves your client's needs.

As part of this discussion, go over negotiating strategy with the client. It may seem premature, as you have not yet drafted the contract, but this is exactly the right time for the first of these discussions. A contract's first draft opens the bidding for the next round of the negotiations, so how you write its provisions affects how the other side responds. Does the client want to start with extreme positions, on the theory that you cannot get what you do not ask for? Or does the client want to start with more moderate positions, to possibly get to a final agreement more quickly? If the latter, the message to the other side is that the moderate provisions are close to final, leaving little room for negotiation. In practice, the negotiation strategy will most likely differ depending on the deal and the provision.

As part of the discussion of negotiating strategy, look at the contract from the other side's perspective. What does the other side need to make a deal? Much of this will already have been discovered in the earlier negotiations between the principals. But as you discuss the business issues with your client, discuss whether your client will be more likely to get what it needs if the contract's first draft reflects the other side's needs. At the same time, discuss how the other side may react to specific provisions. If you think that it will have a strong negative reaction, it may be more strategic for the client to raise the issue directly with the other side's principal.

Next, ask the client how sophisticated the agreement should be. Should you "pull out all the stops" and address every business point that you can think of? If not, should you draft a "down and dirty" contract—that is, a contract that covers only the salient business terms? If the latter, the answer may reflect concerns as to both timing and cost. If cost matters, discuss with your client the consequences of not dealing with certain issues. The associated risks may convince her that you should draft a more detailed contract. You could also decide that some terms should be dealt with summarily, and others, such as the endgame provisions, should be drafted in detail. Of course, these decisions may change during the negotiations.

With these preliminary matters concluded, begin asking specific questions about the transaction. Be sure to keep accurate notes, as you will discuss too many issues to rely on your memory.

Use your checklist as a guide for what needs to be discussed. Although the client will need to answer your specific questions, encourage expansive answers. The more you know, the better you can tailor the contract to the client's needs. If the client raises matters that are not on your checklist, explore them or add them to a list for follow-up. Also, add to that list any questions that the client cannot answer.

As you go through the specific issues on your checklist, the client may instruct you *not* to address a specific business or legal matter. If so, explore the client's rationale. It may be a negotiating strategy. The client may lack negotiating leverage and fear that raising the issue means losing it. By omitting the issue from the contract, the client postpones the problem until a time when he may be in a stronger position.

The client may also see the risk as sufficiently remote or small that she does not want to spend time and money on it. If so, provide the client with the information needed to knowledgeably decide what to do, and then respect that business decision.

Alternatively, the client may tell you that she has established a terrific working relationship with the other side and can rely on their good faith to work out any issues. If so, gently remind the client that her contact person on the other side could change jobs or otherwise be removed from the process, leaving her with just the contract and its provisions.

As you discuss this matter with the client, keep in mind that her focus on the relationship reflects a legitimate approach to negotiating and drafting contracts. Indeed, this approach can often prevail in Japan, for example. When the parties focus on the relationship, they usually put less emphasis on memorializing the deal and will agree to a much less detailed, shorter contract. Nonetheless, U.S. contracts are negotiated in a different culture, where failing to address an issue can be dangerous. Again, your client ultimately must decide.

Finally, a client may want to avoid contentious or unpleasant issues. This can be particularly true with endgame provisions. When putting together a deal, clients often want to focus on its success, not its potential failure. They will resist attempts to address the consequences of the deal foundering. Here, your objectivity can be quite valuable to a client. You can lay out the advantages and disadvantages of including the endgame provisions, as well as the relative merits of specific provisions. Again, the client must decide, but that decision will be a considered one if you do your job right.

As part of this interview, you may also want to ask whether you or the client will take the lead in the negotiations. Although lawyers often negotiate contracts, some business executives are excellent negotiators and want to take the lead on key business terms.

Before the meeting concludes, discuss timing. When does the client want to see a draft, and how quickly does he want to distribute it to the other side? In addition, review what you are to do and any matters on which the client should follow up.

The initial meeting will give you plenty of information with which to work. As you start using it and other information that you gather, you will think of more questions. This is as it should be.

B. LEARNING ABOUT A TRANSACTION FROM A SUPERVISOR

Learning about a new transaction from a supervisor resembles, but is not the same as, learning about it from a client. As a junior drafter, you should consider more senior drafters in your office to be your first clients. Therefore, your interactions with them will in many ways mirror the interaction that you will have with a client. However, receiving an assignment is often a more passive interaction than meeting with a client. When you learn about a transaction from a supervisor, she will probably have already discussed the transaction with the client. Or, if you are working *in house* at a company or the client is the entity where you work, there may have been someone above your supervisor who passed the information to your supervisor about the contracts that need to be drafted and the negotiation that needs to be finalized. When you meet with your supervisor, your job is to ensure that she thoroughly and accurately transfers all that information to you.

Listen carefully to confirm that you understand the nature of the transaction. Are you to draft a sublease or a lease assignment? If you are to draft an employment agreement, should you also draft a noncompetition agreement? You should leave the meeting with all the information and documents that you would have had if you had been in a client meeting, including deal memos, letters of intent, correspondence, previous contracts, and notes. If you need other information, ask for it. Also, ask questions if you do not understand something. Do not be embarrassed. As a junior drafter, you can ask almost any question without others thinking it is dumb. Senior drafters expect you to ask questions at the initial meeting and to return later with even more questions.

Before you leave, find out the deadline and, as much as possible, establish a timeline for the entire transaction. You should ask your supervisor at the very least about the following deadlines and the timing of any other related transactions:

- The date by which you must submit your draft to the supervisor.
- The date by which the supervisor must submit a draft to the client or their own supervisor.
- The date by which your office must deliver the agreement to the other party.

V. PREPARING TO DRAFT A CONTRACT

A. RESEARCHING THE LAW AND OBTAINING THE ADVICE OF SPECIALISTS

Before beginning to draft, determine what legal issues the transaction raises. For example, what are possible endgame scenarios, and will any of them require you to include a liquidated damages provision? If so, you may need to research the law and the industry to help you and your client choose a dollar amount that adequately compensates the injured party but does not convert the provision into an unenforceable penalty provision. Similarly, you must also consider whether any statute affects the agreement. Must you deal with securities regulations, environmental laws, or **Uniform Commercial Code (UCC)** provisions?

You cannot—and should not—research all of an agreement's legal issues before you begin drafting. First, you may not know about an issue until you are working on a specific provision. Second, the client may want to distribute a draft to the other side as quickly as possible. Third, others in your office may have subject matter expertise. Speaking with those lawyers will often save you time and the client money.

In any transaction, you *must* obtain the advice of an accountant, a tax lawyer, or both, unless you are sure that you understand the subtleties of all the issues raised. Almost always, these issues require a specialist's expertise because of their implications. In more sophisticated transactions, these issues might require the transaction's structure to be changed or the deal to be abandoned. Because of these consequences, talk with the accountants and tax lawyers as early as possible in the transaction, if relevant.

B. RESEARCHING THE PARTIES AND THE INDUSTRY

As this book repeatedly explains, before drafting a contract, you must fully understand the business deal and everyone involved. Often, to do this, you must research the client, the other side, and their industry. What you learn will enable you to add value to the deal because of your ability to find and resolve issues that you might otherwise have missed.

For example, assume that your client, a bank, has agreed to lend $5 million to a jewelry manufacturer. As part of the transaction, the borrower has agreed to grant the bank a security interest in their inventory. Taking the security interest may be more complicated than you would expect. In the jewelry industry, manufacturers often consign individual pieces of jewelry to their customers, which are often retail stores. Sometimes these consignments are properly documented with UCC filings. Frequently, however, a manufacturer and their customer operate on a more informal basis. The manufacturer gives the retailer the jewelry "on memo," a short document that recites that the manufacturer has transferred the jewelry to the retailer. The parties file no UCC forms. Without knowing how the borrower's industry functions, you could not draft the proper papers to document the bank's security interest.

With the development of the Internet and libraries and databases that are easy to access at any time, researching a client, the other side, and the parties' industry has become much easier. By going online, you can find annual reports, recent articles, and research analysts' reports. As you sift through this information, try to determine the issues with which the industry — and the parties — are grappling. Then, assess the information and how you can use it to your client's advantage.

If the other side is a public company, also check the **Securities Exchange Commission's (SEC)** EDGAR database for agreements that the public company has entered into that may be related or relevant.[2] If you find one for a transaction similar to the one that you are working on, you may be able to use it against the other side during the negotiations. For example, if the other side insists on a materiality qualifier for a specific representation and warranty, but previously gave it flat, without qualifying it in any way, you can argue more forcefully that no qualifier is required.

VI. DRAFTING WITH AND WITHOUT PRECEDENT OR A STANDARD FORM

A. CHOOSING PRECEDENT OR A STANDARD FORM

Lawyers use precedent or a standard form as the basis of a new agreement. In the drafting context, **precedent** refers to a contract from an earlier transaction. A **standard form**, also known as a **model** or **template**, usually has different possible provisions that you can choose from and that can be adjusted to a real transaction, even possibly annotated with brief explanations and instructions.

Almost all drafting done today begins with precedent or a standard form for two reasons. First, it is efficient. They save time and money. Rather than reinventing the wheel for each new deal, a lawyer gets a head start. Second, if the precedent or standard form is a good one, using it will reduce errors and improve a contract's quality.

There are precedent and standard forms available for almost any type of transaction now, and, generally, you should not have a problem finding one that is on point for your transaction. The more difficult task will be choosing the right one. If you are working directly with a client, ask whether they have a preferred form that they would like you to use. However, carefully review their precedent to confirm that it is appropriate for the new transaction. Clients generally are not lawyers and may not understand why a particular form is inappropriate.

If you are working for a supervisor, ask that person to recommend a precedent or standard form. Drafters tend to use the same precedent or standard form again and again because they are familiar with it and comfortable with its quality. If you use a different one, your supervisor may compare your draft to hers, which may only result in your needing to change the draft so it more closely resembles your supervisor's.

---

2. U.S. Sec. and Exch. Comm'n, *Fillings & Forms* (accessed May 5, 2023), http://www.sec.gov /edgar.shtml.

If no one gives you a precedent or standard form to use, you will need to look for one. If you work in a firm or a general counsel's office (the lawyer for a corporation or similar type of entity), ask your colleagues whether they have a contract from an earlier deal that would work for your transaction. In addition, find out whether your firm or company has a form bank. Many firms and general counsel offices create forms for each type of transaction they handle. Some even annotate the forms' provisions with explanations and instructions on how to tailor them. These forms and contracts should be your first choice because of their quality. In addition, you may have ready access to the precedent's or standard form's drafter, who can explain the purpose behind provisions that you do not understand.

If you do not obtain a precedent or standard form from someone in your office or from the client, you can obtain forms from industry associations, treatises, continuing legal education materials, and online. Be wary of all of these since the quality can vary.

In addition to finding forms online from various vendors, you can search the SEC's EDGAR database, which includes contracts that public companies have entered into and then filed to comply with their disclosure obligations.

When choosing between precedent and standard forms, follow these guidelines:

Guidelines for Choosing Precedent or a Standard Form

1. Choose an agreement that is for the same type of transaction. Do not choose a share purchase agreement if your transaction is a merger.

2. Choose an agreement where the party in your client's position had the greater negotiating leverage and where conditions were as similar as possible. For example, assume that you represent the landlord in the lease of a 35-story building at a time when demand for space is high and first-class space is generally unavailable. In this case, you would want to avoid leases that were negotiated when the real estate market was not doing well, because there were many properties on the market and tenants had the negotiating leverage. A lease from a time when the market was thriving, with fewer properties available on the market, would probably include more landlord-friendly provisions.

3. Look at annotated precedent or standard forms with different options or different drafts of agreements instead of a final executed agreement. Final, executed agreements include all the concessions that the party in your client's position made, so they may not be a good place from which to start. However, a final, executed agreement that has been approved or analyzed by a court in your jurisdiction with relevant provisions could be useful. Most of the time, you will probably want to focus on annotated precedent or standard forms with different options for provisions with explanations and instructions, since they will provide you with various alternatives to consider. Then, you can choose one of the provisions in the annotated precedent or standard form or put together different provisions based on your circumstances. Otherwise, look at drafts of an agreement. Sometimes the first draft sent to the other side under similar circumstances makes a good precedent since it will include your colleagues' and the client's comments and will reflect your side's opening positions.

Keep track of good precedents and standard forms that you find so you can use them in future transactions as additional resources. Analyzing multiple versions of the same type of provision will help you assess the precedent's or standard form's provision and give you ideas about the various ways to draft its substance.

B. USING PRECEDENT AND STANDARD FORMS

Precedent in case law guides the court as it decides how to rule. But because a case is rarely exactly the same as another case, judges must find the similarities and the differences and tailor their opinions accordingly. You should approach a precedent's or standard form's contract provisions in the same way. They should *guide* you as you draft the agreement for your transaction. A precedent's or standard form's words are not engraved in stone. If you are using a form, it represents what others have considered a good starting place. Those who created it intended drafters to modify it for each new transaction. Similarly, if you are using a contract from an earlier deal, the provisions are not specific to your deal, so you must change them.

Using a contract from an earlier deal can be a nightmare when you first begin working as a lawyer. At this stage in your career, you may have trouble figuring out whether a provision is deal-specific or is simply something you do not understand. You cannot ignore it and just leave it in the contract, assuming that it must be correct. You also cannot just delete it, assuming that it is wrong or inapplicable. You must determine its purpose and then actively decide whether to keep, modify, or delete it. If you have access to an annotated precedent or several drafts of the agreement that you are using as a precedent, comparing them may help you determine a provision's role. Having a treatise at hand while drafting may also be helpful.

You will confront one other problem with precedents and standard forms: Many are poorly drafted from a stylistic perspective, even those whose substance is top-notch. In a perfect world, you would redraft each of these provisions, using what you have learned in your law school drafting course and your practice experience. Unfortunately, you generally will not have that option. Redrafting a provision is time-consuming, and you probably will not have that time in a fast-paced transaction. In addition, your firm will want to bill that time to the client, who may resist paying the firm for work that it considers unnecessary.

When at a firm and confronted with a poorly drafted provision, determine whether the existing language creates ambiguity. If it does, redraft it, but mention your changes in the e-mail to your supervisor. Her perspective may differ from yours. If the provision is unambiguous but otherwise poorly drafted, use the provision as is and then deal with its problems after the transaction finishes. Then, consult with the firm's *keeper of the forms*, who will probably appreciate your input. Do not change the firm's master form without permission.

You may be able to change your approach to redrafting poorly drafted provisions as you become a more experienced drafter. As you gain the confidence of your supervisor, she may give you greater latitude to rework a form's provisions.

If you have your own firm, you will probably be unable to clean up a precedent or standard form all at once, even if you want to, because of the other demands on your time. Instead, redraft one or two provisions each time you use the precedent or standard form. By spreading out the work over time, you will be able to manage the task more readily.

C. DRAFTING WITHOUT PRECEDENT OR A STANDARD FORM

Occasionally, you may need to draft a contract for which you can find no precedent or standard form. If this occurs, take a step back and think about the substantive provisions that the contract will need. Do other contracts have similar provisions, even if they are not exactly on point? Can you draft the contract by patching together relevant provisions from different agreements?

For example, suppose that a shareholder requests a new share certificate to replace the one that he has lost. Your client, the corporation that issued the share certificate, is willing to replace it but does not want to be liable if someone subsequently presents the original. The corporation asks that you draft something to protect them. You agree to do so but then cannot find a precedent or standard form.

Although you lack a complete, exact one, you can borrow and modify the substantive provisions of other contracts. From a business perspective, your client has two goals. First, they want the shareholder's assurance that he still owns the shares and that the reason the share certificate is missing is that he lost it, not because he transferred it to a third party. Second, your client wants to be able to sue the shareholder for damages if someone else presents the original certificate.

To accomplish these business goals, you can borrow substantive provisions from two agreements. To address your client's first concern, you could modify a representation and warranty on share ownership from a share purchase agreement.

> *Example — Modifying a Representation and Warranty on Shared Ownership from a Share Purchase Agreement*
>
> **Shareholder's Representations and Warranties**. The Shareholder represents and warrants to the Corporation the following:
>
> (a) The Shareholder owns the shares represented by Certificate No. 3345.
> (b) The Shareholder has not transferred to any third party the shares represented by Certificate No. 3345.
> (c) The Shareholder has lost Certificate No. 3345.

To deal with your client's second concern, you could draft an indemnity provision, tailoring the subject matter performance provision of almost any indemnity agreement, as follows:

> *Example — Tailoring the Subject Matter Performance Provision of an Indemnity Agreement*
>
> **Indemnification**. The Shareholder shall indemnify and defend the Corporation against any liabilities and losses arising from the Shareholder's loss of Certificate No. 3345.

With these key business provisions in place, you can draft the remainder of the contract. However, remember to make sure that you are aware of any relevant issues relating to these issues in the jurisdiction in question.

VII. THE LOGISTICS OF DRAFTING A CONTRACT

If you are drafting a contract using precedent or a standard form, first copy the agreement and put the original aside. Always keep the original agreement unchanged so it can be used again.

If you are going to hand mark changes on a hard copy of the agreement for someone else to input into the electronic version, photocopy the original onto 8½-by-14-inch paper and reduce the size of the photocopy to 90 percent. This allows more room for your markup and makes it easier for you and others to read the changes to be made. Sometimes it can be easier to make changes on the hard-copy version of the document because that allows you to flip back and forth easily from one provision to another.

Every draft of the contract that you distribute, whether internally where you work, to the client, or to third parties, should be numbered and dated in the right or left header, similar to the following example:

Example—Numbering and Dating the Contract in the Header

Draft 1
June 13, 20__

This information not only distinguishes one draft from the next, but it also may be evidence that the draft was not intended as a final and binding agreement.[3]

Be sure to distinguish internal drafts from those sent to third parties. If you distribute two drafts at your firm before sending the agreement outside the firm, those distributions could be *Internal Draft 1* and *Internal Draft 2*. The first distribution outside the firm would be *Draft 1*. There are other numbering variations that can be used to differentiate internal drafts from outside drafts, such as using 1A and 1B for the two internal drafts and simply 1 for the outside draft.

Next, set up electronic file systems to keep track of the internal and external drafts. With respect to the electronic copies of the agreement, create a folder for each draft and keep in it the draft that was distributed and any electronic comments that you receive. By keeping a copy of each draft, you can always easily reinsert into Draft 4, for example, the provision that you deleted from Internal Draft 2C. In addition, you will have electronic precedents available for future transactions.

You may also want hard-copy files. If so, use one accordion-type, expandable folder for each draft and label it with the appropriate draft number and date. In the folder, store a hard copy of the draft, along with all the comments that you received from your colleagues, whether electronically or on a hard copy of the agreement.

In addition to helping you stay organized, keeping electronic and hard-copy files in good condition will show your supervisors that you are organized and in control of the task. Supervisors worry about every aspect of a transaction, including whether you know what you are doing. If you can reduce their worry, that will reduce the pressure on you.

VIII. DRAFTING A CONTRACT

A. COORDINATING WITH OTHER DRAFTERS

Although you may draft most of the contract, others in your office may be responsible for drafting portions of it. For example, when drafting a bank loan agreement, you might need inserts drafted by members of the environmental, labor, tax, and real estate departments. Those lawyers will appreciate your giving them as much lead time as possible.

B. TRANSLATING THE BUSINESS DEAL INTO CONTRACT CONCEPTS

Before beginning to draft, list or outline all the business terms of the deal that you will have to draft. Use the letter of intent, term sheet, or memorandum of understanding

---

3. *See In re Windsor Plumbing Supply Co., Inc.*, 170 B.R. 503, 522-523 (Bankr. E.D.N.Y. 1994); *Girardi v. Shaffer*, 2003 WL 23138445 at *7 (Bankr. E.D. Va. Jan. 17, 2003).

as a starting point. Then check your notes from discussions with your client or supervisor and go through the precedent and secondary materials. (You may have already done the latter if you created your own checklist or added to one that you obtained from your firm or elsewhere.) In addition, consider whether the cascade effect will require you to draft any new provisions or change any existing provisions. Also, use the five-area framework (discussed in Chapter 30 on page 459) to analyze whether the contract must address any other deal-specific business issues. Finally, review the different ways that the parties' relationship could evolve, and confirm that you and the client have settled on a way to deal with each of them (particularly endgame scenarios)—ask "What if?" All of this is time-consuming but critical to the drafting process.

Once you have listed all the business terms of the deal, translate them into contract concepts to make them into provisions. Then, reorganize the list so that what used to be business terms of the deal and are now provisions appear in the order in which they will appear in the contract. Use your precedent or standard form and the organizing principles that you learned in Chapter 31 on page 485 to help you order the list. As an aid for organization, consider having a separate piece of paper or space on an electronic document for each aspect of what you are organizing. If you are drafting an acquisition agreement, then gather all the needed representations and warranties on one page, covenants on a second page, and conditions on a third. As you are doing this, keep asking yourself if there is a cascade effect—a covenant that you need because you added a representation and warranty. If you are organizing the contract by subject matter, each subject should have its own page. When you have finished all this, you are ready to input all these provisions into the contract and draft further directly in the contract. Setting out what you will need and properly organizing those provisions will help you make sure that you have covered everything that you need to and will help you recognize how the various parts and provisions may be related. After you have practiced for a while, you should be able to shorten this process, but, in the beginning, it will help you to go through all the steps.

C. DRAFTING THE FIRST DRAFT

1. How to Begin

Where do you begin? You have your list of provisions to add from the section above, but how do you actually decide what to write first? Drafters differ in their approach, and your approach may change depending on the agreement. You may not want to start with the introductory provisions (title, preamble, recitals, and words of agreement) because you may have an idea for a tough provision and want to try drafting it right away. But absent a good reason to start somewhere else, start with the introductory provisions. Drafting these provisions first will establish the defined terms for the parties and will begin to put words on the page. Writer's block can be as much of a problem when writing contracts as when writing memos and briefs, and beginning with the introductory provisions will help ease you into the rest of the drafting process.

2. Definitions

Although the definitions article generally follows the words of agreement, drafting *all* the definitions is usually *not* the next thing to do. Many drafters prefer to skip the definitions article entirely and deal with a definition only when they need the defined term to draft a provision. This practice works well because it forces the drafter to see how the definition will really be used and fine-tune it accordingly. Also, it helps drafters see better if a definition can be fully included in the definitions section or whether the defined term will have to be defined in context and simply listed in the definitions section.

Some drafters do draft some of the definitions before they turn to the contract's substantive provisions. Those who do so generally work on definitions that they know they need to revise. The ability to do this develops as you work on multiple deals and become familiar with the regularly used definitions. These drafters then deal with the remaining definitions as needed.

Whether you skip the definitions or draft some of them early, stay sensitive to the need to draft new ones as you continue through the drafting and negotiation process. Draft the definitions while you are working on the relevant provisions. As you work with the definitions, remember that they are being incorporated into substantive contract provisions and they will have substantive consequences. They are standards that, when changed, affect the business deal and the parties' rights and obligations. Accordingly, make sure that each definition works each time that its defined term is used.

3. Business Provisions

After the definitions, turn to your list of business terms from Section VIII.B in this chapter. If you have already organized that list so that it coordinates with the sequence of the contract's provisions, you have a road map for working through the contract. But you will probably not stay on a straight path to the signature lines. Drafting is often not linear.[4] Contracts evolve, and the process is often messy.

As you work through the contract, you will constantly refine your ideas and what you have drafted. You will see issues that were not apparent when you started drafting. You may decide on a new provision or do complete redrafts of provisions that you thought you had finished. You may also decide not to revise all of the provisions your first time through the contract. You may prefer to make the easy changes in one round of revisions and then, in the next, return to the more sophisticated provisions. On the other hand, you may draft all the terms in the letter of intent in the first markup and turn to all the other provisions in the next. Most drafters go through at least three or four rounds of revisions before they have a first draft to distribute.

Some provision hopping should be part of your planned approach to drafting. Indeed, it is good practice to work on related provisions at the same time. For example, if you are drafting an acquisition agreement, you should draft the seller's representation and warranty about its equipment and the related covenant about maintaining that equipment at the same time. This will decrease the possibility that the provisions will have different standards and violate the *Say the same thing in the same way* rule. Similarly, provision hopping makes sense if you add a new provision that causes a cascade effect. If you choose not to draft related provisions at the same time, make a margin note in the precedent at the intended location of the second provision to remind yourself of what you still must do.

As you work through the contract, you will have questions. Do not stop drafting and wait to get an answer. Instead, do one or more of the following:

- Create a list of questions to ask your client or supervising lawyer.
  - ◆ Do not call or e-mail every time you have a question.

- Put the provision about which you have a question in brackets.
  - ◆ This option works well if you will not be able to ask a question before submitting your draft.

---

4. Scott J. Burnham, *Drafting and Analyzing Contracts* 318 (3d ed. 2003).

- Craft two or more versions of the provision, putting each in brackets.
    - This shows the reader the options.
- Describe the issue in an e-mail to your supervisor or client.
    - By explaining the issue, you may help the reader decide how to handle it.

Also, set up a system to deal with cross-references. As you draft, you may find that one provision needs to refer to another. Because provisions will change their location as you work through the drafting process, you need to track the cross-references so you can update them properly when you finalize the contract. To deal with this, insert the correct cross-reference at the time of the initial drafting in a large, bold font inside a set of brackets or highlight it. Then, later, you can search for a bracket or the bold reference and insert the revised cross-reference. Alternatively, most word-processing programs can keep track if you properly code the cross-reference.

Choosing the right words to express the deal is challenging — but fun. As you have seen throughout this book, the smallest change in a word or a phrase affects the parties' rights and obligations. Use your knowledge of the business and legal consequences of the contract concepts to guide you in tailoring the provisions. For example, draft a representation and warranty broadly and with no qualifiers if your client will receive the representations and warranties. Keep the following guidelines in mind while you are drafting the rest of the business provisions:

Guidelines for Drafting the Business Provisions

1. Do not recut the deal. Although you are more than a simple writer, you are not a principal. Do not draft a provision so that it favors your client more than the agreed-on deal intended. Doing so could be an ethical violation.

2. Determine whether one party will have more control. If you represent the less-powerful party, you may be able to protect them better with detailed provisions that spell out their rights.

3. Determine whether vagueness or specificity will benefit your client. The answer usually depends on the specific provision.

4. If the contract establishes a relationship that will exist for a term of years, build in flexibility so each change in circumstances does not create a contractual crisis.

5. Use the canons of construction (some discussed in Chapter 27 on page 432) to give you insight into how a court might interpret a provision, and rewrite the provision as needed. For example, rewrite the provision if the parties' intent differs from that possible interpretation and clarify any unclear or ambiguous provisions. If you have to raise a problem with a provision and the other party has superior negotiating leverage, that party may try to strengthen the provision so that it favors them even more. If so, remember that the canons of construction are only a last resort — something to give you and your client comfort if a provision cannot be clarified because of the client's weak negotiating position (e.g., *contra proferentem*, the principle that a contract should be construed against the party who drafted it). Therefore, address such issues as much as possible in the negotiation and drafting process, even if you have to insist on particularly important terms.

6. Draft the contract to deal with all the possibilities of an *if/then* scenario. As you have seen, covenants, discretionary authority, and declarations can be subject to conditions. When you draft a provision that sets out an *if/then* business term, think through what happens if the opposite fact pattern occurs. Does the contract already provide for this possibility? If not, discuss with your client how to handle this new situation. For example, the endgame provisions of most employment agreements deal with the possibility of a termination for cause.

> ### Example — Endgame Provisions with Termination for Cause
>
> **Termination for Cause.** If the Company terminates the Executive for Cause, the Company shall pay the Executive . . .

This *if/then* scenario should make you think of another: termination without cause.

7. Draft a real-world, pragmatic contract that reflects how the parties will interact. Good writing alone does not make a good contract. If a contract's provisions are impractical and will not work on a day-to-day basis, redraft them.

As noted earlier, it may take three or four rounds of revisions to produce your first draft. As you refine it to reflect the business deal as accurately as possible, also look at the contract from a good writing perspective and do the following, as described in Part D:

- Eliminate legalese. (Chapter 22)
- Create clarity through format. (Chapter 23)
- Create clarity through sentence structure. (Chapter 24)
- Eliminate ambiguity. (Chapter 25)

4. Finalizing the Contract

To finalize the contract, do the following:

- Run your word-processing program's spell check.
- Check that all cross-references are correct.
- Print out a hard copy and proofread it carefully.
  - ◆ No matter how good you are at reviewing a document on an electronic device, you will find substantive errors and glitches when reviewing a hard copy that you will not find when looking at the contract on a screen.
  - ◆ Read the contract slowly; look at what you wrote and see if it coincides with what you thought you wrote.

D. REDRAFTING THE CONTRACT

No contract is ever finished after the first draft. Most lawyers are constant revisers and cannot read through a contract without making at least one change. Anyone who reads your draft, whether a supervisor or client, will have comments. Receiving comments does not mean that you did a poor job. It is part of the drafting process. Even senior drafters will have other lawyers review their drafts. In a large firm, you may need to take comments from several lawyers — generally lawyers in other departments who did not give you their input as you were working on your first draft. By working through all these comments, the contract will improve, and you will learn a great deal about drafting.

You will receive comments in several ways. Some readers will talk through their comments with you. This can be helpful because it gives you an opportunity to ask questions. You can take notes on these conversations in two basic ways: by hand or on your computer. You can use a word processor's comment function, taking notes in a balloon adjacent to the applicable draft language. On the other hand, you may prefer to take handwritten notes. If you prefer the latter, create extra room for note-taking by photocopying the draft onto 8½-by-14-inch paper and reducing the copy to 90 percent. When you take notes, consider using a different color for each person or some kind of system for differentiating between them. Then, you will find it easier to report who made which comments. Your supervisor or client may need this information to reconcile conflicting comments.

Some of the people reviewing your draft may mark their comments on a hard copy of the draft and then give you the draft. Others will use a word-processing program's comment function or input changes on an electronic copy of the contract and give you a redlined version, which shows changes by underlining new language and striking through deleted language.

Increasingly, drafters and reviewers are working on a common online platform, and everyone has different levels of access to the contract on that platform. Often, even both sides of the transaction will have access to the contract on that platform and changes can be made at any time. This makes it harder to keep track of drafts and who may have included *what* and *where* in the contract. You may want to consider designating one person from each party to be the one to input changes in the document. By taking on that role yourself, you will be better able to keep track of changes and make sure that nothing slips by you.

Always follow up if you cannot figure out what a reviewer means. Also, as you receive or read through comments, think through whether they are correct. They may not be. You may have already dealt with a point elsewhere, or the comment may be inconsistent with your understanding of the business deal or another comment that you have received. If you disagree with a comment, discuss it with the person who made the comment.

Look carefully at each provision before you modify it. You may need to change additional language in that provision so the requested change works properly. You may also need to change another provision or draft a new one because of the cascade effect. If you cut and paste in a new provision from another agreement, check that the relevant standards in the revised contract are consistent. Sometimes you will introduce a new standard without intending to do so.

When you finish making the requested changes, read the entire contract. Inevitably, you will find glitches and substantive issues that you and others did not see. You may be the only one readily able to spot these problems because of your familiarity with the contract. You will also have to print it out once more to do the final review.

With that, you have completed your first draft for external distribution.

E. MESSAGE TO SUPERVISOR OR CLIENT

Your communications with supervisors and clients about business transactions will mostly be over e-mail. If your firm or workplace uses a different system for transmitting messages and documents, you would put together the same type of message that we describe here and send it through that system. When you distribute the first draft of the contract (indeed, any draft), send it in an e-mail with a message that includes the following:

- Tell the reader where to find the provisions that deal with hot-button issues.
- Explain the risks and benefits of provisions not previously discussed.
- Describe open issues and propose ways of resolving them.

If you take notes on these points as you draft, writing this message will be much easier. Spend time on this message. Keeping your supervisor and client informed is part of your job. Indeed, you have an ethical obligation to keep the client informed, as discussed further in Chapter 35 on page 551. A short, well-written message that highlights the most important issues will help you do that.

Choose the recipients of your message carefully. If it contains privileged information, sending it to the wrong person could destroy the attorney-client privilege. You can find more information online about drafting messages to the client and writing to the other side after reviewing their draft on the CasebookConnect Resources page and at www.aspenpublishing.com.

If you are in a practice setting or working with a client that is more formal, you may need to draft a memorandum for your supervisor or client on these issues. You can find guidelines online about how to draft that memorandum on the Casebook Connect Resources page and at www.aspenpublishing.com.

IX. EXERCISES

A. Exercise 32A: Checklist of Questions for a Client

Your client has called and wants to come in for a meeting. She has decided to create a website for her business and must sign a contract with a marketing company. Create a checklist of questions to ask her. As a starting place, you can find the Website Development Agreement (Version 1) on the CasebookConnect Resources page and at www.aspenpublishing.com. In addition, find at least two other website development agreements and use their provisions to create additional checklist questions.

B. Exercise 32B: Diagram a Transaction

Diagram the following transaction: A corporation ("**Parent**") is the sole shareholder of Subsidiary A ("**Sub A**") and owns 51 percent of the outstanding shares of Subsidiary B ("**Sub B**"). The target ("**Target**") is a wholly owned subsidiary of Target-Parent. Target is to merge into Sub A, with Sub A being the surviving corporation. Sub A will pay Target-Parent with funds Sub A borrows from Big Bank. Sub A has agreed to secure Sub A's debt by granting a security interest in all Sub A's assets to Big Bank. Parent will guarantee Sub A's debt and will back up the guaranty by pledging the shares Parent owns in Sub A and Sub B.

In your diagram, make sure you include all the parties referred to in the description, use their shorthand names, and explain *briefly* what is most important (e.g., the relationship between the parties, what is given or transferred from one party to the other, and vice versa). You do not have to come up with any additional acronyms, but if you do, make sure to include a key with what those acronyms stand for in your diagram.

C. Exercise 32C: Research and Draft Language for Letter of Intent

Research letters of intent and then draft the language that you would use to clarify that a letter of intent did not bind the parties to consummate the transaction.

CHAPTER THIRTY-THREE

How to Review and Comment on a Contract

I. INTRODUCTION

Every contract has at least two primary drafters: the one who writes the initial draft and the one who reviews that draft and suggests changes. In some ways, reviewing a contract is more difficult than writing it. Not only must a reviewing drafter prepare for that review in the same way that a drafter prepares to draft the first draft, but the reviewing drafter must also try to determine what the first drafter was thinking when the provision was written. If a provision is not clear or has problems, the reviewing drafter has to try to figure out the intent of the initial drafter by reverse engineering. They must look at the finished product and figure out the thinking process that created it.

In this chapter, you will learn how to analyze a contract, identify key issues, and give comments. Just as drafting requires more than changing the names and dates in a precedent, analyzing a contract requires more than reading it. The following five steps that you can follow when reviewing and commenting on a contract will be covered in the rest of this chapter:

1. Prepare.
2. Review the contract briefly for a quick overview.
3. Read and analyze the key business provisions.
4. Read and analyze the entire contract.
5. Mark up the contract and give comments.

The ability to analyze a contract and its provisions is an important drafting skill. To **analyze a contract** means to disassemble it to understand the other side's objectives; the contract's business, legal, and drafting nuances; and the issues raised. A drafter protects their client by determining what must be negotiated after reading the other side's draft contract. Each point found is to be negotiated and finalized as much as possible in favor of the client.

You have spent the semester learning how to analyze a contract, even though you may not have been aware of it. The lessons were integrated into learning to draft. First, you learned the contract concepts and their respective business and legal purposes. Then you practiced reading a contract and recognizing what contract concepts were used to memorialize the business terms. You also learned **the close reading skill**: What did individual words mean, and what was the client's business perspective on these words? This skill helps you add further value to the deal. Finally, you engaged in **guided reading**, where you reviewed unfamiliar contracts but you worked your way through them with the help of annotations that explained new concepts and others that asked *thinking* questions. Now that you have this expertise, you are ready to analyze a contract's provisions.

II. PREPARE

Prepare in exactly the same way that you would have if you had been the drafter, before you even read the other side's draft. As we discussed in Chapter 32 on page 495, you must do the following:

- Obtain all available information about the business deal.
- Create a checklist of questions for your supervisor or client.
- Draw a diagram of the transaction if necessary.
- Interview your supervisor or client thoroughly.
- Research the law, the parties, and the industry.
- Obtain the advice of specialists if necessary.
- Find appropriate precedents.
- Create a list of the business terms of the deal (both those that the parties have agreed to and any new ones to be incorporated).
- Translate the business terms of the deal into contract concepts to make them into provisions.
- Organize what are now provisions representing the business terms of the deal in the sequence in which you expect that they will appear in the contract, and try to figure out in which part of the agreement you would put them.

Without this preparation, you cannot effectively review a contract because you will not have the knowledge or the tools to determine whether the draft appropriately memorializes that deal.

III. REVIEW THE CONTRACT TO GET A QUICK OVERVIEW

The first time you look at a contract, take a quick look through it to get a simple overview. This means doing even less than skimming it, and you should not be reading any of the provisions. You should mainly be looking at the headings of articles and titles of subsections to get a sense of the following: How is the contract organized? By subject matter? By contract concept? Is the organization similar to the precedent that you are familiar with? How does it differ? Where are the action sections? Do the captions look familiar, or does the contract contain provisions that you had not expected?

With this information, you will gain a sense of the contract in the same way that you would gain the sense of a history textbook by looking at its table of contents and flipping through the pages. You will not have the details, but you will know where the details are and whether the contract at least appears to be within the expected norm.

IV. READ AND ANALYZE THE KEY BUSINESS PROVISIONS

A. GENERAL APPROACH

Once you have a sense of how the contract is generally organized from your quick overview, review the key business provisions to see if the contract has correctly stated the most significant business terms. Clients or supervisors frequently call shortly after you receive a contract—often before you could have reasonably been expected to have reviewed it fully. By looking at the key business provisions first, you will be able to follow what they are saying, ask some of the first follow-up questions, and even possibly address your client's immediate concerns.

Generally, you should read the payment provisions in the action sections first. Clients often consider these to be a contract's most important provisions. Has the other side gotten the money terms right? If not, the contract has either been poorly drafted or the parties have had a serious misunderstanding. As you look at the payment provisions, analyze each provision using either the short list or the long list of contract analysis included in Section IV.B, which follows.

Next, look at the endgame provisions. Look at them from two perspectives: When does the other side have rights against your client, and when does your client have rights against the other side? Also, confirm that the contract ties up all the loose ends—for example, look to see if the contract provides for the return of deposits and post-termination payments. Finally, remember that endgame and money provisions often go hand in hand. Under what circumstances will your client lose the benefits of the contract, and how much will that cost? As you look at the endgame provisions, like the payment provisions, analyze each provision using either the short list of the long list of contract analysis included in Section IV.B.

Then, turn to the provisions dealing with the most significant other business terms. These may not be intuitively obvious. Sometimes these points reflect concerns specific to your client. For example, assume that you represent an executive in connection with the negotiation and drafting of her employment agreement. The executive may have a special interest in a charity because of her family's circumstances (an illness, for example). As a partial inducement, the employer may have agreed to donate $50,000 a year to that charity. This issue probably does not appear on any treatise checklist or in any precedent, but it may matter greatly to your client. Again, use either the short list or the long list of contract analysis included in Section IV.B.

B. HOW TO ANALYZE EACH PROVISION

When reading the key business provisions detailed in Section IV.A, focus on the substance of the business deal, not on how you might change specific wording. You will deal with possible changes that you might make when you do the markup.

Break down and analyze each key business provision separately. You must ask and answer the six questions that follow for each provision. These six questions make up the suggested short list of questions for the analysis of provisions:

Short Checklist for Analysis of Provisions

1. What is the business purpose of the provision?
2. Does the provision properly incorporate the agreed-on business deal?
3. Can the provision be changed to better protect the client and reduce the risk?
4. Can the provision be changed to further advance the client's goals?
5. Are there legal issues?
6. Are there drafting issues?

If you want to go into more depth in your analysis and ensure you cover all the areas addressed in this text's Parts D and E, use the long list of questions for the analysis of provisions, which has seven questions with subparts, and can be found on the following page. Note that you can also use the short or long list of questions to analyze any other provision in the contract.

Long Checklist for Analysis of Provisions

1. **Provision's Business Purpose.**
   (a) What is the provision's business purpose?
      (i) What does your client want from this provision?
      (ii) How does the other side perceive this provision? What will be its most significant issue with it?
   (b) From a neutral perspective, as drafted, does the provision accomplish its purpose?
      (i) Does it properly state the business deal? Stated differently, are the business terms incorporated correctly?
      (ii) Does the provision follow the guidelines for drafting this type of provision? (For example: If it is a monetary payment, does the provision include both a statement of the amount and the obligation to pay for each type of consideration? If it is a covenant, has it answered the *who, what, when, where, why, how,* and *how much* questions?)
2. **Client's Business Goal.** As drafted, does the provision accomplish the client's business goal? Does this provision hurt the client? Can the client's interests be further advanced or protected?
3. **Legal Issues.** Does the provision implicate any legal issues?
4. **Industry and Practice.** Are there any industry- or practice-specific points to be considered?
5. **Implicate Other Provisions.** Does the provision implicate any other provision (cascade effect)?
6. **Other Business Issues — Add Value.** Does analysis reveal any other business issues? Use the five-area framework from Chapter 30 on page 459 to see how you can add more value.
   (a) Money — Does the contract follow the cash?
   (b) Risk — Has risk been allocated appropriately?
   (c) Control — Who is the decision maker? Can the right to decide be expanded or limited? How can the client control risk?
   (d) Standards — Can the standards be made more client-friendly? What kind of standard is best, one that is vague or one that is specific?
   (e) Endgame — Does the agreement include the appropriate defaults, remedies, exit provisions, and provisions for a happy ending?
7. **Drafting Issues.** Are there other drafting issues?
   (a) Is there ambiguity?
   (b) Does the statement of each business term use the right contract concept and the right signal for that contract concept?
   (c) Is there legalese to be deleted?
   (d) Can clarity be created through formatting?
   (e) Can clarity be created through a change in sentence structure?

V. READ AND ANALYZE THE ENTIRE CONTRACT

A. GENERAL APPROACH

After reading the key business provisions, read and analyze the entire contract from the beginning. Imagine right now that you are drafting the contract and marking up a precedent. As you look at each provision, think about what changes you would make. These provisions are not engraved in stone. Many are merely the other side's opening bid with respect to issues that the parties did not discuss. You cannot recut the business deal, but you can negotiate how it is memorialized.

If the contract includes a definitions article, you may take two different approaches to its review. If you have not previously drafted or reviewed this type of contract, consider initially skipping the article entirely, but then returning to it each time that you confront a defined term. If you have previously drafted or reviewed this type of contract, look for key definitions and skim them to see if they seem relatively standard. If not, pay special attention to the provisions that include the related defined terms. The drafter may have made substantive changes to relatively standard provisions by changing the definitions instead of changing the language in the provisions themselves. In either event, physically separate the definitions article from the rest of the contract. This will enable you to place it and the contract side by side so you can look at a definition and a provision at the same time.

As you continue going through the contract, do not be tied to the order of the contract provisions. Instead, mimic the drafting process. Provision-hop as necessary so that you review related provisions at the same time. Once you deal with a point, go back to where you left off so that you cover every provision. Some drafters check off each provision after they have read it.

In this review, you will analyze provisions as simple as the introductory provisions and as substantive as the action sections. To help you focus on the business issues, use the five-area framework from Chapter 30 on page 459 the same way that you would have had you been the drafter. Review the contract slowly or you will miss issues.

You may have stylistic comments: legalese, lack of formatting, and so on. Generally, you should defer to the drafter on these matters. If she still drafts as if she were in eighteenth-century England, so be it. Do not spend negotiating capital on whether the contract should say *aforesaid* or *previously* (unless there is ambiguity created because of this language). Although stylistic comments are generally inappropriate, some drafters appreciate them. However, it is generally bad form to raise these points at a negotiating session, especially if clients are present. Instead, mark up the relevant provisions and give them to the drafter privately. You may appropriately note in these comments any misspellings, missing, or incorrect words, or other glitches.

Look not only at what is in the contract, but for what is missing. Reviewing lawyers tend to focus on the words on the page, not on what is absent. Use your checklist to determine whether all the business terms were included. Also, step back and think about your client's goals. Does the contract achieve those goals, or are other provisions needed?

As you go through the contract, make notes in the margin, circle problem language, or otherwise indicate any concern that you have with the language. Write your comments simply and clearly, especially if the contract is long, so that you will not have trouble recalling your point. Also, do not do a detailed markup or draft inserts as you go through the contract this time. Subsequent provisions may affect your view of a provision. In addition, you will need the client's input.

B. QUESTIONS TO ASK WHEN REVIEWING THE ENTIRE CONTRACT

As we have already discussed, you can use the short or long list of questions introduced in Section IV.B to analyze any other provision in the contract. Apart from the key business provisions, there may be other provisions for which you may also want to go in more depth and analyze further using those lists.

Separately from your analysis of specific provisions at that deeper level, here are some questions that you should ask each time you review a contract. Note that some are pure drafting issues, while others are part of your overall contract analysis. The list below incorporates some of the issues that we cover in the short and long lists of questions introduced in Section IV.B. Our goal is to give you different options on how to approach your review of the entire contract and its provisions. As you move forward in your career, you will develop and continue to refine your own system.

Questions to Ask When Reviewing the Entire Contract

1. Preamble. Are the parties' names and other information in the preamble correct? Are the correct parties being bound? (See Chapter 14 on page 155.)

2. Recitals. Are the recitals accurate? What would be the effect on your client if they became stipulated facts in a lawsuit? Did the drafter put any substantive provisions in the recitals? (See Chapter 14 on page 168.)

3. Definitions. Does each definition work each time a provision uses its defined term?[1] Are any substantive provisions in the definitions? (See Chapter 15 on page 183.)

4. Action Sections. Are the provisions in the action sections correct? (See Chapter 16 on page 209.)

(a) *Payment Provisions.* Carefully analyze the monetary provisions. Do they work? Does the contract appropriately restrict your client's obligation to pay? Should the other party be paying your client more? Is the other party creditworthy? Should the conditions to the other party's obligation to pay be more easily satisfied? In all instances, do the payment provisions answer the following questions: *who, what, when, where, why, how,* and *how much*? (See Chapter 16 on page 211.)

(b) *Effective Date.* Does the contract include an effective date? If it does, is the trigger for the effective date properly stated? (See Chapter 14 on page 156 and Chapter 19 on page 298.)

(c) *End of Term.* If the contract is for a stated term, what could prematurely terminate it?[2] Should the contract term automatically renew? (See Chapter 16 on page 219.)

5. Representations and Warranties. (See Chapter 3 on page 13 and Chapter 8 on page 55.)

(a) *Your Client.* Are the representations and warranties that your client is being asked to make accurate? Do they allocate too much risk to your client? How can they be qualified to reduce the risk? Does the contract ask your client to make representations and warranties that are unrelated to the transaction?

(b) *Other Side.* Has the other side made representations and warranties? Are they too weak? If so, how can they be strengthened? What additional representations and warranties should they make?

---

1. Check the use of each defined term by using your word-processing program's *Find* function to look for every time the defined term in question is used. Go through each use of the defined term that you are checking. To check each use of the defined term, substitute the definition for that defined term in your reading of the provision to make sure it makes sense. If it does not, you may have to either refine the definition and start your checking all over again or use a different defined term or normal phrase in that particular provision.

2. Most contracts deal with this issue in the endgame provisions. However, sometimes drafters deal with it in the action sections.

6. **Covenants.** (See Chapter 4 on page 25 and Chapter 9 on page 71.)
   (a) *Your Client.* Can your client perform their covenants? Are they too difficult? Does your client have control over the outcome of each of their covenants? What would decrease the degree of obligation? Should any of the covenants instead be conditions to the other party's obligation to perform? Should any of the covenants include an exception?
   (b) *Other Side.* Has the other side made the necessary covenants? If not, what additional or different covenants are needed? How should the degree of obligation be changed? Should any of the covenants include an exception?
7. **Conditions.** (See Chapter 6 on page 39 and Chapter 11 on page 107.)
   (a) *Your Client.* Should the conditions to your client's obligation to perform be more demanding? Should any of your client's covenants be recast as a condition?
   (b) *Other Side.* Are any conditions to the other side's obligation to perform inappropriate? Should any condition to the other side's obligation to perform be recast as a covenant?
8. **Endgame Provisions.** Have you carefully examined the endgame provisions? Do they provide for early termination? What constitutes *default* or *cause*? What are the remedies? Does the contract provide for a friendly termination? Are all the loose ends tied up? Should one or more provisions survive the contract's termination? If an endgame provision involves money, does it answer the *who, what, when, where, why, how,* and *how much* questions? Should disputes be litigated, arbitrated, or mediated? (See Chapter 17 on page 229.)
9. **General Provisions.** Does the contract include all the appropriate general provisions? If any are omitted, what are the consequences? Has each provision been tailored to reflect the parties' agreement? (See Chapter 16 on page 263.)
10. **Signatures.** Are the signature blocks properly set up? Are the names correct? Are they the same names as those in the preamble? If a party is an entity, does its signature line indicate the signatory's title? (See Chapter 19 on page 295.)
11. **Other Drafting Considerations.**
    (a) *Legalese.* Is there legalese that should be deleted? (See Chapter 22 on page 331.)
    (b) *Clarity Through Format.* Does the contract use formatting to enhance clarity? (See Chapter 23 on page 339.)
    (c) *Clarity Through Sentence Structure.* Does each sentence's structure enhance its clarity? (See Chapter 24 on page 361.)
    (d) *Ambiguity.* Is any provision ambiguous? Are two or more provisions ambiguous when read together? (See Chapter 25 on page 371.)
    (e) *Saying the Same Thing in the Same Way.* Do the contract provisions say the same thing in the same way? If the standards differ, should they? (See Chapter 25 on page 380.)
    (f) *Formulas.* With respect to each mathematical formula, have you created hypotheticals to check whether the formula is properly stated? Have you received accounting and tax advice? (See Chapter 26 on page 403.)
    (g) *Adding Value.* Have you used the five-area framework to analyze the contract's provisions? (See Chapter 30 on page 459.)
    (h) *Organization.* Does the contract's organization facilitate its reading? (See Chapter 31 on page 483.)

12. Business Terms, Parties, and Industry. (See Chapter 32 on page 493.)

(a) *All Terms Incorporated.* Has each business point been incorporated? Does the contract deal with all the scenarios that you and the client discussed? If not, do you need to include any of the missing scenarios, or has the client reached a business judgment not to deal with them? Is your client adequately protected?

(b) *Understanding of Parties and Industry.* Do the contract's provisions reflect an understanding of the parties and their industry?

13. Legal Issues. Does the contract raise any legal issues? Are all the provisions enforceable? Have the parties received all the required governmental approvals? (See Chapter 32 on page 499.)

14. Future Performance.

(a) *Realistic Contract.* Is the contract realistic—one that the parties can actually perform?

(b) *Flexibility to Address Changes.* Does the contract have built-in flexibility to address changes in circumstances?

VI. MARK UP THE CONTRACT AND GIVE COMMENTS

Once you have been through the contract and conferred with your supervisor and client, you must prepare your comments for the other side. You have the following three choices when it comes to how you give the other side comments, listed in order of preference:

- A detailed markup of the contract with an accompanying message or memorandum: The markup will show the changes that you want, while the message or memorandum will explain proposed changes and raise issues.
- A message or memorandum discussing the major points, plus a markup of small issues, glitches (typographical errors), and stylistic points (if appropriate).
- Oral comments, conveyed by telephone or at an online or in-person meeting.

Before concluding which approach to take, talk with your client about the time, cost, and strategic benefits of one approach rather than another. Also, you may end up using a combination of the options above. For example, it is common to send to the other side a detailed markup of the contract with an accompanying message or memorandum,[3] which is then followed up with oral comments or a discussion by telephone or at an online or in-person meeting.

A. MARKUP

If you mark up the contract, you regain some of the leverage that you lost when the other side took on the role of initial drafter. Now, you and your client can shape the contract in ways both obvious and subtle. In addition, by making the comments in writing, you permit the drafter to concede the point without doing so in front of you, your client, and the drafter's client. It is easier on the ego, and the need to look tough in front of the client is not directly put into play. It also gives the other side time to

---

3. For more detailed guidelines on how to draft a memorandum, *see* the CasebookConnect Resources page and www.aspenpublishing.com.

think through your side's comments. A point that it might have rejected in person may be easier to win this way. You will not settle all the points with your markup. Key business issues will remain, but you may narrow down the issues, making it easier to complete the negotiations.

If your client is worried about the markup's cost, explain its strategic advantage. Point out that the markup allows you to shape the negotiation and the deal through drafting.

Markups are usually done by making changes in an electronic copy of the agreement. Before marking up a contract electronically, check your firm's or company's procedures. Most firms and companies have a specific procedure they want you to use to make changes and create redlined and clean copies of contracts for your team and for the other side. Also, they have special software to prevent the other side from reviewing the metadata created during the drafting process. Most firms and companies use a word processor that can track changes as you go and create redlines by comparing two different documents. We are also starting to see more often that all the members of the team for one party or all the parties to the contract are working together on the same platform at the same time. In such cases, it does become harder to keep track of changes, but you can usually go back to different versions of the document to verify changes and figure out who made them.

While markups are usually done electronically, you should also know how to mark up a document by hand. The reason for this is that you will often print out a contract to review a hard copy, and it is helpful to make comments to that document by hand and give those comments to someone else at your firm or company with whom you are working to input in the electronic version. You will still want to check and make sure that the changes were inputted correctly, but it will save you time and the client money to delegate tasks like these to employees who do not bill for their time or have a lower billing rate per hour.

An example of how to mark up a document by hand follows these instructions. To indicate that you wish to delete one or more words, put a straight line through those words. To indicate that you wish to insert words, put a **caret** where you want the words. (A caret is a proofreading mark that looks like an upside down "v.") Then, write the words that you want inserted in the margin, circle them to create a balloon, and connect the balloon to the caret by a line.

If an insert consists of more than a few words, write it down on a separate page. Use a caret, a line, and a balloon to indicate where the insert goes. Rather than putting the proposed language in the balloon, put an insert number there. An **insert number** consists of the page number on which the change is to be made and a capital letter to distinguish multiple inserts on the same page. Use the capital letters in alphabetical order. For example: *Insert 5A, Insert 5B,* and *Insert 5C.*

If you wish to move language to another page, circle it, draw a line from it to the margin, and attach it to a balloon. Inside the balloon, give the circled language an insert number, just as if you were adding language. Then, indicate the page to which the language should be moved: *Insert 7A to page 5.* On the page where the language is to be inserted, put a caret at the insertion point and attach it to a balloon in the margin. Inside the balloon, put language along the following lines: *Insert 7A from page 7.*

When you add language or move it, the numbering of sections and subsections may change. Mark those changes too, or write a general comment so that the person inputting the changes can make them.

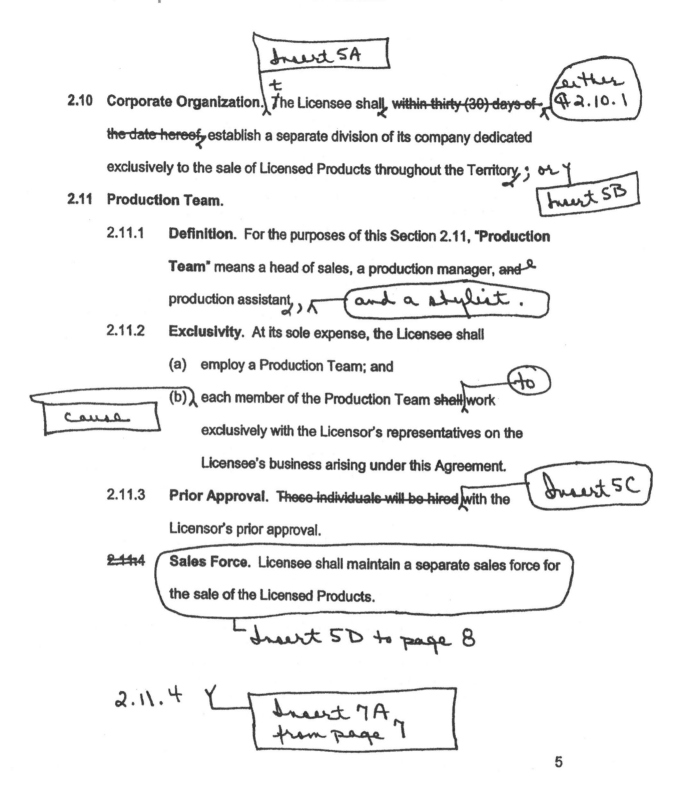

2.10   **Corporate Organization.** The Licensee shall ~~within thirty (30) days of the date hereof,~~ establish a separate division of its company dedicated exclusively to the sale of Licensed Products throughout the Territory;

2.11   **Production Team.**

    2.11.1   **Definition.** For the purposes of this Section 2.11, "Production Team" means a head of sales, a production manager, ~~and~~ a production assistant,

    2.11.2   **Exclusivity.** At its sole expense, the Licensee shall

        (a)   employ a Production Team; and

        (b)   each member of the Production Team ~~shall~~ work exclusively with the Licensor's representatives on the Licensee's business arising under this Agreement.

    2.11.3   **Prior Approval.** ~~These individuals will be hired~~ with the Licensor's prior approval.

    ~~2.11.4~~   **Sales Force.** Licensee shall maintain a separate sales force for the sale of the Licensed Products.

B. MESSAGE OR MEMORANDUM

Until recently, drafters were more formal, and most communications to the other side were in the form of a memorandum. Now there are drafters who still choose to keep the formalities by sending a memorandum to the other side in the form of an e-mail attachment. Increasingly, especially with the development of e-mail, texting, and other modern forms of communication, parties are choosing to communicate more informally.

> *Example — Comments Listed in Ascending Section Number Order*
>
> 1. **Section 2.4** — [title of section]
> 2. **Section 3.6** — [title of section]
> 3. **Section 8.7** — [title of section]

Regardless of which method you prefer to use, you can use a message or memorandum to the other side in two ways: as a stand-alone document or as a supplement to a markup. If you use it as a stand-alone document, use it to explain the changes that you want and why. List the comments in ascending section number order and include the section's title and include an introduction that directs the reader to the numbered paragraphs that have the most important changes.

Use the message or memorandum as a negotiating tool, explaining the business and legal reasons for each change. Laying out the issues for the other side gives them the opportunity to think through the issues privately, without time pressure and without ceding the point in front of you or the client. A message or memorandum is similar to a markup in this regard.

Tone is important, as in any negotiation. A diplomatic tone is generally best, but use a more aggressive tone if appropriate in the context of the transaction.

Although a message or memorandum allows you to argue your position, unfortunately it does not generally allow you to propose specific language changes. If you are hoping to propose specific language, then, you should also send the other side a markup. By not drafting the language, you cede a strategic advantage to the other side. But you may be able to regain some of the advantage in two ways. First, you may include proposed inserts as attachments to the message or memorandum. Second, as you draft the message or memorandum, phrase the discussion so that it uses words or phrases that you think should be incorporated into the agreement. The drafter might just use them as an easy way to make agreed-on changes.

As mentioned above in the beginning of this section, some drafters accompany a stand-alone message or memorandum with a markup of glitches and minor points. This will advance the later negotiation by permitting the parties to clean up the document right away and focus on the primary business issues.

If you use a message or memorandum with a markup, do not elaborate on every change. Instead, use it as a negotiating tool, just as you would with a stand-alone message or memorandum.[4]

C. ORAL COMMENTS

Oral comments on their own are generally the least preferred option to provide comments from a strategic perspective because you do not propose specific language. However, you can compensate for that to some degree. In preparing for the negotiation, draft inserts for key business provisions. This way, you know not only the substance of what you are asking for, but also the details. During the negotiation, make specific comments using words and phrases from your inserts. As the other side takes notes, it may pick up your language and then, later, incorporate it into the contract. Having the draft inserts also enables you to offer them to the other side if they agree to a proposed change.

---

4. For more detailed guidelines on how to draft a memorandum, *see* the CasebookConnect Resources page and www.aspenpublishing.com.

VII. EXERCISES

A. Exercise 33A: Redraft an Employment Agreement

This exercise requires you to redraft and, perhaps, negotiate an employment agreement between Carrie Richards, a junior television reporter, and her soon-to-be new employer, a television station. You can find all the documents for this exercise on the CasebookConnect Resources page and at www.aspenpublishing.com.

CHAPTER THIRTY-FOUR

Amendments, Consents, and Waivers

I. INTRODUCTION

Business deals change. An existing provision no longer works, a new business issue arises, a party fails to perform, or a one-time event requires special handling. As the relationship between the parties evolves, so must the agreement that memorializes their transaction. To deal with these changes, drafters rely on amendments, consents, and waivers.

II. AMENDMENTS

An **amendment** is an instrument that changes a contract, and it can be on any topic covered or not covered by the contract. Under common law, new consideration is generally necessary for an amendment to be enforceable.[1] Nonetheless, courts have frequently overcome this requirement by not asking about the adequacy of consideration and instead deferring to the parties regarding this matter, with only nominal consideration being necessary.[2] In addition, courts have shown a willingness to enforce amendments if the contract is executory (meaning that obligations have not been performed by both parties).[3] Statutes can also play a role in determining an amendment's enforceability. The Uniform Commercial Code (UCC)[4] and other statutes in some jurisdictions[5] include provisions that override common law. These statutes can provide that an amendment is enforceable without consideration—although a writing may be required. Bottom line: the law is a bit of a mix in this area, and knowing the law of the relevant jurisdiction is a must.

As was discussed in Chapter 18 on page 274, amendments can be either oral or written, and oral amendments are often enforceable, despite a *no oral amendments* provision. Because of this, discussions about possible amendments, or what could be construed as discussions about possible amendments, can be delicate. In the appropriate situation, consider sending a message to the other side acknowledging

---

1. *Alaska Packers Ass'n v. Domenico*, 117 F. 99 (9th Cir. 1902).
2. Brian A. Haskel, Amendment and Waiver, in *Negotiating and Drafting Contract Boilerplate* 507-509 (Tina Stark ed. 2003).
3. *Id.*; *see also Restatement (Second) of Contracts* § 89 (1981).
4. UCC § 2-209(1) (an agreement modifying a contract need not have consideration to be binding).
5. *See, e.g.*, Mich. Comp. L. Ann. § 566.1.

negotiations with respect to an amendment but stating, for the record, that the parties did not reach an agreement (if that is the case).

Generally, an amendment can be drafted as either a full, formal agreement or as a letter or other form of informal communication. A letter or similar form of communication can be less formal and quicker but just as binding. This book refers to amendments stated in a full, formal agreement as **inside-the-contract amendments** and amendments made in letter agreements and other more informal communications as **outside-the-contract amendments**.

Even though you have the option to do separate inside- or outside-the-contract amendments, when you amend an agreement, we encourage you to do a **restated agreement** or an **amended and restated agreement** when possible. In a restated agreement, and in an amended and restated agreement, you would include both the parts of the existing agreement that you are not changing and the new amended provisions, so you can have all the provisions together again in one agreement. No matter which of the three options you use, make sure that you are clear about what is going to remain the same as the existing agreement and what is changing with the amendment.

The sections that follow discuss inside-the-contract amendments, outside-the-contract amendments, and restated agreements and amended and restated agreements in more detail.

A. INSIDE-THE-CONTRACT AMENDMENTS

This section details how to draft **inside-the-contract amendments,** which are amendments made in a formal agreement format. The actual inside-the-contract amendments are usually in the action sections, and the other contract parts play their usual roles. In the next section, you will see an example of an inside-the-contract amendment.

1. Introductory Provisions and Definitions

If the parties have previously amended the existing agreement, the amendment's title should reflect the number of amendments: for example, *Second Amendment.* The preamble should also state which agreement is being amended by including that agreement's name, its parties, and the original signing date or *as of* date. By properly titling the amendment and including the information about the existing contract, a drafter quickly conveys to the reader the contract's purpose. Some drafters exclude the information about the existing agreement from the preamble and put it in the recitals. But that style of preamble delays giving the reader critical information. The better style is to include all the information about the existing agreement in the preamble.

Although recitals may be omitted from some agreements, they are often helpful in an amendment. Use them to explain why the parties are amending their agreement. This puts the amendment in context for the reader. If the parties are not exchanging consideration for the amendment, do not state that they have. Keep the words of agreement simple. The introductory provisions (title, preamble, recitals, and words of agreement) in our example of an inside-the-contract amendment are typical.

Example — Inside-the-Contract Amendment

Second Amendment[6]

Second Amendment, dated January 17, 20_7, to the Employment Agreement, dated February 23, 20_5, as amended, between Buckeye Pharmaceuticals Inc., an Ohio corporation (the "**Company**"), and Mohammed Ahmed (the "**Executive**").

Background

The Company has employed the Executive as Executive Vice President of Research for approximately two years and now desires to promote him to President. The parties desire to amend the Employment Agreement, dated February 23, 20_5, as amended (the **Existing Agreement**), to reflect the Executive's new duties, compensation, and other matters.

Accordingly, the parties agree as follows:

1. **Definitions.**
   (a) Terms defined in the preamble and recitals of this Amendment have their assigned meanings, and capitalized terms used in this Amendment without definition have the meanings assigned to them in the Existing Agreement.
   (b) "**Amendment**" means this Second Amendment.
2. **Amendments.**
   (a) Section 2.2 (a) of the Existing Agreement is amended by deleting "Executive Vice President for Research" and inserting in its place "President."
   (b) Section 2.2 (b) of the Existing Agreement is amended by deleting the period at the end of the sentence and inserting in its place the following:

   > ,except if the Company consents, and the Company shall not unreasonably withhold their consent.

   (c) Section 2.3 of the Existing Agreement is amended by deleting the period at the end of the sentence and inserting in its place the following:

   > ,except that the Executive may perform volunteer work for the March of Dimes without violating this provision.

   (d) Section 2.4 of the Existing Agreement is amended by deleting that section and inserting in its place the following:

   > **2.4 Term.** The term of employment under this Agreement is from March 1, 20_5, through December 31, 20_9, (the "**Employment Term**").

   > *(The employment term of the existing agreement was from March 1, 20_5, through December 31, 20_6.)*

---

6. This fact pattern was inspired by one created by the author's colleague, Alan Shaw.

(e) Section 2.5 is amended to read as follows:

2.5 Salary.

    (a) **March 1, 20_5, through December 31, 20_6.** The Company shall pay the Executive at a rate of $140,000 a year during the Employment Term. The annual salary is to be prorated for the period from March 1, 20_5, through December 31, 20_6. The Company shall pay the annual salary in approximately equal monthly payments on the last business day of each month. *(This is the original provision, now recast as a subsection with a caption.)*

    (b) **January 1, 20_7, through December 31, 20_9.** For the period beginning on January 1, 20_7, through December 31, 20_9, the Company shall pay the Executive at a rate of $180,000 a year. *(This is the new provision.)*

(f) The Existing Agreement is amended by deleting Section 3 and inserting in its place "Section 3 has been intentionally omitted."

(g) The Existing Agreement is amended by inserting the following provision as Section 6 after the end of the Existing Agreement's Section 5:

    6. The Company's Location. The Company shall not locate their headquarters outside of the greater metropolitan Cleveland, Ohio, region without the Executive's consent, which consent the Executive shall not unreasonably withhold.

(h) The Existing Agreement is amended to change the section numbers of Sections 6, 7, 8, 9, and 10 to Sections 7, 8, 9, 10, and 11, respectively.

3. **Continuation of Existing Agreement.** Except for the amendments made in this Amendment, the Existing Agreement remains unchanged and in full effect.

4. **General Provisions.**

    (a) **Choice of Law.** [Intentionally omitted.]

    (b) **Choice of Forum.** [Intentionally omitted.]

    (c) **Counterparts.** [Intentionally omitted.]

    (d) **Merger.** [Intentionally omitted.]

    (e) **Severability.** [Intentionally omitted.]

To evidence their agreement to this Amendment's terms, the parties have executed and delivered this Amendment on the date set forth in the preamble.

Buckeye Pharmaceuticals Inc.

By: _____

Betsy Rice, Chief Executive Officer

_____

Mohammed Ahmed

The amending agreement may need to distinguish between the agreement as it exists before it is amended and the agreement that exists after it is amended. *Existing Agreement* is a good defined term to use for the agreement before the amendment. The definition of *Existing Agreement* should incorporate all previous amendments, whether the term is defined in context, as in the example, or in a separate definition.

Amendment or *Amending Agreement* works for the agreement that sets out the amendments, and *Resulting Agreement* can be used to refer to the Existing Agreement as amended by the Amendment.

Other definitions may also be necessary. If so, follow the same drafting guidelines that we discussed in Chapter 15 on page 189. If the amendment uses terms defined in the existing agreement, do not redefine them. Instead, incorporate them into the amending agreement, using the provision that you see in the definitions of the example.

2. Deciding What to Amend

When discussing a proposed amendment with a client, focus on the business goal rather than on specific provisions. Once you understand the goal, carefully review the *entire* contract for provisions that will need to be changed. Often a change in one section leads to a change in another — the *cascade effect*, which we discussed in Chapter 27 on page 420. You may need to change a cross-reference, rewrite a provision, delete a provision, or add a provision.

3. Action Sections

The action sections of an amending agreement are composed of the provisions that implement the changes to the existing agreement — that is, the inside-the-contract amendments. These provisions explicitly state what language is to be deleted from the existing agreement and what language is to be inserted. If a reader wanted to, she could cut and paste the changes into the existing agreement and end up with an amended agreement that could be read from beginning to end.

The Inside-the-Contract Amendment example earlier in this section from an employment agreement demonstrates different ways to draft inside-the-contract amendments. (Although the form of these amendments is correct, they include substantive drafting errors. You will analyze these errors as part of an exercise at the end of this chapter. For now, though, focus on the style of the amendments.)

Note the different ways in which an amendment can be drafted in Section 2 of the example, which is titled *Amendments*. Note that (a), (b), and (c) are short. None of them includes the full amended provision — just the changes. This lack of context can obscure the amendment's effect, which is most apparent in (b).

Subsections (d) and (e) take a different approach and include the entire provision, as amended. This method makes it easier for the reader but results in a longer Amending Agreement.

The amendment in (f) deletes a section and inserts as a placeholder the statement that Section 3 was intentionally omitted. This language reduces a drafter's work by eliminating the need to renumber successive provisions and to revise cross-references that would become incorrect because of the renumbering.

Subsection (g) amends the existing agreement by adding a new section. It has the effect of throwing off the numbering of the subsequent sections. The amendment in Paragraph 8 corrects that problem by renumbering the subsequent sections.

Some drafters put a new provision as the last provision of the existing agreement.[7] This keeps the numbering intact and avoids the need to change cross-references. Similarly, if a new subsection is added to a tabulated enumeration, drafters put it last. Then, the other changes to that provision will be limited to changes to the punctuation of the tabulated items. Here is an example:

Example — Put Last a New Tabulated Subsection

Section 4 of the Existing Agreement is amended by

(a) deleting "and" at the end of subsection (c);

(b) deleting the period at the end of subsection (d) and inserting in its place "; and"; and

(c) *adding the following as a new subsection (e): "[insert new language]."*

---

4. Other Provisions

Amending agreements occasionally include representations and warranties. For example, each party might represent and warrant to the other all of the following:

- Their board of directors has authorized the amendments.
- They have duly executed and delivered the amending agreement.
- The amending agreement is enforceable against them in accordance with its terms.
- The representations and warranties made at the signing of the existing agreement are also true as of the signing of the amending agreement.[8]

In addition to representations and warranties, amending agreements may include conditions. These are usually directed toward postponing an amendment's effectiveness until certain conditions have been satisfied. (Note that the amending agreement itself is effective, but not the actual amendments to the existing agreement.) Here is an example:

Example — Conditions That Postpone an Amendment's Effectiveness

Amendments' Effectiveness. The amendments in this Second Amendment are effective on the satisfaction of the following condition: The Borrower's counsel must have delivered to the Bank an opinion that the Borrower's board of directors has duly authorized this Second Amendment and the amendments set forth in this Second Amendment. If this condition is not satisfied before June 1, 20__, this Second Amendment terminates, and the Existing Agreement continues unchanged and in full force.

Drafters differ as to which of the general provisions should be included in an amending agreement. Some drafters incorporate all of them by reference, but others restate all the governing law provisions (even if they do not restate other provisions).

---

7. However, this should not be done if you are restating the agreement or amending and restating it. *See* Section C on page 534 of this chapter.

8. This may not always be true, so do not simply assume that it is true. Carefully review, check with your client, if needed, and accurately state the then-current facts in the amending agreement.

Another set of drafters restate only some of the general provisions, particularly the following: governing law, choice of forum, counterparts, severability, and merger. The governing law and choice of forum provisions are included to ensure that the amending agreement and the existing agreement are governed by the same law and can be adjudicated in the same court. The reason for including the last three provisions is that they deal directly with the amending agreement's creation. The language of all these provisions should duplicate the language in the existing agreement (*say the same thing the same way*), but with a tweak for the merger provision. It should refer not to the existing agreement but the amending agreement.

Example — Merger Provision with Slight Change for Amending Agreement

Merger. This Second Amendment constitutes the final and exclusive agreement between the parties on the matters contained in this Second Amendment. All earlier and contemporaneous negotiations and agreements between the parties on the matters contained in this Second Amendment are expressly merged into and superseded by this Second Amendment.

Once the amending agreement is executed, the resulting agreement must reflect that the final and exclusive agreement consists of what was the existing agreement plus the amending agreement. You can approach the drafting in one of two ways. If the existing agreement's definition of *Agreement* includes *as amended,* the original merger provision necessarily takes into account the amendment.

Example — Existing Agreement's Definition of Agreement

"Agreement" means this Website Development Agreement, as amended from time to time.

If the existing agreement's definition of *Agreement* does not include *as amended*, then that definition or the merger provision must be amended. That way, each time the defined term *Agreement* is used in a general provision, or any other provision, it refers to the resulting agreement.

Following this approach, the other general provisions do not need to be restated in the amending agreement. Once the parties execute and deliver the amending agreement, each of the general provisions applies to the resulting agreement — that is, the existing agreement after the amendments.

If you decide to incorporate by reference into the amending agreement all the general provisions from the existing agreement, you may need to address a technical drafting issue. Specifically, when those provisions are incorporated, they will probably bring with them references to *this Agreement*. But those references will be wrong because they will refer to the existing agreement. Instead, they should refer to the amending agreement because the general provisions are being incorporated so they become part of the amending agreement. Therefore, to make the incorporation by reference work, add a sentence to the following effect in the provision that incorporates the general provisions from the existing agreement:

> *Example — Sentence Signaling the Incorporation of the General Provisions from the Existing Agreement*
>
> Each reference to "this Agreement" in the provisions incorporated by reference from the Existing Agreement into this Amendment is deemed a reference to "this Amendment."

Amending agreements generally conclude with a provision along the following lines, which makes clear that the Existing Agreement is still valid and enforceable except for the amendments:

> *Example — Concluding Provision of an Amending Agreement*
>
> **Continued Effectiveness of the Existing Agreement**. Except as amended by the amendments in this Amendment, the Existing Agreement continues unchanged and in full force.

This declaration prevents any party from inferring that the amendments have caused a change to any provision in the existing agreement, other than those changed in the amending agreement.

B. OUTSIDE-THE-CONTRACT AMENDMENTS

Outside-the-contract amendments are made in a more informal format, like in a letter, but can be just as binding. An outside-the-contract amendment usually does the following:

- Begins with the typical features of a letter—the addressee's name and address and a salutation
- States that, when signed, the letter constitutes an amendment to the existing agreement
- Incorporates by reference the defined terms from the existing agreement
- Amends the existing agreement
- Requests that the addressee indicate their agreement to the amendments by signing the letter and the enclosed duplicate original (if hard copy is used, rather than PDFs).
- Requests that the addressee return one of the two originals to the sender (if hard copy is used rather than PDFs)

An outside-the-contract amendment primarily differs from an inside-the-contract amendment with respect to the material that surrounds the amending provisions. See the example that follows of an outside-the-contract amendment in letter format.

In an outside-the-contract amendment, the amending provisions can be the same as those of an inside-the-contract amendment or they can differ. If they differ, it is generally because the parties and the drafter are taking a shortcut and trying to save transaction costs, or they are being strategic and trying to make the changes seem insignificant when they are not. In these instances, rather than amending specific words, the amendments state the effect of the amendment. This leaves the parties to the contract, any relevant third parties, and possibly the court in the future (if there are problems) to figure out which words were actually changed. These amendments lack precision and invite problems. You should avoid using them.

Here is an example of a letter of agreement that uses outside-the-contract amendments that only state the amendments' consequences.

Example—Outside-the-Contract Amendment in Letter Format

January 17, 20_7

Mr. Mohammed Ahmed
322 Westland Road
Shaker Heights, OH 12345

Dear Mr. Ahmed:

Please refer to the agreement dated February 23, 20_5, between Buckeye Pharmaceuticals Inc. (the "**Company**") and you relating to your employment by the Company (that agreement, as amended, the "**Existing Agreement**"). When signed by you, this letter constitutes an amendment of the Existing Agreement.

Capitalized terms used in this letter without definition have the meanings assigned to them in the Existing Agreement.

1. You are promoted to President.
2. You may do volunteer work for the March of Dimes without breaching our agreement.
3. All references to December 31, 20_6 are changed to December 31, 20_9.
4. Your annual salary for the period January 1, 20_7, through December 31, 20_9, is $180,000.
5. As you will be President, you no longer have to report to the President.
6. The Company promises not to relocate their headquarters outside of Cleveland, Ohio, without your consent. You have agreed not to withhold your consent unreasonably.
7. Once you have signed this letter, the amendments are effective as of January 1, 20_7.
8. Except as stated in this letter, the Existing Agreement remains unmodified and in full force.

To indicate your agreement to these amendments, please sign this letter and the enclosed duplicate original in the space provided at the end of the letter. In addition, please return [one original to the Company by [a recognized national courier] in the enclosed, pre-paid envelope] [a PDF of the signed original by e-mail to glawyer@gmail.com].

Very truly yours,

Buckeye Pharmaceuticals Inc.

By: _____

Betsy Rice, Chief Executive Officer

Agreed to on _____

_____

Mohammed Ahmed

C. RESTATED AGREEMENTS

Occasionally, parties enter into so many amendments that the then-existing agreement becomes difficult to read. Imagine trying to analyze a section of a contract that has its subsections in four different amending agreements! Therefore, whenever possible, and especially when you anticipate future amendments and have a contract that involves multiple parties, we encourage you to do a **restated agreement** or an **amended and restated agreement**.

To create a restated agreement, the drafter inserts the existing agreement and all the previous amendments into a master document, which then is the exclusive expression of the parties' agreement. An amended and restated agreement not only restates the agreement but also amends one or more provisions at the same time.

In a restated agreement and in an amended and restated agreement, you would have all the provisions that the parties have agreed to again in one place, and the parties would not have to sift through the existing agreement and the subsequent amendments to figure out the various provisions that apply. By taking the time to draft everything into one agreement, there is usually less of a chance of drafting provisions in an amendment that would conflict with still enforceable provisions in the existing agreement or creating other types of ambiguity.

When restating an agreement, move any provisions that were added to the end of the existing agreement — to keep the numbering intact — to their appropriate places within the contract. Now that the agreement will exist on a stand-alone basis (without amendments), the contract's structural integrity should be restored. This will facilitate the reading and analysis of the contract because when a reader looks for a provision in its logical place, it will be there.

Before deciding to restate or amend and restate an agreement, consider whether the benefits of the restated or amended and restated agreement outweigh the following disadvantages:

- The time and cost of preparing the restatement.
- The possibility of introducing errors into the existing agreement.
- The risk that the other side will see the restatement as an opportunity to renegotiate points that they conceded during the original negotiations.

When drafting a restated or an amended and restated agreement, think through the effect of changing the date in the preamble from the date that the parties signed the existing agreement to the date that the parties sign the new agreement. One problem that this change causes relates to the representations and warranties. As you have learned, representations and warranties speak as of a moment in time, generally the date that the parties sign the contract. When a restatement is signed, the date in the preamble is the date of that signing, but the existing agreement's representations and warranties should not speak as of the day of the restatement's signing. Instead, they should continue to speak as of the day of the existing agreement's signing. To prevent disputes on this matter, the introductory language to these representations and warranties should state explicitly that they continue to speak as of the original signing date of the existing agreement, as in the following example:

Example — Representations and Warranties Speak as of Date of Original Signing of Existing Agreement

The Borrower represents and warrants to the Bank that the following statements were true as of [insert date of original signing of the existing agreement]:

If the parties also want to add new representations and warranties or to have the existing representations and warranties also speak as of the date of the restatement's signing, additional language can be inserted, as in the following example:

Example — Representations and Warranties Speak as of the Date of Original Signing of Existing Agreement and Restated Agreement

The Borrower represents and warrants to the Bank that the following statements were true as of the [insert date of original signing of the existing agreement] and are true on the date of this Restated Agreement:

Be careful about the passage of time. The facts underlying some of the representations and warranties may have changed. For example, a statement of the level of the inventory on the date of the restatement is unlikely to be the same as the level of inventory on the date of the signing of the existing agreement. If the parties agree to representations and warranties both as of the original signing date and the restatement date and the facts differ, create separate subsections for each date as of which the representations and warranties speak. Move representations and warranties to their own section and introduce them with language along the following lines:

Example — Representations and Warranties in Separate Subsections

The Borrower represents and warrants to the Bank that the statements in subsection (a) were true as of the [insert date of original signing of the existing agreement] and that the statements in subsection (b) are true on date of this Restated Agreement.

(a) **Inventory Representations and Warranties as of Signing**. [Provision intentionally omitted.]

(b) **Inventory Representations and Warranties as of this Restated Agreement**. [Provision intentionally omitted.]

Also, know the relevant law for the area you are working in and the relevant jurisdiction when restating or amending and restating an agreement. For example, if you are amending and restating a credit agreement, you should be particularly careful and state that the amended and restated agreement is not a novation.[9] Additional language may be appropriate, depending on the jurisdiction. If it is a novation, the lender's security interest taken at the time of the signing of the existing agreement may be deemed terminated and replaced with a new security interest at the time of the signing of the amended and restated agreement, ending the continuity of a security interest in the collateral, which could have other consequences.

---

9. *See, e.g., In re Fair Fin. Co.*, 834 F.3d 651, 667-669 (6th Cir. 2016); Mayer Brown, Amended and Restated Financing Agreement Should Clearly State if Not Intended as Novation, *Lexology* (Nov. 29, 2016), https://www.lexology.com/library/detail.aspx?g=54268073-ed7e-4d9a-8dcf-a6e03002da5a.

III. CONSENTS

A. DEFINITION

Sometimes a party may not want the other party to be able to do something at the time of the signing of the contract but may be open to that action in the future, so long as it is possible only if they give their permission at that future time. In these circumstances, a drafter would want to draft a provision requiring that if one party wants to take that action, then they must get the **consent** of the other party. For example, many contracts contain an anti-delegation provision, which prohibits a party from delegating their performance to a third party without the other party's consent, as in the following example:

> *Example — Prohibiting Delegation Without the Other Party's Consent*
>
> **Delegation.** The Contractor shall not delegate any of the Work without the Owner's prior written consent.

If the Contractor wants to delegate the painting of the house to a different subcontractor without violating this covenant, the Contractor must obtain the Owner's consent.

B. DRAFTING THE CONSENT

When the time comes to ask for a consent from the other party, always do so in writing and keep the following guidelines in mind:

1. The first paragraph of the consent should refer to the agreement requiring the consent and the parties' defined terms:

> *Example — First Paragraph of Request for Consent Referring to Agreement*
>
> We refer to the Credit Agreement, dated November 12, 20_6, between Big Bank N.A. ("**Big Bank**") and Worldwide Shipping Inc., a Florida corporation ("**Worldwide**").

2. The second paragraph should state what your client wants and why. Waiting to include this information later in the document will frustrate the other side — keep it simple and be direct and up-front. Use the subsequent paragraphs to provide details.

3. Track the language in the agreement that prohibits the act for which your client is seeking consent. Say the same thing the same way.

4. Draft the scope of the requested consent so it meets your client's needs. While your client might like the latitude of a broadly drafted consent, requesting that may not be the best strategy. If the other side perceives the consent as overreaching, it may reject the request.

5. Make it as easy as possible for the other side to consent. Explain clearly the process that they need to follow to consent. If you are asking them to return a hard copy of the consent, include the materials for return by overnight courier. If an original, hard copy is not required, request that the signed copy be returned by e-mail as a PDF or in another appropriate format (e.g., by signing the consent on a particular platform for the execution of electronic documents).

IV. WAIVERS

A. DEFINITION

A party may want to continue with a contract, even though an event has occurred that would allow them to have access to other remedies and/or walk away from that contract. Such a party would grant the other party a **waiver,** in which they would agree to keep performing as if the event had not occurred and to not exercise their remedies or walk-away rights.[10]

Waivers typically arise in response to one or more of the following three events:

- The failure of a condition.
- The occurrence of a misrepresentation, breach of warranty, or breach of covenant.
- The likely breach of a covenant.

If any of these offending events occurs, the party entitled to a remedy or walk-away right may choose to waive the event's occurrence.

A waiver does not amend a contract. All of the agreement's provisions, including the provision that relates to the offending event and waiver, remain unchanged and enforceable. If the offending event occurs again, the party entitled to the remedy or walk-away right may once again choose whether to waive.

For example, imagine that a buyer of a house has bargained for the receipt of the house's architectural plans as a condition to closing. If the seller cannot deliver the plans, the buyer may decide not to close and to exercise his walk-away right, or he may waive the failure of the condition and purchase the house. If the seller also promised to deliver the plans, the seller's nondelivery would be a breach of covenant. The buyer would then need to decide whether he also wanted to waive the breach and forgo any remedies available to him.

As noted, a party may waive the application of a provision in anticipation of a breach. A bank might do this if their borrower announces that they will be unable to comply with one of their financial covenants. The pre-breach waiver would be advantageous to both parties. The bank would avoid having a borrower in default, and the borrower would avoid the additional consequences of a breach, such as a cross-default or disclosure obligations if they are a publicly held corporation.

B. DRAFTING THE WAIVER

Waivers can be drafted in the form of a letter or as a stand-alone agreement. In either case, the subject matter performance provision is the waiver and is a self-executing provision,[11] effective on the waiver's execution.

---

10. For an example of a waiver of a condition to an obligation, *see* Chapter 6 on page 43. In that example, if Bob does not get the mortgage that he needs to buy the house (the condition), Bob has the choice to (1) not perform and not buy the house, or (2) to waive the condition and perform by buying the house, even though he does not have the obligation to do so.

11. *See* Chapter 16 on page 210.

Example — Waiver

Waiver. [By signing this Waiver] [By countersigning this letter], the Landlord waives the Tenant's failure to comply with Section 6.8 of the Lease.

To establish that the waiver is a one-time event, most waivers include language to the following effect:

Example — Language Limiting the Waiver to a One-Time Event

Limited Waiver. This Waiver is effective only on this occasion and only for the purpose given and is not to be construed as a waiver on any other occasion, for any other purpose, or against any other Person.

If the contract between the parties has a general provision dealing with waivers with language to this effect, use that same language in the waiver. Remember: *Say the same thing the same way.*

V. CHOOSING BETWEEN A CONSENT AND A WAIVER

Consents and waivers are similar, and sometimes it may be hard to determine which one you should use. Which one is appropriate depends on the contract's language. If a covenant absolutely prohibits something without exception, the piece of paper to be obtained is a *waiver*. A waiver will make that prohibition unenforceable on that one occasion or, in other words, it would allow that one party to do what they are not allowed to do for that one time. If a covenant provides for an exception to the prohibition with the other party's consent, then, in accordance with the contract, the piece of paper to be obtained is a *consent*. In that case, one party may give their consent so the other party is allowed to do something.

VI. EXERCISES

A. Exercise 34A: Identify Issues in Inside-the-Contract Amendments

Review the inside-the-contract amendments in Section A.1 on pages 527-528 of this chapter. What business and drafting issues do the amendments in Sections 2(d) and (e) raise? Read both provisions before trying to answer the question.

B. Exercise 34B: Identify Issues in Outside-the-Contract Amendments

Review the Outside-the-Contract Amendment in Letter Format in Section II.B of this chapter. What business and drafting issues might there be because of the way that the amendments are written? Use the information in the inside-the-contract amendments in Section II.A of this chapter as well to help you with your analysis.

C. Exercise 34C: Mark Up or Redraft a Consent to Assignment

Using the information in the letter that follows and everything you have learned relating to best practices in contract drafting, mark up the *Consent to Assignment* that follows the letter. Alternatively, redraft the consent using the consent that you can find online on the CasebookConnect Resources page and at www.aspenpublishing.com.

January 26, 20_9

Mr. James Smith
425 West Haven Corp.
425 West Haven Avenue
El Paso, Texas 79905

Re: Request for Consent to Assignment and Release

Dear Mr. Smith:

We refer to the Lease (the "**Lease**"), dated July 1, 20_6, between 425 West Haven Corp. ("**West Haven**") and Maria's Muffins Inc. ("**Muffins**"). In accordance with Section 7.8 of the Lease, we request that West Haven consent to Muffins's assignment of their rights under the Lease to Sammy's Sweets Inc. ("**Sweets**").

Muffins is going out of business and desires to assign their rights under the Lease to Sweets. Sweets has agreed to assume all of Muffins's obligations under the Lease that arise and are due and payable on and after March 1, 20_9, the date that Muffins will assign their rights under the Lease to Sweets (the "**Assignment Date**").

Sweets manufactures and distributes chocolate truffles to candy stores in Texas. Enclosed for your information are (a) a description of Sweets's business and (b) Sweets's audited financial statements for the period ended December 31, 20_8.

Section 7.8 of the Lease prohibits the assignment of the Lease without West Haven's consent. Thus, in accordance with the Lease, Muffins requests that West Haven

(a) consent to Muffin's assignment to Sweets, on March 1, 20_9, of all Muffins's rights under the Lease; and

(b) release Muffins from all of their obligations under the Lease that arise and are due and payable on and after March 1, 20_9.

Muffins also requests that you acknowledge that no other consent or consideration is required for the assignment to be effective. Your consent and release will apply only to the transaction described in this letter and is subject to Sweets's assumption of all of Muffins's obligations under the Lease that arise and are due and payable on and after March 1, 20_9. We will mail you a copy of the assumption promptly after Sweets signs it.

To consent to the assignment and to grant the release, please

- sign the two duplicate original consent forms accompanying this letter; and
- return the duplicate original by [national courier in the enclosed, prepaid envelope] [PDF by e-mail to lawyer@gmail.com], as soon as possible, but in no event later than February 20, 20_9.

If you desire any further information concerning the transaction, please do not hesitate to call me at (915) 555-5555. We appreciate your assistance in this matter.

Very truly yours,
Maria's Muffins Inc.

By: _____
Maria Rodriguez, President

Consent to Assignment

Subject to the proviso set forth in the last sentence hereof, West Haven Rental Corp. (the "**Lessor**")

hereby consents to the assignment by Maria's Muffins Inc. ("**Muffins**") of all their rights, title, and interest

under the Lease, dated July 1, 20_6, (the "**Lease**") to Sammy's Sweets Inc. ("**Assignee**"), and Lessor hereby

releases Muffins from all their obligations and liabilities under the Lease arising and due and payable on and

after the date that Muffins assigns their rights under the Lease to the Assignee (the "**Assignment Date**").

Notwithstanding the foregoing, the consent and the release granted herein shall only be effective if, on the

Assignment Date, Assignee shall have assumed all of Muffins's obligations and liabilities under the Lease

arising and due and payable on and after the Assignment Date.

425 West Haven Corp.

By: _____

James Smith, President

Dated: _____

D. Exercise 34D: Amend the Aircraft Purchase Agreement

Amend the Aircraft Purchase Agreement in accordance with the instructions that you can find on the CasebookConnect Resources page and at www.aspenpublishing .com.

CHAPTER THIRTY-FIVE

Professional Responsibility

I. OVERVIEW

This chapter focuses primarily on the duties and responsibilities of lawyers when negotiating and drafting contracts. First, in this section, we provide a general overview of the regulation of lawyers and professional responsibility laws, regulations, and possible consequences, relating to drafters of contracts.

Then, in Section II, we walk through typical scenarios that come up for lawyers before they begin to work on a transaction and as they negotiate and draft agreements. Instead of covering generally all areas of professional responsibility, we focus on the most relevant ethical issues that drafters face in those scenarios and what drafters can do to better resolve them, using the model rules of professional conduct put forth by the American Bar Association.

The American Bar Association (the **ABA**) is a legal trade organization known as the largest national bar association in the United States. The ABA has developed and continues to update model rules of professional conduct, which have been adopted by the states in whole or in part (the "**ABA Model Rules**").[1] The ABA Model Rules include 58 rules, organized into eight areas. After each rule, there are comments providing guidance and illustrating the meaning and purpose of each rule. Since ethical rules vary from state to state and most states have adopted some form of the ABA Model Rules, we use them in Section II to guide our analysis of common ethical scenarios for drafters.

In the United States, lawyers are admitted to the bar of a particular state and are granted a license to practice law in that state. In most states, they have to have a Juris Doctor degree from a U.S. law school accredited by the ABA, pass a bar exam to be admitted to that particular state, pass the Multistate Professional Responsibility Exam, and establish through a character and fitness board that they have the requisite character and fitness to be admitted to the practice of law in that state.

---

1. *Model Rules of Prof'l Conduct,* https://www.americanbar.org/groups/professional_responsibility/publications/model_rules_of_professional_conduct/model_rules_of_professional_conduct_table_of_contents/. The ABA Model Rules are the latest version of model ethical rules created by the ABA. Previously, in 1908, the ABA created the first version, the *Canons of Professional Ethics.* In 1969, the ABA presented a new model for jurisdictions, known as the *ABA Model Code of Professional Responsibility*, which was updated from time to time and was eventually replaced in 1983 by the ABA Model Rules. Cornell Law School, *Model Rules of Professional Conduct*, Legal Information Institute, https://www.law.cornell.edu/wex/model_rules_of_professional_conduct (last visited Aug. 1, 2023).

Once a lawyer is admitted to practice in a state, their license is regulated by a governmental entity, often the state supreme court or a commission designated by that court. Federal court admission is a separate process, as well as federal regulation of the lawyers that practice in those courts. Most transactional lawyers are not admitted to practice in a federal jurisdiction because a lawyer's state bar license is usually all that is needed to draft agreements as a lawyer.

In considering issues of lawyer professional responsibility, the following are some of the laws and regulations that could be applied in cases of lawyer misconduct: legal malpractice law, ethics regulations, criminal law, constitutional law, procedural law, agency law, and securities law. For example, if you are representing a public company, you will have to make sure that your client's practices conform with the Sarbanes-Oxley Act, a federal law that imposes specific financial and accounting requirements on public companies. Some of the provisions also apply to private companies. More specifically, according to Section 307 of the Sarbanes-Oxley Act, as a lawyer, you have a duty to report material violations of securities law or a breach of fiduciary duty.[2]

The possible consequences for the lawyer accused of misconduct may vary, depending on the type of proceedings initiated against the lawyer (e.g., civil, criminal, state discipline, or other) and the types of laws that apply. Here are some of the possible consequences that lawyers can face in professional responsibility cases:

TYPE OF CONSEQUENCE	EXPLANATION
■ Civil liability	■ Possible claims in a court for civil liability include claims for malpractice, breach of fiduciary duty, and/or breach of contract. ■ A plaintiff would be awarded money damages. Jury verdict awards can be the largest in conflict cases with improper use of confidential information.
■ Criminal liability	■ Possible claims in court for criminal liability include claims for malpractice and/or fraud. ■ The court would impose criminal sanctions, which can include a jail or prison sentence.
■ Other court sanctions	■ Depending on the type of matter, a lawyer may have to answer a rule to show cause and justify, explain, or prove something to the court. ■ A motion can be filed in court against a lawyer to disqualify them from serving as counsel for a particular client based on a number of issues, such as a perceived conflict of interest. ■ A motion for sanctions can be filed for failure to comply with discovery or filing frivolous pleadings. ■ A lawyer may be subject to fee disgorgement by a court, which means that the former client would be returned the attorney's fees that they paid.
■ State discipline	■ A lawyer can be subject to state disciplinary proceedings in front of the highest state court based on a violation of that state's ethical rules. Most states' ethical rules are based on the ABA Model Rules. ■ The lawyer could be disbarred (their license to practice law would be taken away permanently), suspended, or publicly or privately reprimanded.

2. Sarbanes-Oxley Act of 2002, Pub. L. No. 107-204, § 307, 116 Stat. 745 (2002).

Since the laws and regulations applied in professional responsibility cases can vary from state to state, it is most important to know the relevant laws in your jurisdiction. For example, if you get an e-mail message from the other side that was meant for their client and not for you, what are you supposed to do according to your jurisdiction?[3] Different jurisdictions have different standards and actions allowed. You should probably know at the very least whether you may or may not continue reading the communication, whether you must notify the other side immediately, or whether you must delete the information and from where. Therefore, make sure that you know your professional duties and responsibilities, particularly according to the jurisdiction that would apply.

While there are many areas of state law involved in professional responsibility matters, there are two primary areas of law that come into play in these issues: legal malpractice and ethics regulations. Legal malpractice is "a lawyer's failure to render professional services with the skill, prudence, and diligence that an ordinary and reasonable lawyer would use under similar circumstances."[4] A common example of legal malpractice in contract drafting is if you do not include an important provision in the contract that you should have included. To prove that a lawyer committed legal malpractice, in most jurisdictions the plaintiff must show that (1) there was an attorney-client relationship, (2) the acts by the attorney were negligent or breach of contract, (3) that the acts by the attorney were the proximate cause of the plaintiff's damages, and (4) the plaintiff would have been successful if it had not been for the lawyer's acts.[5] Each jurisdiction has its own standard of care and precedent relating to legal malpractice claims.

Likewise, violations of the rules of professional conduct are governed by the state rules. A common example of a legal ethics violation in contract drafting is using former client information while representing a different client. That type of conduct could be a violation of the ethical rules in the relevant jurisdiction. If we use the ABA Model Rules as a guide, this type of conduct could be a violation of ABA Model Rules 1.6, 1.8, 1.9, and 1.10. Not every violation of the ethics rules is a legal malpractice claim, and vice versa.

II. PROFESSIONAL RESPONSIBILITY ISSUES IN CONTRACT DRAFTING

In this section, we will analyze common scenarios that present ethical challenges for drafters before beginning a transaction and later while negotiating and drafting an agreement. We will use the ABA Model Rules mostly as a guide. For more information on the ABA Model Rules that you may want to be familiar with as a drafter, go to the Casebook Connect Resources page or the Aspen website product page for this book. Once you begin to practice, you will learn and keep up with developments in your jurisdiction. However, taking the time to review these ABA Model Rules now will help you start to understand and learn how to approach some of the most common ethical issues that come up when contract drafting.

Remember that in the scenarios included in this section, whether it is mentioned or not, the parties would also consider possible legal malpractice claims, apart from

---

3. *Model Rules of Prof'l Conduct* R. 4.4(b) (2023).
4. "Legal Malpractice," *Black's Law* Dictionary, 11th ed. (2019).
5. *Viehweg v. Mello*, 5 F. Supp. 2d 752 (E.D. Mo. 1998); *Schweizer v. Mulvehill*, 93 F. Supp. 2d 376 (S.D.N.Y. 2000); *Kilpatrick v. Wiley, Rein & Fielding*, 909 P.2d 1283 (Utah Ct. App. 1996).

possible violations of the ethical rules. Furthermore, there may be other laws or regulations that come into play, like criminal law, constitutional law, procedural law, agency law, and securities law, which would allow the parties injured by the lawyer to bring forward other types of claims.

A. BEFORE DRAFTING

Before you start drafting, some of the most common issues that come up relating to professional responsibility involve determining who is your client, who is the other side, whether you are competent in this area of law or will need support, and whether the transaction and its different steps are legal. In this section, we explore each of these scenarios in more detail and refer to the ABA Model Rules that would be relevant. Note that liability for the lawyer in every situation will depend on the jurisdiction in question and the laws and regulations that apply there for that client, industry, and transaction. We are simply using the ABA Model Rules as a guide in our discussion, especially since almost all states have adopted a version of these guidelines for their ethical rules.

1. Who Is Your Client?

You must always be clear on who your client is and make that clear to them and any other parties involved from the beginning and throughout the transaction as necessary. Some of the easiest ways for a transactional lawyer to get into trouble are to not make clear who their lawyer is and continue with their representation of a client without resolving potential or existing conflicts, especially when representing more than one party at a time.

According to the Restatement of the Law Governing Lawyers, which compiles and summarizes ethics laws and regulations from the different jurisdictions:

> A relationship of client and lawyer arises when:
> 1. a person manifests to a lawyer the person's intent that the lawyer provide legal services for the person; and either
>   (a) the lawyer manifests to the person consent to do so; or
>   (b) the lawyer fails to manifest lack of consent to do so, and the lawyer knows or reasonably should know that the person reasonably relies on the lawyer to provide the services; or
> 2. a tribunal with power to do so appoints the lawyer to provide the services.[6]

In most jurisdictions, forming a lawyer-client relationship does not require having a formal, written agreement or being paid a fee. The relationship may be implied from how the parties behave. The test is typically what is the reasonable belief in the mind of the client, and, as noted in the Restatement section above, the lawyer is responsible, and it is incumbent on the lawyer to clarify the nature of the relationship. Third parties may believe you are acting as their lawyer when you talk about their interests and do not make it clear that you are not their lawyer.

When your client is an individual in a transaction, client identification is straightforward because there is only one person you have to communicate with, and they can easily speak for themselves. Determining who your client is and whom you should be communicating with gets trickier when your client is an organization. If your client is a business entity, you will have to determine and make clear whether your client is only the business entity or if you are also

---

6. *Restatement of the Law Governing Lawyers* § 14 (Am. Law Inst. 3d ed. 2000).

representing any of the officers individually in the transaction. For example, if you are representing a corporation in the sale of that corporation and you are also drafting an employment agreement for the Chief Financial Officer (**CFO**) to continue working with the buyer after the transaction, are you also representing the CFO? What if the CFO is separately negotiating with the other side, does that make a difference?[7] Also, if a business entity is part of a larger structure, you will have to clarify whether you are representing the parent company, a subsidiary, or more than one party.[8]

You may represent more than one party in a transaction and drafters often do, whether when putting together a purchase agreement, a settlement agreement, a divorce agreement, or an agreement to form any type of business involving various individuals. There are many ABA Model Rules and case law in each jurisdiction that relate to joint clients and what lawyers must do to properly represent them.[9] For example, if you represent more than one client, all material information needs to be shared with each client and, if interests diverge, you cannot represent any of them because you cannot use confidential information of one client to harm the other. To better protect yourself and your clients, get a written waiver from each of the parties that you are representing describing the matter and having them consent to the joint representation.

Before formalizing your lawyer-client relationship, make sure to do a conflicts check including your potential client, the other side, and any third parties to make sure that you do not already have potential conflicts. You need to check to see if anyone else in your law firm has represented this potential client, the other side, or any other third parties involved. For example, if a co-worker worked extensively on another matter for the other side, you may have to consider putting up a screen between you and the other lawyer, to make sure that there is no interaction between you and the other lawyer, including any of your work.[10] Screening is not always possible and often involves elaborate methods, including that: it be set up from the beginning, lawyers be isolated, no confidential information be discussed among lawyers, procedures and rules be established to prevent access to confidential information and files, lawyers not share profits from this representation, lawyers not be supervised by the same persons, and notice be given to the former client.

Generally, if you interview a prospective client and you do not end up representing them, know that you cannot use any confidential information you learned from them going forward.[11] You also cannot use any confidential information from previous clients unless it is information that is generally known.[12]

Here are some best practices when determining who your client is:
- Do a conflicts check before agreeing to represent a party, including your potential client, the other side, and any third parties, to make sure that you do not already have potential conflicts.
- If you identify a conflict and the conflict is not waivable, you may not be able to represent that potential client.

---

7. *Model Rules of Prof'l Conduct* R. 1.13 cmt. 10, 12 (2023).

8. *Model Rules of Prof'l Conduct* R. 1.13 (2023).

9. *Model Rules of Prof'l Conduct* R. 1.7 (2023); *Model Rules of Prof'l Conduct* R. 1.8 (2023); *Model Rules of Prof'l Conduct* R. 1.9 (2023); *Model Rules of Prof'l Conduct* R. 1.13 (2023); *Model Rules of Prof'l Conduct* R. 1.18 (2023).

10. *Model Rules of Prof'l Conduct* R. 1.10 (2023).

11. *Model Rules of Prof'l Conduct* R. 1.18 (2023).

12. *Id.*; ABA Formal Op. 479, 35 ABA/BNA Law. Man. on Prof. Conduct 343 (2018).

> - If you identify a conflict and the conflict is waivable, get a waiver from each of the affected parties.[13]
> - Enter into a formal, written retainer agreement with your client.
> - Make clear in writing to all the other parties involved who your client is at the beginning of the transaction and throughout as necessary.
> - If you are representing more than one client in the same transaction, get a written waiver to conflicts signed by each client.

2. Who Is on the Other Side?

The professional responsibility issues that come up most often when determining who is on the other side of the transaction are conflicts issues, which we started discussing in the previous section. If the party on the other side is a current client, the conflict is probably not waivable, so you will not be able to represent that party in this new transaction.[14] If the party on the other side is a former client, you can usually cure the conflict by getting a waiver.[15] The conflict may only be more problematic if there is the same or substantial relationship between the work done for the former client and the new matter.[16]

If the other side was ever a prospective client but you did not end up representing them, you cannot represent the client that you want to represent if it is the same or a substantially related matter and you previously received information from the prospective client that could be significantly harmful to that person in that matter.[17]

In transactional matters, in many jurisdictions, under limited circumstances, you may enter into a business transaction with a client or acquire an interest adverse to the client.[18] For example, ABA Model Rule 1.8 provides that, to do so, the lawyer must make sure that (1) the transaction and terms are fair and reasonable to the client and fully disclosed in writing in a way that the client can reasonably understand, (2) the client is advised about seeking independent legal counsel in writing and is given a reasonable opportunity to do so, and (3) the client gives informed consent, signed and in writing, to the essential terms of the transaction, making clear whether the lawyer is representing the client in the transaction.[19]

Apart from determining who the other side is and resolving any potential conflicts, you will have to learn whether the other side is represented by counsel. As a lawyer, you cannot reach out to another party directly knowing that they are represented by counsel.[20] Knowledge requires actual knowledge but can be inferred from the circumstances.[21] You cannot close your eyes to the obvious, but there is no requirement to ask if the other side has a lawyer in the matter.[22] However, to avoid any potential issues, it is probably safer for you to ask if they are already represented by counsel and if you should contact them instead. Note, though, that the two parties to the transaction can speak to each other without their lawyers.

---

13. Make sure that you know exactly what you need to include in the waiver based on your jurisdiction. ABA Model Rule 1.7 has guidelines on what to include. *Model Rules of Prof'l Conduct* R. 1.7 (2023).

14. *Id.*

15. *Model Rules of Prof'l Conduct* R. 1.9 (2023).

16. *Id.*

17. *Model Rules of Prof'l Conduct* R. 1.18 (2023).

18. *Model Rules of Prof'l Conduct* R. 1.8 (2023).

19. *Id.*

20. *Model Rules of Prof'l Conduct* R. 4.2 (2023).

21. *Model Rules of Prof'l Conduct* R. 4.2, cmt. 8 (2023).

22. *Id.*

If a party is not represented or you do not know if they are represented, make sure that you are clear in what you say to them and take reasonable efforts to correct any misunderstanding.[23] Also, if the other side is a business entity, keep in mind that you should probably not be in contact with anyone who "supervises, directs or regularly consults with the organization's lawyer concerning the matter or has authority to obligate the organization with respect to the matter or whose act or omission in connection with the matter may be imputed to the organization for purposes of civil or criminal liability."[24]

3. Are You Competent in This Area of Law?

Before negotiating a deal and starting to draft, you will also have to make sure that you are competent in the area of law with which you are about to engage.[25] You may have some challenges and concerns if you are a new lawyer or you are working on a transaction that is in an area that is less familiar to you. However, the ABA Model Rules and most jurisdictions provide some guidance in such circumstances. For example, Comment 2 of ABA Model Rule 1.1 states that you "can provide adequate representation in a wholly novel field through necessary study. Competent representation can also be provided through the association of a lawyer of established competence in the field in question."[26] Therefore, you are able to provide competent representation if you take additional measures, such as studying the subject matter and/or pairing up with an experienced lawyer in the field. However, you usually cannot charge a client for time spent having to educate yourself on the subject.[27]

If you still feel you and your firm cannot provide competent representation, you can retain or contract with other lawyers outside of your firm to better serve your client, but you should probably get your client's informed consent, and you must make sure "that the other lawyers' services will contribute to the competent and ethical representation of the client."[28] Keep in mind that this may be a necessary option for you to exercise in limited cases, since you cannot contract with your client to provide less than competent representation on a matter simply because you do not have the knowledge and skills.[29] There is also an exception allowing lawyers to provide reasonable assistance in emergency situations, but this rarely comes up in transactions since most transactions are planned ahead of time.[30]

The most recent developments relating to competency impose on lawyers the duty to keep up with relevant technology. In 2012, the ABA changed Comment 8 to Model Rule 1.1 to include the phrase here emphasized in italics: "To maintain the requisite knowledge and skill, a lawyer should keep abreast of changes in the law and its practice, *including the benefits and risks associated with relevant technology,* engage in continuing study and education and comply with all continuing legal education requirements to which the lawyer is subject." Since 2012, most of the states have adopted this revised comment and/or issued opinions with guidance on these issues. Materials and updates on the CasebookConnect Resources page and at www.aspenpublishing.com consider even more recent developments in technology, especially relating to artificial intelligence, the impact that they have already had on the profession, and how they will continue to develop going forward.

---

23. *Model Rules of Prof'l Conduct* R. 4.3 (2023).
24. *Model Rules of Prof'l Conduct* R. 4.2, cmt. 7 (2023).
25. *Model Rules of Prof'l Conduct* R. 1.1 (2023).
26. *Model Rules of Prof'l Conduct* R. 1.1 cmt. 2 (2023).
27. *Model Rules of Prof'l Conduct* R. 1.1 (2023); *Model Rules of Prof'l Conduct* R. 1.5 (2023).
28. *Model Rules of Prof'l Conduct* R. 1.1 cmt. 6 (2023).
29. *Model Rules of Prof'l Conduct* R. 1.1 (2023).
30. *Model Rules of Prof'l Conduct* R. 1.1 cmt. 3 (2023).

4. Is the Transaction Legal?

You must make sure that your client is engaging in a legal transaction before you even start drafting. While you must determine and investigate any issues as to the legality of the deal as a whole or in part at the beginning, this is something that may become an issue later once you have already agreed to represent the client and you are in the middle of the transaction.

You cannot ever counsel or assist a client in conduct that you know is criminal or fraudulent, even though you may discuss the legal consequences of any possible actions with your client.[31] If your client is already engaging in criminal or fraudulent activity when you find out, you have "to avoid assisting the client, for example, by drafting or delivering documents that the lawyer knows are fraudulent or by suggesting how the wrongdoing might be concealed."[32] Furthermore, you may be required to withdraw from representing the client, especially if you originally thought the actions were legally proper but then discover that they are criminal or fraudulent.[33] All jurisdictions make it clear that a lawyer cannot commit a criminal act and engage in dishonesty, fraud, deceit, or misrepresentation.[34]

Note that one of the primary exceptions to the attorney-client privilege in most jurisdictions is in cases of criminal activity or fraud. A lawyer may disclose confidential information "to prevent a client from committing a crime or fraud that is reasonably certain to result in substantial injury to the financial interests or property of another and in furtherance of which the client has used or is using the lawyer's services"[35] and "to prevent, mitigate or rectify substantial injury to the financial interests or property of another that is reasonably certain to result or has resulted from the client's commission of a crime or fraud in furtherance of which the client has used the lawyer's services."[36]

You cannot close your eyes to these issues and pretend that you do not know what is happening.[37] You must make sure that you do your own due diligence on your client, the other side, and the transaction in question.[38] In fact, more recent amendments to ABA Model Rule 1.16 and its comments establish that you have an obligation "to inquire into and assess the facts and circumstances before accepting it" and that obligation "continues throughout the representation. A change in the facts and circumstances relating to the representation may trigger a lawyer's need to make further inquiry and assessment."[39] Furthermore, if you come to know or reasonably should know that your client expects you to help them with an action not permitted by the ABA Model Rules, or if you intend to act against your client's instructions, you must consult with your client and may have to withdraw from representing them.[40]

What can also happen is that you give advice to your client on how to proceed on a matter, but they decide not to follow your advice. Instead, they decide to do something else that could be deemed to be criminal or fraudulent activity. They do

---

31. *Model Rules of Prof'l Conduct* R. 1.2(d) (2023).
32. *Model Rules of Prof'l Conduct* R. 1.1 cmt. 10 (2023).
33. *Model Rules of Prof'l Conduct* R. 1.1 cmt. 3 (2023); *Model Rules of Prof'l Conduct* R. 1.6(b)(2) (2023).
34. *Model Rules of Prof'l Conduct* R. 8.4 (2023).
35. *Model Rules of Prof'l Conduct* R. 1.6(b)(2) (2023).
36. *Model Rules of Prof'l Conduct* R. 1.6(b)(3) (2023).
37. ABA Formal Op. 491, 36 ABA/BNA Law. Man. on Prof. Conduct 333 (2020).
38. ABA Formal Op. 463, 35 ABA/BNA Law. Man. on Prof. Conduct 177 (2017).
39. *Model Rules of Prof'l Conduct* R. 1.16 cmt. 1 (2023).
40. *Model Rules of Prof'l Conduct* R. 1.2 cmt. 13, 1.16 (2023).

not tell you, and you do not know or even guess that something may be wrong based on what they *have* told you. However, later, while representing them after some time or on a different matter, you find out. Common examples are creating and providing invoices to third parties or keeping track of financials in ways that are not ethical. Clients sometimes do this because they may think one or more of the following: they may not be found out, what they are doing may not be completely unethical but more of a gray area, and they can make more of a profit by doing this. Your client may want to take the risk, particularly because, in many cases, if the actions are found to be a problem and they have to pay any additional amounts, they can settle for a smaller fee. You cannot be a party in any way to such a transaction, give legal advice furthering fraud or a crime, or simply close your eyes or look the other way.[41] More important, you have an obligation to inquire further and do more due diligence, and you may even have to withdraw from such representation.

Therefore, if you have any questions regarding the legality of part of a transaction, you should investigate, ask questions, and communicate clearly with your client. You may also need to consult with a litigator or other relevant type of attorney and/or withdraw from representing your client.

B. DURING DRAFTING

Once you start negotiating with the other side and drafting an agreement, there are a number of issues you want to keep in mind to make sure that you are complying with professional responsibility laws and regulations. In this section, we explore some of the most important ones.

1. You as an Agent of Your Client

You are an agent of your client as part of the lawyer-client relationship.[42] This means that you must abide by your client's decisions and consult with your client as to the transaction and the agreements that you are drafting.[43] You must follow your client's instructions as much as possible unless you would be assisting your client in a criminal or fraudulent matter.[44] If a client asks you to put something in a contract that does not constitute a crime or fraud but that you have advised him against for different reasons, you must still put it in because that is what your client wants. Also, you could face an ethics violation or a legal malpractice claim if you put in terms that the client instructed you not to add. In addition, there are other areas, such as agency law, that would apply in these circumstances. For example, under agency law, you would be liable as an agent who has gone rogue instead of following your client's instructions.[45]

2. Communicate with Your Client

As a legal agent, you must keep your client informed about what you are drafting[46] and "act with reasonable diligence and promptness."[47] Beginner lawyers sometimes

---

41. *Model Rules of Prof'l Conduct* R. 1.2(d), 1.16 (2023).
42. *Restatement (Third) of Agency* § 1 (Am. Law Inst. 2006).
43. *Model Rules of Prof'l Conduct* R. 1.2, 1.4 (2023).
44. *Model Rules of Prof'l Conduct* R. 1.2 (2023).
45. *Restatement (Third) of Agency* § 8.09 (Am. Law Inst. 2006).
46. *Restatement (Third) of Agency* § 8.11 (Am. Law Inst. 2006); *Model Rules of Prof'l Conduct* R. 1.4 (2023).
47. *Model Rules of Prof'l Conduct* R. 1.3 (2023).

do not want to keep bothering their client, but it is essential that you check in with them throughout a transaction as needed. If you do not want to be constantly e-mailing or calling your client, keep a running list of questions for your client and send them together or set up a time to go over them over the phone or via a different platform.

Make sure to take the time to explain matters clearly and promptly to your client and consult with them to get their input. Furthermore, set clear expectations with your client about how much they want to be involved in the negotiation and drafting. For example, do you need to send a draft of an agreement for them to review every time before you send it to the other side? Will your client be reviewing drafts and giving you feedback, and if so, at what level and how often? In conjunction with this, also make sure to set the other side's expectations clearly as to how final and binding drafts are. Will you need the client's approval at the end so that nothing is quite set in stone, or is the proposed language meant to be more final?

3. Maintain Confidentiality

As a lawyer, you are bound by the ethical responsibility of confidentiality and the evidentiary rules of attorney-client privilege, so you cannot reveal any of your client's confidential information when you are drafting agreements or negotiating the transaction.[48] Ethical regulations and agency law, for example, along with other areas, make it clear that a lawyer cannot use confidential information against the interests of a current or former client.[49] The client is the holder of the privilege and the only person who can waive it, even though they can do so by disclosing information unintentionally in a careless manner.[50] You cannot waive the privilege and can only reveal confidential information of a client if you have a legal obligation, such as if it relates to criminal activity or fraud.[51]

Remember that for a communication to be covered by the attorney-client privilege, it must be in private between you and your client. Therefore, if possible, do not draft in public places (such as on an airplane) where people can possibly see your documents and electronic screens, and do not talk on the telephone while there are others nearby (such as in an elevator, the lobby of a building, or a coffee shop). If you do have to draft or speak in more public spaces, make sure to take the precautions necessary so no one can see your documents or hear you.

Along with the attorney-client privilege, you should also be familiar with the attorney work product rule or doctrine, which allows lawyers to not have to turn over in discovery any materials prepared by them as lawyers in view of litigation.[52] Many transactional lawyers do not realize that the attorney work product doctrine does not apply in most transactions because you are not working in view of litigation. Therefore, the e-mail messages and other communications that you put together for other team members could be discoverable later if a litigation matter arises from the transaction. Your materials are not protected by the attorney work product doctrine. Transactions where the doctrine would apply would be litigation-based, such as in a settlement agreement.

---

48. *Model Rules of Prof'l Conduct* R. 1.6 (2023).
49. *Id.*; *Restatement (Third) of Agency* § 1 (Am. Law Inst. 2006).
50. *Model Rules of Prof'l Conduct* R. 1.6 (2023).
51. *Id.*
52. "Work Product Rule," *Black's Law Dictionary*, 11th ed. (2019); Fed. R. Civ. P. 26(b)(3); *Restatement (Third) of the Law Governing Lawyers* § 87 (Am. Law Inst. 2000).

4. Figure Out What You Can Disclose and Verify Information from the Other Side

One of the most common ethical dilemmas in contract negotiations and drafting is trying to figure out what to disclose and not disclose to the other side. There is often a tension between maintaining your client's information confidential[53] and being truthful in any statement that you make during the negotiation or in the agreement to other parties.[54]

In practice, your primary responsibility is to your client, to whom you must provide competent representation. During negotiations, you also must protect confidential and privileged information unless you are authorized to make disclosures. You usually have "no affirmative duty to inform an opposing party of relevant facts."[55] At the same time, in most jurisdictions, you are required to be truthful to others and not misrepresent material facts. However, during negotiations, you are not required to disclose "estimates of price or value placed on the subject of a transaction and a party's intentions as to an acceptable settlement of a claim are ordinarily in this category, and so is the existence of an undisclosed principal except where nondisclosure of the principal would constitute fraud."[56] In negotiations, these statements "ordinarily are not taken as statements of material fact."[57] Of course, at the very least, you want to make sure that you disclose what you need to disclose to avoid assisting in a crime or any type of fraud by your client.[58]

Other countries, particularly some civil law jurisdictions, have a higher standard for disclosure in negotiations and drafting. Lawyers in these other countries may have to provide more information to the other parties than they would in the United States and more responsibilities to other parties may exist, such as a duty to negotiate in good faith.

Determining what to disclose or not disclose can be especially difficult when you are negotiating and drafting release provisions[59] or your client's representations and warranties in an agreement. For example, imagine that you are drafting a settlement agreement in the context of a litigation matter and you are drafting release provisions that would or would not allow you to bring another claim against the same party. What if you know that there could be additional litigation against your client or that your client has done something else wrong? You would want to draft the release generally to make sure that it would cover anything else without disclosing that information. What if your client could possibly go bankrupt? You would want to draft the release in such a way that the other party has limited rights if there is a bankruptcy or other change in the entity (so long as you and your client do not have a legal obligation to disclose any of this information).

The same issues of whether to disclose or not disclose come up when you are drafting representations and warranties for your client, and you will want to minimize

---

53. *Model Rules of Prof'l Conduct* R. 1.6 (2023).
54. *Model Rules of Prof'l Conduct* R. 4.1 (2023).
55. *Model Rules of Prof'l Conduct* R. 4.1 cmt. 1 (2023).
56. *Model Rules of Prof'l Conduct* R. 4.1 cmt. 2 (2023).
57. "Estimates of price or value placed on the subject of a transaction and a party's intentions as to an acceptable settlement of a claim are ordinarily in this category, and so is the existence of an undisclosed principal except where nondisclosure of the principal would constitute fraud." *Model Rules of Prof'l Conduct* R. 4.1 cmt. 2 (2023).
58. *Model Rules of Prof'l Conduct* R. 4.1(b) (2023).
59. Release provisions are also known as "waiver of liability provisions."

your client's risk, as discussed in Chapter 8 on page 61. You may offer simple representations and warranties to the other side, such as that the company is duly organized and has full authority to enter into the agreement, but not include specific financial, tax, or inventory-related provisions. Even if you do agree to more specific representations and warranties, you may make them extremely general with various qualifiers throughout, such as using *material, to the Company's Knowledge*, and others, or you may make them very specific to carve out what your client is specifically willing to represent and warrant.

If you are selling a house, you may include representations and warranties about the state of the house and limit them to state that the material components are in fair condition, instead of including the whole house, and that all its parts are in good or excellent condition. You may happen to know or be afraid that there are some material items that are broken or not working properly and would need significant repairs (e.g., the fireplace or an appliance like the dryer).

In larger or more complex transactions, if you are consulting with other attorneys in more specific practice areas (e.g., environmental, intellectual property, employment), they may have a higher or lower threshold when determining what to disclose in representations and warranties, based on specific regulations or that practice area, so you need to learn what would be appropriate.

The risk in representations and warranties and the issues relating to how much you want to disclose on behalf of your client have changed with the development of **representation and warranty insurance**, which is a type of insurance policy that entities can purchase in relation to corporate transactions and through which the insurance company covers particular breaches of the representations and warranties. This insurance is more common now, particularly in mergers and acquisitions, where the buyer will usually be the party that purchases it. Before the use of this insurance, the risk was on the buyer because they did not know as much about the seller, and it was harder for the buyer to verify the information they received from the seller. Therefore, the buyer would ask the seller to include more specific and thorough representations and warranties in the agreement and that the buyer be indemnified if they were not true. With the insurance, the risk has now shifted from the buyer to the insurance company, so the parties may not go back and forth as much on what to draft or they may more easily be able to find common ground. However, many transactions still do not involve such types of insurance because these policies are costly. Clients can sometimes limit due diligence on a transaction as well, and take a greater business risk for this same reason.

What if the other side does not ask you about something specifically that you know will be an issue—do you have to tell them? This will depend on the matter at hand, the jurisdiction, and what other laws and regulations apply to that client and industry. Therefore, you must know the industry that you are working in and what applies to your client and the other side, and keep up with developments.

At the same time, how do you know that the information you are receiving from the other side is accurate, and how can you verify it? Again, you must know the industry, how to properly research the parties and the transaction, and the jurisdiction. You must do your due diligence on the transaction and ask follow-up questions. If you are not getting answers or something seems wrong, there is probably a problem that you need to be aware of before finalizing the transaction—you should probably not back down until you get the information that you need.

Some transactional lawyers believe that due diligence can be a waste of time and money at times, since you only really know what the other side provides or tells you. For example, accounting inaccuracies are common. A company may inflate their revenue or sales numbers, so that it seems that the company is doing better than they are, a concept known as **channel stuffing**. The company may count on their books as sales orders for customers who have said that they are interested in buying in the next year but have not yet made any payment or completed any order form, which means they may not necessarily make that purchase in the next year. It is difficult at times to verify this type of information, but if it is important, you should follow up with the other side and ask more specific questions, such as: What are the sales orders recorded? What process do you go through to record a sales order? Have customers paid for these orders, and, if not all, which ones?

5. Know How Far You Can Go in Your Statements to the Other Side

In the previous section, we discussed ABA Model Rule 4.1 relating to *Truthfulness in Statements to Others* and the tension between that rule and the attorney-client privilege. In addition to that ethical dilemma, you may already know that parties in a negotiation often exaggerate their positions or possible consequences. But how far is too far? ABA Model Rule 4.1 requires that you not make a false statement of material fact to another party. What is and is not a false statement of material fact?

ABA Formal Opinion 06-439 provides the following guidance for how to approach negotiations and what is a false statement of material fact:

> It is not unusual in a negotiation for a party, directly or through counsel, to make a statement in the course of communicating its position that is less than entirely forthcoming. For example, parties to a settlement negotiation often understate their willingness to make concessions to resolve the dispute. A plaintiff might insist that it will not agree to resolve a dispute for less than $200, when, in reality, it is willing to accept as little as $150 to put an end to the matter . . .
>
> A party in a negotiation also might exaggerate or emphasize the strengths, and minimize or deemphasize the weaknesses, of its factual or legal position. A buyer of products or services, for example, might overstate its confidence in the availability of alternate sources of supply to reduce the appearance of dependence upon the supplier with which it is negotiating. Such remarks, often characterized as "posturing" or "puffing," are statements upon which parties to a negotiation ordinarily would not be expected justifiably to rely, and must be distinguished from false statements of material fact. An example of a false statement of material fact would be a lawyer representing an employer in labor negotiations stating to union lawyers that adding a particular employee benefit will cost the company an additional $100 per employee, when the lawyer knows that it actually will cost only $20 per employee.[60]

Also, note that in some contexts, like in the sale of securities, material omissions and incomplete truths can be found to be fraudulent.[61]

Furthermore, as with the disclosure ethical dilemmas discussed in the previous section, *posturing* and *puffery* often come up in negotiations and drafts of an agreement. Keep in mind that how often and to what level you engage in these tactics will be part of your reputation as a negotiator and drafter, so you may want to avoid them.

6. Be Careful with Redlines

When you are drafting an agreement, you often send drafts back and forth between the parties. When you send the latest draft to the other side, you usually send a clean version of the agreement and a redline, showing the changes that you are

---

60. ABA Formal Op. 06-439, 22 ABA/BNA Law. Man. on Prof. Conduct 285 (2006).
61. *Model Rules of Prof'l Conduct* R. 4.1 (2023).

suggesting. A common issue that comes up when drafting and sending drafts back and forth is that you receive a clean version with new language that is not highlighted in the redline, so you do not realize that there are words that have been added in a particular provision.

Every lawyer has a duty to be truthful,[62] so sending out a redline intentionally that does not reflect all the changes suggested could be a violation of such duties, along with others. Jurisdictions vary on whether this type of action is a violation of the ethical rules.[63] Make sure to send a redline that includes all the changes that you made to the clean version. When you receive new clean and redlined versions from the other side, run your own redline comparing the new clean version of the agreement to the version that you previously sent to them. Do not rely on the other side's redline. Unfortunately, you could find that the other side's redline is not the same as the one you ran and there are changes to the agreement not reflected in their redline. If this happens, keep in mind that the other side may have done it on purpose or unintentionally and that it is often hard to prove that it was done on purpose by the other lawyer. However, you may have to report the other lawyer if they violated an ethical rule "that raises a substantial question as to that lawyer's honesty, trustworthiness or fitness as a lawyer in other respects."[64] Note that this type of intentional conduct may be hard to prove.

It is harder now to keep track of changes because more often, parties are working together on an online platform. You can go back and look at different versions and see who put in which changes, but it is hard to find the time to do this. The reality is that drafters are finding working together on online platforms can make it harder to keep track of changes, since changes may be constantly made. You may want to try downloading that version when you have done substantive changes, so you can use it to create a redline against a future version of the agreement when more changes are made.

7. Communications to the Wrong Party and Metadata

At the beginning of this chapter, we raised the issue of what happens if you receive an electronic message that you know was not meant for you and is from the other side's lawyer to their client. According to ABA Model Rule 4.4, you need to "promptly notify the sender."[65] However, whether the document will continue to be covered by the attorney-client privilege and whether the lawyer who received it or sent it is required to take additional steps (e.g., returning or deleting the message), is considered beyond the scope of the ABA Model Rules.

In addition, the ABA Model Rules provide limited guidance on whether you can check a document's **metadata**, the data embedded in an electronic document that provides more data on that document, such as when the document was created and when and how it has been altered.[66]

While the ABA Model Rules provide limited guidance on these topics, states vary on what you should do if you get a message that is not meant for you and what is acceptable to do with a document's metadata. Therefore, know your responsibilities for your jurisdiction and, when something of this nature occurs, get informed and consult with a lawyer if needed.

---

62. *Model Rules of Prof'l Conduct* R. 8.4 (2023).
63. *See generally Stonebridge Capital, LLC v. Nomura Int'l PLC,* 897 N.Y.S.2d 672 (2009); *Braga Inv. & Advisory, LLC v. Yenni,* 2023 Del. Ch. LEXIS 134.
64. *Model Rules of Prof'l Conduct* R. 8.3(a) (2023).
65. *Model Rules of Prof'l Conduct* R. 4.4(b) (2023).
66. ABA Formal Ethics Op. 06-442, 22 ABA/BNA Law. Man. on Prof. Conduct 459 (2006).

III. CONCLUSION

This chapter has provided you with some of the most common issues that can come up in contract drafting and in negotiations relating to professional responsibility. However, artificial intelligence and new technological developments are dramatically changing the legal landscape and giving rise to new challenges in professional responsibility. Materials and updates on using artificial intelligence and technology in contract drafting can be found on the CasebookConnect Resources page and at www.aspenpublishing.com.

IV. EXERCISES

A. Exercise 35A: Legal Opinion and Representations and Warranties in a Credit Agreement

1. Assume that you are Sandy Plage, an up-and-coming corporate partner at Good Ethics & Law, a New York City law firm with 450 lawyers in the United States and abroad. Over time, you have developed an excellent business relationship with Bob Hansell. Bob has sent you substantial business from whatever company was his then-current employer. Currently, he is general counsel at Speedskates, Inc. ("**Speedskates**"). Speedskates is the U.S. operating subsidiary of Speedskates International, Inc. ("**International**"), a privately held multinational corporation with its headquarters in Singapore, which manufactures, distributes, and sells different types of skates (e.g., ice skates, rollerblades) and related equipment (e.g., snowboards, skateboards, water skiing materials) for recreational and professional use.

    The sole shareholders of International are two siblings (Robert and Sara Marlat), who are also the directors and officers of Speedskates. At the moment, your law firm is representing International in connection with tax and corporate issues relating to International's operations both in the United States and worldwide. In addition, you are the primary outside counsel in connection with a loan agreement that Speedskates is negotiating.

    Bob just called sounding somewhat distressed. He first reviewed the following deal facts with you:

    a. Speedskates is in the midst of negotiating for a $50 million line of credit from Big Bank NA ("**Big Bank**"). International will guarantee the debt. (Speedskates already has $200 million in long-term debt from a multi-bank group.) The new line would provide Speedskates with some badly needed additional working capital. (See the diagram on page 560.)

    b. As a condition to the consummation of the Credit Agreement, Big Bank has requested Bob, as in-house counsel, to deliver a legal opinion on certain corporate matters. (This is common practice. The theory is that in-house counsel can deliver these opinions more cheaply than outside counsel because in-house counsel has superior knowledge.) Bob wants you to review the Credit Agreement and his overall opinion and to advise him whether the individual opinions that he is being asked to give are appropriate. His initial inclination is that he should be able to give the opinions, as they are all true. Those opinions are as follows:

    (i) Speedskates is duly incorporated and in good standing and the Credit Agreement is duly authorized, executed, and delivered.

    (ii) The consummation of this transaction does not violate any existing agreements to which Speedskates is a party.

    Is it appropriate for you to discuss these matters with Bob?

2. In your preliminary review of the Credit Agreement, you discover two representations and warranties that raise concerns:

a. The draft of the Credit Agreement states that Speedskates has complied with all the covenants in the other loan agreement. That agreement requires Speedskates and its affiliates to meet certain net worth tests. Because of operating losses incurred during the past two years, Speedskates has failed to meet the net worth tests and has breached the loan agreement. Therefore, leaving the representation and warranty as is in the Credit Agreement would result in an untrue statement.

b. In Section 5.7 of the Credit Agreement, Speedskates represents that International and each of its subsidiaries (including Speedskates) has filed the tax returns required to be filed and has paid all required taxes, other than those that could not have a material adverse effect.

Based on the work that your firm has done, you know that Speedskates France, one of International's subsidiaries, may owe some taxes to the United States. No one yet knows whether the amount at stake is material as the detailed review and analysis that would be required to make such an assessment has not been done. An assessment of materiality would need to contemplate not only the consequences of any payment on International's net worth, but also on its liquidity. Neither the firm nor Speedskates' auditors has the time to finish the assessment before the loan closes. Of course, Bob Hansell knows all about the tax issues as he has been acting as International's point person.

After reviewing these representations and warranties with several of your colleagues, you call Bob back.

Answer the following:

(i) What do you advise Bob about the legal consequences of Speedskates making the representation and warranty with respect to no violation of other agreements? Why does this matter? If Speedskates makes the representation and warranty and you continue with your representation, will you violate your ethical duties?

(ii) What do you advise Bob about the legal consequences of Speedskates making the representation and warranty with respect to the tax payments and the financial statements? Why does this matter? If Speedskates makes the representation and warranty and you continue with your representation, will you violate your ethical duties?

(iii) May Bob deliver his opinion without violating any ethical rules?

(iv) Assume that you and Bob have raised grave concerns about the tax returns with the president of International, who tells Bob that the amount at stake with regard to the tax returns is not material, and that the materiality exception in the representation and warranty permits Speedskates to make the representation and warranty without further disclosure. Can you and Bob rely on what the president has said?

(v) Assume that Bob tells International's president that he will not deliver his opinion without changes to the representations and warranties; and the president responds by telling Bob that if he fails to deliver the opinion, he will be in breach of his employment agreement with International. Bob then calls you and asks what his rights are if he quits, or in the alternative, if International fires him. What do you tell Bob?

(vi) Bob goes home to think over his options. The next morning, he calls to report that the deal has closed, the bank having decided to waive the condition requiring Bob's opinion. May you tell the bank? What are your ethical obligations in terms of reporting this matter to the local disciplinary authority?

Diagram of the Speedskates Transaction

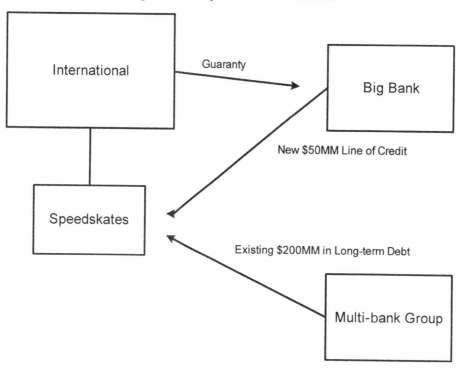

B. Exercise 35B: Inaccurate Representation and Warranty

You have received the following e-mail message:

To: Exhausted, but Still Going, Associate

From: Compassionate, but Demanding, Corporate Partner

As you know, I am representing HiTech Inc. in the sale of substantially all of its assets. Unfortunately, in connection with that deal, I now have an ethical dilemma: The Buyer's lawyers have crafted a provision that is too generous to our client. Specifically, they have drafted the representation and warranty with respect to defaults under existing contracts as follows:

"No material defaults exist under any material agreements."

According to my recollection of the negotiation (and also the recollection of our client), the representation and warranty was supposed to provide that no defaults exist under any material agreement. (No double dip on materiality.)

Our client insists that we say nothing. I am thinking that maybe we should say something. What are our ethical obligations? Do you have any suggestions as to how we should deal with our client on this matter?

Attached is ABA Informal Opinion 86-1518, which may be helpful. Do not do any other research on this matter; our client does not want to pay.

ABA Informal Opinion 86-1518
Notice to Opposing Counsel of Inadvertent Omission of Contract Provision
February 9, 1986

Where the lawyer for [A] has received for signature from the lawyer for [B] the final transcription of a contract from which an important provision previously agreed upon has been inadvertently omitted by the lawyer for [B], the lawyer for [A], unintentionally advantaged, should contact the lawyer for [B] to correct the error and need not consult [A] about the error.

A and B, with the assistance of their lawyers, have negotiated a commercial contract. After deliberation with counsel, A ultimately acquiesced in the final provision insisted upon by B, previously in dispute between the parties and without which B would have refused to come to overall agreement. However, A's lawyer discovered that the final draft of the contract typed in the office of B's lawyer did not contain the provision which had been in dispute. The Committee has been asked to give its opinion as to the ethical duty of A's lawyer in that circumstance.

The Committee considers this situation to involve merely a scrivener's error, not an intentional change in position by the other party. A meeting of the minds has already occurred. The Committee concludes that the error is appropriate for correction between the lawyers without client consultation.[1]

A's lawyer does not have a duty to advise A of the error pursuant to any obligation of communication under Rule 1.4 of the ABA Model Rules of Professional Conduct (1983). "The guiding principle is that the lawyer should fulfill reasonable client expectations for information consistent with the duty to act in the client's best interests and the client's overall requirements as to the character of representation." Comment to Rule 1.4. In this circumstance there is no "informed decision," in the language of Rule 1.4 that A needs to make; the decision on the contract has already been made by the client. Furthermore, the Comment to Rule 1.2 points out that the lawyer may decide the "technical" means to be employed to carry out the objective of the representation, without consultation with the client.

The client does not have a right to take unfair advantage of the error. The client's right pursuant to Rule 1.2 to expect committed and dedicated representation is not unlimited. Indeed, for A's lawyer to suggest that A has an opportunity to capitalize on the clerical error, unrecognized by B and B's lawyer, might raise a serious question of the violation of the duty of A's lawyer under Rule 1.2(d) not to counsel the client to engage in, or assist the client in, conduct the lawyer knows is fraudulent. In addition, Rule 4.1(b) admonishes the lawyer not knowingly to fail to disclose a material fact to a third person when disclosure is necessary to avoid assisting a fraudulent act by a client, and Rule 8.4(c) prohibits the lawyer from engaging in conduct involving dishonesty, fraud, deceit, or misrepresentation.

The result would be the same under the predecessor ABA Model Code of Professional Responsibility (1969, revised 1980). While EC 7-8 teaches that a lawyer should use best efforts to ensure that the client's decisions are made after the client has been informed of relevant considerations, and EC 9-2 charges the lawyer with fully and promptly informing the client of material developments, the scrivener's error is neither a relevant consideration nor a material development and

---

1. Assuming for purposes of discussion that the error is "information relating to [the] representation," under Rule 1.6 disclosure would be "impliedly authorized in order to carry out the representation." The Comment to Rule 1.6 points out that a lawyer has implied authority to make "a disclosure that facilitates a satisfactory conclusion" — in this case completing the commercial contract already agreed on and left to the lawyers to memorialize. We do not here reach the issue of the lawyer's duty if the client wishes to exploit the error.

therefore does not establish an opportunity for a client's decision.[2] The duty of zealous representation in DR 7-101 is limited to lawful objectives. *See* DR 7-102. Rule 1.2 evolved from DR 7-102(A)(7), which prohibits a lawyer from counseling or assisting the client in conduct known to be fraudulent. *See also* DR 1-102(A)(4), the precursor of Rule 8.4(c), prohibiting the lawyer from engaging in conduct involving dishonesty, fraud, deceit, or misrepresentation.

---

2. The delivery of the erroneous document is not a "material development" of which the client should be informed under EC 9-2 of the Model Code of Professional Responsibility, but the omission of the provision from the document is a "material fact" which under Rule 4.1(b) of the Model Rules of Professional Conduct must be disclosed to B's lawyer.

C. Exercise 35C: Disclosing a Problem and Working with Supervisors

You are Lydia Grant, a junior associate at Good Ethics & Law, a New York City law firm with 450 lawyers in the United States and abroad. Your client is Acquisitions Inc. ("**Acquisitions**"), a privately held investment firm. One of Acquisitions' subsidiaries, Newco, is purchasing substantially all the assets of a candy manufacturer. To finance the purchase, Newco is borrowing the necessary funds from Megabank USA. You have been representing the subsidiary in connection with the loan negotiations. You have been working with Henry Loew, Vice President of Acquisitions.

The terms of the borrowing are fairly standard and include mandatory prepayments as determined by a formula.[67] Unfortunately, the formula does not work properly according to your understanding of the provision from earlier discussions with the bankers and their lawyers. It seems as if the formula's results significantly understate the amount Newco must prepay. As the parties did not draft a term sheet, you have no statement of terms with which to compare the provision. Moreover, as Acquisitions and Megabank have not done a deal before, you can't even look at an earlier deal for guidance.

Loew is adamant that you say nothing. To obtain an additional perspective, you speak with Ralph Adams, the firm's partner responsible for legal ethics. He gives you the attached case, thinking that it might provide you with some guidance.

Answer the following:

1. Must you disclose the problem with the prepayment provision?
2. Assume that you conclude that you must disclose the problem with the prepayment provision. On hearing your conclusion, Loew marches into Ralph Adams's office and declares you to be a coward. Ralph tells you and Loew that, although it is a close question, he thinks that the deal can go forward without disclosing the problem with the prepayment formula. What are your ethical obligations? May you follow your superior's instructions without violating your ethical obligations?

---

67. Mandatory prepayment provisions generally provide that a borrower must repay the bank a percentage of any cash that the borrower receives from an additional bank borrowing, the issuance of equity or debt securities, or the sale of substantially all of their assets. The bank insists on the prepayment because a lower outstanding loan balance reduces the credit risk.

Stare v. Tate

21 Cal. App. 3d 432, 98 Cal. Rptr. 264 (2d Dist. 1971)

KAUS, [Presiding Justice].

Plaintiff appeals from an adverse judgment in an action to reform a property settlement agreement with her former husband, the defendant, and to enforce the agreement as reformed.

Facts

The agreement in question was signed by both parties [who were divorcing] on February 21, 1968. It was the culmination of protracted negotiations which had been going on for several years. Both sides were represented by counsel at all times.[1]

In the negotiations both sides apparently agreed that the community property was to be evenly divided. They did not agree, however, on the value of certain items and on the community property status of certain stocks that stood in the husband's name alone.

These disagreements centered principally on items which, it was understood, were to be retained by the husband. . . .

To sum up: if Joan was correct with respect to the value of the Holt property, her community property interest in it was about $25,000 higher than Tim conceded; if she were to succeed on her contentions with respect to the stock, Tim would have had to pay her roughly $40,000 more than he was willing.

In January, 1968, Joan's attorney prepared a document entitled "SECOND PROPOSAL FOR A BASIS OF SETTLEMENT — TATE v. TATE" which, among other things, arrived at a suggested figure of $70,081.85 for the value of Joan's share in the Holt property. This value was arrived at by a computation set forth in the proposal. It is copied in the footnote.[4]

It is obvious that Joan's attorney arrived at the figure of $70,081.85 for the community equity in the property only by making two substantial errors. First, the net value after deducting the encumbrances from the asserted gross value of $550,000 is $241,637.01, not $141,637.01; second, one-half of $141,637.01 is substantially more than $70,081.85. The correct figure for the equity should have been $120,818.50 or, roughly $50,000 more.

The mistake did not escape Tim's accountant who discovered it while helping Tim's attorney in preparing a counteroffer. He brought it to the attention of the attorney who, in his own words, reacted as follows:

> I told him that I had been arguing with (the wife's attorney) to use the value that was on the — on the real property tax statement, but I knew that that was low and (he) would never go for it, that the appraisal had been $425,000.00 when the building had been purchased by said owners, and I thought that until we got it, that we would use something like a $450,000.00 value, and he said, "Fine." It is

---

1. The attorneys who represent the husband on this appeal did not act for him in the negotiations.

4. "888 East Holt Avenue, Pomona

(Note: value as per previous offer)		
Total value	$550,000.00	
Less encumbrance	− 308,362.99	
Net value	$141,637.01	
One-half community		$70,081.85"

my recollection that I said to him, "You know, you might as well use the figure that Walker [the wife's attorney] has there because his mistake is a hundred thousand dollars and we value it at a hundred thousand dollars less, so it is basically the same thing, so give it a $70,000.00 equity," and that is what he did and that is how it came about.

A counteroffer was then submitted to Joan and her lawyer. It lists all of the community assets, with the property in question being valued at $70,082.00, rounding up the erroneous figure in Joan's offer to the nearest dollar. There can be no reasonable doubt that the counteroffer was prepared in a way designed to minimize the danger that Joan or her attorney would discover the mistake. While all other encumbered properties are listed at an agreed gross value, with encumbrances shown as a deduction therefrom, the only figure that appears next to the Holt property is the equity!

. . .

The rule that the party who misleads another is estopped from claiming that the contract is anything but what the other is led to believe, appears to be quite generally accepted. Citing many cases from other jurisdictions and noting no contrary authority Corbin says: "Reformation may be a proper remedy even though the mistake is not mutual. If one of the parties mistakenly believes that the writing is a correct integration of that to which he had expressed his assent and the other party knows that it is not, reformation may be decreed. The conduct of the other party in permitting the first to execute the erroneous writing and later attempting to enforce it may be regarded as fraudulent; but it is enough to justify reformation that he knows the terms proposed by the first party and the meaning thereof and leads that party reasonably to believe that he too assents to those terms. This makes a contract; and the writing may be reformed to accord with it. The fact that the first party was negligent in failing to observe that the writing does not express what he has assented to does not deprive him of this remedy. The ground for estoppel is against the other and non-mistaken party, not against the mistaken party even though he is negligent." (3 Corbin on Contracts, § 614, pp. 730-732.) The rule is also in accord with the Restatement of Contracts.

. . .

Stephens, J., and Aiso, J., concurred.

D. Exercise 35D: Possible Conflict with Previous Agreement, Unaddressed Issues, and Unenforceable Provisions

You are Pat E. Kake, a partner at Good Ethics & Law, a New York City law firm with 450 lawyers in the United States and abroad. You have a broad-ranging corporate practice, having successfully resisted several attempts by the firm to pigeonhole you into a niche practice.

1. One of your clients is WCBA, one of New York City's premier television stations. Your contact at WCBA is Lila Bartley, senior vice president and general counsel.

    Lila just called and related the following: WCBA's longtime sportscaster, Ray Statler, passed away recently. His death has created a significant business problem for WCBA, as its ratings for the evening broadcasts have fallen precipitously since he died. Lila tells you that all is not lost, however. WCBA has learned through the grapevine that Bob Jacobs, WXYZ's longtime sportscaster, is disaffected with his present employer and wants to jump ship as soon as possible. As a result of the intervention of an intermediary, Bob gave his employment agreement to another employee of WCBA, and that agreement has been passed to Lila.

Lila tells you that she has reviewed the contract, and one provision gives her pause. It states the following:

Noncompete. During the Term and for a period of 90 days afterward, Employee shall not

(a) accept employment from,

(b) negotiate for employment with, or

(c) solicit any proposal from

any Person in connection with a position as a radio or television sportscaster.[68]

She then states the obvious: If Bob were to sign a contract with WCBA, he will have violated his contract with WXYZ, and WCBA may be subject to a suit for tortious interference with contract. Lila then continues that WCBA is willing to accept the business risk of the lawsuit. Lila is worried, however, about the risk to herself. Is she somehow acting unethically by participating in the negotiation and drafting of Bob's employment contract with WCBA?

Answer the following:

(i) What do you advise Lila? Should she alert Bob to the issue?

(ii) How (if at all) does this differ from aiding a client who intends to violate a law?

2. Lila calls you and informs you that WCBA has made the business decision to employ Bob. She asks that you negotiate the contract. You are, of course, delighted to do so. (Your hours this month have been a little low.) Lila tells you that Dave Winslow will be negotiating on behalf of Bob.

After marking up an employment agreement from the firm's precedents files, you send a copy to Lila, who blesses it. You then send a copy of the agreement by e-mail to Bob Jacobs and Dave Winslow.

About three days later, Dave calls to give you comments on the draft. Most of his comments are reasonable, while others give you pause.

Answer the following:

(i) Dave asks for a bonus if ratings improve 5 percent or more within the first 30 days of the employment term. Lila approves the bonus. When you go to draft the bonus provision, you note that the parties did not address whether a pro rata bonus should be payable on death or disability. Are you ethically obligated to provide for the pro rata bonus in the revised contract? What nonethical reason could you give to encourage Lila to raise the issue with Dave?

(ii) Dave states that the proposed noncompete provision is probably unenforceable both in terms of time and geographic scope. You agree to a reasonable, shorter time period but insist on a larger geographic scope, arguing that it is the industry standard. It is, but it is also highly unlikely that a court would enforce it. Will you be violating your ethical duties if the contract includes an unenforceable geographic scope provision? Would your answer change if you were drafting a standard-form contract that all of WCBA's employees would sign and you knew that the courts had previously held the provision unenforceable?

---

68. For the purposes of this exercise, assume that this contract provision is enforceable.

E. Exercise 35E: Redlines and Messages Regarding Changes

In addition to WCBA, one of your long-time clients is By'em Inc. ("**By'em**"). By'em buys undervalued companies and sells off the subsidiaries and divisions at prices that are, in the aggregate, greater than the value of the company as a whole. You have strong relationships with both the in-house counsel, Stanley Leech, and the executive vice president, Reena Pixley.

Reena called about two weeks ago to tell you about a new deal. By'em plans to purchase Conglomerate Inc. ("**Conglomerate**"). She asked that you mark up and distribute By'em's standard-form purchase agreement. The deal is on a fast track. Negotiations and due diligence are moving quickly, and the closing is scheduled for the end of the month. The transaction is basically friendly. You even established a good working relationship with Roger Pine, president of Conglomerate.

As part of the negotiations, By'em and Conglomerate agree to a term. When drafting the insert, you craft it in such a way that Conglomerate arguably takes on more of the risk than had been agreed to. You redline the entire provision so that Conglomerate's counsel will know that it has been changed. In your e-mail message, as has been your practice, you point out the significant changes in the revised draft—except this one provision.

Answer the following:

1. Did you violate your ethical duties by drafting the provision in the way that you did, or by failing to note the change in your cover letter?
2. Does your answer change if the client instructs you to make the change? Consider *In re Rothwell*, 296 S.E.2d 870 (S.C. 1982).

In re ROTHWELL
296 S.E.2d 870 (S.C. 1982)

PER CURIAM:

The Hearing Panel and the Board of Commissioners on Grievances and Discipline recommend respondent Donald Erwin Rothwell be publicly reprimanded for professional misconduct. We agree.

Respondent was retained by Richard Mowery to represent him in negotiations with Mowery's former employer, W.W. Williams Company, who had transferred Mowery from Columbus, Ohio to Columbia. To facilitate the transfer, Williams Company loaned Mowery $47,000 to purchase a house in Columbia.

Mowery was discharged from Williams Company after he moved to Columbia, but before he had repaid the $47,000. Williams Company offered to buy Mowery's Ohio house and apply the equity to the debt, leaving a deficiency of $7,201.04.

Williams Company prepared and mailed to respondent a deed along with a letter requesting that respondent have his client, Mowery, execute and return the deed to Williams Company for filing. The letter also stated, "[w]e will expect your call if there are any questions."

Respondent surreptitiously altered the deed by inserting a paragraph satisfying the entire debt from Mowery to Williams Company, and mailed the deed to Williams Company with a letter which stated only:

> We are returning herewith your package to you duly executed. Once you have filed the deed of record, please forward on a clocked copy of same for our files. Thank you.

> No notice was given Williams Company that the deed had been altered.

Williams Company filed the deed and sued Mowery for the deficiency. Respondent raised the altered deed as a defense.

Respondent contends the deed prepared by Williams Company was merely an offer, and his alteration of the deed constituted a counteroffer. Clearly, Williams Company expected respondent to either (1) have his client execute the deed or (2) telephone Williams Company. Respondent's letter to Williams Company gave no notice of the alteration, but rather, led Williams Company to believe he had complied with their request.

We agree with the Panel that respondent engaged in conduct involving dishonesty, fraud, deceit, and misrepresentation which is prejudicial to the administration of justice and adversely reflects on his fitness to practice law, all in violation of DR1-102(A)(1), (4), (5) and (6); DR7-102(A)(3); and sections 5(b) and (d) of the Rule on Disciplinary Procedure of the Supreme Court of the State of South Carolina. Accordingly, respondent Donald Erwin Rothwell stands publicly reprimanded for his acts of professional misconduct.

CHAPTER THIRTY-SIX

Summary of Putting a Contract Together and Important Considerations

The following chart summarizes the material in Chapters 30 through 35. Reading it does not replace reading the chapters. Use it as a handy, quick reference tool.

CHAPTER	TOPIC	GUIDANCE
Adding Value to the Deal (Chapter 30, page 459)	Money—Amount to Be Paid or Received	▪ Usually, the first money issue to consider is whether a client is entitled to receive more money or to pay less. ▪ You may be able to identify other types of consideration in the transaction, whether monetary or not, due to your experience with similar types of transactions. ▪ As you determine the amount to be paid or received in a transaction, consider whether any of the payment should be contingent, as in the case of an earnout (future payment based on formula tied to the business's performance), and try to identify other types of consideration, whether monetary or not.
	Money—Timing of Payment	▪ Clients usually want to pay later but receive money sooner. ▪ If your client must pay the other party, ask whether it can spread out the payments over time or whether the other party will give your client a discount for immediate payment. ▪ If the other side must pay your client, negotiate for receipt of the payment as soon as possible. If the other side objects, find out from your client whether they could benefit from an immediate but smaller payment.
	Money—Credit Risk	▪ Credit risk is always a business issue when the other party is obligated to pay your client in the future. ▪ Whenever your client has agreed to receive a delayed payment, consider whether the risk of a payment default is significant. If it is, then negotiate a mechanism to secure the payment.

CHAPTER	TOPIC	GUIDANCE
	Money—Issues Relating to Payment Formulas	■ Parties often use a formula to determine a contract's consideration. ■ When reviewing a formula, begin by analyzing whether the formula is neutral or whether it favors your client or the other party in some way. ■ Confirm that the formula is properly stated. Is any aspect or variable in the formula ambiguous? Taken as a whole, is the formula ambiguous in any way? Be as specific as possible in drafting a formula. ■ After running the numbers, send the hypotheticals to your client and other experts involved to make sure that they understand how the formula will work, both when the transaction succeeds and when it fails. ■ Once your client approves the formula and hypotheticals, send them to the other side for their review and approval. ■ With the approval of the clients, you may want to add the hypotheticals as an exhibit to the contract so they can better set forth and give examples of the parties' understanding of the formula at the time of contracting.
	Money—Transaction Expenses	■ You and your client should think through whether each party should pay their own expenses or whether the expenses should be shifted from one party to the other from the beginning or at a particular point in the transaction. ■ Then you should make sure that you and/or your client has the discussion with the other side about the transaction expenses.
	Money—Accounting and Tax Issues	■ The accounting and tax issues may determine the structure of the transaction and sometimes even whether the transaction can be done. ■ If you do not have the background to address these issues, you *must* obtain the assistance of a qualified practitioner.
	Risk—Types of Risk and Evaluating the Risk	■ Risk can manifest itself in multiple ways in a transaction: tort liability, contract law risk, statutory liability, inherent in the transaction, and litigation risk. ■ You have to identify risks and then assess the probability that the risk will occur. You should try to quantify the risk and do a risk/reward analysis, possibly with the assistance of the client. The client could decide that the benefits do not justify the risk.

	Risk—Methods to Mitigate Risk	■ Security interest:
		   ■ Determine which assets are the most valuable and which will be the easiest to liquidate. Be sure that the security interest applies to these assets.
		   ■ A third party's credit can be added to the credit of the party with the payment obligation (e.g., as co-obligor, guarantor). This third party must be creditworthy.
		■ Escrow agreement:
		   ■ To create an escrow, the parties deposit cash or other property with a neutral third party, who agrees to release it only in accordance with the terms of the escrow agreement.

CHAPTER	TOPIC	GUIDANCE

		■ Indemnity agreements:
		   ■ In an indemnity agreement, one party promises to pay the other party for certain losses, even if the indemnified party did not cause the loss.
		 ■ Letter of credit:
		   ■ In a letter of credit transaction, a bank substitutes its credit for that of another party's credit.
		 ■ Insurance:
		   ■ In reviewing a counterparty's insurance coverage, learning that a party has insurance is insufficient. You must know, among other things, the following:
		     ■ What constitutes an event of loss and the number of events covered
		     ■ What is excluded from the policy
		     ■ Whether there are any specific additional policies for a particular risk (e.g., key person insurance, through which an employer can receive a death benefit if that employee passes away)
		     ■ The deductible (the amount the insured must pay before the insurer is liable)
		     ■ The insurer's maximum obligation
		     ■ Whether the maximum obligation has been reduced by earlier payments
		     ■ Whether the insurer is creditworthy (Can the insurer pay up?)
		 ■ Deal-specific methods:
		   ■ For example, the parties could reduce a buyer's risk by changing the structure from a stock acquisition to an asset acquisition.
		 ■ Opinion letters:
		   ■ In some transactions, a party may ask for an opinion letter on a specific legal issue relating to the transaction from the other side's lawyer, even though the other side's lawyer is not their lawyer. Lawyers do not like giving opinion letters, and they negotiate relentlessly to limit their scope. Lawyers do not want to be liable to a third party on issues that they cannot fully control.

	Control	■ The first question must be whether having control is good or bad from your client's perspective and what implications control has on them and the transaction. ■ For example, when you are drafting your client's covenants, with respect to each promise that your client makes, you will have to determine whether your client can control and ensure the outcome. To protect your client, negotiate a covenant that reduces the risk by changing the degree of obligation. ■ When thinking about control issues, think through which party is in control, whether that is the correct party, or whether control should be shared, and if so, how. ■ Once controls are in place, they do not need to remain at the same level throughout a relationship.

CHAPTER	TOPIC	GUIDANCE
	Standards	▪ Almost every word or phrase in a contract establishes a standard. For example, every representation and warranty establishes a standard of liability, and the time or duration of an event or an action can also be a standard. ▪ Once you determine what the standard is for a particular issue, determine whether the standard favors your client, and, if not, how it can be modified. ▪ Do not start drafting with a preconceived notion that vagueness is good or bad. Instead, each time that a provision establishes a vague standard, analyze whether it helps your client or whether a more specific, concrete standard would improve the client's position.
	Endgame	▪ The parties must try to anticipate the different options going forward and think through the consequences. ▪ When drafting endgame provisions, think through what the monetary consequences of the contract's end should be. Follow the cash. ▪ Monetary endgame issues also include whether the prevailing party in a litigation should be contractually entitled to recover their attorneys' fees and other litigation expenses.
Organizing a Contract and Its Provisions (Chapter 31, page 483)	Introduction	▪ A well-written contract has an organizational framework that makes it easy to read. A contract is easy to read if the reader knows where to look for a provision and understands how the contract's provisions relate to each other. ▪ There is no single way to organize a contract. Nonetheless, over time, through custom and practice, we have standardized how we organize some types of contracts. ▪ In practice, you will draft very few contracts from scratch. Instead, you will use a precedent—either one from your firm or one that you find in a secondary resource.
	Organizing a Contract at the Macro Level	▪ At the macro level, the organization of contracts rarely differs, so, again, see the overall structure of most contracts on page 484.

	Organizing Provisions at the Micro Level	▪ When you are organizing individual provisions in a contract at the micro level, you can use one of the primary organizing principles listed below. Most contracts use more than one of these principles. See the example on page 487 for more details on how these organizing principles would be used.
		▪ Subject matter:
		  ▪ Organizing a contract's business provisions by subject matter is the most common way to put together a contract.
		  ▪ The drafter begins grouping together business terms on the same or similar topics and creating subject matter groups. These groups will become provisions that must be further organized, often using one or more of the other organizing principles.

CHAPTER	TOPIC	GUIDANCE
		■ Relative importance: 　■ You always want to think about which provisions are most important and place them, if possible, at the top of a section so they are immediately visible and are read first. 　■ In determining the relative importance of provisions, consider, among other things, how important that provision is to your client and whether the parties will need to refer to that provision frequently (more important) or infrequently (less important). 　■ The statement of a rule should precede its exception to facilitate understanding of the exception. 　■ Put provisions that are broader and more comprehensive first, while you place the more specific provisions on that same subject matter afterward. ■ Chronology: 　■ Drafters can use chronology to organize provisions, especially in situations where one party's actions depend on the occurrence—or nonoccurrence—of the other party's actions. 　■ A well-drafted provision will need to provide a timetable for the process. Putting these provisions in chronological order provides the reader with an easy road map to follow. ■ Party: 　■ Organization by party is often a secondary level of organization. ■ Contract concepts: 　■ Contract concepts rarely provide the overarching organizational scheme of a contract's provisions. Acquisition and financing agreements are the exception. Nonetheless, a drafter will sometimes use a contract concept to organize part of a contract that is otherwise organized by subject matter.
The Drafting Process (Chapter 32, page 493)	Agreeing to the Business Terms	■ In a transaction, the parties generally negotiate the key business terms, including price.[1] Once they have done so, each party contacts their lawyers. One of the lawyers will probably draw up a list of the key business points to which all parties have agreed. Then the parties will review and confirm those key business terms. ■ The parties may decide to enter into a more formal, written agreement, such as a letter of intent, term sheet, or memorandum of understanding. All three of these options have the following in common: (1) they include the key business terms that the parties have agreed to for that transaction, (2) they could be binding or nonbinding depending on what the parties decide, and (3) they would be preliminary to the parties doing their due diligence and agreeing to a more final business contract.

---

1. Other scenarios are possible. Sometimes a client will meet with a lawyer at the very beginning of a deal, and the lawyer, with other experts, will help the client structure and negotiate the transaction's material terms.

CHAPTER	TOPIC	GUIDANCE
		■ If you negotiate letters of intent, term sheets, or memoranda of understanding, you should make sure that you are very familiar with the case law and how to best make clear what is binding and not binding.
	Determining Who Drafts the Contract	■ Custom and negotiating leverage often determine who takes the lead and whose precedent is used. ■ If custom does not dictate who drafts the contract, and, if the other side gives you the opportunity to draft the contract, take it, because your client will gain a strategic advantage, and if you control the agreement and the drafting process, you may be able to control the deal's pace.

	Learning About a Transaction from a Client	■ When a client calls, listen carefully to the details. Ask the questions you can and suggest a meeting. Ask the client to bring any relevant documents, including any deal memos, letter of intent, correspondence, previous contracts, and notes.
		■ To prepare for the client meeting, create a checklist of the questions that you want to ask. The checklist should cover all the business terms to be incorporated into the agreement.
		■ As part of your preparation for the meeting, draw a diagram of the transaction.
		■ At the client meeting, begin by getting an overview of the transaction and the client's attitude toward it.
		  ■ If the client is eager to discuss the details of the transaction, then bypass the preliminary overview discussion or integrate it into the discussion of deal points.
		■ Assuming that you begin with a general discussion about the transaction, some of the questions that you might ask are as follows:
		  ■ What is the reason for the transaction?
		  ■ What are the client's business goals and expectations?
		  ■ What would constitute a big win?
		  ■ What does the client want to avoid?
		  ■ What are the hot-button issues and the deal breakers?
		  ■ Is the transaction necessary to the company's survival?
		  ■ Is timing a factor? Is time of the essence?
		  ■ Do the parties have a previous business relationship? If so, are they parties to any other agreements that will affect the new transaction?
		  ■ Is the price a bargain, is it steep, and how was it determined?
		  ■ Is it a good deal but one that the client will pass up if the other side is unreasonable or inflexible?
		  ■ Which party has negotiating leverage, and what is it?
		  ■ How much risk is the client willing to take in different areas?
		■ As part of the client meeting, go over negotiating strategy with the client.
		■ As part of the discussion of negotiating strategy, look at the contract from the other side's perspective.

CHAPTER	TOPIC	GUIDANCE
		▪ Ask the client how sophisticated the agreement should be. ▪ With these preliminary matters concluded, begin asking specific questions about the transaction. Be sure to keep accurate notes. ▪ As part of this interview, you may also want to ask whether you or the client will take the "laboring oar" in the negotiations. ▪ Before the meeting concludes, discuss timing.

	Learning About a Transaction from a Supervisor	▪ Learning about a new transaction from a supervisor resembles, but is not the same as, learning about it from a client. As a junior drafter, you should consider more senior drafters in your office to be your first clients.
		 ▪ Listen carefully to confirm that you understand the nature of the transaction. Also, ask questions if you do not understand something.
		 ▪ You should leave the meeting with all the information and documents that you would have had if you had been to a client meeting, including deal memos, letters of intent, correspondence, previous contracts, and notes. If you need other information, ask for it.
		 ▪ Before you leave, find out the deadline and, as much as possible, establish a timeline for the entire transaction. You should ask your supervisor at the very least about the following deadlines and the timing of any other related transactions:
		   ▪ The date by which you must submit your draft to the supervisor
		   ▪ The date by which the supervisor must submit a draft to the client or their own supervisor
		   ▪ The date by which your office must deliver the agreement to the other party

	Preparing to Draft a Contract	▪ Researching the law and obtaining the advice of specialists:
		   ▪ Before beginning to draft, determine what legal issues the transaction raises. But, you cannot—and should not—research all of an agreement's legal issues before you begin drafting.
		   ▪ In any transaction, you *must* obtain the advice of an accountant, a tax lawyer, or both, unless you are sure that you understand the subtleties of all the issues raised.
		 ▪ Researching the parties and the industry:
		   ▪ Before drafting a contract, you must fully understand the business deal and everyone involved.
		   ▪ Often, to do this, you must research the client, the other side, and their industry.
		   ▪ If the other side is a public company, also check the Securities Exchange Commission's (SEC) EDGAR database for agreements that the public company has entered into that may be related or relevant.

CHAPTER	TOPIC	GUIDANCE

	Drafting With and Without Precedent	■ *Precedent* refers to a contract from an earlier transaction. A *standard form,* also known as a *model* or *template,* usually has different possible provisions you can choose from and that can be adjusted to a real transaction, even possibly annotated with brief explanations and instructions.
		■ If you do not obtain a precedent or standard form from someone in your office or from the client, you can obtain forms from industry associations, treatises, continuing legal education materials, and online. Be wary of all these precedents and standard forms since the quality can vary.
		■ Guidelines for choosing precedent or a standard form:
		  ■ Choose an agreement that is for the same type of transaction.
		  ■ Choose an agreement where the party in your client's position had the greater negotiating leverage and where there were as similar conditions as possible.
		  ■ Look at annotated precedent or standard forms with different options or different drafts of agreements instead of a final executed agreement.
		■ Keep track of good precedents and standard forms that you find so you can use them in future transactions as additional resources. Analyzing multiple versions of the same type of provision will help you assess the precedent's or standard form's provision and give you ideas on the different ways to draft its substance.
		■ Using precedent and standard forms:
		  ■ When at a firm and confronted with a poorly drafted provision, determine whether the existing language creates ambiguity. If it does, redraft it, but mention your changes in the e-mail to your supervisor.
		  ■ If the provision is unambiguous, but otherwise is poorly drafted, use the provision as is and then deal with its problems after the transaction finishes. Then, consult with the firm's keeper of the forms, who will probably appreciate your input. Do not change the firm's master form without permission.
		■ Drafting without precedent or a standard form:
		  ■ If you must create a document without using precedent or a standard form, take a step back and think about the substantive provisions that the contract will need. Do other contracts have similar provisions, even if they are not exactly on point? Can you draft the contract by patching together relevant provisions from different agreements?

	The Logistics of Drafting a Contract	■ If you are drafting a contract using precedent or a standard form, first copy the precedent or standard form and put the original aside. Always keep the precedent or standard form unchanged so it can be used again. ■ Every draft of the contract that you distribute, whether internally where you work, to the client, or to third parties, should be numbered and dated in the right or left header.

CHAPTER	TOPIC	GUIDANCE
		■ Be sure to distinguish internal drafts from those sent to third parties. ■ Next, set up electronic file systems to keep track of the internal and external drafts. You may also want hard-copy files. If so, use one accordion-type expandable folder for each draft and label it with the appropriate draft number and date.
	Drafting a Contract—Coordinating with Other Drafters and Translating the Business Deal into Contract Concepts	■ Give others in your office responsible for drafting certain parts as much lead time as possible. ■ Before beginning to draft, list or outline all the business terms of the deal that you will have to draft. ■ Once you have listed all the business terms of the deal, translate them into contract concepts to make them into provisions. Then reorganize the list so that what used to be business terms of the deal and are now provisions appear in the order in which they will appear in the contract. Use your precedent and the organizing principles to help you order the list. ■ As you are doing this, keep asking yourself if there is a cascade effect—a covenant that you need because you added a representation and warranty.
	Drafting a Contract—Drafting the First Draft	■ How do you actually decide what to write first? Drafters differ in their approach, and your approach may change depending on the agreement. Absent a good reason to start somewhere else, start with the introductory provisions. ■ Whether you skip the definitions or draft some of them early, stay sensitive to the need to draft new ones as you continue through the drafting and negotiation process. Draft the definitions while you are working on the relevant provisions. Make sure that each definition works each time its defined term is used. ■ As you work through the contract, you will have questions. Do not stop drafting and wait to get an answer. Instead, do one or more of the following: ■ Create a list of questions to ask your client or supervising lawyer. ■ Put the provision about which you have a question in brackets. ■ Craft two or more versions of the provision, putting each in brackets. ■ Describe the issue in an e-mail to your supervisor or client. ■ Set up a system to deal with cross-references. ■ Guidelines for drafting the business provisions: ■ Do not recut the deal. ■ Determine whether one party will have more control. ■ Determine whether vagueness or specificity will benefit your client. ■ If the contract establishes a relationship that will exist for a term of years, build in flexibility so each change in circumstances does not create a contractual crisis.

CHAPTER	TOPIC	GUIDANCE

		■ Use the canons of construction to give you insight into how a court might interpret a provision, and rewrite the provision as needed.
		■ Draft the contract to deal with all the possibilities of an *if/then* scenario.
		■ Draft a real-world, pragmatic contract that reflects how the parties will interact.
		■ To finalize the contract, do the following:
		  ■ Run your word-processing program's spell check.
		  ■ Check that all cross-references are correct.
		  ■ Print out a hard copy and proofread it carefully.
		    ■ No matter how good you are at reviewing a document on an electronic device, you will find substantive errors and glitches when reviewing a hard copy that you will not find when looking at the contract on a screen.
		    ■ Read the contract slowly and look at what you wrote and see if it coincides with what you thought you wrote

	Drafting a Contract—Redrafting the Contract	■ Always follow up if you cannot figure out what a reviewer means. ■ Look carefully at each provision before you modify it. You may need to change additional language in that provision so the requested change works properly. You may also need to change another provision or draft a new one because of the cascade effect. ■ When you finish making the requested changes, read the entire contract.

	Drafting a Contract—Message to Supervisor or Client	■ When you distribute the first draft of the contract (indeed, any draft), send it in an e-mail with a message that does the following:
		  ■ Tells the reader where to find the provisions that deal with hot-button issues.
		  ■ Explains the risks and benefits of provisions not previously discussed.
		  ■ Describes open issues and proposes ways of resolving them.
		■ Choose the recipients of your message carefully. If it contains privileged information, sending it to the wrong person could destroy the attorney-client privilege.
		■ If you are in a practice setting or working with a client that is more formal, you may need to draft a memorandum for your supervisor or client on these issues.

How to Review and Comment on a Contract (Chapter 33, page 513)	Prepare	■ Prepare in exactly the same way that you would have if you had been the drafter, before you even read the other side's draft. Do the following:
		  ■ Obtain all available information about the business deal.
		  ■ Create a checklist of questions for your supervisor or client.
		  ■ Draw a diagram of the transaction if necessary.
		  ■ Interview your supervisor or client thoroughly.
		  ■ Research the law, the parties, and the industry.
		  ■ Obtain the advice of specialists if necessary.

CHAPTER	TOPIC	GUIDANCE
		■ Find appropriate precedent. ■ Create a list of the business terms of the deal (both those that the parties have agreed to and any new ones to be incorporated). ■ Translate the business terms of the deal into contract concepts to make them into provisions. ■ Organize what are now provisions representing the business terms of the deal in the sequence in which you expect that they will appear in the contract, and try to figure out in which part of the agreement you would put them.
	Review the Contract to Get a Quick Overview	■ The first time you look at a contract, take a quick look through it to get a simple overview. ■ You should mainly be looking at the headings of articles and titles of subsections to get a sense of the following: 　■ How is the contract organized? By subject matter? By contract concept? Is the organization similar to the precedent that you are familiar with? How does it differ? Where are the action sections? Do the captions look familiar, or does the contract contain provisions that you had not expected?
	Read and Analyze the Key Business Provisions—General Approach	■ Once you have a sense of how the contract is generally organized from your quick overview, review the key business provisions to see if the contract has correctly stated the most significant business terms. ■ Generally, you should read the payment provisions in the action sections first. ■ Next, look at the endgame provisions. ■ Then turn to the provisions dealing with the most significant other business terms.
	Read and Analyze the Key Business Provisions—How to Analyze Each Provision	■ Break down and analyze each key business provision separately. You must ask and answer the six questions that follow for each provision: 　■ What is the business purpose of the provision? 　■ Does the provision properly incorporate the agreed-on business deal? 　■ Can the provision be changed to better protect the client and reduce the risk? 　■ Can the provision be changed to further advance the client's goals? 　■ Are there legal issues? 　■ Are there drafting issues? ■ If you want to go into more depth in your analysis, use the long list of questions for the analysis of provisions on page 516.
	Read and Analyze the Entire Contract	■ After reading the key business provisions, read the entire contract. Start from the beginning. ■ Physically separate the definitions article from the rest of the contract. This will enable you to place it and the contract side by side so you can look at a definition and a provision at the same time.

CHAPTER	TOPIC	GUIDANCE
		<ul><li>As you continue going through the contract, do not be tied to the order of the contract provisions. Instead, mimic the drafting process.</li><li>Look not only at what is in the contract, but also for what is missing.</li><li>As you go through the contract, make notes in the margin, circle problem language, or otherwise indicate any concern that you have with the language.</li><li>See questions that you should ask each time you review a contract on page 518.</li></ul>
	Prepare Comments	<ul><li>Once you have been through the contract and conferred with your supervisor and client, you must prepare your comments for the other side.</li><li>You have the following three choices when it comes to how you give the other side comments, listed in order of preference:<ul><li>A detailed markup of the contract with an accompanying message or memorandum: The markup will show the changes you want, while the message or memorandum will explain proposed changes and raise issues.</li><li>A message or memorandum discussing the major points, plus a markup of small issues, glitches (typographical errors), and stylistic points (if appropriate).</li><li>Oral comments, conveyed by telephone or at an online or in-person meeting.</li></ul></li><li>Before concluding which approach to take, talk with your client about the time, cost, and strategic benefits of one approach rather than another. Also, you may end up using a combination of the options above.</li></ul>
Amendments, Consents, and Waivers (Chapter 34, page 525)	Amendments	<ul><li>An amendment is an instrument that changes a contract and can be on any topic covered or not covered by the contract.</li><li>As was discussed in Chapter 18 on page 274, amendments can be either oral or written, and oral amendments are often enforceable, despite a "no oral amendments" provision.</li><li>When you amend an agreement, do a restated agreement or an amended and restated agreement when possible.</li></ul>
	Amendments— Inside-the-Contract Amendments	<ul><li>Inside-the-contract amendments are amendments made in a full, formal agreement format.</li><li>If the parties have previously amended the existing agreement, the amendment's title should reflect the number of amendments.</li><li>The preamble should also state which agreement is being amended by including that agreement's name, its parties, and the original signing date or *as of* date.</li><li>Use recitals to explain why the parties are amending their agreement.</li><li>*Existing Agreement* is a good defined term to use for the agreement before the amendment. The definition of *Existing Agreement* should incorporate all previous amendments, whether the term is defined in context, as in the example, or in a separate definition.</li></ul>

CHAPTER	TOPIC	GUIDANCE
		▪ *Amendment* or *Amending Agreement* works for the agreement that sets out the amendments, and *Resulting Agreement* can be used to refer to the Existing Agreement, as amended by the Amendment.
		▪ If the amendment uses terms defined in the existing agreement, do not redefine them. Instead, incorporate them into the amending agreement, using the provision that you see in the definitions of the example.
		▪ The action sections of an amending agreement are composed of the provisions that implement the changes to the existing agreement — that is, the inside-the-contract amendments. These provisions explicitly state what language is to be deleted from the existing agreement and what language is to be inserted.
		▪ Some drafters put a new provision as the last provision of the existing agreement. This keeps the numbering intact and avoids the need to change cross-references. Similarly, if a new subsection is added to a tabulated enumeration, drafters put it last.
		▪ Determine what and how other provisions should be included, such as representations and warranties, conditions, and any specific general provisions. If the existing agreement's definition of *Agreement* does not include *as amended,* then that definition or the merger provision must be amended.
	Amendments— Outside-the-Contract Amendments	▪ Outside-the-contract amendments are made in a more informal format, like in a letter, but can be just as binding.
		▪ In an outside-the-contract amendment, the amending provisions can be the same as those of an inside-the-contract amendment or they can differ. If they differ, it is generally because the parties and the drafter are taking a shortcut and trying to save transaction costs, or they are being strategic and trying to make the changes seem insignificant when they are not.
		▪ Avoid using an outside-the-contract amendment that only state the effect of the amendment. Be precise about what you are amending.
	Amendments— Restated Agreements	▪ Whenever possible, and especially when you anticipate future amendments and have a contract that involves multiple parties, do a restated agreement or an amended and restated agreement.
		▪ An amended and restated agreement not only restates the agreement but also amends one or more provisions at the same time.
		▪ When restating an agreement, move any provisions that were added to the end of the existing agreement—to keep numbering intact—to their appropriate place within the contract.
		▪ To prevent disputes on representations and warranties, the introductory language to these representations and warranties should state explicitly that they continue to speak as of the original signing date of the existing agreement.

CHAPTER	TOPIC	GUIDANCE
		■ If the parties agree to representations and warranties both as of the original signing date and the restatement date and the facts differ, create separate subsections for each date as of which the representations and warranties speak.
	Consents	■ Sometimes a party may not want the other party to be able to do something at the time of the signing of the contract but may be open to that action in the future, so long as it is possible, only if they give their permission at that future time. In these circumstances, a drafter would want to draft a provision requiring that if the one party wants to take that action, then they must get the consent of the other party.
		■ Guidelines for drafting consents:
		■ The first paragraph of the consent should refer to the agreement requiring the consent and the parties' defined terms.
		■ The second paragraph should state what your client wants and why.
		■ Track the language in the agreement that prohibits the act for which your client is seeking consent.
		■ Draft the scope of the requested consent so it meets your client's needs.
		■ Make it as easy as possible for the other side to consent.
	Waivers	■ A party may want to continue with a contract, even though an event has occurred that would allow them to have access to other remedies and/or walk away from that contract. Such a party would grant the other party a waiver, in which they would agree to keep performing as if the event had not occurred and to not exercise their remedies or walk-away rights.
		■ Waivers typically arise in response to one or more of the following three events:
		■ The failure of a condition
		■ The occurrence of a misrepresentation, breach of warranty, or breach of covenant
		■ The likely breach of a covenant
		■ A waiver does not amend a contract.
		■ Waivers can be drafted in the form of a letter or as a stand-alone agreement. In either case, the subject matter performance provision is the waiver and is a self-executing provision, effective on the waiver's execution.
		■ If the contract between the parties has a general provision dealing with waivers with language to this effect, use that same language in the waiver. Remember: *Say the same thing in the same way.*
	Choosing Between a Consent and a Waiver	■ Consents and waivers are similar and sometimes it may be hard to determine which one you should use. Which one is appropriate depends on the contract's language.

CHAPTER	TOPIC	GUIDANCE
		■ If a covenant absolutely prohibits something without exception, the piece of paper to be obtained is a waiver. A waiver will make that prohibition unenforceable on that one occasion or, in other words, would allow that one party to do what they are not allowed to do that one time. If a covenant provides for an exception to the prohibition with the other party's consent, then, in accordance with the contract, the piece of paper to be obtained is a consent. In that case, one party may give their consent so the other party is allowed to do something.
Professional Responsibility (Chapter 35, page 543)	Overview	■ This chapter focuses primarily on the duties and responsibilities of lawyers when negotiating and drafting contracts. ■ In considering issues of lawyer professional responsibility, the following are some of the laws and regulations that could be applied in cases of lawyer misconduct: legal malpractice law, ethics regulations, criminal law, constitutional law, procedural law, agency law, and securities law. ■ The possible consequences for the lawyer accused of misconduct may vary, depending on the type of proceedings initiated against the lawyer (e.g., civil, criminal, state discipline, or other) and the types of laws that apply. See the chart on page 544 for some of the possible consequences. ■ Since the laws and regulations applied in professional responsibility cases can vary from state to state, it is most important to know the relevant laws in your jurisdiction. ■ While there are many areas of state law involved in professional responsibility matters, there are two primary areas of law that come into play in these issues: legal malpractice and ethics regulations. ■ Legal malpractice is "a lawyer's failure to render professional services with the skill, prudence, and diligence that an ordinary and reasonable lawyer would use under similar circumstances."[2] A common example of legal malpractice in contract drafting is if you do not include an important provision in the contract that you should have included. To prove that a lawyer committed legal malpractice, in most jurisdictions, the plaintiff must show that (1) there was an attorney-client relationship, (2) the acts by the attorney were negligent or breach of contract, (3) that the acts by the attorney were the proximate cause of the plaintiff's damages, and (4) the plaintiff would have been successful if it had not been for the lawyer's acts. Each jurisdiction has its own standard of care and precedent relating to legal malpractice claims.

---

2. "Legal Malpractice," *Black's Law Dictionary,* 11th ed. (2019).

CHAPTER	TOPIC	GUIDANCE
		▪ Likewise, violations of the rules of professional conduct are governed by the state rules. A common example of a legal ethics violation in contract drafting is using former client information while representing a different client. That type of conduct could be a violation of the ethical rules in the relevant jurisdiction. If we use the ABA Model Rules as a guide, this type of conduct could be a violation of ABA Model Rules 1.6, 1.8, 1.9, and 1.10. ▪ Not every violation of the ethics rules is a legal malpractice claim and vice versa.

	Professional Responsibility Issues in Contract Drafting—Before Drafting	▪ This section primarily uses the ABA Model Rules to analyze common scenarios that present ethical challenges for drafters before beginning a transaction.
		▪ **1. Who Is Your Client?**
		  ▪ You must always be clear on who your client is and make that clear to them and any other parties involved from the beginning and throughout the transaction as necessary.
		  ▪ In most jurisdictions, forming a lawyer-client relationship does not require having a formal, written agreement or being paid a fee. The relationship may be implied from how the parties behave. The test is typically what is the reasonable belief in the mind of the client, and, as noted in the Restatement section above, the lawyer is responsible, and it is incumbent on the lawyer to clarify the nature of the relationship.
		  ▪ If your client is a business entity, you will have to determine and make clear whether your client is only the business entity or if you are also representing any of the officers individually in the transaction.
		  ▪ If a business entity is part of a larger structure, you will have to clarify whether you are representing the parent company, a subsidiary, or more than one party.
		  ▪ If you represent more than one client, all material information needs to be shared with each client and, if interests diverge, you cannot represent any of them because you cannot use confidential information of one client to harm the other. Also, to better protect yourself and your clients, get a written waiver from each of the parties that you are representing describing the matter and having them consent to the joint representation.
		  ▪ Before formalizing your lawyer-client relationship, make sure to do a conflicts check including your potential client, the other side, and any third parties to make sure that you do not already have potential conflicts.
		  ▪ If you interview a prospective client and you do not end up representing them, know that you cannot use any confidential information you learned from them going forward. You also cannot use any confidential information from previous clients unless it is information that is generally known.

CHAPTER	TOPIC	GUIDANCE
		▪ Best practices when determining who your client is include the following: ▪ Do a conflicts check before agreeing to represent a party, including your potential client, the other side, and any third parties, to make sure that you do not already have potential conflicts. ▪ If you identify a conflict and the conflict is not waivable, you may not be able to represent that potential client. ▪ If you identify a conflict and the conflict is waivable, get a waiver from each of the affected parties. ▪ Enter into a formal, written agreement with your client. ▪ Make clear in writing to all the other parties involved who your client is at the beginning of the transaction and throughout as necessary. ▪ If you are representing more than one client in the same transaction, get a written waiver to conflicts signed by each client. ▪ **2. Who Is on the Other Side?** ▪ If the party on the other side is a current client, the conflict is probably not waivable, so you will not be able to represent that party in this new transaction. If the party on the other side is a former client, you can usually cure the conflict by getting a waiver. ▪ If the other side was ever a prospective client but you did not end up representing them, you cannot represent the client that you want to represent if it is the same or a substantially related matter and you previously received information from the prospective client that could be significantly harmful to that person in that matter. ▪ In transactional matters, in many jurisdictions, under limited circumstances, you may enter into a business transaction with a client or acquire an interest adverse to the client. ▪ As a lawyer, you cannot reach out directly to another party knowing that they are represented by counsel. ▪ If a party is not represented or you do not know if they are represented, make sure that you are clear in what you say to them and take reasonable efforts to correct any misunderstanding. ▪ **3. Are You Competent in This Area of Law?** ▪ You are able to provide competent representation if you take additional measures, such as studying the subject matter and/or pairing up with an experienced lawyer in the field. However, you usually cannot charge a client for having to educate yourself on the subject.

CHAPTER	TOPIC	GUIDANCE
		▪ If you still feel that you and your firm cannot provide competent representation, you can retrain or contract with other lawyers outside of your firm to better serve your client, but you should probably get your client's informed consent, and you must make sure "that the other lawyers' services will contribute to the competent and ethical representation of the client."[3] ▪ **4. Is the Transaction Legal?** 　▪ You must make sure that your client is engaging in a legal transaction before you even start drafting. 　▪ You cannot ever counsel or assist a client in conduct that you know is criminal or fraudulent, even though you may discuss the legal consequences of any possible actions with your client. 　▪ You cannot close your eyes to these issues and pretend that you do not know what is happening. You must make sure you do your own due diligence on your client, the other side, and the transaction in question. In fact, more recent amendments to ABA Model Rule 1.16 and its Comment 1 establish that you have an obligation "to inquire into and assess the facts and circumstances before accepting it" and that obligation "continues throughout the representation. A change in the facts and circumstances relating to the representation may trigger a lawyer's need to make further inquiry and assessment."[4] Furthermore, if you come to know or reasonably should know that your client expects you to help them with an action not permitted by the ABA Model Rules or if you intend to act against your client's instructions, you must consult with your client and may have to withdraw from representing them. 　▪ If you have any questions regarding the legality of part of a transaction, you should investigate, ask questions, and communicate clearly with your client. You may also need to consult with a litigator or other relevant type of attorney and/or withdraw from representing your client.
	Professional Responsibility Issues in Contract Drafting — During Drafting	▪ **1. You as an Agent of Your Client** 　▪ You are an agent of your client as part of the lawyer-client relationship. This means that you must abide by your client's decisions and consult with your client as to the transaction and the agreements that you are drafting. 　▪ You must follow your client's instructions as much as possible unless you would be assisting your client in a criminal or fraudulent matter. ▪ **2. Communicate with Your Client** 　▪ As a legal agent, you must keep your client informed about what you are drafting and, according to ABA Model Rule 1.13, you must "act with reasonable diligence and promptness."

---

3. *Model Rules of Prof'l Conduct* R. 1.1 cmt. 6 (2023).
4. *Model Rules of Prof'l Conduct* R. 1.16 cmt. 1 (2023).

CHAPTER	TOPIC	GUIDANCE
		■ If you do not want to be constantly e-mailing or calling your client, keep a running list of questions for your client and send them together, or set up a time to review them by phone or via a different platform.
		■ Set clear expectations with your client about how much they want to be involved in the negotiation and the drafting. In conjunction with this, also make sure to set the other side's expectations clearly as to how final and binding drafts are.
		■ **3. Maintain Confidentiality**
		■ As a lawyer, you are bound by the attorney-client privilege and cannot reveal any of your client's confidential information when you are drafting agreements or negotiating the transaction.
		■ The client is the holder of the privilege and the only person who can waive it, even though they can do so by disclosing information unintentionally in a careless manner.
		■ If possible, do not draft in public places (such as on an airplane) where people can possibly see your documents and electronic screen, and do not talk on the telephone while there are others nearby (such as in an elevator, the lobby of a building, or a coffee shop).
		■ The attorney work product doctrine does not apply in most transactions because you are not working in view of litigation.
		■ The e-mail messages and other communications that you put together for other team members are discoverable if a litigation matter arises from the transaction.
		■ **4. Figure Out What You Can Disclose and Verify Information from the Other Side**
		■ You usually have "no affirmative duty to inform an opposing party of relevant facts."[5] At the same time, in most jurisdictions, you are required to be truthful to others and not misrepresent material facts. However, during negotiations, you are not required to disclose "estimates of price or value placed on the subject of a transaction and a party's intentions as to an acceptable settlement of a claim are ordinarily in this category, and so is the existence of an undisclosed principal except where nondisclosure of the principal would constitute fraud."[6] In negotiations, these statements "ordinarily are not taken as statements of material fact."[7] Of course, at the very least, you want to make sure that you disclose what you need to disclose to avoid assisting in a crime or any type of fraud by your client.[8]

---

5. *Model Rules of Prof'l Conduct* R. 4.1 cmt. 1 (2023).
6. *Model Rules of Prof'l Conduct* R. 4.1 cmt. 2 (2023).
7. "Estimates of price or value placed on the subject of a transaction and a party's intentions as to an acceptable settlement of a claim are ordinarily in this category, and so is the existence of an undisclosed principal except where nondisclosure of the principal would constitute fraud." *Model Rules of Prof'l Conduct* R. 4.1 cmt. 2 (2023).
8. *Model Rules of Prof'l Conduct* R. 4.1(b) (2023).

CHAPTER	TOPIC	GUIDANCE
		■ What if the other side does not ask you about something specifically that you know will be an issue—do you have to tell them? This will depend on the matter at hand, the jurisdiction, and what other laws and regulations apply to that client and industry. Therefore, you must know the industry that you are working in and what applies to your client and the other side, and keep up with developments. ■ How do you know that the information you are receiving from the other side is accurate, and how can you verify it? Again, you must know the industry, how to properly research the parties and transaction, and the jurisdiction. You must do your due diligence on the transaction and ask follow-up questions. If you are not getting answers or something seems wrong, there is probably a problem that you need to be aware of before finalizing the transaction—you should probably not back down until you get the information that you need. ■ Some transactional lawyers believe that due diligence can be a waste of time and money at times, since you only really know what the other side provides or tells you. ■ **5. Know How Far You Can Go in Your Statements to the Other Side** ■ ABA Model Rule 4.1 requires that you not make a false statement of material fact to another party. ■ Keep in mind that how often and to what level you engage in tactics that involve *posturing and puffery* will be part of your reputation as a negotiator and drafter, so you may want to avoid these tactics. ■ **6. Be Careful with Redlines** ■ Make sure to send a redline that includes all the changes that you made to the clean version. ■ When you receive new clean and redlined versions from the other side, run your own redline comparing the new clean version of the agreement to the version that you previously sent to them. Do not rely on the other side's redline. ■ It is harder now to keep track of changes because often parties are working together on an online platform. ■ **7. Communications to the Wrong Party and Metadata** ■ While the ABA Model Rules provide limited guidance on these topics, states vary on what you should do if you get a message that is not meant for you and on what is acceptable to do with a document's metadata. Therefore, know your responsibilities for your jurisdiction and, when something of this nature occurs, get informed and consult with another lawyer, if needed.

Index